T0213973

Lecture Notes in Computer Science   11524

Commenced Publication in 1973
Founding and Former Series Editors:
Gerhard Goos, Juris Hartmanis, and Jan van Leeuwen

More information about this series at http://www.springer.com/series/7412

Jesús Ariel Carrasco-Ochoa ·
José Francisco Martínez-Trinidad ·
José Arturo Olvera-López ·
Joaquín Salas (Eds.)

Pattern Recognition

11th Mexican Conference, MCPR 2019
Querétaro, Mexico, June 26–29, 2019
Proceedings

Springer

Editors
Jesús Ariel Carrasco-Ochoa
National Institute of Astrophysics,
Optics and Electronics
Puebla, Mexico

José Francisco Martínez-Trinidad
National Institute of Astrophysics,
Optics and Electronics
Puebla, Mexico

José Arturo Olvera-López
Autonomous University of Puebla
Puebla, Mexico

Joaquín Salas
National Polytechnic Institute of Mexico
Querétaro, Mexico

ISSN 0302-9743   ISSN 1611-3349 (electronic)
Lecture Notes in Computer Science
ISBN 978-3-030-21076-2   ISBN 978-3-030-21077-9 (eBook)
https://doi.org/10.1007/978-3-030-21077-9

LNCS Sublibrary: SL6 – Image Processing, Computer Vision, Pattern Recognition, and Graphics

This Springer imprint is published by the registered company Springer Nature Switzerland AG
The registered company address is: Gewerbestrasse 11, 6330 Cham, Switzerland

Preface

The Mexican Conference on Pattern Recognition 2019 (MCPR 2019) was the 11th event in the series organized by the Computer Science Department of the National Institute for Astrophysics Optics and Electronics (INAOE) of Mexico and the National Polytechnic Institute (IPN) of Mexico, under the auspices of the Mexican Association for Computer Vision, Neurocomputing and Robotics (MACVNR), which is a member society of the International Association for Pattern Recognition (IAPR). MCPR 2019 was held in Queretaro, Mexico, during June 26–29, 2019.

This conference aims to provide a forum for the exchange of scientific results, practice, and new knowledge, as well as promoting collaboration among research groups in pattern recognition and related areas in Mexico and around the world.

In this edition, as in previous years, MCPR 2019 attracted not only Mexican researchers but it also included worldwide participation. We received contributions from ten countries. In total, 86 manuscripts were submitted, out of which 40 were accepted for publication in these proceedings and for presentation at the conference. Each of these submissions was strictly peer-reviewed by at least two members of the Program Committee, all of them experts in their respective fields of pattern recognition, resulting in these excellent conference proceedings.

Beside the presentation of the selected contributions, we were very honored to have three outstanding invited speakers:

- Prof. Roberto Manduchi, Department of Computer Engineering, University of California at Santa Cruz, USA.
- Prof. Sertac Karaman, Laboratory of Information and Decision Systems, Massachusetts Institute of Technology, USA.
- Prof. Adolfo Guzmán Arenas, Center for Computing Research, National Polytechnic Institute, Mexico.

These distinguished researchers gave keynote addresses on various pattern recognition topics and also presented enlightening tutorials during the conference. To all of them, we express our appreciation for these presentations.

We would like to thank all the people who devoted so much time and effort to the successful running of the conference. In particular, we extend our gratitude to all the authors who contributed to the conference. We are also very grateful for the efforts and the quality of the reviews of all Program Committee members and additional reviewers. Their work allowed us to maintain the high quality of the conference and provided a conference program of high standard.

We are sure that MCPR 2019 provided a fruitful forum for the Mexican pattern recognition researchers and the broader international pattern recognition community.

June 2019   Jesús Ariel Carrasco-Ochoa
                                      José Francisco Martínez-Trinidad
                                         José Arturo Olvera-López
                                                   Joaquín Salas

Organization

MCPR 2019 was sponsored by the Computer Science Department of the National Institute of Astrophysics, Optics and Electronics (INAOE) and the National Polytechnic Institute (IPN) of Mexico.

General Conference Co-chairs

Jesús Ariel Carrasco-Ochoa — National Institute of Astrophysics, Optics and Electronics (INAOE), Mexico

José Francisco Martínez-Trinidad — National Institute of Astrophysics, Optics and Electronics (INAOE), Mexico

José Arturo Olvera-López — Autonomous University of Puebla (BUAP), Mexico

Joaquín Salas — Research Center on Applied Science and Advanced Technology (CICATA) of National Polytechnic Institute (IPN) of Mexico, Mexico

Local Arrangements Committee

Brenda Cervantes
Marisol Alvarado
Daniela Basurto
Lucero Flores
Alejandro Gómez
Héctor Hernández
Alejandro Lozano
Pedro Martínez
Omar Montoya
Edith Muñoz
Dagoberto Pulido
Héctor Sánchez
Pablo Vera

Scientific Committee

Alexandre, L. A. — Universidade da Beira Interior, Portugal
Alonso-Fernandez, F. — Halmstad University, Sweden
Araujo, A. — Universidade da Beira Interior, Brazil
Asano, A. — Kansai University, Japan
Benedi, J. M. — Universidad Politécnica de Valencia, Spain
Borges, D. L. — Universidade de Brasília, Brazil
Calderita-Estévez, L. V. — University of Extremadura, Spain

Camargo, J.	Universidad Nacional de Colombia, Colombia
Castellanos, G.	Universidad Nacional de Colombia, Colombia
Chellappa, R.	University of Maryland, USA
Das, A.	Inria Sophia Antipolis, France
Díaz, M.	Universidad del Atlántico Medio, Spain
Dos-Santos, J. A.	Universidade Federal de Minas Gerais, Brazil
Escalante-Balderas, H. J.	INAOE, Mexico
Facon, J.	Pontifícia Universidade Católica do Paraná, Brazil
Fontanella, F.	Università degli studi di Cassino e del Lazio Meridionale, Italy
Furnari, A.	Università degli Studi di Catania, Italy
Gatica, D.	Idiap Research Institute, Switzerland
Godoy, D.	UNICEN, Argentina
Goldfarb, L.	University of New Brunswick, Canada
Gomez-Barrero, M.	Darmstadt University of Applied Sciences, Germany
Graña, M.	University of the Basque Country, Spain
Grau, A.	Universitat Politécnica de Catalunya, Spain
Guevara, M. R.	Universidad de Playa Ancha, Chile
Haindl, M.	Institute of Information Theory and Automation, Czech Republic
Heutte, L.	Université de Rouen, France
Hurtado-Ramos, J. B.	CICATA-IPN, Mexico
Jiang, X.	University of Münster, Germany
Kampel, M.	Vienna University of Technology, Austria
Klette, R.	University of Auckland, New Zealand
Kober, V.	CICESE, Mexico
Laurendeau, D.	Université Laval, Canada
Lazo-Cortés, M. S.	INAOE, Mexico
Levano, M. A.	Universidad Católica de Temuco, Chile
Lorenzo-Ginori, J. V.	Universidad Central de Las Villas, Cuba
Malmberg, F.	Uppsala University, Sweden
Marfil, R.	Universidad de Málaga, Spain
Mendoza, M.	Universidad Técnica Federico Santa María, Chile
Menotti, D.	Universidade Federal do Paraná, Brazil
Montes-Y-Gomez, M.	INAOE, Mexico
Morales, A.	Universidad Autónoma de Madrid, Spain
Morales, E.	INAOE, Mexico
Moreno, S.	Universidad Adolfo Ibáñez, Chile
Nappi, M.	Università degli Studi di Salerno, Italy
Oliveira, J. L.	Universidade de Aveiro, Portugal
Palagyi, K.	University of Szeged, Hungary
Pedrosa, G. V.	Universidade de Brasília, Brazil
Perez-Suay, A.	Universitat de València, Spain
Pina, P.	Instituto Superior Técnico, Portugal
Pinho, A.	University of Aveiro, Portugal
Pinto, J.	Instituto Superior Técnico, Portugal

Pistori, H.	Dom Bosco Catholic University, Brazil
Ponzoni, I.	Universidad Nacional del Sur, Argentina
Quiros-Ramirez, M. A.	University of Konstanz, Germany
Raducanu, B.	Universitat Autònoma de Barcelona, Spain
Real, P.	University of Seville, Spain
Ross, A.	West Virginia University, USA
Ruiz-Shulcloper, J.	UCI, Cuba
Sanchez-Cortes, D.	HES-SO Valais-Wallis, Switzerland
Sánchez-Salmerón, A. J.	Universitat Politècnica de València, Spain
Sansone, C.	Università di Napoli, Italy
Sappa, A.	Universitat Autònoma de Barcelona, Spain
Sossa-Azuela, J. H.	CIC-IPN, Mexico
Spyridonos, P.	University of Ioannina, Greece
Sucar, L. E.	INAOE, Mexico
Tolosana, R.	Universidad Autónoma de Madrid, Spain
Turki, T.	King Abdulaziz University, Saudi Arabia
Valev, V.	University of North Florida, USA
Velastin, S. A.	Universidad Carlos III de Madrid, Spain
Vitria, J.	University of Barcelona, Spain
Yera-Toledo, R.	UCI, Cuba

Additional Reviewers

Aragon, M. E.	Molina-Abril, H.
Cilia, N. D.	Oliveira, H.
Dhiman, A.	Ortega-Mendoza, R. M.
Diaz-Del-Rio, F.	Pereira, E.
Ferreira-Soares, J.	Pereira, M.
Fouzia, S.	Pérez-Sansalvador, J. C.
García-Hernández, R. A.	Rivas, J. J.
Hernández-Farias, D. I.	Saleem, N.
Laroca, R.	Solorio, S.

Sponsoring Institutions

Instituto Nacional de Astrofísica, Óptica y Electrónica (INAOE)
Instituto Politécnico Nacional of Mexico (IPN)
Mexican Association for Computer Vision, Neurocomputing and Robotics (MACVNR)
National Council of Science and Technology of Mexico (CONACYT)
Queretaro State Council of Science and Technology (CONCYTEQ)

Contents

Computer Vision

Industrial and Medical Applications of Pattern Recognition

Image Processing and Analysis

Pattern Recognition Techniques

Signal Processing and Analysis

Natural Language Processing and Recognition

Artificial Intelligence Techniques and Recognition

A Supervised Filter Feature Selection Method for Mixed Data Based on the Spectral Gap Score

Saúl Solorio-Fernández[✉], José Fco. Martínez-Trinidad,
and Jesús Ariel Carrasco-Ochoa

Computer Sciences Department, Instituto Nacional de Astrofísica,
Óptica y Electrónica, Luis Enrique Erro # 1, Santa María Tonantzintla,
72840 Puebla, Mexico
sausolofer@inaoep.mx

Abstract. Feature Selection for supervised classification plays a fundamental role in pattern recognition, data mining, machine learning, among other areas. However, most supervised feature selection methods have been designed for handling exclusively numerical or non-numerical data; so, in practical problems of fields such as medicine, economy, business, and social sciences, where the objects of study are usually described by both numerical and non-numerical features (mixed data), traditional supervised feature selection methods cannot be directly applied. This paper introduces a supervised filter feature selection method for mixed data based on the spectral gap score and a new kernel capable of modeling the data structure in a supervised way. To demonstrate the effectiveness of the proposed method, we conducted some experiments on public real-world mixed datasets.

Keywords: Supervised feature selection · Spectral feature selection ·
Mixed data · Feature ranking · Feature subset selection

1 Introduction

In areas such as pattern recognition, data mining, machine learning, statistical analysis, and in general, in tasks involving data analysis or knowledge discovery from datasets, it is common to process collections of objects[1] characterized by many features. In this situation, it is reasonable to assume that by retaining all features we will get better knowledge about the objects of study. However, in practice, this is usually not true, because many features could be either irrelevant or redundant. Indeed, it is well-known that irrelevant and redundant features may have an adverse impact on learning algorithms, decreasing the performance

---

[1] Also called instances, samples, tuples or observations.

© Springer Nature Switzerland AG 2019
J. A. Carrasco-Ochoa et al. (Eds.): MCPR 2019, LNCS 11524, pp. 3–13, 2019.
https://doi.org/10.1007/978-3-030-21077-9_1

of supervised classifiers and producing biases or even incorrect models [1]. Feature selection methods [2,3] have shown to be a useful tool for alleviating this problem; where the aim is to identify and eliminate irrelevant and/or redundant features in the data without significantly decreasing the prediction accuracy of a classifier built using only the selected features. Moreover, feature selection, not only reduces the dimensionality of the data facilitating their visualization and understanding; but also, it commonly leads to more compact models with better generalization ability [4].

In the literature of feature selection for supervised classification most feature selection methods (selectors) have been designed for either numeric or non-numeric data. However, these methods cannot be directly applied to mixed datasets where objects are simultaneously described by both numerical and non-numerical features. Mixed data [5] is very common, and it appears in many real-world problems; for example, in biomedical and health-care applications, socio-economic and business, software cost estimations, and so on.

In practice, for using supervised feature selection methods developed exclusively for numerical or non-numerical data on mixed data problems, it is common to apply feature transformations. The process of transforming non-numerical features to numerical ones is called encoding; nevertheless, this transformation has as a main drawback that the categories of a non-numerical feature should be coded as numerical values. This codification introduces an artificial order between feature values which does not necessarily reflect its original nature. Moreover, some mathematical operations such as addition and multiplication by a scalar do not make sense over the transformed data [6,7]. Conversely, when the feature selection methods require non-numerical data as input, an a priori data discretization for converting numerical features into non-numerical ones is needed. However, this discretization brings with it an inherent loss of information due to the binning process [7], and consequently, the results of feature selection become highly dependent on the applied discretization method. Another solution that has been considered in some supervised feature selection methods [7,8] is to analyze the numerical and non-numerical features separately, and then to merge the two set of results. However, as [5] have noted, using this solution, the associations that exist between numerical and non-numerical features are ignored.

Based on the results reported in [9], where the *spectral gap* score combined with a kernel function was successfully used for feature selection in unsupervised mixed datasets. In this paper, we propose an extension of the aforementioned method and show how using a supervised kernel and a simple leave-one-out search strategy results in a filter feature selection method useful to be applied for selecting relevant features in supervised mixed datasets. The proposed method does not transform the original space of features or process the data separately, and it can produce both a feature raking or a feature subset composed of only relevant features. Experimental results on real-world datasets show that the proposed method achieves outstanding performance compared to the state-of-the-art methods.

The rest of this paper is organized as follows. In Sect. 2, we provide a brief review of the related work, in Sect. 3, we describe the proposed method. Experiments will be presented and discussed in Sect. 4. Finally, Sect. 5 will conclude this paper and enunciate further research on this topic.

2   Related Work

In the literature, many supervised feature selection methods have been proposed [10,11], and according to the feature selection approach they can be categorized as filter, wrapper, or hybrid. Among the more classical and relevant filter feature selection methods for supervised classification we can mention: Information Gain (IG) [12], Fisher Score [13], Gini index [14], Relieff [15], and CFS [16]. IG, Fisher score, Gini index, and Relieff are univariate filter methods (also called ranking-based methods) that evaluate features according to some quality criterion that quantifies the relevance of features individually; meanwhile, CFS is a multivariate feature selection method that quantifies the relevancy of features jointly, therefore it provides a feature subset as a result. IG was designed to work on non-numerical features, while Fisher score and Gini index can only process numerical features. On the other hand both CFS and Relieff, according to their respective authors, can process mixed data, CFS processes numerical and non-numerical features as non-numerical (numerical features are discretized). Meanwhile, Relief deals with this problem by using the Hamming distance for non-numerical features and the Euclidean distance for numerical ones.

On the other hand, some supervised feature selection methods developed exclusively for mixed data have also been introduced, and they can be classified into four main approaches: Statistic/Probabilistic [8,17,18], Information Theory [7,19–22], Fuzzy/Rough set theory [23–26], and kernel-based [27,28] methods. In the former, the basic idea is to evaluate the relevancy of features using measures such as the join error probability or using different correlation measures (one for each type of feature) to quantify the degree of association among features. Information theory based methods, evaluate features using measures such as mutual information or entropy. On the other hand, Fuzzy/Rough set theory methods evaluate features based on fuzzy relations or equivalence classes (also called granules). Finally, kernel-based methods perform feature selection using three components: a dedicated kernel that can handle mixed data, a feature search strategy, and a classifier (usually SVM) which allows quantifying the importance of each feature through the objective function using the dedicated kernel.

3   Proposed Method

The proposed method is inspired by the previous Unsupervised Spectral Feature Selection Method for mixed data (USFSM) introduced in [9], which is based on

Spectral Feature Selection [1]. USFSM proposes to quantify the feature consistency[2] by analyzing the changes in the spectrum distribution (spectral gaps) of the Symmetrical Normalized Laplacian matrix when each feature is excluded separately.

Formally, given a collection of m objects $X_F = \{x_1, x_2, \ldots, x_m\}$, described by a set of n numerical or non-numerical features $F = \{f_1, f_2, \ldots, f_n\}$, a target concept $T = \{t_1, t_2, \ldots, t_m\}$ indicating the object's class labels, and a $m \times m$ similarity (kernel) matrix S, containing the similarities $s_{ij} \geq 0$ between all pairs of objects $x_i, x_j \in X_F$. Structural information from X_F can be obtained from the eigensystem of the Symmetrical Normalized Laplacian matrix $\mathcal{L}(S)$ [29] (Laplacian graph) derived from S. Specifically, the first $c + 1$ eigenvalues of $\mathcal{L}(S)$ (arranged in ascending order) and the corresponding eigenvectors contain information for separating the data X_F in c classes [1]. Nevertheless, to quantify the feature consistency using the *spectral gap* score [9] in a supervised context, we need to specify a good similarity function that uses both, the information contained the features in F, and the information provided by the target objective T. For doing this, we propose to build the object's similarity matrix S using the following supervised kernel function:

$$s_{ij} = \frac{K(x_i, x_j) + D(t_i, t_j)}{2} \tag{1}$$

where $D(t_i, t_j) = 1$ if $t_i = t_j$; otherwise $D(t_i, t_j) = 0$, and $K(x_i, x_j)$ is the Clinical kernel defined as in [9]. With this kernel function, we are modeling the data structure in a supervised way, and at the same time, we are taking into account the contribution of each feature in the objects' similarity.

To quantify the consistency of each feature $f_i \in F$, we measure the changes that could be produced when f_i is eliminated from the dataset X_F using a leave-one-out search strategy, i.e.:

$$\varphi(f_i) = \gamma(X_F, c) - \gamma(X_{F_i}, c) \tag{2}$$

where X_{F_i} denotes the dataset described by the set of features F_i, which contains all features except f_i, and $\gamma(\cdot, \cdot)$ is the *spectral gap* score defined as:

$$\gamma(X, c) = \sum_{i=2}^{c+1} \sum_{j=i+1}^{c+2} \left| \frac{\lambda_i - \lambda_j}{\tau} \right| \tag{3}$$

where λ_i, $i = 2, \ldots c + 2$ are the first $c + 1$ nontrivial eigenvalues of the spectrum of $\mathcal{L}(S)$, being S the similarity matrix from X, c the number of classes in the dataset, and $\tau = \sum_{i=2}^{c+2} \lambda_i$ a normalization term. In this score, the bigger the gap of the first $c + 1$ eigenvalues of $\mathcal{L}(S)$, the best will be the separation between the classes.

Our proposed method begins with the construction of the similarity matrix S from the original dataset X_F along with the class label information contained

---

[2] A feature is consistent (relevant), if it takes similar values for objects that are close to each other, and takes dissimilar values for objects that are far apart.

Input : X_F : an $m \times n$ dataset, with m objects and n features
  T : label information for each object
  c: the number of classes in the dataset
Output: F_{Rank}, F_{Sub}: Feature ranking and feature subset respectively

1 $F = \{f_1, f_2, \ldots, f_n\}$;
2 Build S, the similarity matrix from X_F using (1);
3 Compute $\mathcal{L}(S)$ and get its spectrum;
4 $\gamma_F \leftarrow \gamma(X_F, c)$//Computing the *spectral gap* score for X_F using 3;
5 **for** $i \leftarrow 1$ **to** n **do**
6    $\quad F_i \leftarrow F \backslash f_i$;
7    $\quad$ Build S', the similarity matrix from X_{F_i} using (1);
8    $\quad$ Compute $\mathcal{L}(S')$ and get its spectrum;
9    $\quad$ Compute the feature relevancy of f_i ($\varphi(f_i)$) using (2);
10   $\quad w[i] \leftarrow \varphi(f_i)$;
11 **end**
12 Sort w in descending order and build F_{Rank} according this order;
13 Get the feature subset F_{Sub} consisting of those feature with $w[i] > 0$;

Algorithm 1: Supervised Spectral Feature Selection Method for mixed data (SSFSM).

in T using 1. Then, we construct the Symmetrical Normalized Laplacian matrix $\mathcal{L}(S)$ and obtain its spectrum. Afterwards, using (3), the *spectral gap* score $\gamma(\cdot, \cdot)$ for X_F is computed. This procedure is repeated n times using a leave-one-out feature elimination strategy over F to quantify the relevance of each feature f_i through (2). Finally, features in F are ranked from the most to the least consistent according to the feature weights $w[i]$, $i = 1, 2, \ldots, n$ corresponding to each feature $f_i \in F$, and a feature subset F_{Sub} consisting of those features with $w[i] > 0$ (relevant features) is obtained. The pseudocode of our filter method, named Supervised Spectral Feature Selection method for Mixed data (SSFSM), is described in Algorithm 1.

4   Experiment Results

In this section, we first describe the experimental setup in Sect. 4.1, and later, the results obtained from the evaluation of the supervised filter methods over the used datasets are presented in Sect. 4.2.

4.1   Experimental Setup

To evaluate the effectiveness of our method, some experiments were done on real-world mixed datasets taken from the UCI Machine Learning repository [30]; detailed information about these datasets is summarized in Table 1. We have compared our proposal against two feature subset selectors of the state-of-the-art that can handle mixed data, namely, CFS [16] and the Fuzzy Rough Set theory-based method introduced by Zhang et al. in [24]. Moreover, in order to contrast our method against more classical and relevant based-on-ranking filter supervised feature selection methods of the state-of-the-art, we also have made a comparison with IG [12], Relieff [15], Fisher [13], and Gini index [14].

Following the standard way for assessing supervised feature selection methods, for the comparison among all selectors, we evaluate the quality of feature selection results using the classification accuracy (ACC) of the well-known and broadly used SVM [31] classifier. For the evaluation against the feature subset selectors (CFS and Zhang et al. method), we applied stratified ten-fold cross-validation, and the final classification performance is reported as the average accuracy over the ten folds. For each fold, each feature selection method is first applied on the training set to obtain a feature subset. Then, after training the classifier using the selected features, the respective test sets are used for assessing the classifier through its accuracy. Meanwhile, for the comparison against the ranking-based methods (IG, Relieff, Fisher, and Gini), we compute the *aggregated accuracy* [32]. The aggregated accuracy is obtained by averaging the average accuracy achieved by the classifiers using the top $1, 2, \ldots, n-1, n$ features according to the ranking produced by each selector, in this way, we can evaluate how good is the feature ranking obtained by each selector. In order to measure the statistical significance of the results of our method, the Wilcoxon test [33] was employed over the results obtained in each dataset, and we have marked with the "+" symbol those datasets where there is a statistically significant difference of the results of the corresponding method against the results of our method.

The implementation of ranking-based methods was taken from the Matlab Feature Selection package available in the ASU Feature Selection repository [34]. Meanwhile for CFS and Zhang et al. methods we used the author's implementation with the parameters recommended by their respective authors. For SSFSM, the Apache Commons Math[3] library was used for matrix operations and eigensystem computation. All experiments were run in Matlab® R2018a with Java 9.04, using a computer with an Intel Core i7-2600 3.40 GHz × 8 processor with 32 GB DDR4 RAM, running 64-bit Ubuntu 16.04 LTS (GNU/Linux 4.13.0-38 generic) operating system.

4.2   Experimental Results and Comparisons

In Tables 2 and 3, the classification accuracy reached by using the evaluated feature subset methods and the aggregated accuracy of ranking-based methods using SVM on the datasets of Table 1 are shown, respectively. In these tables, the last row shows the overall average results obtained on all tested datasets. Additionally, in the last column of Table 2, the classification accuracy using the whole set of features of each dataset is included.

As we can see in Table 2, regarding the methods for mixed data that select subsets of features, the best average results were obtained by our method, out-

---

[3] http://commons.apache.org/proper/commons-math/.

Table 1. Details of the real-world mixed datasets used in our experiments.

#	Dataset	No. of objects	Numerical	Non-numerical	All	No. of classes
1	Acute-inflammations	120	1	5	6	2
2	Automovile	205	15	10	25	6
3	Flags	194	10	19	29	8
4	Horse-colic	368	7	16	23	2
5	Post-operative	90	1	7	8	3
6	Teaching-assistant-evaluation	151	1	4	5	3
7	Thoracic-surgery	470	3	13	16	2
8	Credit-approval	690	6	9	15	2
9	Cylinder-bands	540	18	21	39	2
10	Heart-statlog	270	6	7	13	2

Table 2. Classification accuracy of SVM on the feature subsets produced by SSFSM, CFS, and Zhang et al. on the mixed datasets of Table 1.

Dataset	SSFSM	CFS	Zhang et al.	Original
Acute-inflammations	1.000	1.000	1.000	1.000
Automovile	0.683	0.5892+	0.698	0.717
Flags	0.624	0.692	0.3094+	0.603
Horse-colic	0.831	0.823	0.826	0.810
Post-operative	0.711	0.678	0.689	0.678
Teaching-assistant-evaluation	0.530	0.458	0.543	0.543
Thoracic-surgery	0.845	0.845	0.845	0.845
Credit-approval	0.858	0.858	0.849	0.849
Cylinder-bands	0.804	0.7240+	0.774	0.815
Heart-statlog	0.844	0.830	0.833	0.833
Average	**0.773**	**0.750**	**0.737**	**0.769**

performing the CFS and Zhang et al. selectors, and having a statistically better performance in Automovile, Cylinder-bands, and Flags datasets. Moreover, as we can observe in this table, our method was the only one that got an average result better than those obtained using the whole set of features.

On the other hand, regarding the ranking-based methods, in Table 3, we can observe that again our method got the best results on average (average aggregated accuracy), and it was significantly better than Gini index, and Fisher score on the Acute-inflammation, Horse-colic, credit-approval, and Automovil datasets. This indicates that the ranking produced by our method is, on average,

Table 3. Aggregated accuracy of SVM on the feature ranking produced by SSFSM, IG, Gini index, Relieff and Fisher score on the datasets of Table 1.

Dataset	SSFSM	IG	Gini index	Relieff	Fisher score
Acute-inflammations	0.9583	0.9569	0.9013+	0.9444	0.9569
Automovile	0.6830	0.6496	0.6419	0.6753	0.6015+
Flags	0.6223	0.6215	0.6457	0.6250	0.6320
Horse-colic	0.8253	0.8217	0.7193+	0.8266	0.8305
Post-operative	0.7069	0.6833	0.6889	0.6986	0.6819
Teaching-assistant-evaluation	0.5033	0.5062	0.4833	0.4880	0.4836
Thoracic-surgery	0.8464	0.8454	0.8507	0.8456	0.8460
Credit-approval	0.8537	0.8539	0.7598+	0.8517	0.8240
Cylinder-bands	0.8067	0.7934	0.6686	0.7905	0.7946
Heart-statlog	0.8165	0.8128	0.8145	0.8148	0.8131
Average	**0.7623**	**0.7545**	**0.7174**	**0.7561**	**0.7464**

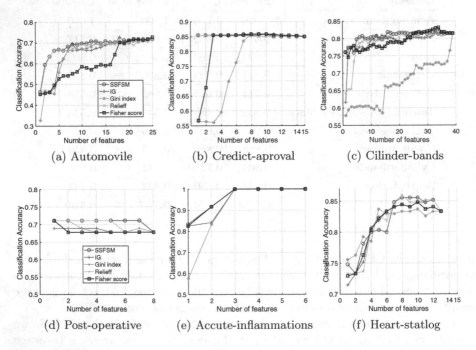

(a) Automovile   (b) Credict-aproval   (c) Cilinder-bands

(d) Post-operative   (e) Accute-inflammations   (f) Heart-statlog

Fig. 1. Classification accuracy of SVM on the feature ranking produced by SSFSM, IG, Gini index, Relieff and Fisher score on six datasets of Table 1. The x-axis is the number of selected features. The y-axis is the classification accuracy.

better than the ranking produced by the other evaluated ranking-based selectors, as we can corroborate in most of the feature ranking plots[4] shown in Fig. 1.

5 Conclusions and Future Work

To solve the feature selection problem in mixed data, in this paper we introduce a new supervised filter feature selection method. Our method is based on Spectral Feature Selection (*spectral gap* score) combined with a new supervised kernel and a simple leave-one-out search strategy. It results in ranking-based/feature subset selector that can effectively solve feature selection problems in supervised mixed datasets. To show the effectiveness of our method, we tested it on several public mixed datasets. The results have shown that our method, is better than CFS [16] and the method introduced by Zhang et al. in [24], two filter feature subset selectors that can handle mixed data. Furthermore, our method achieves better results than popular filter based-on raking feature selection methods of the state-of-the-art, such as IG, Relieff, Fisher score and Gini index.

A comparison using other classifiers and selectors is mandatory, and it is part of the future work of this research. Another interesting research direction is to perform a broader study about wrapper strategies that combined with our method allow to improve its performance in terms of accuracy.

Acknowledgements. The first author gratefully acknowledges to the National Council of Science and Technology of Mexico (CONACyT) for his Ph.D. fellowship, through the scholarship 224490.

References

1. Zhou, Z., Liu, H.: Spectral Feature Selection for Data Mining, pp. 1–216 (2011). 20111464
2. Liu, H., Motoda, H.: Feature Selection for Knowledge Discovery and Data Mining. Springer, Heidelberg (1998). https://doi.org/10.1007/978-1-4615-5689-3
3. Liu, H., Motoda, H.: Computational Methods of Feature Selection. CRC Press, Boca Raton (2007)
4. Pal, S.K., Mitra, P.: Pattern Recognition Algorithms for Data Mining, 1st edn. Chapman and Hall/CRC, Boca Raton (2004)
5. De Leon, A.R., Chough, K.C.: Analysis of Mixed Data: Methods & Applications. CRC Press, Boca Raton (2013)
6. Ruiz-Shulcloper, J.: Pattern recognition with mixed and incomplete data. Pattern Recogn. Image Anal. **18**(4), 563–576 (2008)
7. Doquire, G., Verleysen, M.: An hybrid approach to feature selection for mixed categorical and continuous data. In: Proceedings of the International Conference on Knowledge Discovery and Information Retrieval, pp. 394–401 (2011)
8. Tang, W., Mao, K.: Feature selection algorithm for data with both nominal and continuous features. In: Ho, T.B., Cheung, D., Liu, H. (eds.) PAKDD 2005. LNCS (LNAI), vol. 3518, pp. 683–688. Springer, Heidelberg (2005). https://doi.org/10.1007/11430919_78

---

[4] Due to limitations of space, in Fig. 1 we only show six mixed datasets of Table 1.

9. Solorio-Fernández, S., Martínez-Trinidad, J.F., Carrasco-Ochoa, J.A.: A new unsupervised spectral feature selection method for mixed data: a filter approach. Pattern Recogn. **72**, 314–326 (2017)
10. Kotsiantis, S.B.: Feature selection for machine learning classification problems: a recent overview. Artif. Intell. Rev. **42**, 157–176 (2011)
11. Tang, J., Alelyani, S., Liu, H.: Feature selection for classification: a review. In: Data Classification, pp. 37–64. CRC Press, 1 January 2014. https://doi.org/10.1201/b17320. ISBN: 9781466586741
12. Battiti, R.: Using mutual information for selecting features in supervised neural net learning. IEEE Trans. Neural Netw. **5**(4), 537–550 (1994)
13. Duda, R.O., Hart, P.E., Stork, D.G.: Pattern Classification. Wiley, Hoboken (2012)
14. Gini, C.: Variabilità e mutabilità. Reprinted in Memorie di metodologica statistica (Ed. Pizetti E, Salvemini, T). Libreria Eredi Virgilio Veschi, Rome (1912)
15. Kononenko, I.: Estimating attributes: analysis and extensions of RELIEF. In: Bergadano, F., De Raedt, L. (eds.) ECML 1994. LNCS, vol. 784, pp. 171–182. Springer, Heidelberg (1994). https://doi.org/10.1007/3-540-57868-4_57
16. Hall, M.A.: Correlation-based feature selection for discrete and numeric class machine learning. In: Proceedings of the Seventeenth International Conference on Machine Learning, ICML 2000, pp. 359–366. Morgan Kaufmann Publishers Inc., San Francisco (2000)
17. Tang, W., Mao, K.: Feature selection algorithm for mixed data with both nominal and continuous features. Pattern Recogn. Lett. **28**(5), 563–571 (2007)
18. Jiang, S.Y., Wang, L.X.: Efficient feature selection based on correlation measure between continuous and discrete features. Inf. Process. Lett. **116**(2), 203–215 (2016)
19. Peng, H., Long, F., Ding, C.: Feature selection based on mutual information: criteria of max-dependency, max-relevance, and min-redundancy. IEEE Trans. Pattern Anal. Mach. Intell. **27**(8), 1226–1238 (2005)
20. Doquire, G., Verleysen, M., et al.: Mutual information based feature selection for mixed data. In: 19th European Symposium on Artificial Neural Networks, Computational Intelligence and Machine Learning (ESANN 2011) (2011)
21. Liu, H., Wei, R., Jiang, G.: A hybrid feature selection scheme for mixed attributes data. Comput. Appl. Math. **32**(1), 145–161 (2013)
22. Wei, M., Chow, T.W., Chan, R.H.: Heterogeneous feature subset selection using mutual information-based feature transformation. Neurocomputing **168**, 706–718 (2015)
23. Hu, Q., Liu, J., Yu, D.: Mixed feature selection based on granulation and approximation. Knowl.-Based Syst. **21**(4), 294–304 (2008)
24. Zhang, X., Mei, C., Chen, D., Li, J.: Feature selection in mixed data: a method using a novel fuzzy rough set-based information entropy. Pattern Recogn. **56**, 1–15 (2016)
25. Kim, K.J., Jun, C.H.: Rough set model based feature selection for mixed-type data with feature space decomposition. Expert Syst. Appl. **103**, 196–205 (2018)
26. Wang, F., Liang, J.: An efficient feature selection algorithm for hybrid data. Neurocomputing **193**, 33–41 (2016)
27. Paul, J., Dupont, P., et al.: Kernel methods for mixed feature selection. In: ESANN. Citeseer (2014)
28. Paul, J., D'Ambrosio, R., Dupont, P.: Kernel methods for heterogeneous feature selection. Neurocomputing **169**, 187–195 (2015)
29. Luxburg, U.: A tutorial on spectral clustering. Stat. Comput. **17**(4), 395–416 (2007)

30. Lichman, M.: UCI Machine Learning Repository (2013)
31. Cortes, C., Vapnik, V.: Support-vector networks. Mach. Learn. **20**(3), 273–297 (1995)
32. Zhao, Z., Wang, L., Liu, H., Ye, J.: On similarity preserving feature selection. IEEE Trans. Knowl. Data Eng. **25**(3), 619–632 (2013)
33. Wilcoxon, F.: Comparisons by ranking methods. Biometrics Bull. **1**(6), 80–83 (1945)
34. Li, J., et al.: Feature selection: a data perspective. ACM Comput. Surv. **50**(6) (2017). https://doi.org/10.1145/3136625. ISSN: 0360-0300

Motor Imagery Task Classification in EEG Signals with Spiking Neural Network

Carlos D. Virgilio G[1], Humberto Sossa[1,2]($\boxtimes$), Javier M. Antelis[2],
and Luis E. Falcón[2]

[1] Centro de Investigación en Computación, Instituto Politécnico Nacional,
Av. Juan de Dios Bátiz and M. Othón de Mendizabal, 07738 Mexico City, Mexico
danielvg92@gmail.com, hsossa@cic.ipn.mx
[2] Tecnológico de Monterrey, Escuela de Ingeniería y Ciencias,
Av. General Ramón Corona 2514, Zapopan, Jalisco, Mexico
mauricio.antelis@itesm.mx, luis.eduardo.falcon@tec.mx

Abstract. We report the development and evaluation of brain signal classifiers, specifically Spiking Neuron based classifiers. The proposal consists of two main stages: feature extraction and pattern classification. The EEG signals used represent four motor imagery tasks: Left Hand, Right Hand, Foot and Tongue movements. In addition, one more class was added: Rest. These EEG signals were obtained from a database provided by the Technological University of Graz. Feature extraction stage was carried out by applying two algorithms: Power Spectral Density and Wavelet Decomposition. The tested algorithms were: K-Nearest Neighbors, Multilayer Perceptron, Single Spiking Neuron and Spiking Neural Network. All of them were evaluated in the classification between two Motor Imagery tasks; all possible pairings were made with the 5 mental tasks (Rest, Left Hand, Right Hand, Tongue and Foot). In the end, a performance comparison was made between a Multilayer Perceptron and Spiking Neural Network.

Keywords: EEG signals · Motor Imagery · Power Spectral Density · Wavelet Decomposition · Neural networks · Multi layer perceptron · Spiking Neural Network

1 Introduction

Spiking Neural Networks (SNN) are a special class of artificial neural network, where neurons communicate by sequences of pulses. This type of neuron models provide a powerful tool for spatio-temporal analysis due to its functionality based on neuronal biological models. It has been shown that SNN can be applied not only to all problems solvable by non-spiking neural networks, also SNN are in fact computationally more powerful than perceptrons and sigmoidal gates

J. A. Carrasco-Ochoa et al. (Eds.): MCPR 2019, LNCS 11524, pp. 14–24, 2019.
https://doi.org/10.1007/978-3-030-21077-9_2

[10]. Although they offer solutions to different problems in applied engineering, as is such as fast signal-processing, event detection, classification, speech recognition, currently, they are not very popular in the field of pattern recognition. Brain-Computer Interfaces (BCI) is a promising research field which provides a communication between humans and computers by analyzing electrical brain activity, recorded at the surface of the scalp with electroencephalography. The key part of a BCI system is how to recognize the mental tasks that a subject performs by analyzing EEG signals.

In this work we propose using SNN models in the classification of Motor Imagery (MI [12]) EEG signals. SNN are models with a high degree of realism and with the advantage of performing an analysis of spatio-temporal information. A systematic evaluation procedure was carried out to assess the performance of SNN to differentiate two motor imagery tasks from EEG signals. The results show that the proposed model achieves an accuracy on average of 81.36% which is 11.14%, 0.82%, 1.91% superior to the accuracy achieved with MLP (2,1), MLP $(2n + 1, 1)$, and KNN, respectively.

1.1   Acquisition of EEG Signals

The dataset used in this work was provided by the Institute for Knowledge Discovery (Laboratory of Brain-Computer Interfaces) of the Graz University of Technology, in the event called "BCI Competition IV" (www.bbci. de/competition/iv/). Figure 1 shows the location of the monopolar electrodes, in addition to the selection of the 12 channels that were used to carry out the classification process mentioned in this work. Likewise, detailed information of the used dataset is shown.

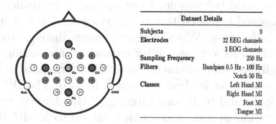

Dataset Details	
Subjects	9
Electrodes	22 EEG channels
	3 EOG channels
Sampling Frequency	250 Hz
Filters	Bandpass 0.5 Hz - 100 Hz
	Notch 50 Hz
Classes	Left Hand MI
	Right Hand MI
	Foot MI
	Tongue MI

Fig. 1. Technical details of the EEG dataset from the BCI competition IV used in this work

The dataset is made up of 144 trials from each of the four classes: Left Hand MI, Right Hand MI, Foot MI and Tongue MI. In addition to this, we took the initial time window with a duration of 2 s to generate a fifth class, this is called Rest. MI EEG were extracted from $t = 3$ s to $t = 5$ s while Rest were extracted from $t = 0$ s to $t = 2$ s. Having at the end five mental tasks with which the process of classification will be carried out.

2   Feature Extraction

In this work, two feature extraction methods were used: Power Spectral Density (PSD) and Wavelet Decomposition (WD). Each trial is composed of 22 EEG channels. From these we selected only 12. The theoretical basis of each of these methods is explained below.

2.1   Power Spectral Density (PSD)

The Power Spectral Density (PSD) of the EEG signals have been used as features to recognize among movement phases. This is because it has been well established the spectral power changes in the motor-related brain rhythms during execution, imagination o attempt to perform movements [2,11,14]. In addition, PSD is one of the most robust methods to estimate the spectral power and one of the standard approaches to compute frequency-based features from EEG signals recorded during motor tasks [13]. The PSD was computed based on the Welch's averaged modified periodogram method in five band of frequency: 1–4 Hz, 5–8 Hz, 9–12 Hz, 13–30 Hz and 1–30 Hz at a resolution of 1 Hz using Hanning-windowed. After this, a PSD matrix is obtained where the number of rows corresponds to each frequency analyzed and each column corresponds to each electrode ($P_{FreqNoXChannelsNo}$). The values of this matrix were normalized in a range of 0 to 1. To reduce the number of PSD values, the following operation was performed: $features = P^T f$; where f is a vector that contains the frequency values (f_{FreqNo}). Therefore, the number of the features for each electrode is 60.

2.2   Discrete Wavelet Transform (DWT)

The DWT method is a method of decoding subbands using a wavelet type function, in this work we used the wavelet function known as Symlet 5. The discrete signal to be decomposed is passed through filters with different frequency of cut and a process of decimation. When a signal passes through these filters, it is split into two bands. The low pass filter extracts the common information of the signal. The high pass filter extracts the detail information of the signal. The output of the low pass filter is then decimated by two. The DWT is computed by successive low pass and high pass filtering of the discrete time-domain signal. This decomposition process was carried out up to level 5 to each channel in each of the trials. At the end, 6 new signals were obtained from each of the channels (D1, D2, D3, D4, D5 and A5), so 72 signals were obtained. In order to reduce the number of features, the variance was calculated in each of these signals, obtaining at the end, 72 features.

3   Classification

Five different classification models were employed in this work, K-Nearest Neighbors (KNN), two models of Multilayer Perceptron (MLP), Single Spiking Neuron (SSN) and Spiking Neural Network (SNN). Below we explain how the SNN works, it is a method that is not commonly used with brain signals.

3.1   Spiking Neurons

At present, it is known that biological neurons communicate through the generation and propagation of electrical pulses also called action potentials or spikes. This feature is the central paradigm of a theory of spiking neural models (SNN). In the work of Ponulak et al. [15] show that the spiking models present three main properties: (1) Information coming from many inputs and only produce a single spiking output; (2) Their probability of firing is increasing by excitatory inputs and decreased by inhibitory inputs; (3) Its dynamics are characterized by state variables, when they reach a certain state, the model generates one or more pulses. The spiking neuron model described by Izhikevich (IZ) was selected for the SNN. This model has a good biological realism as well as low computational cost. The IZ model is described by two differential equations as [7], Euler's method was used for solving the model and its parameters were set in order to reproduce the behaviour of regular spiking neurons:

$$v' = \frac{k(v - v_r)(v - v_t) - u + I}{C} \tag{1}$$

$$u' = a(b(v - v_r) - u) \tag{2}$$

$$\text{if } v > v_{peak}, \text{ then } v \longleftarrow c, u \longleftarrow u + d$$

where v is the membrane potential, u is the recovery current, I is a vector with the input current arriving to the neuron, C is the membrane capacitance, v_r is resting membrane potential, v_t is the instantaneous threshold potential, k is the rheobase resistance, v_{peak} is the spike cutoff value, a is a recovery time constant, b is the input resistance, c is the voltage reset value and d is the outwards minus inwards currents during spike which affect the after-spike behavior of the model [7]. In this work, a behavior of regular spiking neurons is used for the SN model [7]. In order to achieve this, IZ parameters are set according to Fig. 2.

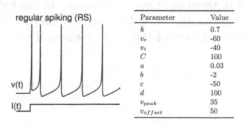

Parameter	Value
k	0.7
v_r	-60
v_t	-40
C	100
a	0.03
b	-2
c	-50
d	100
v_{peak}	35
v_{offset}	50

Fig. 2. Description of the Izhiquevich model parameters

In this type of neuronal models, the simulation must be performed using numerical methods to solve the differential equations that compose it.

Two of the proposed classification models use Spiking Neurons: the model called Single Spiking Neuron uses only one neuron to perform classification

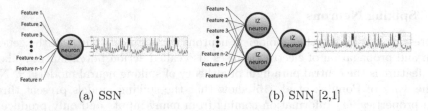

(a) SSN   (b) SNN [2,1]

Fig. 3. Arquitecture of the two Spiking models used to classify MI from EEG

(Fig. 3a), the second model called Spiking Neural Network uses a small network of neurons formed by a hidden layer with two neurons and a single output neuron (Fig. 3b).

These models were optimized using the Particle Swarm Optimization (PSO) algorithm [8]. In this method each particle of a population is taken as a set of possible weights for the SNN model, with this we proceed to make a certain number of iterations and at the end we take the best solution (set of weights) found during this process.

3.2   Multilayer Perceptron (MLP)

The multilayer perceptron is an artificial neural network formed by multiple layers, this allows solving non-linear separable problems. The MLP consists of L layers, without counting the input layer, each layer contains a certain number of perceptrons, it is not necessary that all the layers have the same number of perceptrons, this is known as the structure of the neural network, It is considered a hyperparameter. Each perceptron is consists of two parts: (1) The dot product and (2) The activation function. This transfer function can be different in each layer and when using the delta rule as a base, this function must be differentiable without having to be linear. We used two models of MLP, both with a single hidden layer, the first of them only has two neurons in the hidden layer and the second uses $2n + 1$ neurons in the hidden layer, n is the number of features. Figure 4 shows the configuration of the proposed neural network models.

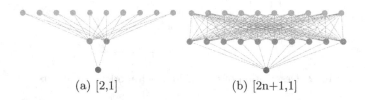

(a) [2,1]   (b) [2n+1,1]

Fig. 4. Arquitecture of the two MLP models used to classify MI from EEG

3.3   Evaluation Procedure

For each subject, the set of trials was randomly partitioned in 75% for training and 25% for testing. To measure performance, the metrics Accuracy, Cohen's Kappa score and F1-score were computed. Accuracy was computed as:

$$Acc = \frac{TP + TN}{TP + TN + FP + FN}$$

where TP, TN, FP and FN are true positives, true negatives, false positives, and false negatives, respectively. F1 is the weighted average of the precision and recall and was computed as [5]:

$$f1 = 2 \times \frac{precision \times recall}{precision + recall}$$

where $precision = TP/(TP + FP)$ and $recall = TP/(TP + FN)$.

Cohen's kappa measures the agreement between two raters who each classify N items into C mutually exclusive categories. The definition of k is: $k = \frac{P_o - P_e}{1 - P_e}$ where P_o is the relative observed agreement among raters (identical to accuracy), and P_e is the hypothetical probability of chance agreement, using the observed data to calculate the probabilities of each observer randomly seeing each category.

4   Recognition of Motor Imagery Tasks from EEG Signals

The binary classification process was implemented with the four mentioned classifiers, in all possible pairs using the five mental tasks. This dataset consists of 9

Table 1. Classification results for subject "A09"

Classes		MLP [2,1] PSD Acc	Kappa	F1	Wavelet D Acc	Kappa	F1	MLP [2n+1,1] PSD Acc	Kappa	F1	Wavelet D Acc	Kappa	F1
Rest	vs Left H.	83.33	0.67	0.83	77.78	0.56	0.80	84.72	0.69	0.85	79.17	0.58	0.77
Rest	vs Right H.	80.56	0.61	0.81	65.28	0.31	0.72	83.33	0.67	0.84	72.22	0.44	0.73
Rest	vs Foot	86.11	0.72	0.86	70.83	0.42	0.70	84.72	0.69	0.85	72.22	0.44	0.70
Rest	vs Tongue	70.83	0.42	0.68	59.72	0.19	0.59	75.00	0.50	0.74	61.11	0.22	0.60
Left H.	vs Right H.	77.78	0.56	0.78	87.50	0.75	0.89	79.17	0.58	0.79	75.00	0.50	0.75
Left H.	vs Foot	84.72	0.69	0.85	93.06	0.86	0.93	81.94	0.64	0.82	84.72	0.69	0.85
Left H.	vs Tongue	86.11	0.72	0.85	87.50	0.75	0.88	86.11	0.72	0.84	88.89	0.78	0.90
Right H.	vs Foot	73.61	0.47	0.72	75.00	0.50	0.74	76.39	0.53	0.74	69.44	0.39	0.72
Right H.	vs Tongue	86.11	0.72	0.86	76.39	0.53	0.77	86.11	0.72	0.86	75.00	0.50	0.76
Foot	vs Tongue	70.83	0.42	0.72	75.00	0.50	0.74	73.61	0.47	0.74	72.22	0.44	0.75

Classes		SSN PSD Acc	Kappa	F1	Wavelet D Acc	Kappa	F1	SNN [2,1] PSD Acc	Kappa	F1	Wavelet D Acc	Kappa	F1
Rest	vs Left H.	84.72	0.69	0.85	87.50	0.75	0.86	90.28	0.81	0.90	83.33	0.67	0.84
Rest	vs Right H.	83.33	0.67	0.83	68.06	0.36	0.63	90.28	0.81	0.90	68.06	0.36	0.68
Rest	vs Foot	79.17	0.58	0.76	87.50	0.75	0.87	86.11	0.72	0.86	87.50	0.75	0.87
Rest	vs Tongue	83.33	0.67	0.84	76.39	0.53	0.69	86.11	0.72	0.84	79.17	0.58	0.77
Left H.	vs Right H.	83.33	0.67	0.81	80.56	0.61	0.83	83.33	0.67	0.84	88.89	0.78	0.90
Left H.	vs Foot	93.06	0.86	0.93	91.67	0.83	0.92	93.06	0.86	0.93	94.44	0.89	0.95
Left H.	vs Tongue	90.28	0.81	0.90	86.11	0.72	0.85	93.06	0.86	0.93	91.67	0.83	0.91
Right H.	vs Foot	63.89	0.28	0.63	65.28	0.31	0.60	66.67	0.33	0.66	66.67	0.33	0.63
Right H.	vs Tongue	79.17	0.58	0.75	73.61	0.47	0.68	77.78	0.56	0.76	77.78	0.56	0.75
Foot	vs Tongue	73.61	0.47	0.72	76.39	0.53	0.75	75.00	0.50	0.76	76.39	0.53	0.76

subjects (A01 to A09). In this stage, the performance of the SSN and SNN was compared against accuracy of the MLP models.

In the BCI area, it has been found that the best way to perform the recognition of MI tasks in EEG signals is to carry it out for each of the subjects [16]. At present, the way to generalize the recognition of patterns in signals of this type has not been found. This can be attributed to the differences in the neural connections that the brain of each subject presents. Therefore, it is important to start with the analysis of a test subject. Table 1 shows the accuracy values obtained with the EEG signals of the A01 Subject for each pair of classes in the four classification methods.

The best results obtained for each pair of classes are highlighted, in most of the classification scenarios an accuracy above 90% was obtained, the best results are observed with the SNN models; only in the Left H. vs Right H. scenario the MLP showed the best performance. The best result obtained with the Spiking Neuron was 97.22% for the Right H. vs Tongue scenario, this occurs when a single neuron or a network of neurons of the Spiking type is used. In the case of the data from this test subject it can be seen that the feature extraction algorithm called PSD shows better results, however this does not always happen.

The same classification process was carried out with the data of each one of the test subjects. Table 2 shows a summary of the accuracy results obtained with each proposed method. The best results obtained in each test subject are again highlighted in this table.

In most scenarios, the models based on Spiking neurons presented the best results, in 7 of the 9 participants they surpass the performance of the MLP models, however, in the two remaining subjects the Spiking Neurons show results close to MLP models. It should be noted that in this work a basic Spiking neuron model is used, since it does not receive pulse trains, only the features in a constant way over the simulation time of the neuronal activity.

Below is the average across all subjects (Table 3) for each classifier in each classification scenario.

Similarly, in 7 of 10 classification scenarios, the SNN exceeded the MLP models, in most cases with the 80% accuracy. The best classification scenario was Rest vs. Right Hand where an average performance of 89.20% was obtained with the Single Spiking Neuron.

One aspect to highlight is that state of the art just reports the classification of two specific mental tasks: Left Hand VS. Right Hand [1,3,4,6,9]. So the binary classification of each possible pair with the five mental tasks together with the using of the SNN in the area of the classification of biological signals, are the two main contributions of this paper, we want to emphasize that there is the possibility of using another type of MI tasks, not only of the superior members.

Below in Table 4 is a comparison with the classification results presented in the state of the art, it is necessary to clarify that the subject in each work is not the same, therefore the performance of the proposed models can not be compared directly. The same thing happens with the number of trials used to train and evaluate.

Table 2. Classification results for each subject

Accuracy (%)

A01

Classes	KNN (K=9)	MLP [2,1]	MLP [2n+1,1]	SSN	SNN [2,1]
R vs LH	77.78	88.89	86.11	95.83	88.89
R vs RH	72.22	86.11	87.50	94.44	90.28
R vs F	69.44	87.50	90.28	93.06	84.72
R vs T	70.83	86.11	87.50	95.83	95.83
LH vs RH	54.17	75.00	76.39	65.28	68.06
LH vs F	80.56	91.67	86.11	93.06	94.44
LH vs T	72.22	94.44	87.50	91.67	94.44
RH vs F	86.11	87.50	86.11	90.28	93.06
RH vs T	86.11	94.44	88.89	97.22	97.22
F vs T	59.72	63.89	63.89	70.83	75.00
Mean	72.92	85.56	84.03	88.75	88.19

A02

Classes	KNN (K=9)	MLP [2,1]	MLP [2n+1,1]	SSN	SNN [2,1]
R vs LH	68.06	73.61	77.78	90.28	87.50
R vs RH	73.61	84.72	83.33	95.83	90.28
R vs F	68.06	83.33	80.56	90.28	88.89
R vs T	79.17	80.56	80.56	93.06	91.67
LH vs RH	55.56	55.56	50.00	65.28	61.11
LH vs F	51.39	66.67	72.22	69.44	66.67
LH vs T	51.39	66.67	66.67	62.50	69.44
RH vs F	59.72	75.00	75.00	73.61	65.28
RH vs T	54.17	69.44	68.06	70.83	59.72
F vs T	66.67	65.28	69.44	63.89	74.72
Mean	62.78	72.08	72.36	77.50	74.72

A03

Classes	KNN (K=9)	MLP [2,1]	MLP [2n+1,1]	SSN	SNN [2,1]
R vs LH	83.33	94.44	91.67	95.83	97.22
R vs RH	87.50	94.44	94.44	98.61	97.22
R vs F	83.33	90.28	88.89	97.22	95.83
R vs T	79.17	90.28	90.28	97.22	94.44
LH vs RH	75.00	93.06	90.28	88.89	90.28
LH vs F	73.61	91.67	93.06	84.72	84.72
LH vs T	83.33	90.28	87.50	90.28	88.89
RH vs F	76.39	86.11	86.11	88.89	90.28
RH vs T	66.67	84.72	84.72	91.67	94.44
F vs T	79.31	80.56	73.61	73.61	72.22
Mean	79.31	90.28	88.06	90.69	90.56

A04

Classes	KNN (K=9)	MLP [2,1]	MLP [2n+1,1]	SSN	SNN [2,1]
R vs LH	66.67	86.11	84.72	87.50	84.72
R vs RH	73.61	88.89	80.56	83.33	81.94
R vs F	76.39	81.94	80.56	86.11	87.50
R vs T	77.78	84.72	81.94	88.89	88.89
LH vs RH	56.94	65.28	68.06	66.67	63.89
LH vs F	68.06	79.17	75.00	81.94	86.11
LH vs T	73.61	77.78	77.78	84.72	84.72
RH vs F	70.83	80.56	77.78	81.94	79.17
RH vs T	69.44	75.00	77.78	65.28	77.78
F vs T	55.56	69.44	70.83	65.28	62.50
Mean	68.89	78.89	77.50	80.83	79.31

A05

Classes	KNN (K=9)	MLP [2,1]	MLP [2n+1,1]	SSN	SNN [2,1]
R vs LH	72.22	77.78	76.39	84.72	81.94
R vs RH	69.44	75.00	83.33	81.94	77.78
R vs F	66.67	73.61	73.61	87.50	83.33
R vs T	77.78	73.61	73.61	86.11	87.50
LH vs RH	54.17	66.67	56.94	62.50	68.06
LH vs F	55.56	66.67	72.22	65.28	68.06
LH vs T	61.11	72.22	59.72	75.00	70.83
RH vs F	62.50	61.11	59.72	59.72	55.56
RH vs T	52.78	63.89	65.28	66.67	62.50
F vs T	63.33	69.17	68.75	66.67	62.50
Mean	63.33	69.17	68.75	73.75	72.50

A06

Classes	KNN (K=9)	MLP [2,1]	MLP [2n+1,1]	SSN	SNN [2,1]
R vs LH	65.28	88.89	81.94	84.72	84.72
R vs RH	66.67	84.72	87.50	84.72	75.00
R vs F	66.67	80.56	76.39	86.11	88.89
R vs T	66.67	86.11	84.72	87.50	88.89
LH vs RH	66.67	70.83	63.89	68.06	65.28
LH vs F	66.67	65.28	59.72	66.67	65.28
LH vs T	65.28	68.06	63.89	68.06	66.67
RH vs F	61.11	68.06	73.61	68.06	68.06
RH vs T	65.28	73.61	61.11	73.61	73.61
F vs T	62.50	62.50	72.78	66.67	74.72
Mean	65.28	74.58	72.78	74.58	74.72

A07

Classes	KNN (K=9)	MLP [2,1]	MLP [2n+1,1]	SSN	SNN [2,1]
R vs LH	83.33	90.28	90.28	90.28	88.89
R vs RH	88.89	93.06	93.06	91.67	88.89
R vs F	76.39	87.50	86.11	90.28	88.89
R vs T	80.56	84.72	86.11	81.94	87.50
LH vs RH	58.33	75.00	73.61	73.61	73.61
LH vs F	68.06	87.50	88.89	83.33	79.17
LH vs T	62.50	84.72	84.72	75.00	76.39
RH vs F	68.06	86.11	86.11	73.61	83.33
RH vs T	76.39	80.56	80.56	80.56	79.17
F vs T	66.67	83.33	90.28	80.56	79.17
Mean	72.92	85.28	85.97	82.36	83.33

A08

Classes	KNN (K=9)	MLP [2,1]	MLP [2n+1,1]	SSN	SNN [2,1]
R vs LH	77.78	91.67	90.28	80.56	87.50
R vs RH	69.44	87.50	87.50	88.89	88.89
R vs F	68.06	76.39	77.78	81.94	84.72
R vs T	73.61	84.72	83.33	75.00	75.00
LH vs RH	77.78	91.67	81.94	86.11	86.11
LH vs F	75.00	84.72	81.94	84.72	81.94
LH vs T	79.17	91.67	91.67	88.89	88.89
RH vs F	56.94	90.28	80.56	76.39	76.39
RH vs T	75.00	87.50	77.78	73.61	86.11
F vs T	73.61	79.17	77.78	73.61	70.83
Mean	72.64	86.53	83.89	80.83	82.08

A09

Classes	KNN (K=9)	MLP [2,1]	MLP [2n+1,1]	SSN	SNN [2,1]
R vs LH	81.94	83.33	84.72	87.50	84.72
R vs RH	69.44	80.56	83.33	83.33	90.28
R vs F	73.61	86.11	84.72	87.50	87.50
R vs T	63.89	70.83	75.00	83.33	86.11
LH vs RH	68.06	87.50	84.72	83.33	88.89
LH vs F	86.11	93.06	84.72	93.06	93.06
LH vs T	87.50	87.50	88.89	90.28	94.44
RH vs F	63.89	75.00	76.39	65.28	66.67
RH vs T	70.83	86.11	86.11	79.17	77.78
F vs T	73.61	75.00	73.61	76.39	76.39
Mean	73.89	82.50	81.67	82.92	85.14

LH: Left Hand , RH: Right Hand, F: Foot, T: Tongue

Table 3. Mean Accuracy across all subjects

Classes			Accuracy (%)				
			KNN (K=9)	MLP [2,1]	MLP [2n+1,1]	SSN	SNN [2,1]
Rest	vs	Left H.	75.15	86.11	84.88	**88.58**	87.96
Rest	vs	Right H.	74.54	86.11	86.73	**89.20**	86.73
Rest	vs	Foot	72.07	83.02	82.10	**88.89**	87.81
Rest	vs	Tongue	74.38	82.41	82.56	87.65	**88.43**
Left H.	vs	Right H.	62.96	**75.62**	71.76	72.84	73.92
Left H.	vs	Foot	69.44	**80.71**	79.32	80.25	**80.71**
Left H.	vs	Tongue	71.30	81.17	78.70	80.09	**81.64**
Right H.	vs	Foot	66.51	**78.86**	78.24	75.31	73.77
Right H.	vs	Tongue	71.60	79.94	78.40	79.94	**80.56**
Foot	vs	Tongue	64.20	71.45	**71.76**	70.83	70.22
	Mean		70.22	80.54	79.44	**81.36**	81.17

Table 4. State of art (Motor Imagery)

	Left Hand vs Right Hand		
	Feature extraction	Classifier	Accuracy (%)
Ahangi2013 [1]	Wavelet Decomposition	KNN	84.28%
		Naive Bayes	68.75%
		MLP	74%
		LDA	87.86%
		SVM	88.57%
Han2013 [6]	Wavelet + CSP (10 channels)	FLDA	93%
		SVM	90.9%
		KNN	92.9%
AsensioCubero2013 [3]	LDB + CSP	FLDA	75%
		DBI	63%
	LDB + LCT	FLDA	64%
		DBI	71%
Belhadj2016 [4]	CSP (2 features)	FLDA	89.4%
	CSP (10 features)		89.4%
Ma2016 [9]	RCSP	Decision Tree	79.8%
		KNN	92.5%
		LDA	95.4%
		PSO - SVM	**97%**
Virgilio2018 [16]	**CSP**	KNN	90.6%
		SVM	87.8%
		MLP	93.3%
		DMNN	87.2%
Proposal methods (A09)	**PSD/DWT**	MLP [2,1]	87.50%
		MLP [2n+1,1]	79.17%
		SSN	83.33%
		SNN	**88.89%**

One of the main objectives of this work is to show the potential of the SNN as a model for classifying signals of this type. As can be seen, the performance of Spiking neural models competes with the results shown in the state of the art, although they do not have patterns with enough spatio-temporal information. It is important to note that these models are conformed with a neuron (SSN) and with 3 neurons (SNN).

5 Conclusions and Further Work

This work provides an approach to perform the classification of five different mental tasks, showing the binary discrimination between each pair of classes using two methods of feature extraction commonly used in the BCI area. Also, the use of SNN provided favorable results, showing that with a small number of neurons, an acceptable discrimination process can be obtained for the efficiently implementation of systems controlled by EEG signals.

It was observed that it is not possible to distinguish which feature extraction method provides better results. The cause of this may be the characteristics of each test subject, each test subject responds differently to the mental tasks evaluated. Another point to emphasize is that this type of neurons show acceptable results even when the features used do not contain enough spatio-temporal information, which, as mentioned above, this kind of neurons have the ability to analyse spatial-temporal information.

Acknowledgements. We would like to express our sincere appreciation to the Instituto Politécnico Nacional and the Secretaria de Investigación y Posgrado for the economic support provided to carry out this research. This project was supported economically by SIP-IPN (numbers 20180730 and 20190007) and the National Council of Science and Technology of Mexico (CONACyT) (65 Frontiers of Science, numbers 268958 and PN2015-873).

References

1. Ahangi, A., Karamnejad, M., Mohammadi, N., Ebrahimpour, R., Bagheri, N.: Multiple classifier system for EEG signal classification with application to brain-computer interfaces. Neural Comput. Appl. **23**(5), 1319–1327 (2013). https://doi.org/10.1007/s00521-012-1074-3
2. Antelis, J.M., Gudiño-Mendoza, B., Falcón, L.E., Sanchez-Ante, G., Sossa, H.: Dendrite morphological neural networks for motor task recognition from electroencephalographic signals. Biomed. Sig. Process. Control **44**, 12–24 (2018). https://doi.org/10.1016/j.bspc.2018.03.010
3. Asensio Cubero, J., Gan, J.Q., Palaniappan, R.: Extracting optimal tempo-spatial features using local discriminant bases and common spatial patterns for brain computer interfacing. Biomed. Sig. Process. Control **8**(6), 772–778 (2013). https://doi.org/10.1016/j.bspc.2013.07.004
4. Belhadj, S.A., Benmoussat, N., Krachai, M.D.: CSP features extraction and FLDA classification of EEG-based motor imagery for Brain-Computer Interaction. In: 2015 4th International Conference on Electrical Engineering, ICEE 2015, pp. 3–8 (2016). https://doi.org/10.1109/INTEE.2015.7416697

 5. Goutte, C., Gaussier, E.: A probabilistic interpretation of precision, recall and F-score, with implication for evaluation. In: Losada, D.E., Fernández-Luna, J.M. (eds.) ECIR 2005. LNCS, vol. 3408, pp. 345–359. Springer, Heidelberg (2005). https://doi.org/10.1007/978-3-540-31865-1_25
 6. Han, R.X., Wei, Q.G.: Feature extraction by combining wavelet packet transform and common spatial pattern in brain-computer interfaces. Appl. Mech. Mater. **239**, 974–979 (2013). https://doi.org/10.4028/www.scientific.net/AMM.239-240.974
 7. Izhikevich, E.M.: Dynamical Systems in Neuroscience Computational Neuroscience (2007). https://doi.org/10.1017/S0143385704000173
 8. Kennedy, J., Eberhart, R.: Particle swarm optimization, vol. 4, pp. 1942–1948 (1995). https://doi.org/10.1109/ICNN.1995.488968
 9. Ma, Y., Ding, X., She, Q., Luo, Z., Potter, T., Zhang, Y.: Classification of motor imagery EEG signals with support vector machines and particle swarm optimization. Comput. Math. Methods Med. **2016**(5), 667–677 (2016). https://doi.org/10.1155/2016/4941235
10. Maass, W.: Networks of spiking neurons: the third generation of neural network models. Neural Netw. **10**(9), 1659–1671 (1997). https://doi.org/10.1016/S0893-6080(97)00011-7
11. McFarland, D.J., Miner, L.A., Vaughan, T.M., Wolpaw, J.R.: Mu and beta rhythm topographies during motor imagery and actual movements. Brain Topogr. **12**(3), 177–186 (2000)
12. Mulder, T.: Motor imagery and action observation: cognitive tools for rehabilitation. J. Neural Transm. **114**(10), 1265–1278 (2007). https://doi.org/10.1007/s00702-007-0763-z
13. Herman, P., Prasad, G., McGinnity, T.M., Coyle, D.: Comparative analysis of spectral approaches to feature extraction for EEG-based motor imagery classification. IEEE Trans. Neural Syst. Rehabil. Eng. **16**(4), 317–326 (2008). https://doi.org/10.119/TNSRE.2008.926694
14. Pfurtscheller, G., Brunner, C., Schlögl, A., Lopes da Silva, F.H.: Mu rhythm (de)synchronization and EEG single-trial classification of different motor imagery tasks. NeuroImage (2006). https://doi.org/10.1016/j.neuroimage.2005.12.003
15. Ponulak, F.: Allen - 2011 - Introduction to spiking neural networks Information processing, learning and applications, January 2011
16. Virgilio Gonzalez, C.D., Sossa Azuela, J.H., Rubio Espino, E., Ponce Ponce, V.H.: Classification of motor imagery EEG signals with CSP filtering through neural networks models. In: Batyrshin, I., Martínez-Villaseñor, M.L., Ponce Espinosa, H.E. (eds.) MICAI 2018. LNCS (LNAI), vol. 11288, pp. 123–135. Springer, Cham (2018). https://doi.org/10.1007/978-3-030-04491-6_10

A Comprehensive Methodology to Find Closed Mathematical Models from Experimental Data

Angel Kuri-Morales[(✉)]

Instituto Tecnológico Autónomo de México,
Río Hondo No. 1, 01000 México, D.F., Mexico
akuri@itam.mx

Abstract. A method which allows us to find a polynomial model of an unknown function from a set of tuples with n independent variables and m tuples is presented. A plausible model of an explicit approximation is found. The number of monomials of the model is determined by a previously trained neural network (NNt). The degrees of the monomials are bounded from the Universal Approximation Theorem yielding a reduced polynomial form. The coefficients of the model are found by exploring the space of possible monomials with a genetic algorithm (GA). The polynomial defined by every training pair is approximated by the Ascent Algorithm which yields the coefficients of best fit with the L_∞ norm. The L2 error corresponding to these coefficients is calculated and becomes the fitness function of the GA. A detailed example for a well known experimental data set is presented. It is shown that the model derived from the method yields a classification error of <7% for the cross-validation data set. A detailed description of the NNt is included. The approximation to 46 datasets tackled with our method is discussed. In all these cases the approximation accuracy was better than 94%. The tool described herein yields general models with explanatory characteristics not found in other methods.

Keywords: Universal Approximation Theorem · Neural networks · Genetic algorithms · Non-linear regression

1 Introduction

In this paper we address the problem of obtaining a general algebraic model for a set of given data pairs $(\vec{x}, y)$. By "model" we mean a function $F(\vec{x})$ derived from a set of n independent variables and m given data pairs assumed to stem from an unknown function $y = f(\vec{x})$, such that the error $\varepsilon = \|f(\vec{x}) - F(\vec{x})\|_2$ is minimized.

In a previous work [1] a methodology is proposed to find a multivariate polynomial model to fit a dataset in which, instead of generating the full range of terms in (1), generates the combination of a preselected number of them. This is accomplished by the ensemble of a genetic algorithm and a regression algorithm, where the individuals of the genetic algorithm represent a set of monomials with different combination of variables and their exponents. The regression algorithm computes the coefficients of the terms in such way that the minimax error norm (or L_∞) is minimized. The current work

© Springer Nature Switzerland AG 2019
J. A. Carrasco-Ochoa et al. (Eds.): MCPR 2019, LNCS 11524, pp. 25–36, 2019.
https://doi.org/10.1007/978-3-030-21077-9_3

is based on this methodology. We complement it by finding a neural network (NNt) which yields the minimum needed number of terms.

The rest of the paper is organized as follows. In Sect. 2 we describe

1. How to select the model's form
2. How to approximate, from an arbitrary training set of pairs $(\vec{x}, y)$, a polynomial model.
3. How to avoid the exponential number of terms as the number of variables and the maximum degrees considered increases
4. How to determine the degrees d_1, ..., d_n of (1) needed for $F(\vec{x})$ to be a universal approximator.

In Sect. 3 we focus on the problem of how to determine the minimum number of terms in $F(\vec{x})$. In Sect. 4 we present the application of the methodology to a case of study. In Sect. 5 we present our conclusions.

2 Previous Results

In order to obtain a comprehensive methodology leading to the goal of finding closed mathematical (polynomial) models from experimental data we rely, at the offset, on previous works. The reader interested in the details is encouraged to dwell on the references.

2.1 Selecting the Model's Form

A basic issue to be considered is how to select the form of $F(\vec{x})$. One possible approach to determine such form is suggested by the Weierstrass approximation theorem (WAT), which states that every continuous function defined on a closed interval [a, b] can be uniformly approximated as closely as desired by a polynomial function [2].

From the WAT we assume that there exists a full polynomial approximation

$$F(\vec{x}) = \sum_{i_1=0}^{d_i} \sum_{i_2=0}^{d_2} \cdots \sum_{i_n=0}^{d_n} c_{i_1 i_2 \ldots i_n} x_1^{i_1} x_2^{i_2} \ldots x_n^{i_n} \tag{1}$$

We consider all possible linear combinations of the products of the independent variables x_1, ..., x_n raised to a given degree d_1, ..., d_n. The set of allowed degrees d_1, ..., d_n will be denoted with **D,** the set of coefficients $c_{i_1 i_2 \ldots i_n}$ will be denoted with **C,** the number of terms of the polynomial will be denoted by **T**. The purpose of the algorithm we implemented is to express $F(\vec{x})$ as a more compact polynomial. By "algebraic model", therefore, we mean a function of the form

$$F(\vec{x}) = \sum_{i=0}^{t} K_i x_1^{t_1} x_2^{t_2} \ldots x_n^{t_n} \tag{2}$$

2.2 Approximation of a Polynomial Model

The number of monomials in (1) is $M = (d_1 + 1)...(d_n + 1)$. Consider, for example, the well known (number of web hits = 1,020,829) classification problem in [3]. The data pairs in it ($n = 13$ and $m = 178$) may be accommodated in a 178 $\times$ 14 data base. This is a classification problem where the values of the tuples determine one of three classes. For convenience we shall assume that the number of the class (the dependent variable y) is denoted with 0, 1 and 2 and, furthermore, that it is placed on the last column of the matrix. Even assuming the conservative $d_1 = ... = d_{13} = 2$ we find that $M = 4^{13} = 67,108,864$. The exponential growth of M has been referred to as "the curse of dimensionality" [4]. With the development of NNs this problem has been successfully circumvented [5] albeit without yielding an explicit model, i.e. one in which the relation between the independent variables is exposed. NNs are frequently cited as suffering from the "black box" disadvantage. The main motivation in this work is to solve this kind of problems without losing the explanatory advantages of an algebraic model. To achieve this we apply a method where the model of (1) is replaced by the one in (3), where the monomials (or "terms") in (1) are selectively retained/discarded.

$$F(\vec{x}) = \sum_{i_1=0}^{d_i} \sum_{i_2=0}^{d_2} \cdots \sum_{i_n=0}^{d_n} \mu_{i_1 i_2...i_n} c_{i_1 i_2...i_n} x_1^{i_1} x_2^{i_2} \cdots x_n^{i_n} \tag{3}$$

where

$$\mu_{i_1 i_2...i_n} = \begin{cases} 0 & \text{if } c_{i_1 i_2...i_n} \text{ is not retained} \\ 1 & \text{if } c_{i_1 i_2...i_n} \text{ is retained} \end{cases} \tag{4}$$

The basic idea is to set $\mathbf{T}$ and $\mathbf{D}$ which, immediately, allows us to avoid the curse of dimensionality. The way in which $\mathbf{T}$ and $\mathbf{D}$ are determined is discussed in what follows.

2.3 Determining the Coefficients of the Monomials

Once $\mathbf{D}$ and $\mathbf{T}$ are determined we may determine the $\mu_{i_1 i_2...i_n}$ indirectly by applying the genetic algorithm (EGA) described in [6], as follows. The individuals of the population of the EGA represent the combination of powers $i_1, \ldots, i_n$ corresponding to each of the T monomials in (2) for which the $\mu_{i1i2...i_n}$ are retained. This is exemplified in Fig. 1 where $n = 3$, $0 \leq d_i \leq 9$ and $T = 5$. For simplicity, the coefficients $c_{i_1 i_2...i_n}$ in (2) have been replaced with $C_1, ..., C_5$.

Every individual of the EGA represents a polynomial consisting of T monomials. From them we find a data base of size $T \times m$ where every one of its tuples is a map from the original $\vec{x}$ into the monomials proposed by the EGA *plus* the value of the dependent variable, as illustrated in Fig. 2. The data base from which this figure is originated consists of 50 $(\vec{x}, y)$ pairs, in this case of the form (x_1, x_2, x_3, F).

From the original data a mapping analogous to the one illustrated in Fig. 2 is obtained.

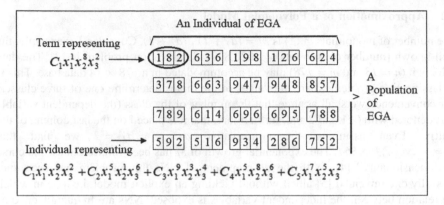

Fig. 1. Illustration of a set of polynomials in EGA

X01	X02	X03	F
0.0000000000	0.0000000000	0.0000000000	0.0000000000
0.1597251943	0.1882374524	0.0203109439	0.2284581703
0.3794620567	0.4380551846	0.0975920321	0.5122464288
0.4967739374	0.5636662255	0.1601940713	0.6413400278
0.7053214735	0.7675612701	0.3020630466	0.8268563958
0.9102004392	0.9370630039	0.4696313041	0.9571192230
1.0000000000	1.0000000000	0.5484344673	1.0000000000
0.0012676177	0.0015023254	0.0000378156	0.0018435801

Original Data (partial view) ($n = 3$)

Variable	Degree
X01	2
X02	2
X03	2

Maximum allowed Degrees

d01	d02	d03
0	0	2
0	2	0
0	2	1
1	1	2
1	2	1
2	0	0

Selected Powers for one hypotetical individual with T=6

T002	T020	T021	T112	T121	T200	F
0.0000000000	0.0000000000	0.0000000000	0.0000000000	0.0000000000	0.0000000000	0.0000000000
0.0004125344	0.0354333385	0.0007196846	0.0000124034	0.0001149518	0.0255121377	0.2284581703
0.0095242047	0.1918923448	0.0187271639	0.0015831640	0.0071062481	0.1439914525	0.5122464288
0.0256621405	0.3177196138	0.0508967985	0.0071857763	0.0252842030	0.2467843449	0.6413400278
0.0912420841	0.5891503034	0.1779605355	0.0493964065	0.1255193872	0.4974783810	0.8268563958
0.2205535618	0.8780870733	0.4123771773	0.1881134759	0.3753458879	0.8284648395	0.9571192230
0.2912322078	0.9869929824	0.5326948504	0.2865475769	0.5274597676	0.9804414902	0.9956892589

Data mapping for the selected monomials (partial view)

Fig. 2. Example of mapping for one individual of the EGA

To find **C** we implemented an approximation algorithm known as the Ascent Algorithm (*AA*) [7]. C_{ij} is the coefficient induced by the *i-th* individual during the *j-th* generation. Using the AA, we find C_{ij} and its associated fit error ε_{ij}. After the evolutionary process the coefficients of the best individual (corresponding to ε_{ij}) will yield $F(\vec{x})$. The $\mu_{i_1 i_2 \ldots i_n}$ are never explicitly obtained. The **C** resulting from the EGA tacitly determines the **T** retained monomials whose coefficients minimize ε.

2.4 Degree of the Terms in the Polynomial

In [1] it was shown that, from the Universal Approximation Theorem [8], any unknown function $f(\vec{x})$ may be approximated with a polynomial of the form of (5)

$$F(\vec{x}) = k + \sum_{i=1}^{T} ci \left(\prod_{j=1}^{n} x^{dj} \right) \tag{5}$$

if

$$\sum dj \in L \;\; \forall j \tag{6}$$

where $\sum dj \in L$ means that the maximum degree (*maxdeg*) of any term (the summation of the degrees associated to each of the independent variables) must belong to set $L = \{1, 3, 5, 7, 9, 11, 15, 21, 25, 33, 35, 37, 45, 49, 55, 63, 77, 81, 99, 121\}$.

The way in which L was arrived at may be found in [1]. Notice, however, that even if *maxdeg* of the *i-th* monomial is odd, the powers of the variables in it may take any value leading to one of those in L.

The algebraic model of (1) is thusly simplified and the EGA can be made to include in its population only individuals whose coefficients comply with (6). To illustrate this fact, the data of Fig. 1 [consisting of 50 pairs $(\vec{x}, y)$] was approximated with the EGA now considering Eq. (5). The resulting coefficients are as shown in Fig. 3. In an "indexed coefficient" like $Ci_1, \ldots, i_n$, the indices denote the degrees associated to the *i-th* variable. The degree of the term is shown on the first column.

Degree of the Term	Indexed Coefficient	Coefficient
1	C00,00,01	-0.05065249
1	C00,01,00	1.22841977
3	C01,01,01	0.02744421
3	C01,02,00	-0.31612161
5	C05,00,00	0.25105819
Δ 5	C00,03,02	-0.40850124
7	C00,02,05	-0.56140460
ε		0.00000015

Fig. 3. Approximation coefficients for the data in Fig. 2

3 Minimum Number of Terms

Once we have a method to determine, via EGA, the most adequate coefficient for every term in (5) it only remains to specify the most adequate value for **T**. The solution to this problem completes the specification of the method. An attempt to solve this problem is to appeal to statistical criteria.

The first step was to set lower and upper practical limits on the number of terms. We reasoned that we were not interested in very small values for **T**. Very low values are hardly prone to yield good models. Therefore, we set a lower value of **T** = *3*. On the other side of the spectrum we decided to focus on **T** ≤ *13*. Higher values are seldom of practical interest since large sets of coefficients are cumbersome and difficult to analyze. At the end of the day algebraic models allow us to search for patterns in the relations which are exposed by the monomials and the possible relations embedded. Very large **T**s will make this search too complex in general.

Therefore, we collected 46 datasets from the University of California Machine Learning dataset repository [9] and the Knowledge Extraction Evolutionary Learning dataset repository [10]. To begin with, 32 of these datasets were chosen and were subjected to the procedure outlined above. For every $\mathbf{T} \in [3, 13]$ a polynomial was found and the number of terms corresponding to the best fit was recorded. A total of 352 (11×32) polynomials, therefore, were calculated. Table 1 shows the values of best **T** from the 32 selected data sets. For every one of the 32 datasets 11 polynomials $(\mathbf{T} = 3, ..., 13)$ were found. From these the lower bound of the number of terms was determined. The best values of **T** were then used to train NNt. The polynomials were calculated as a function of the following variables: (a) Number of attributes, (b) Number tuples, (c) Optimally encoded size, (d) Compression ratio [the quotient of the (dataset's original size)/(optimally compressed size)]. These attributes were selected from a much larger original subset of such attributes. The ones we selected were shown to be the more relevant from a Principal Components Analysis.

The remaining 14 datasets were used as cross validation data for the trained NN model. The corresponding results are shown in Table 2. From the results a statistically highly significant lower bound on T may be inferred. NNt may be fully specified from: (a) Its architecture, (b) The associated weights, (c) The definition of the activation function.

We can calculate the average RMS error and the standard deviation. From $P(\mu T - k\sigma T \leq T \leq \mu T + k\sigma T) > 1 - 1/k^2$ (Chebyshev's theorem [13]). Making $k = 3$, the probability of finding the smallest expected value of **T** above the average value at $k = -3$ standard deviations is $\approx 88\%$. Thereafter the mathematical model for the minimum number of terms as a function of the RMS error within the indicated limits may be calculated. We trained a NN from these data yielding NNt. The architecture of NNt is shown in Fig. 4.

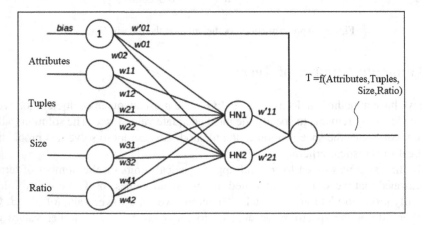

Fig. 4. Architecture of NNt (the NN which yields the value of T)

Table 1. Table of the best values of T for the selected datasets

ID	Dataset name	# Attributes	# Tuples	Size	Comp size	Comp ratio	Expected T
1	Breast cancer wisconsin	10	364	38121	1003	38.007	8
2	Protein localization sites	7	336	28140	7548	3.7281	7
3	Servomechanism	13	167	22610	771	29.3256	6
4	Yeast	9	1484	140066	32021	4.3742	7
5	Abalone	11	3133	360864	39891	9.0463	6
6	Car evaluation	22	1728	216384	34636	6.2474	10
7	CPU	36	209	28398	5348	5.31	9
8	Hepatitis	16	125	30384	5906	5.1446	7
9	Wine	14	125	25986	8876	2.9277	13
10	IRIS	4	150	9120	2685	3.3966	5
11	Facebook	21	500	55200	14521	3.8014	6
12	Whole sale	10	440	46112	13649	3.3784	8
13	3D rood network	2	871	53261	15941	3.34	10
14	Air quality	8	1200	217522	52252	4.16	6
15	Air foil self noise	5	1503	182089	43915	4.15	4
16	Concrete strength	8	1030	18752	52062	3.59	8
17	Auto mpg	6	398	64368	14798	4.35	5
18	Credit approval	15	690	215937	42663	5.06	6
19	Gas turbine propulsion	2	1000	966816	259129	3.73	5
20	Energy efficiency	11	768	185506	36553	5.07	9

NNt was trained using the backpropagation algorithm. To improve convergence the learning rate is set in the hidden and output layers. The learning rate was tested in the hidden layer with the values .1, .2, .3 and .25; the learning rate in the output layer was tested for the values .1, .01 and .001.

Activation Function. Every neuron is a perceptron whose activation function is $1/(1 + e^{-x})$.

Momentum. A momentum term was added, which allows the adjustments on the weights to depend also on the previous changes. If the momentum is equal to 0, the change depends only on the error gradient, while a value of 1 means that the change will only depend on the last change. The value of the momentum in the hidden and output layers was tested for values 0.3, 0.5 and .8. The weights were initialized with uniform random numbers in the range $[-0.1, 0.1] \in R$. The learning strategy used was stochastic in which each input creates a weight adjustment. The NN was trained for 10,000 epochs with a test every 100 epochs. NNt was validated vs. the remaining 14 data sets.

Table 2. Validation stage models

ID	DB name	# Attributes	# Tuples	Compressed size	Compression ratio
1	Pima indian diabetes database	8	768	32,360	3.227688
2	Yacht hydrodynamics	6	308	9,174	3.558752
3	Image segmentation	20	2310	2,13,221	3.42
4	Analizing categorical data	7	900	25,627	4.249424
5	Appendicitis	7	106	3,024	3.189815
6	Balance	4	625	10,881	4.365407
7	Baseball salaries	13	337	21,125	3.366011
8	Hayes-roth	4	160	298	22.013422
9	House prices	15	1300	1,11,601	2.807322
10	Laser	4	993	21,357	3.533642
11	Mv synthetic	10	1300	75,388	2.862524
12	Phonems	5	1200	38,677	2.823383
13	Treasury	5	1049	36,651	2.60454
14	Weather izmir	7	1461	53,229	3.32114

The above information was fed to NNt to get **T**. In Table 3 we see the estimated **T** which are expected to be near the optimum fit. RMS(T-i) denotes the RMS error when NNt yields i for the value of **T**. The actual best value of **T** was always within $i \pm 2$ of the **T** suggested by NNt.

Table 3. Terms calculated by NNt for the validation sets

ID	Estimated T	Rounded T	RMS(T−2)	RMS(T−1)	RMS(T)	RMS(T+1)	RMS(T+2)
1	8.6634990936	9	0.412718594	**0.406120106**	0.4200713649	0.410491696	0.418528407
2	7.4266991038	7	0.037526053	0.061839319	0.03250066	**0.031067453**	0.032766126
3	2.8167562596	3	**0.207598173**	0.214679407	0.229129966	0.224681547	0.225307872
4	8.477513871	8	0.067469116	0.050167953	**0.04093897**	0.043811914	0.04796777
5	7.2928672806	7	0.337443754	0.319763624	0.318348383	0.313419036	**0.313209334**
6	7.7389574277	8	0.340522415	0.325661129	0.334526005	**0.308926934**	0.324996133
7	7.7052644686	8	0.119055026	0.11559727	**0.108739684**	0.124787914	0.117380777
8	6.2126030641	6	0.258552437	0.245556743	**0.241290077**	0.26038423	0.269854381
9	8.0014918908	8	0.101553883	**0.096687173**	0.101330919	0.102006909	0.100162057
10	8.5616749213	9	0.086605404	0.0839230232	0.082046364	0.078676946	**0.076810137**
11	7.5255321089	8	0.074918077	0.063573936	0.076393697	**0.056997275**	0.06215833
12	7.0866960532	7	0.395806995	0.400738082	0.405261065	**0.392372343**	0.399877438
13	8.6697108438	9	0.068657151	0.068666017	0.062620414	**0.061057446**	0.062685869
14	5.7585208346	6	0.14429961	0.137041337	**0.130248103**	0.140362715	0.135891573

The weights of NNt are shown in Fig. 5. Every neuron is, as stated, a perceptron whose activation function is $1/(1 + e^{-x})$. Because of this the input values were scaled into [0, 1). Given the values of the 4 input attributes a simple spreadsheet may easily calculate the suggested number of terms. An example is shown in Fig. 6.

- Since the values must be scaled the upper and lower values of the variables are needed. These are shown in the lines titled "Max" and "Min". The corresponding scaled values are shown in the line "Scaled_01".
- "Compressed size" refers to the size (bytes) of the original dataset after it is compressed using the PPMZ Algorithm [11]. This yields a practical approximation to the information contained in the dataset[1].

First Layer

Weights	Values
$w_{0,1}$	9.93878
$w_{0,2}$	−1.277238
$w_{1,1}$	12.794103
$w_{1,2}$	2.149855
$w_{2,1}$	−32.754846
$w_{2,2}$	9.336392
$w_{3,1}$	1.290772
$w_{3,2}$	−8.214893
$w_{4,1}$	8.711606
$w_{4,2}$	−21.087847

Second Layer

Weights	Values
$w'_{0,1}$	−0.018833
$w'_{1,1}$	0.452167
$w'_{2,1}$	0.531239

Fig. 5. Weights of NNt

B11		f_x =B5*B7+C5*C7+D5*D7+E5*E7+F5*F7				
A	**B**	**C**	**D**	**E**	**F**	**G**
1	Bias	Number of Tuples	Number of Attributes	Compressed Size	Compression Ratio	Terms
2 Original	1.00000	400	13	27,442	2.67	**9**
3 Max		3,134.5324	36.2564	258,920.2939	38.0070	13.02073
4 Min		59.4136	1.35639	5,305.1796	2.26812	1.00635
5 Scaled_01	1.00000	0.11076	0.33363	0.08729	0.01124	
6	w01	w11	w21	w31	w41	
7	9.93878	12.794103	-32.754846	1.290772	8.711606	
8	w02	w12	w22	w32	w42	
9	-1.277238	2.149855	9.336392	-8.214893	-21.087847	
10	Input to HN1		Input to HN2			
11	0.63851394		1.121575388			
13	Output from HN1		Output from HN2			
14	0.65441745748		0.75428081777			
15	w'01	w'11	w'21			
16	-0.018833	0.452167	0.531239			
17		Input to OutN				
18		0.677776366				
20		Output From OutN				
21		0.663242225				
22		8.974794649				

Fig. 6. Calculation of **T** from a spreadsheet's implementation of NNt

---

[1] The true amount of information in a data set is exactly expressible by Kolmogorov's Complexity (KC) which corresponds to the most compact representation of the set under scrutiny. Since KC is known to be incomputable [12] we have chosen the PPM (Prediction by Partial Matching) algorithm as our compression standard; a good practical approximation to KC.

4   Case of Study

To illustrate the process we take the data base from the U.S. Census [14]. From the web page we get the data illustrated in Fig. 7.

Census Income Data Set

Abstract: Predict whether income exceeds $50K/yr based on census data. Also known as "Adult" dataset.

Data Set Characteristics:	Multivariate		
Attribute Characteristics:	Categorical, Integer		
Associated Tasks:	Classification		
Number of Instances:	48842	Area:	Social
Number of Attributes:	14	Date Donated	1996-05-01
Missing Values?	Yes	Number of Web Hits:	319785

Fig. 7. Characteristics of the census database

A partial view of the data set is shown in Fig. 8. This data is both numerical and categorical (i.e. non-numerical). The numerical attributes are scaled into [0, 1) and, subsequently, the non-numerical attributes were encoded into [0, 1) using the CESAMO algorithm [15]. The original DB is illustrated in Fig. 8. The corresponding encoded DB is illustrated in Fig. 9. This DB was further divided into a training data (TRN) set and a test data set (TST).

TRN was used to train (find) a polynomial and cross validated with TST. The number of terms T of the polynomial, as illustrated in Fig. 6, was originally determined to be 9. The actual resulting polynomial is illustrated in Fig. 10.

EpsiTh denotes the worst case approximation error in TST. In every column starting with the second row we find (a) The degree of the monomial, (b) The powers of the independent variables in every monomial, (c) The coefficient associated to the monomial. The value of T is 7 because the EGA may yield monomials of identical

Age	Workclass	Fnlwgt	Education	Edunum	Marstat	Occup
37	Private	146398.000000000	Bachelors	13.000000000000	Never-married	Prof-specialty
42	Private	255667.000000000	Some-college	10.000000000000	Married-civ-spouse	Craft-repair
44	Private	188331.000000000	Some-college	10.000000000000	Divorced	Exec-managerial
35	Private	54953.0000000000	HS-grad	9.000000000000	Married-civ-spouse	Craft-repair
43	State-gov	30824.0000000000	Some-college	10.000000000000	Divorced	Adm-clerical
38	Private	187069.000000000	HS-grad	9.000000000000	Married-civ-spouse	Transport-moving
20	Private	41356.0000000000	Some-college	10.000000000000	Never-married	Prof-specialty
43	State-gov	167298.000000000	HS-grad	9.000000000000	Divorced	Exec-managerial
17	Self-emp-inc	181608.000000000	10th	6.000000000000	Never-married	Sales
26	Private	160300.000000000	HS-grad	9.000000000000	Married-spouse-absen	Protective-serv
38	Private	136137.000000000	Some-college	10.000000000000	Married-civ-spouse	Exec-managerial
62	Self-emp-not-inc	204085.000000000	Some-college	10.000000000000	Married-civ-spouse	Sales
50	Self-emp-not-inc	176867.000000000	Doctorate	16.000000000000	Married-civ-spouse	Prof-specialty

Fig. 8. Partial view of the data base

Age	Workclass	Fnlwgt	Education	Edunum	Marstat	Occup
0.2739726027400000	0.73971	0.0943676131440000	0.28353	0.8000000000000000	0.84681	0.88829
0.3424657534250000	0.73971	0.1754988424570000	0.81658	0.6000000000000000	0.57252	0.17091
0.3698630136990000	0.73971	0.1255024806620000	0.81658	0.6000000000000000	0.54126	0.35263
0.2465753424660000	0.73971	0.0264705401920000	0.60314	0.5333333333330000	0.57252	0.17091
0.3561643835620000	0.81183	0.0085549792180000	0.81658	0.6000000000000000	0.54126	0.85300
0.2876712328770000	0.73971	0.1245654572480000	0.60314	0.5333333333330000	0.57252	0.02011
0.0410958904110000	0.73971	0.0163748925240000	0.81658	0.6000000000000000	0.84681	0.88829
0.3561643835620000	0.81183	0.1098856712640000	0.60314	0.5333333333330000	0.54126	0.35263
0.0000000000000000	0.61321	0.1205107148850000	0.25855	0.3333333333330000	0.84681	0.11727
0.1232876712330000	0.73971	0.1046897205120000	0.60314	0.5333333333330000	0.71390	0.95631
0.2876712328770000	0.73971	0.0867489148500000	0.81658	0.6000000000000000	0.57252	0.35263
0.6164383561640000	0.65325	0.1371996810260000	0.81658	0.6000000000000000	0.57252	0.11727

Fig. 9. Partial view of the encoded data base

monomials are odd (1, 3, 5, 7). The genetic algorithm was allowed to choose from any combination of the degrees in set L. It may be seen that it picked terms whose highest power for any one variable is 3 and the corresponding highest degree is 7.

degrees and these are merged in the end. As specified, the degrees of every one of the are odd (1, 3 ,5, 7). The genetic algorithm was allowed to choose from any combination of the degrees in set L. It may be seen that it picked terms whose highest power for any one variable is 3 and the corresponding highest degree is 7.

When the polynomial was evaluated on the test data we determined that, of the 235 tuples of TST, 231 were correctly classified for an effectiveness ratio of 93.83%.

	EpsiTh	0.385073
1	C00,00,00,00,00,00,00,00,01,00,00	0.067318
1	C01,00,00,00,00,00,00,00,00,00,00	0.602544
3	C00,02,00,00,00,00,00,01,00,00,00	0.232134
3	C00,00,00,00,03,00,00,00,00,00,00	0.362339
5	C00,00,01,01,00,00,02,00,01,00,00	3.821144
5	C00,00,00,00,03,00,00,00,00,02,00	-0.233319
7	C01,00,03,00,00,00,00,03,00,00,00	-3.679192

Fig. 10. Coefficients and degrees of the multivariate polynomial.

5 Conclusions

A method allowing us to find a polynomial model of an unknown function from a set of experimental tuples was explored. The allowed powers of the monomials in such polynomial were derived from the Universal Approximation Theorem. The coefficients of the monomials were gotten by exploring the space of such monomials with the EGA. Every individual's represented polynomial is found by the Ascent Algorithm. The AA yields the coefficients of best fit with the $L\infty$ norm. From these coefficients the L2 error is calculated and becomes the fitness function of the GA. In it, every individual represents a plausible polynomial in which the number of terms (**T**) is determined by a trained neural network (NNt) with the best value of **T** ($3 \leq$ **T** ≤ 13) for 32 representative real world data sets, i.e. 352 (11×32) polynomials were calculated. NNt yields **T** when the number of tuples, the number of attributes, the size of the compressed data set and the compression ratio are input. The method was used to solve a case study where the evaluated polynomial over the test data set yielded an effectiveness ratio of 93.83%. This illustrates a method which yields the number of terms and the coefficients and degree of every one of the independent variables for each term purely by machine learning.

References

1. Kuri-Morales, A., Cartas-Ayala, A.: Polynomial multivariate approximation with genetic algorithms. In: Sokolova, M., van Beek, P. (eds.) AI 2014. LNCS (LNAI), vol. 8436, pp. 307–312. Springer, Cham (2014). https://doi.org/10.1007/978-3-319-06483-3_30
2. Cotter, N.E.: The Stone-Weierstrass theorem and its application to neural networks. IEEE Trans. Neural Netw. **1**(4), 290–295 (1990)
3. https://archive.ics.uci.edu/ml/datasets/wine. Wine Data Set: Accessed 27 Nov 2018
4. Haykin, S.: Neural Networks: A Comprehensive Foundation. Prentice Hall PTR, Upper Saddle River (1994)
5. Bastian, M., Heymann, S., Jacomy, M.: Gephi: an open source software for exploring and manipulating networks. In: ICWSM, vol. 8, no. 2009, pp. 361–362 (2009)
6. Kuri-Morales, A.F., Aldana-Bobadilla, E., López-Peña, I.: The best genetic algorithm II. In: Castro, F., Gelbukh, A., González, M. (eds.) MICAI 2013. LNCS (LNAI), vol. 8266, pp. 16–29. Springer, Heidelberg (2013). https://doi.org/10.1007/978-3-642-45111-9_2
7. Cheney, W., Kincaid, D.: Linear Algebra: Theory and Applications. The Australian Mathematical Society, p. 110 (2009)
8. Cybenko, G.: Approximation by superpositions of a sigmoidal function. Math. Control Signals Syst. **2**(4), 303–314 (1989)
9. Dheeru, D., Karra Taniskidou, E.: UCI machine learning repository (2017). http://archive.ics.uci.edu/ml
10. Alcalá-Fdez, J., et al.: Keel data-mining software tool: data set repository, integration of algorithms and experimental analysis framework. J. Multiple-Valued Logic Soft Comput. **17** (2011)
11. Moffat, A.: Implementing the PPM data compression scheme. IEEE Trans. Commun. **38** (11), 1917–1921 (1990)
12. Vitányi, P.M.B., Li, M.: An Introduction to Kolmogorov Complexity and Its Applications. TCS, vol. 34. Springer, New York (2008). https://doi.org/10.1007/978-0-387-49820-1
13. Saw, J.G., Yang, M.C.K., Mo, T.C.: Chebyshev inequality with estimated mean and variance. Am. Stat. **38**(2), 130–132 (1984)
14. Kohavi, R., Becker, B.: Data Mining and Visualization. Silicon Graphics. https://archive.ics.uci.edu/ml/datasets/Census+Income
15. Kuri-Morales, A.: Transforming mixed data bases for machine learning: a case study. In: Batyrshin, I., Martínez-Villaseñor, M., Ponce Espinosa, H. (eds.) MICAI 2018. LNCS (LNAI), vol. 11288, pp. 157–170. Springer, Cham (2018). https://doi.org/10.1007/978-3-030-04491-6_12

Novel Leak Location Approach in Water Distribution Networks with Zone Clustering and Classification

Marcos Quiñones-Grueiro[1(✉)], Cristina Verde[2], and Orestes Llanes-Santiago[1]

[1] Departamento de Automática y Computación,
Universidad Tecnológica de la Habana, Havana, Cuba
marcosqg88@gmail.com
[2] Instituto de Ingeniería, Universidad Nacional Autónoma de México,
Mexico City, Mexico

Abstract. A novel leak location approach for large-scale water distribution networks (WDNs) is discussed in this paper. The location task is formulated as a classification problem, and it is simplified by applying a clustering strategy. Data from each class are formed by measurements associated with leakages that occur within a specific zone of the WDN. A zone is defined as a set of nodes that share similar topological properties. Therefore, clustering is performed for network partitioning. Sensors are then placed within the network for maximizing leak detection coverage, and data of each class are generated by using the EPANET hydraulic simulator. The robustness of the proposal is demonstrated for different kinds of uncertainties and measurements' noise. A real-life network is used as case study with synthetically generated field data. The proposal achieves an improved performance for the different scenarios in comparison with the node location approach.

Keywords: Leak location · Clustering · Classification · Uncertainties

1 Introduction

Water preservation is important for the future of humanity. Water distribution networks are complex nonlinear dynamic systems continuously delivering drinking water to different types of consumers. Leakages cause a significant loss in the fluid transportation system as well as additional effects, such as low pressure, for final consumers. Therefore, leakage monitoring has stimulated many researchers in recent years [9,10,13,14].

Leak location approaches have been proposed by using analytic, data-driven and mixed models. Leakages are located by analyzing the difference between measurements and synthetic data generated through a model. Analytic models of the network consider the main physical laws that describe the system's operation. Data-driven models capture the network behavior from a representative

© Springer Nature Switzerland AG 2019
J. A. Carrasco-Ochoa et al. (Eds.): MCPR 2019, LNCS 11524, pp. 37–46, 2019.
https://doi.org/10.1007/978-3-030-21077-9_4

sample of measurements obtained over varying conditions. Mixed approaches are formalized by using an analytic model and a data-driven decision tool. The latter has shown promising results recently [9].

Since it is usually considered that leaks occur in nodes, the goal of traditional location approaches is to find the leakage node [9]. Depending on the number of sensors, there can be many indistinguishable leak signatures for different nodes because of uncertainties of the model and measurement noise. As a consequence, the location problem may require many sensors for achieving a satisfactory performance in large-scale networks. Researchers have proposed as an alternative solution forming the classes by grouping nodes into zones of the network [10,13,14]. The idea of locating leaks in predefined network zones is appealing from a practical point of view because it allows the operators to narrow down the leakage location to a bounded area. Therefore, leakage search with specialized equipment is faster because there is certainty about the zone where the leak is located.

Wachla et al. proposed a set of classifiers for locating leaks in sub areas [10]. In their work, flow meters are installed at different nodes, and areas are defined by domain experts. Zhang et al. solved the zone location problem with support vector machines by considering pressure measurements [14]. Network zones are defined according to the network variables' response to leakages in different nodes. Therefore, their results depend on the network operating conditions. A similar approach was put forward by Xie et al., but linear classifiers are combined with a sparse representation for improved results [13]. The latter research explores the influence of uncertainty in the measurements and concludes that selecting the sensors' number depends on the measurement precision for a desired location accuracy. In realistic conditions, there are several sources of uncertainty associated with the hydraulic model parameters, consumers' demand and measurements' noise. None of the previously mentioned works, however, explores the impact of all these uncertainties in the location performance. Moreover, the zone partitioning results depend on the network operating conditions and leakage sizes simulated.

The main contribution of this paper is a novel leak location approach for WDNs that combines a topological clustering strategy with classification tools. Operational zones are defined by using the k-medoids method, which considers the topological parameters of the network nodes. Pressure sensors are placed for guaranteeing the detection of small leakages. Classification tools selected for the leak location task are Random Forests (RFs) and Support Vector Machines (SVMs). Both classifiers were selected because of their successful results in many papers and their different working principles. The proposed approach allows selecting a reliable and robust leak location by setting the trade-off among the number of zones, the number of sensors and the location accuracy under realistic conditions. A real large-scale network, the Modena WDN, is considered for demonstrating the advantages of the proposal against different uncertainties in comparison with recent node location approaches.

The structure of the paper is the following. The modeling framework of the WDN is introduced in Sect. 2. The zone clustering strategy is described in Sect. 3. The classification approach is outlined in Sect. 4. For demonstrating the advantages of the proposal, the Modena WDN is introduced, and the uncertain scenarios considered are detailed in Sect. 5. The results and discussion are presented in Sect. 6. Finally, conclusions and directions for future work are proposed.

2   Water Distribution Networks

Water networks are formed by n_1 junctions and n_2 nodes spatially distributed across a geographical area. Two main physical laws that govern the behavior of demand-driven WDNs are as follows: (1) the net inflow must be equal to the net outflow for any node of the network, and (2) the sum of pressure heads around any loop of the network is equal to zero. In general, leakages are considered as extra demands that occur at existing nodes according to the following equation

$$\sum_{ni=1}^{Ni} q_{ni}(t) = d_i(t) + l_i(t); \quad l_i(t) = C_e h_i(t)^\gamma \tag{1}$$

where $h_i(t)$ is the pressure head, l_i is the leakage outflow, d_i is the total demand, Ni is the number of branches connected to the node i, $q_{ni}(t)$ denotes the flow of the branch ni, C_e is the emitter coefficient size and $\gamma = 0.5$ [7]. To distinguish a leak from a demand deviation, some properties for the demand must be known. Therefore, leakage location is generally performed by monitoring flows or pressure heads during minimum night flow conditions because the demand behavior is easy to characterize.

3   Zone Clustering

The zone partitioning for WDNs is performed for many purposes. In particular, it is commonly formulated to establish district metered areas (DMAs). Clustering is usually applied to define the shape and dimension of network zones. Given a data set of topological parameters $D = \{\mathbf{c}\}_{i=1}^n$ of n nodes with $\mathbf{c} \in \Re^m$, the clustering task can be formulated as finding the z clusters of nodes $G_{j=1}^z = \mathbf{c}_1, ..., \mathbf{c}_{n_j}$ that maximize/minimize an optimization function. The three main variables considered for the $\mathbf{c}$ vector are the geographical coordinates (X,Y) and the topological height of each node. Different methods have been applied for zone division in WDNs [5]. Since uniformity is the main concern within the scope of this paper, the k-medoids clustering algorithm will be used. The optimization problem is the following

$$\min(SSE(G)) = \sum_{i=1}^z \sum_{j=1}^{n_j} \|\mathbf{c}_{n_j} - \mathbf{c}^*_i\|^2 \tag{2}$$

where $\mathbf{c}^*_i$ is the vector of parameters of a specific node and $\sum_{j=1}^{z} |G_j| = n$. Partitioning around medoids is the algorithm used in this paper for solving this optimization problem. Further details can be found in [4].

Network partitioning can be performed by using hydraulic and topological indicators to form the $\mathbf{c}$ vector. Hydraulic indicators require a hydraulic model of the network [5]. Topological indicators are normally easy for computation and use. Moreover, the shape of the network partitions obtained by employing topological indicators does not depend on the simulated network operating conditions. Therefore, the topological parameters considered for each node are its coordinates and elevation. Hence, nodes are grouped together according to their geographical locations. There are many indicators used for assessing the quality of network partitioning algorithms. Nonetheless, the criterion considered in this paper is the uniformity: a similar number of nodes throughout all the clusters. In addition, it is recommended to visually evaluate the results since the partitioning and the linkage among clusters can be analyzed intuitively [6].

4   Classification Tools

A mixed model/data-driven leak location strategy is described next. The estimated consumer demands $\tilde{\mathbf{x}} = \tilde{\mathbf{d}} \in \Re^N$ are used for generating the system's response $\tilde{\mathbf{y}} \in \Re^p$ by using the nominal analytic hydraulic model. The measured variables from the real network can be flows $\mathbf{q} \in \Re^{n_1}$ in n_1 pipes and pressure $\mathbf{h} \in \Re^{n_2}$ at n_2 nodes such that $\mathbf{y} = [\mathbf{q}, \mathbf{h}] \in \Re^{p=n_1+n_2}$. It is considered that single leaks $\Omega = \{\mathbf{l_1}, \mathbf{l_2}, ..., \mathbf{l_z}\}$ can occur at any of the z network nodes. Thus, a residual vector $\mathbf{r} \in \Re^p$ (with p as the number of sensors installed in the network) provides a leakage signature according to the leakage location. From a pattern recognition point of view, the classification task consists of mapping the feature space ($\mathbf{r}$) onto a set of z classes (leak location $\tilde{\mathbf{l}}_i$) by using a decision function: $g(\mathbf{r}): \Re^p \rightarrow \Omega$. The parameters of $g(\mathbf{r})$ are then estimated off-line by sampling from the classes population according to the *learning from examples* paradigm [3]. Two classification tools selected in this paper are described next.

4.1   Random Forests

Random forests is a machine learning method used for classification and regression [1]. In the former task, an ensemble of decision trees is used for making the class decision. A single decision tree is a recursive and partition-based classifier. This classifier splits the data space into regions by using axis-parallel hyperplanes

$$g(\mathbf{r}) = \mathbf{w}^T \mathbf{r} + b \tag{3}$$

where $\mathbf{w}$ and b (bias) are used to define the hyperplane position; and $\mathbf{r} \in \mathbb{R}^p$ denotes a measurement vector. The value of $\mathbf{w}$ is restricted *a priori* to one of the standard basis vectors $\mathbf{e_1}, ..., \mathbf{e_p}$, where $\mathbf{e_1} \in \mathbb{R}^p$ has a 1 for the j dimension and 0 for the others. A hyperplane specifies a decision or split point. The selection of split points is made in this work by minimizing the measure known as the Gini diversity index.

The ensemble is formed by a number of decision trees built by applying two preprocessing operations on the original data set: bootstrapping and random feature selection. The former consists of generating training sets by randomly sampling with replacement from the original data set. The latter is randomly selecting a limited number of features at each node when building the tree without pruning. Once a large number of trees are built, new data are classified by aggregating the outputs of all trees by applying a majority voting strategy. While individual decision trees tend to overfit, random forests present a good generalization performance thanks to the previous two operations. The number of variables randomly selected for each tree in this work is the square root of the number of variables.

4.2 Support Vector Machines

The objective behind the support vector machine method is defining the optimal separating hyperplane that maximizes the margin w among the closest observations of two different classes that form a data set. These observations are called support vectors [8]. The separating hyperplane $g(\mathbf{r})$ of two classes is defined with Eq. (3), but the values of w are not restricted as in decision trees. Conversely, w and b are defined by solving the following dual optimization problem

$$\max \ W(\mathbf{a}) = \left(\sum_{i=1}^{m} a_i - \frac{1}{2} \sum_{i,j=0}^{m} a_i a_j g_i g_j \, K(\mathbf{r_i}, \mathbf{r_j}) \right)$$

$$\text{subject to} \ \sum_i g_i a_i = 0; \quad 0 \leq a_i \leq C \tag{4}$$

where C represents the error penalty, $\mathbf{a} \in \Re^m$ are the Lagrange multipliers, m is the number of training examples that form the data set $X \in \{\mathbf{r_i}, \mathbf{y_i}\}^m$ with the label vector $\mathbf{y} \in \{1, -1\}$, and $K(\mathbf{r_i}, \mathbf{r_j})$ is a kernel function that allows access to spaces of higher dimensions. The Radial Basis Function kernel is selected in this work because of its generality and successful results. The extension of this method to multi-class classification problems is developed by applying discriminant strategies. The one-against-one approach is selected in this work.

5   Case Study: Modena Network

The Modena network is a reduced version of the WDN of the medium-sized Italian city. It is formed by 317 pipes and 268 demand nodes with a required minimum pressure head of 20 m. The network is gravity-fed by four reservoirs, and it is completely looped as shown in Fig. 1. The pipe diameters are set according to [11]. Pressure head sensors are used here because they are cheaper and easier to install and maintain than flow meters. The location of the sensors is selected by maximizing the leak detection coverage. The *Darwin Sampler* tool was used for placing a specific number of sensors [12]. Single leakage events are generated by considering the minimum leak size that is desired to be located. This occurs for an emitter coefficient at each node with a magnitude of 0.1. The sensitivity selected for pressure head sensors is 0.01 m. The number of leakage scenarios is selected as three times the number of network nodes (1000 leakage scenarios) according to the software's recommendation.

5.1 Uncertainty Simulation for Realistic Scenarios

A steady-state simulation of the network is performed with the package EPANET [7] coupled with $MATLAB^©$. A sampling period of 15 min is considered, and hourly average values of the measurements are used for leak location, which aims to reduce the uncertainty effect [9]. A total of 120 samples (hourly averages) are generated for each node by considering minimum night flow conditions, but the final data set is formed by grouping the nodes' data corresponding to each class according to the zones' distribution. The uncertainty effects are obtained by using the following equation

$$\theta_r = \theta_t + \theta_u \tag{5}$$

where θ_r represents the uncertain parameter and θ_t and θ_u are the true and the added uncertainty, respectively. All values of θ_u are generated from a uniformly sampled distribution. The following unknown disturbances are all simulated for resembling real conditions

1. Leak size variability. Uncertainty is related to the emitter coefficient size that is considered within the range $C_e \in [0.1, 2]$. The outflow of leakages is between 0.5 lps and 12 lps (approximately 0.1% to 3% of the network's total demand).
2. Measurements uncertainty. Measurements are corrupted with 5% noise amplitude.
3. Pipe roughness uncertainty. Hazen-Williams coefficient (CHW) uncertainty is simulated for $CHW \in [125, 130]$.
4. Estimated demand uncertainty. An uncertain demand is considered with 10% amplitude around the nominal consumption of each node.

6 Results and Discussion

Performance measures for classification problems are usually calculated by using a confusion matrix $A = [A(i,j)]$. The element (i,j) of A represents the observations with the true class label i, which are classified as class j. Location performance is estimated by considering the identification of leaky nodes within the specific predefined zone where they belong. Thus, the percentage of data that has been correctly classified determines the overall accuracy (Ac). Given z zones, Ac is computed according to $Ac = \frac{1}{m} \sum_{i=1}^{z} A(i,i)$ where m is the number of observations.

The parameters of the classifiers are set by using 10-fold cross validation. The accuracy displayed in the figures is estimated by using the test data that have not been used for adjusting the parameters. For the RFs classifier, the number of trees is adjusted to 100 by analyzing the out-of-bag error improvement. This large number of trees may take a long time to prepare off-line, but the classifier will not overfit [1]. For the SVM classifier, the parameters $\{C, \sigma\}$ were adjusted for each scenario by using a grid search for the interval $C \in 2^{\eta}$, $\eta \in [-2, 5]$ and $\gamma \in 2^{\eta}$, $\eta \in [-5, 3]$. The LIBSVM library was used for this purpose [2]. Since minimum night flow (MNF) conditions usually last for six hours (12 a.m. to 6 a.m.), the Bayes rule can be applied to the probable leak locations throughout a time window of up to six observations to obtain the leak location decision [9].

Zone clustering results for 5 and 25 zones are presented in Fig. 1. As it is observed, the network partitioning is reasonable from a practical point of view. The number of nodes per zone for the clustering of 5 and 25 zones is observed in Fig. 2. When the number of zones increases, the uniformity of the node distribution improves. The performance of the proposed approach depends on two elements: the number of pressure sensors and the number of zones. The desired result is a satisfactory accuracy of over 90% to guarantee the reliability of the location method for the network operators. It is useless to implement a method with poor performance because operators will ignore its results in the long term. There is a trade-off among the sensors, zones and accuracy that is shown in Fig. 3.

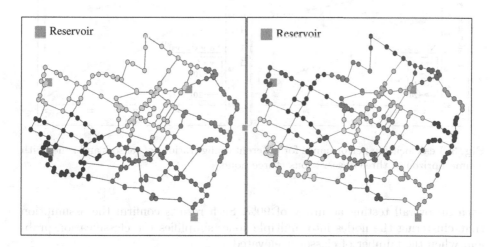

Fig. 1. Zone clustering results with topological parameters and the k-medoids method for 5 (left) and 25 zones (right)

Leak location performance degrades depending on the number of pressure sensors available. When 5 sensors are placed, only 5 leakage zones can be distinguished with a satisfactory performance by using both classifiers. When the number of sensors increases to 10, up to 15 leakage zones can then be isolated

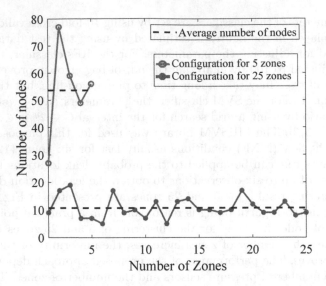

Fig. 2. Node uniformity with respect to the number of zones

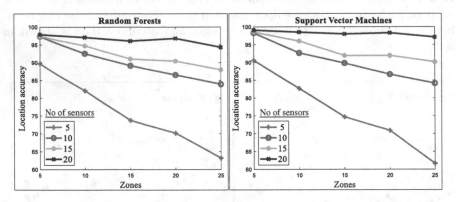

Fig. 3. Leak location performance for different configurations of sensors and zones with a time horizon of three observations (three hours)

with an overall testing accuracy of 90%. Such results confirm the assumption that clustering the nodes into multiple zones simplifies the classification problem when the number of classes is elevated.

To compare the results obtained by using the proposal presented in this paper with the node location approach proposed in [9], some simulations are developed by employing the SVM classifier. The leak location results are shown in Fig. 4. For 5 sensors only 58% accuracy can be achieved by considering a time horizon of 24 observations. Even for 25 sensors, the top performance is 83% for 24 observations. This implies requiring data from four days (considering that minimum night flow conditions last six hours in the best case) for making a decision. With the proposal only 10 sensors are required for making a decision with 90% location accuracy. Therefore, it presents a superior reliability and lower cost. Moreover, since only data from one day are required, the location decision is performed in less time than with the node location approach where data from four days are necessary.

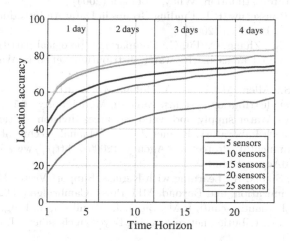

Fig. 4. Leak node location performance for a varying time horizon under MNF conditions by using the SVM classifier with the approach proposed in [9]

7 Conclusions

In this paper, a novel leak location method based on network zones is presented. The proposal uses a topological clustering strategy to divide the WDN in logical zones from a practical point of view and combines this clustering strategy with classification tools for obtaining a satisfactory performance in the leak location against uncertainties. The proposal allows establishing an adequate relation between the number of zones and the number of sensors to be used in the leak location assessment. The simulated experiments with a real network demonstrate that it is possible to obtain a reliable leak location with fewer sensors and within a shorter time horizon than other recently proposed leak location methods. The latter represents superior reliability and lower costs in the leak location task.

Acknowledgments. This work is supported by IT100519-DGAPA-UNAM and 280170conv2016-3 SENER-CONACYT, Fondo Sectorial CONACyT-Secretaría de Energía-Hidrocarburos.

References

1. Breiman, L.: Random forests. Mach. Learn. **45**(1), 5–32 (2001)
2. Chang, C., Lin, C.: LIBSVM: a library for support vector machines. ACM Trans. Intell. Syst. Technol. **2**(3), 1–27 (2011)
3. Heijden, F.V.D., Duin, R., Ridder, D.D., Tax, D.: Classification, Parameter Estimation and State Estimation. Wiley, Hoboken (2004)
4. Kaufman, L., Rousseeuw, P.J.: Finding Groups in Data: An Introduction to Cluster Analysis. Wiley, Hoboken (2009)
5. Liu, H., Zhao, M., Zhang, C., Fu, G.: Comparing topological partitioning methods for district metered areas in the water distribution network. Water **10**(4), 368 (2018)
6. Perelman, L.S., Allen, M., Preis, A., Iqbal, M., Whittle, A.J.: Automated subzoning of water distribution systems. Environ. Model. Softw. **65**, 1–14 (2015)
7. Rossman, L.A.: Water supply and water resources division. National Risk Management Research Laboratory. Epanet 2 User's Manual. Technical report, United States Environmental Protection Agency (2000). http://www.epa.gov/nrmrl/wswrd/dw/%0Aepanet.html
8. Scholkopf, B., Smola, A.: Learning with Kernels: Support Vector Machines, Regularization Optimization, and Beyond. MIT Press, Cambridge (2002)
9. Soldevila, A., Fernandez-canti, R.M., Blesa, J., Tornil-sin, S., Puig, V.: Leak localization in water distribution networks using Bayesian classifiers. J. Process Control **55**, 1–9 (2017)
10. Wachla, D., Przystalka, P., Moczulski, W., Wachla, D., Przystalka, P., Moczulski, W.: A method of leakage location in water distribution networks using artificial neuro-fuzzy system. IFAC-PapersOnLine **48**(21), 1216–1223 (2015)
11. Wang, Q., Guidolin, M., Savic, D., Kapelan, Z.: Two-objective design of benchmark problems of a water distribution system via MOEAs: towards the best-known approximation of the true pareto front. J. Water Resour. Plan. Manag. **141**(3), 1–14 (2015)
12. Wu, Z., Wang, Q., Butala, S., Mi, T., Song, Y.: Darwin optimization user manual. Technical report, Bentley Systems, Incorporated, Applied Research Group (2012)
13. Xie, X., Hou, D., Tang, X., Zhang, H.: Leakage identification in water distribution networks with error tolerance capability. Water Resour. Manag. **33**(3), 1233–1247 (2019)
14. Zhang, Q., Wu, Z.Y., Zhao, M., Qi, J.: Leakage zone identification in large-scale water distribution systems using multiclass support vector machines. J. Water Resour. Plan. Manag. **142**(11), 04016042 (2016)

Convolutional Genetic Programming

Lino Rodriguez-Coayahuitl$^{(\boxtimes)}$ ⓘ, Alicia Morales-Reyes ⓘ,
and Hugo Jair Escalante ⓘ

Instituto Nacional de Astrofísica, Óptica y Electrónica,
Sta. Ma. Tonantzintla, 72840 Puebla, Mexico
{linobi,a.morales,hugojair}@inaoep.mx

Abstract. In recent years Convolutional Neural Networks (CNN) have come to dominate many machine learning tasks, specially those related to image analysis, such as object recognition. Herein we explore the possibility of developing image denoising filters by stacking multiple Genetic Programming (GP) syntax trees, in a similar fashion to how CNNs are designed. We test the evolved filters performance in removing additive Gaussian noise. Results show that GP is able to generate a diverse set of feature maps at the 'hidden' layers of the proposed architecture. Although more research is required to validate the suitability of GP for image denoising, our work set the basis for bridging the gap between deep learning and evolutionary computation.

Keywords: Deep Genetic Programming ·
Evolutionary machine learning · Genetic Programming ·
Image filtering · Deep Learning

1 Introduction

Convolutional Neural Networks (CNN) are a type of connectionist machine learning (ML) algorithms particularly adept at image processing tasks [9]. This is thanks to a clever architectural design that allows them to scale well to high dimensionality problems. In recent years, CNN and Deep Neural Networks (DNN) in general have achieved record performance in typical ML tasks such as classification and regression, outclassing both systems handcrafted by human experts of the problem's domain and ML systems based on techniques other than CNN [8]. DNN have achieved this performance thanks to an ever increasing number of stacked convolutional layers [7,13].

Herein we explore the possibility to implement the fundamental architecture of CNN through a different algorithmic paradigm, Genetic Programming (GP) [6]. GP is an evolutionary algorithm typically used for ML tasks. In GP a population of solutions (often encoding models) is evolved by using mutation and crossover operators. GP is known to be suitable for modeling highly complex functions, hence we think it is appealing to mimic tasks approached by CNN.

The motivation to follow CNNs' architectural design through GP is twofold: first, we wish to explore the idea of replacing neurons in CNNs with GP syntax

J. A. Carrasco-Ochoa et al. (Eds.): MCPR 2019, LNCS 11524, pp. 47–57, 2019.
https://doi.org/10.1007/978-3-030-21077-9_5

trees, as we believe they have the same, or even higher, computational power than that of CNN's neurons; and secondly due to the fact that GP does not scale well to high dimensionality problems [3], and we suspect it might benefit from CNNs' architectural design.

In order to test the proposed approach, we tackle the problem of image denoising. The purpose of image denoising is to recover a clean image from a contaminated one. The contamination model may be of different kinds. In this work we attempt to clean images from additive Gaussian noise, which is a fairly standard problem targeted by CNN models.

The main contributions of this work are as follows:

- We introduce a novel GP-based method for image denoising filters that operates at pixel level.
- We propose a multi-layer convolutional GP architecture.
- We propose different training/evolution mechanisms to suit the proposed multi-layer convolutional GP architecture.
- We compare the performance of the evolved GP filters to that of recent DNN.

The implicit relevance of this work lies in the fact that for the first time, to the best of the authors' knowledge, we establish in a quantitative manner, the performance gap between evolutionary algorithms/GP and Deep Learning. Many other works related to this subject have avoided such direct comparison.

2   Background

2.1   Genetic Programming

GP is an evolutionary algorithm that iteratively modifies a population of candidate solutions to the problem at hand. These candidate solutions are called individuals. Each individual's performance is tested against a training dataset; the best individuals are selected to reproduce through the use of genetic operations, i.e. generate slightly modified versions of themselves; these new solutions are also evaluated and the best performing replace the worst from current ones, leading to a new generation of individuals. This process repeats until a stop criterion is met. Canonical individuals in GP are syntax trees that represent a mathematical function or simple computer programs [6,10]. Internal nodes in these trees are basic functions called primitives, while leaf nodes are constants or feature variables from the instance being processed. In this way, data flows from bottom nodes to the top root node where the final output is generated. Figure 1 shows an example of a tree structure that represents the function $f(x, y) = (2.2 - (\frac{x}{11})) + (7 * \cos(y))$ [2].

Problems with high dimensionality inputs, such as in the case of image processing tasks, are challenging for ML algorithms for several reasons, such as time complexity issues, the *curse of dimensionality* [1], and the large number of parameters that need to be tuned within algorithms to work properly when faced with such high dimensionality problems.

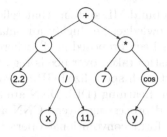

Fig. 1. Typical tree structures used in GP to represent candidate solutions.

In the case of GP, high dimensionality issues arise due the nature canonical individual representation itself. Notice how trees depth has to increase in order to accommodate more input features at leaf nodes. Larger trees means an exponentially growing search space of candidate solutions, that eventually becomes intractable.

2.2 Image Denoising

The problem of image denoising is defined as follows: extract a clean image $\mathbf{x}$ from a noisy observation $\mathbf{y}$ such that $\mathbf{y} = \mathbf{x} + \mathbf{v}$, where $\mathbf{v}$ is a contamination process; a typical example is when $\mathbf{v}$ follows a Gaussian distribution with some given σ, which case is known as Additive Gaussian Noise (AWGN). Figure 2 shows a noisy image contaminated with AWGN, as well as a clean version of it we wish to recover through image denoising.

Fig. 2. (a) Image contaminated with AWGN; (b) clean image.

3 Related Work

GP has been successfully used in the past to synthesize image filters. Examples of those works can be found in [5,16]. However, they rely on a modified version of the canonical GP individual such that primitive functions may include already specialized image filters or at least well known image processing functions. This is undesirable if we wish to build ML systems that relies as little as possible on domain human expert's knowledge, i.e. highly automated learning systems. A more agnostic approach has been proposed in [4], where terminals of the syntax trees consist of simple statistics taken over pixels regions.

It is relevant to contrast such specialized GP approaches with recent developments in the area of Deep Learning (DL). DNN are artificial neural networks composed by several stacked processing layers. CNN are a type of DNN where these processing layers perform convolutional operations. Each convolutional layer is made of linear approximators coupled with a non-linear transformation. There is really nothing specialized regarding image processing in the architecture of DNN other than the use of convolution to efficiently process images. DnCNN [17] is a recent DNN designed to tackle image denoising; its flexibility is such that, by just switching the dataset with which is trained, the same network can learn to remove vastly different types of noises such as Gaussian noises with different or unknown levels of deviation, deblocking artifacts, and can even perform super resolution. DnCNN is competitive with fully and partially handcrafted image filters designed by human experts.

In more general terms, high dimensionality issues have been long acknowledged in the GP community [3]. Standard approaches to tackle such issues generally involve grouping input features in one way or another, process each cluster separately, and then attempt to assemble a joint global solution [11,15]. In [11], authors proposed a GP autoencoder that generated a compact representation of an input image and could decode the original image from the compact representation. The proposed autoencoder relied on the canonical GP individual representation. In order to use the proposed GP autoencoder on images, it was required to partition the input images in small groups of neighboring pixels that are processed independently in isolated GPs. Even though this approach allowed GP to process a large enough input such as images, it is still not the most efficient approach, since isolated GPs did not share information with neighboring GP processes and such many independent GP required vast amounts of memory and processing power.

Our work draws inspiration from CNN and propose a single sliding GP window that swipes an input image for processing, instead of many multiple independent GP processes.

4   A Convolutional GP for Image Denoising

Our approach to evolve image denoising filters through GP is to leverage from the CNN architecture, where we replace neurons with GP syntax trees. Initially we propose to evolve a single syntax tree that acts as image filter by sliding over a noisy input image and cleaning it pixel by pixel. Thereafter, we propose to stack multiple layers of these GP filters. We explain the theoretical advantages of stacking filters in this manner further below in this section.

4.1   Single Layer Convolutional GP Filter

We propose to use a standard GP individual representation, i.e. a syntax tree, to act as an image filter. This filter operates over a small window region of $d \times d$ pixels, with d an odd number, receiving as input pixels within such region, and returning as output a single value that is the level of noise of the central pixel in the operating window. In order to filter a whole image, the window is slid over the entire image, generating a residual image with the same size of the input image that we want to clean of noise. Figure 3a shows a depiction of the proposed GP filter. This residual image represents the (estimated) level of noise of each pixel that composes the input image. In order to retrieve an approximation of the clean image, we subtract the residual image from the noisy input.

The leaf nodes of the GP individual should be the individual pixels in the region being processed, or constants values within some range. The primitives can be any function that can operate at this individual pixel level. This is done in this way to avoid the use of any image filtering expert's knowledge.

4.2   Multi-layer Convolutional GP

Additionally, we also propose to stack multiple of these sliding GP filters, both in parallel and in series, since DNN are actually designed this way. That is, instead of using a single GP syntax tree that filters the image, we can slide multiple, different, GP syntax trees that generate as output several *feature maps*, which are intermediate transformations of the input that may be useful for generating the desired output. All these feature maps form a volume of codified information that is further processed by another GP tree that generates the final output, i.e. the residual image. Figure 3b shows a GP filter architecture composed of two stacked filter in series, while Fig. 3c depicts an architecture with multiple GP filters both in series and in parallel.

Stacking these convolutional filters in series carries the advantage of increasing the *receptive field*. This means that if we use two sliding filter with windows of 3×3 in series, when we reconstruct the central pixel at the output of the second filter, we are actually using information of a 5×5 window size around it (this is as along as the first filter did manage to codify information at feature map it outputs). On the other hand, stacking filters in parallel per layer allows to generate more than one feature map at each layer. Each feature map might codify different information useful for the next layer of processing.

The canonical form of GP contemplates individuals that are composed of a single syntax tree. In our proposed method, in the case of multiple stacked filters, we would need to evolve more than a single GP tree. Although there do exists GP individual representations based on forests (multiple trees), in this type of representations the trees are loosely dependent on each other, whereas in the multilayer architecture we are proposing here, the filter trees series rely completely on the output generated by the previous trees in the structure.

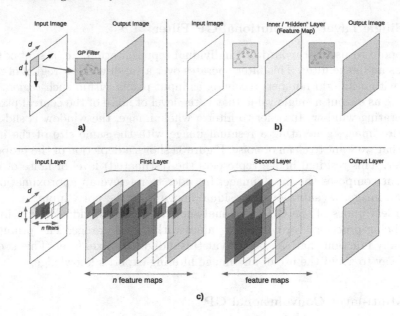

Fig. 3. Multilayer GP architecture. (a) Single layer, single filter; (b) Two layer, one filter per layer; (c) Three layer, first and second layers with n filters, third layer with only 1, output, filter.

4.3   Evolving Multiple Layers of Convolutional GP Filters

In order to train this complex architecture, we propose three different approaches: (**straightforward**) define the GP individual as the entire set of trees across all layers, evolve individuals by applying genetic operations layer-wise; (**sequential**) evolve the multi-layer structure sequentially, i.e. evolve the first layer for fixed number of generations; once this first evolution is finished, the second layer of filters are evolved, which take as input a cleaner version of the noisy image generated by the first layer, and so on; (**ensamble**) the third approach is based on the idea that the multiple feature maps at the penultimate layer might actually act as ensamble learner, with the last layer only performing the mean function, so in this architecture we enforce this behavior by taking as output the mean over the feature maps of the last layer. Figure 4 illustrates these three variants.

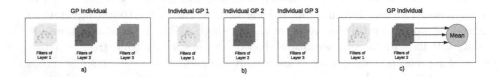

Fig. 4. Different possible GP individual representations for multilayer GP filters.

5   Experimental Results and Analysis

In this section we present and discuss experimental results of different variants of the proposed method.

5.1   Training and Testing Datasets

We generated the training data following the work of [17]. From the Berkeley Segmentation Dataset [12] we extracted 19,200 unique 40×40 image patches for training purposes. For testing, we use the same classic image processing set used in [5,16,17], composed of well-known pictures such as "Lena" and "Boats". A total of 12 (seven 256×256 and five 512×512) pictures were used for testing. We contaminated both training patches and testing images by adding them noise masks generated with a Gaussian distribution of $\sigma = 25$. All training and testing was performed on grayscale images.

5.2   Evolutionary Algorithm Setup

For all experiments we used a multi-population, island based, model [14]. We used a population of 500 individuals split across 5 islands each with 100 individuals. We used an heterogeneous and asynchronous [14] model where each island had different crossover/mutation probabilities, and every 10 generations send their top 10 performing individuals to another, randomly selected, island (migration). Crossover/mutation probabilities were set as follow for each island: [0.9/0.1, 0.7/0.3, 0.5/0.5, 0.3/0.7, 0.1/0.9]. The set of primitives used consist on binary arithmetic operators, $[+, -, \times, \div]$, binary functions max, min, $mean$, and unary functions x^2, x^3, and Rectifier Linear Units (ReLUs).

We used an on-line form of learning defined in [11]. We partitioned the entire training dataset into mini-batches of 60 samples, and use one mini-batch per evolutionary cycle for evaluating both individuals and offspring generated. We used a steady state population replacement policy. As fitness function we used the minimization of the mean square error (MSE) between the predicted noise level and the actual noise level to drive the evolution of all systems proposed.

5.3   Results

We tested two Single Layer Convolutional GP, one consisting in a sliding window of 3×3 pixels, and another with a window of 5×5 pixels. We tested three different Multi-layer Convolutional GP, each under one of the three different proposed methods for evolving multi-layer GPs. All Multi-layer architectures consisted in only 2 layers (2 layers + mean, for the ensemble method). Both straightforward and sequential architectures were composed of 3 filters at the first layer, and 1 filter in the second layer (3 filters in both layers for the ensemble method). All filters were 3×3 windows. Table 1 shows results obtained by different tested approaches. We include in Table 1 unfiltered noisy images values (to understand how much the proposed approaches actually denoise images), as well as DnCNN network performance [17], to fully appreciate how far GP is from modern DNN. These results were obtained on the same testing dataset for all approaches (including DnCNN), and using the same training dataset (also applies for DnCNN). All GP approaches were given the same computational time[1]. Therefore these results are based on a comparison as fair as possible. For completion, Fig. 5 shows the performance of a 2-Layer, sequentially evolved variant GP, on ten training patches. We found no visually appreciable difference between this output and the one from a single layer GP.

Table 1. Average performance of all convolutional GP architectures tested. Values expressed in decibels. Higher is better.

Noisy Image	Single GP, 3×3	Single GP, 5×5	Strfwd-GP (2 Layers)	Sequential GP (2 Layers)	Ensamble (2L + Mean)	DnCnn
20.32	25.96	25.07	25.22	25.93	23.60	30.43

5.4 Additional Results and Discussion

We also performed experiment using 10 filters per layer for the Multi-layer GP architectures. Although we found them to be consistently inferior in performance to the 3 filters per layer reported above, we found that these GP variants generated interesting patterns in the hidden layer. Figure 6 shows feature maps generated by ten filters for ten different training patches. Some feature maps appear to be signaling borders or other points of interest.

Fig. 5. Visual results of the output generated by a 2-Layer convolutional, sequentially evolved, GP. From top to bottom: original images, noisy samples, filtered images.

Results shows that GP can successfully synthesize image denoising filters, even though none of the proposed methods allows GP to benefit from a multi-layer convolutional architecture, thus positioning a single layer GP filter as the

---

[1] DnCNN runs in less time than GP, due to being accelerated in GPU and implemented in highly optimized DL software libraries.

reference method-to-beat in future works based on GP. Results also confirm that GP struggles with high dimensionality problems. In this case, a single layer 5×5 window GP filter does not performs any better, if not worse, than a 3×3 window one, even though the first one has more than twice context information that theoretically should allow it to perform a better filtering.

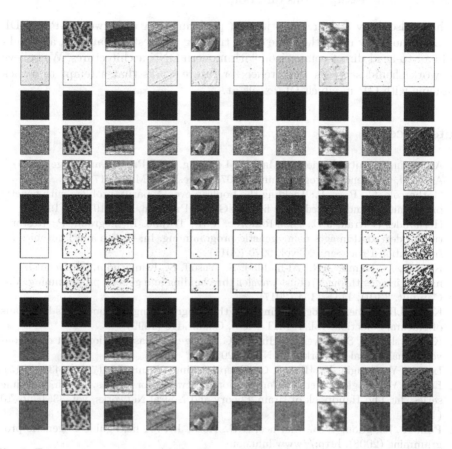

Fig. 6. Feature maps generated by a 2-layer GP in the hidden layer given 10 different input patches and 10 evolved GP filters in the hidden layer. From top to bottom: first row, 10 different noisy patches; rows 2 to 10, feature maps generated; last row, filtered final output.

6 Conclusions

We introduced a method to evolve image denoising filters with GP, through an architecture inspired by CNN. Our results have confirmed that:

– GP is a viable method to synthesize image denoising filters, even when processing images at individual pixel level.
– GP struggles with high dimensionality problems, since it cannot make use of input samples with as low as 25 features.
– GP cannot directly benefit from a stacked convolutional architecture. More research is necessary in this direction.

We have also draw a clear, quantitative, performance gap between GP and DL based methods, by using the same exact training and testing datasets, and making head-to-head direct comparison with modern DNN architectures. We believe this work should serve as a reference for future works that attempt to attack problems with GP in which DL excels at.

References

1. Alpaydin, E.: Introduction to Machine Learning. MIT Press, Cambridge (2009)
2. Axelrod, B.: Genetic programming (2007). Accessed 5 May 2017
3. Gathercole, C., Ross, P.: Tackling the boolean even N parity problem with genetic programming and limited-error fitness. Genet. Program. **97**, 119–127 (1997)
4. Hernández-Beltrán, J.E., Díaz-Ramírez, V.H., Trujillo, L., Legrand, P.: Restoration of degraded images using genetic programming. In: Optics and Photonics for Information Processing X, vol. 9970 (2016)
5. Khmag, A., Ramli, A.R., Al-haddad, S., Yusoff, S., Kamarudin, N.: Denoising of natural images through robust wavelet thresholding and genetic programming. Vis. Comput. **33**(9), 1141–1154 (2017)
6. Koza, J.R.: Genetic Programming: On the Programming of Computers by means of Natural Selection, vol. 1. MIT Press, Cambridge (1992)
7. Krizhevsky, A., Sutskever, I., Hinton, G.: ImageNet classification with deep convolutional neural networks. In: NIPS (2012)
8. LeCun, Y., Bengio, Y., Hinton, G.: Deep learning. Nature **521**(7553), 436 (2015)
9. LeCun, Y., Bengio, Y., et al.: Convolutional networks for images, speech, and time series. In: The Handbook of Brain Theory and Neural Networks, vol. 3361, no. 10 (1995)
10. Poli, R., Langdon, W.B., McPhee, N.F., Koza, J.R.: A field guide to genetic programming (2008). http://www.lulu.com
11. Rodriguez-Coayahuitl, L., Morales-Reyes, A., Escalante, H.J.: Structurally layered representation learning: towards deep learning through genetic programming. In: Castelli, M., Sekanina, L., Zhang, M., Cagnoni, S., García-Sánchez, P. (eds.) EuroGP 2018. LNCS, vol. 10781, pp. 271–288. Springer, Cham (2018). https://doi.org/10.1007/978-3-319-77553-1_17
12. Roth, S., Black, M.J.: Fields of experts: a framework for learning image priors. In: Null, pp. 860–867. IEEE (2005)
13. Szegedy, C., et al.: Going deeper with convolutions. In: Proceedings of CVPR, pp. 1–9 (2015)
14. Tomassini, M.: Spatially Structured Evolutionary Algorithms: Artificial Evolution in Space and Time. Springer, Heidelberg (2006). https://doi.org/10.1007/3-540-29938-6

15. Tran, B., Xue, B., Zhang, M.: Using feature clustering for GP-based feature construction on high-dimensional data. In: McDermott, J., Castelli, M., Sekanina, L., Haasdijk, E., García-Sánchez, P. (eds.) EuroGP 2017. LNCS, vol. 10196, pp. 210–226. Springer, Cham (2017). https://doi.org/10.1007/978-3-319-55696-3_14
16. Yan, R., Shao, L., Liu, L., Liu, Y.: Natural image denoising using evolved local adaptive filters. Sig. Process. **103**, 36–44 (2014)
17. Zhang, K., Zuo, W., Chen, Y., Meng, D., Zhang, L.: Beyond a gaussian denoiser: residual learning of deep CNN for image denoising. TIP **26**(7), 3142–3155 (2017)

Methods for Procedural Terrain Generation: A Review

Luis Oswaldo Valencia-Rosado$^{(\boxtimes)}$ and Oleg Starostenko

Department of Computing, Electronics and Mechatronics,
Universidad de las Américas Puebla, San Andrés Cholula, 72810 Puebla, Mexico
{luis.valencia, oleg.starostenko}@udlap.mx

Abstract. Advances in computer graphics allow to simulate ever growing virtual worlds with a higher level of realism which can even be created in real time. An integral part of these worlds are the terrains which are the physical features of the land. Despite the capabilities of modern computer systems, the creation process still demands high amounts of man-hours. To automatically generate coherent, realistic-looking and useful content is still and open problem, and research focuses on how to automatize these processes while allowing users to exert a certain degree on control over the generated content. This survey goes over the different techniques used for the automatic generation of terrains, which include different land formations such as mountains, valleys, rivers, shores, etc. These terrains have different uses such as simulation or entertainment which translates on different needs over the desired realism of the terrain and the degree of control that users have. Through time, different approaches have been proposed: repeating patterns that resemble those seen in nature; using software agents that imitate geological processes; using artificial intelligence techniques for pattern recognition and imitation of landscapes; or allowing users to interact with the system to draw desired terrain features. This review presents an overview of the area and discusses how different techniques adapt to the different needs and different stages of terrain creation.

Keywords: Automatic · Virtual · Landscape · Simulation · Videogames

1   Introduction

Procedural generation started as a solution for the constraints on memory availability when programming videogames: instead of saving all assets, just seeds and instructions would be saved. During the 80s, studies about the mathematical behavior of natural occurrences kicked-off several works, among them was the simulation of terrains, this is the inception of the area of Procedural Terrain Generation (PTG). Procedural generation refers to assets being automatically produced by a computer system, or with limited human input. The goal is to save time and resources through automatization [1].

The aim of this review is to provide an updated general overview of the procedural terrain generation area; without being too specific as in [2] where only evolutionary algorithms are presented or [3] which is focused on noise based methods; or too ample like in [4] and [5] where full videogames or virtual worlds are considered.

© Springer Nature Switzerland AG 2019
J. A. Carrasco-Ochoa et al. (Eds.): MCPR 2019, LNCS 11524, pp. 58–67, 2019.
https://doi.org/10.1007/978-3-030-21077-9_6

As noted in [2] the evaluation of the terrains is difficult. Execution-time comparisons are not always reported and depend not only on hardware, but on the size of the generated terrain and level of detail. Also, authors use different rendering algorithms, some do not use textures and only present the geometrical features of the terrains. Therefore, comparisons over quality cannot be objective. Hence, instead of a direct comparison, a taxonomy focusing on the generative capabilities of the algorithms is proposed.

In Sect. 2 the uses of the terrains, the generation methods and the taxonomy will be presented. In Sect. 3 there will be a discussion about the uses the methods. Finally, in Sect. 4 are the conclusions.

2 Terrain Classification

2.1 Uses of Terrains

Virtual terrains are used for videogames, simulations, movies and animations [6]. For simulations, real-world accuracy is necessary in terms of positions and spatial relations between features. If the simulation will be used for training, such as in self-driving cars, the level of detail needs to be as high as possible. In the case of movies only a single angle needs to be created, but it needs to look as realistic as possible. For animation, the above is true, but instead of realism, the terrain should be able to adapt to a desired aesthetic. In videogames the traversability is a desirable feature, this is that the players are able to traverse the terrain [7]. This is true for most games as there should be at least one route that the player can follow.

2.2 Generation Methods

There are four different families of generation techniques, they are the stochastic methods, the simulation methods, leaning methods and sketch-based methods. As shown in Table 1 each family comprises several methods.

Stochastic Methods. These methods use construction rules and parameters that try to imitate natural randomness, these rules could be applied recursively to increase detail. Control is exerted through these parameters and rules. Although these methods are very fast, they lack enough control and features are generated at random positions.

Fractal Methods. Fractals are geometric figures where each one of its parts has the same statistical character as the whole. These are created by repeating an instruction over an initial figure. The work of Prusinkiewicz [8] is one of the earliest fractal methods that could produce more than one type of landscape feature, it uses the midpoint displacement algorithm for generating mountains and squig curves for rivers. Chaotic fractals or noise can be used to create heightmaps that resemble natural terrains. Approximations of Perlin noise and fractional Brownian motion (fBm) functions are used in [9], and in [10] two approximations of pink noise are proposed.

Grammar-Based Methods. Grammars are rules for creation of formal languages in which growing sequences are applied to an initial state, in the work of Márak [11] these rules are used for deforming terrains and thus imitating the actions of erosion.

Table 1. Techniques for terrain generation.

Families	Stochastic	Simulation	Learning	Sketches
Techniques	Fractals	Geomorphological	Example-based	2D sketch
	Grammars	Ecosystem	Search-based	3D sketch
	Tiling	Agent-based	Inverse procedural generation	
	Parametrization			

Tiling. Tiling is a technique that improves terrains by dividing them into smaller areas. One of them is the Voronoi diagrams which divide the surface in cell-like structures. A different set of parameters can be used at each cell, in this way the monotony of noise algorithms is broken and transition between areas look more natural. Tiling is only able to make subdivision, for this reason it is used in combination with other methods [10].

Parametrization Methods. These techniques revolve around having building instructions which are controlled by the user, who adjusts their parameters. The variability of the results is limited by the number of controllable parameters. In [12] a method based on parametrization of tiles is presented. The authors present a terrain generator with latitude and dispersion parameters. The former controls the type of generated biomes and the later the size of the transition area between two biomes. Yin [13] proposes a method for creating mountain ridges, parameters are altitude, slope and influence area.

Simulation Methods. These methods try to emulate natural occurrences that generate terrains. There are three approaches: geomorphological simulations, ecosystem simulations, and agent-based simulations.

Geomorphological Simulation. Erosion is one of the main drivers of terrain formation and these approaches focus on its simulation for creating realistic and natural shapes. These methods are posterior to fractal ones [14]. In [15] the authors propose to use a layered representation which has information on the type of terrain. Upper layers provide material to lower ones, this simulates erosion of flowing water, and this is repeated until a slope threshold is reached. Erosion creates cliffs and canyons, while deposition generates plains. In the case of [16] tectonic uplift is also taken into consideration. This process elevates the whole terrain over time and thus can create higher mountain ranges.

Ecosystem Simulation. Two terrains with the same geomorphological formations can look very different by introducing vegetation and climate. Ecosystem simulation methods alter existing terrains. A layered model that includes vegetation is presented in [17]. There are four types of layers: bedrock, granular material, vegetation and dead vegetation. Elevation is determined by the sum of the first two layers. Vegetation is controlled by moisture and sun exposure. There are trees and shrubs, which have density, height and age; and grass which only has density. In [18] the focus is over the accuracy of vegetation distribution. It needs two types of data: a heightmap and a biomass map. The later shows were vegetations is present and the former is the base terrain. Plants have the following data: species, spacing, relative size, closeness and coverage.

Agent-Based Simulation. These methods are considered separately as the agents do not base their actions on geomorphological events, usually they are divided into constructive and destructive. Doran and Parberry [19] define five types of agents: coastline agents which create initial landmass; smoothing agents that create plains; beach agents that flatten coastal areas; mountain generation agents; and river creation agents. Creation and smoothening are done randomly. Flattening and the creation of mountains are random but also include rules for certain control. The river agents connect a point in mountain areas with another in the coast following the lowest uphill gradient.

Learning Methods. Learning methods use real-world data, mostly in the form of images and digital elevation models (DEM) and try to imitate how real terrains look.

Example Methods. Terrain features are extracted from a set of examples. Zhou [20] proposes a method where small patches of mountains and canyons, extracted from real-world heightmaps, are copied and pasted over a sketch. Then, splines are used to create continuity between patches. In [21] extracted features and generated ones are combined to form full terrains. The construction of terrains is represented as a tree, where the leaves generated terrain parts and nodes are combination operators. When going further on the three, the level of detail increases, and these parts come from real-world images. In [22] Argudo creates a dictionary of atoms. The dictionary includes information on elevation, vegetation, light and water flow. To obtain an atom the terrain is divided into patches which are decomposed using sparse representation. When decomposing a new patch, if no combination of the existing atoms can recreate it a new atom is added to the dictionary. New terrains are created by combining the atoms.

Search-Based Methods. Most works are based on evolutionary algorithms (EAs), which rely on a set of examples that are evaluated using a fitness function. There are open problems with EAs: codification of terrains into chromosomes, fitness function design and improving variation of terrains. In the work of Frade [7] terrains are automatically evaluated by accessibility and obstacle length, but resulting terrains are too plain in comparison to real ones. On the other hand, Walsh [23] proposes a method where the user selects the parents for recombination, in this case the problem is the user fatigue.

Inverse Procedural Generation. This method recovers the idea of parameters, in here the system learns the parameters from examples. Emilien [24] proposes learning the distribution of objects such as trees. The number of objects in a radius will be reflected in a density function and stored in a brush, when this brush is used in another part of the map it will create a distribution of trees with the same density.

Sketch Methods. These methods improve the control over the generated terrains by giving the user the ability to place terrain features with painting-like interfaces. The disadvantage is that there is less realism in comparison with other methods.

2D Sketch. The method proposed in [13] the user draws a sketch map. Plains, mountains, canyons, rivers and lakes have color codes, and a skeleton is built upon a standard height that depends on the feature type. In [25] prevents the user draws a map that represents the altitude of areas, the system will then select adequate features. These features have areas of influence defined through Voronoi diagrams. Other works like [26] use sketches in the Y-axis, this allows to make changes in the terrain from a camera perspective that allows to see the horizon. The user draws silhouettes of the mountain features they want to make visible from that camera angle.

3D Sketch. Instead of making 2D strokes that will be later transformed into 3D features, some authors propose working with vectors that are 3D from the beginning. In the case of [27] curves are used. Once these curves are placed, the system will proceed to the voxelization, which is transforming the vectors into discrete approximations. Emilien [28] uses these 3D vectors to allow users to create river networks. Angle, position and length is decided by the user. If angles are too steep waterfalls are generated. The type of river depends on water flow and slope.

2.3   Taxonomy

A direct comparison between generation methods is difficult, generation speed and quality of generated terrains are not always reported or are subjective. This usually leads to comparisons that do not tell the potential uses of the generative methods, for this reason, the proposed taxonomy focuses on the generative capabilities of the algorithms and their needed inputs. As presented in Table 2, the taxonomy is composed of 7 categories that have mutually exclusive options.

Needed Input. There are algorithms that need pre-existing terrains to work on them, they can erode an existing terrain [11, 14, 29], can add vegetation or ecological behaviors [17, 18, 24], or can add volumetric features to terrains that did not have them [27, 30]. When a previous terrain is not needed, the user may input a map [25, 31], or a sketch [13, 20, 21, 32]. There may be a database which is used to create terrains [22, 33, 34], or the algorithm may create a terrain from nothing more than parameters input by the user [8, 10, 12, 16, 35–37].

Terrain Representation. The most used representations in literature are the height-maps, sometimes referred as heightfields or digital elevation maps, these are grayscales images where the white color represent the highest altitude while the black is the lowest. This representation is compact but has the inability to show volumetric features, such as caves or overhangs. It also represents relative altitude relations and not absolute heights. In the opposite way, there are methods that represent the terrain differently, like multilayers that allow to represent materials [15, 29]; vegetation and water presence [22]; graphs [34]; volumetric pixels, or voxels, [30] and 3D curves [27].

Table 2. Taxonomy of terrain generation methods

Category	Options		
Needed input	Pre-existing terrain [11, 14, 17, 18, 24, 27, 29, 30]	No terrain needed [8, 10, 12, 13, 16, 20–22, 32–37]	
Terrain representation	Heightmap [8–14, 16–21, 23–26, 28, 30–40]	Other representation [15, 22, 27, 29, 34]	
Controllability	Random [8, 10, 14, 18, 29, 38]	Suggested control [7, 12, 17, 19, 21, 22, 31, 33, 37]	Precise control [13, 20, 24, 26–28, 32, 34, 39]
Terrain evaluation	User evaluated [8–40]	Automatic [7]	
Number of features	Single feature [24, 26, 29–31, 33]	Multiple features [16, 17, 19, 20, 25, 27, 28, 34, 40]	
Vegetation presence	Yes [12, 17, 18, 22, 24]	None/Texture only [7–11, 13–16, 19–21, 23, 25–40]	
Water presence	None/Flooding [7, 9–15, 17, 18, 22–27, 29–31, 33, 35–39]	Rivers [8, 16, 19–21, 32, 34, 40]	Others [19, 28]

Controllability. Earlier works, and those that are focused on a fast generation do not allow the user to control the position where the terrain features would be placed, positioning is random. These methods may be used to generate base terrains that would be used as input for other methods [8, 14, 29, 38], or when the terrains would be used as backgrounds and further editing is not needed [10, 18]. Suggested control is when the methods allow a certain degree of control over the positioning of the features. This may be achieved by subdividing the terrain in tiles and having inputs for each individual tile [12], by selecting examples for evolutive algorithms [7, 31]; by giving the system examples from real-world terrains [21, 22, 33]; by adjusting agents [19]; simulation parameters [12, 17]; or by adding constraints [37]. Finally, methods that provide a precise control over the position of the generated features are those that use sketches [13, 20, 26, 32, 39]; that allow for a three dimensional positioning of the features [27, 28, 30]; or that use brushes [24].

Terrain Evaluation. There are few proposals that aim to do an automatic evaluation of the terrains such as [7] where the terrains are evaluated according the distribution of ledges and the connectivity of the plain spaces. This is still a challenge in the area, as evaluation is done by users and is subjective.

Number of Features. There are algorithms that only allow to generate a single terrain feature, being the most common the generation of mountains [26, 29, 31, 33], others generate features such as caves [30] or vegetation that covers terrains [24]. It is noted that the mountain algorithms often flood areas below an altitude threshold, but these methods are not considered to be specialized in the generation of water bodies. On the other hand there are methods that are able to generate multiple types of terrain features, combining mountains with rivers [16, 34, 40], canyons [20], arches and overhangs [27], vegetation [17] and plateaus [25]. There is also a specialization in the multiple features that a river network has including waterfalls [28]. And finally those that generate many features such as mountains, plains, plateaus, rivers and coastal plains [19].

Vegetation Presence. The presence of vegetation is important, because terrains would look very different depending on the plant types or if there is no vegetation at all. Many methods only include green textures that only work when looking at the terrains from afar, but when making a close-up they rapidly lose realism. Vegetation can be generated over an existing terrain [18, 24], or along with the terrain generation [12, 17, 22].

Water Presence. Other important feature are water bodies, these include rivers, lakes and shores. It is noticeable that most works that generate water bodies only generate rivers [8, 16, 19, 32, 34, 40] and canyons generated by those rivers [20, 21]. Those that generate other types of water bodies are not as common, in [28] waterfalls are generated, and in [19] shorelines are created using agents. Many works only flood lower areas, but there are no algorithms for specifically creating water bodies.

3   Discussion and Evaluation

Terrain generation methods have evolved in many ways during the last 30 years. Stochastic methods are the oldest ones and they produce terrains with basic features which are placed randomly. They are used for quickly generating base terrains that are altered using other methods or when trying to achieve real-time generation. By using GPUs, it is possible to create very big terrains during execution time with these methods.

When terrains need high geomorphological realism the simulation methods are the best ones, even if they are slow, the generated terrains are accurate. The most simulated event is erosion, specially water erosion. For this reason, the simulation of rivers and is common in the literature. Methods that use patches from real-world heightmaps and evolutive methods have proven to be close in terms of realism, but this depends on the used databases, which need to be big for improving results.

For videogames, the placement of assets or the use of pre-made maps is important, sketch methods perform the best to achieve this, as they allow to control the placing of the terrain features. Also, methods that can generate realistic water bodies and vegetation are preferred when using them for videogames because the player will traverse the terrain. The exception is flight simulators where the stochastic methods are enough because the terrain only serves as background.

When generating a terrain, the heightmap is the most common form of representation because of its low dimensionality which uses little memory, although it lacks the capability of representing hollow formations they can be later added with other algorithms.

Nowadays a highly competitive generator is one that would allow for high precision in the position of generated features; that allows to create several terrain features and that is capable to generate vegetation and water bodies. Automatic evaluation of terrains would be ideal as this would save more time to users, but this is still a problem that needs more attention because the proposals are limited to specific uses of the terrain.

4   Conclusion

In this paper the generation techniques and uses of the procedurally generated terrains were presented, and a taxonomy based on generative capabilities was proposed.

There are still many open research challenges in the area, such as the automatization of the evaluation methods, which has only been applied as a fitness function for evolutive methods. This is part of a bigger issue in the area: there is no standardized way of reporting results. Important data such as execution times or size of terrains is often missing. Also, the chosen render makes terrains look with different quality and geometrical characteristics are thus not properly evaluated, as a result, evaluations are subjective. Finding a way of making an objective comparison between generation methods is of interest in the area.

There are features that research has neglected such as coastal environments, cliffs, lakes, river deltas, wetlands, swamps, glaciers and glacial eroded terrains such as fjords. As research has advanced, the focus is now on adding more detail to the terrain through the simulation of ecological and weather processes, in the same way vegetation and water became important features of the terrains instead of just add-ons, it is possible that future research would require these simulations as an integral part of terrains.

References

1. Smith, G.: An analog history of procedural content generation. Presented at the Foundations on Digital Games (2015)
2. Raffe, W.L., Zambetta, F., Li, X.: A survey of procedural terrain generation techniques using evolutionary algorithms. In: 2012 IEEE Congress on Evolutionary Computation, pp. 1–8 (2012)
3. Rose, T.J., Bakaoukas, A.G.: Algorithms and approaches for procedural terrain generation - a brief review of current techniques. In: 2016 8th International Conference on Games and Virtual Worlds for Serious Applications (VS-GAMES), pp. 1–2 (2016)
4. Hendrikx, M., Meijer, S., Van Der Velden, J., Iosup, A.: Procedural content generation for games: a survey. ACM Trans Multimed. Comput. Commun. Appl. 9, 1:1–1:22 (2013)
5. Smelik, R.M., Tutenel, T., Bidarra, R., Benes, B.: A survey on procedural modelling for virtual worlds. Comput. Graph. Forum 33, 31–50 (2014). https://doi.org/10.1111/cgf.12276
6. Smelik, R.M., Tutenel, T., de Kraker, K.J., Bidarra, R.: A declarative approach to procedural modeling of virtual worlds. Computational Graphics 35, 352–363 (2011)
7. Frade, M., de Vega, F.F., Cotta, C.: Automatic evolution of programs for procedural generation of terrains for video games. Soft Computing 16, 1893–1914 (2012)
8. Prusinkiewicz, P., Hammel, M.: A fractal model of mountains and rivers. In: Graphics Interface, pp. 174–180. Canadian Information Processing Society (1993)
9. Helsing, J.K., Elster, A.C.: Real-time editing of procedural terrains (2015)
10. Olsen, J.: Realtime procedural terrain generation (2004)
11. Marák, I., Benes, B., Slavik, P.: Terrain erosion model based on rewriting of matrices. In: WSCG 1997, Winter School of Computer Graphics and Visualisation, pp. 341–350 (1997)
12. Choros, K., Topolski, J.: Parameterized and dynamic generation of an infinite virtual terrain with various biomes using extended voronoi diagram. J UCS. 22, 836–855 (2016)

13. Yin, H.F., Zheng, C.W.: A practical terrain generation method using sketch map and simple parameters. IEICE Trans. Inf. Syst. **96**, 1836–1844 (2013)
14. Roudier, P., Peroche, B., Perrin, M.: Landscapes synthesis achieved through erosion and deposition process simulation. Comput. Graph. Forum **12**, 375–383 (1993)
15. Šťava, O., Beneš, B., Brisbin, M., Křivánek, J.: Interactive terrain modeling using hydraulic erosion. In: Proceedings of the 2008 ACM SIGGRAPH/Eurographics Symposium on Computer Animation, pp. 201–210. Eurographics Association (2008)
16. Cordonnier, G., et al.: Large scale terrain generation from tectonic uplift and fluvial erosion. Comput. Graph. Forum **35**, 165–175 (2016)
17. Cordonnier, G., et al.: Authoring landscapes by combining ecosystem and terrain erosion simulation. ACM Trans. Graph. TOG **36**, 134 (2017)
18. Onrust, B., Bidarra, R., Rooseboom, R., van de Koppel, J.: Ecologically sound procedural generation of natural environments. Int. J. Comput. Games Technol. **2017**, 17 (2017)
19. Doran, J., Parberry, I.: Controlled procedural terrain generation using software agents. IEEE Transactions on Computational Intelligence in AI and Games **2**, 111–119 (2010)
20. Zhou, H., Sun, J., Turk, G., Rehg, J.M.: Terrain synthesis from digital elevation models. IEEE Trans. Vis. Comput. Graph. **13**, 834–848 (2007)
21. Génevaux, J.-D., et al.: Terrain modelling from feature primitives. Comput. Graph. Forum **34**, 198–210 (2015)
22. Argudo, O., et al.: Coherent multi-layer landscape synthesis. Vis. Comput. **33**, 1005–1015 (2017)
23. Walsh, P., Gade, P.: Terrain generation using an interactive genetic algorithm. In: 2010 IEEE Congress on Evolutionary Computation (CEC), pp. 1–7. IEEE (2010)
24. Emilien, A., et al.: WorldBrush: interactive example-based synthesis of procedural virtual worlds. ACM Trans. Graph. TOG **34**, 106 (2015)
25. Mangra, A.P., Sabou, A., Gorgan, D.: TSCH algorithm-terrain synthesis from crude heightmaps. Rom. J. Hum.-Comput. Interact. **9**, 119 (2016)
26. Tasse, F.P., Emilien, A., Cani, M.-P., Hahmann, S., Dodgson, N.: Feature-based terrain editing from complex sketches. Computational Graphics **45**, 101–115 (2014)
27. Becher, M., Krone, M., Reina, G., Ertl, T.: Feature-based volumetric terrain generation. In: Proceedings of the 21st ACM SIGGRAPH Symposium on Interactive 3D Graphics and Games, p. 10. ACM (2017)
28. Emilien, A., et al.: Interactive procedural modelling of coherent waterfall scenes. Comput. Graph. Forum **34**, 22–35 (2015)
29. Beneš, B., Forsbach, R.: Parallel implementation of terrain erosion applied to the surface of mars. In: Proceedings of the 1st International Conference on Computer Graphics, Virtual Reality and Visualisation, pp. 53–57. ACM, New York (2001)
30. Dey, R., Doig, J.G., Gatzidis, C.: Procedural feature generation for volumetric terrains using voxel grammars. Entertain. Comput. **27**, 128–136 (2018)
31. Antoniuk, I., Rokita, P.: Procedural generation of adjustable terrain for application in computer games using 2D maps. In: Kryszkiewicz, M., Bandyopadhyay, S., Rybinski, H., Pal, S.K. (eds.) PReMI 2015. LNCS, vol. 9124, pp. 75–84. Springer, Cham (2015). https://doi.org/10.1007/978-3-319-19941-2_8
32. Gain, J., et al.: Terrain sketching. In: Proceedings of the 2009 Symposium on Interactive 3D Graphics and Games, pp. 31–38. ACM, New York (2009)
33. Cruz, L., et al.: Patch-based terrain synthesis. In: International Conference on Computer Graphics Theory and Applications, Berlin, France (2015)
34. Génevaux, J.-D., Galin, É., Guérin, E., Peytavie, A., Benes, B.: Terrain generation using procedural models based on hydrology. ACM Trans. Graph. TOG **32**, 143 (2013)

35. Backes, G.C., Engel, T.A., Pozzer, C.T.: Real-time massive terrain generation using procedural erosion on the GPU (2018)
36. Golubev, K., Zagarskikh, A., Karsakov, A.: Dijkstra-based terrain generation using advanced weight functions. Procedia Comput. Sci. **101**, 152–160 (2016)
37. Stachniak, S., Stuerzlinger, W.: An algorithm for automated fractal terrain deformation. Comput. Graph. Artif. Intell. **1**, 64–76 (2005)
38. Pi, X., Song, J., Zeng, L., Li, S.: Procedural terrain detail based on Patch-LOD algorithm. In: Pan, Z., Aylett, R., Diener, H., Jin, X., Göbel, S., Li, L. (eds.) Edutainment 2006. LNCS, vol. 3942, pp. 913–920. Springer, Heidelberg (2006). https://doi.org/10.1007/11736639_111
39. Bradbury, G.A., Choi, I., Amati, C., Mitchell, K., Weyrich, T.: Frequency-based controls for terrain editing. In: Proceedings of the 11th European Conference on Visual Media Production, pp. 15:1–15:10. ACM, New York (2014)
40. Zhang, J., Wang, C., Qin, H., Chen, Y., Gao, Y.: Procedural modeling of rivers from single image toward natural scene production. Vis. Comput. **35**, 223–237 (2017)

Some Variations of Upper Confidence Bound for General Game Playing

Iván Francisco-Valencia[✉], José Raymundo Marcial-Romero,
and Rosa María Valdovinos-Rosas

Facultad de Ingeniería, Universidad Autónoma del Estado de México,
Cerro de Coatepec S/N Ciudad Universitaria,
50100 Toluca, Estado de México, Mexico
if.valencia@hotmail.com, {jrmarcialr,rvaldovinosr}@uaemex.mx

Abstract. Monte Carlo Tree Search (MCTS) is the most used method in General Game Playing, area of the Artificial Intelligence, whose main goal is to develop agents capable of play any board game without preview knowledge. MCTS requires a tree which represents the states and moves of the board game which is visited and expanded using an iterations method. In order to visit the tree, MCTS requires a selection policy which determines which node is visited in each level. Nowdays, Upper Confidence Bound (UCB), is the most popular policy in MCTS due to its simplicity and efficiency. This policy was propose for the Multi-Armed Bandit Problem (MABP) which consists in set of slot machines each of which has a certain probability of give a reward. The goal is to maximize the accumulative reward that is obtained when a machine is played in a series of rounds. Other policy proposed for MCTS is Upper Confidence Bound$_{\sqrt{}}$ (UCB$_{\sqrt{}}$) whose goal is to identify the machine with the highest probability to give a reward. This paper shows a comparative between five modifications of UCB and one of UCB$_{\sqrt{}}$, this comparative has the goal of finding a policy which be able to identify the optimal machine as quickly as possible, this goal in MCTS is equals to identify the node with the highest probability to leading to a victory. The results show that some policies find the optimal machine before UCB, however, with 10,000 rounds UCB is the policy who plays the optimal machine more often.

Keywords: General game playing · Selection policy ·
Upper confidence bound

1 Introduction

For Bjornsson and Finnsson [5], General Game Playing (GGP) is the area of Artificial Intelligence of which the objective is to create intelligent agents who can learn, automatically, how to play a wide variety of board games, based only on the descriptions of the rules of the games. The foregoing implies that without prior knowledge about the game and while playing, the agent must be able to

© Springer Nature Switzerland AG 2019
J. A. Carrasco-Ochoa et al. (Eds.): MCPR 2019, LNCS 11524, pp. 68–79, 2019.
https://doi.org/10.1007/978-3-030-21077-9_7

develop strategies that allow it to win. Since its inception GGP makes use of methods based on MinMax or Alpha-Beta tree [11], this is due to the nature of boardgames, to which tree can be associated, where the root node represents the initial state of the game and each child node represents the status of the game after some movement has been made. Due to the above, the leaf nodes of the game tree correspond to the statuses where the game has ended, whereby the agent must only find a leaf node where he achieves a win; this is the reason for using methods based on search trees.

Monte Carlo Tree Search (MCTS) is the search method based on the most popular tree in GGP, as it has a better performance in game trees [6]. MCTS consists of four steps that are repeated cyclically, until a stop criterion is met: Selection, Expansion, Simulation, and Back Propagation. The stop criterion can be a limit number of simulations, execution time or number of iterations [6].

Selection In this step the method crosses the tree from the root node until it finds a node that still has children to add to the tree, once this node is found the Expansion step is reached. The route taken by this step is guided by a Selection Policy, which indicates which node should be explored in each level; an example of this policy is to choose the node that has the highest ratio between wins and visits.

Expansion In this step, a corresponding child node is added to the node found in the selection step.

Simulation Starting from the status represented by the newly added node, the method simulates playing the game by performing the movements of the players randomly until a result is obtained.

Back Propagation In this step, the result of the simulation step is propagated in all the nodes visited, updating the number of wins and the number of visits of each node.

Once the method ends, the movement that the agent must perform is chosen among the children of the root node which could be: the node with the highest number of wins, the node with the highest number of visits, the node that meets the two previous criteria, or the node is chosen based on the selection policy. MCTS has the advantage of being able to be used at any time during the game since the root of the tree can be any status of the game, another feature of MCTS is to be efficient by not having to completely expand the tree as it resorts to probability to choose the movement that has the highest chance of leading to a win, so it is also known as a probabilistic method.

In recent years efforts have been made to improve MCTS, mainly in the Simulation Step where attempts have been made for the simulation to reflect movements of real adversaries without being completely deterministic, highlighting the works of Cazenave [8–10], whose idea is to make use of online knowledge, by identifying the movements of previous iterations that led to wins to be used, with a greater probability, in future iterations.

Another step of MCTS where efforts are made to improve it is the Selection Step specific to the Selection Policy; in the beginning the average of wins of each node was used as selection policy. However, new policies have been proposed, such as Upper Confidence Bound. In the Selection Step, at each level of the tree, MCTS has to make the following decision: Which node should be explored? The one in which the highest number of wins is obtained so far, or should we explore less promising nodes that may turn out to be better in future iterations? This decision is an instance of the Explore-Exploit Dilemma, which Auer et al. [3] describe as the search for a balance between exploring the environment to find profitable actions while taking the best empirical action as frequently as possible.

Another instance of the Explore-Exploit Dilemma is the Multi-Armed Bandit Problem (MABP), which consists in set of slot machines each of which has a certain probability of give a reward. The goal is to maximize the accumulative reward that is obtained when a machine is played in a series of rounds.

An algorithm that allows to decide which machine to activate in each round in MABP is known as Activation Policy, where Upper Confidence Bound (UCB) is the most popular, mainly because it is efficient, simple to implement and can be used at any time [3,4]. However, there are other policies that achieve performance close to UCB such as UCB2, ϵ-greedy, UCB-Tuned, UCB-Normal [3], UCB-Improved [4], UCB-V [2], UCB-Minimal [13] and Minimax Optimal Strategy in the Stochastic Case [1].

Because MABP and the decision made by MCTS in the Selection Step are instances of the Explore-Exploit Dilemma, it is possible to use Activation Policies as Selection Policies. In this case, each level of the tree is treated as a MABP where each node is equivalent to a slot machine; this idea was used for the first time by the agent Cadiaplayer, which made use of UCB as a selection policy, giving good results to such an extent that the combination of MCTS and UCB, known as Upper Confidence Bound Applied to Trees (UCT), became the state of the art of GGP.

The approach of activation policies like UCB and its similar ones is to minimize Cumulative Regret which is defined as the loss that is obtained due to the fact that the policy does not always choose the best machine [3]. However, this approach is not necessarily suitable for MCTS since in this the idea is to identify the node that is most likely to lead to a win. Another approach known as Simple Regret [7,14] has been proposed, and is more suited to MCTS [12], and which is defined as the difference between the expected reward of the optimal machine (the machine with the highest probability of giving a reward) and the expected reward of the machine that has been identified as the optimal machine, from this approach emerge $UCB_{\sqrt{\cdot}}$.

This paper presents a comparison between five modifications of UCB and one of $UCB_{\sqrt{\cdot}}$. In order to find a selection policy that is able to identify the machine as quickly as possible, the above would be equivalent in MCTS to identifying the node that has the highest chance of leading to a win at each level of the tree. The comparison was made in the regarding MABP in two scenarios: the first consists of the scenario proposed by Auer et al. [3], in the second one the use of the branching factor of the game tree of different board games is used to generate sets of machines where the proposed policies were tested. The results show that certain policies find the optimal machine in the first iterations, although at close to 10,000 iterations it is UCB that activates the optimal machine.

2 Upper Confidence Bound

Auer et al. [3,4] formally define MABP by the random variables $X_{i,n} \in \{0,1\}$ with $1 \le i \le K$ and $n \ge 1$, where each i is the index of a slot machine, and K the machines available. By successively activating the i machine, the rewards $X_{i,1}, X_{i,2}, \cdots$ are obtained, which are independent and identically distributed according to an unknown law with unknown expectation μ_i.

UCB is the most widely used policy in MABP because it achieves logarithmic and uniform regret as n increases, and does not require information about probability distributions and is easy to implement.

UCB consists in the following:

1. Play each machine once.
2. Play the machine j that maximize $\bar{x}_j + \sqrt{\frac{2 \ln n}{n_j}}$
   where $\bar{x}_j$ is the average reward obtained by the j machine, n_j is the number of the times that the j machine has been played and n is the total number of plays done so far.
3. The previous step is repeated until a certain number of rounds is reached.

3 Upper Confidence Bound$_{\sqrt{}}$

Proposed by Tolpin and Shimony [14], the UCB$_{\sqrt{}}$ policy is the one used in MCTS and is focused on minimizing simple regret, and consists of:

1. Play each machine once
2. Play the machine j that maximize

$$\bar{x}_j + \sqrt{\frac{c\sqrt{n}}{n_j}} \tag{1}$$

where $\bar{x}_j$ is the average reward obtained by the j machine, n_j is the number of the times that the j machine has been played and n is the total number plays done so far.
3. The previous step is repeated until a certain number of rounds is reached.

4 Policies Proposals

UCB is the most used policy in MABP and consequently in Monte Carlo Tree Search; in this section five modifications to this policy are presented:

$$UCB\text{-}A = \bar{x}_j + \sqrt{\frac{2 \log n}{n}} \tag{2}$$

$$UCB\text{-}B = \overline{x}_j + \sqrt{\frac{2\log n_j}{n_j}} \tag{3}$$

$$UCB\text{-}C = \overline{x}_j + \sqrt{\frac{2\log n_j}{n}} \tag{4}$$

$$UCB\text{-}D = \overline{x}_j \tag{5}$$

$$UCB\text{-}E = \overline{x}_j + \frac{n_j}{n} \tag{6}$$

The $UCB\text{-}A$ policy makes use only of the total number of Machine Activations (number of simulations of the parent node in MCTS). The $UCB\text{-}B$ policy makes use of the number of activations of the machine (number of simulations in the child node). The policy $UCB\text{-}C$ is similar to UCB but with n_j y n exchanged. The $UCB\text{-}D$ policy only takes the average of rewards obtained in the machine (the average of wins per node in MCTS) that means that this policy is only for exploitation. The $UCB\text{-}E$ policy requires the average of the plays. Finally, $UCB\text{-}F$ is a modification of the policy UCB$_{\sqrt{.}}$ with n_j y n exchanged.

$$UCB\text{-}F = \overline{x}_j + \sqrt{\frac{2\sqrt{n_j}}{n}} \tag{7}$$

5   Comparative of Policies

In this section we compare the performance of the proposed policies with respect to UCB and UCB$_{\sqrt{.}}$. Specifically, we can see how good the policies are in choosing the optimal machine. The choice to measure how much a policy chooses the optimal machine is because in the MCTS field it is equivalent to choosing the child node in which the highest number of wins is given.

The policies were compared in the MABP in two scenarios; the first is the one proposed by Auer et al. [3] and the second scenario is where the branching factor of a set of board games is used.

5.1   First Scenario

This scenario is the one proposed by Auer et al. [3] to prove the policies UCB, $UCB\text{-}T$, $UCB2$, $UCB\text{-}Normal$ and ϵ-greedy. Auer et al. propose that the policies should be proven in 7 sets of machines, the Table 1 shows these sets with the probabilities of giving a reward of each of their machines.

For Auer et al. the sets A and D are easy to contrast because the reward of the optimal machine has low variance and the difference between the expected value of the optimal machine and suboptimal is wide. Sets C and G are hard sets because the reward of the optimal machine has high variance and the difference between the expected value of the optimal machine and suboptimal is small.

The policies were compared with the following conditions:

- Each of the sets proposed by Auer et al. were used.
- Each policy was tested 100 times in each set, from which the average of activation of the optimal machine was obtained.
- The policies were limited to 100,000 rounds.

Table 1. Sets of slots machine

Set	Probability of giving a reward									
A	0.9	0.6								
B	0.9	0.8								
C	0.55	0.45								
D	0.9	0.6	0.6	0.6	0.6	0.6	0.6	0.6	0.6	0.6
E	0.9	0.8	0.8	0.8	0.7	0.7	0.7	0.6	0.6	0.6
F	0.9	0.8	0.8	0.8	0.8	0.8	0.8	0.8	0.8	0.8
G	0.55	0.45	0.45	0.45	0.45	0.45	0.45	0.45	0.45	0.45

Results. This Figs. 1, 2, 3 and 4 show the results obtained in each set and the Table 2 shows the average percentage of plays of the optimal machine. We can note at 100,000 rounds, UCB is the best policy because it has the best performance due it activates the optimal machine over 95.8% on average, the same happens at 10,000 rounds where the optimal machine is activated 80.6%. However, in lower rounds UCB-A and UCB-B are the policies that activate the optimal machine more frequently, over 71% at 1,000 rounds and over 57% at 100 rounds. It is worth highlighting that $UCB - B$ has performance similar to the performance of UCB, and it is the second-best performance at 100,000 and 10,000 rounds. The other policies have a performance bellow UCB, UCB-A, UCB-B and UCB-D, and it is UCB-E the worst policy due it only reaches 37% of the activation of the optimal machine. From the figures we can note that UCB in the first rounds it is dedicated to exploration in order to find the optimal machine without underestimate any other suboptimal machine, in these same rounds UCB-A and UCB-D are the polices that most quickly activate the optimal machine in all sets except for the set C. However, both policies tend to stagnate after 1,000 rounds and they do not overcome to UCB.

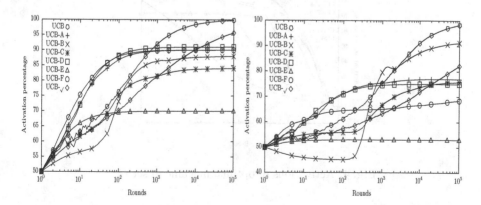

Fig. 1. Activations of optimal machine in sets A (left) and B (right)

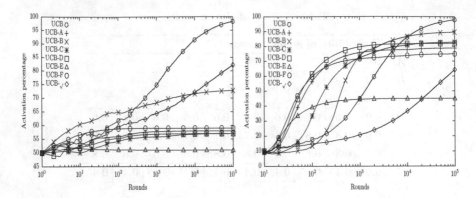

Fig. 2. Activations of optimal machine in sets C (left) and D (right)

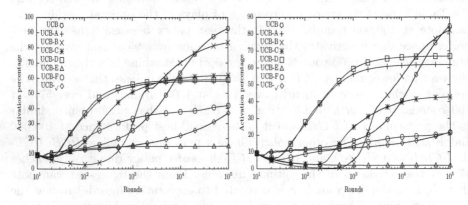

Fig. 3. Activations of optimal machine in sets E (left) and F (right)

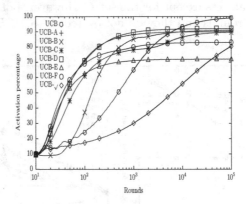

Fig. 4. Activations of optimal machine in set G

Table 2. Activation percentage of optimal machine

Rounds		UCB	UCB − A	UCB − B	UCB − C	UCB − D	UCB − E	UCB$_\sqrt{}$	UCB − F
100,000	$\bar{x}$	**95.8182**	73.3904	85.4395	70.5138	74.6906	37.5698	66.1962	62.6921
	σ	4.9840	13.0925	6.1034	15.8557	13.3010	28.8866	25.0811	22.2657
10,000	$\bar{x}$	**80.5987**	73.0574	78.3030	68.7177	74.4771	37.5555	51.9887	61.2636
	σ	19.4140	13.1107	12.1342	15.9161	13.3509	28.8716	26.0406	23.3561
1,000	$\bar{x}$	56.2810	71.0549	61.1777	61.4323	**72.3633**	37.4120	41.1454	58.9154
	σ	25.9311	13.8878	28.8332	18.1425	14.0022	28.7228	25.7844	24.7352
100	$\bar{x}$	37.9771	57.4729	33.8329	42.8214	**58.6314**	35.9771	34.7229	52.6000
	σ	25.1655	19.6814	26.9652	23.8225	19.3466	27.3797	24.2615	25.9624

5.2 Second Scenario

In this scenario the proposal policies were tested in the field of the MABP problem however we used the branching factor of the games that we show in the Table 3.

Table 3. Branching factor of games

Game	Branching factor	Game	Branching factor
Tic-Tac-Toe	4	Connect 4	4
Draughts (10 × 10)	4	Domineering (8 × 8)	8
Nine Men's Morris	10	Reversi	10
Fanorona	11	Lines of Action	29
Chess	35	Chinese chess	38
Japanese chess	40	Korean chess	92
Gomoku	210		

The branching factor is used because this will be the number of machines the polices will face if implemented in the Monte Carlo Tree Search

For this scenario the following conditions are required:

- The game branching factor is used.
- For each branching factor, five sets of machines with random probabilities were created.
- The policies were tested 100 times in 10,000 rounds in these sets, of which the average was obtained.
- We obtained the average of activations of the optimal machine.

Results. From the Table 4 we can note that when we have a branching factor under 11, it is *UCB-B* the policy with the best performance due it reaches between 74% and 83% of activations of the optimal machine, except when we have a branching factor of 4 where *UCB* is the best policy. For the rest of branching factors, we can note that *UCB-A* and *UCB-B* have the best performance due to these are the policies that activate the optimal machine more frequently. Form the Table 5 we can note that in all games the best policies are *UCB-A* and *UCB-B* given that in average they activate the optimal machine more frequently. From the Table 6 we can note that the behavior of the policies changes with *UCB-A* and *UCB-D* the best policies when we have a branching factor under 11. Surprisingly, in the Table 6, we can note for the branching factors 29, 35, 38 and 40, *UCB-F* has the best performance.

Table 4. Activation percentage of optimal machine in games at 10,000 rounds

BF		UCB	UCB − A	UCB − B	UCB − C	UCB − D	UCB − E	UCB$_\checkmark$	UCB − F
4	$\bar{x}$	**65.6611**	59.6806	57.9441	51.5995	56.9357	49.5891	50.3142	51.0588
	σ	15.3476	5.5503	11.2091	5.9047	11.1973	4.3158	11.6598	8.2216
8	$\bar{x}$	74.9371	75.1826	**82.8859**	74.4210	74.9500	52.5614	44.2984	63.2555
	σ	18.3563	16.9671	13.5736	14.5467	17.8437	16.2887	16.1516	19.9180
10	$\bar{x}$	67.8768	69.5031	**74.8487**	65.4245	69.7310	38.7614	33.7844	59.9355
	σ	13.2718	14.9729	15.1556	15.4648	16.5656	8.5786	7.7511	12.9619
11	$\bar{x}$	74.3563	77.8430	**80.1822**	73.1342	76.8665	34.9542	36.9537	65.4115
	σ	22.1472	24.4220	22.8700	23.0606	25.0331	17.8814	12.6490	28.0763
29	$\bar{x}$	37.2920	**76.8383**	55.7563	62.7048	74.1868	36.8889	10.1818	46.2529
	σ	11.0098	15.4155	29.1863	18.5392	14.9992	22.8625	1.4704	21.5763
35	$\bar{x}$	24.5105	**67.4117**	43.2063	53.0103	66.6836	29.6829	7.4822	40.0294
	σ	3.1729	21.0204	33.6807	28.1489	21.6409	23.6254	0.7376	29.2565
38	$\bar{x}$	22.7111	57.6530	30.0124	41.6675	**57.7975**	14.9365	7.0274	25.8340
	σ	3.9723	12.0977	25.3554	16.9108	13.0974	14.9539	0.5625	16.7117
40	$\bar{x}$	30.0559	72.9773	50.1235	59.0959	**73.6321**	26.2777	7.0432	34.8555
	σ	9.0977	19.1200	30.1434	25.1066	20.2007	29.5561	1.0251	31.7675
92	$\bar{x}$	6.3170	**36.9091**	7.3637	17.1300	33.3640	7.5018	2.0843	9.1248
	σ	0.9060	6.4753	14.5398	14.8989	8.0411	10.6270	0.0996	13.7220
210	$\bar{x}$	1.8606	45.1294	0.0100	1.5039	**45.8125**	0.9766	0.7544	0.3475
	σ	0.1406	18.3626	0.0000	2.0300	18.6298	1.9332	0.0139	0.5902

Table 5. Activation percentage of optimal machine in games at 1,000 rounds

BF		UCB	$UCB-A$	$UCB-B$	$UCB-C$	$UCB-D$	$UCB-E$	$UCB_{\sqrt{}}$	$UCB-F$
4	$\bar{x}$	52.2936	**59.2170**	54.3214	49.6422	56.3692	49.4910	42.3852	50.4402
	σ	13.0574	5.6605	10.1968	7.0983	11.2702	4.3013	7.1777	7.7528
8	$\bar{x}$	49.5066	72.8488	66.7468	66.7380	**72.9586**	52.2142	30.2922	59.5674
	σ	17.5118	17.3604	16.4454	15.3563	18.0711	16.1459	9.3635	19.8535
10	$\bar{x}$	38.6312	67.0240	54.7670	55.4538	**67.3690**	38.4144	22.1458	56.6776
	σ	9.4914	14.8311	10.2368	13.3721	16.0270	8.4904	3.4105	10.7863
11	$\bar{x}$	43.2396	**75.2802**	50.4530	62.3224	74.4496	34.5416	22.0318	59.9800
	σ	15.5835	24.9104	27.2729	23.6197	25.5042	17.6155	5.0195	27.1612
29	$\bar{x}$	11.9900	**66.7928**	35.8372	41.6526	65.1450	35.8894	6.4858	40.4814
	σ	2.1578	12.6583	27.1850	26.1605	11.9942	22.2133	0.4633	22.3180
35	$\bar{x}$	8.5186	**57.5004**	14.1398	28.7188	56.5842	28.6292	5.0170	35.1438
	σ	0.8929	16.3202	17.7661	20.9094	17.1572	22.8657	0.3096	28.2344
38	$\bar{x}$	8.0218	**47.9556**	12.4592	22.5314	47.5542	14.3646	4.6864	21.3432
	σ	0.7405	11.1791	23.7481	18.1138	11.8451	14.4796	0.2377	17.1685
40	$\bar{x}$	8.2068	63.0024	16.8792	25.9206	**63.4442**	25.1766	4.5156	30.2384
	σ	1.4715	17.5381	31.2955	32.3617	17.9930	28.4204	0.3370	31.4916
92	$\bar{x}$	2.2336	**21.1234**	0.1284	4.7348	21.0182	6.6180	1.5626	6.0978
	σ	0.1456	1.8250	0.0568	8.0212	4.5364	9.4044	0.0389	10.3251
210	$\bar{x}$	0.7472	9.4600	0.1000	0.3362	**9.6454**	0.7658	0.5976	0.2388
	σ	0.0323	9.6418	0.0000	0.3081	9.8170	1.3316	0.0017	0.2776

Table 6. Activation percentage of optimal machine in games at 100 rounds

BF		UCB	$UCB-A$	$UCB-B$	$UCB-C$	$UCB-D$	$UCB-E$	$UCB_{\sqrt{}}$	$UCB-F$
4	$\bar{x}$	39.2640	**55.5520**	47.0840	46.8160	53.2960	48.5100	35.7300	49.0280
	σ	6.3660	6.3454	10.9596	7.6774	10.9542	4.1571	3.9259	6.9773
8	$\bar{x}$	26.3080	57.5320	35.6840	44.2320	**58.5100**	48.7420	21.0560	52.1900
	σ	6.6413	17.6117	15.9314	13.6677	17.8331	14.7257	3.7780	16.2202
10	$\bar{x}$	18.9140	49.7680	17.6100	31.4280	**50.2840**	34.9440	15.7100	47.1020
	σ	2.5276	11.3634	6.3259	6.6079	11.6234	7.6148	1.2526	7.8605
11	$\bar{x}$	18.0800	55.9120	10.0180	23.9920	**56.6580**	30.4160	14.6320	45.0880
	σ	3.6091	20.0240	4.3396	12.7578	19.7044	14.9594	1.8329	18.9701
29	$\bar{x}$	5.3460	20.1220	16.8800	23.3360	19.4020	25.8940	4.6920	**27.5820**
	σ	0.3909	7.6491	13.6249	18.3071	7.6527	15.7421	0.2729	15.6954
35	$\bar{x}$	4.0440	16.0360	7.3080	11.5380	16.5060	18.0920	3.6740	**20.2440**
	σ	0.0739	9.3594	9.3838	12.6745	9.2657	15.3353	0.2782	18.6115
38	$\bar{x}$	3.7960	8.6560	6.7820	9.3140	8.8000	8.6460	3.0820	**10.1560**
	σ	0.0736	4.3635	11.5640	12.8030	4.8589	9.8454	0.0937	12.0551
40	$\bar{x}$	3.5040	11.7760	4.2520	11.4960	11.8560	14.1660	2.9740	**15.4960**
	σ	0.2938	8.9449	6.4641	17.5303	8.9641	17.1619	0.0372	19.4871

6   Conclusions and Future Work

From the first scenario we could note that *UCB* is the policy with the best performance due to it activates the optimal machine over 80% of the time after 10,000 rounds. *UCB-B* had a similar performance to *UCB* however it did not reach the percentage of *UCB*. In this scenario we could note that *UCB-A* and *UCB-B* are the policies that activate the optimal machine as quick as possible, however, in the last rounds they are outperformed by *UCB*. This behavior was repeated when we used set of machines based in branching factor of games and we could note that the performance of *UCB* decreased as the number of rounds increased, probably in late rounds *UCB* can outperformed the other polices.

Because *UCB-A* and *UCB-D* are policies that only use exploitation and due to the results that we got, we can conclude that when we have low number of rounds below 10,000, it is better to use exploitation polices but with a high number of round is better use *UCB*. However, we need to apply these policies in MCTS and GGP in order to get the real behavior. In both scenarios *UCB*$_{\sqrt{}}$ had the worst performance, this may be due to the wrong choice of the value of its constant, so we leave as future work to tune this value and compare its performance with the exploitation polices.

References

1. Audibert, J.Y., Bubeck, S.: Minimax policies for adversarial and stochastic bandits. In: COLT, pp. 217–226 (2009)
2. Audibert, J.-Y., Munos, R., Szepesvári, C.: Tuning bandit algorithms in stochastic environments. In: Hutter, M., Servedio, R.A., Takimoto, E. (eds.) ALT 2007. LNCS (LNAI), vol. 4754, pp. 150–165. Springer, Heidelberg (2007). https://doi.org/10.1007/978-3-540-75225-7_15
3. Auer, P., Cesa-Bianchi, N., Fischer, P.: Finite-time analysis of the multiarmed bandit problem. Mach. Learn. **47**(2–3), 235–256 (2002)
4. Auer, P., Ortner, R.: UCB revisited: improved regret bounds for the stochastic multi-armed bandit problem. Periodica Math. Hungarica **61**(1–2), 55–65 (2010)
5. Bjornsson, Y., Finnsson, H.: Cadiaplayer: a simulation-based general game player. IEEE Trans. Comput. Intell. AI Games **1**(1), 4–15 (2009)
6. Browne, C.B., et al.: A survey of Monte Carlo tree search methods. IEEE Trans. Comput. Intell. AI Games **4**(1), 1–43 (2012)
7. Carpentier, A., Valko, M.: Simple regret for infinitely many armed bandits. In: International Conference on Machine Learning, pp. 1133–1141 (2015)
8. Cazenave, T.: Playout policy adaptation for games. In: Plaat, A., van den Herik, J., Kosters, W. (eds.) ACG 2015. LNCS, vol. 9525, pp. 20–28. Springer, Cham (2015). https://doi.org/10.1007/978-3-319-27992-3_3
9. Cazenave, T.: Playout policy adaptation with move features. Theoret. Comput. Sci. **644**, 43–52 (2016)
10. Cazenave, T., Diemert, E.: Memorizing the playout policy. In: Cazenave, T., Winands, M.H.M., Saffidine, A. (eds.) CGW 2017. CCIS, vol. 818, pp. 96–107. Springer, Cham (2018). https://doi.org/10.1007/978-3-319-75931-9_7

11. Genesereth, M., Thielscher, M.: General Game Playing. Synthesis Lectures on Artificial Intelligence and Machine Learning. Morgan & Claypool Publishers, San Rafael (2014)
12. Liu, Y.C., Tsuruoka, Y.: Modification of improved upper confidence bounds for regulating exploration in Monte-Carlo tree search. Theoret. Comput. Sci. **644**, 92–105 (2016)
13. Maes, F., Wehenkel, L., Ernst, D.: Automatic discovery of ranking formulas for playing with multi-armed bandits. In: Sanner, S., Hutter, M. (eds.) EWRL 2011. LNCS (LNAI), vol. 7188, pp. 5–17. Springer, Heidelberg (2012). https://doi.org/10.1007/978-3-642-29946-9_5
14. Tolpin, D., Shimony, S.E.: MCTS based on simple regret. In: AAAI (2012)

Dendrite Ellipsoidal Neuron Trained by Stochastic Gradient Descent for Motor Imagery Classification

Fernando Arce[1]([⊠]), Omar Mendoza-Montoya[2], Erik Zamora[1],
Javier M. Antelis[2], Humberto Sossa[1,2], Jessica Cantillo-Negrete[3],
Ruben I. Carino-Escobar[3], Luis G. Hernández[2], and Luis Eduardo Falcón[2]

[1] Instituto Politécnico Nacional - CIC,
Av. Juan de Dios Batiz S/N, Gustavo A. Madero, 07738 Mexico City, Mexico
fernando.arce.vega@gmail.com, ezamorag@ipn.mx, hsossa@cic.ipn.mx
[2] Tecnológico de Monterrey Campus Guadalajara, Av. Gral Ramón Corona 2514,
45201 Zapopan, Jalisco, Mexico
{omendoza83,luisg.hernandez,luis.eduardo.falcon}@tec.mx,
mauricio.antelis@itesm.mx
[3] Division of Medical Engineering Research, Instituto Nacional de Rehabilitación,
14389 Mexico City, Mexico
{jcantillo,ricarino}@inr.gob.mx

Abstract. Dendrite ellipsoidal neurons are a novel and different alternative for classification tasks, giving competitive results compared with typical classification methods. Based on k-means++ algorithm, the network allows each dendrite to build a hyperellipsoidal in order to assign each incoming pattern $x_i = (x_1, x_2, \ldots, x_n)^T$ to its respective C class. The main disadvantage of this training algorithm is the lack of accuracy in high dimensional datasets. In this research, we solved this problem by training the dendrite ellipsoidal neuron using stochastic gradient descent. Furthermore, electroencephalography data were acquired during two mental conditions (imaginary movements of the left and right hand) in order to test the new training algorithm. The proposed algorithm outperformed the accuracy acquired by a dendrite ellipsoidal neuron based on k-means++ obtaining 76.02% and 62.77%, respectively. Also, the algorithm was compared with multilayer perceptrons and support vector machines which are some of the most common classifiers used to detect motor-related information in brain signals. These achieved an accuracy of 72.38% and 65.81%, respectively.

Keywords: Dendrite Ellipsoidal Neuron · Motor Imagery ·
Electroencephalography · Multilayer perceptrons · Support vector
machines · Stochastic Gradient Descent · k-means++

1 Introduction

The main objective about pattern classification is to stablish a mathematical function that associate input patterns $x_i = (x_1, x_2, \ldots, x_n)^T$ to their

© Springer Nature Switzerland AG 2019
J. A. Carrasco-Ochoa et al. (Eds.): MCPR 2019, LNCS 11524, pp. 80–88, 2019.
https://doi.org/10.1007/978-3-030-21077-9_8

corresponding classes $C^1, C^2, \ldots, C^j$. This assignation must be as strong as possible to reduce potential variations in incoming data and must be capable to find elemental relationships between patterns.

Since 60 years ago, many types of neural networks have been presented for solving classification tasks and the most common approach is a group of classical perceptrons which create hyperplanes to divide and associate data by using synaptic weights, biases and activation functions.

In a common neural network, each neuron can divide the input search space into two parts. Thereby, appending more neurons in a single layer, the network has the capacity to learn any complex function [1].

Other type of neural networks less known are Dendrite Morphological Neural Networks (DMNN) which separate data employing hyperboxes. These neurons group patterns using minimum or maximum operators to generate the piecewise boundaries for classification tasks. DMNN have the advantage of being easily implemented in logic devices.

This research proposes an improvement to a specific type of morphological neural networks called Dendrite Ellipsoidal Neuron (DEN) trained with k-means++ algorithm [2,3]. DEN has shown good performance in low dimensional datasets, requiring few training parameters and it is easy to implement in logic devices. Although DEN has shown to be efficient, it also has poor performance with high dimensional datasets. All these DEN advantages motivated us to explore new ideas in order to improve DEN accuracy in high dimensional datasets.

In this paper, we trained a DEN using Stochastic Gradient Descent (SGD) [4] implemented as a neural network layer of the Keras library [5] in Python. Furthermore, in order to test the proposed training algorithm in a high dimensional dataset, Electroencephalography (EEG) data were adquired from eight able-bodied subjects for classifying Motor Imagery (MI) of the hands into binary classes (Left vs Right). Contributions of this research are:

- This is the first time that a DEN is trained by SGD.
- Through a series of experiments, we show that the new training algorithm outperforms the actual DEN accuracy for our dataset, and the accuracy achieved by some of the most common classifiers for MI.

The rest of the paper is structured as follows: Sect. 2 provides a chronological list of publications related to previous literature with a comprehensive explanation. Section 3 describes the methods and materials used to obtain and characterize the EEG signals. Section 4 shows the DEN and the proposal architecture. Section 5 describes the general details of the used classifiers and the experimental results. In Sect. 6, we give our conclusions and future work.

2 Related Works

Morphological Neural Networks MNN were originally besought by Ritter and Davidson as a combination between neural networks and image algebra [6–9].

After this, Arbib published a book where it was taken into account that biological neurons process the information not only in the neuron cells but also in the dendrites [10]. Other related works resumed this research [11]. And several approaches have been proposed based on heuristics to manipulate hyperboxes not taking into account the dendrite fitness function.

All these techniques create hyperboxes to divide the input space into rectangular segments. In addition, in 2017 we presented DEN which changes the operations performed for MNN dendrites by using the Mahalanobis distance [12]. The main advantage of the ellipsoidal model is that it creates smoother decision boundaries and not rectangular regions.

Some other similar approaches to the k-means++ [13] clustering algorithm and the Mahalanobis distance [12] are elliptical k-means clustering algorithms, Gaussian Mixture Models (GMM), and classifiers based on the Mahalanobis distance.

Authors in [14,15] employed elliptical k-means clustering algorithm to discriminate between human and nonhuman faces. For this, they altered k-means by modifying the normalized Mahalanobis distance to achieve six face pattern clusters.

GMM is a probabilistic technique focused to approximate almost any continuous density by using an enough number of Gaussian [16].

3   Methods and Materials

This section describes the experiments carried out to obtain EEG signals from subjects whom performed MI of both hands and the preprocessing and feature extraction procedure.

3.1   Experiment Setup

For this study, eight healthy people (three males and five females) aged 25 to 30 participated in an experiment designed to obtain EEG recordings for two mental tasks:

1. Imagined movements of the left hand and,
2. Imagined movements of the right hand.

These experimental conditions consisted of flexion and extension of the fingers of the right and left hand mentally without performing the actual movements. A graphical user interface developed by our team provided the instructions of the experiment and indicated when the subject had to carry out the mental imaginations.

The experiment was divided into 16 blocks of a duration of 28 s each. A block started with a fixation cross shown on the screen for 5 s, followed by a visual cue of the action to be performed by the participant (3 s). White arrows and a sphere that moved from the center of the screen to the left or right side of the monitor represented the different types of tasks, Fig. 1 (Right). Then, the participant had to execute for 15 s the imagined movement specified by the interface. Finally, the word "Rest" was shown on the screen for 5 s, indicating that the subject could relax or move freely until the beginning of the next block. The software selected the task of each block randomly. Also, both conditions were balanced, i.e., the subject performed eight times the "left" task and eight times the "right" task. In total, an experiment lasted around seven and a half minutes. Fig. 1 (Left) illustrates the different stages of this paradigm.

During the experiment execution, a g.USBamp amplifier recorded EEG signals from 12 active electrodes at a sampling rate of 256 Hz (g.tec medical engineering GmbH, Austria). Data were band-pass filtered from 0.1 to 100 Hz, and a built-in notch filter removed the power supply noise. According to the international 10/20 system, the electrode positions used in this experiment were FC3, FCz, FC4, C3, Cz, C4, CP3, CPz, CP4, P3, Pz, and P4. This arrangement was selected to cover scalp locations that are close to the motor cortex. Additionally, the ground electrode was located at AFz, and the reference electrode was placed over the right earlobe.

3.2 Preprocessing and Feature Extraction

The Common Spatial-Pattern (CSP) algorithm was used to characterize the brain activity of both experimental conditions. This algorithm finds linear combinations of the original EEG signals (or band-limited components of the EEG) so that the variances of the new signals of one condition are maximized, whereas the variances of the signals of the other condition are minimized. In this way, if the log-variances of the signals in the projected space are used as features, the separability between conditions is optimal. In this study, the CSP algorithm was applied over band-limited components extracted by a filter bank. This strategy is commonly known as Filter Bank Common Spatial-Pattern (FBCSP).

In the preprocessing stage, a filter bank of gaussian bandpass filters with a bandwidth of 4 Hz extracted 22 components from the EEG signals (4, 5, 6, ..., 25 Hz). Then, the data was separated into epochs or trials of 1 second of time samples. Trials contaminated by visual or muscular artifacts were identified and rejected from this study. Finally, the CSP algorithm was used to compute a new set of signals for each frequency component to increase the separability between conditions. For each band, the three best spatial filters that maximize the variances of the "Left" conditions were calculated. Likewise, the three best spatial filters that maximize the variances of the "Right" conditions were also computed, associated to a class label y {Left, Right}. The features used in the classification stage were the log-variances of these time-series. In total, each trial consisted of 132 new projected signals, $x \in \Re^{132 \times 256}$.

4 Den Architecture

DEN has the same structure as any other neural network architecture: an input, a hidden and an output layer, Fig. 2.

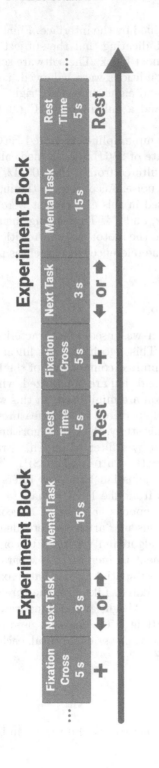

Fig. 1. Left: The experiment starts with **Fixation Cross**, which indicates the beginning of the experiment. After this, **Next Task** just indicates the action that will be carried out. **Mental Task** shows the mental task needed to be carried out. And **Rest Time** indicates relaxing time. Right: Visual cues. + Fixation Cross. ← Imagined movements of the left upper limb. → Imagined movements of the right upper limb. **Reset**.

The input layer receives the incoming $x_i = (x_1, x_2, \ldots, x_n)^T$ patterns. The hidden layer calculates the Mahalanobis distance between the input patterns and all the hyperellipsoids placed by the dendrites with Eq. 1. Lastly, the output layer assigns patterns to their nearest dendrites which are related to their corresponding $C^1, C^2, \ldots, C^j$ classes with Eq. 2:

$$\tau_K = [x_i - \mu_k]^T \sum_k^{-1} [x_i - \mu_k], \tag{1}$$

$$y_i = argming(\tau_K), \tag{2}$$

where x_i is a n dimensional vector, τ_K is a vector with k Mahalanobis distances and y_i is the output vector of each x_i pattern. $\sum_k^{-1}$ is the covariance matrix and μ_k is the centroid vector both related with the k hyperellipsoids.

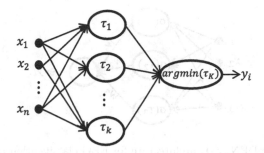

Fig. 2. DEN architecture with an input, a hidden and an output layer.

Once we experimentally observed that DEN has a good performance with small dimensional datasets but not with high dimensional datasets, we occurred to the task of setting the hyperellipsoids by using SGD as an optimization method [4].

To do this, we first implemented the hidden layer (Eq. 1) in a Keras custom layer [5]. Keras computes gradients by using automatic differentiation which automatically calculate the function derivatives of a computer program [17]. And then, we removed the output layer (Eq. 2) which could be replaceable by one or more neurons.

5   Classifiers and Results

This section shows the general details of the used classifiers for the MI classification task and the results achieved by them.

The first technique was a Support Vector Machine (SVM) [18] which is one of the most widespread methods for Brain-Computer Interface (BCI) based on EEG, as previously mentioned. It is formed by two layers: depending on the kernel, the first layer is employed for feature extraction and the second layer creates a hyperplane to separate patterns into two different classes. The goal of the second layer is to create a hyperplane with optimal margins among the support vectors.

In the experiment, we implemented the SVM with a Radial Basis Function (RBF) kernel; so commonly utilized on BCI based on EEG [19,20]. And we selected the γ gamma and the C compensation factor by doing a grid sweep in order to choose the best parameters.

The second classifier was a Multilayer Perceptron (MLP) [21]. This was implemented with two hidden layers, each layer with 100 ReLU neurons and an output layer with a sigmoid neuron (σ). To decrease the overfitting problem, we applied dropout with a rate of 0.2 between each layer.

The last classifiers were DEN and DEN trained by SGD (DEN_SGD). DEN_SGD architecture was composed by three hyperellipsoids with sigmoid activation functions in the input layer and a sigmoid neuron in the output layer, Fig. 3.

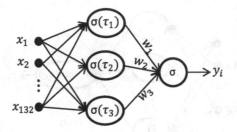

Fig. 3. DEN_SGD architecture for EEG classification task.

Table 1 presents the accuracy achieved by the four classifiers. It can be appreciated that the SVM always obtained a 100% of accuracy in the training stage. However, it computed a 65.81% in testing. As can be seen, the SVM has a high overfitting problem.

Table 1. Experimental results acquired by the SVM, MLP, DEN and SGD_DEN classifiers using our EEG dataset.

	SVM		MLP		DEN		SGD_DEN	
Participant	Train	Test	Train	Test	Train	Test	Train	Test
P1	100.00	62.99	96.73	70.66	76.02	62.76	91.48	74.50
P2	100.00	64.45	99.42	68.49	83.82	62.70	91.09	72.86
P3	100.00	72.97	98.51	78.96	80.79	64.19	93.46	81.27
P4	100.00	63.24	96.47	68.28	83.36	64.02	94.81	72.60
P5	100.00	62.46	97.74	68.61	92.61	63.66	90.52	73.65
P6	100.00	64.35	98.40	71.54	84.28	63.55	90.94	75.44
P7	100.00	75.59	96.84	82.53	70.34	63.50	97.94	85.03
P8	100.00	60.48	98.40	69.96	75.34	57.79	95.19	72.80
Average	100.00	65.81	97.81	72.38	80.82	62.77	93.18	76.02
STD	0.00	5.06	0.98	5.02	6.41	1.94	2.47	4.31

DEN achieved the lowest accuracy in training and in testing, 80.82% and 62.77%, respectively.

The best classifiers for this task were the MLP and the SGD_DEN. The MLP acquired an accuracy of 72.38% in testing and the SGD_DEN slightly acquired an improvement with 76.02%. Both presented the overfitting problem, but it was less with SGD_DEN.

Finally, as a comparison of the proposed method with the other classifiers in statistical terms, it was performed a paired t-test with a significance level of $\alpha = 0.05$. Table 2 gives the p-values acquired in the test. The comparisons between SGD_DEN and SVM, MLP and DEN achieved a less value than α, which indicates that for this dataset SGD_DEN has a significantly better performance.

Table 2. $P - values$ of a paired t-test with $\alpha = 0.05$.

Classifiers	$P - values$
SVM	0.000000136
MLP	0.000007950
DEN	0.000028302

6   Conclusions

In this research, we have implemented SGD to train a DEN and acquired an EEG dataset from eight healthy participants to test the performance of the proposed training algorithm. The besought model achieved an enhancement of 13.25% over the DEN training algorithm and an improvement of 3.64% and 10.21% compared with the MLP and the SVM, respectively. We invite the reader to regard an improvement obtained with a shallow architecture which can be easily implemented in embedded electronic devices. Future work will be the evaluation of DEN_SGD using standard datasets and the implementation of this network to control external electronic devices.

Acknowledgments. H. Sossa and E. Zamora would like to acknowledge the support provided by CIC-IPN and M. Antelis to Tecnológico de Monterrey, in carrying out this research. This work was economically supported by SIP-IPN (grant numbers 20180180, 20180730, 20190007 and 20190166) and CONACYT grant numbers 65 (Frontiers of Science), 268958 and PN2015-873. F. Arce and O. Mendoza-Montoya acknowledge CONACYT for the scholarship granted towards pursuing their PhD and post-PhD studies, respectively.

References

1. Leshno, M., Lin, V.Y., Pinkus, A., Schocken, S.: Multilayer feedforward networks with a nonpolynomial activation function can approximate any function. Neural Netw. **6**(6), 861–867 (1993)

2. Arce, F., Zamora, E., Sossa, H.: Dendrite ellipsoidal neuron. In: 2017 International Joint Conference on Neural Networks (IJCNN), pp. 795–802, May 2017
3. Arce, F., Zamora, E., Fócil-Arias, C., Sossa, H.: Dendrite ellipsoidal neurons based on k-means optimization. Evolving Syst. 1–16 (2018). https://app.dimensions. aion2019/02/18
4. Montavon, G., Müller, K.-R.: Big learning and deep neural networks. In: Montavon, G., Orr, G.B., Müller, K.-R. (eds.) Neural Networks: Tricks of the Trade. LNCS, vol. 7700, pp. 419–420. Springer, Heidelberg (2012). https://doi.org/10.1007/978-3-642-35289-8_24
5. Chollet, F., et al.: Keras (2015). https://keras.io
6. Ritter, G.X., Li, D., Wilson, J.N.: Image algebra and its relationship to neural networks (1989)
7. Davidson, J.L., Ritter, G.X.: Theory of morphological neural networks (1990)
8. Davidson, J.L., Sun, K.: Template learning in morphological neural nets (1991)
9. Davidson, J.L., Hummer, F.: Morphology neural networks: an introduction with applications. Circ. Syst. Sig. Process. **12**(2), 177–210 (1993)
10. Segev, I.: The Handbook of Brain Theory and Neural Networks, pp. 282–289. MIT Press, Cambridge (1998)
11. Ritter, G.X., Iancu, L., Urcid, G.: Morphological perceptrons with dendritic structure. In: The 12th IEEE International Conference on Fuzzy Systems, FUZZ 2003, vol. 2., pp. 1296–1301, May 2003
12. Mahalanobis, P.C.: On the generalised distance in statistics. Proc. Natl. Inst. Sci. India **2**(1), 49–55 (1936)
13. Arthur, D., Vassilvitskii, S.: K-means++: the advantages of careful seeding. In: Proceedings of the Eighteenth Annual ACM-SIAM Symposium on Discrete Algorithms, SODA 2007, pp. 1027–1035. Society for Industrial and Applied Mathematics, Philadelphia (2007)
14. Sung, K.-K., Poggio, T.: Learning human face detection in cluttered scenes. In: Hlaváč, V., Šára, R. (eds.) CAIP 1995. LNCS, vol. 970, pp. 432–439. Springer, Heidelberg (1995). https://doi.org/10.1007/3-540-60268-2_326
15. Sung, K.K., Poggio, T.: Example-based learning for view-based human face detection. IEEE Trans. Pattern Anal. Mach. Intell. **20**(1), 39–51 (1998)
16. Bishop, C.M.: Pattern Recognition and Machine Learning. Information Science and Statistics. Springer, New York (2006)
17. Rall, L.B.: Automatic computation of gradients, Jacobians, Hessians, and applications to optimization. In: Rall, L.B. (ed.) Automatic Differentiation: Techniques and Applications. LNCS, vol. 120, pp. 91–111. Springer, Heidelberg (1981). https://doi.org/10.1007/3-540-10861-0_6
18. Cortes, C., Vapnik, V.: Support-vector networks. Mach. Learn. **20**(3), 273–297 (1995)
19. Lotte, F., Congedo, M., Lécuyer, A., Fabrice, L., Arnaldi, B.: A review of classification algorithms for EEG-based brain-computer interfaces. J. Neural Eng. **4**, R1 (2007)
20. Ali, A.B.M.S., Abraham, A.: An empirical comparison of kernel selection for support vector machines. In: Soft Computing Systems: Design, Management and Applications, pp. 321–330 (2002)
21. Rumelhart, D.E., Hinton, G.E., Williams, R.J.: Parallel Distributed Processing: Explorations in the Microstructure of Cognition, vol. 1, pp. 318–362. MIT Press, Cambridge (1986)

An Improved Convolutional Neural Network Architecture for Image Classification

A. Ferreyra-Ramirez, C. Aviles-Cruz, E. Rodriguez-Martinez[✉],
J. Villegas-Cortez, and A. Zuñiga-Lopez

Departamento de Electrónica, Universidad Autónoma Metropolitana,
Unidad Azcapotzalco, Av. San Pablo 180, Col. Reynosa-Tamaulipas,
02200 Mexico City, Mexico
{fra,caviles,erm,jvc,azl}@azc.uam.mx

Abstract. This manuscript presents the design and implementation of an improved convolutional neural network (CNN) for image classification which was carefully crafted to avoid overfitting. Contrary to most CNNs which apply normalization before pooling, our proposed architecture reverse the order of such tasks. The performance of the proposed architecture, named ACEnet, was evaluated using a hold-out method over five selected databases: Olivia, Paris, Oxford Buildings, Caltech-101, and Caltech-256. We present three main results: processing time, training performance and testing performance for each database. Also, we present a comparison versus the well-known Alexnet architecture, where our CNN proposal improves 5.11% the mean testing performance over the selected databases.

Keywords: Convolutional neural network · Image classification · Mini-batch size · Epochs number · Overfitting

1 Introduction

Nowdays, convolutional neural networks are a central topic in computer vision, specifically in applications such as video and image processing, where deep learning architectures have proven to outperform traditional image classification approaches. A CNN is a variation of a multilayer perceptron, but its performance makes it much more effective in machine vision tasks because each stage models one part of the visual cortex. Theoretical foundations of CNNs are based on the Neocognitron introduced by Fukushima in 1980 [13], improved by LeCun in 1998 [19] and fine-tuned by Ciresan in 2011 [11].

As classifiers, CNNs have an incredible generalization capability, which increases with the size of the training set, because the greater the amount of information available, the better the millions of parameters contained in its structure will be trained [3,12]. For databases with limited number of labeled images, it has been suggested that fine-tuning a trained architecture with a robust database is better than training the same architecture from scratch [10,14,21,27].

© Springer Nature Switzerland AG 2019
J. A. Carrasco-Ochoa et al. (Eds.): MCPR 2019, LNCS 11524, pp. 89–101, 2019.
https://doi.org/10.1007/978-3-030-21077-9_9

One of the key issues for a successful CNN is choosing the structure and parameters that represent image information accurately and uniquely. These structure is comprised of stages, where each stage is conformed by *convolution, rectification, pooling and normalization* tasks. When the CNN is used in classification problems, there is also a classification stage comprised of fully connected layers followed by an output layer, where the number of neurons is equal to the number of classes.

The configuration parameters in a CNN are divided into two categories: (a) those concerning the architecture –such as kernel size, stride and padding– and (b) those concerning the training algorithm –such as mini-batch size, regularization type, number of training epochs, learning-rate drop period, learning-rate drop factor, learning-rate schedule, and initial learning rate.

In this paper, we present the design and implementation of an improved convolutional neural network for image classification which was carefully crafted to avoid overfitting. The performance of the proposed architecture, which we named *ACEnet*, was compared against that of *Alexnet* [18], achieving a 5.11% increase in classification accuracy.

ACEnet consists of six feature extraction (FE) stages, instead of five as proposed in [17, 18]. The additional stage is comprised of convolution, rectification and pooling tasks. Another important difference between Alexnet and our proposal is on the second FE stage, where in the sequence of tasks: *convolution, rectification, normalization and pooling*, proposed by *Alexnet*, the order of the last two task is inverted.

To compare the performance of both architectures, each was trained from scratch using five databases: Oliva and Torralba (Oliva) [4], Paris [6], Oxford [5], Caltech-101 [1] and Caltech-256 [2]. For each selected database we present processing time and classification accuracy for both training set and testing set.

The rest of the paper is organized as follows. Section 2 describes the state of the art. Section 3 presents a general convolutional neural network architecture. The proposed architecture is presented in Sect. 4. Section 5 presents the employed methodology. Results are described in Sect. 6. Finally, Sect. 7 summarizes the main conclusions and briefly talks about future directions.

2   State of the Art

The classical techniques to avoid over-fitting in CNNs have been dropout and data augmentation, first proposed in [18]. Recently, several works have shifted the attention into other regularization forms that attempt to modify the loss function used by the gradient descent algorithm or its variants. An intermediate layer between pooling and convolution layers is proposed in [23], such layer is a *micro network* which can be modelled as a small classifier, such as SVM or softmax classifiers. Each micro network adds a regularization term to the CNN's loss function, which simultaneously minimize final classification error while enforcing hidden layers to learn more discriminative features.

The term *micro network* was introduced in [20] and refers to a modification in the architecture of a CNN where a multi-layer perceptron (MLP), or other small network, is used instead of a linear filter at each convolutional layer. Each patch of the input volume is fed to the MLP, and the MLP output forms a voxel of the output matrix. The feature maps are build by sliding the MLP over the whole input volume. The architecture using micro networks is known as *network-in-network* (NiN).

An extension of [20] was proposed in [26], where the output of a NiN is routed into multiple fully-connected layers, each concatenated to a different loss function. The authors of [26] claim that using multiple loss functions drag the training algorithm away from overfitting to one particular single-loss function. The intuition behind using multiple loss functions is that each will model a different aspect of the same task. For instance, the pairwise ranking loss [24] prioritizes learning a given order of labelled pairs, while the LambdaRank loss [9] optimizes the top-k classification accuracy.

A redundancy regularizer was proposed in [25] to reduce the number of correlated kernels at each convolutional layer. Such regularizer showed a slight improvement over dropout, but when combined with it and early stopping the improvement was significant.

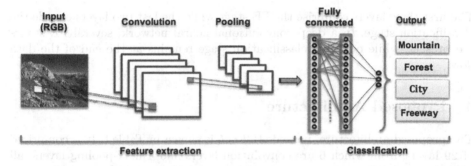

Fig. 1. Hierarchical representation of a convolutional neural network.

3   Convolutional Neural Network

Figure 1 displays a generic CNN architecture. It is a hierarchical structure composed of five principal layers:

Input layer. It is considered as a pre-processing layer, where the input images can be resized, rotated or subsampled.

Convolution layer. It is considered as the basic building block in a CNN, and performs most of the computational work. This layer receives an input volume with H_{in}^c pixels height, W_{in}^c pixels width, D_{in}^c channels deep, and P pixels for padding. The input volume is processed with a set of k filters, which are encoded as weights and connections between neurons. Such filters are based on convolutional masks, called *kernels*, and are defined with the following parameters: spatial extension $(E, [W_f, H_f])$ and stride (S_x, S_y), where

E is the kernel depth along D_{in}^c, $[W_f, H_f]$ is the area size where convolution will be computed, and (S_x, S_y) define the number of pixels that will be skipped between consecutive convolutions. The output volume size is defined as $(H_{out}^c, W_{out}^c, D_{out}^c)$, where each dimension is defined in terms of the input volume as $W_{out}^c = (W_{in}^c - E + 2P)/S_x + 1$, $H_{out}^c = (H_{in}^c - E + 2P)/S_y + 1$, and $D_{out}^c = k$.

Pooling layer. Its purpose is to shrink the convolution layer output so that the dimensionality of the extracted features can also be reduced, while keeping the information they encode. The pooling layer receives an input volume of size $(W_{in}^p, H_{in}^p, D_{in}^p)$, which is processed with a set of filters with the following parameters: spatial extension $(F, [W_f, H_f])$ and stride (S_x, S_y). The output volume size is defined as $(H_{out}^p, W_{out}^p, D_{out}^p)$, where each dimension is defined in terns of the input volume as $W_{out}^p = (W_{in}^p - F)/S_x + 1$, $H_{out}^p = (H_{in}^p - F)/S_y + 1$, and $D_{out}^p = D_{in}^p$.

Fully connected layer. This layer computes the weighted sum of the pooling layer output, or of the convolution layer when no pooling layer is present.

Output layer. This layer holds one neuron per category in the classification task.

The first three layers comprise the FE stage while the last two layers encode the classification stage. In a deep convolutional neural network, several FE stages are present, while only one classification stage remains at the end of the data flow.

4   Proposed Architecture

The proposed architecture, named *ACEnet*, is shown in Table 1. It is comprised of 29 layers, from which 6 are convolution layers and 4 max-pooling layers, all of them using different kernels and strides. Some of the convolutional layers use padding to make their output conform with the input size needed for the next feature-extraction stage. *ACEnet* uses six FE stages. Each of the first three FE stages comprises of four layers: a convolution layer, a rectification layer, a pooling layer, and a normalization layer. The next two FE stages only have two layers: a convolution layer followed by a rectification layer, while the last FE stage also have a pooling layer at the top of the previously mentioned layers. Layers 20–25 form two generalization stages, intended to avoid overfitting in the network. Each generalization stage calculates the weighted sum of its inputs and rectifies it, to subsequently apply a regularization technique known as drop-out. In the following we describe some characteristics of our proposed architecture.

Convolution layers: They were designed using small kernels (i.e. $E \in \{7, 5, 3\}$) to get highly representative features and decrease the number of training parameters. The first convolution layer gets low-level features (i.e. edges, lines and curves), while subsequent convolution layers get high-level features.

Rectification layers: These layers have neurons with the non-linear, non-saturating activation function $f(x) = \max(0, x)$. They are known as Rectified Linear Units (ReLU) because their behavior is similar to the half-wave rectifier in electrical engineering. They provide a better model of biological neurons, with similar or better performance than the logistic-sigmoid function and the hyperbolic-tangent function. It has been proved that ReLU units reach good performance without resorting to unsupervised pre-training and, although their training requires large amounts of labeled data, there is no negative effect to their performance [15]. The CNNs with ReLU layers are trained several times faster then their equivalent with hyperbolic-tangent units [18].

Pooling layers with overlap: Pooling in CNNs is highly disruptive. If the filters do not overlap, the pooling layers loose information about objects localization on the image, which is needed to detect the precise relation among them. The most popular pooling layers use 2×2 filters with a stride of 2, shrinking the input image size by half, discarding about 75% of the activations generated by the previous layer. To avoid information loss and overfitting, the pooling layers used in the proposed architecture consist of 3×3 filters with a stride of 2, also called pooling with overlap; if pooling windows overlap enough, location information will be preserved.

Normalization layers: Their propose is to add generalization ability to the network. Normalization of a neuron's output implements a kind of lateral inhibition much more like the found in real neurons, promoting competition among several neurons output at times of great neural activity [18].

Drop-out layer: These layers were included to force fully connected layers to learn more robust features. Drop-out is a highly recommended technique to cope with overfitting [22], in which the output of some randomly-selected neurons are set to zero so they can't contribute with the backpropagation of the error at training, reducing complex coadaptation of neurons; in this way, every time a new example is fed for training, the neural network shows a different architecture, however all the different architectures share their weights.

5 Methodology

In this section we provide a detailed description of three important experiments that allow us to justify the proposed architecture, as well as the training parameters. In the first subsection, we describe the model selection method used to set the mini-batch size and epochs number in the training algorithm for *ACEnet*. In the last subsection, we provide the settings for the numerical comparison of the classification performance between *ACEnet* and *Alexnet*.

We used the algorithm Stochastic Gradient Descent with Momentum (SGDM) to train the compared architectures. Let θ_i be the vector with all the weights of the network at the i-th iteration of the SGDM algorithm, which are updated by the rule $\theta_{i+1} = \theta_i - \eta \nabla E(\theta_i) + \mu(\theta_i - \theta_{i-1})$, where η is the initial

Table 1. Architecture of the proposed convolutional neural network

No.	Layer	Output volume size			Kernel	Stride	Padding
		Width	Hight	Deep			
0	Input	227	227	3	-	-	-
1	Convolution1	111	111	50	7	2	-
2	ReLu1	111	111	50	-	-	-
3	Pooling1	55	55	50	3	2	-
4	Normilization1	55	55	50	-	-	-
5	Convolution2	55	55	100	5	1	2
6	ReLu2	55	55	100	-	-	-
7	Pooling2	27	27	100	3	2	-
8	Normalization2	27	27	100	-	-	-
9	Convolution3	27	27	256	3	1	2
10	ReLu3	27	27	256	-	-	-
11	Pooling3	13	13	256	3	2	-
12	Normalization3	13	13	256	-	-	-
13	Convolution4	13	13	400	3	1	1
14	ReLu4	13	13	400	-	-	-
15	Convolution5	13	13	400	3	1	1
16	ReLu5	13	13	400	-	-	-
17	Convolution6	13	13	256	3	1	1
18	ReLu6	13	13	256	-	-	-
19	Pooling6	6	6	256	3	2	-
20	Fully connected	1	1	4800	-	-	-
21	ReLu	1	1	4800	-	-	-
22	Drop-out	1	1	4800	-	-	-
23	Fully Connected	1	1	2400	-	-	-
24	ReLu	1	1	2400	-	-	-
25	Drop-out	1	1	2400	-	-	-
26	Fully connected	1	1	NC	-	-	-
27	Softmax	1	1	NC	-	-	-
28	Classification	1	1	1000	-	-	-

learning rate, μ is the momentum, and $E(\theta_i)$ is the loss function described as $E(\theta_i) = \frac{1}{\beta} \sum_{k=1}^{\beta} E_k(\theta_i) - \frac{\lambda}{2} \theta_i^T \theta_i$, where $E_k(\theta_i)$ is the loss function value at the k-th training example in the mini-batch of size β, and λ is the regularization coefficient. The SGDM parameters used to train Alexnet were set as recommended in [18]. Some other parameters were kept in common for both architectures and were set as follows: the initial weights at every layer were randomly drawn from the gaussian distribution $N(0, 0.01)$; the activation thresholds at each layer were initialized to zero; finally, the number of neurons in the output layer was adjusted to match the number of classes in each database. Both architectures were trained on a GPU NVIDIA GeForce GTX TITAN X with 3072 cores and 12 GB of memory, using MatLab and the Deep Learning Toolbox.

Table 2. SGDM parameters used for training of ACEnet and Alexnet

Parameter	Value	
	ACEnet	*Alexnet*
Initial learn rate (η)	0.001	0.01
Learn rate schedule	Piecewise	Piecewise
Learn rate drop factor	0.1	0.1
Learn rate drop period	30	30
Max epochs	100	100
Momentum (μ)	0.9	0.9
L2 regularization (λ)	0.0005	0.0005
Mini batch size (β)	25	128

In case of *ACEnet*, we decided to set the learning rate at 0.001 to get a finer control over the steps given by the SGDM algorithm, and by setting $\lambda = 0.0005$, we reduced the probability of overfitting and the complexity of the CNN [16]. We performed a sequential search to find the optimal value for the mini-batch size and epoch number. In each step of the search the classification error was computed using the hold-out method and the optimal was found in the minimum value of the classification error.

To test the ACEnet generalization performance, we selected five complex databases with real-world images in JPEG format. Relevant statistics for each database are displayed on Table 3. A sixth database was build by combining all selected databases, and used only for performance comparison against

Table 3. Summary of the selected databases for image classification. "Min p. class" and "Max p. class" refer to the minimum and maximum images per class, respectively.

Database	Categories	Dimensions			No. images		
		Width	Hight	Depth	Total	Min p. class	Max p. class
Oliva [7]	8	256	256	3	2,668	260	410
Paris [6]	12	1024	768	3	6,412	147	1,497
Oxford [5]	17	1024	768	3	5,063	59	1,502
Caltech-101 [1]	101	300	200	3	8,677	31	800
Caltech-256 [2]	256	300	200	3	29,780	80	798

Alexnet. Both, model selection and performance comparison was completed for each database. In every experiment, we estimated the classification performance by means of hold-out, where each database was split into training and testing sets. We used 70% of the total number of images as training set and the rest as testing set.

5.1 Training Parameters

Mini-batch Size. The mini-batch size is one of the parameters that directly impacts CNNs performance. It indicates the number of images from the training set that are considered at each iteration of the SGDM algorithm. The optimal mini-batch size was found by means of sequential search in the interval [10, 120] with increments of 10 units. At each point in the search, we recorded the classification accuracy and training time, and selected the optimal mini-batch size as the point in the search with minimum training time and maximum accuracy. In this experiment, every time we run the SGDM algorithm we fixed the epochs number to 100.

Epochs Number and Overfitting. Besides drop-out layers, controlling the epochs number in the training algorithm is an efficient way to avoid overfitting in a CNN [18]. We trained ACEnet with different values for the epochs number, ranging from 10 to 100 with increments of 10. We recorded the classification error for the training set and testing set at the end of the training algorithm. It is well known that the training and testing errors steadily decrease before overfitting, and they diverge when the CNN has been overfitted [8]. Thus, the optimal epochs number is the point before the classification errors diverge.

5.2 Performance Comparison

We compared the classification performance of ACEnet against that of the well-known Alexnet architecture. The training parameters for Alexnet and for ACEnet were the same except for the mini-batch size, which was set using the results of the model selection method for our proposed architecture. The mini-batch size as well as the rest of the training parameters for Alexnet were taken from [18] and are listed in Table 2. For each of the five selected databases, we trained both architectures using 70% of the total number of images until the SGDM converged. After reaching convergence, we recorded training time and classification accuracy on the training set. Next, we computed and recorded the classification accuracy on the testing set.

6 Results

In this section we start by describing the results of the parameter selection experiment and then we will proceed to the comparison with the well-known Alexnet architecture.

6.1   Training Parameters

Mini-batch Size. Figure 2 shows the recorded training times and classification accuracies for every mini-batch size tested in the model selection method described in Sect. 5.1 for Oliva database. It can be seen in Fig. 2 that the best accuracy is located between 1 and 50 images per batch, while the minimum training time is located between 20 and 40 images per batch. So, having a trade-off between accuracy and training time, we propose to use a mini-batch size of 25 for Oliva database. The same results were found for other image datasets.

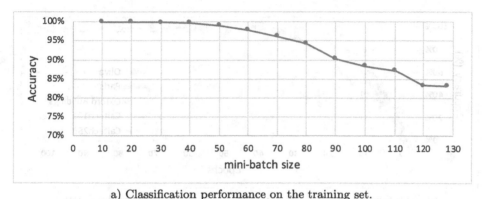

a) Classification performance on the training set.

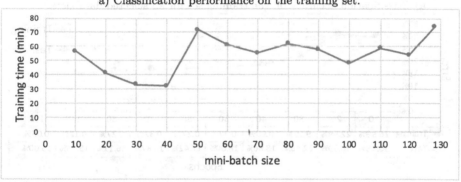

b) Training time as a function of mini-batch size.

Fig. 2. Mini-batch size selection for olivaba database.

Epoch Number and Overfitting. We can observe in Fig. 3a the classification accuracy reached when ACEnet is trained using different number of epochs for each of the selected databases. Clearly, our proposed architecture correctly learns the training set in about 60 epochs, regardless of the database used. Thus, setting the number of epochs to 100 give a good training margin for future databases, however it must be tested if ACEnet does not overfit to the training set with such large number of epochs. Figure 3b displays training and testing errors recorded for different values of the epochs number using the Oliva database. It is worth noting that although the testing error has a light increment when setting the epochs number to 20, both training and testing errors keep decreasing steadily until the 50 epochs point. Such increment could be considered as an overfitting indicator, however in the next point along the grid we see both errors decrease again, which points towards the ability of our architecture to recover from overfitting. The training error can be considered stable after the 50 epochs point, however the testing error keeps decreasing until the 100 epochs point. Therefore, we can safely train ACEnet for 100 epochs without incurring in overfitting.

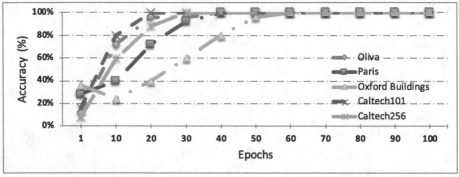

a) Classification accuracy on the training set for all selected databases.

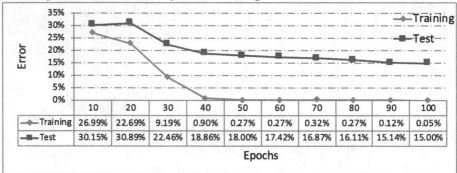

b) Overfitting test for Oliva-Torralba database.

Fig. 3. Epoch number selection based on overfitting analysis.

6.2   Performance Comparison

Table 4 shows an overview of the experimental results from the performance comparison against Alexnet. In the following we elaborate further on the three aspects shown in Table 4, namely training time T_{tr}, and classification accuracy for the training A_{tr} and testing A_{te} set. ACEnet required consistently less time to reach a 100% of classification accuracy on the training set than Alexnet.

The achieved speed up for Oliva, Paris, Oxford, Caltech-101, and Caltech-256 databases was 1.4x, 1.2x, 1.3x, 1.9x, 1.8x and 1.4x, respectively. Although ACEnet has one more stage than Alexnet, such increase in model complexity did not directly impacted on the time needed for training. Regarding classification accuracy on the test set, ACEnet performed better than Alexnet for all selected databases. The performance improvement for Oliva, Paris, Oxford, Caltech-101, and Caltech-256 databases was 9.58%, 8.60%, 4.35%, 12.05%, and 17.60%, respectively. On average, our proposal improves 5.11% the mean testing performance over the five selected databases. For the artificially build database, our proposal outperformed Alexnet by 6.65%.

Table 4 also shows other measures of classification performance for both networks, namely F1-score, G-measure, and Matthews correlation coefficient. While F1-score provides the harmonic mean of precision and recall, G-measures is their geometric mean. On the other hand, Matthews correlation coefficient indicates the disagreement between predicted and true labels, and it is robust to the imbalanced-class problem. As can be seen, ACEnet generally outperforms Alexnet in all the mentioned measures. Additionally, we performed the nonparametric Friedman's test to prove the statistical difference in the results obtained by the two architectures. The resulting p-values for all the selected performance measures are given in the bottom of Table 4. From such tests, we can say that the results obtained with ACEnet are statistically different from those obtained with Alexnet with 97% of confidence.

Table 4. Time and performance comparison between ACEnet and Alexnet. Training time T_{tr} is given in hours, while classification accuracy for the training A_{tr} and testing A_{te} set are given in percentages. F1 is the harmonic mean of precision and recall, while G is their geometric mean. MCC displays Matthew correlation coefficient.

Database	ACEnet						Alexnet					
	T_{tr}	A_{tr}	A_{te}	F1	G	MCC	T_{tr}	A_{tr}	A_{te}	F1	G	MCC
Oliva	0.58	100	85.11	0.86	0.86	0.84	0.83	98.83	77.67	0.81	0.81	0.79
Paris	4.36	98.93	46.09	0.43	0.46	0.41	5.27	97.61	42.44	0.41	0.43	0.37
Oxford	3.36	99.49	31.42	0.25	0.30	0.20	4.35	99.97	30.11	0.20	0.26	0.15
Caltech-101	1.82	99.95	71.51	0.59	0.69	0.71	3.45	99.51	63.83	0.01	0.50	0.64
Caltech-256	7.68	99.99	36.99	0.01	0.14	0.37	13.57	99.60	31.20	0.01	0.08	0.30
All	18.63	96.81	35.51	0.01	0.23	0.35	26.88	96.64	28.95	0.01	0.14	0.28
p-value			0.0143	0.030	0.030	0.030						

7 Conclusions and Future Works

We have presented an improved convolutional neural network architecture for image classification. Designing a CNN for image classification involves setting properly the feature extraction layers, the classification stage, and the parameters of the learning algorithm. The architecture of a CNN can be empirically designed if the behavior and purpose of each stage are clearly understood, however, the parameters of the learning algorithm must be fine-tuned by a model selection method. The proposed architecture can be trained from scratch with any database, which avoids reusing pre-trained networks.

The results presented show that the proposed architecture do not suffer from overfitting, allowing us to increase the number of epochs in the training algorithm. We showed that while the training error reaches stability, the testing error keeps decreasing as the number of epochs increases, however the training time will also increase. In order to keep a low training time, we must sacrifice generalization performance, however we obtained testing errors comparable to those in the state-of-the-art.

Comparing our proposal with the well-known Alexnet architecture. Our proposal improves 5.11% the mean testing performance over five real-world databases. Regarding mean processing time, our proposal required 17.8 h to process all five databases, while Alexnet needed 27.47 h. Our proposal is faster due to the use of a smaller mini-batch and kernel size, and due to the reduction in the number of epoch. However we empirically demonstrated that such size reduction do not affect the classification accuracy. While Alexnet was specifically designed to get a low classification error on the ILSVRC-2012 database, our proposed architecture does not depend on a specific database and has a better generalization performance due to the extra processing stage. As future work, we would like to use more complex image databases, beside we would like to use the weights of intermediate layers in pretrained CNN as a set of features for image classification/identification, where the final aim is to conform a content-based image retrieval (CBIR) system.

References

1. Caltech-101 dataset. http://www.vision.caltech.edu/Image_Datasets/Caltech101
2. Caltech-256 dataset. http://www.vision.caltech.edu/Image_Datasets/Caltech256
3. Imagenet dataset. http://www.image-net.org/
4. Labelme dataset. http://cvcl.mit.edu/database.html
5. The Oxford Buildings dataset. http://www.robots.ox.ac.uk/~vgg/data/oxbuildings
6. The Paris dataset. http://www.robots.ox.ac.uk/~vgg/data/parisbuildings
7. Oliva, A., Torralba, A.: Modeling the shape of the scene: a holistic representation of the spatial envelop. Int. J. Comput. Vis. **42**(3), 145–175 (2001)
8. Bishop, C.M.: Neural Networks for Pattern Recognition. Clarendon Press, Glouces- tershire (1996)
9. Burges, C., et al.: Learning to rank using gradient descent. In: 22nd International conference on Machine Learning. ACM Press (2005)
10. Chatfield, K., Simonyan, K., Vedaldi, A., Zisserman, A.: Return of the devil in the details: delving deep into convolutional nets. In: proceedings of ECCV (2014)
11. Ciresan, D.C., Meier, U., Masci, J., Gambardella, L., Schmidhuber, J.: Flexible high performance convolutional neural networks for image classification. In: Pro- ceedings of the Twenty-Second International Joint Conference on Artificial Intel- ligence, vol. 2, pp. 1237–1242 (2011)

12. Deng, J., Dong, W., Socher, R., Li, L., Li, K., Li, F.F.: ImageNet: a large-scale hierarchical image database. In: IEEE Computer Vision and Pattern Recognition, pp. 248–255 (2009)
13. Fukushima, K.: Neocognitron: a self-organizing neural network model for a mechanism of pattern recognition unaffected by shift in position. Biol. Cybern. **36**(4), 193–202 (1980)
14. Girshick, R.B., Danahue, J.: Rich features hierarchies for accurate object detection and semantic segmentation. In: Proceedings of the IEEE Conference on Computer Vision and Pattern Recognition, pp. 580–587 (2014)
15. Glorot, X., Bordes, A., Bengio, Y.: Deep sparse rectifier neural networks. In: Proceedings of the International Conference on Artificial Intelligence and Statistics, vol. 15, pp. 315–323 (2011)
16. Goodfellow, I., Bengio, Y., Courville, A.: Deep Learning. The MIT Press, Cambridge (2016)
17. Hertel, L., Barth, E., Kaster, T., Martinetz, T.: Deep convolutional neural networks as generic feature extractor. In: Proceedings of the IEEE International Joint Conference on Neural Networks, pp. 1–4, July 2015
18. Krizhevsky, A., Sutskever, I., Hinton, G.: Imagenet classification with deep convolutional neural networks. In: Advances in Neural Information Processing Systems, vol. 25, pp. 1097–1105 (2012)
19. LeCun, Y., Bottou, L., Bengio, Y., Haffner, P.: Gradient-based learning applied to document recognition. Proc. IEEE **86**, 2278–2324 (1998)
20. Lin, M., Chen, Q., Yan, S.: Network in network. In: Proceedings of the 2nd International Conference on Learning Representation (2014)
21. Razavjan, A.S., Azizpour, H., Sullivan, J., Carlsson, S.: CNN features off-the-shelf: an astounding baseline for recognition. In: Proceedings of the IEEE Conference on Computer Vision and Pattern Recognition, pp. 512–519 (2014)
22. Srivastava, N., Hinton, G., Krizhevsky, A., Sutskever, I., Salakhutdinov, R.: Dropout: a simple way to precent neural network from overfitting. J. Mach. Learn. Res. **15**, 1929–1958 (2014)
23. Sun, W., Su, F.: A novel companion objective function for regularization of deep convolutional neural networks. Image Vis. Comput. **60**, 58–63 (2017)
24. Usunier, N., Buffoni, D., Gallinari, P.: Ranking with ordered weighted pairwise classification. In: Proceedings of the 26th Annual International Conference on Machine Learning, ACM Press (2009)
25. Wu, B., Liu, Z., Yuan, Z., Sun, G., Wu, C.: Reducing overfitting in deep convolutional neural networks using redundancy regularizer. In: Lintas, A., Rovetta, S., Verschure, P.F.M.J., Villa, A.E.P. (eds.) ICANN 2017. LNCS, vol. 10614, pp. 49–55. Springer, Cham (2017). https://doi.org/10.1007/978-3-319-68612-7_6
26. Xu, C., et al.: Multi-loss regularized deep neural network. IEEE Trans. Circ. Syst. Video Technol. **26**(12), 2273–2283 (2016)
27. Yosinski, J., Clune, J., Bengio, Y.: How transferable are features in deep neural networks? In: Advances in Neural Information Processing Systems, vol. 27, pp. 3320–3328 (2014)

Computer Vision

Estimation of Forest Carbon from Aerial Photogrammetry

Dagoberto Pulido[1], Klaus Puettmann[2], and Joaquín Salas[1]([✉])

[1] CICATA Querétaro, Instituto Politécnico Nacional,
Cerro Blanco 141, Cimatario, 76030 Querétaro, Mexico
dagopuar@hotmail.com, jsalasr@ipn.mx
[2] Oregon State University, Corvallis, USA
klaus.puettmann@oregonstate.edu

Abstract. Quantifying tree biomass is a critical process for carbon stock estimation at the stand, landscape, and national levels. A major challenge for forest managers is the amount of effort involved to document carbon storage levels, especially in terms of human labor. In this paper, we propose a method to quantify the amount of carbon in forest stands. In our approach, we obtain aerial images from where we build 3D reconstructions of the terrain. Using the resulting orthomosaics, we identify individual trees and process their point clouds to extract information to estimate tree the height and to infer the diameter, which we employ in allometric equations to compute carbon content. We compare our results with carbon estimates obtained from allometric equations applied to manual tree diameter and height measurements.

Keywords: Tree detection · Carbon estimation · Deep learning · Remote sensing

1 Introduction

As part of the natural carbon cycle, trees absorb carbon dioxide from the atmosphere, store carbon in wood and bark, and release oxygen back into the atmosphere [8]. Thus, information about carbon stock and forest biomass is crucial for the development of sustainable forest management programs, including those aiming to mitigate climate change. However, standard procedures to estimate the carbon stored in trees require knowledge about specific features, such as the trunk diameter at breast height (DBH) (typically measured at 1.3 m height) and the height of trees. There have been some efforts to undertake these tasks using remote sensing technologies, particularly LiDARs [11,16], or its combination with cameras [15]. Nevertheless, these approaches make use devices which may require correspondingly robust infrastructure. More commonly, estimation of the overall carbon content of vegetation is still a labor-intensive, costly, error-prone and lengthy task, which includes the need to deploy personnel in the field.

© Springer Nature Switzerland AG 2019
J. A. Carrasco-Ochoa et al. (Eds.): MCPR 2019, LNCS 11524, pp. 105–114, 2019.
https://doi.org/10.1007/978-3-030-21077-9_10

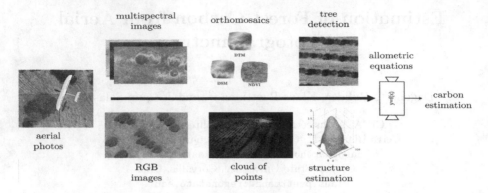

Fig. 1. Estimating carbon content in a forest stand. We process multispectral photos from Unmanned Aerial Systems (UAS) to obtain orthomosaics. Our tree detector algorithm uses these orthomosaics as input for determining bounding boxes. We use RGB images to generate a sparse point cloud for each tree. Once located a tree and measured its structure, we obtain conventional allometric equations to estimate carbon content.

Thus, there is a need to develop reliable, economical, and fast strategies for the efficient management of forest resources.

In this paper, we describe a methodology to estimate carbon stocks by detecting and measuring trees in forest stands via an Unmanned Aerial System (UAS) automatically (see Fig. 1). To identify individual trees, we employ a deep learning based approach where we create synthetic images for training. To estimate carbon content, we use aerial photos to reconstruct the scenario applying structure from motion techniques [12]. From the resulting point cloud, we determined the tree height and crown diameter, and predicted DBH of the identified trees. We implemented these methods for tree detection and used allometric equations to predict carbon content in the forest stand. Finally, we compared with estimates obtained from manual measurements of tree height and DBH. Although the focus of this paper is the determination of forest carbon, we briefly describe the tree detection method, which receives full attention in a different document.

We structure the rest of the document as follows. In Sect. 2, we review the literature covering the problem of carbon estimation in forests. Then, in Sect. 3, we provide an overview of our deep learning strategy for tree detection. Next, in Sect. 4, we introduce a model to estimate DBH from height measurements and the allometric model that computes carbon from estimated and measured DBHs. Finally, we conclude the document and delineate directions for future research.

2   Related Research

We examine the scientific literature in the areas of carbon estimation, automatic tree detection, and synthetic images generation, as related to our problem.

Carbon Estimation. Conventionally, measuring trees for biomass estimation requires field DBH measurements [4] using tools such as diameter tapes or calipers while one utilizes Clinometers or laser hypsometers for measuring tree height [13]. One inputs the measurements into allometric models, which require ground truth data to solve for parameters. Commonly, predictive models use these equations to generalize to other trees in similar conditions of soil and fertility, having conventional measures as input parameters [13]. One could calculate carbon as the product of aboveground biomass and the amount of carbon per biomass unit in the studied species of tree. Official carbon estimation methods vary for each country [10]. Escalona *et al.* [2] estimate the carbon contained by a stand of *Pinus greggii* using field measurements. They measure DBH and height for a tree stand, cut off a dry sample of trees from their study field, and obtain the total organic carbon using a combustion catalytic oxidation method.

Tree Detection. Automatic tree detection is experiencing a radical change as researchers explore deep learning approaches as opposed to classical ones [9]. Classical methods for detecting trees relied on the use of crafted features, including local maxima filtering, template matching, valley-following, watershed, region growing, and marked point processes [6]. Lately, there has been a surge in methods to detect and count plants using convolutional neural networks (CNNs). So far, researchers have employed well-established architectures such as LeNet, VGG, AlexNet or GoogleNet for classification or regression.

Synthetic Dataset Generation. Deep learning commonly requires vast amounts of labeled data to train a CNN. As the manual labeling of images is very demanding, the creation of synthetic datasets is attractive for researchers working in machine learning. Ubbens *et al.* [17] render 3D models of *Arabidopsis thaliana* rosettes and use them to create data sets for training. Han and Kerekes [7] review simulation methods for multispectral images. To verify models for biomass estimation, Fassnacht *et al.* [3] simulate canopy height and cover type combining the SILVA individual-tree forest simulator [14] with real LiDAR point clouds of individual trees.

3   Tree Detection Using Deep Learning

Our approach to detect trees consists of using multispectral images captured from UAS to generate the input for a CNN. As a by-product, we obtain the Digital Elevated Vegetation Map (DVEM), a representation for tree stands. One problem in deep learning is the existence of a sizable database with exemplary samples. We solve this problem with the use of synthetic datasets for training.

3.1   The Digital Elevated Vegetation Model

Digital Surface Models (DSMs) and Digital Terrain Models (DTMs) are 2.5D representations, but while the former gives information about the objects over the terrain, the latter gives the bare surface without vegetation or human-made structures. Also, one could generate indices, such as the Normalized Difference Vegetation Index (NDVI), to filter out no vegetal elements from the images. One could calculate the NDVI [18] with the red and near-infrared radiation, for $\mathbf{x} = (x, y)$, where $x \in [1, w]$ and $y \in [1, h]$, as

$$\text{NDVI}(\mathbf{x}) = \frac{\text{NI}(\mathbf{x}) - \text{RE}(\mathbf{x})}{\text{NI}(\mathbf{x}) + \text{RE}(\mathbf{x})}. \tag{1}$$

In our method, we combine the DSM, DTM and NDVI models to define the Digital Elevated Vegetation Model (DEVM) as

$$\text{DEVM}(\mathbf{x}) = (\text{DSM}(\mathbf{x}) - \text{DTM}(\mathbf{x}))\text{NDVI}(\mathbf{x}), \tag{2}$$

where the subtraction of the DTM from the DSM leaves the objects over the terrain. The NDVI filters out non-vegetal objects. The DEVM representation facilitates the generation of synthetic images for the training of deep learning classifiers.

3.2   Synthetic Dataset Generation

Using the DVEM representation, we proceed to define synthetic images that closely resemble the treetops (see Fig. 2). We produce a synthetic image $\mathbf{I}(\mathbf{x})$ varying randomly, over uniform distributions, the number n of trees, the position of their center $(\overline{x}_i, \overline{y}_i)$, and their width a_i and b_i. We model each tree as a set of at most m_i randomly overlapping domes. We use the following analytic expression to represent each dome:

$$\mathbf{D}(\alpha, \beta) = h_{ij} \cdot \cos\left(\frac{\alpha\pi}{2a_{ij}}\right) \cdot \cos\left(\frac{\beta\pi}{2b_{ij}}\right), \tag{3}$$

for given values of a_{ij}, b_{ij}, and h_{ij}, where $\alpha \in [-a_{ij}, a_{ij}]$ and $\beta \in [-b_{ij}, b_{ij}]$, and h_{ij} is a random gain variable.

(b) *Synthetic*   (a) *Real*

Fig. 2. Samples of (a) Synthetic and (b) Real DEVM images

3.3 CNN Architecture

To identify trees in DEVM images, we used DetectNet [1], a CNN that predicts the bounding box limits and the class probabilities from images in a single pass. It includes an initial layer that divides an image into a regular cell grid of $S \times S$ elements. Each cell predicts B bounding boxes with their respective confidence score. Correspondingly, each bounding box consists of predictions for (x, y), the center of the bounding box; (w, h), the width and height; and the intersection of the union (IoU) between the predicted and ground truth boxes.

To detect multiple objects in DetectNet during training, we extract the bounding boxes of each image from the annotations overlaid on the *coverage map*. Given the coverage map for object k, $C_k(\mathbf{x})$, for $\mathbf{x} = (x, y)$ and $1 \leq x, y \leq S$, we set to 1 the positions where objects are present and 0 otherwise. We use the following loss function for training

$$loss = \frac{1}{2N} \sum_{i=1}^{N} \left\{ \sum_{\mathbf{x}} \left(C_i^t(\mathbf{x}) - C_i^p(\mathbf{x})\right)^2 + \lambda \left(|\mathbf{u}^t - \mathbf{u}^p| + |\mathbf{l}^t - \mathbf{l}^p|\right) \right\}, \quad (4)$$

where N is the number of objects, λ weights the regularization term, C^t and C^p are the coverage maps, and $\mathbf{u}$ and $\mathbf{l}$ are the upper-left and lower-right corners for the ground truth t and the prediction p.

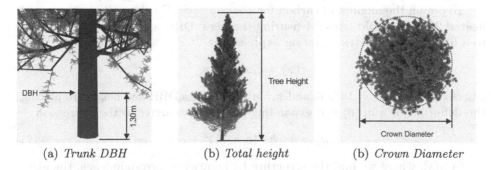

(a) *Trunk DBH*   (b) *Total height*   (b) *Crown Diameter*

Fig. 3. Conventional measures of trees: (a) trunk *DBH* is the diameter of the trunk at a standard height of 1.30 m, also known as diameter at breast height; (b) total height of the tree from the ground to the top; and (c) approximated diameter of the crown from a zenithal viewpoint.

4 Carbon Content Estimation

A common practice in silviculture is to compute the carbon content from the tree trunk DBH using allometric equations (Fig. 3). In our approach, we infer a tree's DBH using the tree height we obtain from the 3D SfM reconstruction and the location information from our tree detector. Using its location bounding box,

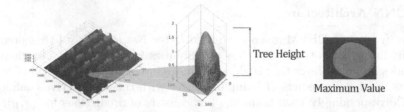

Fig. 4. We use the cloud of points in the resulting bounding boxes to estimate the height from DSM as the difference between the maximum and minimum height values.

we calculate a tree's height from the DSM, computing the difference between the maximum and the minimum height values (see Fig. 4).

To estimate the DBH for a tree, we define an allometric relationship between the DBH and the height. Firstly, we obtain paired ground truth data from field inventorying, where we use a metric tape to measure the height and DBH from a set of trees in a forest stand (see Fig. 5). In our approach, we propose to model the relationship between height, h, and DBH, d, as

$$d(h) = d_1 h^2 + d_2 h. \tag{5}$$

We estimate the value for the coefficients d_1 and d_2 using least squares and forcing a constraint making the DBH zero whenever the height equals zero.

To obtain the amount of carbon for *Pinus greggii*, Escalona *et al.* [2] cut and heated 20 six year old trees. Measuring the trees' DBH and height, they arrived to a quadratic allometric equation expressed as

$$c(x) = c_1 x^2 + c_2 x, \tag{6}$$

where $c_1 = 3287$, $c_2 = 147.36$, and $x = d^2 h$ combines DBH and height. Replacing the definition of x in (6) and expanding d by (5), we arrive to the expression

$$c(h) = hd(h)^2 (c_1 hd(h)^2 + c_2). \tag{7}$$

In SfM, where we find the structure by pointwise correspondence, the algorithms tend to underestimate tree height. Given an estimated tree height h, we correct it using

$$\hat{h} = \alpha h + \beta, \tag{8}$$

where $\alpha = \sigma_g / \sigma_e$ and $\beta = \mu_g - \alpha \mu_e$ are scale and bias factors, and σ_g and σ_e and μ_g and μ_e correspond to the standard deviation and mean of the distribution of measured and estimated heights, respectively. A summary of the data flow is described in the Algorithm 1.

5   Experimental Results

For our experiments, we mounted a Parrot-Sequoia Micasense camera on a 3DR Solo quadcopter and flew over *Las Mancañas*, a 0.76 ha leaf-on(*Pinus greggii*)

Call : $c_e \leftarrow$ carbonContent (h_g, d_g, h_e)

Inputs : The ground truth height, h_g, and DBH, d_g, and estimated treetop
height h_e.

Outputs: $\bar{c}_e$, the individual trees' carbon content and e, the RMS value
estimation

```
// calibrate measurement tree height
```
$[\alpha, \beta] \leftarrow$ calibrate (h_g, d_g); // use (8)

for $i = 1; i < n$ **do**

> ```
> // split the data between training and testing
> ```
> $\left[h_g^{\text{train}}, h_g^{\text{test}}\right] \leftarrow$ split (h_g); $\left[d_g^{\text{train}}, d_g^{\text{test}}\right] \leftarrow$ split (d_g);
> $\left[h_e^{\text{train}}, h_e^{\text{test}}\right] \leftarrow$ split (h_e);
> ```
> // Estimate carbon content for the ground true sample
> // Correct treetop height
> ```
> $\hat{h}_e^{\text{test}} \leftarrow \alpha h_e^{\text{test}} + \beta$;
> ```
> // Fit a quadratic equation with null intercept
> ```
> $\mathbf{d} \leftarrow$ fit $\left(h_g^{\text{train}}, d_g^{\text{train}}\right)$; // use (5)
> ```
> // Estimate the DBH for the test set
> ```
> $d_e^{\text{test}} \leftarrow d_1 \left[h_e^{\text{test}}\right]^2 + d_2 h_e^{\text{test}}$;
> ```
> // Estimate carbon content for the test sample
> ```
> $\mathbf{C}_{ei} \leftarrow$ carbon $\left(h_e^{\text{test}}, d_e^{\text{test}}\right)$; // use (7)

end
```
// compute carbon content and rms value
```
$c_g \leftarrow$ carbon (h_g, d_g); // use (7)

$\bar{c}_e \leftarrow \mathbf{C}_e^T \mathbf{1}$; $e = $ rms$(\bar{c}_g, \bar{c}_e)$;

Algorithm 1. A model to estimate carbon content from treetops height.

pine field with a mean distance between the trees of 5.9 m. The sampling area is located in Guanajuato, Mexico in the coordinates 20°58'40."N 100°16'31.2"W. We flew at an altitude of 30 m in a double grid procedure with 85% of overlap between adjacent images along the paths of rows and columns followed by one spiral flight approximating the center of the sampled area. In this landscape, the Parrot-Sequoia produced 2,212 multispectral and RGB images with spectral response peaking in wavelengths of 550 nm (Green), 660 nm (Red), 735 nm (Red Edge, RE) and 790 nm (Near Infrared, NI) (see Fig. 5).

To train DetectNet, we generated a synthetic-labeled dataset of 12,500 synthetic DEVM images. We trained DetectNet through ten epochs, using transfer learning from a model previously trained with the KITTI database [5]. At refinement, we utilized the synthetic dataset, splitting the 12,500 images into a set of 10,000 images for training and 2,500 images for validation.

To test our carbon content measurement model, we obtained ground truth for the sampled area through a field inventorying of 60 trees, measuring their DBH and height. The trees have an average height of 211.53 cm with a standard

(a) *Las Mancañas*, 3D reconstruction representation of the sampled area, highlighted in red.

(b) Using metric tape to measure circumference of tree trunk at a standard height of 1.30 m, which is used to calculate DBH ground truth.

Fig. 5. Ground truth measurement for DBH estimation (Color figure online)

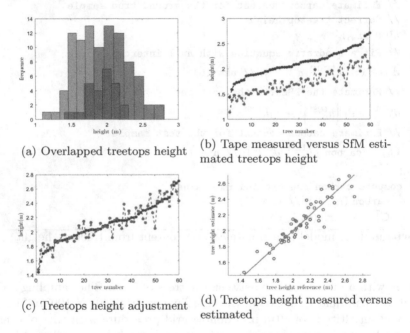

(a) Overlapped treetops height

(b) Tape measured versus SfM estimated treetops height

(c) Treetops height adjustment

(d) Treetops height measured versus estimated

Fig. 6. Tree height adjustment. SfM underestimates tree height (a)–(b). We apply a correction factor based on the offset and spread (c). The linear correlation coefficient (d) with respect to the manual measurements is satisfactory.

deviation of 26.47 cm and an average DBH of 4.64 cm with a standard deviation of 1.70 cm. To measure the height of the detected trees, we automatically extracted sub-images from the DSM for the 60 detected bounding boxes. For each of these sub-images, we calculated the height as the difference of the maximum and the minimal depth values. SfM techniques tend to underestimate the treetops height. Figure 6(a)–(b) illustrates the treetops height distributions and plot for the tape measured and SfM process, respectively. The mean and standard value for the tape measured and the SfM estimated height is (2.12 m, 1.73 m) and (0.26 m, 0.25 m), respectively. We computed adjustment variables α and β, as described in (8), as 1.08 and 0.25, respectively. Figure 6(c)–(d) shows the resulting adjustment. The linear correlation coefficient for the heights is 0.999.

To estimate the carbon content, we iteratively selected random partitions of the data, into training and testing sets, to adjust the coefficients of (5) before computing the carbon content. In the end, we evaluated (7) using both the ground truth values and the estimated ones. In Fig. 7, we illustrate the ground truth carbon content, with the blue dotted line, and the estimated carbon content with a box plot diagram. Our method estimates that the mean carbon content for the tree stand is 0.84 kg (50.4 kg for the forest stand), while the ground truth estimation is 0.94 kg (56.4.4 kg for the forest stand), the RMS value is 0.58 kg.

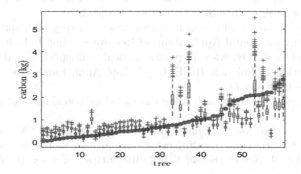

Fig. 7. Carbon estimation. The blue line represents the ground truth carbon content for the sample forest stand, while the boxplot includes the mean values, maximum and minimum value, and standard deviation for the estimated values. (Color figure online)

Conclusion

In this paper, we introduce a methodology to estimate carbon content in a forest stand using the photogrammetry measurements of trees taken by a UAS. We demonstrate that a system built out of this methodology can successfully be scaled up by estimating the carbon content of a parcel of *Pinus greggii*. During the development of this research, we introduce a tree detection method based on the use of a CNN. The DEVM representation made it possible to develop a strategy to construct synthetic ground truth data useful for training, alleviating the need for labeling ground truth data. Our method reduces the resources that are necessary to obtain those measures with classical approaches with on-field personnel.

In the future, we are planning to develop models for carbon estimation circumventing the use of allometric equations based on DBH. As we are aiming to increase the precision of our estimation, we may rely on the use of biomass change over time.

Acknowledgements. Dagoberto Pulido thanks CONACYT for providing a scholarship for his studies. SIP-IPN 20196702 partially funded Joaquín Salas.

References

1. Barker, J., Sarathy, S., Tao, A.: DetectNet: deep neural network for object detection in DIGITS. Nvidia (2016). https://tinyurl.com/detectnet. Accessed 30 Nov 2016
2. Escalona, F., Aldrete, A., Gómez, A., Fierros, A., Cetina, V., Vaquera, H.: Carbon storage in the aboveground biomass of one young Pinus greggii plantation. Rev. Fitotec. Mex. **30** (2007)
3. Fassnacht, F., Latifi, H., Hartig, F.: Using synthetic data to evaluate the benefits of large field plots for forest biomass estimation with LiDAR. Remote Sens. Environ. **213**, 115–128 (2018)
4. Gayon, J.: History of the concept of allometry. Am. Zool. **40**(5), 748–758 (2000). https://doi.org/10.1093/icb/40.5.748
5. Geiger, A., Lenz, P., Stiller, C., Urtasun, R.: Vision meets robotics: the KITTI dataset. Int. J. Robot. Res. **32**(11), 1231–1237 (2013)
6. Gomes, M., Maillard, P.: Detection of tree crowns in very high spatial resolution images. In: Environmental Applications of Remote Sensing. InTech (2016)
7. Han, S., Kerekes, J.: Overview of passive optical multispectral and hyperspectral image simulation techniques. IEEE J. Sel. Top. Appl. Earth Obs. Remote Sens. **10**(11), 4794–4804 (2017)
8. Luyssaert, S., et al.: Old-growth forests as global carbon sinks. Nature **455**(7210), 213 (2008)
9. Mubin, N.A., Nadarajoo, E., Shafri, H.Z.M., Hamedianfar, A.: Young and mature oil palm tree detection and counting using convolutional neural network deep learning method. Int. J. Remote Sens., 1–16 (2019). https://doi.org/10.1080/01431161.2019.1569282
10. Neumann, M., et al.: Comparison of carbon estimation methods for European forests. Forest Ecol. Manag. **361**, 397–420 (2016)
11. Oono, K., Tsuyuki, S.: Estimating individual tree diameter and stem volume using airborne LiDAR in Saga Prefecture, Japan. Open J. For. **8**(02), 205 (2018)
12. Özyeşil, O., Voroninski, V., Basri, R., Singer, A.: A survey of structure from motion. Acta Numer. **26**, 305–364 (2017)
13. Picard, N., Saint-Andre, L., Henry, M.: Manual for building tree volume and biomass allometric equations: from field measurement to prediction (2012)
14. Pretzsch, H., Biber, P., Durskỳ, J.: The single tree-based stand simulator SILVA. Forest Ecol. Manag. **162**(1), 3–21 (2002)
15. Priedītis, G., Šmits, I., Arhipova, I., Daġis, A., Dubrovskis, D.: Tree diameter models from field and remote sensing data. Math. Mod. Meth. Appl. S **6**, 707–714 (2012)
16. Tinkham, W., et al.: Development of height-volume relationships in second growth Abies grandis for use with aerial LiDAR. Can. J. Remote Sens. **42**(5), 400–410 (2016)
17. Ubbens, J., Cieslak, M., Prusinkiewicz, P., Stavness, I.: The use of plant models in deep learning: an application to leaf counting in rosette plants. Plant Methods **14**(1), 6 (2018)
18. Weier, J., Herring, D.: Measuring vegetation (NDVI & EVI) (2000)

Using Synthetic Images for Deep Learning Recognition Process on Automatic License Plate Recognition

Saulo Cardoso Barreto(ID), Jorge Albuquerque Lambert(✉)(ID), and Flávio de Barros Vidal(ID)

Department of Mechanical Engineering, Department of Computer Science, University of Brasília, Brasília 70910-900, Brazil
saulo_cardoso@outlook.com, lambert.jal@dpf.gov.br, fbvidal@unb.br

Abstract. The Automatic License Plate Recognition has been the subject of several studies, given its applicability in real world situations (e.g. toll collection, identification of vehicles in parking lots or even for safety issues in vehicle control that cross borders between countries). In this work, we propose an analysis of the influence to retraining a plate recognition model and a deep neural network for object detection, using synthetic plates image databases from the Brazilian licence plates. The proposed data set uses variations of rotation, size and noise to evaluate the robustness. Thus, the influence of the use of synthetic plates images on the accuracy of systems responsible for locating real plates, segmenting the characters and recognizing them was evaluated and in the tests performed there was an increase in accuracy (considering a system trained with real plates) of three stages: character segmentation, letter recognition and number recognition (2.54%, 1.09% and 2,49% respectively). It stands out the accuracy of 62.47% (in the number recognition step) obtained by a neural network trained exclusively with synthetic data and tested on real plates.

Keywords: Deep neural networks · License plate recognition · Synthetic images

1 Introduction

The task of locating and identifying car cards in real time or in images that have already been captured has received increasing attention in Computer Vision research due to its importance and wide variety of applications such as: traffic accident investigation, image analysis in crime scenes, automated verification of parking tickets and surveillance of speed limits [10]. Automatic License Plate Recognition (ALPR) is defined as a system whose objective is to perform the tasks described above in order to obtain a satisfactory result in the final application: locate a vehicle license plate and recognize each character [14]. In according

© Springer Nature Switzerland AG 2019
J. A. Carrasco-Ochoa et al. (Eds.): MCPR 2019, LNCS 11524, pp. 115–126, 2019.
https://doi.org/10.1007/978-3-030-21077-9_11

Fig. 1. ALPR system steps (the license plate was blurred due to privacy constraints).

to Li et al. [14], an input image of an ALPR system is captured under the influence of several factors: camera resolution, vehicle and camera orientation, presence of light in the environment at the time of capture, camera shutter speed, and climatic conditions among others. The process for recognizing a license plate can be divided into three steps, as illustrated in the Fig. 1: (i) find the region of an image corresponding to the vehicle's plate (ii) from the plate image locate and segment the characters and finally (iii) recognize each letter and number.

Machine Learning techniques have been used for the three steps of recognizing a license plate. The greatest challenge for the ALPR and which prevents it from achieving results close to those of object recognition. For example, is the unavailability of a large-scale annotated database, given the difficulty in collecting and categorizing a data set with real license plates. In a situation where it is not possible to obtain a large scale database, the Data Augmentation method is used to create a synthetic database. Knowing that the license plates of the vehicles have many different standards, depending on the country in analysis, the project described in this paper is limited to the Brazilian standard adopted until 2018, which consists of three letters followed by four numbers (See a license plate sample in Fig. 1).

The general objective of this work is to verify the ability to recognize real license plates from a trained neural network with a synthetic database, as well as to verify the accuracy of a previously trained network with real images, retrained with artificial plates (*transfer learning* and *fine-tuning*). Considering the difficulties of obtaining real databases with annotated vehicle license plates, the possibility of training a network and obtaining a high accuracy in the recognition of the characters, using only artificial plates, would be shown as a promising result in the area of Computer Vision and verify the influence on the accuracy of the system when performing a new training, starting from the initial weights of the previous training, but using artificial data as input.

2   Related Works

ALPR systems are not new in the industry and academy wherein many techniques were developed and improved along the last decades. However, even with a wide variety of techniques available, it is still a relevant research topic. Early works basically used image processing techniques to locate the vehicle's nameplate area and then recognize the data contained (characters and numbers) in the previously bounded area [4].

In recently years, many approaches were developed and used on ALPR systems. In current technical literature, many works can be found using any variation of the AI approach as describe in [19]. All these works (and many others available) using only real images of private license plate data sets, and most of them specific for a country, in the work developed in [6], the authors focused on Brazilian license plates and evaluated data augmentation techniques. Mainly because of the difficulty in achieving a large data set of real labeled images to perform the a good training of these models. Because of this issue, the analysis of the direct impact on the recognition process accuracy of license plates from synthetic images may contribute to the improvement of the entire recognition process, from training and validation to testing of the proposed model.

3 Artificial Neural Networks Models

3.1 Convolutional Neural Networks

LeCun [13] proposed in 1998 the use of convolutional neural networks (CNN) for image, voice, and time series recognition. What differentiates it from other types of neural networks is the use of the convolution operation instead of the multiplication of matrices in at least one of its layers. Two main features of a CNN stand out from other types of neural networks: local receptive fields and shared weights. **Local Receptive Fields:** Each pixel of an image is used as input of a neuron in a convolutional neural network [3]. Considering a fully connected neural network, neurons in one layer are connected to all neurons in the next layer. **Shared Weights:** In a neural network, each connection between neurons has an associate weight while in a convolutional neural network, all weights are shared and used throughout the whole image [12]. Thus, the same filter is applied for each nxn pixels, and a feature can be located in any region of the input image, thus conferring CNN's the properties of **translation and rotation invariance**. Considering that the weights matrix has parameters shared by all the neurons, not one for each, the number of parameters used by a neural network decreases substantially when using the convolutional architecture.

3.2 You Only Look Once (YOLO)

For applications that have the real-time requirement, the execution time of the various stages of the frameworks based on selection of regions of interest becomes a bottleneck of the strategy as stated by Zhao et al. [22] which also observed that systems that have only one step based on global regression directly map the pixels to bounding boxes, reducing the time taken for detection. The first object-recognition architecture to succeed in detection using only one step was proposed by Redmon et al. [16] in 2015, in which was not necessary to propose regions of interest, resulting in a detection up to 6–7 times faster than a Faster R-CNN network, with a detection time of 22 ms [9]. Therefore, such architecture is capable of processing videos in real time, but the disadvantage is a loss in accuracy.

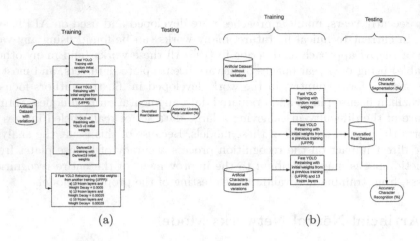

(a)   (b)

Fig. 2. (a) Training and tests stages of plate location architectures. (b) Training and tests stages of character segmentation and recognition architectures.

4   Proposed Methodology

The flowcharts represented in Figs. 2(a) and (b) illustrate the methodology used to verify the proposed approach and more detailed described in the next subsections.

4.1   Data Sets

Artificial Dataset Without Variations: This data set (represented in Fig. 3(a)) consists of license plates created using the OpenCV library [8]. The city and state name were omitted to avoid overfitting by preventing the neural network from extracting a feature from that part of the license which would not contribute to the use with license plate from different locations. The text font used was the mandatory as specified by the Brazilian traffic department. The colors and a gray gradient were also set so as to approach actual license plates. 902 artificial license plate have been created in this database, such amount is justified by the number of unique character sequences of the Diversified Real Data set used in the test step.

Artificial Data Set with Variations: In order to have a more complex data set, the SUN397 database [21], provided by the Massachusetts Institute of Technology, was used as the background image in which a plate was added with random and limited variations of rotation, scaling, Gaussian noise, brightness, perspective and sharpening using the Data Augmentation for Object Detection (YOLO) tool [18].

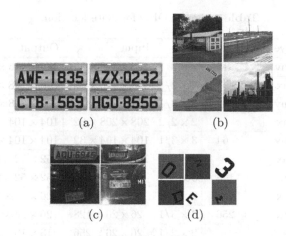

Fig. 3. (a) Artificial dataset without variations. (b) Artificial dataset with variations. (c) Diversified real database. (d) Artificial character data set.

Diversified Real Data Set: In order to have a database that was not used in any training cited in this work, the images available in [1] were used as reference for all the calculated accuracy. This choice is justified because it is a database with real license plates captured in different environments under varying circumstances, as illustrated in Fig. 3(c). It is formed by 1126 images of which 902 are unique sequence of character. The annotation of this database had only the information of which characters were present in each plate, in this way, it was necessary to manually define the bounding box for each license plate.

Artificial Character Data Set: To perform the retraining of the letter and number recognition networks, artificial databases were created for each group using the Data Augmentation for Object Detection (YOLO) tool [18]. In the training stage, 50 variations of each digit were used (totaling 500 images), and 20 variations of each letter (totaling 520 images). The Fig. 3(d) shows sample images of these databases.

4.2   Deep Neural Network Architectures

All the architectures described in this Subsection have been implemented using the neural network framework darknet [15], written in C language which presents optimization for execution in GPUs. The choice of the tool is justified by the fact that the Brazilian work used as reference [11] for the license plate recognition task was developed in this platform. Therefore, compatibility was maintained with the previously generated training files. In addition, the YOLO architecture and its variations used in this work were also created in this framework. The fixed parameters for the training were: $momentum = 0.9$ and learning rate equal to 0.001, 0.0001 and 0.00001 up to the iterations 100, 25000 and 35000 respectively. The ratio used for the training and test data set was 75:25% as done in [7].

Table 1. Fast YOLO for plate location.

	Layer	Filters	Size	Input	Output
0	conv	16	$3 \times 3/1$	$416 \times 416 \times 3$	$416 \times 416 \times 16$
1	max		$2 \times 2/1$	$416 \times 416 \times 16$	$208 \times 208 \times 16$
2	conv	32	$3 \times 3/1$	$208 \times 208 \times 16$	$208 \times 208 \times 32$
3	max		$2 \times 2/2$	$208 \times 208 \times 32$	$104 \times 104 \times 32$
4	conv	64	$3 \times 3/1$	$104 \times 104 \times 32$	$104 \times 104 \times 64$
5	max		$2 \times 2/2$	$104 \times 104 \times 64$	$52 \times 52 \times 64$
6	conv	128	$3 \times 3/1$	$52 \times 52 \times 64$	$52 \times 52 \times 128$
7	max		$2 \times 2/2$	$52 \times 52 \times 128$	$26 \times 26 \times 128$
8	conv	256	$3 \times 3/1$	$26 \times 26 \times 128$	$26 \times 26 \times 256$
9	max		$2 \times 2/1$	$26 \times 26 \times 256$	$13 \times 13 \times 256$
10	conv	512	$3 \times 3/1$	$13 \times 13 \times 256$	$13 \times 13 \times 512$
11	max		$2 \times 2/1$	$13 \times 13 \times 512$	$13 \times 13 \times 512$
12	conv	1024	$3 \times 3/1$	$13 \times 13 \times 512$	$13 \times 13 \times 1024$
13	conv	1024	$3 \times 3/1$	$13 \times 13 \times 1024$	$13 \times 13 \times 1024$
14	conv	30	$1 \times 1/1$	$13 \times 13 \times 1024$	$13 \times 13 \times 30$
15	detection				

Fast YOLO for Plate Location: Considering that the analysis of the training of a neural network with synthetic database involves several training with variations of parameters, it was decided to use the Fast YOLO because it presents a smaller number of layers, and consequently, a shorter convergence time (for training) and detection (for the test). Thus, two parameters were analyzed in order to observe their influence on the network accuracy: (i) Freezing of 13 or 10 layers and (ii) Decay of Weights equal to 0.0005 or 0.00025 as described in Table 1. Such an architecture reduces accuracy, but it is able to recognize objects in sampled images at a rate of 155 frames per second [9]. The YOLOv2 (with its 32 layers) and Darknet19 (25 layers) architectures were omitted due to space limitation but can be obtained in [2].

Modified YOLO-VOC for Character Segmentation and Recognition: As verified by Gonçalves et al. [5], the separation of the neural networks responsible for identifying the numbers and letters reduces the incorrect classifications. The size of the image of the network responsible for segmenting the characters (240×80) is justified by the ratio of the dimensions of the Brazilian car plates (3: 1). It is important to note that the segmented characters are sorted in descending order according to their coordinates on the horizontal axis, thus separating the first 3 that are letters, of the last 4 that are the numbers. The Table 2 represents the architecture used for character segmentation. For letter recognition the same architecture was used, adjusting only the size of the layers

Table 2. Modified YOLO-VOC for character segmentation and recognition.

	Layer	Filters	Size	Input	Output
1	conv	32	$3 \times 3/1$	$240 \times 80 \times 3$	$240 \times 80 \times 32$
2	max		$2 \times 2/1$	$240 \times 80 \times 32$	$120 \times 40 \times 32$
3	conv	64	$3 \times 3/1$	$120 \times 40 \times 32$	$120 \times 40 \times 64$
4	max		$2 \times 2/2$	$120 \times 40 \times 64$	$60 \times 20 \times 64$
5	conv	128	$3 \times 3/1$	$60 \times 20 \times 64$	$60 \times 20 \times 128$
6	conv	64	$1 \times 1/1$	$60 \times 20 \times 128$	$60 \times 20 \times 64$
7	conv	128	$3 \times 3/1$	$60 \times 20 \times 64$	$60 \times 20 \times 128$
8	max		$2 \times 2/2$	$60 \times 20 \times 128$	$30 \times 10 \times 128$
9	conv	256	$3 \times 3/1$	$30 \times 10 \times 128$	$30 \times 10 \times 256$
10	conv	128	$1 \times 1/1$	$30 \times 10 \times 256$	$30 \times 10 \times 128$
11	conv	256	$3 \times 3/1$	$30 \times 10 \times 128$	$30 \times 10 \times 256$
12	conv	512	$3 \times 3/1$	$30 \times 10 \times 256$	$30 \times 10 \times 512$
13	conv	256	$1 \times 1/1$	$30 \times 10 \times 512$	$30 \times 10 \times 256$
14	conv	512	$3 \times 3/1$	$30 \times 10 \times 256$	$30 \times 10 \times 512$
15	conv	30	$1 \times 1/1$	$30 \times 10 \times 512$	$30 \times 10 \times 30$
16	detection				

and the amount of filters. However for number recognition the first four layers were removed since the network performance would not be affected [11].

4.3 Accuracy Criteria

Considering the network responsible for locating the license plate in a image, if the Intersection over Union of the predicted bounding box is equal or greater to 70% ($IoU \geq 0.7$) when compared to the ground truth bounding box, the license plate defined by the neural network is considered accurate. The choice of this value is justified by the protocol developed by Li et al. in 2017 (using 0.7 for the anchor box definition) [14], who stated that this value would better evaluate the detection performance. For the character segmentation network, it is considered as a hit the segmentation of exact 7 characters, and for the character recognition the matching between the predicted and expected character.

5   Results and Discussion

In this Section, the results for the proposed methodology in Figs. 2(a) and (b) will be presented. The relation between the terms are: **Epoch:** When a neural network received all the elements of the training set as input and updated the weights, it is said that an epoch was finalized; **Batch:** The amount of images used in a training step is defined by the batch size; **Iteration:** Number of steps performed with the defined batch.

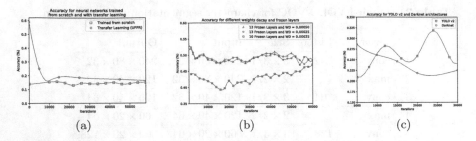

(a)   (b)   (c)

Fig. 4. (a) Comparison between two trainings: without transfer learning and with initialized weights from another training. (b) Influence of the freezing layers and the variation of the weight decay. (c) Comparison between two trainings: YOLO v2 and Darknet.

5.1   Trained Networks to Find a License Plate in an Image

Random Initial Weights Vs. Initialized Weights: The Fig. 4(a) illustrates the accuracy of neural networks in intermediate stages of their respective training, in which it is verified that the final results are similar after 60 thousand iterations (a difference of 0.62% exists between the final values). It is also worth mentioning the decreasing behavior of the transfer learning carried out with initial non-random weights, because during the training its accuracy was reduced by 44.76%. It is also possible to verify the low values obtained by the training indicated in green in Fig. 4(a) in which the highest value obtained was after 14 thousand interactions and was equal to 15.63% which represents 176 correctly located plates, given the 1126 images of database.

Different Weights Decay and Frozen Layers: Considering the three trainings performed in this stage (Fig. 4(b)), the accuracy values for the two trainings with the same number of frozen layers were similar, since the average accuracy of the intermediate stages for $WeightDecay = 0.0005$ and $WeightDecay = 0.00025$ were equal to 49.51% and 49.32%, respectively, evidencing that for this case, the change in weight decay did not significantly influence the accuracy of the models. There is also a difference between the obtained values for the same value of Weight Decay (with a change in the layer freeze strategy), since the 13-layer frozen network located 557 of the 1126 license plates, while the 10-layer frozen network correctly located 474 vehicle license plates (difference of 7.37%). The highest standard deviation was for the architecture with 13 frozen layers being equal to 1.46% for the training with the decay of weights equal to 0,00025. When the network was analyzed with decay of 0.0005, the standard deviation was 1.25%. Finally, the only network with 10 frozen layers had a standard deviation of 1.40%.

Yolo v2 Vs. Darknet: Comparing the results of both trainings performed with initial weights of neural networks trained to recognize the most varied objects, it

Table 3. Accuracy for neural networks trained to segment characters.

Training	Accuracy (%)
Fast YOLO (UFPR initial weights)	78,42
UFPR training	75,84
Fast YOLO (UFPR initial weights and 13 frozen layers)	67,50
Fast YOLO (Random initial weights)	25,13

Table 4. Accuracy for neural networks trained to recognize letters.

Training	Accuracy (%)
Fast YOLO (UFPR initial weights)	84,53
Fast YOLO (UFPR initial weights and 13 frozen layers)	83,71
UFPR training	83,44
Fast YOLO (Random initial weights)	11,57

is noted that the transfer learning performed with the YOLO v2 had an average accuracy of 2,23% greater than the Darknet architecture (26.26% and 24.03%, respectively) for the 30 thousand iterations. The accuracy of the analyzed networks begin to distance themselves from the $20,000^{th}$ iteration, presenting a difference of approximately 10% when the accuracy of *YOLO* v2 reaches its maximum value and locates 359 of 1126 plates correctly (31.88%) as described in Fig. 4(c), which is justified by the fact that Yolo v2 has the first 23 layers identical to Darknet-19 but has 7 additional layers, as described in [15].

5.2 Trained Networks to Segment Characters

Considering the neural networks trained to segment the characters, it is observed that only one of them exceeded the result obtained previously with the UFPR Training: the transfer learning performed with the UFPR initial weights made the accuracy increase by 2.58%, causing the number of correctly-located license plates to increase by 30 (going from 854 to 884). Both the YOLO training with 13 frozen layers (since the architecture of the network responsible for segmenting the characters is identical to the one responsible for locating a license plate) and training with random initial weights showed inferior performance: respectively 760 and 283 plates recognized, out of 1126 (67.50 and 25.13%).

5.3 Trained Networks to Recognize Characters

Letter Recognition: This was the network that presented the worst performance for the scenario with random initial weights: only 307 letters out of 2652 were correctly recognized (11.57%). As for the improvements in initial UFPR training, both transfer learning and fine-tuning made the accuracy increase by 1.09 and 0.27%, respectively (Table 4).

Table 5. Accuracy for neural networks trained to recognize digits.

Training	Accuracy (%)
Fast YOLO (UFPR initial weights and 9 frozen layers)	92,76%
Fast YOLO (UFPR initial weights)	92,44%
UFPR training	90,27%
Fast YOLO (Random initial weights)	62,47%

Number Recognition: In the stage of recognizing the numbers, the fine-tuning obtained a higher accuracy than the network that was submitted to *transfer learning*: the first recognized 10 more numbers than the second one 3278 in a set of 3536 numbers-92.76%. The freezing of the first 9 layers of the net (which has 12 layers) caused the accuracy to increase by 2.49%. Thus, the network was able to recognize 88 additional characters in relation to the amount previously recognized by UFPR training (without any training with artificial databases). Considering all the trained networks with random initial weights, the person responsible for recognizing the numbers presented the best result, since 2209 numbers of actual plaques among the 3536 evaluated (62.47 %) were correctly classified by a neural network that did not receive numbers captured in real-world situations at any stage of your training, as described in Table 5.

6   Conclusions

Initially, by analyzing the performance of all trained neural networks with random initial weights and artificial database, our proposed approach was partially proved since 62 out of 100 numbers were recognized by a neural network trained exclusively with a synthetic database, proving that there is no need to use large annotated real databases for this task of a ALPR system. The character segmentation performed by the model initialized with random weights was able to correctly segment 25.13% characters of the real license plates. Considering that the training of this networks was done with a database without variations (Fig. 2(b)), it did not extract features from license plates in different perspectives or angles, thus restricting its ability to correctly extract the expected 7 characters, nonetheless, a reasonable learning ability of the network with this result is noted. The second approach was fully confirmed by the results obtained for all the neural networks, but with different aspects since the influence in the segmentation (Table 3), letter and number recognition networks (Tables 4 and 5) is positive, that for all these steps there was an increase in accuracy caused by transfer learning. It should be noted the effect of applying the freezing layers strategy, since it is possible to verify the largest accuracy variation in this work: the transfer learning with UFPR initial weights and all free layers achieved an accuracy of 14,20% at the end of the iterations (Fig. 4(a)), while the same architecture with 13 frozen layers and weight decay equal to 0.0005 achieved an average accuracy of 49.51% (Fig. 4(b)) in the step of finding a license plate.

Evidencing that the performed fine-tuning resulted in an increase of 35.31% in the model accuracy.

Finally, the results in the Fig. 4(c) show that deep neural networks previously trained to recognize different objects can be used as a starting point for a specific training, knowing that the strategy has already been used to recognize plants [17], medical images [20] and Norwegian car plates [9]. The strategy made the maximum accuracy of the YOLO v2 architecture equal to 31.88% (Fig. 4(c)) with only 24000 iterations, implying that features extracted from other training (edge information, color, position in the image, etc.) can be useful in developing a model to recognize a smaller number of classes. Analyzing the obtained results, it is verified that the use of synthetic databases for the license plate recognition task can improve the performance of some stages of the process. All presented results achieved improvements for the training step (less epochs and improved the accuracy) when synthetics labeled image are used.

References

1. Plates BR - GitHub. https://bit.ly/2TEG2e5. Accessed 10 Nov 2018
2. YOLO: Real-time object detection. https://bit.ly/2fXFbXS. Accessed 06 Aug 2018
3. Bojarski, M., et al.: VisualBackProp: visualizing CNNs for autonomous driving. CoRR abs/1611.05418 (2016). http://arxiv.org/abs/1611.05418
4. Du, S., Ibrahim, M., Shehata, M., Badawy, W.: Automatic license plate recognition (ALPR): a state-of-the-art review. IEEE Tran. Circuits Syst. Video Technol. **23**(2), 311–325 (2013). https://doi.org/10.1109/TCSVT.2012.2203741
5. Gonçalves, G.R., Menotti, D., Schwartz, W.R.: License plate recognition based on temporal redundancy. In: 2016 IEEE 19th International Conference on Intelligent Transportation Systems (ITSC), November, pp. 2577–2582 (2016). https://doi. org/10.1109/ITSC.2016.7795970
6. Gonçalves, G.R., Diniz, M.A., Laroca, R., Menotti, D., Schwartz, W.R.: Real-time automatic license plate recognition through deep multi-task networks. In: 2018 31st SIBGRAPI Conference on Graphics, Patterns and Images (SIBGRAPI), pp. 110–117 (2018)
7. Hamori, S., Kawai, M., Kume, T., Murakami, Y., Watanabe, C.: Ensemble learning or deep learning? Application to default risk analysis. Discussion Papers 1802, Graduate School of Economics, Kobe University, January 2018
8. Itseez: Open source computer vision library (2015). https://github.com/itseez/ opencv
9. Jorgensen, H.: Automatic license plate recognition using deep learning techniques (2017). https://brage.bibsys.no/xmlui/handle/11250/2467209
10. Kim, J., Kim, S., Lee, S., Lee, T., Lim, J.: License plate detection and recognition algorithm for vehicle black box. In: 2017 International Automatic Control Conference (CACS), November, pp. 1–6 (2017). https://doi.org/10.1109/CACS.2017. 8284273
11. Laroca, R., et al.: A robust real-time automatic license plate recognition based on the YOLO detector. In: 2018 International Joint Conference on Neural Networks (IJCNN), July, pp. 1–10 (2018). https://doi.org/10.1109/IJCNN.2018.8489629
12. LeCun, Y., et al.: Backpropagation applied to handwritten zip code recognition. Neural Comput. **1**(4), 541–551 (1989). https://doi.org/10.1162/neco.1989.1.4.541

13. LeCun, Y., Bengio, Y.: Convolutional networks for images, speech, and time series. In: The Handbook of Brain Theory and Neural Networks, pp. 255–258. MIT Press, Cambridge (1998). http://dl.acm.org/citation.cfm?id=303568.303704
14. Li, H., Wangy, P., Shen, C.: Towards end-to-end car license plates detection and recognition with deep neural networks. IEEE Trans. Intell. Transp. Syst. (2017)
15. Redmon, J.: Darknet: open source neural networks in C. https://pjreddie.com/darknet/. Accessed 23 Nov 2018
16. Redmon, J., Divvala, S.K., Girshick, R.B., Farhadi, A.: You only look once: unified, real-time object detection. CoRR abs/1506.02640 (2015). http://arxiv.org/abs/1506.02640
17. Reyes, A.K., Caicedo, J.C., Camargo, J.E.: Fine-tuning deep convolutional networks for plant recognition. In: CLEF (2015)
18. Shreeraman: Data augmentation for object detection (YOLO). https://github.com/srp-31/Data-Augmentation-for-Object-Detection-YOLO
19. Silva, S.M., Jung, C.R.: Real-time Brazilian license plate detection and recognition using deep convolutional neural networks. In: 2017 30th SIBGRAPI Conference on Graphics, Patterns and Images (SIBGRAPI), October, pp. 55–62 (2017)
20. Tajbakhsh, N., et al.: Convolutional neural networks for medical image analysis: full training or fine tuning? IEEE Trans. Med. Imaging **35**(5), 1299–1312 (2016)
21. Xiao, J., Hays, J., Ehinger, K., Oliva, A., Torralba, A.: SUN database: large-scale scene recognition from abbey to zoo. In: IEEE Conference on Computer Vision and Pattern Recognition abs/1703.06870 (2010)
22. Zhao, Z.Q., Zheng, P., Xu, S.-T., Wu, X.: Object detection with deep learning: a review. CoRR abs/1807.05511 (2018)

A Review of Local Feature Algorithms and Deep Learning Approaches in Facial Expression Recognition with Tensorflow and Keras

Kennedy Chengeta[✉]

Computer Science Department, University of KwaZulu Natal, Durban, South Africa
216073421@ukzn.ac.za
http://www.kaributechs.com/

Abstract. In facial expression identification classification and lower processing times are key in choosing the algorithms to use in the facial detection, preprocessing, feature extraction or classification step. Facial expression recognition is based on deep learning, feature and holistic algorithms. Feature based algorithms like local binary patterns, local directional patterns (LDP) extract features from various facial components like nose, mouth or ears into a histogram. Deep learning involves using convolutional neural networks for image analysis with several hidden layers as opposed to artificial neural or shallow networks. The most popular models are AlexNet, VGG-Face and GoogleNet. The study evaluates computational accuracy and efficiency of deep learning algorithms and compares them to local feature based algorithms. The FER2013, Yale Faces, AT&T Database of Faces, JAFFE and CK+ datasets were used for analysis. Popular frameworks deep learning frameworks called Keras and Tensorflow backends are used to classify data and give better accuracy than a variant of local binary patterns. The processing time is shorter for feature based algorithms than the deep learning algorithms. To improve time on the deep learning approaches the study used pretrained models to achieve greater accuracy with low execution times as well. A combination of preprocessed multi block binary patterns, PCA, multilayer perceptron, support vector machines and extra trees classifier gave competitive results to the superior established convolutional network for small datasets within a percentage range. Preprocessing used canny edge detection and histogram equalization.

Keywords: Keras · Tensorflow · Multi-block local binary patterns

1 Introduction

Use of automated facial expression has relied on improved classification methods like deep learning in order to reduce human bias and dependency. Wide scale

© Springer Nature Switzerland AG 2019
J. A. Carrasco-Ochoa et al. (Eds.): MCPR 2019, LNCS 11524, pp. 127–138, 2019.
https://doi.org/10.1007/978-3-030-21077-9_12

use has been witnessed in hospitals, social media, manufacturing with lean systems, oil industry as well as security, search and rescue operations [4,6]. One's facial expressions is depicted in 7 different facial expressions namely surprise, fear, joy, contempt, sadness, neutral and anger. The recognition process involves facial detection, facial alignment, feature extraction, feature selection and classification [4,6,15,17,19]. Facial detection involves use of software and hardware systems to identify facial images from a human image from a video or static picture. There has been wide interest in facial recognition using deep learning as opposed to using feature based approaches [2,8,17]. The emergency of convolutional neural networks through use of GPUs has had a multiplier effect on their processing timelines and accuracy [1,2,20]. Transfer learning techniques have also been used on the facial expression datasets to reduce the training time by reusing trained data [7].

The study used a deep neural network to compare its accuracy with a feature based algorithm. The MB-Local Binary Pattern variant or multi-block local binary patterns approach classified the features using an ensemble of neural networks (multi-layer perceptron), extra-trees classifier and support vector machines [17]. The former has an input module, recognition module and output module. The study used popular frameworks Keras and Tensorflow as the backend.

2   Related Work

Facial expression recognition research has exceeded expectations in different fields like medical, travel, education, security and manufacturing [8,14,18]. The key expressions include sadness, anger, fear, neutral and disgust. The key stages include image detection using Viola Jones and Haar Cascade, preprocessing of images using histogram equalization and edge detection algorithms [9,14]. The popular edge detectors to have been used with great popularity include canny edge detector, kirsch and LoG detectors. Deep learning algorithms or local feature based algorithms are then used to retrieve features and classify emotions from images [4,12] and videos [8]. Local descriptors are good on images with varying illumination changes due to their use of grey scale images [1,10,13,17]. Some of the popular feature based algorithms include local binary patterns and their variants like central-symmetric local binary patterns, multi-block local binary patterns, local directional patterns and rotational local invariant local binary patterns. Deep learning algorithms accuracy and performances have risen due to better processing power including Nvidia GPUs and other better processing devices. Deep learning algorithms use loss functions through the use of softmax function. Activation functions are also more varied from sigmoid function to rectifier RELu and Tanh function [2,4].

2.1   Local Feature Extraction Methods

Feature based algorithms analyze facial components as separate components like mouth, nose or forehead and the features are aggregated using a histogram. Local Binary and Directional Patterns are popular algorithms to have been used in facial expression recognition [12,14]. Different LBP variants were successfully used in facial expression recognition that include, TLBP or Ternary Local Binary Patterns, Over-Complete Local Binary Patterns (OCLBP) and ELBP or elliptical local binary patterns and rotational local binary patterns [3,12,17,20]. These eliminated the challenges of basic LBP algorithm like illumination or rotation [13,14]. **Multi-Block Local Binary Patterns (MB-LBP)** uses rectangular regions in encoded format to derive their local binary operator to enable local structure image diversity [10–12]. The block regions are used in place of one pixel. The algorithm divides the input as horizontal/spawn processes (Fig. 1).

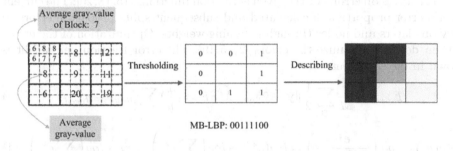

Fig. 1. Multi-Block Local Binary Patterns (MB-LBP) [14,17]

The algorithm also encodes the image's micro and macrostructures. The average of sub-region blocks is used to remove locality disadvantages [11,12]. The algorithm is based on the Haar-like rectangular features and represented in the form below [10,14,17]:

$$MB - LBP(X,Y)(x_c, y_c) = \sum_{X=1}^{X=8} 2^X s(g_x - g_c), s(x) = \begin{cases} 1, & (x \geq 0) \\ 0, & x < 0 \end{cases} \quad (1)$$

2.2 Artificial Neural Networks

Artificial neural networks have been used to recognize facial expression with relative success. The ANN is a black box model with labelled inputs and output with set of predicted vectors grouped as probability distribution labels. It consists of artificial neurons based on biology [15,16]. The data is fed through dense networks that include hidden layers [15,16]. The initial layer is given as a parameter of the initial dense layer and hidden layer can be one or more layers. Single layers are termed shallow networks and deep networks for multiple hidden layered networks [15,16]. The algorithm has the output layer where data is returned from the network. Several activation functions successfully used in deep networks include RELu, Tanh and sigmoid functions. Inputs are assumed standard and standardization to a mean of zero and variance of 1 is always recommended [16]. The output values from the neural network are in either in binary, continuous or categorical/multiple values form. Popular algorithms include the feed forward and backpropagation algorithms [15,16,18,20].

Feed Forward and Backpropagation. Feed forward or multi-layer perceptron neural networks are shown as linear (regression) and nonlinear (classification) models and have generalized activations functions. The layers undergo affine transforms and normally they contain a single hidden layer represented with a continuous function as shown in the following equation [2,15,19,20].

$$y(x,w) = f(\sum_{j=1}^{m} w_j \theta_j(x)) \quad \mathbf{z}^{(l)} = \mathbf{W}^{(l)} \cdot \mathbf{a}^{(l-1)}, \quad \mathbf{a}^{(l)} = \sigma(\mathbf{z}^{(l)}). \quad (2)$$

Backpropagation networks handle nonlinear problems through use of partial derivatives on errors for the given activation functions [15,18,20]. The current layer's error proportion is calculated and subsequent splits propagate errors to previous layers and nodes through assigning weights. Optimization of the errors is then done to minimize the errors [2,15,19]. The error fraction per weight is shown in the equations below:

$$E_{mse} = \frac{1}{M} \sum_{\mathcal{D}} \frac{1}{2} \|\mathbf{y} - \hat{\mathbf{y}}\|_2, \quad MSE = (\frac{1}{n}) \sum y_{true} - y_{pred}^2 \quad (3)$$

$$log(\hat{y}_j) = log\left(\frac{e^{z_j}}{\sum_{i=1}^{n} e^{z_i}}\right) = log(e^{z_j}) - log\left(\sum_{i=1}^{n} e^{z_i}\right) = z_j - log\left(\sum_{i=1}^{n} e^{z_i}\right) \quad (4)$$

3 Deep Learning

Deep learning convolutional neural networks produced exceptional results in image classification to create a boom in classification. This was aided by rise of GPU machines as well as improved processing power. The rise of cognitive cloud solutions like AWS Cognitive solution, Microsoft Azure Cloud and other cloud solutions [1] allowed for cheaper infrastructure models based on per use basis to execute deep learning models. Key advantages include huge storage advantages for readily available web data. With CNN one or more convolutional layers are used together with a pooling and fully connected layers [5]. Key deep learning models include AlexNet, VGG-Face and GoogleNet [1,2] and a fusion with feature based algorithms has improved accuracy [3]. Deep learning enables feature extraction and classification together based on multilayer networks (hidden, input and output) as well use of Softmax to allow for classification using a probability function model [1,5] and this is depicted in the following equation:

$$S(a,b) = (V * Z)(a,b) = \sum_x \sum_y Z(a-x, b-y)V(x,y) \quad (5)$$

Convolutional neural networks are based on mathematical convolutions for several layers of filters and kernels(k) and for an image in two dimensional format the neural network at time t given values u and s, the value s(t) is shown as below: [2,4]

$$s(t) = (x * w)(t) = \sum_{a=-\infty}^{\infty} x(a)w(t-a) \quad (6)$$

$$i \otimes k = \sum_{y=0}^{c} (\sum_{x=0}^{r} i(x-a, y-b)k(x,y)) \tag{7}$$

The convolutional neural networks are made up of one or more pooling layers and output layers [2,4]. Key pooling options include max pooling, L2 norm pooling as well as average pooling. The output layers receive features from a multitude of hidden layers to generate output classes and error predictions are based on given loss functions [5,6] in a single forward and backward pass cycle [2,3].

Convolutional Layers. The convolution filters denoted f(k) are determined through sharing weights of nearby neurons allowing for smaller weights to be trained. Through max pooling, the input is reduced by applying the maximum function on the input.

Activation Function. Activation functions map a node's inputs to its outputs through transformations in hidden layers. They derive the weighted sum and also enhance it though bias in a nonlinear functional model. Key hidden layer activation functions include Rectified Linear Unit (ReLU), Sigmoid and Tanh [5] and are key in deciding whether a neuron can be activated or not [6,8]. The sigmoid function or logistic denoted with 'S' shaped graph has smooth edges in some parts [1,22]. The tanh function allows for back propagation through a hyperbolic function. The Rectifier function (ReLU) allows for back propagation of errors and activates neurons on different layers [2]. The activation function allows non-linearity into the key functions as shown in the following equations.

$$o(x) = \sigma(w_0 + \sum_h \sigma(w_o^h + \sum_i w_i^h x_i)) \quad Y = activation(\sum(W*I) + b) \tag{8}$$

$$sigm_{f(x)} = (1 + e^{-x})^{-1} \quad tanh(x) = 2\,sigm\,(2x) - 1 \quad reluf(x) = max(0, x) \tag{9}$$

Softmax Function. Softmax is used in the output layer based on the sigmoid function or multiclass regression to classify images in computer vision. The layer's nodes match the output layer nodes where the classifier returns class probabilities that add up to 1 in a probability distribution and in normalized form [1,2,21,23]. In cases of binary classification, a logistic regression model is applied as $yk = \sigma(ak)$ and multiclass models(Maximum Entropy Classifier) softmax based on an extended multi-class logistic regression model is applied [4,21]. The latter uses decimal probability models whose sum is 1 and follows $[1, -2, 0] \rightarrow [e^1, e^{-2}, e^0] = [2.71, 0.14, 1] \rightarrow [0.7, 0.04, 0.26]$.

$$\sigma_x = \Pr(Y_i = k) = \frac{e^{\beta_k \cdot \mathbf{X}_i}}{\sum_{0 \le c \le K} e^{\beta_c \cdot \mathbf{X}_i}} \quad for\ i = 1....k\ \ and\ \ z = (z_1....z_k) = R^k \tag{10}$$

3.1   TensorFlow, Theano and Keras

The Google Open Source library, Tensorflow is Python and C++ language driven [21,22]. The framework is used to recognize facial expressions using GPU or CPUs. The mathematical operations are defined as nodes and edges are used to define node input and output and association. The data is transferred using tensors, a multi layered array. Execution is done asynchronously and in parallel [21,23] (Fig. 2).

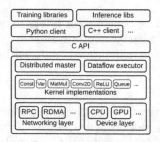

Fig. 2. TensorFlow architecture diagram [21,23]

The input node values and their connected proportions/weights are used as the aggregate inputs. where y takes values $y = f(\sum_{i=1}^{D} w_i * x_i) \ldots y = f(w_1 * x_1 + w_2 * x_2 + \ldots w_D * x_D)$.

– # Define predictions based on slope and intercept variables
– pred = tf.add(tf.multiply(m,x), b)
– loss_x = tf.reduce_mean(tf.pow(pred - y, 2)) # Create loss function
– optim = tf.train.AdamOptimizer(learning_rate = 0.01).minimize(loss_x) # optimizer
– with tf.Session() as sess:sess.run(init) # Initialize TensorFlow session

An optimizer like Stochastic Gradient Descent (SGD), ADAM and RMSprop is required and the loss algorithm MSE used to minimize errors in the model.

Keras on TensorFlow. Whilst tensorflow uses graph execution based on sessions and maintains state using variables, Theano based programs train and run simple neural networks based on fully connected layers (with, convolutional, max pooling and softmax) [3,21–23,23]. They activate neurons using activation functions (sigmoid, tanh, and rectified linear units). Keras is a modular high level framework that runs open neural networks on top of Tensorflow or Theano backends [21,23]. The latter is a high level framework and the former are low level complex apis. The Keras model has multiple layers with a defined network graph and the sequence is shown as below [21,23]:

– Import 'Sequential' from 'keras.models' from keras.models import Sequential
– Import 'Dense' from 'keras.layers' from keras.layers import Dense

- *Initialize a constructor sequential model*
- *Add an input layer model.add(Dense(12, activation is relu, input_shape=(11,)))*
- *Add a hidden layer model.add(Dense(8, activation is relu))*
- *Add an output layer model.add(Dense(1, activation is sigmoid)), Dropout(0.5)(x)*
- *Compile model.compile(optimizer is rmsprop' and loss is mse)*

Transfer Learning. Speed of execution is based on resources and data availability challenges for neural networks which rely on huge datasets. To reuse previous models, transfer learning has been used in facial expression recognition based on pre-trained models. Transfer learning enables pre-trained feature extractors in deep learning using convolutional layers and only the output layers are replaced/altered based on the data available [7].

4   Implementation Framework

The study used a Keras on Tensorflow approach on facial expression images and compares the results to a proposed local binary pattern variant, MB-LBP which is preprocessed with Gabor Filters, histogram equalization, edge detection and also feature reduction with PCA algorithm. The proposed approach used a classification approach based on support vector machines, stochastic gradient descent (SGD), multilayer perceptron and an extra trees classifier with a 3:1:2:2 classifier ratio. The 2 approaches were compared in terms of accuracy and processing time. The Keras deep learning approach uses GPUs. The SGD classifier is based on the *sklearn.linear_model.SGDClassifier python implementation*. The stochastic gradient descent also acts as an optimizing algorithm hence the choice and the support vector machine enables loss derivation.

Tools. The study used python to implement both the deep learning approaches and feature based approaches. Flask a mini web python framework was used to design the frontend for the solution. The implementation used python running on a docker engine based on linux. The docker was configured and run on an Amazon AWS cloud environment to take advantage of GPU use. Other popular frameworks considered included other popular frameworks like Apache MXNet, PyTorch and Microsoft Cognitive Toolkit but Amazon cloud environment was chosen due to the easiness of use.

Approach and Databases. The study compared the MB-LBP with PCA and Gabor Filters as well as the deep learning CNN algorithm in terms of accuracy of classification of the FER-2013 dataset, AT&T Database of Faces, Yale Faces, Cohn-Kanade (CK) and JAFFE databases. Facial detection was done using the Viola Jones Open CV detection algorithm. Feature extraction for the local feature approach was done using the algorithms MB-LBP algorithm. Classification was through machine learning classifiers namely multilayer perceptron, support vector machines (SVM), SGD classifier and extra trees classifier all in weighted proportions [2]. The first step involved using histogram equalization and canny edge detector to preprocess the images. Gabor filters were then used for filtering before the feature based algorithm was used to extract expression features for classification (Fig. 3).

Fig. 3. Example expression images: JAFFE dataset. [24,25]

The study used FER-2013 dataset, AT&T Database of Faces, Yale Faces, Cohn-Kanade (CK) AU-coded expression dataset and JAFFE (Japanese Female Expression) datasets. The latter is made up of 10 Japanese subjects with 213 expression images giving 7 different expressions namely anger, sadness, neutral, fear, disgust and happiness. The Yale Faces has 165 grayscale images in GIF format and the CK+ dataset is based on a mixture of images of American, Latin and Asian descent. The AT & T Database of Faces is composed of 10 unique images of each of 40 distinct subjects. The deep learning computation involved using decay factor, a learning rate of 0.00001 and 3000 epochs which indicates when all queued images have been successfully processed. The deep learning datasets were normalized using *preprocessing. MinMaxScaler()* preprocessor. The pooling layers reduce spatiality of data and dense layers used the features from the convolution layers. The drop out layers remove some neurons to cater for overfitting and normalization is done using batch normalization by subtracting the mean and dividing with the batch mean [1].

Deep Learning Facial Expression Analysis Results. The deep learning algorithm executed was executed against the FER-2013 dataset, AT&T Database of Faces, Yale Faces, Cohn-Kanade (CK) AU-coded expression dataset and JAFFE (Japanese Female Expression) datasets and had accuracy values as shown in the following tables where 7 different expressions were the output class layers. The batch size was 64 and number of epochs varied but best results was found when 3000 epochs were used.

The Keras model was based on a 5 dense layers value 512, softmax activation and an input of 4624 compiled based on Stochastic gradient descent (SGD) with values $SGD(lr = 0.0001, decay = 1e-6, momentum = 0.9)$. The optimiser was extended with the adaptive learning rate based on the Adam(Adaptive Moment Estimation) optimiser with value of *keras.optimizers.Adam(lr = 0.00001).*

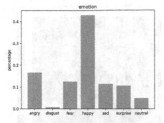

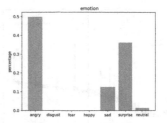

Fig. 4. Selected CK+ image (a)-happy mood

Fig. 5. Selected JAFFE image (b)-angry mood

The other options include Adaptive Gradient Algorithm (AdaGrad) and the Root Mean Square Propagation (RMSprop). The different optimisers *optimizers.Adadelta(), optimizers.Adagrad(), optimizers.Adam(), optimizers.Adamax(), optimizers.SGD(), optimizers.RMSprop()* were executed and the best results came by using the SGD and the Adam optimiser.

Deep Learning Vs Feature Based MB-LBP Algorithm		
Feature	MB-LBP	Keras backed TensorFlow
Design	Uses local facial regions, mouth, nose,eyes	Based on whole image
Speed	Faster, runs in sub minute times	Slower but speeds improving due to use of GPUs and Cloud, from days to hours
Light	Gray scale images reduce light impact	Affected by light
Error Detection	Use SVM to reduce loss impact	Use MSE to detect losses and rectify
Preprocesing	Edge Detection,HE, Gabor Filters, PCA	Images normalised to mean of 0 and a norm of 10
Dataset Size	Good for small and large datasets	Very good on large data sets and good on small datasets

The FER2013 dataset has 3 convolutional Conv2D(128) layers, dropout at 0.2, two FC dense(1024) layers all based on RELU activation function and softmax for the classification based on an input of (48, 48, 1). The Figs. 4, 5, 6 and 7 show the emotion distribution and confusion matrices for the 7 different expressions namely angry, fear, disgust, neutral, surprise, fear and happy.

The deep learning accuracy losses are shown in the following training loss against number of epochs executed. The deep learning algorithm gave an accuracy of 87.88%, 88.38% on the FER2013, Yale Faces, CK+ and JAFFE datasets. The loss function is shown in Figs. 6 and 8 as shown where the graph shows the number of epochs against the loss averaging at 1.5. The following diagram shows the loss function for both the training and testing phase for the deep learning test based on 100 images in this case and the training phase averaged just above zero from 1.5 and 0.7. For one facial image the distribution predicted showed high frequency on the happy class image (Fig. 9).

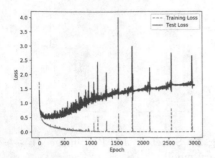

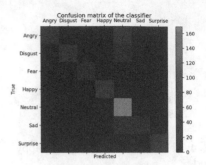

Fig. 6. Epochs = 3000, lr = 0.0001 loss function

Fig. 7. 3000 epochs confusion matrix

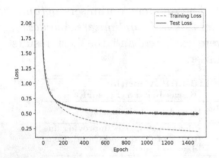

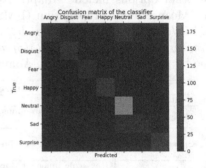

Fig. 8. Epochs = 1600, lr = 0.00001 loss function

Fig. 9. 1600 epochs confusion matrix

The MB-LBP algorithm showed high accuracy with preprocessing with percentages of 87%, 85% and 86% respectively for CK+ and JAFFE, Yale and AT&T Faces on small datasets. Deep learning approaches showed better accuracy but with more processing power and execution time was longer. The accuracy of the deep learning algorithm was better than the feature based algorithm MB-LBP on the CK+ and JAFFE databases. For smaller datasets, the MB-LBP algorithm accuracy was almost the same as the convolutional neural network approach since deep learning algorithms work better on bigger datasets. This convolutional neural network approach was executed over 50, 100, 500, 1000, 2000 and 3000 epochs on the FER2013, Yale Faces, AT&T Faces, CK+ and JAFFE datasets.

4.1   Conclusion

Deep learning approaches showed much better accuracy than feature based local algorithms like local binary patterns and their variants. For smaller datasets as in this study, the accuracy was almost closely matched between the 2 approaches but on big datasets, the deep learning approach showed much improved accuracy compared to the local based approach. The Keras implementation

Accuracy and Performance Results				
Algorithm	Dataset	Preprocessors	Layers/Classifier	Accuracy(%)
Keras with Tensorflow	CK+JAFFE	Histogram Equalization		88.38%
	Yale Faces	Histogram Equalization		87.78%
	AT&T Faces	Histogram Equalization		89.33%
	FER2013	Histogram Equalization		75.09%
TensorFlow	FER2013	Histogram Equalization		76.43%
MB-LBP	CK+JAFFE	Histogram Equalization Canny Detector/GF	SVM,ExtraTrees, MLP,SGDClassifier	87.56%
	Yale Faces	Histogram Equalization Canny Detector/GF	SVM,ExtraTrees, MLP,SGDClassifier	85.33%
	AT&T Faces	Histogram Equalization Canny Detector/GF	SVM,ExtraTrees, MLP,SGDClassifier	86.64%
	FER2013 Kaggle	Histogram Equalization Canny Detector/GF	SVM,ExtraTrees, MLP,SGDClassifier	73.77%

is simpler and high level than the tensorflow alone approach but classification results are similar. Changing the learning rates to smaller values improves the results. The proposed approach in this study of MB-LBP, Gabor Filters, canny edge detector and Histogram Equalization classified by a weighted classifier of support vector machines, extra trees classifier and multi-layer perceptron showed a marked improvement of 4–5% points compared to a basic local binary pattern (LBP) on the FER2013 dataset. The feature based approach executes with much faster processing times than the Keras/Tensorflow approach. The deep learning approach showed improved processing times when executed on GPUs on the Amazon AWS cloud environment and also when transfer learning was used in the case of the FER2013 dataset. The study concludes that feature based approaches like local binary patterns' accuracy was marginally less compared deep learning approaches but processing times favour the feature based approaches.

References

1. Pramerdorfer, C., Kampel, M.: Facial expression recognition using convolutional neural networks: state of the art (2016). arXiv preprint arXiv:1612.02903
2. Tang, Y.: Deep learning using linear support vector machines. arXiv preprint arXiv:1306.0239 (2013)
3. Levi, G., Hassner, T.: Emotion recognition in the wild via convolutional neural networks and mapped binary patterns. In: ACM International Conference on Multimodal Interaction, pp. 503–510. ACM, November 2015
4. Mollahosseini, A., Chan, D., Mahoor, M.H.: Going deeper in facial expression recognition using deep neural networks. In: IEEE Winter Conference on Applications of Computer Vision (WACV), pp. 1–10. IEEE, March 2016
5. Zhao, X., Shi, X., Zhang, S.: Facial expression recognition via deep learning. IETE Tech. Rev. 32(5), 347–355 (2015)

6. Hemalatha, G., Sumathi, C.P.: A study of techniques for facial detection and expression classification. Int. J. Comput. Sci. Eng. Surv. **5**(2), 27 (2014)

7. Xu, M., Cheng, W., Zhao, Q., Ma, L., Xu, F.: Facial expression recognition based on transfer learning from deep convolutional networks. In: 11th International Conference on Natural Computation (ICNC), pp. 702–708. IEEE, August 2015

8. Kahou, S.E., et al.: Emonets: multimodal deep learning approaches for emotion recognition in video. J. Multimodal User Interfaces **10**(2), 99–111 (2016)

9. Tripathi, S., Acharya, S., Sharma, R.D., Mittal, S., Bhattacharya, S.: Using deep and convolutional neural networks for accurate emotion classification on DEAP dataset. In: Twenty-Ninth IAAI Conference, February 2017

10. Cai, Z., Gu, Z., Yu, Z.L., Liu, H., Zhang, K.: A real-time visual object tracking system based on Kalman filter and MB-LBP feature matching. Multimedia Tools Appl. **75**(4), 2393–2409 (2016)

11. Girish, G.N., CL, S.N., Das, P.K.: Face recognition using MB-LBP and PCA: a comparative study. In 2014 International Conference on Computer Communication and Informatics, pp. 1–6. IEEE, January 2014

12. Dhavalikar, A.S., Kulkarni, R.K.: Face detection and facial expression recognition system. In: 2014 International Conference on Electronics and Communication Systems (ICECS), pp. 1–7. IEEE, February 2014

13. Zhou, S., Yin, J.: Face detection using multi-block local gradient patterns and support vector machine. J. Comput. Inf. Syst. **10**(4), 1767–1776 (2014)

14. Zhang, L., Chu, R., Xiang, S., Liao, S., Li, S.Z.: Face detection based on multiblock LBP representation. In: Lee, S.-W., Li, S.Z. (eds.) ICB 2007. LNCS, vol. 4642, pp. 11–18. Springer, Heidelberg (2007). https://doi.org/10.1007/978-3-540-74549-5_2

15. Iftikhar, S., Younas, R., Nasir, N., Zafar, K.: Detection and classification of facial expressions using artificial neural network. J. Inf. Technol. Electr. Eng. **3**, 18–22 (2014)

16. Chaudhari, M.V., Student, M.E., Bhusaval, S.S.G.B.C.O.E.T., Patil, Y.S., Patil, D.D.: Facial expression recognition using ANN & Gabor filter **1**(6) (2017)

17. Pietikinen, M., Hadid, A., Zhao, G., Ahonen, T.: Computer Vision Using Local Binary Patterns, vol. 40. Springer, Heidelberg (2011). https://doi.org/10.1007/978-0-85729-748-8

18. Poornima, P., Radhapriya, S.: Survey of automatic facial recognition based on classification schemes **4**(10) (2017). ISSN: 2454-6933

19. Ruiz, L.Z., Alomia, R.P.V., Dantis, A.D.Q., San Diego, M.J.S., Tindugan, C.F., Serrano, K.K.D.: Human emotion detection through facial expressions for commercial analysis. In: Conference on Humanoid, Nanotechnology, (HNICEM) (2017)

20. Han, J., Kamber, M.: Data Mining: Concepts and Techniques. Morgan Kaufmann, San Francisco (2001)

21. Gulli, A., Pal, S.: Deep Learning with Keras. Packt Publishing Ltd., Birmingham (2017)

22. Breuer, R., Kimmel, R.: A deep learning perspective on the origin of facial expressions (2017)

23. Xia, X.L., Xu, C., Nan, B.: Facial expression recognition based on tensorflow platform. In: ITM Web of Conferences, vol. 12, p. 01005. EDP Sciences (2017)

24. The Japanese Female Facial Expression (JAFFE) Database. http://www.kasrl.org/jaffe.html

25. Kanade, T., Tian, Y., Cohn, J.F.: Comprehensive database for facial expression analysis. In: IEEE International Conference Automatic Face GestureRecognition (2000)

Detection and Tracking of Motorcycles in Congested Urban Environments Using Deep Learning and Markov Decision Processes

Jorge E. Espinosa[1](✉) [iD], Sergio A. Velastin[2,3,4] [iD], and John W. Branch[5] [iD]

[1] Politécnico Colombiano Jaime Isaza Cadavid,
Carrera 48 No. 7-151 El Poblado, Medellín, Colombia
jeespinosa@elpoli.edu.co
[2] Cortexica Vision Systems Ltd., London, UK
sergio.velastin@ieee.org
[3] Queen Mary University of London, London, UK
[4] University Carlos III Madrid, Madrid, Spain
[5] Universidad Nacional de Colombia – Sede Medellín,
Calle 59 A N 63-20, Medellín, Colombia
jwbranch@unal.edu.co

Abstract. This research describes "EspiNet", a Deep Learning Convolutional Neural Network model, in conjunction with a Markov Decision Process (MDP) tracker for detection and tracking of occluded motorcycles in urban environments. The model is trained and evaluated, using a new public dataset with up to 10,000 annotated images, created for this research, and captured in real urban traffic scenes. Images were captured using a moving camera mounted in a drone, where more than 60% of the motorcycles are affected by occlusions. The network design involves many tests, where a promising result of 88.84% in average precision (AP) is achieved, despite the considerable number of occluded vehicles, the movement of the camera and the low angle used for capture. The model predictions are used as input to an MDP tracker, reaching results up to 85.2% in Multiple Object Tracking Accuracy (MOTA). The proposed network architecture outperforms state of the art YOLO (You Look Only Once) v3.0 and Faster R-CNN (VGG16 based) detection models, producing also better tracking results in comparison with the use of the other two models as detector base for the MDP tracker.

Keywords: Motorcycle detection · Motorcycle tracking ·
Faster R-CNN · Region based detector · CNN · Deep learning ·
Occluded images · Markov Decision Process

© Springer Nature Switzerland AG 2019
J. A. Carrasco-Ochoa et al. (Eds.): MCPR 2019, LNCS 11524, pp. 139–148, 2019.
https://doi.org/10.1007/978-3-030-21077-9_13

1   Introduction

1.1   Motorcycles as Part of Urban Traffic

Motorcycles are currently one of the most popular means of transport in emerging countries, which results in important fatality rates [4] and a significant environmental impact due to emissions (e.g. P.M. 2.5) [19].

As an example of conditions in emerging countries, the annual report of Traffic Accidents of the Andean Community 2007–2016 [1], indicates that in 2017, for Bolivia, Colombia, Ecuador and Perú, of the 347,642 road accidents 88% correspond to urban occurrences. Colombian road users most affected by traffic accidents are motorcyclists, representing 49.82% of reported deaths and 56.36% of non-fatal injuries. Of the total drivers, motorcyclists represented 78.81% of the dead and 80.51% of the injured and for their passengers the figures were 50.69% and 48.99%, respectively [2].

Therefore, it is important to implement traffic management techniques or strategies starting from the detection and tracking of motorcycles to reduce accidents. The use of Intelligent Transportation Systems (ITS) and video analysis in particular, could be one way of helping address issues affecting road safety.

In this research we introduce EspiNet, a CNN model inspired on Faster R-CNN [15] combining it with a Markov Decision Process (MDP) tracker for the tasks of detecting and tracking motorcycles in urban traffic video sequences, especially under occlusion, characteristic of road conditions in emerging countries. General vehicle detection, under this condition, has been studied by many authors, benchmarking their results mainly using the KITTI dataset [10], which unfortunately lacks a motorcycle category. For this reason we have created and used a new public motorbike dataset of 7,500 and 10,000 annotated images, captured on a public road using a camera mounted in a drone.

The main contributions of this work are

1. The publication of a realistic annotated video dataset of motorcycle traffic, presenting realistic occlusion conditions;
2. The proposal of a new convolutional model, EspiNet, inspired by Faster R-CNN to detect motorcycles;
3. The combination of EspiNet and an MDP tracker that obtains competitive results and that provides a baseline for other researchers to improve upon.

This paper is organized as follows: Sect. 1.2 describes works related with vehicle and motorbike detection. Section 2 describes the motorcycles dataset created for this research. Section 3 shows the EspiNet model, describing its main improvements w.r.t to Faster R-CNN, and providing an insight about the advantages of its architecture. Section 4 the MDP tracking strategy used in this research. Section 5 shows the experimentation done for detection and tracking, and a comparative study with state of the art detectors trained end-to-end for this purpose. Finally, Sect. 6 presents the conclusions around the proposed model and the directions for future research.

1.2   Motorcycle Detection

Traditionally, video technique analysis requires reliable methods for object feature extraction to obtain accurate classification results. Video detection systems in the last decade are implemented through discrimination capabilities on appearance features. Motorcycle detection and classification using appearance features include the construction of 3D models [5], dimensions of the vehicles [8], there is also used colour, symmetry, shadows, texture and geometrical features (e.g. circles) as wheel contours [7]. Description of features as histogram of oriented gradients (HOG) used for detection of helmet in motorcycle riders [16]. There are also variations of HOG [6] and the use of scale-invariant feature transform (SIFT), DSIFT and speeded up robust features (SURF) [17].

Deep learning theory (DL) has emerged as an important breakthrough in the field of computer vision in the last nine years, with astonishing results in image processing. This theory has been successfully used in vehicle detection, mainly based on DL general object detectors. These detectors can be divided into region based stage detectors and single stage detectors. Region based detectors involve two general components, the region proposal step (RPN) and the classification step. R-CNN [11], combines selective search algorithm for region proposal (RPN) and CNN features to perform object detection. This model was used in [3] to classify motorcycles according to the USA Federal Highway Administration (FHWA) scheme. There is also work based on single stage detectors, where a single convolutional architecture simultaneously predicts bounding boxes and class scores associated. Huynh et al. [13] designed a network for this purpose, working on top-view captured images, that significantly reduces occlusion between urban objects. Other approaches based their detection of moving objects on background subtraction methods using a pre-trained network (AlexNet) for feature extraction for helmet detection [18]. However there are no reports using an open dataset of motorcycles on congested urban environments.

2   The Dataset

Real urban traffic present occlusions between vehicles or with regular urban furniture (Fig. 1). Despite that there had been effort to construct a dataset such as KITTI [10], where occluded vehicles are annotated, and state of the art algorithms benchmark their performance, there is not motorcycle category created on this dataset or any dataset public available explicitly oriented to occluded motorcycles in urban environments.

This is why we have created an annotated motorcycle public dataset, which contains images taken from a camera mounted in a drone, subject to subtle unstable conditions. To speed up processing analysis, images were resized to one-third of their original size, reaching 56,975 ROI (Region of Interest) annotated motorcycles, and 25 pixels as the minimal height size. 60% of the annotated motorcycles has a level of occlusion. Objects partially occluded smaller than 25 pixels were discarded. The ground truth generated is specified in an XML file that describes the class, frames covered by the object, Name, Id, height

Fig. 1. Original dataset image vs. annotated image. Note the small object size of some annotated objects and the variate level of occlusions.

Table 1. Details of the new dataset

Dataset	Classes	Objects	Min. vertical size	Occlusion	Format
MotorBikes7,500	1	221	25 px	>60%	XML
MotorBikes10,000	1	317	25 px	>60%	XML

and width of the bbox surrounding the object. Table 1 describes these datasets, available on the internet[1].

3   EspiNet

The EspiNet model is based on Faster R-CNN. The difference here is that we create a more compact model, hence with faster inference, with just 4 layers of convolution. EspiNet is the evolution of the architecture described in [9]. Now, the number of convolutional layers has been increased to four, to capture more discriminating features. All the convolutional filters implemented are of size [3 3]. The first convolutional layer includes 64 filters, used to work with the three image channels and capturing primitive features. These primitive features are fed to a second convolutional layer, with 32 filters to create more complex features, which are aggregated even more in the third (64 filters) and fourth (128 filters) layer. As in [9], this architecture is used simultaneously as a region proposal network (RPN) and detection network. Figure 2 shows the described model able to identify motorcycles even under occluded scenarios.

The optimization algorithm used for training the model is Stochastic Gradient Descent with Momentum (SGDM). The training comprises four steps learning shared parameters for the RPN and detector networks. The RPN and the detector network are trained separately. EspiNet uses a learning rate of 1e-5 for these two steps since they require a quicker convergence. In the last two steps, the shared convolutional layers are fixed, fine-tuning the layers unique to RPN and detector network. In these last steps, the learning rate is set to 1e-6 for a smooth fine-tuning process.

---

[1] http://videodatasets.org/.

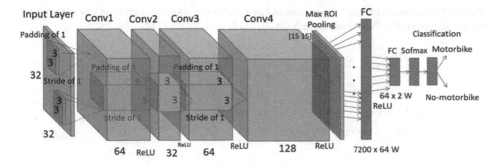

Fig. 2. The EspiNet CNN model. Used simultaneously for RPN and for classification

For RPN training, positives image examples patches are those which have 0.6 to 1.0 overlapping with the ground truth boxes. Negative ones have overlapping of 0 to 0.3. The overlapping criteria used is IoU (Intersection over Union) or Jaccard coefficient.

4   Multi-Object Tracking (MOT)

Multiple object tracking (MOT) is a challenging task, since it implies localizing and following multiple objects in the same scene during their life in the sequence, even under occlusion.

4.1   Online Multi-Object Tracking by Decision Making

We adopt the work proposed for online multi-object tracking based on Markov Decision Processes (MDP) [20], where the object tracked lifetime is modeled by using a MDP with four state subspaces: Active, Tracked, Lost and Inactive. With the state transitions the appearance/disappearance of objects is modeled in the MDP tracking process. Data association is performed by learning (reinforcement learning) a similarity function within the MDP policy scheme. The modular architecture of the framework can be combined with different object detection approaches, single object tracking and data association techniques which could be used for learning the MDP policy. We tested this tracking framework on the challenging new dataset (Sect. 2), and evaluated tracking performance for Faster R-CNN (VGG16 based), YOLO v3, and EspiNet, all models are trained end to end.

The framework is categorized as a hybrid learning model, implementing off-line learning using supervision from ground truth trajectories, and online-learning method while tracking objects on training examples, making the MDP able to decide supported on the history and the current status of the target.

Table 2. Comparative detection results EspiNet model against a state of the art trained network Faster-R-CNN (based on VGG16) [12] and YOLO [14]

Metrics	EspiNet	Faster R-CNN	YOLO
Precision (%)	**93.7**	57.3	93.0
Recall (%)	**90.0**	76.3	81.0
F1 score (%)	**91.8**	65.4	86.6
AP (Average Precision)	**88.84**	68.75	80.72

5   Experiments

5.1   Detection

For comparative purposes, we chose state of the arts models, representative of single stage detectors (YOLO [14]) and the region based Faster-R-CNN (VGG16 based) [12]. For a fair comparison, all these models were trained end-to-end using the challenging 10,000 examples dataset (Sect. 2). Evaluating the model we achieved an Average Precision (AP) of 88.84% and an F1-score of 91.8%, outperforming results of Faster-R-CNN (based on VGG16) and YOLO (Table 2).

In all metrics, EspiNet outperforms the other two detectors, the closet best performance is achieved by YOLO that showed almost the same precision but poorer recall because the single stage model lacks RPN and thus it can fail to detect objects that appear too close or too small. Video results can be viewed in the following link[2].

5.2   Tracking

The tracking algorithm is evaluated also in the new dataset described in Sect. 2. For comparative purposes, we used the detection results of EspiNet, YOLO and Faster R-CNN (VGG-16 based) described in Sect. 5.1.

Tracking Performance Metrics. Based on the metrics defined in the MOT challenge[3], we evaluated the results of the modified MDP, tracking detections from the new dataset. Two main performance metrics were used:

Multiple Object Tracking Precision (MOTP) $MOTP = \dfrac{\sum i, td_t^i}{\sum t, C_t}$ which calculates the total error for matched pairs of ground truth-tracker pairs over all frames, averaged by the total number of matches found.

Multiple Object Tracking Accuracy (MOTA) $MOTA = 1 - \dfrac{\sum_t (m_t + fp_t + mme_t)}{\sum_t g_t}$ where m_t, fp_t and mme_t are the number of misses, of false positives, and of mismatches, respectively, for time t.

---

[2] https://goo.gl/RSZQGz.
[3] https://motchallenge.net/.

Additionally, other metrics are used that allow understanding tracking behaviour: Mostly Track targets (MT), percentage of ground truth tracks covered by the tracking mechanism for at least 80%. Mostly Lost targets (ML, percentage of ground truth tracks covered by the tracking mechanism less than 20%. ID Switches (IDS) ID of the tracks that are erroneously changed by the algorithm. Fragmentation (Frag) corresponds to the total number of times a trajectory appears fragmented.

Tracking Results. For training proposes, the 7,500 section of the dataset 2 was used. For data association in the Lost state, we use $K = 10$ as trade off as suggested in [20]. The tracking results described in Table 3 show the importance of using a quality detector for the MDP tracking process. According to the results presented 5.1, the use of EspiNet as a detector for the MDP tracker offers the best results achieving a MOTA of 85.2% or tracking accuracy, which evaluates how many mistakes the tracker made in terms of misses, false positives, mismatches and failures to recover tracks. This result is consistent with a good recall result (90.0), reflected in a low false alarm rate (0.24) and a relative low number of ID switches (89). The use of EspiNet as a base detector reports also a better MOTP (82.5%), or tracking precision which expresses how well the exact position of the motorcycles is estimated. These results are consistent with a slightly better precision compared to YOLO and Faster R-CNN, which allows the MDP tracker to obtain less fragmentations (341). Video tracking results can be viewed via the following link[4].

Figure 3 shows an annotated frame and the results of the MDP tracker using the above mentioned detectors. In this comparative figure, it is possible to see the difference between the detectors and the ground truth, where the motorcycle tracking is annotated with a different count number that the one generated by different detectors. The more approximate numbers of the tracker objects to the ground truth are in this order Espinet: (d), YOLO (c) and Faster R-CNN (b).

An Nvidia Titan X (Pascal) 1531 Mhz GPU is used for training the EspiNet model and the Faster R-CNN model (VGG 16 based), both installed on a Windows 10 Machine with a CPU core i7 7th generation 4.7 GHz, with 32 GB of RAM. The training process on the dataset in EspiNet model took 32 h for training, and 57 h for Faster R-CNN (VGG 16). For YOLO training a Titan Xp 1582 Mhz GPU was used, running with Ubuntu 16.04.3, with a Xeon E5-2683 v4 2.10 GHz CPU, and 64 GB of RAM, taking 18 h for training. All models were trained from scratch. Meanwhile the training of the MDP tracker took 18 h on the Windows environment.

6   Discussion

This research has combined EspiNet and an MDP Tracker for motorcycle detection and Tracking in urban scenarios. The model can deal with highly occluded

---

[4] https://goo.gl/rLL2Le.

Table 3. Comparative results for MDP tracking using detectors EspiNet (Sect. 3), Faster-R-CNN (based on VGG16) [15] and YOLO [14]

Metrics	EspiNet	Faster R-CNN	YOLO
Recall	**90.0**	76.3	81.0
Precision	**93.7**	57.3	93.0
False Alarm Rate	**0.24**	2.04	0.38
GT Tracks	318	318	318
Mostly Tracked	**283**	113	142
Mostly Lost	2	7	2
ID Swiches	**89**	808	111
Fragmentations	**341**	1766	420
MOTA	**85.2**	34.1	71.4
MOTP	**82.5**	72.7	77.8

Fig. 3. Different detector effects on the MDP tracker. (a) Ground truth. (b) MDP tracker using Faster R-CNN as a base detector. (c) MDP tracker using YOLO as a base detector. (d) MDP tracker using EspiNet(Ours) as a base detector.

images and achieves in detection an Average Precision of nearly 90% and an F1 score of 91.8% for a newly annotated motorcycle urban dataset. Results can be compared with state of the art algorithms benchmarked in sites such as KITTI [10].

We have illustrated the importance of the use of an accurate detector in the implementation of the Multi-object tracking frameworks based on Markov decision process [20]. The tracker modeled the life time of the tracked object using four sub-space states (Active, Tracked, Lost and Inactive). The state transition handled by the MDP algorithm is now improved by the quality of the detections to handle incoming and leaving objects, as well as birth and death of the object being tracked.

Several tests were carried out to evaluate the influence of the detector in the MDP tracking. Lower quality of detections also produce poorer tracking, losing the tracking of some objects or forcing some tracks to drift.

Nevertheless the MDP tracking algorithm helped to preserve the identity of the detected object and the results showed performance close to the state of the art achieving a Multiple Object Tracking Accuracy of 85.2%, using a well trained EspiNet as base detector for the MDP tracker.

We have defined a model capable of detecting and following motorcycles in urban scenarios with a high level of occlusion, which represents an important aid to CCTV surveillance centers in emerging countries, where this type of vulnerable road users exceeds 50% of the vehicular park.

Results of the use of EspiNet + MDP tracker in CCTV surveillance center, can be retrieved from[5].

As future work we plain to move to an integrate deep learning model for simultaneously detect and track objects exploiting spatio-temporal features for improve detection and speed up tracking.

Acknowledgments. This work was partially supported by COLCIENCIAS project: Reduccion de Emisiones Vehiculares Mediante el Modelado y Gestion Optima de Trafico en Areas Metropolitanas - Caso Medellin - Area Metropolitana del Valle de Aburra, codigo 111874558167, CT 049-2017. Universidad Nacional de Colombia. Proyecto HERMES 25374. The authors gratefully acknowledge the support of NVIDIA Corporation with the donation of GPUs used for this research.

References

1. Accidentes de tránsito en la Comunidad Andina, 2007–2016. http://intranet. comunidadandina.org/Documentos/DEstadisticos/SGDE800.pdf
2. Mortalidad por accidentes de tránsito, June 2018. https://www.asivamosensalud. org/salud-para-ciudadanos/mortalidad-por-accidentes-de-transito
3. Adu-Gyamfi, Y.O., Asare, S.K., Sharma, A., Titus, T.: Automated vehicle recognition with deep convolutional neural networks. Transp. Res. Rec.: J. Transp. Res. Board **2645**, 113–122 (2017)
4. Bazargani, H.S., Vahidi, R.G., Abhari, A.A.: Predictors of survival in motor vehicle accidents among motorcyclists, bicyclists and pedestrians. Trauma Mon. **22**(2) (2017). https://doi.org/10.5812/traumamon.26019. http://traumamon.neoscriber. org/en/articles/13364.html. Accessed 26 Sept 2017

---

[5] https://goo.gl/8N5iZM.

5. Buch, N., Orwell, J., Velastin, S.A.: Urban road user detection and classification using 3D wire frame models. IET Comput. Vis. **4**(2), 105–116 (2010). https://doi.org/10.1049/iet-cvi.2008.0089

6. Chen, Z., Ellis, T., Velastin, S.A.: Vehicle detection, tracking and classification in urban traffic. In: 2012 15th International IEEE Conference on Intelligent Transportation Systems, September, pp. 951–956 (2012). https://doi.org/10.1109/ITSC.2012.6338852

7. Duan, B., Liu, W., Fu, P., Yang, C., Wen, X., Yuan, H.: Real-time on-road vehicle and motorcycle detection using a single camera, pp. 1–6. IEEE (2009). http://ieeexplore.ieee.org/xpls/abs_all.jsp?arnumber=4939585

8. Dupuis, Y., Subirats, P., Vasseur, P.: Robust image segmentation for overhead real time motorbike counting. In: 2014 IEEE 17th International Conference on Intelligent Transportation Systems (ITSC), October, pp. 3070–3075 (2014). https://doi.org/10.1109/ITSC.2014.6958183

9. Espinosa, J.E., Velastin, S.A., Branch, J.W.: Motorcycle detection and classification in urban Scenarios using a model based on Faster R-CNN. arXiv preprint arXiv:1808.02299 (2018)

10. Geiger, A., Lenz, P., Urtasun, R.: Are we ready for autonomous driving? The KITTI vision benchmark suite, p. 3354–3361. IEEE (2012). http://ieeexplore.ieee.org/xpls/abs_all.jsp?arnumber=6248074. Accessed 27 Oct 2016

11. Girshick, R., Donahue, J., Darrell, T., Malik, J.: Rich feature hierarchies for accurate object detection and semantic segmentation. In: 2014 IEEE Conference on Computer Vision and Pattern Recognition, June, pp. 580–587 (2014). https://doi.org/10.1109/CVPR.2014.81

12. Huang, J., et al.: Speed/accuracy trade-offs for modern convolutional object detectors. arXiv:1611.10012, November 2016

13. Huynh, C.K., Le, T.S., Hamamoto, K.: Convolutional neural network for motorbike detection in dense traffic. In: 2016 IEEE Sixth International Conference on Communications and Electronics (ICCE), July, pp. 369–374 (2016). https://doi.org/10.1109/CCE.2016.7562664

14. Redmon, J., Farhadi, A.: YOLOv3: an incremental improvement. arXiv:1804.02767, April 2018

15. Ren, S., He, K., Girshick, R., Sun, J.: Faster R-CNN: towards real-time object detection with region proposal networks, pp. 91–99 (2015). https://goo.gl/A3FHD7

16. Silva, R.R., Aires, K.R., Veras, R.M.S.: Detection of helmets on motorcyclists. Multimed. Tools Appl. **77**, 1–25 (2017)

17. Thai, N.D., Le, T.S., Thoai, N., Hamamoto, K.: Learning bag of visual words for motorbike detection. In: 2014 13th International Conference on Control Automation Robotics Vision (ICARCV), December, pp. 1045–1050 (2014). https://doi.org/10.1109/ICARCV.2014.7064450

18. Vishnu, C., Singh, D., Mohan, C.K., Babu, S.: Detection of motorcyclists without helmet in videos using convolutional neural network. In: 2017 International Joint Conference on Neural Networks (IJCNN), May, pp. 3036–3041 (2017)

19. Walsh, M.P.: PM 2.5: global progress in controlling the motor vehicle contribution. Front. Environ. Sci. Eng. **8**(1), 1–17 (2014)

20. Xiang, Y., Alahi, A., Savarese, S.: Learning to track: online multi-object tracking by decision making. In: Proceedings of the IEEE International Conference on Computer Vision, pp. 4705–4713 (2015)

Rock Detection in a Mars-Like Environment Using a CNN

Federico Furlán[1]([⊠]), Elsa Rubio[1], Humberto Sossa[1,2], and Víctor Ponce[1]

[1] Instituto Politécnico Nacional - Centro de Investigación en Computación,
Av. Juan de Dios Bátiz and M. Othón de Mendizabal, 07738 Mexico City, Mexico
ffurlan_b11@sagitario.cic.ipn.mx, {erubio,hsossa,vponce}@cic.ipn.mx
[2] Escuela de Ingeniería y Ciencias, Tecnológico de Monterrey,
Av. General Ramón Corona 2514, Zapopan, Jalisco, Mexico

Abstract. In this paper we study the problem of rock detection in a Mars-like environment. We propose a convolutional neural network (CNN) to obtain a segmented image. The CNN is a modified version of the U-net architecture with a smaller number of parameters to improve the inference time. The performance of the methodology is proved in a dataset that contains several images of a Mars-like environment, achieving an F-score of 78.5%.

Keywords: Convolutional neural networks · Rock detection · Mars exploration

1 Introduction

The ability to get information from the environment is crucial for robot navigation, this field has been broadly studied and is yet growing. Particularly in the case of space exploration robots, thecomplexity is higher because objects like rocks do not have a regular morphology and have similar features, like color or texture compared to other objects like soil, gravel or sand. The challenge is to select the features that differentiate rocks from the rest of the objects. Rocks are the principal obstacles present in environments like Mars or the Moon; an exploration robot could end up damaged while colliding or by trying to climb them.

Space exploration robots need to cope with problems like sporadic communication with the Earth, missing data transmission and a limited quantity of on-board sensors. A way to overcome those problems is to give some autonomy to the robot by using an algorithm that can localize obstacles and provide this information to a path planner to reduce human interaction required for navigation.

The use of cameras is preferred over other types of sensors because they can acquire broader information about the environment. In some articles such as [4], some techniques are introduced to detect objects in planetary terrain based in

© Springer Nature Switzerland AG 2019
J. A. Carrasco-Ochoa et al. (Eds.): MCPR 2019, LNCS 11524, pp. 149–158, 2019.
https://doi.org/10.1007/978-3-030-21077-9_14

image processing. In Thomson and Castaño [16] conducted a comparative study of different methodologies developed for rock detection.

They compared seven methodologies Rockfinder [2], Multiple Viola-Jones [17], Rockster [1], Stereo Height Segmentation [7] and a SVM that classify each pixel in the image. Each method is tested in 4 different datasets, two of them composed by images taken from the Navcams and Pancams from the Spirit Mars Exploration Rover. Another form by images taken in an outdoor rover environment conditioned to be similar to Mars. Moreover, the last set is form by synthetic images made by a simulation program. None of these methods can find the actual contour of the rock; they only make approximations or find just a part of the rock. The methodologies are measured using Precision and Recall, but none of them achieve a good F-score because some algorithms like Stereo and Rockfinder obtain high precision and low recall, the Rockster algorithm gets the best recall but presents inter-image variation. They concluded that "None of the detectors we evaluated can yet produce reliable statistics about the visual features of rocks in a Mars image." [16] and suggest that autonomous detections are still away to replace manual analysis. Since the problem of rock detections can be consider still an open problem, we will examine some works that solve the problem of terrain classification or rock segmentation through different methodologies.

1.1   Related Work

Gong and Liu [5] reports a methodology to segment rocks in grayscale images from the Moon. First, they divide the images in superpixels, then obtain features from every superpixel like size, position, intensity, texture, and degradation. Using those features, they proposed an algorithm based in cut-graphs and Adaboost optimization. The total runtime cost is 12 s, and the F-score report is 81.95%.

Shang and Barnes [14] presented a way to select the most representative features extracted from Mars images, using Fuzzy-rough feature selection and an SVM (Support Vector Machine) to classify the pixels into nine classes. Their best classification result is 87.18%, it does not report a runtime cost, although it is expensive since it requires to obtain features from the image and evaluate the SVM as in the next work.

Rashno et al. [11] extracted 50 features from each pixel to form a vector that is used to classify seven types of terrains in Mars images. They used two methods based on ACO (Ant Colony Optimization) to reduce the number of parameters needed for classification. The subsets of features are processed by SVM and ELM (Extreme Learning Machine) to assign a class. They report an F-score of 91.72% in a 90 images dataset, with a runtime cost of 353 s per class, resulting in 2471 s for features extraction and 1428 ms of ELM evaluation.

Xiao et al. [18] solve the problem of rock detection using superpixels. Its technique consists in dividing the image into several regions called superpixels and calculate the variance and intensity to get a contrast value, after that they compare the contrast values among all regions and through a dynamic threshold algorithm they obtain a segmentation of rocks and background. They test the algorithm with 36 images taken during the MER's mission. They report an F-score of 70.52%, taking 3.4 s to run the algorithm while generating 600 superpixels per image.

2   Methodology

Convolutional Neural Networks (CNN) have proven to obtain good results in segmentation and localization through obtaining characteristic features from the target objects. Hence trying to use a CNN model to locate rocks in a Mars-like environment could overcome the disadvantages of other techniques. The objective is to propose a CNN architecture capable of segmenting rocks. The methodology proposed uses a U-net architecture with a different configuration aimed to reduce the number of parameters that will result in faster computing time.

2.1   Convolutional Neural Networks (CNN)

CNNs as proposed by LeCun in 1989 [8] are a type of neural network that uses convolutional layers to filter useful information from their inputs. A convolution operation is a matrix multiplication between a kernel (filter) and an input, resulting in a feature map that can become the input for another convolution or pass through an activation function to add non-linearity. The CNN's are suitable to process images, achieving excellent results for image classification [3] and image segmentation [20] only to mention a few.

Mathematically the convolution operation is defined as:

$$s(t) = (x * w)(t) \tag{1}$$

where x is the input, w is the kernel, and s are the feature maps [6].

2.2   U-Net

The U-net, view Fig. 1, is a CNN architecture that was created to segment grayscale biomedical images, was design in Freiburg University [12]. This architecture function similar to Auto-encoders, which are a two-part process, first a coding phase that reduces the dimensionality of the input and then a decoding or reconstruction phase that tries to recover the input information, but for the U-net what it recovers is a binary mask. The coding phase works as follows: the input (an image in RGB or grayscale) is passed through a series of convolutions and activation functions (usually ReLU), then applying a max-pooling operation to code the information while reducing the dimension of the input matrix by half. The decoding phase takes the features maps and by applying an up-sampling process tries to recover a binary mask that segment the target objects from the background. A unique characteristic of the U-net is that it shares feature maps from convolutions in the code phase with the output of the up-sampling operation of the decoding phase. The U-net has a symmetric architecture for each coding convolution and max-pooling operation; there must be a decoding convolution and up-sampling operation.

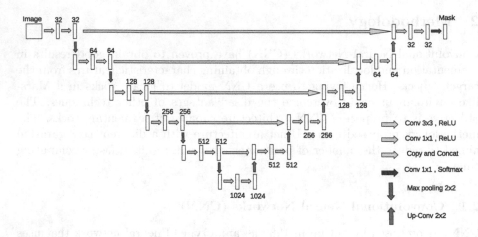

Fig. 1. U-net architecture as presented in [12].

2.3   Metrics

The F-score metric was presented in 1992 in MUC-4 as a way to evaluate data extraction [13] and is the harmonic mean of the precision (P) and recall (R); the next formula defines the metric:

$$F = \frac{2PR}{P + R} \tag{2}$$

where the precision also called predicted positive value is the percentage of correct predictions from all predictions, and the recall or sensibility is the percentage of positive predictions from the expected predictions define by the ground truth. It is preferred to use this metric rather than the arithmetic mean because it is more intuitive over percentages.

3   Methodology

3.1   Dataset

Due to the reduced amount of images available from Mars, it was decided to use images taken on Earth from a region with similar characteristics. Accordingly to NASA's Analog Missions [10], the Haughton Crater, located in Devon Island, resembles the Mars surface in more ways than any other place on Earth, because it has a landscape of dry, unvegetated, rocky terrain and extreme environmental conditions. The most significant project developed in this area is The Haughton-Mars Project that combines human and robotics research like the K-10 robotic rover [9]. So the images to train the CNN were taken from [15], that is a collection of data gathered in the Devon Island by the Autonomous Space Robotics Lab (ASRL) from the University of Toronto, an example of the terrain is in Fig. 2.

Fig. 2. Example of an image from the dataset.

The dataset is formed by 400 images that contain rocks with different sizes, shapes, and textures. The images were manually labeled resulting in a total of 2467 rocks segmented. The dataset was divided randomly into 300 images for training and 100 for validation.

3.2 Proposed CNN

The architecture used to segment the rocks is a modified version of U-net. We chose the U-net because it can converge to excellent results with a small training set in few epochs. Several CNN configurations were trained to evaluate the performance; the most important factors were the best F-score achieved and the number of parameters that are strictly related to the inference time. Table 1 shows the comparison of different U-net configurations. Usually, a characteristic of the U-net is that the number of filters increases as the U-net grow deeper. However, for rock segmentations, it turns out to work better if the number of filters decreases with the depth of the U-net. We show the modified U-net configuration in Fig. 3, where the number placed on top or at bottom of every rectangle, represents the number of filters per convolution.

However, data augmentation was used to improve the results by producing a bigger training set to avoid over-fitting and obtain a better generalization. We

Table 1. Comparison of the number of parameters and performance among different U-net versions.

U-net Model	Parameters	F1-score
1	123,362,282	71.9%
2	45,987,842	73.8%
3	16,660,482	74.9%
4	**1,939,170**	**78.5%**

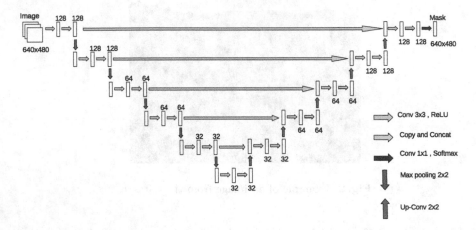

Fig. 3. U-net architecture proposed.

applied seven transformations to the images and labels from the training set, in Table 2 we list each transformation and show an example image. After the data augmentation and including the original images the training dataset contains 2400 images.

The methodology is implemented in Python using Keras and Tensorflow as back-end. We base our code in the one developed by Zamora [19]; we made some changes to the generator function and the network model. The CNN trained in a computer with an Intel i9 CPU and GTX 1080Ti graphic card. The CNN used binary cross entropy, a learning rate of 0.0001 and an Adam optimizer. At the beginning of the training process, all the U-net weights are randomly initialized in Fig. 4 is shown the loss function and the F-score for training and validation sets. The weights reported in this work are taken from the 67 epoch, because achieved the best performance for the F-score in the validation set.

Table 2. Data augmentation transformations.

Transformation	Original	Image Transform
Flip right-left		
Flip up-down		
Translate up		
Scale		
Rotate clockwise		
Rotate counterclockwise		
Shear		

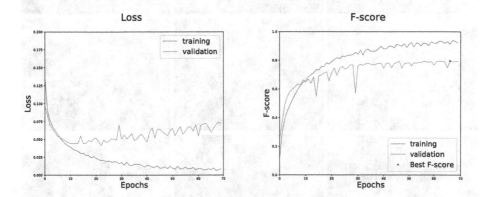

Fig. 4. F-score and loss graphics.

4   Results

The average F-score for the validation set is 78.5%, in Fig. 5 we show some results where the first image is the original image, the images with rocks segmented in green are the ground truth and the proposed CNN infers the images with rocks segmented in red.

Original   Ground truth   CNN inference

Fig. 5. Results of the trained CNN. (Color figure online)

The performance of the net is good, but there is still room for improvement. If we compare it with [18] and [5] the results are better in runtime cost and competitive in F-score, see Table 3. However, compare with [11] our methodology underperformed, but it is not a fair comparison because object segmentation is different from classification. The inference time of the CNN using the GPU is around 0.06 s which is 16 frames per second. Nevertheless, if the CNN uses only the CPU it takes 1.6 s per image, that is a huge increment of time, but it still surpasses the time reported in papers that solve rock segmentation.

Table 3. Results comparison.

Methodology	Best F-score	Runtime cost (seconds)
Gong (2012)	**81.95%**	12
Xiao (2017)	70.52%	3.4
Furlan (2019)	78.5%	**1.6**

5   Conclusions

We proposed a new solution for the problem of rock segmentation using CNN's with an improvement in the processing time and competitive F-score. Hence it could be a key element for a navigation system in an autonomous robot as a way to detect obstacles in a Mars-like environment. Further investigation will focus on growing the size of the dataset to make it more homogeneous and to improve the generalization performance. Also, we are trying to improve the performance by designing a specialize CNN architecture for rocks segmentation that optimizes the number of parameters and the F-score metric while not increasing the processing time.

Acknowledgments. We would like to express our sincere appreciation to the Instituto Politécnico Nacional and the Secretaría de Investigación y Posgrado for the economic support provided to carry out this research. This project was supported economically by SIP-IPN (numbers 20180730, 20190007, 20195835 and 20195882) and the National Council of Science and Technology of Mexico (CONACyT) (65 Frontiers of Science). F. Furlán acknowledges CONACyT for the scholarship granted towards pursuing his Ph.D. studies.

References

1. Castano, R., et al.: Onboard autonomous rover science. In: 2007 IEEE Aerospace Conference, pp. 1–13, March 2007. https://doi.org/10.1109/AERO.2007.352700
2. Castano, R., et al.: Current results from a rover science data analysis system. In: 2005 IEEE Aerospace Conference, pp. 356–365, March 2005. https://doi.org/10.1109/AERO.2005.1559328

3. Chollet, F.: Xception: Deep learning with depthwise separable convolutions. CoRR (2016)
4. Gao, Y., Spiteri, C., Pham, M.T., Al-Milli, S.: A survey on recent object detection techniques useful for monocular vision-based planetary terrain classification. Robot. Auton. Syst. **62**(2), 151–167 (2014)
5. Gong, X., Liu, J.: Rock detection via superpixel graph cuts. In: 19th IEEE International Conference on Image Processing (2012)
6. Goodfellow, I., Bengio, Y., Courville, A.: Deep Learning. MIT Press, Cambridge (2016)
7. Gor, V., Manduchi, R., Anderson, R., Mjolsness, E.: Autonomous rock detection for mars terrain. In: Space 2001 (AIAA), August 2001. https://doi.org/10.2514/6.2001-4597
8. LeCun, Y.: Generalization and network design strategies. University of Toronto, Technical report (1989)
9. NASA: K10 robots: scouts for human explorers (2010). https://www.nasa.gov/centers/ames/K10/
10. Olson, J., Craig, D., National Aeronautics and Space Administration, Langley Research Center: NASA's Analog Missions: Paving the Way for Space Exploration. National Aeronautics and Space Administration (2011). https://books.google.com.mx/books?id=-6hVnwEACAAJ
11. Rashno, A., Saraee, M., Sadri, S.: Mars image segmentation with most relevant features among wavelet and color features. In: AI & Robotics (IRANOPEN) (2015)
12. Ronneberger, O., Fischer, P., Brox, T.: U-net: convolutional networks for biomedical image segmentation. In: Navab, N., Hornegger, J., Wells, W.M., Frangi, A.F. (eds.) MICCAI 2015. LNCS, vol. 9351, pp. 234–241. Springer, Cham (2015). https://doi.org/10.1007/978-3-319-24574-4_28
13. Sasaki, Y.: The truth of the F-measure. School of Computer Science, University of Manchester, Technical report (2007)
14. Shang, C., Barnes, D.: Fuzzy-rough feature selection aided support vector machines for mars image classification. Comput. Vis. Image Underst. **117**, 202–213 (2013)
15. Furgale, P., Carle, P., Enright, J., Barfoot, T.D.: The Devon Island rover navigation dataset. Int. J. Robot. Res. **31**, 707–713 (2012)
16. Thompson, D., Castaño, R.: Performance comparison of rock detection algorithms for autonomous planetary geology. In: IEEE Aerospace Conference (2007)
17. Viola, P., Jones, M.: Rapid object detection using a boosted cascade of simple features. In: Proceedings of the 2001 IEEE Computer Society Conference on Computer Vision and Pattern Recognition, CVPR 2001, vol. 1, pp. I, December 2001. https://doi.org/10.1109/CVPR.2001.990517
18. Xiao, X., Cui, H., Yao, M., Tian, Y.: Autonomous rock detection on mars through region contrast. Adv. Space Res. **60**, 626–635 (2017)
19. Zamora, E.: Minitaller-aprendizaje-profundo (2017). https://github.com/ezamorag/Minitaller-Aprendizaje-Profundo/blob/master/codigos/path_segmentation_training.ipynb
20. Zhao, H., Shi, J., Qi, X., Wang, X., Jia, J.: Pyramid scene parsing network. In: IEEE Conference on Computer Vision and Pattern Recognition (CVPR) (2017)

Towards a Rodent Tracking and Behaviour Detection System in Real Time

José Arturo Cocoma-Ortega[1]([envelope]) and Jose Martinez-Carranza[1,2]

[1] Instituto Nacional de Astrofísica, Óptica y Electrónica, Cholula, Mexico
{cocoma,carranza}@inaoep.mx
[2] University of Bristol, Bristol, UK

Abstract. To analyze rodent behaviors in non-conditioned animal models is an important task that enables a researcher to elaborated conclusions about the effects in the behavior after drug application. Because the amount of data generated in the use of this kind of test, an automatized system that can record these behaviors becomes relevant. There are several proposals aiming at identifying and tracking the rodent in the open field maze, however, behavior identification is a highly desirable feature that is not included. Other works can identify behaviors, but due to high computational costs, special computers or devices are required. In this work, we propose an automatic system based on features computed by a stochastic filter that allows the development of rules to detect specific behaviors exhibited in the open field maze. We demonstrate that it is possible to track a rodent and identify behaviors in real-time (30 fps) and also in high speed (>100Hz) without the need of powerful devices or special conditions for the environment.

Keywords: Rodent tracking · Behavior detection ·
Extended Kalman Filter

1 Introduction

Neuro-pharmacology is an important field that studies the effect of some drugs in the neural system. To prove this kind of effects, animals are used before a drug can be given to a human. The most common animals for the test are rodents specifically rats, that is because we know entirely its biology, also they are easy to breed and feed. There are mainly two ways to verify the effects in the neural system of the animal test: an invasive one in which is necessary to check the brain chemistry by a surgical that involves sacrificing the animal; the other one is a non-invasive method that uses behavioral animal models to observe the behaviors of the animal and compare before and after a drug application.

One of the most important tests is the Open Field Maze [16] (OFM, OFT). This test consists of a square box, it has a base and four walls. The typical sizes are between 50 cm to 100 cm. Inside the box, in the base, are painted a grid to identify zones in where the rodent stays. This test can be around 15 min long

© Springer Nature Switzerland AG 2019
J. A. Carrasco-Ochoa et al. (Eds.): MCPR 2019, LNCS 11524, pp. 159–169, 2019.
https://doi.org/10.1007/978-3-030-21077-9_15

or a few hours. Usually the researchers in the field put the animal in the maze and record a video of all the test, next they watch the video to identify one or more behaviors, this process is repeated many times as necessary, so this causes that a systematic error is present in the results, also the measures can become variable depending of the personal interpretation.

Given this problem, one solution is the aid of an automatic system that can detect and account for the behaviors present during the open field test. There is some commercial system that is too expensive and leaves out the possibility of being acquired by those who need it. It is from here that many approaches have been proposed to give a solution to this need, The next section gives a review of the works proposed in the last years to approach an automatic system for behaviors and tracking.

2   Related Work

The task to analyze the rodent's behavior when is placed in a test like the open field maze has been tried to solve in different ways since the early 80s when computer capabilities were still weak, a combination of algorithms and electronics were the first attempts reported [6, 7].

More recent approximations that can successfully track the rodent in the test [5, 8, 19, 21, 23] have not behavior detection available and that limits the potential results of the open field maze.

There are special cases where controlled conditions of light are necessary to remark a high contrast between the animal and the scenario to performs the identification of the rodent [1, 13], but these conditions are not always possible to set by the researchers in the neuroscience.

We found some cases where invasive techniques are used to track the rodent. In the works presented in [2, 4, 11, 14] a surgical implant to the animal is done to identify the rodent and track it, but this is not ideal because the animal is exposed to an unusual conditioning and could affect its behavior, in the other hand, invasive techniques changes the animal's welfare.

In addition to the identification of the rodent, is important to detect some specific behaviors that are commonly presented during the test. For this reason, some works try to identify behaviors in the rodent using special devices (infrared camera, touch-panel, sensors) or more powerful computers (faster CPU, GPU) [8, 9, 12, 15, 22].

Other approximations are the uses of depth cameras to identify the rodent position and also gets its orientation, besides they can analyze more than one rodent, are not capable to identify behaviors like spinning or freezing and only detects rearing [10, 18, 20].

The research developed in [8, 15] can identify many behaviors of the rodent in the open field maze in a successful way, but a high-cost computer is used to performs this results and these devices are not accessible for many researchers in the field.

In not all cases the results are processed in real-time, in the others 30 fps system are developed but an especial dimension is set mainly 320 × 240 pixel frame is used [1,9,17,19,23]. The better approximations that perform real-time and behavior identification are limited to open field maze are [3,20], and have not probed in other mazes that can result of interest for researchers.

As we view a system that can perform the identification and tracking of the rodent in real-time and also can identify behaviors is needed with the use of no high-cost computer. In this work, we propose a system in real-time that can track the rodent efficiently and also detect some specific behavior presents in the execution of the open field test.

3   Methods

To achieve the goal to develop a system that can perform the behaviors detection and rodent tracking, we propose the methodology described in the next sections.

3.1   System Calibration

The position of the camera and the characteristics of the box test (color, illumination, position, etc.) are the initial problems to solve. The system will not require a specific color in the arena and neither a specific position of the camera, instead a calibration process is implemented. When the test is ready, before put the rat inside the box, it is necessary to mark manually the corners of the box by click on them in the image showing by the system. This calibration removes the need to adjust the position of the camera to match a specific area. Thus, a time of 5 s of the camera recording the scenario allows the system to learn the characteristics of the arena without the need of use a particular box with some special color or illumination.

3.2   Rodent Segmentation and Tracking

Before we can do the rodent's tracking, an observable parameter is needed in order to use the EKF, the parameter used is the centroid of the rat (*ratCentroid*). Based on the *bgMean*, each pixel of the current frame is analyzed by calculating its standard deviation and verifying if it is under the Gauss bell in about four standards deviations, classifying by background and non-background each pixel.

By the use of Eq. 1, we calculated the centroid of the rat from the segmentation.

$$ratCentroid = (\sum \frac{x}{totalPixels}, \sum \frac{y}{totalPixels}) \tag{1}$$

3.3   Features Extraction

As mentioned in the previous section, the EKF is used to extract dynamic information from the rodent. We propose the dynamical model described in Eq. 2, from this model we obtain position (x, y), velocity (r), orientation (θ), acceleration $(\dot{r})$ and angular velocity $(\dot{\theta})$.

$$X = (x, y, r, \theta, \dot{r}, \dot{\theta}) \tag{2}$$

$$x = \Delta t \cdot \dot{r} \cdot cos(\dot{\theta} \cdot \Delta t) + \Delta W \tag{3}$$

$$y = \Delta t \cdot \dot{r} \cdot sin(\dot{\theta} \cdot \Delta t) + \Delta W \tag{4}$$

$$r = \Delta t \cdot r + \Delta W \tag{5}$$

$$\theta = \Delta t \cdot \theta + \Delta W \tag{6}$$

$$\dot{r} = \Delta W \tag{7}$$

$$\dot{\theta} = \Delta W \tag{8}$$

For the predicted step (Eq. 9) we use the model from above and we use the rodent centroid calculated from segmentation as the observable parameter in 10

$$X_k = f(X_{k-1}, U_k, W_k) \tag{9}$$

$$Z_k = h(X_k, V_k) \tag{10}$$

We need additional information about the rat-like shape, i.e., every time the rat is moving and present some behaviors its body shape changes. For example, when the rat is rearing its body stretches, or when it is grooming usually its body shrinking forming a circle form. For this reason, we calculate its body shape deformations by Principal Component Analysis (PCA). This let us reduce data and only have two lines that represent the height and width of the rat. With this we can know when the rat's body looks like an ellipse or a circle, bringing us information about the things the rat is probably doing. Joining all these characteristics information we develop rules that can identify what are the rat's behaviors. The Fig. 1 shows the features extracted from the rat.

Fig. 1. Features obtained from the rat.

3.4   Behaviors Detection

At this point we have identified the rodent and we know its position, velocity, direction (angle) and shape. Till now we can track the rodent motion, the next is know what the rodent is doing in every frame. The behaviors required for this test are wall rear, path distance, walking and freezing.

For wall rearing detect, we generated rules to classify if the rodent is rearing or not, taking the shape and orientation of the rodent. We observed in the test that when the rat is wall rearing two important characteristics are present, the body of the rat is over a defined limit that we can estimate, and when this occurs, its body stretches and the ellipse that is formed has the principal diagonal greater than the secondary one, with this analysis we estimate when a rearing is happening.

By the use of the features extracted we can detect the *freezing*, this means the absence of movement of the rodent. Using the velocity, we can estimate when the rodent is quiet and can label this behavior as freezing.

We estimate the distance traveled by rodent using *velocity* parameter, the velocity is given as the total pixels moved from the previous frame, this means we don't calculate the velocity in terms of meters over seconds, instead is calculate how many pixels the rodent is moving in every time recorded. So, with this measure, and applying a rule based on the known size of the box we estimate the distance that the rodent has covered during the test.

4   Results

We present the analysis and the proposed solution in the section above. For the implementation, we use c++ with OpenCV library for video and image operations (opening, math operations), all programmed under Linux Ubuntu distribution with no special characteristics in the computer. We count with a data set to test the proposed solution, each video was tested with the system, then the result of every algorithm implemented is shown in order to verify the correct function of the system.

Supplementary video: https://youtu.be/6Smkff19r14.

4.1   Segmentation

For our propose, the first step is the system calibration, next the extraction of the rodent from the frames is required, by applying the algorithm explained in Sect. 3.2, we can separate the rodent from the rest of the background and we use the segmentation to calculate the centroid of the rodent, as we can see even the tail is not complete segmented (see Fig. 2a) the centroid is positioned correctly compared when the system preserves the complete tail in the segmentation (see Fig. 2b).

4.2   Tracking

As we explained early, the observable parameter for the EKF is the centroid obtained from segmentation. To estimate the accuracy of the centroid calculated, we compare the data resulting from the system with hand-labeled data for the centroid (see Fig. 3). We calculated the RMSE for the coordinates x and y. For

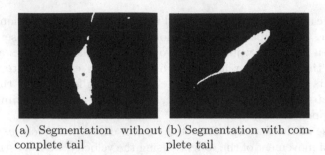

(a) Segmentation without complete tail

(b) Segmentation with complete tail

Fig. 2. Segmentation of the rodent

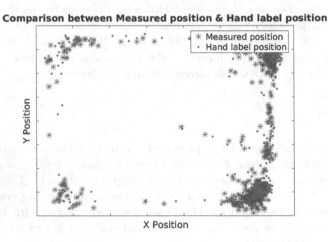

Fig. 3. Comparison plot of centroid calculated from segmentation and hand label centroid.

x we obtain RMSE of 2.4, and 6.82 for y. With this, we make sure that the centroid calculated is good for EKF measurement, also we have to considerate that the hand-labeled data is not always in the exact center of the rodent.

In the Fig. 4, we observe the tracking of the rat estimated by EKF (red circles), We show the comparison between the original frame and the segmentation, thus we plot the tracking generate, all this for one representative video.

4.3   Behaviors Identification

The rules generated in the previous sections were applied to the data set. An example of the visual result for the rearing detection is showing in the Fig. 5. The Fig. 5a shows the original frame from video. In the Fig. 5b we paint a blue oval around the rat every time it performs a wall rearing in the box. Additional of this, we count every wall rearing and at the end of the process. Another result we can observe in the Fig. 5c is the information given by PCA, this information is painted in green and blue lines in the rodent segmentation representing the

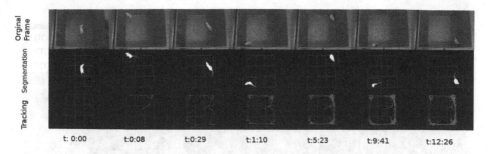

t: 0:00   t:0:08   t:0:29   t:1:10   t:5:23   t:9:41   t:12:26

Fig. 4. Image sequence for a video. First row shows the original frame from video. Second row shows the segmentation for that frame. Last row shows the rat's tracked trajectory. (Color figure online)

tendency of the shape of the rodent. The last result showed is the bounding box marked with a blue square. We do not process all the image, we only work in the area restricted by the bounding box, thus we speed up the process.

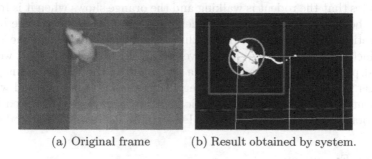

(a) Original frame   (b) Result obtained by system.

Fig. 5. Wall rearing. (Color figure online)

We can observe in the video that the camera position is not completely over the box, the camera has an inclination that causes a box distortion like a trapezoid shape, additionally, the box has not perfect square shape and this increases the distortion effect. Because of this, there are some positions of the rodent that confuse the algorithm and counts it as wall rearing.

4.4 Ethogram Generation

In the previous section, we show examples from the system operation in a specific frame. Given the amount of data generated for the entire video, the system generates a report for every frame of the video specifying what is the rodent activity in that frame. This report is called ethogram and is drawn as a colored graphic representing each behavior with one color. The Fig. 6 shows the Ethogram for video 2. We can observe from the ethogram that the behavior of the rodent is not constant.

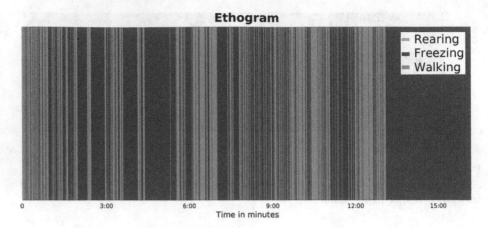

Fig. 6. Ethogram resulting from video 2. (Color figure online)

The blue color represents when the rodent performs a wall rearing, the yellow one indicates that the rodent is walking and the orange shows when it is freezing.

At the beginning of the test, the rodent is not familiarized with the box and an exploration behavior is presented, this means the rodent have the need to sniffing (including wall rearing) and travel for all the box, that is what we found in the first part of the ethogram. After a few minutes, the wall raring is present for a longer time combining with walking. After the rat is familiarized with the environment its activity reduces drastically, this behavior is observed by the freezing (orange color) because the need to explore decreases in the rodent.

4.5   Time Execution

To evaluate the velocity to obtain results by our proposal, we measure the time required for each module. For this test, we divide the complete process into three steps: segmentation, prediction of position (tracking) and behavior detect. The Table 1 shows the mean times for the main blocks for each video. From the table,

Table 1. Time execution per frame in video. The columns segmentation, tracking and behaviors show the mean time needed to process the task. Complete process column is the mean of the time necessary to complete one frame from the video.

Name	Duration	Segmentation	Tracking	Behaviors	Complete process
Video 1	15.36 min	8.7906 ms	0.078536 ms	0.0074666 ms	8.8766 ms
Video 2	15.36 min	9.0582 ms	0.077902 ms	0.0059656 ms	9.1421 ms
Video 3	15.36 min	10.908 ms	0.077804 ms	0.011042 ms	10.9969 ms
Video 4	15.36 min	8.0083 ms	0.095194 ms	0.0127 ms	8.1162 ms
Video 5	15.36 min	9.8927 ms	0.078414 ms	0.00613 ms	9.9772 ms
Video 6	15.36 min	10.9231 ms	0.078756 ms	0.0087033 ms	11.0106 ms

we notice that the process that takes the longest time is rodent segmentation and is the time predominant in the complete process. Computing the average time needed to complete each frame from the video we show that our proposal can run in real time, even more, the max speed is over 100 Hz. This time is better than most reported in the related work.

5   Conclusion and Future Work

In this paper, we have presented a system for rodents tracking and behaviors detection. In our proposal we didn't change the initial conditions in the test, we worked directly on the videos without any prior information of manual adjustments. Even when the camera position was not the best, we correctly segmented and identified the rodent. In addition, our system was able to detect behaviors of particular interest in the test from which an ethogram was also generated, a graph that can be used by the experts to analyze the rodent's behaviors along time and after having a applied a drug to the rodent.

Therefore, we demonstrated that it is possible to do tracking and behavior identification successfully without any special conditions an also our proposal runs in high speed over 100 Hz without requiring special hardware such as a GPU.

For future work, we propose the use of other classification techniques to detect more behaviors and compare with current results in order to improve the behaviors detection. Also, we will expand the work to other mazes like water maze or elevated plus maze and detect the corresponding behaviors presented in each test.

Acknowledgments. We thank Ilhuicamina Daniel Limón Pérez de León, Ph.D., head research of Neuroscience laboratory from Benemérita Universidad Autónoma de Puebla for provided to us the data set for the evaluation and for the guidance about the behaviors that are interesting to detect in the open field maze.

References

1. da Silva Aragão, R., Rodrigues, M.A.B., de Barros, K.M.F.T., Silva, S.R.F., Toscano, A.E., de Souza, R.E., Manhães-de-Castro, R.: Automatic system for analysis of locomotor activity in rodents–A reproducibility study. J. Neurosci. Methods **195**(2), 216–221 (2011)
2. Howerton, C.L., Garner, J.P., Mench, J.A.: A system utilizing radio frequency identification (RFID) technology to monitor individual rodent behavior in complex social settings. J. Neurosci. Methods **209**(1), 74–78 (2012)
3. van Dam, E.A., van der Harst, J.E., ter Braak, C.J., Tegelenbosch, R.A., Spruijt, B.M., Noldus, L.P.: An automated system for the recognition of various specific rat behaviours. J. Neurosci. Methods **218**(2), 214–224 (2013)
4. Sourioux, M., et al.: 3-D motion capture for long-term tracking of spontaneous locomotor behaviors and circadian sleep/wake rhythms in mouse. J. Neurosci. Methods **295**, 51–57 (2018)

5. Chanchanachitkul, W., Nanthiyanuragsa, P., Rodamporn, S., Thongsaard, W., Charoenpong, T.: A rat walking behavior classification by body length measurement. In: The 6th 2013 Biomedical Engineering International Conference, pp. 1–5 (2013)
6. Clarke, R.L., Smith, R.F., Justesen, D.R.: An infrared device for detecting locomotor activity. Behav. Res. Methods Instrum. Comput. 17(5), 519–525 (1985)
7. Gapenne, O., Simon, P., Lannou, J.: A simple method for recording the path of a rat in an open field. Behav. Res. Methods Instrum. Comput. 22(5), 443–448 (1990)
8. Geuther, B.Q., et al.: Robust mouse tracking in complex environments using neural networks. Commun. Biol. 2(1), 124 (2018)
9. Giancardo, L., Sona, D., Scheggia, D., Papaleo, F., Murino, V.: Segmentation and tracking of multiple interacting mice by temperature and shape information. In: Proceedings of the 21st International Conference on Pattern Recognition, ICPR 2012, pp. 2520–2523 (2012)
10. Hong, W., et al.: Automated measurement of mouse social behaviors using depth sensing, video tracking, and machine learning. Proc. Nat. Acad. Sci. 112(38), E5351–E5360 (2015)
11. Jia, Y., Wang, Z., et al.: A wirelessly-powered homecage with animal behavior analysis and closed-loop power control. In: 2016 38th Annual International Conference of the IEEE Engineering in Medicine and Biology Society (EMBC), pp. 6323–6326 (2016)
12. Lai, P.L., Basso, D.M., Fisher, L.C., Sheets, A.L.: 3d tracking of mouse locomotion using shape-from-silhouette techniques (2011)
13. Linares-Sánchez, L.J., Fernández-Alemán, J.L., García-Mateos, G., Pérez-Ruzafa, Á., Sánchez-Vázquez, F.J.: Follow-me: a new start-and-stop method for visual animal tracking in biology research. In: 2015 37th Annual International Conference of the IEEE Engineering in Medicine and Biology Society (EMBC), pp. 755–758 (2015)
14. Macrì, S., Mainetti, L., Patrono, L., Pieretti, S., Secco, A., Sergi, I.: A tracking system for laboratory mice to support medical researchers in behavioral analysis. In: 2015 37th Annual International Conference of the IEEE Engineering in Medicine and Biology Society (EMBC), pp. 4946–4949 (2015)
15. Sebov, K.: Deep rearing. Stanford University, Technical report (2017)
16. Seibenhener, M., Wooten, M.C.: Use of the open field maze to measure locomotor and anxiety-like behavior in mice. J. Vis. Exp. (JoVE) 96, e52434 (2015)
17. Shi, Q., Miyagishima, S., Fumino, S., Konno, S., Ishii, H., Takanishi, A.: Development of a cognition system for analyzing rat's behaviors. In: 2010 IEEE International Conference on Robotics and Biomimetics, pp. 1399–1404 (2010)
18. da Silva Monteiro, J.P.: Automatic Behavior Recognition in Laboratory Animals using Kinect. Master's thesis, Faculdade de Engenharia da Universidade do Porto (2012)
19. Tungtur, S.K., Nishimune, N., Radel, J., Nishimune, H.: Mouse behavior tracker: an economical method for tracking behavior in home cages. BioTechniques 63(5), 215–220 (2017)
20. Wang, Z., Mirbozorgi, S.A., Ghovanloo, M.: Towards a kinect-based behavior recognition and analysis system for small animals. In: 2015 IEEE Biomedical Circuits and Systems Conference (BioCAS), pp. 1–4 (2015)
21. Wilson, J.C., Kesler, M., Pelegrin, S.L.E., Kalvi, L., Gruber, A., Steenland, H.W.: Watching from a distance: A robotically controlled laser and real-time subject tracking software for the study of conditioned predator/prey-like interactions. J. Neurosci. Methods 253, 78–89 (2015)

22. Xie, X.S., et al.: Rodent Behavioral Assessment in the Home Cage using the Smartcage™ System, pp. 205–222. Humana Press, Totowa, NJ (2012)
23. Ziegelaar, M.: Development of an inexpensive, user modifiable automated video tracking system for rodent behavioural tests. Master's thesis, School of Mechanical and Mining Engineering (2015)

Facial Re-identification
on Non-overlapping Cameras
and in Uncontrolled Environments

Everardo Santiago Ramírez[1]([⊠]) [iD], J. C. Acosta-Guadarrama[1] [iD],
Jose Manuel Mejía Muñoz[1] [iD], Josue Dominguez Guerrero[1] [iD],
and J. A. Gonzalez-Fraga[2] [iD]

[1] Instituto de Ingeniería y Tecnología, Universidad Autónoma de Ciudad Juárez,
Ciudad Juárez, Mexico
{everardo.santiago,juan.acosta,jose.mejia,josue.dominguez}@uacj.mx
[2] Facultad de Ciencias, Universidad Autónoma de Baja California,
Ensenada, Mexico
angel_fraga@uabc.edu.mx

Abstract. Face re-identification is an essential task in automatic video
surveillance where the identity of the person is known previously. It
aims to verify if other cameras have observed a specific face detected
by a camera. However, this is a challenging task because of the reduced
resolution, and changes in lighting and background available in surveillance video sequences. Furthermore, the face to get re-identified suffers
changes in appearance due to expression, pose, and scale. Algorithms
need robust descriptors to perform re-identification under these challenging conditions. Among various types of approaches available, correlation
filters have properties that can be exploited to achieve a successful re-
identification. Our proposal makes use of this approach to exploit both
the shape and content of more representative facial images captured by
a camera in a field of view. The resulting correlation filters can characterize the face of a person in a field of view; they are good at discriminating faces of different people, tolerant to variable illumination and
slight variations in the rotation (in/out of plane) and scale. Further, they
allow identifying a person from the first time that has appeared in the
camera network. Matching the correlation filters generated in the field
of views allows establishing a correspondence between the faces of the
same person viewed by different cameras. These results show that facial
re-identification under real-world surveillance conditions and biometric
context can be successfully performed using correlation filters adequately
designed.

Keywords: Face re-identification and recognition · Biometrics ·
Correlation filters

© Springer Nature Switzerland AG 2019
J. A. Carrasco-Ochoa et al. (Eds.): MCPR 2019, LNCS 11524, pp. 170–182, 2019.
https://doi.org/10.1007/978-3-030-21077-9_16

1   Introduction

The goal of person re-identification is to determine if disjoint field-of-views have observed a specific person already detected in another field-of-view (FoV) [9,28]. It can get performed after the events by processing stored videos and (or) images. That is useful, for example, to know where a person has been in previous time. On the other hand, the re-identification can be performed in real time, i.e., while the person crosses a camera network that belongs to a video surveillance system.

Person re-identification (Re-Id) is a primordial task for many critical applications, such as public safety, multi-camera tracking, and legal forensic search [9,28]. However, it is an inherently challenging task because of the visual appearance of a person may change dramatically in camera views from different locations due to unknown changes in human pose, viewpoint, illumination, occlusion, cloth, and background clutter [10,28].

Re-identification task requires person detection, tracking, synthesis, and matching task on digital images. In this sense, computer vision is a feasible technology as it can provide the image of a person in a discrete, remote, and non-intrusive way. The synthesis and matching are the most crucial task for a successful re-identification. Different views of the person in an FoV must be synthesized to generate the descriptor while matching task must compare the descriptors to determinate correspondences.

Descriptors can be generated using cues such as face [19,23]; the full image of the person's body [13,20]; walking pattern (gait) [11]; height and build [5]; and head, torso, and limbs of a person [25]. Although the visual appearance of the whole body is the most exploited in the person re-identification, the face of the person allows a discreet, remote, and non-intrusive re-identification. Furthermore, the face allows a stable re-identification by a long time slot. For this reason, in this work, we propose to perform the re-identification by using correlation filters that synthesize face images detected in the FoVs.

The rest of the paper is organized as follows. Section 2 describes some related works; Sect. 3 presents the basics of correlation filters; Sect. 4 describes the proposed algorithm; Sect. 5 presents the results of experimental evaluation; and finally, the main conclusions of this work.

2   Related Work

Existing approaches for re-identification mainly focus on developing robust descriptors to capture the invariant appearance of a person's face in different camera views. For this purpose, it can be exploited from the face either the full image or a set of features extracted from it.

A significant challenge in re-identification is class imbalance. In some FoVs, the number of faces captured from a person-of-interest gets outnumbered by the face images of other people. Two-class classification systems designed using imbalanced data tend to recognize better the class with the most significant number of samples. A learning algorithm named Progressive Boosting (PBoost) can address this problem, which progressively inserts uncorrelated samples into a Boosting procedure to avoid losing information while generating a diverse pool of classifiers [17].

The face images captured in an FoV could appear in arbitrary poses, resolutions in different lighting conditions, noise and blurriness. That problem got addressed with a Dynamic Bayesian Network (DBN) that incorporates the information from different cameras, proposed in [1]. In [3], given a set of face images captured under realistic surveillance scenarios, they train a Support Vector Machine (SVM) as the descriptor of the person. In [19], the authors proposed to overcome the variability of facial images by embedding a distance metric learning into set-based image matching. The distance metric learning scheme learns a feature-space by mapping to a discriminative subspace. Person identification in video data is naturally performed on tracks, not on individual frames, to average out noise and errors under the assumption that all frames belong to the same person [4]. In [7] they propose a framework based on Convolutional Neural Network (CNN). First, a set of attributes is learned by a CNN to model attribute patterns related to different body parts, and whose output gets fused with low-level robust Local Maximal Occurrence (LOMO) features to address the problem of the large variety of visual appearance.

The person re-identification systems are computationally expensive. In order to obtain results in real-time, powerful computing equipment is a must in the implementation of existing approaches. That allows systems to re-identify a person from hundreds, even thousands, of potential candidates in a matter of seconds.

As can be seen in the related work, the approaches for re-identification focus their effort on characterizing the facial variations into a descriptor. However, no effective re-identification exists in uncontrollable environments. That raises the need to develop new strategies in order to obtain a robust re-identification.

3   Correlation Filters

Correlation pattern recognition is based on selecting or defining a reference signal $h(x, y)$, called a correlation filter, and then on determining the degree of similarity between the reference and test signals [18]. Correlation filters can be designed in either the spatial domain or frequency domain by Fourier Transform (FT). The correlation process using the FT is given by:

$$g(x, y) = \mathcal{F}^{-1}\{F(k, l) \cdot H^*(k, l)\}, \tag{1}$$

where $g(x, y)$ is the correlation output; $\mathcal{F}^{-1}$ is the inverse of FT; $F(k, l)$ and $H(k, l)$ are the FT of the test signal $f(x, y)$ and reference signal $h(x, y)$, respectively; "$\cdot$" is an element-wise multiplication; and "$*$" represents the complex conjugate operation. The correlation output $g(x, y)$ should exhibit a brightness, named correlation peak, when $f(x, y)$ is similar to $h(x, y)$. This process is depicted by Fig. 1a.

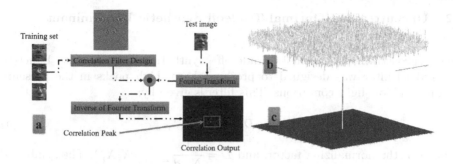

Fig. 1. Scheme of the correlation process the Fourier domain.

The sharpness of the correlation peak indicates a similarity degree between the test and reference signals. A correlation output for signals of the same class could contain a sharp high peak, as in Fig. 1c; while in another case, the correlation output only contains noise and no prominent peak, as in Fig. 1b. The peak-to-sidelobe ratio (*psr*) can measure the sharpness of the peak:

$$psr = \frac{(peak - \mu_{area})}{\sigma_{area}}, \tag{2}$$

where μ_{area} and σ_{area}, respectively, are the mean and standard deviation of some area or neighborhood around, but not including, the correlation peak. Consider *th* as a recognition threshold; thus $psr \geq th$ means that $f(x, y)$ and $h(x, y)$ belong to the same class.

3.1   Synthetic Discriminant Function

A Synthetic Discriminant Function (SDF) filter is a linear combination of MFs [6]. They design this filter by using a training set, T, composed of images with general distortions expected for the object of interest, and it is, therefore, robust at recognizing an object that presents distortions similar to those found in T.

Let $T = \{f_1(x, y), f_2(x, y), \ldots, f_N(x, y)\}$ be the training set, and $\boldsymbol{x}_j$ the column-vector form of $f_j(x, y)$. The vector $\boldsymbol{x}_j$ is constructed by lexicographic scanning, in which each image is scanned from left to right and from top to bottom. Each vector is a column of the training data matrix, $X = [\boldsymbol{x}_1, \boldsymbol{x}_2, \ldots, \boldsymbol{x}_N]$. The SDF correlation filter is given by:

$$\boldsymbol{h} = X(X^+X)^{-1}\boldsymbol{u}, \tag{3}$$

where X^+ is the complex conjugate transpose, and $\boldsymbol{u} = [\boldsymbol{u}_1, \boldsymbol{u}_2, \ldots, \boldsymbol{u}_N]^+$ is a vector of size N that contains the expected values at the origin of the correlation output for each training image. Typical values for $\boldsymbol{u}$ are 1 for *true* class, and 0 for *false* class.

3.2   Unconstrained Optimal Tradeoff Synthetic Discriminant Function

The Unconstrained Optimal Trade-off Synthetic Discriminant Function (UOTSDF) filter was designed to produce sharp, high peaks in the presence of noise and low-light conditions. This filter is given by:

$$h = (\alpha D + \sqrt{-1}\alpha)^{-1}, \tag{4}$$

where α is the normalizing factor, and $D = \dfrac{1}{N \cdot d} \sum_{i=1}^{N} (X_i X_i^*)$. The symbols d and X are the amount of pixels in $f_i(x, y)$ and FT of $f_i(x, y)$.

3.3   Maximum Average Correlation Height

Maximum Average Correlation Height (MACH) filter is designed to be tolerant to noise and distortion while addressing the issue of sensor noise and background clutter. MACH filter is given by:

$$\boldsymbol{h} = \alpha(S + C)^{-1}\boldsymbol{m}, \tag{5}$$

where α is a normalizing coefficient,

$$S = \frac{1}{N \cdot d} \sum_{i=1}^{N} (X_i - \overline{X})(X_i - \overline{X})^*, \tag{6}$$

where X_i is FT of the i-th training image, C is the covariance matrix of the input noise, and $\boldsymbol{m}$ is a vector containing the average of the training images.

In recent years, correlation filters have achieved impressive results in discrimination, efficiency, location accuracy, and robustness [22].

Furthermore, correlation filters could be designed for reliable recognition of partially occluded objects as is described in [14] and [15]. The SDF, UOTSDF, and MACH correlation filters described in this section were used to test the proposed algorithm for re-identifying persons by their facial images captured in disjoints FoVs.

4   Correlation Filters Based Algorithm for Facial Re-identification

This section describes the proposed algorithm for re-identifying a person by their face images by using correlation filters. Since it is all about a video-based person, re-identification must perform in a discreet remote non-intrusive way; the face recognition process makes that possible and allows the proposed algorithm to work in a biometric context.

4.1 Framework for Facial Re-identification

Here is described the proposed framework for facial re-identification in an unconstrained environment. Let $G(V, E)$ be a graph that represents a camera network, where V is the set of FoVs, and E is the set of edges between them. To re-identify a person by their face image on this camera network, necessarily different tasks must work in collaboration: the face detection, identification, tracking, synthesis, and matching.

Figure 2 shows the correlation-filters-based algorithm for re-identifying a person by their face images. A facial descriptor gets synthesized from a set of face images captured in the FoVs, where the person gets last seen. Then, the facial descriptors will correlate (match) for determining correspondence. As one can see in Fig. 2, the person gets identified by using the set of face images, recorded in the FoV, where seen for the first time.

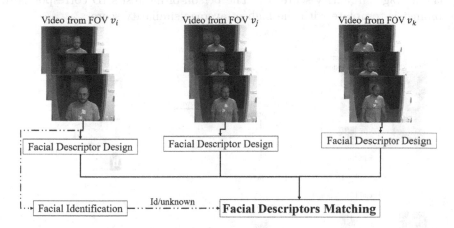

Fig. 2. Basic scheme of proposed algorithm for re-identifying persons by their face images.

The facial identification, synthesis, and matching modules details are in the next subsections.

4.2 Facial Identification

In the traditional face recognition task, only a few samples per subject are necessary to identify face images [2,8]. However, face images in uncontrollable environments are usually accompanied with appearance changes in lighting, pose, expression, resolution, and occlusion. As a result, the person gets identified by using only the most representative face images, i.e., using only the images that contribute to their recognition.

The proposed identification process is depicted in Fig. 3a. Before the identification, we must build a gallery of biometric templates G_{bt}.

Given a sequence S recorded in the i-th FoV, and where appears the person-of-interest, p; each frame is searched for face images to generate the set $F_{p,i}$. This set could contain face images with different distortions, and not all are suitable for using them to generate the biometric template. That raises the need for selecting only the most representative face images from $F_{p,i}$. That is why we used the approach proposed in [16]. The selected set must contain face images that best describe the set $F_{p,i}$. Images with variable illumination and noise may not be considered in the training set since image processing algorithms can remove them successfully.

A UOTSDF filter is synthesized with the set selected from $F_{p,i}$ and used as the biometric template $H(k,l)$ for p. For each known person, a biometric template must get synthesized and stored in G_{bt}. Once the gallery G_{bt} is ready, the identification works as follows. Face images $F_{q,j}$ of person q, detected in the j-th FoV, are correlated with the biometric template $H_i(k,l) \in G_{bt}$ for calculating the average similarity score $\overline{psr}$. The person-of-interest's ID corresponds to the biometric template with the highest average similarity score.

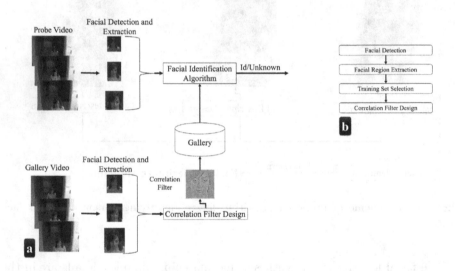

Fig. 3. Facial identification scheme for the proposed re-identification algorithm.

The gallery of biometric templates is generated once and updated eventually to adapt to changes of the face, while the identification performs each time that a person gets detected for the first time. The filters of the identification module are different from those used in the re-identification that we describe below.

4.3   Facial Synthesis

A robust facial descriptor must allow a re-identification either inter/intra FoVs and short/long intervals of time. The algorithm for synthesizing correlation filter as a facial descriptor in the i-th FoV is in Fig. 3b. First, the most frontal faces in each video frame get detected. Second, the region of the detected faces must get extracted from the video frames. Let $F_{p,i} = \{f_1(x,y), \ldots, f_N(x,y)\}$ be a set of those face images. Third, face images in $F_{p,v}$ contain variations concerning illumination conditions, pose, sharpness, as well as size because the person moves away or approaches to the camera. Using all these images may lower the performance of re-identification algorithms, and it is computationally expensive. Therefore, it is more appropriate to choose a subset $T_{p,i} \subset F_{p,i}$ that best describes the faces in i. Fourth, $T_{p,i} \subset F_{p,i}$ is used to train a UOTSDF filter $H_{p,i}(k,l)$, which in turn works as a descriptor of the person. Any correlation filter described in Sect. 3 or another reported in the literature could be suitable for this purpose. This module generates a filter in each FoV, where a person gets viewed and use them in the matching module.

4.4 Descriptors Matching

Descriptors matching could be performed in two ways: (a) once a person has left the camera network, and (b) while a person walks through the network of cameras. In this work, the descriptors matching task runs while the person walks through the camera network for real-time face Re-Id, as depicted by Algorithm 1.

Given the sequence S of the current FoV, a facial descriptor $H_{i-1}(k,l)$ generated in a previous FoV, a recognition threshold th, and a binary vector of matching results; the algorithm works as follows. First, build a facial descriptor $H_i(k,l)$ for faces in S, as described in Sect. 4.3. Later, calculate the psr of the correlation between $H_i(k,l)$ and $H_{i-1}(k,l)$, according to (2). Then, put 1 to vector c if $psr_{i,j} \geq th$, which means that there is a correspondence. Otherwise, put 0 to c. Finally, return $H_i(k,l)$ and c.

Algorithm 1. Facial descriptors matching.

   Data: $video_i, H_{i-1}(k,l), th, c$
   Result: $H_i(k,l), c$
1   $H_i(k,l) = BuildFacialDescriptor(video_i)$
2   $psr_{i,j} = AverageSimilarity(H_i(k,l), H_i(k,l))$
3   **if** $psr_{i,j} \geq th$ **then**
4 | $c = [c, 1]$
5   **else**
6 | $c = [c, 0]$
7   **end**
8   **return** $H_i(k,l), c$

Once the person leaves the camera network, the binary vector c contains all the matches. If all values in c are 1, then it means that the compared facial descriptor belongs to the same person identified in the first FoV. We performed experiments under real-world surveillance conditions to verify the proposed algorithm.

5 Experimental Evaluation

This section presents the performance of the proposed correlation-filter-based algorithm for re-identifying a person by their face images regarding Detection and Identification Rate (DIR), Verification Rate (VR), Mean Reciprocal Rank (MRR), and the correctness of the descriptors matching. In a first experiment, we tested the facial identification module in DIR, VR and MRR metrics by using UOTSDF filter. In a second experiment, the facial descriptors matching module got tested by using UOTSDF, SDF, and MACH correlation filters. In this section, we compare the performances for correlation filters and LBP images [27] at face re-identification. We used the *psr* measure as the similarity score in correlation filters, while for LBP images we used the Structural Similarity (SSIM) in [24]. Both in identification and correspondence modules, the subsets were selected by using the approach proposed in [16].

5.1 Data Set Configuration

The experimental evaluation of the proposed algorithm got conducted on the publicly available ChokePoint[1] video dataset. This dataset consists of 25 subjects (19 males and six females) in Portal 1 and 29 subjects (23 males and six females) in Portal 2 such as described in [26]. The recording of Portal 1 and Portal 2 are one month apart. The dataset has a frame rate of 30 fps, and the image resolution is 800×600 pixels.

Three case studies (see Table 1) were used to evaluate the performance of the proposed algorithm under different environments and time interval between recording. These case studies contain the most frontal faces, and they are from the ChokePoint website. Case Study 1 was recorded in a short time interval and indoor scene, while Case Study 2 got recorded both indoor and outdoor scenes and with short time interval as well. Similarly, Case Study 3 got recorded in both indoor and outdoor scenes although with a long time interval.

Face images in ChokePoint video dataset have variations regarding illumination conditions, pose, sharpness, as well as scale since the person can approach or move away from the camera. For evaluation purpose, we re-sized the face images to 32 by 32 pixels, and we averaged ten executions to achieve the results.

5.2 Numerical Results

Suppose that an operator visually recognizes the person on the video and thus it is only necessary to verify the person's identity. Now suppose that the operator can not visually identify the person, so the algorithm has to search the gallery for the identity of such person. The performance in the first case gets measured by VR metric, while in the second case by the DIR metric.

Table 2 shows the performance of the facial recognition module. Regarding DIR and MRR metrics, the correlation filters obtained the best performance of

---

[1] http://arma.sourceforge.net/chokepoint/.

Table 1. Case studies used in the experimental evaluation.

Case study 1	Case study 2	Case study 3
P1E_S1_C1	P2E_S2_C2	P1E_S1_C1 P1E_S3_C3
P1L_S1_C1	P2L_S2_C2	P1E_S2_C2 P1E_S4_C1
P1E_S3_C3	P2E_S4_C2	P1L_S1_C1 P1L_S3_C3
P1L_S3_C3	P2L_S4_C2	P1L_S2_C2 P1L_S4_C1
P1E_S2_C2	P2E_S1_C3	P2E_S2_C2 P2E_S4_C2
P1L_S2_C2	P2L_S1_C1	P2E_S1_C3 P2E_S3_C1
P1E_S4_C1	P2E_S3_C1	P2L_S2_C2 P2L_S4_C2
P1L_S4_C1	P2L_S3_C3	P2L_S1_C1 P2L_S3_C3

Table 2. Performance of the facial identification module using correlation filters and LBP images.

Case study	Descriptor	DIR	VR	MRR
1	CF	0.85	0.99	0.91
	LBPi	**0.89**	**1.00**	**0.93**
2	CF	**0.86**	0.96	**0.89**
	LBPi	0.80	**0.99**	0.86
3	CF	**0.81**	0.97	**0.91**
	LBPi	0.79	**1.00**	0.85

both indoor/outdoor scenarios and short/long time interval (Case Studies 2 and 3). These results are evidence that the correlations filters are suitable for facial identification under re-identification conditions. The LBP images obtained the best performance under indoor scenarios and in short time interval–Case Study 1. Moreover, regarding VR metric, LBP images obtained the best performance in three case studies of person re-identification.

In the identification task, each element of the set $F_{p,i}$ gets compared against $N = |G_{bt}|$ biometric templates. This process could produce a list of possible matches. Thus, the biometric template must be able to produce a similarity score higher than other possible matches for the authentic person. The MRR metric measures the performance of the correlation filter to produce a similarity score higher than other possible matches.

The performance of facial descriptors matching module was calculated using the UOTSDF, SDF, and MACH filters. We measured the ability of the descriptor generated in the i-th FoV to match with the descriptor generated in the j-th FoV. As one can see in Table 1, each person appears in eight, eight, and 16 FoVs in the case studies 1, 2, and 3, respectively. Thus, $M = |V_p|$ becomes the number of FoVs, where the p-th person appears, so are performed $M - 1$ comparisons.

The performance of the descriptor matching module was calculated in terms of the number of successful matches between the total numbers of matches. We executed a total of seven matches for case studies 1 and 2, while 15 for case study 3. Both correlation filters and LBP images obtained 100% of effectiveness, which shows the competitiveness of the correlation filters against other approaches in face Re-Id.

5.3   Discussion

Although LBP image obtained similar performance to correlation filters in some cases, it does not allow to synthesize a set of images into a single signal. So, both recognition and matching are computationally expensive and thus not suitable for real-time systems. Furthermore, LBP image requires a big set of images for obtaining good performance. On the other hand, correlation filters can synthesize several images into a single signal. This synthesis improves the speed of the proposed algorithm for re-identifying a person by their facial images.

The results achieved by our proposed algorithm in the recognition module are competitive with those reported in the literature. In [26] they tested the LBP+ Multi-Region Histogram (MRH) and Average MRH, obtaining $VR = 86.7\%$ and $VR = 87.7\%$, respectively, on the ChokePoint dataset. Our proposed method outperforms these results in all case studies. In [12] they proposed a covariance descriptor based on bio-inspired features, getting $VR = 87\%$ in the best case; although that result is on a different dataset, our proposed algorithm achieved better results in the same metric. The descriptor matching module achieved results competitive with those approaches that use facial images for re-identification, reported in [17] and [21,23].

6   Conclusion

In this paper, we propose a correlation-filter-based algorithm for re-identifying people by their face images. We tested the proposed algorithm with the UOTSDF filter in the facial identification module, achieving the best performance in the DIR metric for indoor/outdoor scenes. We assessed the matching module by using UOTSDF, SDF, and MATCH filters. Although they all scored perfect matches, we observed that the SDF filter does not affect the speed of the proposed algorithm. On the other hand, the UOTSDF and MATCH filters require a matrix inversion, which slows down the re-identification process.

We can highlight at least four strengths of the proposed algorithm. First, correlation filters can be successfully applied to facial re-identification as shown by the results previously presented. Second, since correlation filters synthesize the training sets into a single signal, it helps to maintain or even to improve the speed of re-identification algorithms. Third, the identification task in the re-identification algorithm avoids the need for using an operator and allows the development of intelligent re-identification systems. Fourth, the selection of a subset of the most representative face images, in the identification and matching modules, improves their precision. Due to these four strengths, the proposed algorithm is suitable for re-identifying a person by their face images in a camera network, and it also promises further results in future work for both intelligent and big-data processes.

References

1. An, L., Kafai, M., Bhanu, B.: Dynamic Bayesian network for unconstrained face recognition in surveillance camera networks. IEEE J. Emerg. Sel. Top. Circ. Syst. **3**(2), 155–164 (2013). https://doi.org/10.1109/JETCAS.2013.2256752
2. Apicella, A., Isgrò, F., Riccio, D.: Improving face recognition in low quality video sequences: single frame vs multi-frame super-resolution. In: Battiato, S., Gallo, G., Schettini, R., Stanco, F. (eds.) ICIAP 2017. LNCS, vol. 10484, pp. 637–647. Springer, Cham (2017). https://doi.org/10.1007/978-3-319-68560-1_57
3. Bäuml, M., Bernardin, K., Fischer, M., Ekenel, H.K., Stiefelhagen, R.: Multi-pose face recognition for person retrieval in camera networks. In: Proceedings–IEEE International Conference on Advanced Video and Signal Based Surveillance, AVSS 2010 (i), pp. 441–447 (2010). https://doi.org/10.1109/AVSS.2010.42
4. Bäuml, M., Tapaswi, M., Stiefelhagen, R.: A time pooled track kernel for person identification. In: Proceedings of the 11th International Conference on Advanced Video and Signal-Based Surveillance (AVSS). IEEE, 26–28 August 2014
5. Bedagkar-Gala, A., Shah, S.K.: A survey of approaches and trends in person re-identification. Image Vis. Comput. **32**(4), 270–286 (2014). https://doi.org/10.1016/j.imavis.2014.02.001
6. Casasent, D., Chang, W.T.: Correlation synthetic discriminant functions. Appl. Opt. **25**, 2343–2350 (1986)
7. Chen, Y., Duffner, S., Stoian, A., Dufour, J.Y., Baskurt, A.: Deep and low-level feature based attribute learning for person re-identification. Image Vis. Comput. **79**, 25–34 (2018). https://doi.org/10.1016/j.imavis.2018.09.001
8. Cui, Z., Chang, H., Shan, S., Ma, B., Chen, X.: Joint sparse representation for video-based face recognition. Neurocomputing **135**, 306–312 (2014). https://doi.org/10.1016/j.neucom.2013.12.004
9. Gong, S., Cristani, M., Loy, C.C., Hospedales, T.M.: The re-identification challenge. In: Gong, S., Cristani, M., Yan, S., Loy, C.C. (eds.) Person Re-Identification. ACVPR, pp. 1–20. Springer, London (2014). https://doi.org/10.1007/978-1-4471-6296-4_1
10. Li, W., Zhu, X., Gong, S.: Person re-identification by deep joint learning of multi-loss classification. CoRR abs/1705.04724 (2017). http://arxiv.org/abs/1705.04724
11. Liu, Z., Zhang, Z., Wu, Q., Wang, Y.: Enhancing person re-identification by integrating gait biometric. In: Jawahar, C.V., Shan, S. (eds.) ACCV 2014. LNCS, vol. 9008, pp. 35–45. Springer, Cham (2015). https://doi.org/10.1007/978-3-319-16628-5_3
12. Ma, B., Su, Y., Jurie, F.: Covariance descriptor based on bio-inspired features for person re-identification and face verification. Image Vis. Comput. **32**(6), 379–390 (2014). https://doi.org/10.1016/j.imavis.2014.04.002
13. Ren, Y., Li, X., Lu, X.: Feedback mechanism based iterative metric learning for person re-identification. Pattern Recognit. **75**, 1339–1351 (2018). https://doi.org/10.1016/j.patcog.2017.04.012

14. Ruchay, A., Kober, V., Gonzalez-Fraga, J.A.: Reliable recognition of partially occluded objects with correlation filters. Math. Probl. Eng. **2018**, 8 p. (2018). https://doi.org/10.1155/2018/8284123. Article ID 8284123
15. Santiago-Ramirez, E., Gonzalez-Fraga, J.A., Lazaro-Martnez, S.: Face recognition and tracking using unconstrained non-linear correlation filters. In: International Meeting of Electrical Engineering Research ENIINVIE (2012)
16. Santiago-Ramirez, E., Gonzalez-Fraga, J.A., Gutierrez, E., Alvarez-Xochihua, O.: Optimization-based methodology for training set selection to synthesize composite correlation filters for face recognition. Signal Process.: Image Commun. **43**, 54–67 (2016). https://doi.org/10.1016/j.image.2016.02.002
17. Soleymani, R., Granger, E., Fumera, G.: Progressive boosting for class imbalance and its application to face re-identification. Expert. Syst. Appl. **101**, 271–291 (2018). https://doi.org/10.1016/j.eswa.2018.01.023
18. Vijaya-Kumar, B.V.K., Mahalanobis, A., Juday, R.: Correlation Pattern Recognition. Cambridge University Press, Cambridge (2005)
19. Wang, G., Zheng, F., Shi, C., Xue, J.H., Liu, C., He, L.: Embedding metric learning into set-based face recognition for video surveillance. Neurocomputing **151**(P3), 1500–1506 (2015). https://doi.org/10.1016/j.neucom.2014.10.032
20. Wang, J., Zhou, S., Wang, J., Hou, Q.: Deep ranking model by large adaptive margin learning for person re-identification. Pattern Recognit. **74**, 241–252 (2017). https://doi.org/10.1016/j.patcog.2017.09.024
21. Wang, J., Wang, Z., Liang, C., Gao, C., Sang, N.: Equidistance constrained metric learning for person re-identification. Pattern Recognit. **74**, 38–51 (2018). https://doi.org/10.1016/j.patcog.2017.09.014
22. Wang, Q., Alfalou, A., Brosseau, C.: New perspectives in face correlation research: a tutorial. Adv. Opt. Photon. **9**(1), 1–78 (2017). https://doi.org/10.1364/AOP.9.000001
23. Wang, Y., Shen, J., Petridis, S., Pantic, M.: A real-time and unsupervised face re-identification system for human-robot interaction. Pattern Recognit. Lett. (2018). https://doi.org/10.1016/j.patrec.2018.04.009
24. Wang, Z., Bovik, A.C., Sheikh, H.R., Simoncelli, E.P.: Image quality assessment: from error visibility to structural similarity. IEEE Trans. Image Process. **13**(4), 600–612 (2004). https://doi.org/10.1109/TIP.2003.819861
25. Watson, G., Bhalerao, A.: Person re-identification using deep foreground appearance modeling. J. Electron. Imaging **27** (2018). https://doi.org/10.1117/1.JEI.27.5.051215
26. Wong, Y., Chen, S., Mau, S., Sanderson, C., Lovell, B.C.: Patch-based probabilistic image quality assessment for face selection and improved video-based face recognition. In: IEEE Biometrics Workshop, Computer Vision and Pattern Recognition (CVPR) Workshops, pp. 81–88. IEEE, June 2011
27. Yang, B., Chen, S.: A comparative study on local binary pattern (LBP) based face recognition: LBP histogram versus LBP image. Neurocomputing **120**, 365–379 (2013). https://doi.org/10.1016/j.neucom.2012.10.032. Image Feature Detection and Description
28. Zheng, L., Yang, Y., Hauptmann, A.G.: Person re-identification: past, present and future. CoRR **14**(8), 1–20 (2016)

Thermal Radiation Dynamics of Soil Surfaces with Unmanned Aerial Systems

Othón González[1], Mariano I. Lizarraga[2], Sertac Karaman[3],
and Joaquín Salas[1](✉)

[1] CICATA Querétaro, Instituto Politécnico Nacional, Cerro Blanco 141,
76030 Cimatario, Querétaro, Mexico
othon.gonzalezc@gmail.com, jsalasr@ipn.mx
[2] Santa Cruz, USA
[3] Massachusetts Institute of Technology, Cambridge, USA
sertac@mit.edu

Abstract. Thermographies are a source of abundant and rapid information, valuable in precision agriculture tasks such as crop stress assessment, plant disease analysis, and soil moisture evaluation. Traditionally, practitioners obtain soil temperature directly from the ground or using satellites and other airborne methods, which are costly and have a low spatial and temporal resolution. In this paper, we introduce a method for short term tracking of thermal radiance inertia with the use of an unmanned aerial system (UAS). In our approach, we retro-project the spatial reconstruction obtained with structure from motion (SfM) to estimate the thermal radiation corresponding to three-dimensional structures. Then, we register the resulting orthomosaics using a pyramidal scheme. We use the first cloud of points as the fixed reference as new orthomosaics become available. Finally, we estimate the dynamics of the thermal radiation using the difference of the registered orthomosaic radiation intensity measurements.

Keywords: Thermographic imaging · Unmanned aerial systems ·
Soil surface temperature · Remote sensing

1 Introduction

Due to the potential benefits, there are significant efforts underway to apply UAS-generated data towards what is known as *precision agriculture* [3,31]. Nowadays, one could conveniently use a UAS to perform tasks such as monitoring the area covered, the volume of biomass, the estimation of crop yield, and the plants' health via the three-dimensional characterization of the vegetation's structure and soil information [28]. The latter is particularly useful as soil surface temperature is a rapid response variable which can be used to monitor the growth and stress of plants. For instance, Hassan-Esfahani *et al.* [10] observe that

© Springer Nature Switzerland AG 2019
J. A. Carrasco-Ochoa et al. (Eds.): MCPR 2019, LNCS 11524, pp. 183–192, 2019.
https://doi.org/10.1007/978-3-030-21077-9_17

soil temperature is related to the spatial distribution of its surface moisture. In this paper, we introduce a UAS to obtain the evolution of soil thermal radiance (see Fig. 1). By using a set of images $\mathcal{I}$, captured with a thermal camera, we estimate the parameters related to camera motion and the scene's structure. Then, using an approximation of the position of a particular point $\mathbf{p}$ in the scene, we estimate its thermal radiance $I(\mathbf{p})$. The radiance values are incorporated into the cloud of points and used to generate an orthomosaic. After their registration, the difference between a fixed orthomosaic, used as a reference, and a current orthomosaic is used to characterize the radiance dynamics $\Delta \mathbf{R}$.

Currently, practitioners estimate soil radiance using direct measurements or satellites and other airborne methods. However, because of the high cost of these approaches and their low spatial and temporal resolution, the use of UASs [6] is an appealing proposition. Indeed, regardless of the platform, the use of thermal cameras remains problematic for both aerial sensors and satellites because a considerable amount of the thermal radiation emitted from the earth's surface is attenuated by energy dispersion and atmospheric absorption. These attenuations become more substantial as the sensor's altitude increases. Contrariwise, a UAS can function as low-altitude atmospheric satellites making the thermal radiance absorption problem, and temperature measurement, less error prone [16,22]. Thermal cameras operate commonly at wavelengths between 8–14 μm. This range of wavelengths is important because water vapor, carbon dioxide molecules, and ozone have a strong absorption capacity and solar radiation has a considerable overlap at other wavelengths [22].

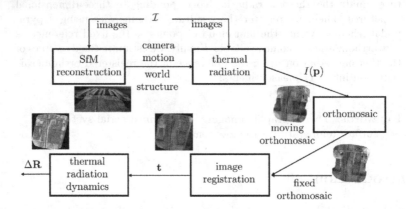

Fig. 1. Thermal radiance dynamics using observation from a UAS. We use structure from motion (SfM) to estimate camera motion and world structure from a sequence of images $\mathcal{I}$. Then, we obtain the corresponding thermal radiation from a world point using the set of images from which such a point is visible. Next, we construct an orthomosaic using such estimates. In our work, we aim to characterize the thermal radiance dynamics $\Delta \mathbf{R}$ from the registered orthomosaics corresponding to a fixed reference and the incoming cloud of points.

Fig. 2. Experimental field. To monitor the thermal radiance dynamics we instruct our UAS to follow an antipodal staggered flight several times over roughly the same area (a). For the flights we describe in this research, we use a 757-3 Ranger EX UAV (b). The FLIR Vue Pro-R camera mounted below the UAV's fuselage.

Our contributions include an end-to-end workflow using a UAS to obtain the dynamics of thermal soil radiance; the introduction of a scheme to robustly estimate 3D world points radiance from the images used during its reconstruction; and the insights resulting of our experiments in a 64 ha experimental area. We structure the rest of the article as follow. In Sect. 2, we review the current state of structure from motion techniques, thermal radiation measurements, orthomosaic registration and thermal radiation dynamics. Then, in Sect. 3, we describe our approach to estimate radiance measurements from 3D reconstructions. Next, the successive registration of orthomosaics is detailed in Sect. 4. In Sect. 5, we describe the experimental setup, our system, and the results we obtained with it. Finally, we present our conclusion and outline future lines of research.

2 Related Literature

In our approach, we characterize thermal inertia measuring the radiance dynamics between registered orthomosaics. We compute orthomosaics as the solution to the problem of extracting the structure from a set of images. This methodology allows us to sample several times the thermal radiation emitted by a point in the scene due to its presence in different thermal images. In this section, we survey the literature related to these issues.

Structure from Motion (SfM). SfM a is family of techniques to recover the three-dimensional geometry of the world and the motion of the camera from the projection of scene features into the images composing a sequence [20]. Some of the problems practitioners ought to solve include extracting relevant features, finding their correspondence, estimating camera motion from geometric constraints, and recovering the three-dimensional structure usually minimizing the retro-projection error [23]. SfM has reached a high level of maturity in recent years, as shown by systems able to make reconstructions even with a hundred million images [11]. Usually, in the solution of the SfM problem there is a large amount of computational resources involved, and the problem of drifting due to accumulated errors is always present. The use of GPS information alleviates both problems by providing geometrical constraints on the search space [13]. The utilization of GPS information into the SfM pipeline has fructified in commercial products specialized on three-dimensional reconstruction from aerial photography, such as Pix4D [21] and Agisoft [1], and some open source community-based developments such as OpenDroneMap [19].

Thermal Radiation Measurements. Recently, there has been an increasing interest on the development of applications based on thermal infrared remote sensing applied to precision agriculture [12]. In particular, Sugiura *et al.* [27] demonstrate that thermal imaging can be used to monitor soil moisture.

Practitioners obtain the images from satellites or other airborne platforms. However, their cost may be a deterrent, and the spatial and temporal resolution may not be adequate. For instance, consider that the satellite images from MODIS have a pixel size of 250, 500 and 1000 m and can be obtained once a day [18], while the images from CBERS have a spatial resolution of 80 m/pixel and observe the same area once every 16 days [6]; notwithstanding the attenuation of thermal radiation due to dispersion and the atmospheric absorption [22]. Therefore, UASs emerge as an attractive alternative [26]. For instance, Hassan-Esfahani *et al.* [10]) compare the temperature obtained with cameras mounted on a UAS and data from soil sampling and conclude that the former accurately estimate the spatial distribution of surface moisture. Distinctly to Hassan-Esfahani *et al.* [10], our interest lies in the feedback loop between the temperature of the land surface, the texture of the soil and the water content in it [15].

Orthomosaic Registration. An orthomosaic is the orthographic projection of a surface, where each pixel is placed on its geographic position and the effects of perspective and lens distortion have been eliminated [8]. An orthomosaic is a by-product of the digital three-dimensional construction of a surface and can be readily obtained using SfM. In addition, the purpose of image registration is to align two images with an overlapping field of view [14]. This process involves detecting and matching corresponding features and resampling the image, based on the transformation computed. In remote sensing applications, it is common to use Ground Control Points (GCP), for which the geo-position is critical [30]. However, obtaining reliable GCPs is costly and time-consuming. Especially when there is a reference image, as in our case, it is appealing to compute the reference points automatically [29].

Thermal Radiation Dynamics. The operation of a thermal camera to obtain the temperature is non-trivial. Radiation measured by a thermal sensor is a function of the surface emissivity of an object and the transmissivity of the atmosphere [12]. For example, Sobrino *et al.* [25]) confirm that the emissivity of the earth's surface varies according to the type of soil, and the emissivity of the sky varies with the conditions of clouds, *i.e.*, temperature and vapor content [2]. Therefore, to correct thermal imaging, we need to consider the effects of emissivity and the consequences of atmospheric transmissivity which may vary depending on relative humidity, ambient temperature, distance and angle of view. One can measure the first two during the mission and approximate the last two from the aircraft position and the camera orientation with respect to the three-dimensional reconstruction reference system. In this paper, we focus on a system that captures and registers surface thermal radiance, and infers its dynamics, leaving its relationship with temperature for further research.

3   Thermal Radiance

We measure the radiance by retro-projecting the three-dimensional scene points to their intensity values in the corresponding images. A property of techniques based on SfM is that, for each point in the scene, there are several images where the corresponding point is projected.

Let $\mathbf{x}$ be a point from a cloud of points $\mathcal{X}$. From SfM we assume that for each of the valid images in the sequence, we can compute a rotation ${}^{w}_{c}\mathbf{R}_i$ and a translation ${}^{w}_{c}\mathbf{t}_i$ corresponding to the i-th position of the camera $\{c\}$ in a global reference system $\{w\}$. Under these circumstances, the point position $\mathbf{y} = (X, Y, Z)^T$ in the camera reference system $\{c\}$ is given by the expression

$$\mathbf{y} = {}^{c}_{w}\mathbf{R}_i(\mathbf{x} - {}^{w}_{c}\mathbf{t}_i). \tag{1}$$

In perspective projection, the point position in the image plane could be expressed by the ratio

$$u = X/Z; \text{ and } v = Y/Z. \tag{2}$$

However, we need to correct for lens distortion. Although there is an ample set of models for lens distortion, arguably the more widespread corresponds to Brown's model [5]. This model integrates terms to correct for radial and tangential distortion, and it is expressed in a polynomial form, for three radial and two tangential distortion coefficients, as

$$
\begin{aligned}
x_d &= -u(1 + \kappa_1 r^2 + \kappa_2 r^4 + \kappa_3 r^6) + 2\tau_1 uv + \tau_2(r^2 + 2u^2), \\
y_d &= -v(1 + \kappa_1 r^2 + \kappa_2 r^4 + \kappa_3 r^6) + 2\tau_2 uv + \tau_1(r^2 + 2v^2),
\end{aligned}
\tag{3}
$$

where $(u, v)^T$ and $(x_d, y_d)^T$ correspond respectively to the undistorted and distorted coordinates, κ_i and τ_i are the radial and tangential coefficients, and $r = \sqrt{u^2 + v^2}$ is the radial distance from the center of distortion to the position of the undistorted pixel. To express the position of a point in the scene in the image plane, we use the parameters corresponding to the focal length and center of projection of the camera. The expression corresponds to

$$
\begin{pmatrix} x \\ y \\ 1 \end{pmatrix} = \begin{pmatrix} f_x & 0 & c_x \\ 0 & f_y & c_y \\ 0 & 0 & 1 \end{pmatrix} \begin{pmatrix} x_d \\ y_d \\ 1 \end{pmatrix}, \tag{4}
$$

where (4) expresses the result in the pixels' coordinate system.

For each point $\mathbf{x}$ in the point cloud $\mathcal{X}$, we obtain the retro-projection for the images in the dataset $\mathcal{I}$, keeping only the subset $\mathcal{I}_s$ where the projection of $\mathbf{x}$ is within the image boundaries. For each image in $\mathcal{I}_s$, we obtain the radiance intensity for $\mathbf{x}$ using bilinear interpolation. Then, we compute the resulting image intensity level ν corresponding to the point $\mathbf{x}$ as the median value of these samples. Our preference for the median as a descriptor for central tendency is due to its relative robustness to outliers compared to other statistics such as the mean.

4   Orthomosaic Registration

In our case, a point cloud $\mathbf{P} = (\mathcal{X}, \mathcal{C})$ is constituted by three-dimensional spatial position elements $\mathcal{X} = \{\mathbf{x}_1, \ldots, \mathbf{x}_m\}$, where $\mathbf{x}_i \in \mathcal{R}^3$, and a property component $\mathcal{C} = \{c_1, \ldots, c_m\}$, where we associate c_i with position $\mathbf{x}_i$. The properties we currently represent are associated with the measurements of soil surface radiance. Let $\mathbf{P}_f = (\mathcal{X}_f, \mathcal{C}_f)$ and $\mathbf{P}_m = (\mathcal{X}_m, \mathcal{C}_m)$ be two point clouds. The components $\mathcal{X}_f$ and $\mathcal{X}_m$ are associated approximately to the same spatial region. However, the reference system under which they are expressed has positional uncertainty. This uncertainty is due to factors such as noise in the geo-positioning measurements and the optical distortions associated with the lenses of the camera. Geo-referencing with regular GPS creates an uncertainty that is between five and ten meters of displacement [17]. Meanwhile lens distortion creates artifacts in the reconstruction, e.g., it creates a *dome effect* on flat surfaces [7].

Our interest is to determine the thermal inertia of the soil for a terrain which has a three-dimensional structure $\mathcal{X}_f$, with respect to later observations, which have correspondingly generated a three-dimensional structure $\mathcal{X}_m$. To simplify the process, we assume that the point clouds are separated by a rotation $_m^f\mathbf{R}$ and a translation $_m^f\mathbf{t}$ of the structure $\mathcal{X}_m$ with respect to $\mathcal{X}_f$. In our approach, we create an orthomosaic by interpolating on a Delaunay triangulation built on the latitude and longitude values of the cloud of points and assign it to the vertices of the triangulation of the intensity values, as computed in Sect. 3. We use the first orthomosaic obtained as a fixed reference. Then, we register subsequent orthomosaics with respect to the reference orthomosaic estimating the relative translation using a multi-scale Lucas-Kanade tracker [4].

5   Experimental Results

Our UAV (Fig. 2) is based on a 2.6 Kg 757-3 Ranger EX model, flown with the Open Source PX4 autopilot. Typically, we operate on visual flight rules (VFR) via Radio Control (RC). The UAV communicates telemetry to the Ground Control Station via a 900 Hz digital modem.

Our test field is located at *La Estacada, Querétaro*, latitude 20° 49' 08.48"N, longitude 100° 24' 50.56"W, at an altitude of 2025 m above Mean Sea Level (MSL). For the experiments we report in this article, we flew seven times over the area depicted in Fig. 2 following an antipodal staggered flight in an area of approximately 800 m × 800 m. During each pass, our camera takes 589, 408, 408,

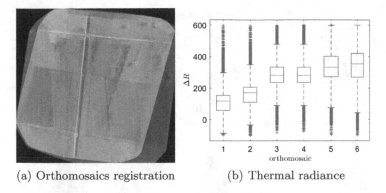

(a) Orthomosaics registration   (b) Thermal radiance

Fig. 3. Experimental Results. In (a), we illustrate the registration of two orthomosaics. The gray color means that both measurements coincide, while green and purple are chosen when the intensity value in one orthomosaic is larger than the corresponding one in the other orthomosaic. In (b), we show the mean value for the thermal radiance differences for the observations illustrated in Fig. 4. (Color figure online)

410, 401, and 475 images respectively. Each pass takes the UAV about 7 min. During the mission, our UAV tries to fly at a constant height of 150 m Above Ground Level (AGL).

To capture the images, we used a FLIR Vue Pro-R camera [9], which weight is about 113gr, with a resolution of 512(rows) × 640(columns). This camera can extract radiometric information at up to 200 m. The camera is mounted below the UAV's fuselage and located on the front so the center of gravity of the UAV is within its aerodynamic limits. This position also guarantees an unobstructed field of view. The calibration of the camera resulted in a focal length of $f = 827.113$ pixels and a center of projection at $\mathbf{c} = (332.12, 242.84)$ pixels with an uncertainty of $\sigma_f = 1.45$ pixels and $\sigma_{\mathbf{c}} = (0.62, 0.69)$ pixels.

For 3D reconstruction, we use Pix4D [21] due to its ability to produce denser cloud points and more accurate Digital Elevation Maps (DEM) relative to other tools such as PhotoScan and OpenDroneMap [24].

Pix4D uses binary descriptors derived from SIFT features which outperforms regular floating-point SIFT in accuracy and hashing speeds, when applied to a large number of possible matches. We process our images on an Intel Core i7-3770 at 3.4 GHz, 16 GB in RAM, and Nvidia GPU GTX 760. Using Pix4D each reconstruction takes approximately 25 min, on average.

Using the point cloud, and the parameters for each camera position and orientation, we obtain, for each flown circuit, the set of image intensities associated with each observable point in the reconstruction. Then, we perform a tessellation on the cloud points to interpolate intensity values on a regular grid with a separation of 0.2 m. We register the orthomosaics using a pyramidal approach with three levels (see Fig. 3(a)). The resulting lateral displacement for each orthomosaic, in meters, resulted in $\{(-12.04, -3.6), (-7.0, -6.8), (-1.6, -4.8), (-2.0, -4.0), (-10.4, -10.3), (-0.03,$

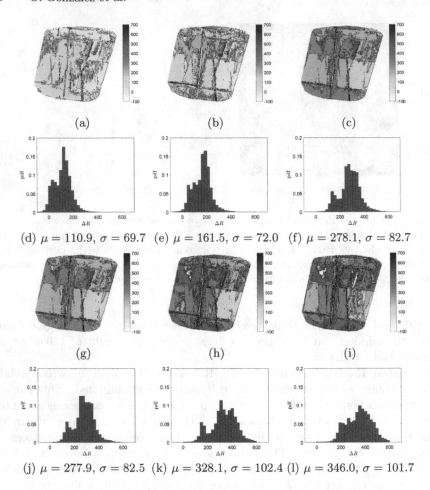

(a)   (b)   (c)

(d) $\mu = 110.9$, $\sigma = 69.7$ (e) $\mu = 161.5$, $\sigma = 72.0$ (f) $\mu = 278.1$, $\sigma = 82.7$

(g)   (h)   (i)

(j) $\mu = 277.9$, $\sigma = 82.5$ (k) $\mu = 328.1$, $\sigma = 102.4$ (l) $\mu = 346.0$, $\sigma = 101.7$

Fig. 4. Thermal inertia for a soil surface. (a–c) and (g–i) show the thermal radiance difference for a patch of soil, while (d–f) and (j–l) show their corresponding distribution.

−0.03)}, respectively. The final difference in intensity corresponds to the subtraction between the registered orthomosaics for each of the circuits with respect to the first one (see Fig. 4). The mean and standard deviation of these differences is {(110.9, 69.7), (161.5, 72.0), (278.1, 82.7), (277.9, 82.5), (328.1, 102.4), (346.0, 101.7)}, respectively. This trend is illustrated in Fig. 3(b).

The increasing mean shows that the overall radiance of the terrain is increasing. On the other hand, the increasing standard deviation shows that the radiances for different patches of terrain do not increase evenly. The latter suggests that different regions of soil will act depending on its thermal radiance dynamics, as expected.

6   Conclusion

In this paper, we introduce a system to assess the thermal inertia of the radiance emitted by a soil surface. Our experiments show that the applied sampling strategy provides a reliable characterization of the radiance dynamics. This sound result reflects the underlying robustness of the technique used to register orthomosaics. Overall, the development presented in this paper provides a foundation for the development of algorithms to measure soil stress, texture, and water content.

For future work, we plan to complement our system with measurements of ambient temperature and relative humidity. In addition, we plan to complement our method with models for surface emissivity and atmosphere transmissivity. These measurements and models together with the use of the aircraft altitude should give a robust base to transform radiance measurements to temperature.

Acknowledgments. This work was partially funded by SIP-IPN 20196702 for Joaquín Salas. Othón González is supported by a grant from CONACyT.

References

1. Agisoft: Agisoft Photoscan (2017). www.agisoft.com
2. Allen, R., Irmak, A., Trezza, R., Hendrickx, J., Bastiaanssen, W., Kjaersgaard, J.: Satellite-based ET estimation in agriculture using SEBAL and METRIC. Hydrol. Process. **25**(26), 4011–4027 (2011)
3. Anderson, K., Gaston, K.: Lightweight unmanned aerial vehicles will revolutionize spatial ecology. Front. Ecol. Environ. **11**(3), 138–146 (2013)
4. Bouguet, J.Y.: Pyramidal implementation of the affine Lucas-Kanade feature tracker description of the algorithm. Intel Corp. **5**(1–10), 4 (2001)
5. Brown, D.: Close-range camera calibration. Photogram. Eng. **37**(8), 855–866 (1971)
6. CBERS: Satelite Sino-Brasileiro de Recursos Terrestres (2017). http://www.cbers.inpe.br
7. Eltner, A., Schneider, D.: Analysis of different methods for 3D reconstruction of natural surfaces from parallel-axes UAV images. Photogram. Rec. **30**(151), 279–299 (2015)
8. Fernandez, E., Garfinkel, R., Arbiol, R.: Mosaicking of aerial photographic maps via seams defined by bottleneck shortest paths. Oper. Res. **46**(3), 293–304 (1998)
9. FLIR: FLIR Vue Pro R, Radiometry from the Air (2017). http://www.flir.com/suas/vuepror/
10. Hassan-Esfahani, L., Torres-Rua, A., Jensen, A., McKee, M.: Assessment of surface soil moisture using high-resolution multi-spectral imagery and artificial neural networks. Remote Sens. **7**(3), 2627–2646 (2015)
11. Heinly, J., Schonberger, J., Dunn, E., Frahm, J.M.: Reconstructing the world* in six days*(as captured by the yahoo 100 million image dataset). In: IEEE Conference on Computer Vision and Pattern Recognition, pp. 3287–3295 (2015)
12. Khanal, S., Fulton, J., Shearer, S.: An overview of current and potential applications of thermal remote sensing in precision agriculture. Comput. Electron. Agric. **139**, 22–32 (2017)

13. Lhuillier, M.: Incremental fusion of structure-from-motion and GPS using constrained bundle adjustments. IEEE Transact. Pattern Anal. Mach. Intell. **34**(12), 2489–2495 (2012)
14. Li, H., Ding, W., Cao, X., Liu, C.: Image registration and fusion of visible and infrared integrated camera for medium-altitude unmanned aerial vehicle remote sensing. Remote Sens. **9**(5), 441 (2017)
15. Mattikalli, N., Engman, E., Jackson, T., Ahuja, L.: Microwave remote sensing of temporal variations of brightness temperature and near-surface soil water content during a watershed-scale field experiment, and its application to the estimation of soil physical properties. Water Resour. Res. **34**(9), 2289–2299 (1998)
16. Minkina, W., Klecha, D.: Atmospheric transmission coefficient modelling in the infrared for thermovision measurements. J. Sens. Sens. Syst. **5**(1), 17 (2016)
17. Misra, P., Enge, P.: Global Positioning System: Signals, Measurements and Performance. Ganga-Jamuna Press, Massachusetts (2006)
18. National Aeronautics and Space Administration: MODIS Web - Data (2017). https://modis.gsfc.nasa.gov/data/
19. OpenDroneMap: OpenDroneMap (2017). https://github.com/OpenDroneMap
20. Özyeşil, O., Voroninski, V., Basri, R., Singer, A.: A survey of structure from motion. Acta Numer. **26**, 305–364 (2017)
21. Pix4D: Pix4D (2017). http://www.pix4d.com
22. Quattrochi, D., Luvall, J.: Thermal infrared remote sensing for analysis of landscape ecological processes: methods and applications. Landscape Ecol. **14**(6), 577–598 (1999)
23. Schonberger, J.L., Frahm, J.M.: Structure-from-motion revisited. In: IEEE Conference on Computer Vision and Pattern Recognition, pp. 4104–4113 (2016)
24. Schwind, M.: Comparing and characterizing three-dimensional point clouds derived by structure from motion photogrammetry. Ph.D. thesis, Texas A&M University-Corpus Christi (2016)
25. Sobrino, J., et al.: Soil emissivity and reflectance spectra measurements. Appl. Opt. **48**(19), 3664–3670 (2009)
26. Stark, B., Smith, B., Chen, Y.: Survey of thermal infrared remote sensing for unmanned aerial systems. In: International Conference on Unmanned Aircraft Systems, pp. 1294–1299. IEEE (2014)
27. Sugiura, R., Noguchi, N., Ishii, K.: Correction of low-altitude thermal images applied to estimating soil water status. Biosyst. Eng. **96**(3), 301–313 (2007)
28. Torresan, C., et al.: Forestry applications of UAVs in Europe: a review. Int. J. Remote Sens. **38**(8–10), 2427–2447 (2017)
29. Tsai, C.H., Lin, Y.C.: An accelerated image matching technique for UAV orthoimage registration. ISPRS J. Photogram. Remote Sens. **128**, 130–145 (2017)
30. Ye, Y., Shan, J., Bruzzone, L., Shen, L.: Robust registration of multimodal remote sensing images based on structural similarity. IEEE Transact. Geosci. Remote Sens. **55**(5), 2941–2958 (2017)
31. Zhang, C., Kovacs, J.: The application of small unmanned aerial systems for precision agriculture: a review. Precision Agric. **13**(6), 693–712 (2012)

Industrial and Medical Applications
of Pattern Recognition

Intra-patient Arrhythmia Heartbeat Modeling by Gibbs Sampling

Ethery Ramírez-Robles, Miguel Angel Jara-Maldonado,
and Gibran Etcheverry(✉)

Universidad de las Américas Puebla, Sta. Catarina Mártir, Cholula, Puebla, Mexico
gibran.etcheverry@udlap.mx

Abstract. Heartbeat modeling allows to detect anomalies that reflect the functioning of the heart. Certain approaches face this problem by using Gaussian Mixture Models (GMMs) and other statistical classifiers by extracting the fiducial points provided by the MIT-BIH database. In this work, MIT-BIH database heartbeats are modeled into different heartbeat types from a single subject by using the Gibbs Sampling (GS) algorithm. Firstly, a data pre-processing step is performed; this step involves several tasks such as filtering the raw signals from the MIT-BIH database and reducing the heartbeat types to five. Secondly, the GS is applied to the resulting signals of one subject. Thirdly, the Euclidean distance between each heartbeat type is calculated, and lastly, the Bhattacharyya distance is used to classify heartbeats. The results obtained by the GS algorithm were also compared to results obtained by applying the Expectation Maximization (EM) algorithm to the same data-set. Results allow to conclude that GS is a proper solution for separating each heartbeat type; by providing a significant difference between each heartbeat type which can be used for classification.

Keywords: Arrhythmia · Electrocardiogram ·
Gibbs Sampling algorithm · Expectation Maximization ·
QRS complex · R programming

1 Introduction

Electrocardiograms (ECG) are measurements of the electricity with which the heart operates. The QRS complex (which is a deflection on the ECG that states ventricular contraction and myocardial depolarization) can be used to analyze the ECGs. According to [1], cardiac disorders can be diagnosed by analyzing the perturbations in the normal electrical patterns. An arrhythmia is "any disturbance in the rate, regularity, site of origin, or conduction of the cardiac electrical impulse" [1]. An arrhythmia can be a single abnormal beat, or a series of different beats that cause rhythm disturbances during the whole lifetime of the patient.

The classification of arrhythmias detected in ECG signals has been investigated in different works. There exist several approaches such as linear discriminant classifiers in [2] and Gaussian Mixture Models (GMMs) in [3–5], among

© Springer Nature Switzerland AG 2019
J. A. Carrasco-Ochoa et al. (Eds.): MCPR 2019, LNCS 11524, pp. 195–205, 2019.
https://doi.org/10.1007/978-3-030-21077-9_18

others. Although their results are promising, accuracy and false positive rates are not yet unerring. This work subscribes to the electrocardiogram ECG raw signal treatment for arrhythmia classification and to the Markov Chain Monte Carlo (MCMC) filtering for ECG nonlinear dynamical modeling; see [6,7]. These approaches are considered given the difficulty encountered when modeling and classifying heart diseases because an ECG signal varies for each person, and "different patients have separate ECG morphologies for the same disease" [8]. Hence, here we consider the intra-patient analysis as a first step, given that the inter-patient protocol considers different patients with the same disease [9].

2   Heartbeat Dataset Description

For this work, the MIT-BIH Arrhythmia Database was used [10]. According to its creators, it was the first open access database that provided standard test material for arrhythmia detection, and it has been used since 1980. This database has a total of 48 records of over 30 min long (including records 201 and 202 which belong to the same subject). There are 25 men subjects, and 22 women subjects; and it includes a wide variety of waveforms, including normal beats, complex ventricular, junctional and supraventricular arrhythmias and conduction abnormalities. All heartbeats from each subject are presented as a collection of amplitudes, along with a file that allows to determine the key positions for the R waves of each heartbeat type. According to [2], the number of possible heartbeat types was reduced to the following five types: N, S, V, F, Q. This types are adopted in this work because they are a recommended standard by the Association for the Advancement of Medical Instrumentation (AAMI) [8]. The mapping procedure to obtain the N, S, V, F, Q nomenclature is shown in Table 1, which was obtained from [2].

3   Methodology

Two different methods were tested in this work; namely the GS algorithm, which is used in this work to generate samples from an ECG; and the EM algorithm suited for cases in which the data-set is not complete. According to [11], the GS can be thought of as a stochastic analog of the EM approach, used to obtain likelihood functions when missing data are present. The difference is that in the GS, random sampling replaces the expectation and maximization steps. For this reason, both methods are compared in this work in order to asses whether a stochastic solution performs better than its iterative analogue.

Before using the MIT-BIH heartbeat dataset, each heartbeat type had to be converted into one of the AAMI classes presented in Table 1. Once that this was achieved, the GS algorithm was used to obtain characteristics of the posterior distribution for each heartbeat type. Then, the obtained characteristics were used to calculate the Euclidean distance from each heartbeat type, and finally, the Bhattacharyya distance was used to classify the signal. This process is discussed in detail in the following sub-sections.

Table 1. MIT-BIH arrhythmia database heartbeat types convertion into AAMI heartbeat classes.

AAMI class	Description	MIT-BIH heart types
N	Non S, V, F, Q class heartbeats	Normal Beat (NOR), Left Bundle Branch Block (LBBB), Right Bundle Branch Block Beat (RBBB), Atrial Escape beat (AE), Nodal/Junctional Escape beat (NE)
S	Supraventricular ectopic beat	Atrial Premature beat (AP), aberrated Atrial Premature beat (aAP), Nodal/Junctional Premature beat (NP), Supraventricula Premature beat (SP)
V	Ventricular ectopic beat	Premature Ventricular Contraction (PVC), Ventricular Escape beat (VE)
F	Fusion beat	Fusion of Ventricular and Normal beat (fVN)
Q	Unknown beat	Paced beat (P), Fusion of Paced and Normal beat (fPN), Unclassified beat (U)

3.1 Pre-processing Step

All heartbeat types were mapped into one of the five AAMI heartbeat classes mentioned in Sect. 2. Each signal was pre-processed by a band-pass filter to reduce the influence of muscle noise, interference, and baseline wander. The chosen values for the filter ranged from 5 Hz to 15 Hz, as suggested by Pan and Tompkins, due to the fact that this is approximately the desirable band-pass to maximize the QRS energy, achieving a 99.3% detection of the QRS complex [12]. Hence, we separated each heartbeat by using the R peak location provided by the MIT-BIH dataset. We followed the Ghorbani et al. statement about separating heartbeats by using samples 225 ms before the R peak, and 400 ms after the R peak; yielding 0.65 s for each heartbeat [4]. Therefore, we divided each beat from 81 samples before the R peak (250 ms interval) to 82 samples before the R peak of the next QRS complex; this is shown in Fig. 1.

3.2 Gibbs Sampling (GS)

GS is an algorithm used to approximate a sequence of observations from a continuously distributed parameter vector Θ [11]. This algorithm was used under the assumption that heartbeats can be modeled by observing to which heartbeat type Probability Density Function (PDF) they approximate better. In order to

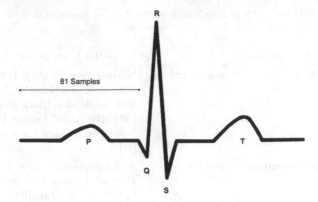

Fig. 1. The P wave (atrial depolarization and contraction) plus the QRS complex and the T wave (repolarization) [13].

achieve this, a Markov Chain (MC) is created to repeatedly sample the parameter sub-vectors $\Theta_1, ..., \Theta_M$, by using the following process. First, the starting value $\Theta^{(0)}$ of the parameter vector Θ is arbitrarily initialized (i.e. all $\Theta_i^{(0)}$ are randomly initialized). Then, the sub-vector $\Theta_0^{(1)}$ is sampled from the full conditional of Θ_0 with the rest of the Θ_i sub-vector values randomized in the previous step. This is done by using Eq. 1 [11]. This process is repeated until each $\Theta_1, ..., \Theta_M$ of the actual sub-vector (i.e. Θ^j) has been updated, yielding a new $\Theta^{(t)}$; where t stands for the current step (thus $t - 1$ is the last calculated step).

$$\Theta_1^t \sim P(\Theta_1 \mid \Theta_2^{t-1}, \Theta_3^{t-1})$$

$$\Theta_2^t \sim P(\Theta_2 \mid \Theta_1^t, \Theta_3^{t-1}) \tag{1}$$

$$\Theta_3^t \sim P(\Theta_3 \mid \Theta_1^t, \Theta_2^t)$$

The subsequent $\Theta^{(2)}$s are calculated using $\Theta^{(1)}$ instead of the arbitrary $\Theta^{(0)}$, and so on until the sequence $\Theta^{(0)}, ..., \Theta^{(N)}$ is obtained, which is a MC whose stationary distribution is the posterior distribution of Θ. Once converged to the stationary distribution, the MC samples the posterior distribution and can be used to obtain different characteristics of it [14]. For this work, those characteristics were used to calculate each heartbeat PDF and this is explained in Sect. 3.3.

In order to apply the GS algorithm to the MIT-BIH signals, the Windows implementation of the Bayesian analysis using GS (*WinBUGS* software)[1] was employed. It consists of a program capable of automatically tuning the most suitable Markov Chain Monte Carlo (MCMC) algorithm for a particular model. A normal distribution was used to explore each heartbeat likelihood type an the

---

[1] https://www.mrc-bsu.cam.ac.uk/software/bugs/the-bugs-project-winbugs/.

mean μ and precision τ variables were used to specify the mean and variance of it. The mean was updated by multiplying the y_{t-1} value by a ϕ normal distribution with zero mean and a variance of 0.0001. Afterwards, τ was updated from a gamma distribution with 0.1 mean and 0.0001 variance. Also, a scale parameter σ was occupied for the gamma distribution and was calculated by using Eq. 2. The WinBUGS software was called from a script developed in the R programming language, by using the *R2WinBUGS* library; and three MCMC chains were used with 2,600 iterations each, and 100 *burn-in* iterations (discarded iterations). No *thinning* was used (a strategy for reducing auto-correlation in the outputs [15]).

$$\sigma = \frac{1}{\sqrt{\tau}} \tag{2}$$

As an example of the posterior distribution characteristics obtained, Table 2 shows the posterior distribution characteristics obtained by applying the GS algorithm to the N-AAMI class heartbeats of subject 208. Three parameters are recovered; ϕ, σ, and deviance, from which the mean and standard deviation are calculated. This values are later used to calculate the proximity between each heartbeat type and to classify a heartbeat in one of the five AAMI classes.

Table 2. Subject 208 posterior distribution characteristics matrix.

Parameter	Mean	Standard deviation
ϕ	0.985	2.941×10^{-4}
σ	0.028	3.524×10^{-5}
Deviance	-1.388×10^{6}	0

3.3   Euclidean Distance

The posterior distribution characteristics obtained with the process explained earlier were used to determine the Euclidean distance between every type of heartbeat. In other words, first the GS was applied to the whole set of heartbeats of each class separately. Then, those characteristics were compared, by using the *Euclidean distance* as shown in Eq. 3 [16].

$$d(u,v) \,=\, \|\, u-v \,\| \,=\, \sqrt{(u_1 - v_1)^2 + (u_2 - v_2)^2 + ... + (u_n - v_n)^2} \tag{3}$$

where u and v are the two vectors to be compared. In this case, each vector would contain the posterior distribution characteristics of the different heartbeat types recorded in the signal. A matrix was generated, containing the distances of each heartbeat type. This allowed to better understand the separability of the data.

3.4   Bhattacharyya Distance

According to [17], the *Bhattacharyya distance* is used as a class separability measure. For this work, the Bhattacharyya distance between the p and q classes (which is applied to the case of two uni-variate normal distributions) was calculated by using Eq. 4.

$$D_{BC}(p,q) = \frac{1}{4}ln\left(\frac{1}{4}\left(\frac{\sigma_p^2}{\sigma_q^2} + \frac{\sigma_q^2}{\sigma_p^2} + 2\right)\right) + \frac{1}{4}\left(\frac{(\mu_p - \mu_q)^2}{\sigma_p^2 + \sigma_q^2}\right) \tag{4}$$

where σ_p^2 and μ_p are respectively the variance and mean of the p-*th* distribution, and p, q are two different distributions.

In this work, the Bhattacharyya distance was used to classify heartbeats and was calculated between the ϕ values previously obtained (i.e. mean and standard deviation values obtained from the posterior distribution characteristics of each heartbeat). In concrete, the ϕ values obtained from applying GS to the whole set of an AAMI class of heartbeats, against the ϕ values obtained from the heartbeat to be classified. In other words, the **patient heartbeat** to be classified is compared against each of the AAMI class values obtained previously, to determine to which class it belongs to.

3.5   Expectation Maximization (EM)

As a means to compare the performance of the GS algorithm against another method, the EM algorithm was implemented and used for the classification of heartbeat arrhythmia. According to [18], the EM algorithm is occupied in those cases where the data set presents incompleteness. In this case, the algorithm was used to generate a model that allowed to separate the heartbeats into different PDFs in order to classify them. The PDF of the incomplete data is given by Eq. 5.

$$p_x(x,\theta) = \int_{Y(x)} p_y(y,\theta)dy \tag{5}$$

where $p_y(y,\theta)$ is the corresponding PDF and y contains the complete data samples, but cannot be directly observed, and θ is an unknown parameter vector. The Maximum Likelihood Estimate (MLE) of θ is given by Eq. 6.

$$\hat{\theta}_{ML} : \sum_k \frac{\delta ln(p_y(y_k,\theta))}{\delta\theta} = 0 \tag{6}$$

Since the y's are not available, the EM algorithm maximizes the expectation of the log-likelihood function, conditioned on the observed samples and the current iteration estimate of θ [12]. The three steps of the algorithm are enunciated next.

- Initialization: the GMM parameters are determined by the k-means clustering algorithm.

– Expectation (E)-step: the initial parameters are used to determine the probability that an observation at the $(t+1)th$ step of the iteration belongs to a component. This is achieved by using Eq. 7.

$$Q(\theta, \theta(t)) = E\left[\sum_k ln(p_y(y_k : \theta \mid X, \theta(t)))\right] \tag{7}$$

– Maximization (M)-step: the component parameters are re-estimated by maximizing $Q(\theta, \theta(t))$ through the use of Eq. 8.

$$Q(\theta + 1) : \frac{\delta Q(\theta, \theta(t))}{\delta \theta} = 0 \tag{8}$$

In order to use the EM algorithm, the pre-processed signals were separated into each heartbeat class (i.e., they were concatenated into a different vector for each heartbeat type). Then, the *cepstrum* vector for each heartbeat was obtained and its mean value was calculated to use it as an *expert* to better separate each heartbeat type. In other words, for each heartbeat contained in a class vector, the cepstrum was obtained, giving a vector of cepstrums of the same type, then the mean was obtained, and that scalar value was considered as an expert. During the classification process, only those amplitudes found in the R point were used, given they offer a better separation. For each heartbeat type, its corresponding R point amplitude vector was multiplied by their corresponding expert, and these vectors were then used by the k-means algorithm to initialize the GMMs. Finally, to classify a new heartbeat, the Bhattacharyya distance between the heartbeat to be classified and each heartbeat type vector was calculated, and the lower distance obtained was then used to decide to which class the heartbeat belonged to.

4   Results and Discussion

From the 48 patients included in the MIT-BIH Arrhythmia Database, 19 patients were selected for this work. The subjects that had more than 100 heartbeat records on two or more heartbeat types were chosen, so that the algorithm had enough data to classify. Those subjects that did not comply with this condition, as well as those with pacemakers were discarded. The chosen records were 106, 116, 119, 200, 201, 203, 207, 208, 209, 210, 213, 214, 215, 221, 222, 223, 228, 232 and 233. Most of the selected subjects had the N, S and V type heartbeats, while only two patients presented the F type too. Almost all analyzed patients presented an Euclidean distance between the mean and the standard deviation of the posterior distribution characteristics greater than 1,000,000 (i.e., the mean and standard deviation of μ, σ and deviance). The shortest distance obtained was 93,000 belonging to the N - V distance of subject 208.

As mentioned before, the Bhattacharyya distances were used to perform the beat by beat classification. Only the mean and standard deviation of the ϕ posterior distribution characteristics parameter were occupied. The accuracy

Table 3. Classification accuracy using GS and the Bhattacharyya distance.

Subject	Accuracy				
	N	V	S	F	Total
116	99.56%	98.16%	-	-	99.50%
119	58.91%	83.55%	-	-	64.41%
200	49.85%	79.17%	73.33%	-	59.44%
201	86.66%	81.81%	21.21%	-	80.78%
203	68.72%	54.27%	-	-	66.56%
207	71.01%	78.73%	88.78%	-	74.08%
208	75.16%	87.29%	-	93.54%	80.01%
209	80.57%	-	65.27%	-	78.62%
210	91.20%	80.51%	-	-	90.40%
213	81.82%	17.27%	-	66.57%	75.70%
214	61.58%	49.21%	-	-	60.18%
215	99.71%	81.70%	-	-	98.8%
221	90.69%	96%	-	-	91.55%
222	65.46%	-	40.06%	-	63.37%
223	74.57%	72.09%	15.06%	-	72.44%
228	98.16%	77.34%	-	-	94.48%
232	64.07%	-	35.09%	-	41.57%
233	72.15%	51.92%	-	-	66.66%

results obtained from using the Bhattacharyya distances with GS are presented in Table 3, where the accuracy was calculated for each heartbeat class, and the total accuracy is also presented. Recall that all the subjects have a different number of heartbeat records for each heartbeat type, being the N type the most frequent in most of the cases. Therefore, the classification performance is mostly influenced by the results obtained for the N heartbeat types. The best result was obtained from subject 116, which had an accuracy percentage of 98.8%. Furthermore, subjects 201 and 223 presented the lowest accuracy in the S heartbeat type classification, where more than 75% of the heartbeats were misclassified. This may be caused by a confusion between the S and V heartbeat types, whose proximity is one of the closest (the S - V Euclidean distance for subject 201 is 110,691.8; whereas the greatest Euclidean obtained is greater than 3,000,000 and corresponds to subject 215). Similarly, subject 213 had a low accuracy in the V class, probably because the V class varies in its morphology, and may resemble to the N class. Finally, in the case of the subject 201, 97 S class heartbeats were classified as V class heartbeats, from a total number of 165; while in the case of the subject 223, the S beats were principally misclassified as N beats.

Table 4. Classification accuracy using the EM algorithm.

Subject	Accuracy				
	N	V	S	F	Total
116	33.17%	87.88%	-	-	47.21%
119	80.10%	1.83%	-	-	76.56%
200	97.64%	83.89%	0%	-	92.15%
201	63.60%	99.49%	62.42%	-	67.06%
203	75.40%	96.62%	-	-	78.57%
207	91.70%	99.26%	0%	-	89.70%
208	48.99%	90.52%	-	94.36%	68.68%
209	7.43%	-	96.34%	-	18.77%
210	93.47%	92.82%	-	-	93.42%
213	19.46%	0%	-	96.96%	26.83%
214	51.39%	60.93%	-	-	52.48%
215	47.23.%	100%	-	-	49.80%
221	60.95%	99.49%	-	-	67.24%
222	97.18%	-	17.22%	-	90.45%
223	75.25%	87.94%	0%	-	75.45%
228	78.25%	98.61%	-	-	81.85%
232	92.71%	-	12.87%	-	30.73%
233	100%	65.66%	-	-	90.68%

In the case of the results obtained by the EM algorithm, some of the accuracy results are shown in Table 4. From this table it can be observed that for subjects 200, 207 and 223, the S type heartbeats were completely misclassified. This is produced by a bad initialization given in the k-means algorithm step. The S heartbeats in subjects 207 and 223, were clustered in the V type cluster (and in the case of subject 223, all the S beats were sent to the V type cluster, while the S type cluster included some heartbeats of type N and V). Furthermore, the performance drop presented in the N type heartbeats for subject 208 (for the EM algorithm), may be caused by the fact that the F type is a fusion heartbeat that occurs when electrical impulses from different sources act upon the same region of the heart at the same time (i.e., the F type is a fusion of the ventricular and the normal heartbeat types, which may cause confusion, generating N type heartbeats to be classified as F type).

5 Conclusions

In the present work we have used the Gibbs Sampling (GS) algorithm to model heartbeats from individuals in the MIT-BIH Arrhythmia Database according to the AAMI classes, and compared its results with the ones obtained by using the Expectation Maximization (EM) algorithm. The posterior distribution characteristics obtained from the GS algorithm were used for each class separability and classification. A possible improvement to the results obtained by the GS algorithm could be the application of an expert to the heartbeat signals to classify.

Acknowledgements. Authors would like to acknowledge the Mexican National Council on Science and Technology (CONACyT) and the Universidad de las Américas Puebla (UDLAP) for their support through the doctoral scholarship program.

References

1. Thaler, M.S.: The Only EKG Book You'll Ever Need. Board Review Series. Lippincott Williams & Wilkins, Philadelphia (2007)
2. de Chazal, P., O'Dwyer, M., Reilly, R.B.: Automatic classification of heartbeats using ECG morphology and heartbeat interval features. IEEE Trans. Biomed. Eng. **51**(7), 1196–1206 (2004)
3. Povinelli, R.J., Johnson, M.T., Lindgren, A.C., Ye, J.: Time series classification using Gaussian mixture models of reconstructed phase spaces. IEEE Trans. Knowl. Data Eng. **16**(6), 779–783 (2004)
4. Ghorbani Afkhami, R., Azarnia, G., Ali Tinati, M.: Cardiac arrhythmia classification using statistical and mixture modeling features of ECG signals. Pattern Recognit. Lett. **70**, 45–51 (2016)
5. Martis, R.J., Chakraborty, C., Ray, A.K.: A two-stage mechanism for registration and classification of ECG using gaussian mixture model. Pattern Recognit. **42**(11), 2979–2988 (2009)
6. Escalona-Moran, M.A., Soriano, M.C., Fisher, I., Mirasso, C.R.: Electrocardiogram classification using reservoir computing with logistic regression. IEEE J. Biomed. Health Inform. **19**(3), 892–898 (2015)
7. Edla, S., et al.: Sequential Markov chain monte carlo filter with simultaneous model selection for electrocardiogram signal modeling. In: 34th Annual International Conference of the IEEE EMBS, August 2012
8. Kaplan Berkaya, S., et al.: A survey on ECG analysis. Biomed. Signal Process. Control **43**, 216–235 (2018)
9. Da, E.J., Luz, S., et al.: ECG-based heartbeat classification for arrhythmia detection: a survey. Comput. Methods Programs Biomed. **127**, 144–164 (2015)
10. Moody, G.B., Mark, R.G.: The impact of the MIT-BIH arrhythmia database. IEEE Eng. Med. Biol. Mag.: Q. Mag. Eng. Med. Biol. Soc. **20**, 45–50 (2001)
11. Walsh, B.: Markov chain monte carlo and gibbs sampling. Lecture Notes Online (2002)
12. Pan, J., Tompkins, W.J.: A real-time QRS detection algorithm. IEEE Trans. Biomed. Eng. **BME–32**(3), 230–236 (1985)
13. Association for the Advancement of Medical Instrumentation and American National Standards Institute. Testing and Reporting Performance Results of Cardiac Rhythm and ST-segment Measurement Algorithms. ANSI/AAMI. The Association (1999)
14. Lambert, B.: A Students Guide to Bayesian Statistics. SAGE Publications, Thousand Oaks (2018)

15. Ruppert, D.: Statistics and Data Analysis for Financial Engineering. Springer Texts in Statistics, 1st edn. Springer, Berlin (2010). https://doi.org/10.1007/978-1-4419-7787-8
16. Anton, H.: Elementary Linear Algebra. Wiley, Hoboken (2010)
17. Kashyap, R.: Combining dimension reduction, distance measures and covariance, November 2016
18. Theodoridis, S., Konstantinos, K.: Pattern Recognition, 4th edn. Academic Press Inc., Orlando (2008)

Non-invasive Glucose Level Estimation: A Comparison of Regression Models Using the MFCC as Feature Extractor

Victor Francisco-García[1], Iris P. Guzmán-Guzmán[2],
Rodolfo Salgado-Rivera[1], Gustavo A. Alonso-Silverio[1] (iD),
and Antonio Alarcón-Paredes[1(✉)] (iD)

[1] Facultad de Ingeniería, Universidad Autónoma de Guerrero,
Av. Lázaro Cárdenas S/N, 39070 Chilpancingo, Guerrero, México
{victor_fg,sarr,gsilverio,aalarcon}@uagro.mx
[2] Facultad de Ciencias Químico-Biológicas,
Universidad Autónoma de Guerrero, Av. Lázaro Cárdenas S/N,
39070 Chilpancingo, Guerrero, México
pao_nkiller@yahoo.com.mx

Abstract. The present study comprises a performance comparison on well-known regression algorithms for estimating the blood glucose concentration from non-invasively acquired signals. These signals were obtained measuring the light energy transmittance of a laser-beam source through the fingertip by means of an embedded light dependent resistor (LDR) microcontroller system. Signals were processed by computing the Mel frequency cepstral coefficients (MFCC) to perform the feature extraction. The glucose concentration in blood was measured by a commercial glucometer in order to evaluate the performance of five well-known regression models. The experimental results revealed comparable values of mean absolute error (MAE) and Clarke grid analysis. The best performance was obtained by the support vector regression with a mean absolute error of 9.45 mg/dl. However, this study serves as a starting point and alludes to the potential application of non-invasive systems in the glucose level estimation. Future experiments measuring the glucose concentration with laboratory standard tests should be conducted, and a model implementation in an embedded device for their use is also mandatory.

Keywords: Non-invasive glucose measuring ·
Mel frequency cepstral coefficients · MFCC · Optical sensing

1 Introduction

Diabetes Mellitus (DM) is a metabolic disorder that occurs when the body is unable to regulate blood sugar levels and has become an increasing major health challenge [1]. There are two types of diabetes mellitus: DM type-1 is a condition caused when the body is unable to produce any insulin, which is used to regulate the blood glucose levels and is essential to convert glucose into energy [2, 3]. DM type-2 occurs when the body has not enough insulin or fails to effectively use it, and it is spreading worldwide

© Springer Nature Switzerland AG 2019
J. A. Carrasco-Ochoa et al. (Eds.): MCPR 2019, LNCS 11524, pp. 206–215, 2019.
https://doi.org/10.1007/978-3-030-21077-9_19

more rapidly than type-1. With 415 million adults having diabetes, it is the most probable cause of one in ten deaths among people 20–59 years old [2]. Currently the international diabetes federation estimates 372 million of people with DM in 2012 and predicts 552 million by 2030 [3]. Diabetes affects the body leading to many serious illnesses such as cardiovascular diseases, eye problems, kidney problems, brain dysfunction, and premature mortality claiming thousands of lives every year [4]. It has also become a common cause for limb amputations which yields disability.

The most common commercially available glucose devices are invasive and require a blood sample to determine the glucose concentration on the human blood [5]. This method poses difficulty for the patients since they need to prick their finger several times a day in order to control the glycaemia. Patients may feel discomfort and distress, depending on the severity of puncturing the skin. Moreover, the needle can induce body infections into the blood stream [6]. In this regard, the development of non-invasive sensors and real-time systems that determine the glucose concentration in blood are highly important.

Several optical technologies have gained attention because of their ability to analyze samples without any prior manipulation [7, 8]. Near infrared spectroscopy [9–11], Raman spectroscopy [7, 8], and Fourier transform infrared (FTIR) spectroscopy [7, 12] have been investigated to develop non-invasive glucose monitoring sensors and systems. Most of the previously reported works use expensive laboratory equipment/software, which are very complex to use, hence limiting the development of an affordable device.

In the state of the art, frequency domain techniques are commonly applied to signal and speech processing, e.g. fast fourier transform (FFT), discrete wavelet transform (DWT), discrete cosine transform (DCT) and the Mel frequency cepstrum coefficients (MFCC). Being very effective and highly reported, we analyze their potential use.

The MFCC [13] is one of the best feature extraction techniques for speech recognition applications [14]. However, MFCC have not only been used in acoustic applications. In [15], the MFCC feature extraction is used for the diagnosis of diseases from corneal 2-D images first converted to 1-D signals, then the extracted features from MFCC are used to train and test a neural network. Dessouky et al. [16] have reported a system based on the identification of most significant features of Alzheimer's disease using the MFCC from MRI images to perform a computer aided diagnosis.

We found MFCC truly interesting for being applied to signals other than voice, due to some aspects: MFCC are the most common technique in speech processing, MFCC combine the use of two aforementioned techniques (FFT and DCT), the incorporation of logarithmic Mel filter banks break the linearity in MFCC analysis.

The aim of this work is to explore the potential of the MFCC as feature extractor for estimating the glucose concentration non-invasively by implementing and comparing five regression models using a low-cost setup: a laser-beam emitting diode was pointed to the user fingertip and a light dependent resistor (LDR) sensor serves as the photodiode for measuring the non-invasive signal with an Arduino microcontroller.

2 Materials and Methods

2.1 Beer – Lambert Law

In optics, the Beer-Lambert law provides a mathematical formulation that allows the calculation of the quantity of a material in a sample by means of its absorbance, *i.e.*, the absorption of light by a material is proportional to the quantity of material, so the absorbance value is also related to the transmittance [17]. The Beer-Lambert law forms a mathematical model of expressing how light is absorbed by matter; (a) the intensity of transmitted light decreases exponentially as concentration of the substance in the solution increases, and (b) the intensity of transmitted light decreases exponentially as the distance travelled through the substance increases. A simplified model of this law is shown in Eq. (1).

$$\text{absorption} = \frac{\text{intensity of incident light}}{\text{intensity of transmitted light}} \tag{1}$$

2.2 Mel Frequency Cepstral Coefficients

The cepstrum is defined as the inverse discrete Fourier transform (IDFT) of the log-magnitude of the discrete Fourier transform (DFT) of a signal, that is:

$$C(n) = F^{-1}(\log|F(X(n))|) \tag{2}$$

where F is the DFT and F^{-1} is the IDFT.

The use of Mel frequency cepstral coefficients (MFCC) is well-known for speech recognition, in which feature vectors are computed to represent speech signals. To this end, the signal is first divided into overlapping frames of n samples filtered with a Hamming window. After that, the fast Fourier transform (FFT) is calculated on each of the frames obtaining thus a frequency representation of the signal. The frequency is scaled logarithmically using the Mel filter bank, and then the logarithm is taken. Finally the MFCC are obtained by computing the discrete cosine transform (DCT) from the log-outputs of the Mel filter banks [13]. This procedure is depicted in the Fig. 1.

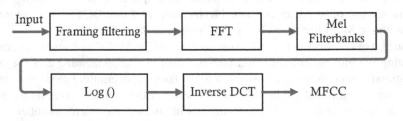

Fig. 1. MFCC feature extraction

3   Experimental Setup

The proposed system considers the interaction of an Arduino microcontroller unit (MCU) for data acquisition, based on the principle of Beer-Lambert law, in which the energy source is represented by a laser-beam emitting diode, and a light dependent resistor (LDR) sensor serves as the photodiode for measuring the light absorbance of the medium, represented by the user fingertip. As hypothesized by previous works [7–12, 17], we also assume that transmitted light may vary according to the glucose concentration in blood. The whole system is fully operated by three main stages: (*i*) signal acquisition, (*ii*) feature extraction and (*iii*) glucose level estimation. Figure 2 illustrates a block-diagram of the proposed system.

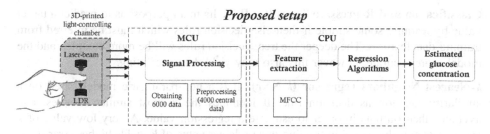

Fig. 2.   Block-diagram of the proposed system

3.1   Signal Acquisition

For signal acquisition stage, a 650 nm wavelength laser-beam was used pointing to the user fingertip. Below fingertip, a light diode resistor (LDR) is used as a photodiode for measuring the transmitted light across the finger. The setup used for this purpose is illustrated on Fig. 2. The Arduino microcontroller unit (MCU) measured the signal, during a 6 s lapse, with a sampling frequency of 1 kHz, obtaining a data vector of size 6000. Nevertheless, with the aim of avoid signal variations caused by initial and final finger placement movements, 1000 data were discarded at the beginning and the end of the measured signal, leaving only the 4000 central data.

3.2   Feature Extraction

The main intention of feature extraction is to transform a complex signal into representative values to be used by the prediction algorithms. Once the signal is fully acquired by the 8-bit MCU, the Mel frequency cepstral coefficients (MFCC) are computed by using the *python_speech_features* library. For this method we considered a window framing of 25 ms, and a Hamming filter for signal smoothing. Then, a fast Fourier transform (FFT) computes the signal spectrum to be filtered with the triangular Mel filter banks. The final cepstral coefficients are obtained by applying the discrete cosine transform (DCT) to the log values of Mel filters. The python mfcc function outputs the first 13 coefficients of the DCT representing the MFCC.

3.3   Glucose Level Estimation

Five regression models were fit and implemented to assess the glucose estimation: *(i)* ordinary-least-squares linear regression, *(ii)* classification and regression tree, *(iii)* k-nearest neighbors regression, *(iv)* random forest regression and *(v)* support vector regression. The five regression algorithms were implemented using the *sklearn* library with Python programming language, leaving the parameters for all regression models as defaults in the library, except for the SVR in which we select a scaled RBF kernel.

Ordinary Least Squares Linear Regression (OLS-LR). It is the simplest model for performing regression tasks. Its importance relies in the ability to represent data behavior with a truly simple model. In this study, the OLS-LR was implemented using the gradient descent algorithm for the error function minimization.

Classification and Regression Trees (CART). Its main purpose is to predict a target value by learning some simple if-then-else decision rules which must be inferred from training data features. The deeper the tree, decision rules will be more complex and the model more accurate; however this also may yield data overfitting.

***k*-Nearest Neighbors regressor (*k*-NNr).** It is a non-parametric model based on a similarity function as decision rule. It identifies the k most similar samples, and averages their outputs in order to estimate a regression value. A very low value of k tends to overfit the model in training data; a larger value of k yields higher error rates.

Random Forest regressor (RFr). It consists of an ensemble of decision trees trained on different sub-samples of training data set. Each sub-sample has the same number of features than the original data, when using bootstrap technique. The result of all decision trees is averaged to improve the predictive power and control over-fitting.

Suppor Vector Regression (SVR). The prediction is made by using a lineal function with a loss parameter representing the maximum tolerance for errors in the prediction with respect to actual output values. Non-linear predictions can be performed by mapping the training data into a higher dimensional data by using a kernel function.

4   Results and Discussion

4.1   Participants

A total of 58 participants were invited to be part of this study. At the same time, a written informed consent was obtained for each of the participants while explaining what the study is about. Participants were selected on a random basis, having an age average 29 ± 1.24 within a range of 25–38 years old.

4.2   Evaluation Metrics

The five regression algorithms were implemented using the *sklearn* library with Python programming language, using the 5-fold cross-validation scheme for model validation. Performance metrics used in this study were the mean absolute error (MAE) (see Eq. 3) and the Clarke error grid. The Clarke error grid is a plot divided into five regions to evaluate the reference glucose concentration versus the estimated. Regions A and B represent a good correlation measures. On the other hand, region C would lead to an unnecessary treatment while regions D and E are potentially dangerous because may confuse hyperglycaemia and hypoglycaemia treatments.

$$\text{MAE} = \frac{1}{n}\sum_{i=1}^{n} |y_i - \hat{y}_i| \tag{3}$$

4.3 Results

The experimental task consisted of a total of 100 repetitions of the 5-fold cross-validation for each regression model, where the average performance was reported. Figure 3 depicts the boxplot error graph resulting for all repetitions. The average of the MAE for all repetitions $\pm$ the standard deviation as well as the Clarke error grid analysis, are reported in Table 1.

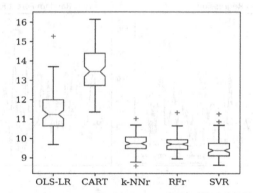

Fig. 3. Regression models boxplot for 100 repetitions of glucose estimation

Table 1. Results for 5-fold cross-validation on regression algorithms

Classifier	Mean absolute error	Clarke grid error region (%) (A – B – C – D – E)
Linear regression	11.4 ± 1.03	(84.5 – 15.5 – 0 – 0 – 0)
CART decision tree	13.52 ± 1.1	(86.2 – 13.8 – 0 – 0 – 0)
k-NN-regression	9.75 ± 0.44	(86.2 – 13.8 – 0 – 0 – 0)
Random forest regression	9.7 ± 0.38	(89.7 – 10.3 – 0 – 0 – 0)
Support vector regression	9.45 ± 0.51	(89.7 – 10.3 – 0 – 0 – 0)

Figure 4 shows graphically the glucose concentration obtained with the algorithms in contrast to the reference values measured with a commercial AccuCheck glucometer.

Finally, Fig. 5 illustrates the Clarke error grid for all algorithms. The best result, both for MAE and Clarke error grid analysis, was achieved by the SVR algorithm, with a MAE = 9.45 ± 0.51 and having 89.7% of estimated values in the region A, and 10.3% in the region B of Clarke error grid.

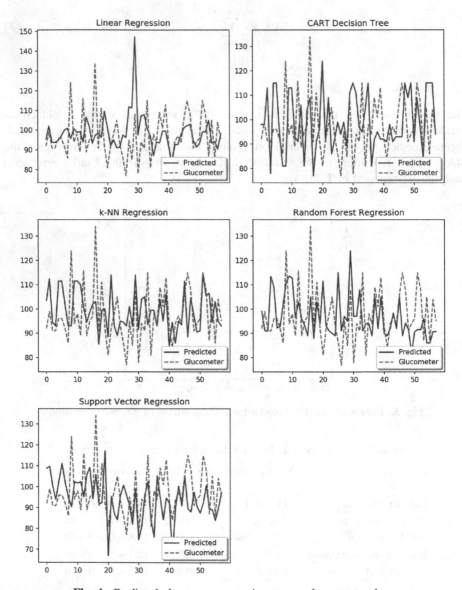

Fig. 4. Predicted glucose concentration versus glucometer values

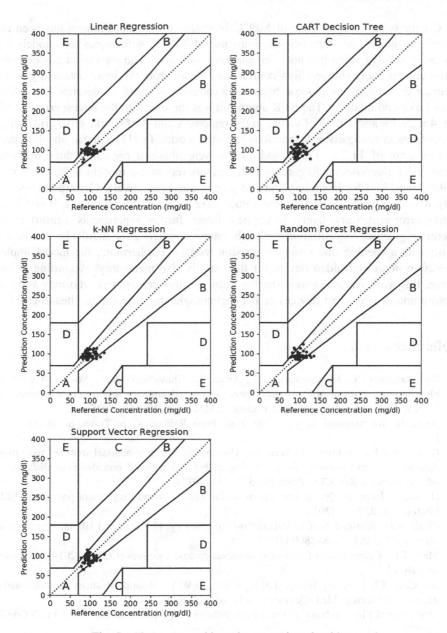

Fig. 5. Clarke error grid on the regression algorithms

5 Conclusions

This study explored the potential of using the MFCC, as feature extractor of non-invasive data, with well-known regression methods for glucose estimation as an alternative to existing models. Besides, the experimental low-cost setup used in the present study allows, and urges, the development of affordable devices for this purpose.

On the other hand, the use of MFCC in different other applications has been reported previously, nevertheless, the joint use of MFCC with regression models for glucose level estimation had not been analyzed until now. The regression models used in the current study showed high confidence to learn from the input data and give an accurate estimate of the glucose blood concentration of users, as described by MAE and Clarke grid analysis. The SVR algorithm was the one with the lowest error (MAE of 9.45; 89.7% and 10.3% of values in the regions A and B of Clarke error grid) being competitive in comparison to previous reported works. In [18] a mean absolute percentage error of 11.2%, 12.7% and 11.6% were obtained regarding three different commercial glucometers. Regarding [19], authors reported a root-mean-squared-error of 9.81 and 15.94 for laboratory test and glucometer, respectively. Correspondingly in [20], results of 87.71%, 10.32% and 1.96% were disclosed for regions A, B and D of Clarke error grid, respectively. In the near future, further experiments measuring the reference glucose concentration with laboratory standard tests should be conducted along with a specific fine tuning regression models. Furthermore, the model implementation in an embedded device for their use is also mandatory. According to the above, this work can serve as a starting point to other researchers who may want to explore and design smart devices or IoT technologies for e-health and health-care.

References

1. Ramasahayam, S., Koppuravuri, S.H., Arora, L., Chowdhury, S.R.: Noninvasive blood glucose sensing using near infra-red spectroscopy and artificial neural networks based on inverse delayed function model of neuron. J. Med. Syst. **39**, 166 (2015)
2. Atlas, D.: International diabetes federation. Press Release, Cape Town, South Africa, 4 (2006)
3. Guariguata, L., Whiting, D., Weil, C., Unwin, N.: The international diabetes federation diabetes atlas methodology for estimating global and national prevalence of diabetes in adults. Diabetes Res. Clin. Pract. **94**, 322–332 (2011)
4. Haxha, S., Jhoja, J.: Optical based noninvasive glucose monitoring sensor prototype. IEEE Photonics J. **8**, 1–11 (2016)
5. Clark, V.L., Kruse, J.A.: Clinical methods: the history, physical, and laboratory examinations. JAMA **264**, 2808–2809 (1990)
6. Mall, T.D.: Comparison of current continuous glucose monitors (CGMs) (2014). Accessed 16 July 14
7. So, C.-F., Choi, K.-S., Wong, T.K.S., Chung, J.W.Y.: Recent advances in noninvasive glucose monitoring. Med. Devices (Auckland, NZ) **5**, 45 (2012)
8. Shao, J., et al.: In vivo blood glucose quantification using Raman spectroscopy. PLoS One **7**, e48127 (2012)
9. Yatim, N.N.M., et al.: Noninvasive glucose level determination using diffuse reflectance near infrared spectroscopy and chemometrics analysis based on in vitro sample and human skin. In: 2014 IEEE Conference on Systems, Process and Control (ICSPC), pp. 30–35. IEEE (2014)
10. Bakker, A., Smith, B., Ainslie, P., Smith, K.: Near-infrared spectroscopy, applied aspects of ultrasonography in humans. Appl. Asp. Ultrason, Humans (2012)

11. Jeon, K.J., Hwang, I.D., Hahn, S.J., Yoon, G.: Comparison between transmittance and reflectance measurements in glucose determination using near infrared spectroscopy. J. Biomed. Opt. **11**, 14022 (2006)
12. Chen, T.-L., Lo, Y.-L., Liao, C.-C., Phan, Q.-H.: Noninvasive measurement of glucose concentration on human fingertip by optical coherence tomography. J. Biomed. Opt. **23**, 47001 (2018)
13. Davis, S., Mermelstein, P.: Comparison of parametric representations for monosyllabic word recognition in continuously spoken sentences. IEEE Trans. Acoust. **28**, 357–366 (1980)
14. Gaikwad, S., Gawali, B., Yannawar, P., Mehrotra, S.: Feature extraction using fusion MFCC for continuous marathi speech recognition. In: 2011 Annual IEEE India Conference (INDICON), pp. 1–5. IEEE (2011)
15. Tawfik, N., Eldin, M., Dessouky, M., AbdEl-samie, F.: Processing of corneal images with a cepstral approach. In: The 23rd International Conference on Computer Theory and Applications (ICCTA 2013), pp. 29–31 (2013)
16. Dessouky, M.M., Elrashidy, M.A., Taha, T.E., Abdelkader, H.M.: Effective features extracting approach using MFCC for automated diagnosis of Alzheimer's disease. Age (Omaha) **63**, 33–94 (2014)
17. Kocsis, L., Herman, P., Eke, A.: The modified Beer-Lambert law revisited. Phys. Med. Biol. **51**, N91 (2006)
18. Segman, Y.: Device and Method for Noninvasive Glucose Assessment. J. Diabetes Sci. Technol. **12**, 1159–1168 (2018)
19. Alarcón-Paredes, A., Rebolledo-Nandi, Z., Guzmán-Guzmán, I.P., Yáñez-Márquez, C., Alonso, G.A.: A non-invasive glucose level estimation in a multi-sensing health care monitoring system. Technol. Heal. Care. **26**, 203–208 (2018)
20. Monte-Moreno, E.: Non-invasive estimate of blood glucose and blood pressure from a photoplethysmograph by means of machine learning techniques. Artif. Intell. Med. **53**, 127–138 (2011)

Non-parametric Brain Tissues Segmentation via a Parallel Architecture of CNNs

Dante Mújica-Vargas[1(✉)], Alicia Martínez[1], Manuel Matuz-Cruz[2], Antonio Luna-Alvarez[1], and Mildred Morales-Xicohtencatl[1]

[1] Tecnológico Nacional de México/CENIDET, Cuernavaca, Morelos, México
{dantemv,amartinez}@cenidet.edu.mx
[2] Tecnológico Nacional de México/ITTapachula, Tapachula, Chiapas, México
mjmatuz@tapachula.tecnm.mx

Abstract. A fully automatic brain tissue segmentation framework is introduced in current paper, it is based on a parallel architecture of a specialized convolutional deep neuronal network designed to develop binary segmentation. The main contributions of this proposal imply its ability to segment brain RMI images of different acquisition modes, it does not require the initialization of any parameter; apart from the foregoing, it does not require any preprocessing stage to improve the quality of each slice. Experimental tests were developed considering BrainWeb and BraTS 2017 databases. The robustness and effectiveness of this proposal is verified by quantitative and qualitative results.

Keywords: Brain RMI segmentation · Parallel architecture · Convolutional deep neuronal network

1 Introduction

Magnetic resonance imaging is a medical modality used to guide the diagnosis process and the treatment planning. To do so, it needs to develop the images or slices segmentation, in order to detect and characterize the lesions, as well as to visualize and quantify the pathology severity. Based on their experiences and knowledge, medical specialists make a subjective interpretation of this type of images; in other words, a manual segmentation is performed. This task is long, painstaking and subject to human variability.

Brain MRIs in most cases do not have well-defined limits between the elements that compose them; in addition, they include non-soft tissues, as well as artifacts that can hinder segmentation. Despite all these inherent conditions, numerous automatic algorithms or techniques have been developed and introduced in state-of-the-art. Among approaches exclusively designed to segment the brain tissues stand out those that are based on the paradigm of fuzzy clustering as well as all its variants [3,4,6,11]. With the same purpose, hybrid methods

© Springer Nature Switzerland AG 2019
J. A. Carrasco-Ochoa et al. (Eds.): MCPR 2019, LNCS 11524, pp. 216–226, 2019.
https://doi.org/10.1007/978-3-030-21077-9_20

based on combinations of different paradigms of machine learning and optimization algorithms have also been presented, e.g. [7,8,10]. On the other hand, methods designed to segment brain tumors or other abnormalities have also been introduced, among which one can refer to [1,2]. For this task it is possible to affirm that in the state-of-the-art the proposals based on Deep Learning are the most novel and have the best results. The majority of these proposals yielded a high performance in the image processing task, specifically when these were brain magnetic resonance images. Nevertheless, after the pertinent analysis it was noted that most methods of them suffer from one or more challenges such as: training need, special handcrafted features (local or global), sensitive to initializations, many parameters that require a tuning, various processing stages, designed to segment just *T1*-weighted brain MRI images, among others. In this research paper, we concentrate on brain tissue image segmentation, the introduced proposal has the following special features in contrast with those abovementioned: (1) it is able to segment RMIs with different relaxation times such as *T1, T2, T1ce* and *Flair*, (2) it does not require the initialization of any parameter, such as the number of regions in which the slice will be segmented, (3) it does not require any preprocessing stage to improve the segmentation quality of each slice and (4) it does not need various processing stages to increase its performance.

The rest of this paper is organized as follow. In Sect. 2, a brief theoretical explanation about Deep Learning and the layers required is given. The parallel architecture of Convolutional Neural Networks is introduced in detail in Sect. 3. Experimental results and a comparative analysis with other current methods in the literature are presented in Sect. 4. In the final section the Conclusions are drawn and future work is outlined.

2 Background

2.1 Convolutional Deep Neural Networks

Deep architectures are conventional neural networks, which share the same common basic property. They process de information by means of hierarchical layers in order to understand representations and features from data in increasing levels of complexity. Among them, there exists different variants that have found success in specific domains. In this regard, *Convolutional Deep Neural Networks* (CNNs) highlight in most computer vision tasks. A CNN is a feedforward neural network with several types of special layers; typically, it has *convolutional* layers interspersed with spatial *pooling* layers, as well as *fully connected* layers such as a standard multi-layer neural network. Lead role is developed by *convolution layers*, since they can detect local features at different positions in the input feature maps by means of learnable kernels.

An explicit mathematical formulation of layers used in most conventional models is given in [12]. Let $x \in \mathbb{R}^{H \times W \times D}$ to be the imput map, K a bank of multi-dimensional filters, $f \in \mathbb{R}^{H' \times W' \times D \times D''}$, b the biases and $y \in \mathbb{R}^{H'' \times W'' \times D''}$ the output, last one is given as:

$$y_{i''j''d''} = b_{d''} + \sum_{i'=1}^{H'} \sum_{j'=1}^{W'} \sum_{d'=1}^{D} k_{i'j'd'} \times x_{S_h(i''-1)+i'-P_h^-,S_w(j''-1)+j'-P_w^-,d',d''}, \quad (1)$$

where $y_{i''j''d}$ is the feature map result after the convolution operation, $b_{d''}$ is the bias value added to convolution result between the $k_{i'j'd'}$ filter and the input neurons x. By other hand, $(P_h^-, P_h^+, P_w^-, P_w^+)$ stand for top-bottom-left-right paddings and (S_h, S_w) are subsampling strides of the output array. In order to obtain features with the attribute of being non-linear transformations of the input, an elementwise non-linearity is applied to the kernel convolution result by means of *activation functions*. There exist modern such as Rectified Linear Unit (ReLU), Leaky ReLU, Exponential Linear Units (ELU), among others; as well as classical ones e.g. step, sigmoid and tanh, that let to develop this process. To obtain a baseline accuracy it is convenient to use the standard ReLU (or its Leaky ReLU variant), which is defined simply as:

$$y_{ijd} = \max\{0, x_{ijd}\}, \quad (2)$$

Most of the time a convolution layer is followed by a spatial pooling layer. In detail, a *pooling layer* takes the feature map that occurred in the convolution layer and performs a condensate of the feature map, by taking small regions of this and performing an operation on it, usually proceeding by obtaining the maximum value (Max-Pooling) of each of these regions. This operator computes the maximum response of each feature channel in a $H' \times W'$ patch in next way:

$$y_{i''j''d''} = \max_{1 \leq i' \leq H', 1 \leq j' \leq W'} x_{i''+i'-1,j''+j'-1,d}, \quad (3)$$

resulting in an output of size $y \in \mathbb{R}^{H'' \times W'' \times D''}$ similar to the convolution operator. For the segmentation process, the so-called *deconvolution layer* is used. It aims at the reconstruction of the entrance maintaining a pattern of connectivity compatible with the convolution, mathematically it is given as:

$$y_{i''j''d''} = \sum_{d'=1}^{D} \sum_{i'=0}^{q(H',S_h)} \sum_{j'=0}^{q(W',S_w)} f_{1+S_h i'+m(i''+P_h^-,S_h),1+S_w j'+m(j''+P_w^-,S_w),d'',d'} \times$$
$$x_{1-i'+q(i''+P_h^-,S_h),1-j'+q(j''+P_w^-,S_w),d'}, \quad (4)$$

where $m(k, S) = (k-1) \bmod S, q(k, n) = \lfloor \frac{k-1}{S} \rfloor, (S_h, S_w)$ are the vertical and horizontal input upsampling factors, $(P_h^-, P_h^+, P_w^-, P_w^+)$ are the output crops, x and f are zero-padded as needed in the calculation.

2.2   U-Net

U-Net is a fully convolutional neuronal network model originally designed to develop a binary segmentation [9]; that is, the main object and the background of the image. This network is divided into two parts, in the first part, the images are subjected to a downward sampling, by means of convolution operations with a kernel of 3×3 each followed by a rectified linear unit (ReLU) and a maximum grouping layer of 2×2. The next part of the model consists of layers of deconvolution and convolution with 2×2 kernel, finally the output will correspond to a specific class of objects to be segmented, in Fig. 1 the U-Net model is shown graphically.

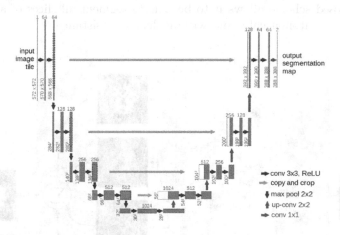

Fig. 1. U-Net model.

3   Parallel Architecture of CNNs for RMIs Segmentation

3.1   Proposed Scheme

Conventionally, it may be assumed that next five different regions can be found in a MRI slice: (1) White Matter (WM), (2) Gray Matter (GM), (3) Cerebral Spinal Fluid (CSF), (4) Abnormalities (ABN) and (5) Background. Nevertheless, it should be clarified that depending on the slice, not all regions may be present or the magnitude of their presence will be variant. Given the complexity that this consideration brings with it, most methods proposed in the state-of-the-art work only with the central slices of medical studies, mainly because they facilitate their segmentation by having a better delimitation in the regions.

To address this issue, a *parallel architecture of CNNs* is introduced in order to develop an automatic soft tissues recognition and their segmentation, for each slice of the whole medical study. The proposal is depicted in Fig. 2; it is basically comprised by four U-Nets models trained to work on a specific soft tissue. The operation of proposed scheme is quite intuitive, in the first instance any slice of a study must be entered into the system, then a binary segmentation is developed by each U-Net model. That is, all of them have to identify the pixels that correspond to the tissue for which it was trained, and therefore must be able to segment it. After that, the binary segmented images are merged in order to obtain the final segmentation. Two remarks must be stated: (1) Depending on the slice number, the different tissues should appear; in this situation, if the input image does not contain certain specific tissue, the U-Net in charge of segmenting it will return the corresponding label to the background of the image as a result. (2) If the study corresponds to a healthy patient, then there will be no abnormality or tumor, in the same way as in the previous remark, the result should be the label of the image background. This adaptive capacity of the proposed scheme allows it to be able to segment all slices of a complete medical study, automatically and without human assistance.

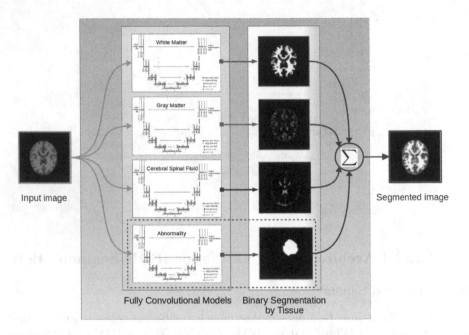

Fig. 2. Proposed parallel architecture of CNNs.

4   Experimental Setup

4.1   Data

In this research paper, two databases specialized in brain magnetic resonance imaging were considered. From BrainWeb [13] a normal anatomical model and one with abnormalities were used for training, while another normal model was used in the validation stage; each of them has 101 images with a size of 256×256 pixels with $8-$bits depth. For a real and objective evaluation of our proposal, tests were done with BraTS 2017 [5], it consists of 210 medical studies with existing Glioblastoma and 75 with Glioma and 47 more without classification. On the other hand, each study has RMIs in modalities T1, T1ce, T2, Flair, as well as their respective ground truth images. For each modality there are 155 images of $8-$bits with a size of 240×240 pixels.

4.2 Tuning

In order to accelerate the training of the four neural networks required to segment the different tissues, all characteristic maps of low and medium level of the original trained U-Net were transferred to each network, and only the high level ones were trained. By other hand, it is a well-known fact that data augmentation is essential to teach the network the desired invariance and robustness properties, when only few training samples are available. In our particular case, BrainWeb was used as a training information source. This repository has only one study with 101 soft tissue images, for which it was required to increase the process of information. In Table 1 all operations carried out to increase the information are summarized. Scale stands out for 3 different image sizes, rotation implies 120 possible images if an angle of 3° is taken into account; besides, 4 quadrants where considered for translating, as well as without translation. In addition to 181, 800 images to train each neural network, their respective ground-truth images were required. During the training phase, several preliminary tests were developed to make the meta parameter tuning for each network. In order to obtain the best results in the test phase it is suggested: (a) color depth of 8−bits, (b) TIFF image format, (c) Adaptive Moment Estimation (ADAM) optimization method, (d) 1000 epochs and (e) learning rate of 0.001.

Table 1. Data augmentation summary.

Scale	Rotation	Translation (quadrants)	No. images
100%	0°, 3°, · · · , 360°	Non-translation	101 × 120 = 12, 120
75%	0°, 3°, · · · , 360°	Non-translation	101 × 120 = 12, 120
50%	0°, 3°, · · · , 360°	Non-translation	101 × 120 = 12, 120
100%	0°, 3°, · · · , 360°	I, II, III, IV	101 × 120 × 4 = 48, 480
75%	0°, 3°, · · · , 360°	I, II, III, IV	101 × 120 × 4 = 48, 480
50%	0°, 3°, · · · , 360°	I, II, III, IV	101 × 120 × 4 = 48, 480
			Total = 181, 800

4.3 Evaluation

In order to evaluate quantitative and objectively the image segmentation performance as well as the robustness three metrics were considered in this study. To measure the segmentation accuracy, we used the Misclassification Ratio (MCR), which is given by:

$$MCR = \frac{misclassified\ pixels}{overall\ number\ of\ pixels} \times 100 \tag{5}$$

where, the values can ranges from 0 to 100, a minimum value means better segmentation. Dice Similarity Coefficient is used to quantify the overlap between segmented results with ground-truth; it is expressed in terms of true positives (TP), false positives (FP), and false negatives (FN) as:

$$Dice = \frac{2 \cdot TP}{2 \cdot TP + FP + FN} \tag{6}$$

where $TP + FP + TN + FN$ = number of brain tissue pixels in a brain MR image. In this metric a higher value means better agreement with respect to ground-truth. In addition to stated metrics, the Intersection-Over-Union (IOU) metric was also considered. This is defined by:

$$IOU = \frac{TP}{TP + FP + FN} \tag{7}$$

The IOU metric takes values in $[0, 1]$ with a value of 1 indicating a perfect segmentation.

5   Results and Discussion

The performance of the proposed scheme (for convenience it will be identified as PA-CNNs) was compared with other methods mentioned previously in the introductory section, such as the Chaotic Firefly Integrated Fuzzy C-Means (C-FAFCM) [4], Discrete Cosine Transform Based Local and Nonlocal FCM (DCT-LNLFCM) [11], Generalized Rough Intutionistic Fuzzy C-Means (GRIFCM) [6], Particle Swarm Optimization - Kernelized Fuzzy Entropy Clustering with Spatial Information and Bias Correction (PSO-KFECSB) [10]. All of them were implemented in the MATLAB R2018a environment, while for ours we used CUDA+CuDNN+TensorFlow+Keras, that is, conventional frameworks and libraries for Deep Learning, as well as a GPU Nvidia Titan X.

5.1   Segmentation of a Simulated BrainWeb Study

In this experiment, a fully study was simulated was simulated using the Brain-Web database (consisting in 181 images). The parameters were established as: T1 modality, normal phantom, 3% of noise level and a non-uniform intensity level of 20%. A quantitative comparison in terms of MCR, Dice and IOU is summarized in Table 2. The results reveal that proposed clustering algorithm has a superior performance in terms of segmentation quality than all compared methods. This is mainly due to the fact that the parallel architecture is robust in the presence of a noise level like the pre-established one. To visually exemplify the results obtained, the slice_071 was taken as sample. As can be seen in Fig. 3, in the presence of Gaussian noise, all comparative methods were affected with loss and gain information phenomenons, which directly impacts their quantitative results. On the other hand, the proposed scheme obtained the result with greater similarity to the ground-truth, which confirms its balance in the quantitative and qualitative results.

Table 2. Average performance on BrainWeb study.

Modality	Metric	C-FAFCM	DCT-LNLFCM	GRIFCM	PSO-KFECSB	PA-CNNs
T1	MCR	8.450	10.681	8.923	9.038	7.667
	Dice	0.912	0.755	0.858	0.836	0.931
	IOU	0.909	0.743	0.884	0.815	0.924

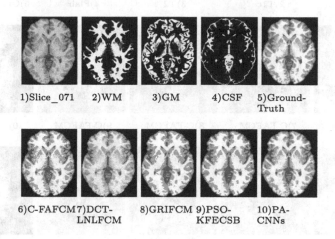

1)Slice_071   2)WM   3)GM   4)CSF   5)Ground-
                                                 Truth

6)C-FAFCM 7)DCT-   8)GRIFCM 9)PSO-   10)PA-
          LNLFCM   KFECSB   CNNs

Fig. 3. BrainWeb segmentation results.

5.2 Segmentation of a Real BraTs-2017 Study

A convincing way to know the true performance of the proposed method is to subject it to the task of tissues segmentation of real brain magnetic resonance images. In this regard, the second experiment is related with the segmentation of images with modalities T1, T1ce, T2 and Flair taken from the BraTS-2017

Table 3. Average performance on BraTS-2017 study.

Modality	Metric	C-FAFCM	DCT-LNLFCM	GRIFCM	PSO-KFECSB	PA-CNNs
T1	MCR	8.450	10.681	9.338	9.423	7.705
	Dice	0.912	0.755	0.863	0.815	0.931
	IOU	0.909	0.743	0.856	0.786	0.924
T1ce	MCR	9.141	11.925	10.434	11.026	7.191
	Dice	0.884	0.705	0.877	0.729	0.948
	IOU	0.905	0.760	0.873	0.848	0.951
T2	MCR	9.743	10.986	9.708	10.003	7.939
	Dice	0.873	0.688	0.812	0.760	0.918
	IOU	0.872	0.667	0.752	0.717	0.911
Flair	MCR	9.743	11.593	9.005	10.986	7.939
	Dice	0.873	0.688	0.760	0.722	0.920
	IOU	0.872	0.667	0.752	0.717	0.909

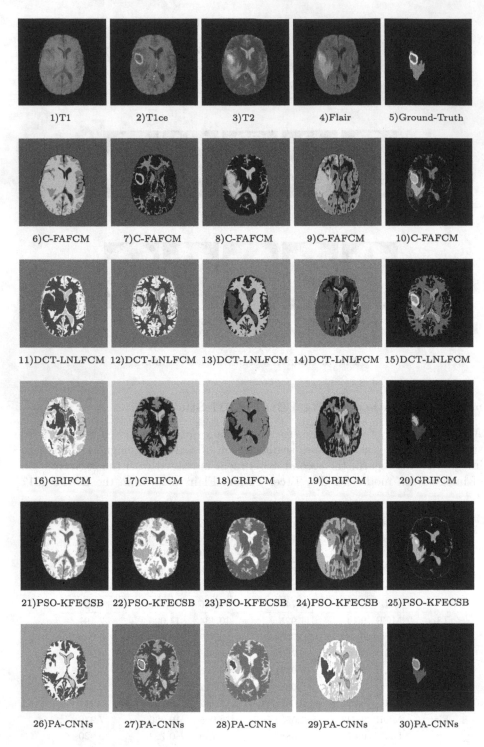

Fig. 4. BraTS17_2013_10_1 segmentation results.

database; specifically, the Glioblastoma Brats17_2013_10_1 study. The quantitative evaluation was done considering the metrics established above, a summary of these is presented in Table 3. The numerical results reveal a superior performance of the segmentation method proposed in all the metrics considered, as well as all exposition modalities.

A sample image and the segmentation provided by all algorithms evaluated in this experiment are depicted in Fig. 4, it is possible to see that just the proposed algorithm was able to segment images with different modalities. On the other hand, all the other methods presented problems of loss of information in the segmented regions, and in some cases they were not even able to segment the images in the 4 established regions. In the BraTS challenge, primary task is the Multimodal Brain Tumor Segmentation, in this regard a good segmentation of the images in these modalities can guarantee the identification and segmentation of brain tumors. With the results obtained by the proposed algorithm and depicted in Figs. 4.26 to 4.30, it is possible to affirm its ability to detect abnormalities in the brain, unlike the comparative methods.

6 Conclusions and Future Improvements

In this research paper, a parallel architecture of Convolutional Neural Networks was stated. The experimentation carried out on simulated and real images allow us to sustain the following qualities: (1) It has the capacity to identify and segment the regions of an MRI without prior specification of the regions, that is, it carries out identification and segmentation autonomously, (2) It has the ability to segment images without prior processing and in different modalities or exposure times such as T1, T1ce, T2 and Flair, (3) It is robust to most artifacts in this type of magnetic resonance imaging of the brain, (4) It has the ability to generalize, that is, although it has been trained with a simulated database, it is capable of segmenting real images. As future work will be done the training using the BraTS database, which is expected to increase the performance of the proposed architecture, as well as to specifically target brain tumors.

Acknowledgement. The authors are grateful to CONACYT, as well as Tecnológico Nacional de México/CENIDET for their support trough the project 5628.19-P so-called "Sistema embebido para asistencia de conducción basado en Lógica Difusa Tipo-2".

References

1. Angulakshmi, M., Priya, G.L.: Brain tumour segmentation from MRI using superpixels based spectral clustering. J. King Saud Univ.-Comput. Inf. Sci. (2018). https://www.sciencedirect.com/science/article/pii/S1319157817303476
2. Charron, O., Lallement, A., Jarnet, D., Noblet, V., Clavier, J.B., Meyer, P.: Automatic detection and segmentation of brain metastases on multimodal MR images with a deep convolutional neural network. Comput. Biol. Med. **95**, 43–54 (2018)

3. Ganesh, M., Naresh, M., Arvind, C.: MRI brain image segmentation using enhanced adaptive fuzzy K-means algorithm. Intell. Autom. Soft Comput. **23**(2), 325–330 (2017)
4. Ghosh, P., Mali, K., Das, S.K.: Chaotic firefly algorithm-based fuzzy C-means algorithm for segmentation of brain tissues in magnetic resonance images. J. Vis. Commun. Image Represent. **54**, 63–79 (2018)
5. Menze, B.H., et al.: The multimodal brain tumor image segmentation benchmark (BRATS). IEEE Trans. Med. Imaging **34**(10), 1993 (2015)
6. Namburu, A., Samayamantula, S.K., Edara, S.R.: Generalised rough intuitionistic fuzzy C-means for magnetic resonance brain image segmentation. IET Image Process. **11**(9), 777–785 (2017)
7. Narayanan, A., Rajasekaran, M.P., Zhang, Y., Govindaraj, V., Thiyagarajan, A.: Multi-channeled MR brain image segmentation: a novel double optimization approach combined with clustering technique for tumor identification and tissue segmentation. Biocybern. Biomed. Eng. **39**(2), 350–381 (2018)
8. Pham, T.X., Siarry, P., Oulhadj, H.: Integrating fuzzy entropy clustering with an improved PSO for MRI brain image segmentation. Appl. Soft Comput. **65**, 230–242 (2018)
9. Ronneberger, O., Fischer, P., Brox, T.: U-net: convolutional networks for biomedical image segmentation. In: Navab, N., Hornegger, J., Wells, W.M., Frangi, A.F. (eds.) MICCAI 2015. LNCS, vol. 9351, pp. 234–241. Springer, Cham (2015). https://doi.org/10.1007/978-3-319-24574-4_28
10. Senthilkumar, C., Gnanamurthy, R.: A fuzzy clustering based MRI brain image segmentation using back propagation neural networks. Cluster Comput., 1–8 (2018). https://link.springer.com/article/10.1007/s10586-017-1613-x
11. Singh, C., Bala, A.: A DCT-based local and non-local fuzzy C-means algorithm for segmentation of brain magnetic resonance images. Appl. Soft Comput. **68**, 447–457 (2018)
12. Vedaldi, A., Lenc, K., Ehrhardt, S., Jaderberg, M.: MatConvNet: CNNs for MATLAB (2014)
13. Brain Web: Simulated brain database. McConnell Brain Imaging Centre, Montreal Neurological Institute, McGill (2004). http://brainweb.bic.mni.mcgill.ca/brainweb

Automatic Detection and Classification of Hearing Loss Conditions Using an Artificial Neural Network Approach

Edgar Mosqueda Cárdenas, José P. de la Rosa Gutiérrez,
Lina María Aguilar Lobo, and Gilberto Ochoa Ruiz$^{(\boxtimes)}$

Universidad Autónoma de Guadalajara, Zapopan Jalisco, Mexico
{lina.aguilar,gilberto.ochoa}@edu.uag.mx

Abstract. The auditory dysfunction is one of the most frequent disabilities, this condition can be diagnosed with an electroencephalogram modality called auditory evoked potentials (AEP). In this paper, we present a machine learning implementation to automatically detect and classify hearing loss conditions based on features extracted from synthetically generated brainstem auditory evoked potentials, a necessity given the scarcity of full-fledged datasets. The approach is based on a multi-player perceptron, which has demonstrated to be a useful and powerful tool in this domain. Preliminary results show very encouraging results, with accuracy results above 90% for a variety of hearing loss conditions; this system is to be deployed as hardware implementation for creating an affordable and portable medical device, as reported in previous work.

Keywords: Hearing loss · Diagnostic · BAEP · Latency · Neural Networks

1 Introduction

The auditory dysfunction is one of the most frequent disabilities and it's usually caused either by genetic characteristics or prenatal factors or by infections that cause damage to the auditory pathways. According to data in the national survey of the demographic dynamics of 2014 (INEGI), 6% of the population (7.2 million) have a disability, of which 33.5% has auditory issues. Therefore, detecting this condition in the early stages, can mitigate the consequences. Several of these problems can be diagnosed using an electroencephalogram modality called auditory evoked potentials (AEP), a study which is usually performed on non-cooperative and/or on pediatric patients. The use of Artificial Neural Networks (ANNs) has shown to be effective in the field of medicine where they have been used to detect various diseases [1, 2]. Given that such systems can help in the diagnosis of diseases such as hearing loss, a great deal of research has been carried in this domain, which have aimed at investigating the use of ANNs to detect hearing loss in neonatal patients [6]. The ANN extracts features in the frequency domain to determine whether or not a hearing condition is present.

Such tools are increasingly necessary for estimating auditory levels in order to assess the degree of hearing loss in pediatric and handicapped patients.

© Springer Nature Switzerland AG 2019
J. A. Carrasco-Ochoa et al. (Eds.): MCPR 2019, LNCS 11524, pp. 227–237, 2019.
https://doi.org/10.1007/978-3-030-21077-9_21

Current technologies could exploit reliable measurement techniques such as EEG, developing an intelligent model for estimation auditory levels. In this paper, we undertake such an approach for proposing a system for automatically detecting a classifying various hearing loss conditions. Several related works have been proposed the automatic or semi-automatic evaluation of hearing loss conditions [13]. Some of these include the Raleigh test, the Watson's U2 test, the Kuiper's test, the Hodges–Ajne's test, the Cochran's Q-test, and the Friedman test. For a more detailed study, the reader is directed an excellent survey in the topic [14].

The present work is not based on the frequency domain, but we use a multilayer perceptron (MLP) trained with time-domain measurements of BAEP signals, since it makes our architecture simpler to implement. For instance, we take into account the absolute values of BAEP features such as the amplitudes and latencies. These are the features used by doctors to assess the severity of various hearing loss conditions and makes the results more intuitive. This article presents a diagnostic model based on a multilayer perceptron (MLP), with synthetic data simulating patients of 6, 12 and 24 months of age, as it will be described later in the article.

This paper is organized as follows: in Sect. 2, we describe the use and characteristics of the BAEP signals. In Sect. 3 we explain the proposed system based on the MLP architecture. In Sect. 4, we delve into the obtained results and in Sect. 5 we conclude the article, pointing at future extensions and other possible directions.

2 Neurophysiological Signal Present in BAEP

The electroencephalography is a non-invasive technique widely used in the diagnosis of many neurological diseases and problems associated with brain dynamics [16]. These signals are indicators of the cerebral electrical activity that can help to interpret several brain conditions. Therefore, understanding the characteristics of the BAEP signals, used as the foundation of this work, is vital. The next section will be devoted to this purpose and to provide more context to their use in hearing loss conditions.

2.1 Auditory Evoked Potential

When an auditory stimulus is provided to the human brain, there is a potential peak referred to as auditory evoked potential (AEP) in the auditory cortex, from which on can assess the auditory capacity of a patient, through the analysis of these evoked responses. Thus, AEP is a modality of electroencephalography that represents variations of voltage in a sensitive nerve pathway after or during extrinsic acoustic stimulation, which captures and the neuroelectric activity generated as responses to a stimulus.

The AEP test consists of the stimulation of the auditory path through a beep signal that stimulates most of the cochlea, i.e. the areas with frequency higher than 1,500 Hz. This mechanical stimulus is transformed by the organ of Corti into an electrical stimulus that travels the auditory path to reach the cerebral cortex. From the moment the organ of Corti is stimulated until the arrival of the information to the cortex, approximately 300 ms pass, and this period known as latency.

The auditory pathway consists of a series of nerve stations as depicted in Fig. 1. Typically, the applied stimulus in BAEP tests goes through to nervous system, producing a signal that can be observed on top of the figure.

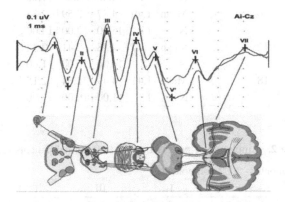

Fig. 1. The wave pattern obtained by AEP and the associated latencies (see Table 1).

The signal is composed of a series of waves, with distinct peaks and valleys. The waves are of clinical interest and can be classified as follows:

- Wave I: electrical activity of the spiral ganglion.
- Wave II: posterior part of the anteroventral cochlear nucleus and behind zone of the posteroventral cochlear nucleus.
- Wave III: anterior part of the anteroventral cochlear nucleus ipsilateral and medial nucleus of the contralateral trapezoid body.
- Wave IV: isolateral and contralateral cells of the olive superior medial.
- Wave V: cells of the lateral lemniscus and/or inferior colliculus.

The latencies of each wave are measured and categorized as I-III, I-V and III-V. The normal latencies at 80 dB for healthy adult individuals in a normal environment are [16, 17]: Wave I (1.5 ms), Wave III (3.75 ms) and Wave V (5.5 ms).

The information contained in those 5 waves are of clinical interest. The waves are presented in time limits clinically known as latencies, as we have described previously and is depicted on Fig. 1. The wave patterns formed by the acoustic stimulus are shown in Fig. 1 as well, whereas Tables 1 and 2 summarize the most important aspects of the latencies and the amplitudes, respectively.

Table 1. Mean latencies of 165 normal patients of different ages [3, 4].

Age in months		Y1: I	Y2: V-I	Y3: I-III	Y4: III-V
0	Mean	1.58	5.18	2.77	2.43
	N	14	14.00	10.00	11.00
6	Mean	1.49	4.87	2.59	2.35
	N	17	16.00	13.00	12.00
12	Mean	1.47	4.58	2.41	2.32
	N	18	16.00	16.00	11.00
18	Mean	1.41	4.49	2.34	2.15
	N	11	11.00	10.00	7.00

(column header note: "Time difference in the waves down shown in milliseconds")

Table 2. Amplitude of peaks in AEP of 50 normal patients [3, 4]

Age in months	AEP components			
	I	II	III	IV-V
1	0.54 ± 0.08	0.45 ± 0.09	0.59 ± 0.08	0.48 ± 0.06
10	0.51 ± 0.04	0.75 ± 0.15	0.86 ± 0.10	0.82 ± 0.07
30	0.35 ± 0.03	0.59 ± 0.10	0.72 ± 0.08	0.68 ± 0.07
50	0.17 ± 0.02	0.35 ± 0.07	0.40 ± 0.07	0.50 ± 0.06

Two typical patterns of the BAEP (Brain-stem auditory evoked potentials) signal are shown in Fig. 2. The recorded signals were classified as normal (a) and abnormal (b) by the physician, based on the information contained of peaks and encoded in the tables.

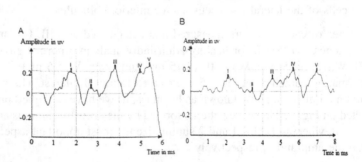

Fig. 2. Typical waveform BAEP: (A) normal patient and (B) subnormal patient [15].

The statistical differences between the age groups is important, since the amplitude of the waves change as the patient gets older. Tables 1 and 2 clearly show those statistical differences. The mean amplitudes and the values of the BAEP components for the 5 age groups are given for stimulation with hearing levels of 80 and 60 dB in the tables.

3 Implementation of the Proposed MLP-Based Architecture

In order to implement a classification system for BAEP signals based on an MLP approach, a data set for training and testing is necessary. Unfortunately, the data collection involves certain obstacles such as the availability of samples of interest or legal restrictions in the collection and handling of patient information.

Our solution to this problem has been to generate synthetic data for training and testing [14], based on characteristics extracted from real samples as shown in Fig. 3.

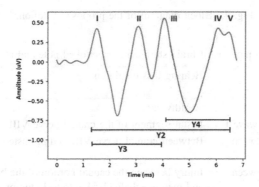

Fig. 3. A synthetically generated signal of a 6-month-old patient at 80 dB

As it can be seen, the generated signals are very similar to the real signals depicted in Fig. 2, as the values of these signals are filtered to obtain the maximum amplitude peaks in the waves I, II, III and V. Once these amplitudes are obtained, the latencies are extracted, using the temporal differences between the different peaks or waves (IV, I-III, III-V) which are subsequently used by our machine learning application.

The proposed solution is divided into two stages, the first part deals with the generation of synthetic data. The generated dataset simulates a BAEP sampled in the time domain with the objective for training and testing our MLP algorithm. The second stage deals with feature extraction (Tables 1 and 2), which are used as inputs to the MLP.

The MLP classifies the extracted data and as output provides a four-bit code according to a condition as shown in Table 3. The block diagram of the proposed solution is shown in Fig. 4, where we have a block that includes three main components. The first block retrieves the synthetically generated BAEP signal. The second block performs some preprocessing on the signal (i.e., since the sampled signal has different values it is necessary to take the values of interest from the BAEP). Once these values have been extracted, we add them to our training dataset. This dataset is then passed to the MLP classifier, which categorizes the hearing condition and codifies its into 4 output bits, where each encoded binary value represents an ailment, as summarized in Table 3.

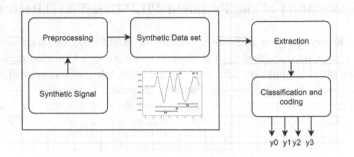

Fig. 4. Block diagram of the proposed solution.

Table 3. Global patterns of brain stem auditory evoked potential abnormalities [4]

Diagnosis	Hearing loss condition	Binary coding
Normal values	Healthy ear	0000
Prolonged latency in wave I	Distal segment of the cranial nerve VIII	0001
Prolonged latency between peaks I-III	Between cranial nerve VIII and brainstem bridge	0010
Prolonged latency between peaks III-V	Injury between the caudal portion of the brainstem and mesencephalon bridge (attack, tumor, multiple sclerosis, intracranial hemorrhage, malformation, etc.)	0011
Prolonged latency between peaks IV-V and III-V	Rostral section of the brainstem or mesencephalon bridge and vestibulocochlear nerve or brainstem bridge	0100
Wave III absent with presence of I and V	Hearing loss at mild and moderate levels	0101
Wave V absent with presence of I and III	Normal variation	0110
Wave V absent with normal of I and III	Probably auditory radiations to the primary auditory cortex	0111
Absence of waves	Severe hearing loss	1000
Excess in amplitude radius V/I	Possible hearing impairment	1001
Absence of waves except I (and possibly II)	Brain death	1010

The proposed MLP architecture is depicted in Fig. 5. The number of neurons in the input layer is 5, in order to encode a vector that includes values for age, latencies and amplitudes of wavelengths that go from wave I to wave IV-V. The number of neurons in the intermediate layer was chosen based on an experimental test that consisted on varying the neurons of this hidden layer with 5 neurons per iteration until reaching 25 neurons within a single hidden layer. The output layer consists of are 4 neurons. The results of these experimental iterations will be discussed later in the paper.

The pathologies tackled by our approach are summarized in Table 3, which contains a description of each of the most important pathologies associated with the average variances described in Tables 1 and 2. The last column shows the associated coding that we have chosen as outputs of MLP algorithm, as will be explained in Sect. 4.

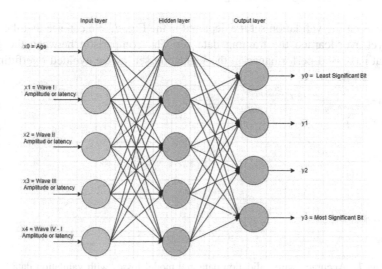

Fig. 5. Implemented MLP algorithm and its relationship with the BAEP signals

According to Cybenko's theorem, the sigmoid function [10–12] is used in the intermediate hidden layer and relu or linear regression [9] in the output layer used for convolutional networks [8] and is used in this classifier for the smallest error generated with the logistic function [7]. In order to validate the designed classifier, cross-validation is usually employed to assess the performance of machine learning models [5]. However, in our particular case, as we counted with limited dataset of synthetically generated feature vectors, we made use of use k-fold cross-validation, as is typical in such scenarios. Figure 6 shows the accuracy and loss plots in the training set; the model could probably be trained a little longer, since the trend of precision continues to increase with more iterations.

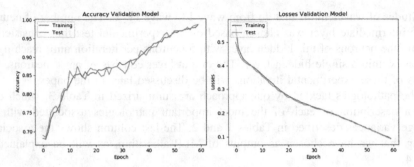

Fig. 6. Accuracy with training data and model losses with training data.

The tests on the validation set are depicted in the Fig. 7. We can see that the model has not yet over-learned the training data set. The comparison between the graphs shows that increased performance in the validation set, as we avoided overfitting.

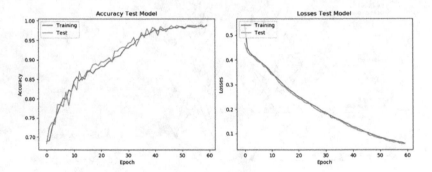

Fig. 7. Accuracy with validation data and model losses with validation data.

4   Results and Discussion

The final MLP implementation through the modification of the number of neurons in the hidden layer, and then comparing the results, gradually increasing the number of training epochs. In Table 4, we go into detail of these variations in the hidden layer of the MLP, showing the associated impact the in the model accuracy.

Table 4. Model selection method through the modification of the MLP architecture.

Neurons in the input layer	Neurons in the hidden layer	Neurons in the output layer	Epochs	Validation accuracy	Test accuracy
5	5	4	60	96.19%	96.38%
5	10	4	60	96.39%	96.91%
5	15	4	60	96.59%	97.19%
5	20	4	60	96.99%	97.79%
5	25	4	60	97.39%	98.19%

After the performance training and validation tests, synthetic signals are generated from patients of 6, 12 and 20 months of age, simulating a healthy patient. As mentioned earlier, the signals are processed in the time domain, although the signs are generated using a combination of Fourier and Wavelet transforms. The data filtered and used by our MPL algorithm, called "experimental values" are the following:

Table 5. Filtered data of the synthetic wave fed to our MLP algorithm

Age (months)	Latency wave I	Latency wave I-V	Latency wave I-II	Latency wave III-V
6	1.51	4.87	2.52	2.35
12	1.4	4.6	2.4	2.2
20	1.4	4.5	2.4	2.1

The similarity of the filtered data shown in Table 5 with respect to real data [3], can be readily observed. Therefore, this signal generation process is an important contribution of our work, but it has not been explored in detail in this paper due to space limitations.

Once the experimental values are entered into our MLP based algorithm, and the training values are compared with the experimental values.

Table 6. Output matrix, expected response by the network zeroes indicate that there are not ailments.

Y_0	Y_1	Y_2	Y_3
0	0	0	0
0	0	0	0
0	0	0	0

After the validation of the model, the perceptron makes the prediction with the experimental values, these values represent a patient without any handicaps or hearing loss conditions, therefore we show the results in Table 6 as expected from those in Table 3.

5 Conclusion

Neural network models have been used in a variety of other clinical medicine settings, but to our knowledge this is the first time it has been used to help diagnose hearing loss. The preliminary results presented in this seem rather promising, as we have obtained very good accuracies using only temporal features. It must be noted that we have undertaken such an approach due to the lack of readily available datasets containing

BAEP signals, although some works like ours are exploring the same feature generation avenue and such datasets should me made public for improving the research in this domain.

As future work, we plan to strength the signal generation process, making a more thorough study as well, to include a validation against noisy measurements. Also, we would like to carry out a comparative study using other machine learning algorithms as KNN or SVM and see how they fare in comparison with the proposed approach.

However, as explained at the beginning of this article, the rationale for this initial research is to use the proposed MLP system as a validation stage, upon which more complex feature combinations can be explored. Furthermore, we plan to integrate the MLP into an SoC FPGA for implementing a full-fledged low-cost diagnosis device and other modules are expected to produce the synthetically generation signals or in the future, to pre-process actual BAEP signals from real patients using an electronic acquisition system and the FPGA for filtering the BAEP signals and extracting the corresponding features. In this sense, the highly parallel architecture and regular architecture of the MLP or other ANNs is especially suited for implementation in reconfigurable devices and for its integration into a signal processing pipeline, which is intended as the next stage of this project.

References

1. Yan, H., Jiang, Y., Zheng, J., Peng, C., Li, Q.: A multilayer perceptron-based medical decision support system for heart disease diagnosis. Expert Syst. Appl. **30**(2), 272–281 (2006)
2. Yan, H., Zheng, J., Jiang, Y., Peng, C., Li, Q.: Development of a decision support system for heart disease diagnosis using multilayer perceptron. In: Proceedings of the 2003 International Symposium on Circuits and Systems, ISCAS 2003, vol. 5, p. pp. V-709–V-712. IEEE, 2003 May
3. Mochizuki, Y., et al.: Developmental changes of brainstem auditory evoked potentials (BAEPs) in normal human subjects from infants to young adults. Brain Dev. **4**(2), 127–136 (1982). https://doi.org/10.1016/s0387-7604(82)80006-5
4. Psatta, D.M., Matei, M.: Age-dependent amplitude variation of brain-stem auditory evoked potentials. Electroencephalography Cli. Neurophysiol./Evoked Potentials Sect. **71**(1), 27–32 (1988). https://doi.org/10.1016/0168-5597(88)90016-0
5. Cover, T.M.: Learning in pattern recognition. In: Watanabe, S. (ed.) Methodologies of Pattern Recognition, pp. 111–132. Academic Press, New York (1969)
6. Sriraam, N.: EEG based automated detection of auditory loss: a pilot study. Expert Syst. Appl. **39**(1), 723–731 (2012)
7. LeCun, Y.A., Bottou, L., Orr, G.B., Müller, K.-R.: Efficient BackProp. In: Montavon, G., Orr, G.B., Müller, K.-R. (eds.) Neural Networks: Tricks of the Trade. LNCS, vol. 1524, pp. 9–50. Springer, Heidelberg (1998). https://doi.org/10.1007/978-3-642-35289-8_3
8. Glorot, X., Bordes, A., Bengio, Y.: Deep sparse rectifier neural networks. In: AISTATS (2011)
9. Hahnloser, R., Sarpeshkar, R., Mahowald, M.A., Douglas, R.J., Seung, H.S.: Digital selection and analogue amplification coexist in a cortex-inspired silicon circuit. Nature **405**, 947–951 (2000)

10. Escolano, F.: Inteligencia Artificial. Editorial Paraninfo, Madrid (2003)
11. Hernández López, L.: Predicción y optimización de emisio-nes y consumo mediante redes neuronales (1 ed, 2 imp edición). Editorial Reverté, S.A., p. 53 (2006)
12. Hadeler, K.: « 42 ». Matemáticas para biólogos (1 ed, 2 imp edición). Editorial Reverté, S. A., p. 138 (1982)
13. Narasingarao, M.R., Manda, R., Sridhar, G.R., Madhu, K., Rao, A.A.: A clinical decision support system using multilayer perceptron neural network to assess well being in diabetes. JAPI **57**, 127–133 (2009)
14. Valderrama, J.T., et al.: Automatic quality assessment and peak identification of auditory brainstem responses with fitted parametric peaks. Comput. Methods Programs Biomed. **114** (3), 262–275 (2014)
15. Jaderberg, M., et al.: Synthetic data and artificial neural networks for natural scene text recognition. ArXiv.org, June 2014
16. Rodríguez Sáenz, E., Otero Costas, J.: Maduración de la respuesta auditiva del troncocerebral. Rev Neurofisiol Clin. **3**, 3–4 (1990)
17. Peters, J.: An Automated infant screener using advanced evoked response technology. Hearing J. **39**, 25–30 (1987)

Asymmetry Level in Cleft Lip Children Using Dendrite Morphological Neural Network

Griselda Cortés$^{(\boxtimes)}$, Fabiola Villalobos , and Mercedes Flores

Tecnológico de Estudios Superiores de Ecatepec,
Av. Tecnológico s/n, Col. Valle de Anáhuac,
55210 Ecatepec de Morelos, Estado de México, Mexico
{gcortes,mflores}@tese.edu.mx, famivica@hotmail.com

Abstract. Approximately 3% of live newborn children suffer from cleft lip syndrome. Technology can be used in the medical area to help treatment for patients with Congenital Facial Abnormalities in cases with oral fissures. Facial dysmorphism classification level is relevant to physicians, since there are no tools to determine its degree. In this paper, a mobile application is proposed to process and analyze images, implementing the DLIB algorithm to map different face areas in healthy pediatric children, and those presenting cleft lip syndrome. Also, two repositories are created: 1. Contains all extracted facial features, 2. Stores training patterns to classify the severity level that the case presents. Finally, the Dendrite Morphological Neural Network (DMNN) algorithm was selected according to different aspects such as: one of the highest performance methods compared with MLP, SVM, IBK, RBF, easy implementation used in mobile applications with the most efficient landmarks mapping compared with OpenCV and Face detector.

Keywords: Facial dystrophy · Cleft lip · Mobile technology ·
Dendrite Morphological Neural Network

1 Introduction

Mobile computing has been developed particularly and emphatically towards practical processes that aim to be 100% functional. In technological contexts, there has been an attempt to improve the indicators of the respective uses of mobile applications in the health sector among the clinical services offered. A concrete example is to present cases of patients with some physical irregularity in the face, known as Facial Dysmorphia (FD), caused by poor fusion in the tissues that generate the upper lip during embryonic development.

Size, shape and location of the separations vary enormously. In some cases, newborns who suffer from this anomaly, have a small nick in the upper lip, others have a separation that goes up to the base of the nose, and such separation in the middle of the lip [1] technological advances of today have given rise to a variety of algorithms that allow us to identify faces of human beings, extract relevant information for facial processing, analysis and *landmarks* [2]. In literature there are techniques of Artificial Intelligence (AI) [3–5] and [6] with technology advances support [7], it is possible to solve problems of this nature [8]; achieving interpretation of properties and comparison

© Springer Nature Switzerland AG 2019
J. A. Carrasco-Ochoa et al. (Eds.): MCPR 2019, LNCS 11524, pp. 238–247, 2019.
https://doi.org/10.1007/978-3-030-21077-9_22

with databases, to recognize objects or people in controlled environments. Thus, participating in the health sector [9–11].

Unfortunately, in the health sector and pediatric clinical services that attend to cases of patients with some Congenital Facial Abnormality (CFA), there is no portable application accurate enough for physiognomic level severity assessment so as not to depend on traditional systems based on subjective clinical observations by physicians. Nor is there a repository with physiognomic information extracted from portraits of newborn children up to the age of 12 months, healthy or with some facial dysmorphia, specifically on the lips. To carry out investigations to address the problem above, we present a mobile application for Android that uses DLIB library, tool that contains a wide range of open source machine learning algorithms, through a C++ API, with a applications diversity (object and face recognition, face pose estimator, and so on) [12].

This algorithm is used mainly to map face dots (*landmarks*) and from them generate a repository with characteristic features of individuals without FD, or with some facial anomaly given the degree of asymmetry present in North and Central America, with which the tool manages to determine if a person presents facial recognition patterns with irregular measurements. In short, the objective of the proposal is that the database be used in future research, that can impact health, technology and science sectors.

This work aims to raise awareness among specialists in different areas (Systems, computing and related areas) about the importance of carrying out relevant studies in this type of diagnostics, thus involving public and private health sector institutions. The rest of this article is structured as follows: Sect. 2 gives state-of-the-art, general and relevant overview of the proposal. Section 3 presents method, phases and repository main components. Section 4 focuses on experimental results where the app with classification method used in the recognition process is tested and compared with other classifiers. Section 5 shows results, discussions and conclusions towards future works.

2   Related Work

OpenCV is a recognized algorithm to solve emotional recognition problems based on facial expressions, object detection, point mapping, and so on. The first task was to find an algorithm to map the face efficiently; it was observed that OpenCV presented irregularities in some adult's face areas. Also, algorithms are used to extract the face features, and another to obtain its value [13–15]. Our research uses an algorithm that map, extract its value and presented the best result compared with other algorithms used in our propose. The AI use techniques such as Support Vector Machine (SVM), k-Nearest Neighbors (KNN), Multilayer Perceptron (MLP), and so on. To classify emotions [3–6, 13, 14, 16], Dendrite Morphological Neural Network (DMNN) to a nontrivial problem (atrophy in upper lip) were used.

Also, landmarks have been used for facial expressions recognition [13, 14, 17], facial asymmetry [17, 18] specifically with cleft lip [19] y [20]; each algorithm considers a different number of points adapted to the problem. However, in [21], it makes a comparison of approach errors to map 37, 68, 84 and 194 points; and it is seen that it will be more precise that with more points in the curves than in the complete form. Other tasks such as [5, 6, 8, 21] besides the anthropometric and geometric points [22], propose implementing morphometric measurements (distances or angles) [6, 22].

Unfortunately, our investigation on Euclidean distance and angles applied to open cleft lip problems was not functional. Most of these investigations merge different techniques (learning, landmarks, distance metrics, analysis methods, among others) to improve response accuracy. The proposed method uses: 68 landmarks, 8 of these are key points, computation of distances in radians and a method to classify facial asymmetry level of infants with open cleft lip.

3 Proposed Method

3.1 Preprocessing and Features Extraction

The requirements of the app, the repository and the descriptive features will be identified to train and classify the type of facial dystrophy of those pediatric individuals who present the diagnosis (cleft lip), described below:

Software and hardware requirements. Android 5.0 Operating System (*Lollipop*), image normalization with: 2-6 Mega pixels (MP) resolution, format (jpg., png., bmp.). *Avoid object saturation, such as:* landscapes, portraits, objects, among others. *Newborns photographs:* healthy ones and others suffering from the syndrome, specifically cleft lip (0 and 12 months). *Areas of interest: Face limit-* It refers to the facial limits, that is. *Nose-* Central axis (lobule) for this analysis purpose. *Lips-* Considering the dividing line between upper and lower lips. *Landmarks map:* The drawing process was made with DLIB facial detection algorithm [12], detecting 68 points on digital image (Table 1), and draws the faces (frontal, inclined or lateral).

Images analysis process. An image will be selected to graph the landmarks using different colors (blue, red, yellow, magenta and green; outer limit of cheeks, eyebrows, eyelid area, nose width and height, lower and upper lip, respectively).

Repository construction will be generated containing records with 142 properties (Table 1), obtained from images of healthy children; plus others with facial dysmorphism and infants who had the disease and who underwent surgery in more than two sessions, depending on the type of condition, which will be used for the normalization, classification and to determine the three levels of asymmetry addressed in this article. The Table 1 first column, represent the total attributes, each point labeled with the recovered landmarks in 2D *P(x, y)*, represented in Cartesian plane (right and upper side (+), left and lower side (−)), and the two subsequent columns indicate the landmark number and its description.

Table 1. Attributes labeled according section of the face

Attrib	Landmark	Labeled	Attrib	Landmark	Labeled
16	1–8	Right face contour	14	49–55	Upper vermillion border
16	10–17	Left face contour	10	56–60	Low vermilion border
10	18–22	Right eyebrow	10	61–65	Upper peristomal border
10	23–27	Left eyebrow	6	66–68	Low peristomal border
12	37–42	Right eye	6	28–30	Dorsum nasal
12	43–48	Left eye	6	51–53	Cupid's bow
10	32–36	Alar rim	10	31,9	Lobulus, Menton

3.2   Normalization and Feature Extraction

The normalization process performs a Cartesian to polar $(x, y) \rightarrow (r, \theta)$. The coordinates (x, y) represent the geometric location of the extracted facial points, $r = \rho$ also known as rho, represents the distance between the origin (landmark 31) and the interest points (upper lip landmarks) and θ is the elevation angle between polar axis (landmark 31) and the object. Then, we get ρ by means of:

$$\rho = \sqrt{x^2 + y^2} \tag{1}$$

Now, we will obtain a vector of θ associated with location of (x, y) corresponding to the interest area points (upper lip) in a range of $-\pi$ to π, thus

$$a_{ji} = atan2_i(y, x) = \begin{cases} arctan\left(\dfrac{y}{x}\right) & x > 0 \\ arctan\left(\dfrac{y}{x}\right) + \pi & y \geq 0, x < 0 \\ arctan\left(\dfrac{y}{x}\right) - \pi & y < 0, x < 0 \end{cases} \tag{2}$$

Where $atan2_i$ obtains the distances (represented in angles as radian unit measurements) between the point 31 and the points of the upper lip (Table 1). Each set is in a_{ji}. After that, pair point differences are computed by Eq. (3).

$$d_{ji} = (a_{jk_1} - a_{jk_2}) \tag{3}$$

Where d_{ji} represents the differences, a has all the measures Eq. (2) with respect to the polo (31), $j = n$ records, $i = n$ pair groups, k_1 y k_2 indicate the landmark number. Finally, We compute by arithmetical mean of differences, thus

$$M_j = \frac{1}{n} \sum_{j=1}^{n} d_j \tag{4}$$

3.3   Training and Classification

The training process of a classifying method requires identifying the attribute C_j to classify properly. Then, we delimit the proper classification ranges of each type by Eq. (4).

$$R_{j_{j=3}} max_{i \to \infty_j}(x_{ji}), min_{i \to \infty_j}(x_{ji}) \tag{5}$$

Where *max* and *min* gets the upper and lower limit of the means M_j. The ranges denoted by R_j (Table 2). To label each record by class name, thus obtains

$$C_{j_{i \to 3}}\{S, M, N\} \tag{6}$$

Table 2 shows the asymmetry level; we consider 3 class (C_j): *Severe* $C_0 = S$: physical features determining notorious facial amyotrophy presence, *Moderate* $C_1 = M$: People who have been surgically treated due to facial disease presence, *almost null* $C_2 = N$: No physical features determining facial amyotrophy. The classification stage uses the ranges (Table 2) obtained from the Eq. (6) to perform and accurate classification.

Table 2. Ranges and assigned class

Asymmetry level	Since	Until
Almost null	0.0034331826	0.0038525829
Moderate	0.0046739103	0.0085488006
Severe	0.0000846416	0.0034320826

The document (.csv) for training, will be composed of 8 attributes: $d_{j1} = (49, 53)$, $d_{j2} = (50, 52), d_{j3} = (61, 63), d_{j4} = (67, 65), a_{j5} = (51), a_{j6} = (62)$, M_j and C_j, each with 105 cases of healthy children, another 35 with facial dysmorphism and 20 infants who had the disease or underwent surgery in more than two sessions depending on the type of condition.

4   Experimental Results and Discussions

The interface GUI is composed of four modules: *picture take.–* in order to capture and store file; *portrait analysis.–* to normalize and analyze photographs using the facial detection algorithm from an intelligent device and save information in the BD; *Create file.–* Retrieve relevant data to create file with the necessary attributes for training. *Files compression.* – The functionality of this module is evaluated by the end user by coordinating the number of documents to be compressed. Finally, modeling controls generated errors and authors involved. With the above, it is possible using the DLIB algorithm [12] to analyze the captured image. For the analysis process first, an image is selected to graph the landmarks (Fig. 1) using different colors (blue, red, yellow, magenta and green; outer limit of cheeks, eyebrows, eyelid area, nose width and height, lower and upper lip, respectively).

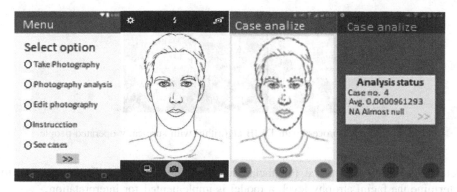

Fig. 1. Interface: (a) menu, (b) camera opening and photo storage, (c) analysis, (d) results (Color figure online)

The estimation stage shows the user the case number examined, the value of the arithmetic mean corresponding to the current image, and the facial severity level of the selected case (Fig. 1). Finally, it generates a file in the indicated format. The drawing process was made using DLIB facial detection algorithm; the selection of this detector was due to its better performance in comparison with OpenCV and Face Detector which showed great instability when working with images with these characteristics.

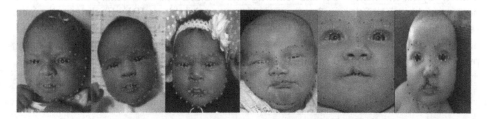

Fig. 2. Drawing process with algorithm in healthy kids and with dysmorphia

The proposed application "Queiloquisis", was tested using point location process and facial detection algorithm (DLIB) generating 68 *landmarks*, on different banks of 140 images [1], from Faces + [23], New México Cleft Palate Center [24], and St. Louis Children's Hospital [25, 26]. The rest of the images used in the investigation were captured from a mobile device. Figure 2 shows the healthy individuals images mapping and who present the disease known as open cleft lip and Fig. 3 cases presenting of the disease with several surgical interventions.

The face axes are stored by coordinates x and y. Therefore, the positions of the points (Fig. 2) cover a dimension of the face from 0 to 100 pixels (left side) and from 0 to 250 pixels (right side), resulting in a very variable proportion, which was controllable. Another aspect of determination when selecting the facial recognition algorithm was based on high performance, reflected when analyzing the total samples, reaching an error margin of 4%, 15% and 18% with the DLIB algorithm, OpenCV and Face

Fig. 3. Drawing process with DLIB algorithm with surgically operated people

Detector, respectively. Since the facial detection algorithm (DLIB) is not able to determine the facial atrophy level, a model is implemented for interpretation.

Experiments are carried out and conjectures of distance between two points are discarded, due to the irregularities of the face (curves impossible to be drawn in Cartesian coordinates). When analyzing a healthy person photograph, the distance between the right corner of the lip and the left side in relation to the nose lobe is $3.459...n$ and $5.686...n$ units, respectively, generating an imbalance that directly alters the result. However, when performing the above analysis (Eqs. 1–4), the result is $1.543...n$ and $1.540...n$ units. With these values it is demonstrated that the normalization process is adequate to the research needs, generating good results.

Table 3 shows the results with Weka and the used classification methods, applying a dataset normalized (Eqs. 1–6). For the MLP, a sigmoid polynomial function, five hidden layers, moment = 0.2 and learning rate = 0.3. For SVM, binary classifier with polynomial kernel of degree 2 was used. K-nearest neighbors IBK, Euclidean distance search algorithm and k = 1. For Radial Basis Function RBF, with 2 Clusters and normalized Gaussian. For DMNN, M = 0.25 and 23 dendrites; technique recently proposed by [27] and used in other experiments such as [28, 29].

Table 3. Classifiers methods performance

% Classification error						
Instances	Train %	MLP	SVM	IBK	RBF	DMNN
160	100%	0,9	3,57	0,7	0	0
130	80%	6,3	6,25	6,3	9,38	5
112	70%	4	2	4	2	6
Average		3,6	4,91	3,5	4,69	2,5

The Table 3 demonstrate the performance on the DMNN improves the results obtained and shows the classification error when manipulating a dataset with these characteristic, to have an estimated error generalization, 100%, 80% and 70% of data for training and the other samples were used for testing on each of the 3 class were used.

The results of most of the algorithms used show a high performance. Therefore, out of the four, the best DMNN is implemented in the application to determine image symmetry level (Fig. 1). In addition, to know the performance of the classification technique, performance metrics are generated, considering 3 classes, see Table 4.

Table 4. Proposed algorithm confusion matrix

		Predicted class			
		A	B	C	n
Current class	A	29	2	0	31
	B	0	10	0	10
	C	0	0	9	9
		29	12	9	50

Table 5 is generated achieving a statistical Kappa of 92.86% and a correct data classification rate of 96% (overall accuracy). To get a better evaluation of the model, different metrics are considered, reaching a true positives rate of 96%, demonstrating a classification model good performance.

Table 5. Proposed algorithm accuracy detail

Performance by class		
Accuracy	Sensibility	Specificity
96.865	100	94.736
100	90	100
98.958	96.666	98.245

We conclude this section, emphasizing that this research focus does not imply representing or showing which side represents more asymmetry, but the level of asymmetry that a case presents.

5   Conclusions and Future Works

This work depends on the medical area, facilitating the analysis process and classification asymmetry level in images of pediatric patients within and without congenital facial diseases, improving the response time, efficiency, capacity, execution level, quality control and above all a control of information to be abundant and accurate. This allowed us to have a broader view of the latent needs in this field.

The relevance of this document lies in four elements: (a) implementation of the facial detector (DLIB), algorithm with better performance compared to OpenCV and Face detector; (b) Images normalization for a better analysis, (c) Distance calculations converted to radians to obtain a high margin of reliability, ensuring useful results, reliable and functional for the health sector and (d) The classifier method DMNN was created recently and this word demonstrated the best performance in infant facial asymmetry classification with cleft lip.

Finally, this article showed the research potential, making feedback possible in: (a) the understanding of training and the pediatric facial dysmorphic syndrome classification, (b) the scarcity of relevant information in this diagnosis; reason for which a repository with features and characteristic patterns of the condition (cleft lip) were built. It should be noted that this research does not only point towards this line of work, but it could also be directed to new investigations such as: (a) address this diagnosis in the bilateral symptom, (b) perform tests with other conjectures, (c) develop a hybrid application, and (d) create a shared information center (server, cloud, etc.) allowing for data linking among mobile devices running the application.

Acknowledgements. Griselda Cortés and Mercedes Flores wish to thank COMECYT and Tecnológico de Estudios Superiores de Ecatepec (TESE) for its support in development of this project. The authors also thank Juan C. Guzmán, Itzel Saldivar and Diana López for their work and dedication to this project with which they aim to obtain the degree in computer systems engineering in TESE.

References

1. Christopher, D.: http://www.drderderian.com. Accessed 11 Feb 2018
2. Liu, M., et al.: Landmark-based deep multi-instance learning for brain disease diagnosis. Med. Image Anal. **43**, 157–168 (2018)
3. Tang, X., et al.: Facial landmark detection by semi-supervised deep learning. Neurocomputing **297**, 22–32 (2018). https://doi.org/10.1016/j.neucom.2018.01.080
4. Li, Y., et al.: Face recognition based on recurrent regression neural network. Neurocomputing **297**, 50–58 (2018). https://doi.org/10.1016/j.neucom.2018.02.037
5. Deng, W., et al.: Facial landmark localization by enhanced convolutional neural network. Neurocomputing **273**, 222–229 (2018). https://doi.org/10.1016/j.patrec.2016.07.005
6. Haoqiang, F., Erjin, Z.: Approaching human level facial landmark localization by deep learning. Image Vis. Comput. **47**, 27–35 (2016). https://doi.org/10.1016/j.imavis.2015.11.004
7. Smith, M., et al.: Continuous face authentication scheme for mobile devices with tracking and liveness detection. Microprocess. Microsyst. **63**, 147–157 (2018). https://doi.org/10.1016/j.micpro.2018.07.008
8. Barman, A., Paramartha, D.: Facial expression recognition using distance and shape signature features. Pattern Recogn. Lett. **000**, 1–8 (2017). https://doi.org/10.1016/j.procs.2017.03.069
9. Josué Daniel, E.: Makoa: Aplicación para visualizar imágenes médicas formato DICOM en dispositivos móviles iPad. http://132.248.52.100:8080/xmlui/handle/132.248.52.100/7749. Accessed 22 Apr 2017
10. Jones, A.L.: The influence of shape and colour cue classes on facial health perception. Evol. Hum. Behav. 19–29 (2018). https://doi.org/10.1016/j.evolhumbehav.2017.09.005
11. Mirsha, et al.: Effects of hormonal treatment, maxilofacial surgery orthodontics, traumatism and malformation on fluctuating asymmetry. Revista Argentina de Antropología Biológica 1–15 (2018). https://doi.org/10.1002/ajhb.20507

12. DLIB: (2008). http://dlib.net/. Accessed 25 Oct 2017
13. Yang, D., et al.: An emotion recognition model based on facial recognition in virtual learning environment. Procedia Comput. Sci. **125**, 2–10 (2018). https://doi.org/10.1016/j.procs.2017.12.003
14. Tarnowski, P., et al.: Emotion recognition using facial expressions. Procedia Comput. Sci. **108**, 1175–1184 (2017)
15. Al Anezi, T., Khambay, B., Peng, M.J., O'Leary, E., Ju, X., Ayoub, A.: A new method for automatic tracking of facial landmarks in 3D motion captured images (4D). Int. J. Oral Maxillofac. Surg. **42**(1), 9–18 (2013)
16. Fan, H., Zhou, E.: Approaching human level facial landmark localization by deep learning. Image Vis. Comput. **47**, 27–35 (2016)
17. Liu, S., Fan, Y.Y., Guo, Z., Samal, A., Ali, A.: A landmark-based data-driven approach on 2.5D facial attractiveness computation. Neurocomputing **238**, 168–178 (2017). https://doi.org/10.1016/j.neucom.2017.01.050
18. Economou, S., et al.: Evaluation of facial asymmetry in patients with juvenile idiopathic arthritis: Correlation between hard tissue and soft tissue landmarks. Am. J. Orthod. Dentofac. Orthop. **153**(5), 662–672 (2018). https://doi.org/10.1016/j.ajodo.2017.08.022
19. Hallac, R.R., Feng, J., Kane, A.A., Seaward, J.R.: Dynamic facial asymmetry in patients with repaired cleft lip using 4D imaging (video stereophotogrammetry). J. Cranio-Maxillo-Fac. Surg. **45**, 8–12 (2017). https://doi.org/10.1016/j.jcms.2016.11.005
20. Al-Rudainy, D., Ju, X., Stanton, S., Mehendale, F.V., Ayoub, A.: Assessment of regional asymmetry of the face before and after surgical correction of unilateral cleft lip. J. Cranio-Maxillofac. Surg. **46**(6), 974–978 (2018)
21. Chen, F., et al.: 2D facial landmark model design by combining key points and inserted points. Expert Syst. Appl 7858–7868 (2015). https://doi.org/10.1016/j.eswa.2015.06.015
22. Vezzetti, E., Marcolin, F.: 3D human face description: landmarks measures and geometrical features. Image Vis. Comput. **30**, 698–712 (2012). https://doi.org/10.1016/j.imavis.2012.02.007
23. Faces +, Faces + (Cirugía plástica, dermatología, piel y láser) de San Diego, California. http://www.facesplus.com/procedure/craniofacial/congenital-disorders/cleft-lip-and-palate/#results. Accessed 02 Mar 2017
24. New Mexico Cleft Palate Center. http://nmcleft.org/?page_id=107. Accessed 02 Mar 2017
25. Pediatric Plastic Surgery: Hospital de niños en St. Louis. http://www.stlouischildrens.org/our-services/plastic-surgery/photo-gallery. Accessed 10 Mar 2017
26. My UK Healt Care: Hospital de niños en Kentucky. http://ukhealthcare.uky.edu/kch/liau-blog/gallery/. Accessed 22 Mar 2017
27. Sossa, H., Guevara, E.: Efficient training for dendrite morphological neural networks. Neurocomputing 132–142 (2014). https://doi.org/10.1016/j.neucom.2013.10.031
28. Vega, R., et al.: Retinal vessel extraction using lattice neural networks with dendritic processing. Comput. Biol. Med. 20–30 (2015). https://doi.org/10.1016/j.compbiomed.2014.12.016
29. Zamora, E., Sossa, H.: Dendrite morphological neurons trained by stochastic gradient descent. Neurocomputing 420–431 (2017). https://doi.org/10.1016/j.neucom.2017.04.044

Novel SSVEP Processing Method Based on Correlation and Feedforward Neural Network for Embedded Brain Computer Interface

Juan Ramírez-Quintana[✉], Jose Macias-Macias, Alma Corral-Saenz, and Mario Chacon-Murguia

PVR Laboratory, Tecnologico Nacional de Mexico/I. T. Chihuahua, Mexico City, Mexico
{jaramirez, jmmaciasm, adcorral, mchacon}@itchihuahua.edu.mx

Abstract. Steady State Visually Evoked Potential (SSVEP) is a successful strategy in electroencephalographic (EEG) processing applied to spellers, games, rehabilitation, prosthesis, etc. There are many algorithms proposed in literature to detect the SSVEP frequency, however, most of them must to be implemented in high processing computers because SSVEP methods require many EEG input channels and the algorithms are computationally complex. Then, this paper proposes a low computational cost method for SSVEP embedded processing (EP-SSVEP) whose input is one EEG channel and is based on Canonical Correlation and a Feedforward Neural Network. Additionally, this paper also proposes an embedded system to implement EP-SSVEP and a dataset composed with the EEG signals from eight subjects. According to the results, EP-SSVEP is one of the best methods in literature to SSVEP embedded processing because it reports an accuracy of 96.09% with the proposed dataset and the EEG input is acquired with one channel.

Keywords: SSVEP · Brain Computer Interface · Canonical Correlation · Feedforward Neural Network

1 Introduction

Steady state visually evoked potential is a strategy that increase the energy in brain activity after the presentation of a visual stimulus modulated at a fixed frequency that can be measure in EEG signal as a magnitude rise at the stimulation frequency. The stimulus is presented as message that a subject must select from a group of stimuli with other messages. This stimuli selection has made SSVEP a successful processing strategy in spellers [1–3], games [4], rehabilitation with robot [5], prosthesis control [6] or any application for communication and control purposes.

The research to develop new processing methods for SSVEP has been generated a wide variety of algorithms reported in literature for feature extraction and classification. The most common models for feature extraction are Discrete Fourier Transform

© Springer Nature Switzerland AG 2019
J. A. Carrasco-Ochoa et al. (Eds.): MCPR 2019, LNCS 11524, pp. 248–258, 2019.
https://doi.org/10.1007/978-3-030-21077-9_23

(DFT) [7, 8], Canonic Correlation Analysis (CCA) [9–13], Spectral Power Density (SPD) [14], Discrete Wavelet transform (DWT) [15] and Principal Component Analysis (PCA) [16, 17]. For classification, the most used methods are based on Artificial Neural Networks (ANN) [18–20] and Support Vector Machine [4, 15, 21].

However, most of the SSVEP methods reported in literature needs many EEG input channels and are computationally complex. Consequently, the Brain Computer Interfaces (BCI) that acquire and process SSVEP signal, require computer systems with high processing capabilities and these BCI may cause discomfort to the users due to electrodes positioned in the scalp. Hence, in order to develop a ubiquitous BCI embedded systems, this paper proposes a low computational cost method for SSVEP processing (EP-SSVEP) that use a single EEG channel and is based on Canonical Correlation Analysis and a Feedforward Neural Network (FFNN). To the experiments, we also propose a ubiquitous and comfortable-to-use BCI embedded system with one EEG channel, a portable acquisition device and a small size embedded processor.

The rest of the paper is organized as follows: Sect. 2 presents the BCI embedded system and the dataset acquired for experiments. Section 3 reports the graphical interface that generates the stimuli to evoke the SSVEP. Section 4 describes the proposed method EP-SSVEP. Section 5 presents the results and finally, Sect. 6 reports the conclusions.

2   BCI Embedded System and Dataset

The design of BCI embedded system for experiments was based on three aspects: acquisition device, number of electrodes and method for SSVEP processing.

The acquisition device for the system is the Cyton board of OpenBCI® and it was selected because of its low cost, portability and its SDK is compatible with commercial embedded boards.

The criterion for the number of electrodes is based on the fact that as the number of channels to acquire EEG signal decreases, the comfort of the system increases, and the complexity of the algorithms falls significantly. Then, we develop an experiment to find the best EEG channels to acquire the SSVEP frequency. In this experiment, we read the EEG signals from eight subjects using electrodes connected to the EEG channels O1, O2, Oz, the ground A1 and the reference Fpz, which are standard positions of 10–20 international system. These channels were selected because according to Lee et al. [22], the occipital lobule is the best part of the brain to detect the SSVEP frequencies when a subject stares a stimulus. Results of our experiments show that the EEG channel Oz generates an SSVEP with the necessary properties to design a system that detects the stimulus that the subject stares.

Thus, the proposed method was designed considering a single EEG channel as input and the method must allow online applications in commercial embedded boards.

These aspects were considered in the design of the BCI embedded system whose components are showed in Fig. 1. The system is composed of a visual interface to evoke the SSVEP, gold cup electrodes placed on the channel Oz, A1 and Fpz, the Cyton acquisition device and the embedded bard. The electrodes were connected to the Cyton board to transform the EEG signals to digital data at a sample frequency (Fs) of

250 Hz. Also, Cyton board sends the EEG data by Bluetooth to an embedded board. The board is a Raspberry Pi that analyzes the EEG data with EP-SSVEP to find the stimulus that subject stares. Finally, the board sends by WiFi the message of the selected stimulus to an Internet of Things network (IoT) for any control or communication purposes.

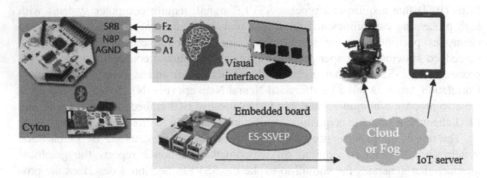

Fig. 1. BCI embedded system scheme.

For the experiments, a dataset was designed considering the regular organization of SSVEP datasets reported in literature [23–25]. Our dataset consists of eight healthy subjects that were selected from a group of male and female persons with an age from 21 to 25 years. All of them have normal or corrected-to-normal vision. None of them were taking medication. The total of EEG dataset signals is 384 (48 signals per subject).

3   Graphical Interface for Visual Stimuli Presentation

The common technology for the stimuli presentation to evoke the SSVEP is a digital monitor because the stimulation methodology can be designed with software, while other technologies would require hardware design.

To design the stimuli, there are two aspects to consider: figure and stimulation frequency.

The common figures are graphics (box, arrow, star, circle) and checkerboard inversion patterns [26]. However, according to the literature, a checkerboard inversion generates better amplitude response in SSVEP than figures because inversion causes the optical illusion that the checkerboard moves [23].

The stimulation frequency is calculated with the monitor refresh rate [3] and commercial monitors have 60 Hz of refresh rate, so the stimulus frequency f_e is given as:

$$f_e = {}^{60}\!/\!Z \tag{1}$$

where Z is an entire number. Another aspect to be considered in frequency stimulation is that f_e greater than 10 Hz can generate secondary effects in photosensitive subjects [26]. Hence, f_e selection includes frequencies less than 10 Hz in Eq. (1).

Then, the interface for visual stimuli presentation is a graphical user interface with four black/white checkerboard patterns distributed as Fig. 2 shows. The f_e of checkerboard are 6, 6.6, 7.5 and 8.5 Hz and they are distributed as Table 1 shows. The red points in the checkboard are used by the subject to stare the center of the selected checkerboard.

Fig. 2. Graphical interface for visual stimuli presentation. (Color figure online)

Table 1. Frequencies distribution for checkerboards

Checkerboard	Right	Left	Down	Up
Frequency (Hz)	6	6.6	7.5	8.5

4   EP-SSVEP Method

This section presents the proposed method EP-SSVEP whose input is an EEG data recorded during 12 s from Oz EEG channel at 250 Hz. This signal is given by $s(n)$, $n = 0,...,2999$, where n is the time index.

EP-SSVEP was developed with a machine learning approach because the SSVEP signals have noise and the amplitude frequencies may change in each session and subject. The modules of EP-SSVEP are preprocessing, feature extraction with DFT and CCA and classification with a FFNN as Fig. 3 shows. The output is the SSVEP frequency related with the f_e that a subject stares.

Fig. 3. EP-SSVEP modules.

4.1   Preprocessing Module

The preprocessing module removes the unnecessary frequencies from the EEG signal using a fifth order bandpass Butterworth filter with cut frequencies of 5.5 Hz and 9 Hz. The filter is expressed as $H(\omega)$: $s \rightarrow s_{f2}$, where $H(\omega)$ is the filter transfer function and s_{f2} is the output of the filter.

4.2   Feature Extraction

This module generates a feature vector to develop an efficient SSVEP detection by reducing the dimension of the frequency components of EEG signal. The first step of this module is the Discrete Fourier Transform given by:

$$S(k) = \sum_{n=0}^{N-1} s_{f2}(n)e^{-i2\pi kn/N} \quad k = 0, \ldots, N-1 \tag{2}$$

where $S(k)$ contains the frequency components of $s_{f2}(n)$, $N = 1500$. DFT is computed with the radix 2 fast Fourier transform algorithm. There are other methods to find the frequency components like SPD and DWT, but the DFT was selected because it finds a correct definition of SSVEP frequencies, the input is defined in one dimension and DFT reports the least processing time in feature extraction. The next step is a normalization defined by:

$$x(k) = (S(k) - \mu_s)/\sigma_s \tag{3}$$

where μ_s is the mean of $S(k)$ and σ_s the standard deviation. This normalization reduces the uncertainty generated by the amplitude levels of SSVEP signals. The final step is the Canonical Correlation Analysis, which was used because is one of the most popular methods to reduce the data dimension in SSVEP. CCA finds four Pearson correlation coefficients that represent similarity between $x(k)$ and four SSVEP signals $\lambda_j(k)$, $j = 1$, ...4 at frequencies of 6, 6.5, 7.5 and 8.5 Hz. Signals of $\lambda_j(k)$ are showed in Fig. 4, and they are the average of signals per subject obtained from training signals of dataset. Table 2 shows the distribution of SSVEP frequencies in each $\lambda_j(k)$ signal. The CCA is defined as follows:

$$\rho_j = \sigma_{x\lambda j}/\sigma_x \sigma_{\lambda j} \tag{4}$$

where $\sigma_{x\lambda j}$ is the covariance between $x(k)$ and each $\lambda_j(k)$ signal, σ_x is the standard deviation of $x(k)$ and $\sigma_{\lambda j}$ is the standard deviation of $\lambda_j(k)$. Thus, the result is a correlation vector $\rho_j = \{\rho_1, \rho_2, \rho_3, \rho_4\}$, where each coefficient is the Pearson correlation between $x(k)$ and each $\lambda_j(k)$ signal. According to the definition of (4), if SSVEP is not presented in $x(k)$, then, the values of ρ_j are close to zero, but if SSVEP is presented, the values of ρ_j have results in the interval from 0 to 1, and they vary according to the SSVEP frequency in $x(k)$ and its quality. The frequency of SSVEP generates a value close to one in the component of ρ_j related to the $\lambda_j(k)$ signal with the most similar frequency to the SSVEP frequency of $x(k)$. However, the quality of the signal causes uncertainty in the results of ρ_j and that quality depends of the conditions of the subject during the BCI sessions. Therefore, the best option in classification module is a supervised algorithm.

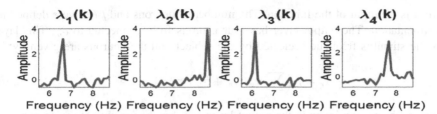

Fig. 4. Frequency signals $\lambda_j(k)$.

Table 2. SSVEP frequency distribution in $\lambda_j(k)$.

Signal	$\lambda_1(k)$	$\lambda_2(k)$	$\lambda_3(k)$	$\lambda_4(k)$
SSVEP frequency (Hz)	6	6.6	7.5	8.5

4.3   Classification

According to experiments and the literature, classifiers with the best results in SSVEP analysis are artificial neural networks. Then, the classification module in this method is a Feedforward Neural Network (FFNN) trained with scaled conjugate gradient back-propagation algorithm. Figure 5 shows the architecture of the network, which includes three layers: input, hidden and output.

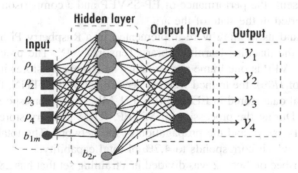

Fig. 5. FFNN architecture.

The input is the vector ρ_j. The second layer has five neurons defined as follows:

$$o_m = f_1\left(\sum w_{jm}\rho_j + b_{1m}\right) \quad m = 1,\ldots,5 \tag{5}$$

where m is the neuron index in the hidden layer, w_{jm} are the weights of the neurons, b_{1m} is the neuron bias and $f_1(u)$ is the *softsign* activation function $f_1(u) = u/(1 + |u|)$, where u is the input of the function. The number of neurons and $f_1(u)$ were defined by experimentation. The output layer has four neurons fully connected to o_m. This layer finds the stimulus frequency selected by the subject and the neurons are given by:

$$y_r = f_2\left(\sum w_{mr}O_m + b_{2r}\right) \quad r = 1,\ldots,4 \tag{6}$$

where r is the neuron index in the output layer, w_{mr} are the weights of the neurons, b_{2r} is the neuron bias and $f_2(.)$ is a *softmax* activation function that generates the best results in the experiments. The output layer has four neurons because each neuron represents each frequency f_e.

4.4 Frequency Stimulation

After propagation of ρ_j in the network, EP-SSVEP determines the selected f_e with:

$$e = \underset{r}{\arg\max} \ y_r \tag{7}$$

where e is the index value of r, which is the stimulus that the subject stares during the SSVEP session.

5   Results

This section presents the performance of EP-SSVEP and a comparison of this method with others reported in the state of the art.

EP-SSVEP and its training were implemented in a Raspberry Pi 3B model using Python 3.4 and the machine learning library TensorFlow™. The processing velocity average of EP-SSVEP is one frame per second. The Raspberry stores in the EEPROM the coefficients of $H(\omega)$, the trained weights per subject of the FFNN, the signals $\lambda_j(k)$ and $\sigma_{\lambda j}$. The total data stored in EEPROM is 171 Mb, which corresponds to 1.06% of total capability. During the processing of SSVEP, RAM memory stores $s(n)$, $s_{f2}(n)$, x (k), $sf2(n)$ signals, σ_x, ρ_j and the propagation of the network. The total data stored in RAM is 41 Mb, which corresponds to 4.7% of total capability.

Dataset described on Sect. 2 was divided in a training set that has 28 signals from 8 subjects, and a test set that has 20 signals from 8 subjects. The signals for training and test was randomly separated by cross-validation with five k-fold iterations. Figure 6 shows the confusion matrix of both sets and the reported performance in these matrices are 98.23% for training set and 96.09% for test set. Additionally, stimulus of 7.5 and 8.5 Hz (up and down) reports the best performance than stimulus 6 and 6.6 Hz (right and left) due vertical checkerboards were placed closer of central area of subject vision than horizontal stimulus.

Training		Objective				Test		Objective			
		6.6 Hz	8.5 Hz	6 Hz	7.5 Hz			6.6 Hz	8.5 Hz	6 Hz	7.5 Hz
Output class	6.6 Hz	374	8	1	1	Output class	6.6 Hz	91	4	1	0
	8.5 Hz	1	379	0	4		8.5 Hz	1	94	0	1
	6 Hz	1	4	378	1		6 Hz	2	1	91	2
	7.5 Hz	0	2	4	378		7.5 Hz	0	1	2	93

Fig. 6. Matrix confusion generated with 5 k-fold cross validation for (a) training set. (b) Test set.

5.1 Comparison with Other SSVEP BCI Systems

To evaluate the performance of EP-SSVEP BCI system, this section presents a comparison with other popular SSVEP BCI focused to embedded applications reported in literature. We do not found a database or methodology for comparisons of BCI embedded systems, thus we design a criterion considering the mainly aspects of BCI operation, which are:

Number of Subjects in the dataset (NS). EEG signals are noisy and they have a response that can be different in each subject. Then, in order to find a better statistical description of the method, it is important to increase as much as possible the number of subjects used for dataset and experiments.

Number of EEG channels (NE). The number of EEG channels is related to the computational cost of the processing methods, i.e., as the number of electrodes reduces, the complexity of the proposed method decreases. Additionally, a large number of electrodes can cause discomfort in the subjects, which affects the performance of the SSVEP sessions. Then, is important to reduce as much as possible the number of EEG channels without compromising the signal quality.

Accuracy (Acc). There are many metrics to compare SSVEP processing methods like Information Transfer Rate (*ITR*) [24], Accuracy (Acc) [2], etc. Among them, Acc is the most used and it refers to the number of SSVEP samples correctly detected divided by the total number of samples.

Table 3 shows the comparison of EP-SSVEP with two state of the art methods for specific purposes [22, 27] and other popular methods implemented in embedded systems [4, 28]. According to the results showed in Table 3, EP-SSVEP has better Acc than the other methods in spite of EP-SSVEP uses a single EEG channel and that method was tested with eight subjects. This Acc is because of the next reasons:

- Subjects reports better concentration during the SSVEP sessions in our BCI system than other systems because our system is comfortable for subjects due to two reasons: the use of just one EEG channel and the card processor allows an ubiquitous embedded system.
- The gold cup electrodes acquire the EEG signal with less noise than other commercial BCI.
- EP-SSVEP needs data from one EEG channel and uses a classifier that is trained considering the natural uncertainty in SSVEP signals.

Table 3. Comparisons between EP-SSVEP and other popular methods.

Method	NS	NC*	Acc (%)
EP-SSVEP	8	1	96.09
Humanoid Robot SSVEP BCI [28]	3	2	75
BCI gaming system [4]	2	4	78.9–80.5
Quadcopter control SSVEP [27]	10	4	78
Attention monitoring system [22]	13	2	72–82

* Electrodes A1 and Fpz are not considered because they are used as ground and reference in all methods.

6 Conclusions

This paper proposes EP-SSVEP, a novel method designed for ubiquitous BCI embedded systems that process SSVEP signals from a single EEG channel. The proposed method is implemented in an embedded board that sends the information of stimulus that the subject stares to an IoT network. A dataset was designed for experimentations and it consists of the EEG signals obtained from eight subjects. EP-SSVEP is composed of three modules: preprocessing to eliminate noise of EEG signal, feature extraction that uses DFT and CCA and a classification with a FFNN. EP-SSVEP reports the best performance in vertical stimulus than horizontal because of the colocation of the checkerboards respect to the user vision. In the comparisons, EP-SSVEP is a method that generates a BCI embedded system that uses the least number of EEG channels and reports the best Acc. Then, based on these results, we conclude that EP-SSVEP is one of the best methods proposed in the literature. Additionally, EP-SSVEP allows the design of ubiquitous BCI embedded systems because this method can be processed in one second in embedded processors, includes the best accuracy in comparisons of Table 3 and uses as input one EEG data channel.

Acknowledgements. This research was funded by TecNM under grant 6418.18-P. The authors thank the volunteer that participate in the dataset elaboration.

References

1. Stawicki, P., Gembler, F., Rezeika, A., Volosyak, I.: A novel hybrid mental spelling application based on eye tracking and SSVEP-based BCI. Brain Sci. **4**(35), 1–17 (2017)
2. Rezeika, A., Benda, M., Stawicki, P., Gembler, F., Saboor, A., Volosyak, I.: Brain – computer interface spellers : a review. Brain Sci. **8**(57), 1–38 (2018)
3. Nezamfar, H., Mohseni Salehi, S.S., Moghadamfalahi, M., Erdogmus, D.: FlashTypeTM: a context-aware c-VEP-based BCI typing interface using EEG signals. IEEE J. Sel. Top. Signal Process. **10**(5), 932–941 (2016)
4. Martišius, I., Damaševičius, R.: A prototype SSVEP based real time BCI gaming system. Comput. Intell. Neurosci. **2016**(1), 1–15 (2016)

5. Zeng, X., Zhu, G., Yue, L., Zhang, M., Xie, S.: A feasibility study of SSVEP-based passive training on an ankle rehabilitation robot. J. Healthc. Eng. **2017**(1), 1–9 (2017)
6. Chen, X., Wang, Y., Gao, X.: Control of a 7-DOF robotic arm system with an SSVEP-based BCI. Int. J. Neural Syst. **28**(8), 1–15 (2018)
7. Tan, F., Zhao, D., Sun, Q., Fang, C., Zhao, X., Liu, H.: Analysis of feature extraction algorithms used in brain-computer interfaces. In: 2016 International Conference on Applied Mechanics, Electronics and Mechatronics Engineering. pp. 1–7. University of Posts and Telecomunications, Chomgqing (2016)
8. Capati, F.A., Bechelli, R.P., Castro, M.C.F.: Hybrid SSVEP/P300 BCI keyboard - controlled by visual evoked potential. In: Proceedings of the 9th International Joint Conference on Biomedical Engineering Systems and Technologies, pp. 214–218 (2016)
9. Vu, H., Koo, B., Choi, S.: Frequency detection for SSVEP-based BCI using deep canonical correlation analysis. In: 2016 IEEE International Conference on Systems, Man, and Cybernetics, pp. 1983–1987. School of interdisciplinary Bioscience and Bioengineering, Pohang (2016)
10. Chen, Y.-J., Chen, S.-C., Wu, C.-M.: Using modular neural network to SSVEP-based BCI. In: International Conference on Applied System Innovation, pp. 1–3. University of Science and Technology, Okinawa (2016)
11. Trigui, O., Zouch, W., Ben Messaoud, M.: A comparison study of SSVEP detection methods using the Emotiv Epoc headset. In: Conference on STA, pp. 48–53. Sfax University, Monastir (2016)
12. Duan, F., Lin, D., Li, W., Zhang, Z.: Design of a multimodal EEG-based hybrid BCI system with visual servo module. In: IEEE Transactions on Autonomous Mental Development, pp. 332–341. IEEE (2015)
13. Aznan, N., Bonner, S., Connolly, J., Al Moubayed, N., Breckon, T.: On the classification of SSVEP-based dry-EEG signals via convolutional neural networks. In: IEEE International Conference on Systems, Man, and Cybernetics (SMC) (2018)
14. Irshad, A., Singh, R.: SSVEP and ANN based optimal speller design for brain computer interface. Comput. Sci. Tech. **2**(2), 338–349 (2014)
15. Heidari, H., Einalou, Z.: SSVEP extraction applying wavelet transform and decision tree with bays classification. Int. Clin. Neurosci. J. **4**(3), 91–97 (2017)
16. Liu, Q., Chen, K., Ai, Q., Xie, S.Q.: Review: recent development of signal processing algorithms for SSVEP-based brain computer interfaces. J. Med. Biol. Eng. **34**(4), 299–309 (2014)
17. Ghassemzadeh, N., Haghipour, S.: A review on EEG based brain computer interface systems feature extraction methods. Int. J. Adv. Biol. Biomed. Res. **4**(2), 117–123 (2016)
18. Turnip, A., Rizgyawan, M.I., Esti, K.D., Yanyoan, S., Mulyana, E.: Real time classification of SSVEP brain activity with adaptive feedforward neural networks. In: 3rd International Conference on Information Technology, Computer, and Electrical Engineering, pp. 1–5. IEEE, Semarang (2017)
19. Turnip, A., Simbolon, A.I., Faizal Amri, M., Sihombing, P., Setiadi, R.H., Mulyana, E.: Backpropagation neural networks training for EEG-SSVEP classification of emotion recognition. Internetworking Indones. J. **9**(1), 53–57 (2017)
20. Kwak, N.S., Müller, K.R., Lee, S.W.: A convolutional neural network for steady state visual evoked potential classification under ambulatory environment. PLoS ONE **12**(2), 1–20 (2017)
21. Chatzilari, E., Liarios, G., Georgiadis, K., Nikolopoulos, S., Kompatsiaris, Y.: Combining the benefits of CCA and SVMs for SSVEP-based BCIs in real-world conditions. In: Proceedings of the 2nd International Workshop on Multimedia for Personal Health and Health Care, pp. 3–10. MMHealth17, Mountain View (2017)

22. Lee, Y., Lin, W., Cherng, F., Ko, L.: A visual attention monitor based on steady-state visual evoked potential. IEEE Trans. Neural Syst. Rehabil. Eng. **24**(3), 399–408 (2016)
23. Zhang, N., Yu, Y., Yin, E., Zhou, Z.: Performance of virtual stimulus motion based on the SSVEP-BCI. In: IEEE International Symposium on Computer, Consumer and Control, pp. 656–659. IEEE, Xi'an (2016)
24. Samima, S., Sarma, M., Samanta, D.: Correlation of P300 ERPs with visual stimuli and its application to vigilance detection. In: Proceedings of the Annual International Conference of the IEEE Engineering in Medicine and Biology Society, pp. 2590–2593. IEEE, Jeju Island (2017)
25. Kuziek, J.W.P., Shienh, A., Mathewson, K.E.: Transitioning EEG experiments away from the laboratory using a Raspberry Pi 2. J. Neurosci. Methods **277**(1), 75–82 (2017)
26. Zhu, D., Bieger, J., Garcia Molina, G., Aarts, R.M.: A survey of stimulation methods used in SSVEP-based BCIs. Comput. Intell. Neurosci. **2010**(1), 1–12 (2010)
27. Wang, M., Li, R., Zhang, R., Li, G., Zhang, D., Member, S.: A wearable SSVEP-based BCI system for quadcopter control using head-mounted device. IEEE Access. **6**(1), 26789–26798 (2018)
28. Guneysu, A., Akın, H.L.: An SSVEP based BCI to control a humanoid robot by using portable EEG device. In: Annual International Conference of the IEEE Engineering in Medicine and Biology Society, pp. 6905–6908. IEEE, Osaka (2013)

Image Processing and Analysis

Polygonal Approximation Using a Multiresolution Method and a Context-free Grammar

Hermilo Sánchez-Cruz[1]([✉]), Osvaldo A. Tapia-Dueñas[1], and Francisco Cuevas[2]

[1] Centro de Ciencias Básicas, Universidad Autónoma de Aguascalientes,
Av. Universidad 940, 20131 Aguascalientes, Aguascalientes, Mexico
hsanchez@correo.uaa.mx, black.osvo@gmail.com
[2] Departamento de Metrología Óptica, Centro de Investigaciones en Óptica, A. C.,
37150 León, Guanajuato, Mexico
fjcuevas@cio.mx

Abstract. An new method to obtain polygonal approximation for object contours is presented. The method consists of coding the contour with the Angle Freeman chain code (AF8), obtaining strings of eight symbols, and looking for patterns of substrings that represent slope changes along the contour. Our strategy for detecting dominant points is to look for the ends of discrete straight lines through patterns of AF8 symbols, which can be produced by a context-free grammar. With a multiresolution method, we present the polygonal approximation for noisy contours. A set of N dominant points is obtained, the integral square error (ISE) is calculated and, finally, based on lost pixels (LP) in decoding process a new error criterion, that we call lost ratio (LR), is proposed. We found that our method produces the lowest ISE, LP and LR regarding the state-of-the-art.

Keywords: Dominant points · Polygonal approximation · Angle Freeman chain code · Contour shapes · Context-free grammar

1 Introduction

The search for optimal methods to find descriptors is a constant task in computer vision and pattern recognition. Particularly regarding the search of methods with polygonal approximation to represent the shape of binary objects, in which the data of the vertices, significantly reduce the memory storage and facilitate the handling of the original shape information. In this work, each vertex is also called dominant point (DP, for short). Of course, it is inevitable to lose data, but this loss is bearable as long as the information of both the main shape features and its original topology are not affected in the least.

Attneave [2] already had noticed that a shape could be recognized when its contour was simplified by means of a set of straight lines. However, many

© Springer Nature Switzerland AG 2019
J. A. Carrasco-Ochoa et al. (Eds.): MCPR 2019, LNCS 11524, pp. 261–270, 2019.
https://doi.org/10.1007/978-3-030-21077-9_24

papers have been written to quantify the error between such straight lines and the original contour.

Given a contour of n cells 8-connected and listed in the clockwise direction, $C = \{(x_i, y_i), i = 1, ..., n\}$, the problem of finding the best polygon of m vertices (*i.e.*, one that allows a tolerable error) is considering the $C_m^n = n!/[m!(n-m)!]$ different possible polygons.

Teh and Chin [13] use Freeman chain code of eight directions [5], that we call F8, to represent contour shapes and proposed a non-parametric method for dominant point detection. In [12], Sarkar used F8 chain code seeking significant vertices by differentiating the code symbols, instead of taking any coordinate into account. Cronin [4] developed a symbolic algorithm using, also, F8 chain code to assign special symbols to detect DPs. Arrebola and Sandoval [1] proposed a hierarchical computation of a multiresolution structure on chain-coded contours allowing detection of shape details at different scales.

Some authors base their method on the iterative elimination of candidates, called *break points*, until final DPs are obtained [3,9,10].

An alternative way to obtain polygonal approximations is presented in this work, which is based on the recognition of chains that are part of a context-free grammar. Also, our method relies on not only to significantly decrease the number of vertices, *i.e.*, the dominant points, but to look for an error criterion that not only implies the integral square error or the compression ratio, but also, on the amount of information that is lost from the original contour, since there are pixels that can not be recovered in a decoding process.

This paper is organized as follows. In Sect. 2 we explain our proposed method by using a context-free garmmar and a multiresolution method to find DPs, whereas in Sect. 3 the proposal for a new error criterion is detailed. The application of our method is presented in Sect. 4. Finally, in Sect. 5 we give some conclusions and further work.

2   Method

Following definitions are used throughout the paper to understand our method.

Definition 1. A 2D *grid*, is a regular orthogonal array, denoted by $\mathbb{G}$, composed of r rows and c columns of resolution cells. A resolution cell is called a *pixel* denoted by p, if the following two properties are considered: its *Cartesian coordinates* (x, y) and its *intensity value* $I_p \in \{0, 1\}$. If $I_p = 0$, we say that the resolution cell is a 0-*pixel*; on the contrary, if $I_p = 1$, the resolution cell is a 1-*pixel*. Unless otherwise stated, and without causing confusion, in this work we often consider 1-pixel simply as pixel.

Definition 2. AF8 is a two-based vector code [6]: a reference and change vector, whose direction changes are labeled by the symbols of the alphabet $\Sigma_{AF8} = \{a, b, c, d, e, f, g, h\}$. See Fig. 1.

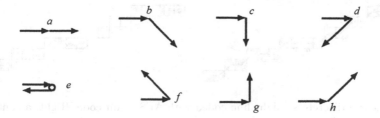

Fig. 1. *AF*8 symbols

We rely on the search for breakpoints where some others can be added carrying out another iteration, such that error criteria are the minimum as possible. The steps of our multiresolution method are:

1. Consider two superimposed grids, $\mathbb{G}$ and $\mathbb{G}'$, so that $\mathbb{G}'$ can be scaled by a parameter $\alpha \geq 1$, with $\alpha \in \mathbb{Z}$. This scaling is done through the origin given by the centroid of the binary object. Start with α as a power of 2.
2. Obtain another contour in $\mathbb{G}'$ with the help of the original in $\mathbb{G}$ by visiting each cell of both grids, and follow the next steps.
   (a) From leftmost and upmost, find the first cell of $\mathbb{G}'$ that contains 1-pixels of the contour in $\mathbb{G}$ and mark it. Cover the set of marked cells in clockwise.
   (b) The next cell to mark in the 8-vicinity of $\mathbb{G}'$ is the one that has the greatest number of 1-pixels of $\mathbb{G}$.
   (c) Repeat last step until all 1-pixels of $\mathbb{G}$ have been covered.
   (d) Given the AF8 chain code of the contour, find strings from the set.

$$L = \{xa^p(bha^q)^r, xa^p(hba^q)^r \mid x \in \{a, b, c, d, e, f, g, h\}\}, \qquad (1)$$

   where p, q, r indicate the number of times the symbol or substring in parentheses is concatenated, x is the label for the breakpoints and $a, b, ..., h$ are symbols of the alphabet AF8.
   (e) Once a cell of $\mathbb{G}'$ has been defined as breakpoint, find the 1-pixel of $\mathbb{G}$ closest to the center of the cell of $\mathbb{G}'$ and define it as a breakpoint.
3. Given two breakpoints (x_k, y_k) and (x_{k+1}, y_{k+1}), a continuous-line segment is defined. The distance between this segment and the points of the contour cells is given by Eq. (2).

$$d^2(p_i, \overline{p_k p_{k+1}}) = \frac{((x_i - x_k)(y_{k+1} - y_k) - (y_i - y_k)(x_{k+1} - x_k))^2}{(x_i - x_{k+1})^2 + (y_k - y_{k+1})^2}. \qquad (2)$$

If $\alpha \geq 1$ and, also, the error between line segments given by breakpoints and the contour is greater than a certain tolerable error, make $\alpha \to \alpha/2$ and go to step 2. Otherwise, consider all breakpoints as DPs and stop.

The main idea of our method is to capture what visually seems to us a digital straight segment (DSS). Of course, there is an error if we consider the continuous straight segment. For contours with high noise, it is not convenient

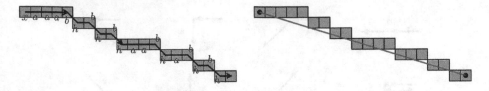

Fig. 2. Left: a discrete straight line coded with AF8 chain code. Right: a continuous straight line is adapted.

to adapt DSS for each pair of abrupt changes, that is why we proceed to expand $\mathbb{G}'$ doing $\alpha > 1$, with this we apply the algorithm on $\mathbb{G}'$ cells, ignoring the details of the noise. Figure 2 presents an example of a visual DSS. As can be observed, the AF8 chain code is $C_{AF8} = xaaabhbhbhbhaabhabhbh$, which can also be written as $C_{AF8} = xa^3 \underbrace{bha^0}\, \underbrace{bha^0}\, \underbrace{bha^2}\, \underbrace{bha^1}\, \underbrace{bha^0}\, \underbrace{bha^0}$. Notice that it is on the form given by L in Eq. (1), where $p = 3$, $0 \le q \le 2$, and $r = 6$.

Figure 3 exemplifies our method. In Fig. 3(a) the contour is immersed in the grid $\mathbb{G}'$ scaled by $\alpha = 4$. The red cells represent the breakpoints. On the other hand, in Fig. 3(b), an approximating polygon was obtained in the first iteration, obtained by applying the CFG. The circumscribed regions are not under a tolerable error. Once our procedure has been carried out iteratively, a final set of DPs is obtained, as shown in Fig. 3(c).

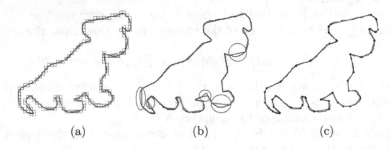

(a)   (b)   (c)

Fig. 3. Example of the method: (a) the grid $\mathbb{G}'$, (b) first iteration, (c) final DPs.

Theorem 1. *L is a subset of a language generated by a context-free grammar, CFG.*

Proof. Let a 4-tuple $G = (V, \Sigma_{AF8}, S, P)$, where the variables V and terminal symbols Σ_{AF8} are disjoint sets, $S \in V$ and P is the set of productions given by the formulas below.

$$S \to xAB | xAC$$
$$B \to bhAB | \epsilon$$
$$C \to hbAC | \epsilon$$

$$A \rightarrow aA \mid \epsilon$$

where ϵ is the empty string. As can be noticed this 4-tuple defines a CFG and produces each of the strings given by L in Eq. (1).

3 Trade Off Between Common Error Criteria

A considerable number of papers have been written to find the best polygonal approximation, proposing a series of error criteria to evaluate the different methods. Some parameters commonly used for assessing the methods are given by the compression ratio (CR, Eq. (3)) and the integral square error (ISE, Eq. (4)).

$$\text{CR} = \frac{n}{N}. \tag{3}$$

$$\text{ISE} = \sum_{i=1}^{n} d_i^2. \tag{4}$$

where n is the number of pixels of the contour shape and N the number of DPs.

As noted by Masood and Haq in [10], the quality of the polygonal approximation should be measured in terms of the data reduction and in the similarity with the original contour, as well. Of course, another primary criterion is the number of DPs. However, sometimes this number is sacrified to obtain minor error distance. In this work we also propose to consider the number of pixels that are lost (LP) when a decoding is carried out to recover the shape. The reasons are given below. Once the DPs are found, if a decoding is performed, the lost pixels can be counted. The approximated polygon is obtained by considering the pixels that contain part of the continuous straight segments given by pairs of DPs. Starting with the first DP, the next pixel to decode is chosen when it contains the longest segment length. If the neighbor cell with the largest segment matches the 1-pixel of the original contour, then the pixel is not lost, otherwise it is a lost pixel.

Figure 4 shows an example of lost pixels when decoding a segment between two DPs, which make a side of a polygonal approximation. Traversing the cells from top to bottom and from left to right, note that the 1-pixels labeled from 1 to 4 contain less length, of the continuous segment, than one of the neighbors (0-pixels) of the previous visited pixel, therefore they are pixels that are lost in decoding, that are mark in yellow. The gray pixels in the right of Fig. 4 are the final decoded approximating polygon. Note, also, that there is an error between the recovered pixels and the continuous segment, given by the coordinates in black dots.

Consider the case in which N DPs are found. Suppose the shape is recovered, and the exact original contour is obtained. In this case there is no loss of information and the method can be considered *lossless*. Something important to note (as depicted to the right of Fig. 4) is that this can happen even if ISE $\neq 0$! If, on the other hand, those N DPs are found in such places where the recovered contour loses pixels, then the method is *lossy*.

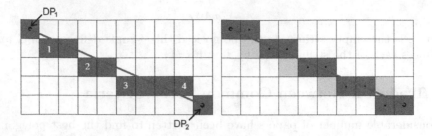

Fig. 4. Lost pixels in a decoding process. Red continous segment is a side of the approximating polygon. Left: some 1-pixels of the original contour in gray cells; right: lost pixels in yellow cells. (Color figure online)

Suppose two solution models (losy and lossles models) that give the same number of DPs, however distributed in different places. Of course, the value of CR is the same!

Once we have analyzed these ambiguities, we propose to consider the importance of N and ISE as a summation in a lost ratio (LR), but weighted by lost pixels (LP), fairly in a single equation, given by Eq. (5).

$$LR = \frac{LP * (N + ISE)}{n}, \tag{5}$$

where LP is the number of pixels lost in the decoding and n the number of pixels of the original contour. Thus, we propose to consider the number of lost pixels as part of the effectiveness of the method: the fewer pixels lose the method, the better. The same is valid for ISE and N, as expressed in Eq. (5).

4   Experiments

We applied our method to a set of samples that commonly appear in the literature. To select the values of the parameters p and q of our proposed L, each string of the AF8 chain code is read, and the maximum number of concatenated a's is obtained, while r is the result of finding repetitions of the form bha^q or hba^q.

4.1   First Set

In this first part, the parameter $\alpha = 1$, *i.e.* no scale is performed due to the very low resolution of sample test. The chain codes of each sample are as presented in Table 1.

Our proposed method was compared and implemented, taking our tolerable errors from those found by Naser *et al.* [11], Masood [8] and Madrid-Cuevas *et al.* [7] methods, using parameters $(p, q, r) = (4, 4, 2)$ for Chromosoma and Leaf and (6,6,1) for Semicircle polygonal approximations, respectively.

Table 1. Chain codes of the sample shapes.

Shape	Chain code
Chromosome	cacabhbahgahbhbbbbaabhaaaaaaaabbcahbhafabhbbbchabhaaaahbahbh
Semicircle	baaaaaaabhabaaaaabahbaaaaaaabgbhbabhchbabhbfaaabhbabhbaaab hbbabhbaaafbhbabhchbabhbgbaaaaaaabhabaaaaabah
Leaf	daabhabafaahbadhabhbafahabcabhbhbaaaahaahbaaaaaaaaccaaaaaaaa aahbagabhbaaaaabhdbhaaafabhbhdbhaaafabhbaaehaafaabhdbaafaaaa

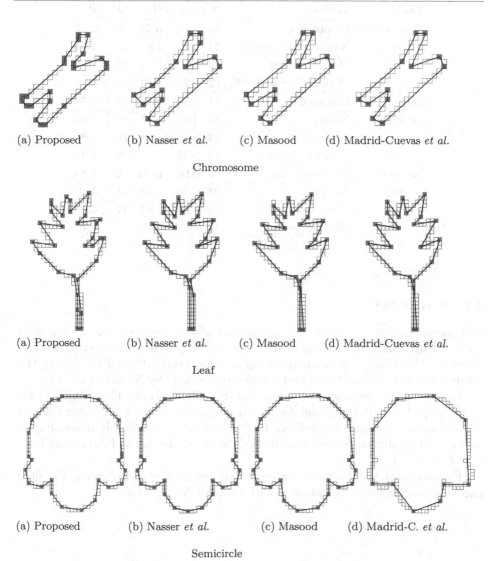

(a) Proposed   (b) Nasser *et al.*   (c) Masood   (d) Madrid-Cuevas *et al.*

Chromosome

(a) Proposed   (b) Nasser *et al.*   (c) Masood   (d) Madrid-Cuevas *et al.*

Leaf

(a) Proposed   (b) Nasser *et al.*   (c) Masood   (d) Madrid-C. *et al.*

Semicircle

Fig. 5. Dominant points of three shapes.

In our experiments, we found an interesting result: the number of pixels that are lost when decoding the shape is lower with our method than with those of the literature. Table 2 shows the results of applying our method comparing with the above mentioned other recent polygonal approximation methods, whereas in Fig. 5 a visual comparison of the different methods is presented.

Table 2. Quantitative comparisons with other polygonal approximation methods.

Shape	Method	N	CR	ISE	LP	LR
Chromosome	Proposed	22	2.73	**3.78**	8	3.44
$n = 60$	Nasser *et al.* (2018)	14	4.28	4.97	10	**3.16**
	Masood (2008)	12	5	7.76	15	4.94
	Madrid-Cuevas (2016)	12	0.2	5.82	13	3.86
Leaf	Proposed	31	3.87	**8.42**	**11**	**3.61**
$n = 120$	Nasser	24	4.95	9.96	15	4.25
	Masood	23	5.22	10.61	18	5.04
	Madrid-Cuevas	22	5.45	11.16	18	4.97
Semicircle	Proposed	25	4.08	**6.32**	**6**	**1.84**
$n = 102$	Nasser	23	4.43	7.63	11	3.30
	Masood	22	4.64	8.61	17	5.10
	Madrid-Cuevas	10	10.2	40.79	47	23.40

4.2   Second Set

In this subsection, we show the application of our method, for objects with greater length in contour shapes. We compare our proposed method with Algorithm 1, APS (applying automatic simplification process) and FDP (fixing the desired number of dominant points) reported recently by Nasser *et al.* [11].

Using Eq. (1), parameters were found. For Shark: $(p, q, r) = (20, 20, 7)$ for Cup: $(p, q, r) = (19, 19, 1)$ and for Stingray: $(p, q, r) = (4, 4, 1)$. Table 3 shows the results in error criteria defined. Cup and Stingray are highly noisy shapes, and a multiresolution process was applied, by using the method iteratively from $\alpha = 4$, to $\alpha = 1$.

Figure 6(a) shows the regions where multiresolution was used, while Fig. 6(b) shows a comparison of our method with those of Nasser *et al.*

Table 3. Quantitative comparisons of second set with other polygonal approximation methods.

Shape	Method	N	ISE	CR	LP	LR
Shark	Proposed	37	**45.46**	7.92	**73**	**20.54**
$n = 293$	Algo 1	23	79.41	12.73	137	47.89
$\alpha = 1$	APS	21	75.52	13.95	133	43.81
	FDP	19	105.09	15.42	135	57.18
Cup	Proposed	20	**93.22**	20.25	**105**	**29.35**
$n = 405$	Algo 1	21	160.70	19.29	167	74.92
$\alpha = 4, 2$	APS	11	238.45	36.82	220	135.50
	FDP	17	159.56	23.82	180	78.47
Stingray	Proposed	37	**84.36**	8.86	**122**	**45.14**
$n = 328$	Algo 1	25	118.66	13.12	180	78.84
$\alpha = 4, 2, 1$	APS	23	121.38	14.26	160	70.43
	FDP	20	165.75	16.40	180	101.94

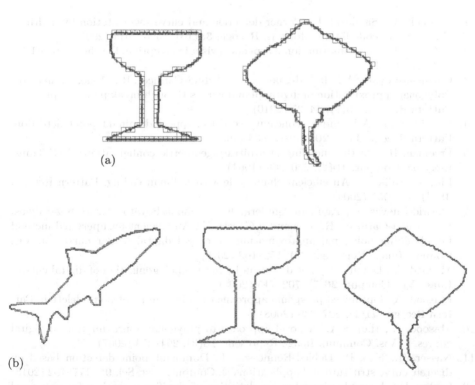

(a)

(b)

Fig. 6. (a) Mutirresolution method applied to Cup and Stringray shapes; (b) polygonal approximation in red is from our proposed method, whereas in green is given by Algorithm 1 from Nasser *et al.*. (Color figure online)

5   Conclusions and Further Work

Without any explicit analysis of curvature changes, we have proposed a new method for detecting dominant points and consequently a polygonal approximation, with an error that improves current models. Although the chain codes already implicitly contain the information of the angles and curvature changes, our method is based on the syntactic search of strings well established by a context-free grammar. In addition, a new evaluation criterion was proposed for the polygonal approach, based on lost pixels in decoding.

As a future work, it is suggested to apply our method to higher resolution shapes, and with greater amount of noise. On the other hand, we decided to find the closest pixel to the center of a $\mathbb{G}'$ cell, however it may not be the optimal. A study through metaheuristic techniques may be appropriate.

Acknowledgements. H. Sánchez-Cruz was supported by CONACyT and Universidad Autónoma de Aguascalientes, under Grant PII18-8.

References

1. Arrebola, F., Sandoval, F.: Corner detection and curve segmentation by multiresolution chain-code linking. Pattern Recogn. **38**(10), 1596–1614 (2005)
2. Attneave, F.: Some informational aspects of visual perception. Psychol. Rev. **61**(3), 183–193 (1954)
3. Carmona-Poyato, A., Madrid-Cuevas, F., Medina-Carnicer, R., Munoz-Salinas, R.: Polygonal approximation of digital planar curves through break point suppression. Pattern Recogn. **43**(1), 14–25 (2010)
4. Cronin, T.M.: A boundary concavity code to support dominant point detection. Pattern Recogn. Lett. **20**(6), 617–634 (1999)
5. Freeman, H.: On the encoding of arbitrary geometric configurations. IRE Trans. Electron. Comput. **10**(2), 260–268 (1961)
6. Liu, Y., Zalik, B.: An efficient chain code with huffman coding. Pattern Recogn. **38**(4), 553–557 (2005)
7. Madrid-Cuevas, F., Aguilera-Aguilera, E., Carmona-Poyato, A., Munoz-Salinas, R., Medina-Carnicer, R., Fernandez-Garcia, N.: An efficient unsupervised method for obtaining polygonal approximations of closed digital planar curves. J. Vis. Commu. Image Represent. **39**, 152–163 (2016)
8. Masood, A.: Dominant point detection by reverse polygonization of digital curves. Image Vis. Comput. **26**(5), 702–715 (2008)
9. Masood, A.: Optimized polygonal approximation by dominant point deletion. Pattern Recogn. **41**(1), 227–239 (2008)
10. Masood, A., Haq, S.A.: A novel approach to polygonal approximation of digital curves. J. Vis. Commun. Image Represent. **18**(3), 264–274 (2007)
11. Nasser, H., Ngo, P., Debled-Rennesson, I.: Dominant point detection based on discrete curve structure and applications. J. Comput. Syst. Sci. **95**, 177–192 (2018)
12. Sarkar, D.: A simple algorithm for detection of significant vertices for polygonal approximation of chain-coded curves. Pattern Recogn. Lett. **14**(12), 959–964 (1993)
13. Teh, C., Chin, R.T.: On the detection of dominant points on digital curves. IEEE Transactions on Pattern Analysis and Machine Intelligence **11**(8), 859–872 (1989)

A Binary Descriptor Invariant to Rotation and Robust to Noise (BIRRN) for Floor Recognition

J. A. de Jesús Osuna-Coutiño[1]([✉]) and Jose Martinez-Carranza[1,2]

[1] Instituto Nacional de Astrofísica, Óptica y Electrónica (INAOE),
Cholula, Mexico
{osuna,carranza}@inaoep.mx
[2] University of Bristol, Bristol, UK

Abstract. Floor recognition is a conventional task in computer vision with several applications in different fields, from augmented reality to autonomous driving. To address this problem, there is a plethora of methods, several of them based on the use of visual descriptors. However, most previous work has low robustness under image degradation. One alternative to address image degradation problems is the use of binary descriptors. Unfortunately, these descriptors are sensitive to noise. In addition, these descriptors use only some pixels within a patch, this limits the floor recognition scope since useful information is available just for a small pixel set. To cope with these problems, we propose a new texture descriptor based on binary patterns suitable for floor recognition. This descriptor is robust to noise, robust to illumination changes, invariant to rotation and it considers a larger number of pixels than the used in the previous LBP-based approaches. Experimental results are encouraging, the proposed texture descriptor reach high performance under several real-world scenarios, 7.4% more *recall* and 3.7% $F - score$ than previous texture descriptors and it has high robustness under image degradation.

Keywords: Binary descriptor · Floor recognition · Urbanized scenes

1 Introduction

Urban structures (lines, planes, etc.) recognition is a useful task for computer vision systems since it provides rich scene information that can be exploited to understand the scene. This is due to the fact that human-made scenes floor have a consistent appearance and they can be used to improve several computer vision applications performance [1–4]. For instance, floor recognition could be used as preliminary cues to infer the road for autonomous vehicle navigation [5]. Currently, there are several trends for floor recognition, for example, some works propose the use of external devices such as Radio-Frequency Identification or pressure sensing to solve the floor recognition problem [6,7]. However, floor

© Springer Nature Switzerland AG 2019
J. A. Carrasco-Ochoa et al. (Eds.): MCPR 2019, LNCS 11524, pp. 271–281, 2019.
https://doi.org/10.1007/978-3-030-21077-9_25

information acquisition can be affected by several environmental factors such as type of material or shape of the road (i.e. if it is uneven, bumpy, etc) [8].

Other approaches focus on the analysis of two or more images captured from different camera views for the same scene, some of these works extend their methodology to the use of Simultaneous Localization And Mapping algorithms, from which cloud points and camera poses can be estimated and used within the floor segmentation problem [9]. More generally speaking, multi-view approaches also rely on fitting algorithms, typically RANSAC and some optimization technique to fit the plane floor within the 3D point clouds (mapping), provided by the SLAM algorithm or any other point cloud generation algorithm based on two or more views. Nevertheless, several thresholds and specialized tuning are required to guarantee high performance for a specific scene. This is an important limitation because in several cases it is difficult to set appropriate threshold values. Also, this approach requires sufficient parallax, i.e., some difference between camera views in order to reach accurate results.

Another approach, which we are interested in this work, is that of carrying out floor recognition from a single image [10]. Unlike the previous approaches (using two views or using external devices) this approach performs floor recognition without thresholds and without parallax constraints. Besides, it has high stability under outdoor scenarios and in most cases, it uses RGB cameras (easy to mobilize and with low size and cost) as the only sensing mechanism. Moreover, there exit several single views available from shots taken from historical images, internet images, personal pictures, holiday photos, etc, which do not have an additional view, hence, floor recognition could not be performed with the conventional methods described before. In contrast, this cases are ideal test benches for an algorithm designed to work with single view images.

Motivated by the high scope of floor recognition from a single image, in this work we are interested in tackling the problem of floor recognition from a single image. In particular, we are interested in how to improve performance under image degradation (i.e., blur, lighting changes, noise, etc.), especially because most of the previous work, also in the domain of single RGB images, fail under high image degradation. Different to previous work we do not classify every pixel in the input image via semantic segmentation. Instead, we propose a novel method that relates image regions with floor patterns. The proposed floor recognition method uses a new binary descriptor which is robust to image degradation, noise and that considers a larger pixels number than previous work, LBP-based solutions [11–14].

Therefore, in order to present our proposal, this paper has been organized as follows: Sect. 2 discusses the related work; Sect. 3 describes the methodology behind our approach; Sect. 4 presents and discusses our results; conclusions are finally outlined in Sect. 5.

2   Related Work

In recent work, important progress under floor recognition from a single image has been made. In particular, the promising result was achieved via learning algorithms that learn the relationship between visual appearance and the floor [15]. In this context, one popular trend is for learning algorithms used in a semantic segmentation core where the aim is for assigning object labels to each pixel of an image. Another approach is direct learning, more efficient regarding computational size and cost. In this case, floor recognition is carried out without segmentation core and therefore input parameters are directly correlated with the image content to recover floor patterns.

For the direct approaches, [16] propose a methodology to estimate the ground plane structure. This methodology uses a supervised learning algorithm with MRF to find the relation between image descriptors (texture and gradient) and its depth information. In order to locate the ground plane boundaries on the depth map, this method divides the input image in similar regions using super-pixels information within depth map. In our case, in recent years we have focused in to develop previous work within the direct learning-based approach. In first manuscript [17], we present a new dominant plane recognition method from a single image that provides five 3D orientation within dominant planar structures to detect (floor, wall and ceiling) on interior scenes. For that, we train a learning algorithm with texture descriptors to predict the 3D orientation in a planar structure. In the second manuscript [18], we present a floor recognition method to integrate virtual information on interior scenes. To detect the floor light variations, we proposed a rule system that integrates three variables: texture descriptors, blurring and superpixels-based segmentation. In order to remove noise, we proposed a remove noise technique that analyzes the consecutive pixels behavior.

Although in our previous works we used descriptors to obtain floor recognition information on interior scenarios. These descriptors have low robustness under image degradations (blur, lighting changes, noise, etc.) that outdoor scenarios provide. To solve these problems, in this work we propose a new floor recognition method that aims for high robustness under image degradations and high density for floor recognition on interior and outdoor scenarios. To solve these problems, we introduce a new texture descriptor based on binary patterns. This descriptor is robust to noise, robust to lighting changes and invariant to rotation. Also, a texture descriptor with these properties (robust to noise, robust to lighting changes and invariant to rotation) is useful considering learning algorithms since would be possible to decrease elements number used within training and it decrease elements number to detect.

3   The Proposed Method

In this section, we present the proposed method to obtain floor recognition using a learning algorithm, a proposed texture descriptor based on binary patterns, a color descriptor using a Gaussian filter and floor recognition analyses.

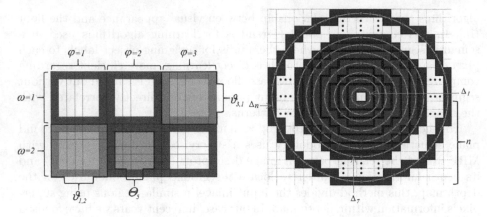

Fig. 1. (a) Grid of 3×2 for the BIRRN; (b) example of n BIRRN circles Δ_j (Color figure online)

3.1 Input Image

In this article, the input image is denoted as I. The image I is used to obtain the texture and RGB color descriptors. We divide the image I in a grid Θ to obtain faster processing. For that, the grid Θ consists of sections Θ_w. Section Θ_w is a finite set of pixels $\Theta_w = \{x_1, ..., x_q\}$, $\Theta_w \in \Theta$, where, q is the number of pixels in one section $\Theta_w \iff q$ is an odd number. Each section Θ_w has a patch $\vartheta_{\varphi,\omega}$. Patch $\vartheta_{\varphi,\omega}$ is a finite set of pixels $\vartheta_{\varphi,\omega} = \{x_1, ..., x_u\}$, $\vartheta_{\varphi,\omega} \in \Theta$, where, u is the number of pixels in one patch $\vartheta_{\varphi,\omega} \iff u$ is an odd number. Pixel $\rho_{\varphi,\omega}$ is the central pixel within patch $\vartheta_{\varphi,\omega}$. Pixel $\varrho_{\varphi,\omega}$ is a pixel within patch $\vartheta_{\varphi,\omega}$. Where, w denotes the w-th section in Θ, φ is the abscissa from grid Θ and ω is the ordinate from grid Θ. Fig. 1(a) shows a grid example Θ of 3×2. Where orange squares are the patches $\vartheta_{\varphi,\omega}$ of 7×7, green square is one section Θ_w of 5×5 and the gray lines are the limits of sections Θ_w.

3.2 Patches Detection with Floor

In this work, to obtain the floor recognition, we use a training system that detects floor patches. The training system is to recognize the floor with its different light intensities using texture and color descriptors.

Training Set. In the patches $\vartheta_{\varphi,\omega}$ we extract the training matrix descriptors. Where, the training labels $\upsilon_{\varphi,\omega}$ are the floor light intensities variations and training matrix descriptors $\psi_{\varphi,\omega}$ are extracted through the pixels of patches $\vartheta_{\varphi,\omega}$. Our training matrix descriptors $\psi_{\varphi,\omega}$ are conformed of the texture descriptor $\Psi_{\varphi,\omega}$ and color descriptor $\chi_{\varphi,\omega}^k$. We obtained the descriptors number for training matrix used the Pareto principle or 80/20 rule [19].

Training Labels. The training labels $v_{\varphi,\omega}$ are the different light intensities of the floor. Where, the different light intensities are a finite set of classes $i = \{1, 2, ..., m\}$ and m correspond to the light intensities number.

Texture Descriptor. We propose a new descriptor to obtain texture based on binary patterns: BIRRN (Binary descriptor Invariant to Rotation and Robust to Noise). The BIRRN descriptor considers a set of neighbor pixels within circular distributions with binary values, where binary values are added in each circular distribution. We defined to Δ_j as the set of neighboring pixels in a circular distribution or BIRRN circle. The BIRRN provides the texture information in a patch $\vartheta_{\varphi,\omega}$, applying Eqs. 1–5.

$$pc_{\varphi,\omega} = \left(\sum_{\tau=1}^{n} \sum_{k=0}^{\varsigma_\tau - 1} p_{(\tau \sin \frac{2\pi k}{\varsigma_\tau}, \tau \cos \frac{2\pi k}{\varsigma_\tau})}\right) / \left(\sum_{\tau=1}^{n} \varsigma_\tau\right) \tag{1}$$

$$\Psi_{\varphi,\omega} = \sum_{\tau=1}^{n} \left(\sum_{k=0}^{\varsigma_\tau - 1} S(pv_{(\tau \sin \frac{2\pi k}{\varsigma_\tau}, \tau \cos \frac{2\pi k}{\varsigma_\tau})} - pc_{\varphi,\omega})\right) f^\tau \tag{2}$$

Where, n is the radios number, τ are the radius of different BIRRN circles $\tau = \{1, 2, ..., n\} \iff \tau > 0$, ς_j is the neighboring pixels number of BIRRN circle Δ_j, ς is a set of the neighboring pixels number ς_j within of different BIRRN circles $\varsigma = \{\varsigma_1, ..., \varsigma_n\}$, $\varsigma \in \vartheta_{\varphi,\omega} \iff \varsigma_1, ..., \varsigma_n > 1$, $pc_{\varphi,\omega}$ is the gray value average within BIRRN circles, $pv_{x,y}$ is the gray value of each neighboring pixel, $p_{\alpha,\beta}$ is gray value of a pixel within BIRRN circles, α is the abscissa of a pixel within BIRRN circles, β is the ordinate of a pixel within BIRRN circles, j denotes the j-th BIRRN circle Δ_j of patch $\vartheta_{\varphi,\omega}$, S is a thresholding function and $\Psi_{\varphi,\omega}$ is the BIRRN value. In addition, f is a factor to discriminate the values of BIRRN circles. The pixels distribution (x, y) used in BIRRN circles are defined as:

$$x = \tau \sin \frac{2\pi k}{\varsigma_\tau} \tag{3}$$

$$y = \tau \cos \frac{2\pi k}{\varsigma_\tau} \tag{4}$$

The threshold function S, which is used to determine the types of local pattern transition, is defined as a characteristic function:

$$S(pv_{x,y} - pc_{\varphi,\omega}) = \begin{cases} 1 & \text{if} \quad pv_{x,y} - pc_{\varphi,\omega} \geq 0, \\ 0 & otherwise, \end{cases} \tag{5}$$

Figure 1(b) shows an image generalized of BIRRN descriptor. Where, this image has n BIRRN circles (green ring) Δ_j, each BIRRN circles has different numbers of neighbor pixels (red circle) $pv_{x,y}$ and the blue squares are the pixels of the BIRRN circles Δ_j.

Color Descriptor. The color descriptor $\chi_{\varphi,\omega}^k$ is obtained using a Gaussian filter on patches $\vartheta_{\varphi,\omega}$. The Gaussian filter information in this work is used to consider uniform RGB values in the training set. To obtain the Gaussian information Eq. 6 the image I is divided in patches $\vartheta_{\varphi,\omega}$ as in the Fig. 1(a). Where, I is the input image, φ is the abscissa from grid Θ, ω is the ordinate from grid Θ, δ is the pixel number of the rows or columns of the patch $\vartheta_{\varphi,\omega}$, σ is the standard deviation of the distribution of the Gaussian function, i' denotes the position of an i'-th pixel, j' denotes the position of a j'-th pixel, a is the abscissa of Gaussian filtering, b is the ordinate of Gaussian filtering, the Gaussian function. is expressed as $g(i',j') = \frac{1}{2\pi\sigma^2}e^{\frac{i'^2+j'^2}{2\sigma^2}}$, $\chi_{\varphi,\omega}^k$ are the RGB gaussian values of a patch $\vartheta_{\varphi,\omega}$ and k is a set with the RGB channel $k = \{R, G, B\}$.

$$\chi_{\varphi,\omega}^k = \sum_{i'=1}^{a} \sum_{j'=1}^{b} (\frac{1}{2\pi\sigma^2}e^{\frac{i'^2+j'^2}{2\sigma^2}})I((\delta * \varphi) + i', (\delta * \omega) + j') \tag{6}$$

Learning Algorithm. We use gradient descent to adjust the parameters θ_0, θ_1, $\theta_2, \theta_3, ..., \theta_n$ of the logistic regression hypothesis [20]. The cost function used in this methodology is shown in Eq. 7. Where, the number of elements is n, the number of examples in training set is m, the i-th elements of the training set are (x^i, y^i) and the regularization parameter is denoted by λ.

$$J(\theta) = -[\frac{1}{m}\sum_{i=1}^{m} y^i \log h_\theta(x^i) + (1 - y^i)\log(1 - h_\theta(x^i))] + \frac{\lambda}{2m}\sum_{j=1}^{n} \theta_j^i \tag{7}$$

Trained System. The proposed method recognizes m different floor light intensities. We use regularized logistic regression with one against all technique to predict the different light intensities [20]. To estimate the light intensities the image I is divided in patches $\vartheta_{\varphi,\omega}$ as in the Fig. 1(a). The logistic regression hypothesis used to recognizes light intensities is presented in Eq. 8. Where, the logistic regression classifier $h_\theta^i(x)$ looks for to find the probability that y is equal to the classes i, i.e., $h_\theta^i(x) = P(y = i|x; \theta)$ be i a finite set of classes $i = \{1, 2, ..., m\}$. Element θ_j is a parameter adjusted of the logistic regression, the element x_j is the texture $\Psi_{\varphi,\omega}$ and color $\chi_{\varphi,\omega}^k$ descriptor of a patch $\vartheta_{\varphi,\omega}$ in the image I.

$$h_\theta^i(x) = g(\theta_j^T x_j) \tag{8}$$

3.3   Floor Recognition Analyses

The first analysis increases the floor recognition and removes the floor recognition with a low connection. For that, the first analysis connects patches with floor recognition and the patches with less connections are removed. The second analysis uses the floor recognition with connection to obtain recognition surface sets. Finally, the set with more connection and more surface is considered the floor.

Fig. 2. Floor and grass recognition using our method and proposed texture descriptor.

4   Discussion and Results

We elaborated a dataset to validate the floor recognition on urban environments. This dataset consists of urban scenes with 1,500 images (720 × 1280 pixels), five different classes (grass, road, smooth carpet, tile and square carpet). These 1,500 images have floor labeled. The dataset images were divided into training images and test images. We use the proposed dataset to compares our floor recognition method using different binary descriptors: [11–14]. To provide quantitative results, we use three measures (*recall*, *precision* and $F - score$). Comparing the *recall*, *precision* and $F - score$ measures of regularized logistic regression (Table 1) and proposed floor recognition method (Table 2), all texture descriptors increase using the proposed method (Table 2). The *recall* has an increase of 21% to 33%, the *precision* has an increase of 7% to 11% and the $F - score$ has an increase of 17% to 28%. In Table 2 our method using proposed texture descriptor (BIRRN) has the best result in the average *recall*, its *precision* has a similar result to the other descriptors (with an average variation of 1%) and its $F - score$ has the best result in the average. In addition, for our floor recognition method using proposed texture descriptor, experimental results demonstrated that it delivers high stability under different scenes, it reaches lower misrecognition and higher *recall* and $F - score$ than previous descriptors under floor recognition domains.

Table 1. Texture descriptors comparison only using regularized logistic regression.

Scene	Descriptor	Recall	Precision	F-score
Grass	LBP [11]	0.339743	0.787709	0.474732
	CsLBP [12]	0.615155	**0.820368**	0.703093
	LBSP [13]	0.323829	0.727545	0.448176
	XcsLBP [14]	0.526395	0.812915	0.639008
	ours	**0.681719**	0.797602	**0.735121**
Road	LBP [11]	0.383351	0.857511	0.529837
	CsLBP [12]	0.583576	**0.890922**	0.705217
	LBSP [13]	0.363858	0.857059	0.510842
	XcsLBP [14]	0.588648	0.81216	0.682573
	ours	**0.650204**	0.860244	**0.74062**
Smooth carpet	LBP [11]	0.334685	0.814794	0.474474
	CsLBP [12]	**0.53772**	**0.872703**	**0.665431**
	LBSP [13]	0.304254	0.809285	0.442244
	XcsLBP [14]	0.22865	0.814368	0.357051
	ours	0.52631	0.846607	0.649097
Tile	LBP [11]	0.391476	0.769171	0.518869
	CsLBP [12]	0.473832	0.794269	0.593565
	LBSP [13]	0.352952	0.773199	0.484663
	XcsLBP [14]	0.552328	**0.815355**	0.658549
	ours	**0.623673**	0.754467	**0.682863**
Square carpet	LBP [11]	0.415673	0.856402	0.559689
	CsLBP [12]	0.486353	0.902816	0.632158
	LBSP [13]	0.388417	0.857615	0.534677
	XcsLBP [14]	**0.933961**	**0.910821**	**0.922246**
	ours	0.588064	0.891786	0.708757
Average	LBP [11]	0.3729856	0.8171174	0.5115202
	CsLBP [12]	0.5393272	**0.8562156**	0.6598928
	LBSP [13]	0.346662	0.8049406	0.4841204
	XcsLBP [14]	0.5659964	0.8331238	0.6518854
	ours	**0.613994**	0.8301412	**0.703291**

We evaluate our approach on proposed dataset, a dataset with multi-class segmentation (MSRC-21) [21] and a dataset that provide different urbanized scenes (Make3D) [22]. Quantitative evaluation is performed using pixels comparisons of the floor recognition with ground-truth. Figure 2 shows floor and grass recognition using our method and proposed texture descriptor. The blue regions show our results on the proposed dataset, Make3D dataset, and MSRC-21 dataset.

Table 2. Texture descriptors comparison using our floor recognition method.

Scene	Descriptor	Recall	Precision	F-score
Grass	LBP [11]	0.645875	**0.94219**	0.766388
	CsLBP [12]	0.881022	0.917091	0.898695
	LBSP [13]	0.608002	0.8642	0.713809
	XcsLBP [14]	0.836078	0.939789	0.884905
	ours	**0.912708**	0.941358	**0.926811**
Road	LBP [11]	0.739093	0.930369	0.823774
	CsLBP [12]	0.895929	0.906249	0.901059
	LBSP [13]	0.701121	**0.935607**	0.801567
	XcsLBP [14]	0.858454	0.870907	0.864636
	ours	**0.935818**	0.906268	**0.920806**
Smooth carpet	LBP [11]	0.623882	0.9596	0.756153
	CsLBP [12]	0.830134	**0.969362**	0.894362
	LBSP [13]	0.550838	0.965192	0.70139
	XcsLBP [14]	0.388786	0.929895	0.548321
	ours	**0.866503**	0.961508	**0.911537**
Tile	LBP [11]	0.7147	0.856645	0.779262
	CsLBP [12]	0.762408	0.859603	0.808094
	LBSP [13]	0.642524	0.878089	0.74206
	XcsLBP [14]	0.844669	**0.883588**	0.863691
	ours	**0.930751**	0.830872	**0.87798**
Square carpet	LBP [11]	0.786115	0.939599	0.856032
	CsLBP [12]	0.836924	0.954079	0.89167
	LBSP [13]	0.746683	0.939989	0.832259
	XcsLBP [14]	**0.958729**	**0.962195**	**0.960459**
	ours	0.933335	0.950606	0.941891
Average	LBP [11]	0.701933	**0.9256806**	0.7963218
	CsLBP [12]	0.8412834	0.9212768	0.878776
	LBSP [13]	0.6498336	0.9166154	0.758217
	XcsLBP [14]	0.7773432	0.9172748	0.8244024
	ours	**0.915823**	0.9181224	**0.915805**

5 Conclusions

In this work, we have introduced a new floor recognition algorithm which is robust enough to provide accurate floor recognition under different urbanized environments. In order addressed the image degradation and improved the floor recognition performance, two different algorithmic improvements were proposed. The first one consists of a new binary texture descriptor (BIRRN) that it is robust to noise, illumination and rotation, and it uses a larger pixel number than the used in the previous LBP-based descriptors. The second improvement consists of two analyses that consider the floor connection and its segmentation in floor surface sets. Regarding the experimental results, it was demonstrated that our binary texture descriptor and the proposed analyses improves the floor recognition performance. For the proposed binary texture descriptor, it reaches high performance under several real world scenarios, more *recall* and $F - score$ than previous texture descriptors and higher robustness under image degradation.

References

1. Okada, K., Inaba, M., Inoue, H.: Walking navigation system of humanoid robot using stereo vision based floor recognition and path planning with multi-layered body image. In: IROS, pp. 2155–2160 (2003)
2. Goncalves, R., Reis, J., Santana, E., Carvalho, N.B., Pinho, P., Roselli, L.: Smart floor: indoor navigation based on RFID. In: WPT (2013)
3. Hoiem, D., Efros, A.A., Hebert, M.: Automatic photo pop-up. ACM Trans. Graph. **24**, 577–584 (2005)
4. Sánchez, C., Taddei, P., Ceriani, S., Wolfart, E., Sequeira, V.: Localization and tracking in known large environments using portable real-time 3D sensors. Comput. Vis. Image Underst. **149**, 197–208 (2016)
5. Martel, J.N., Sandamirskaya, Y., Dudek, P.: A demonstration of tracking using dynamic neural fields on a programmable vision chip. In: ICDSC, pp. 212–213 (2016)
6. Khaliq, A.A., Pecora, F., Saffiotti, A.: Children playing with robots using stigmergy on a smart floor. In: (UIC/ATC/ScalCom/CBDCom/IoP/SmartWorld) (2016)
7. Serra, R., Knittel, D., Di Croce, P., Peres, R.: Activity recognition with smart polymer floor sensor: application to human footstep recognition. IEEE Sens. J. **16**, 5757–5775 (2016)
8. Kang, S.H., et al.: Implementation of Smart Floor for multi-robot system. In: IEEE International Conference ICARA, pp. 46–51 (2011)
9. Zhang, H., Ye, C.: An indoor wayfinding system based on geometric features aided graph SLAM for the visually impaired. IEEE Trans. Neural Syst. Rehabil. Eng. **25**, 1592–1604 (2017)
10. Dai, J., He, K., Sun, J.: Instance-aware semantic segmentation via multi-task network cascades. In: CVPR, pp. 3150–3158 (2016)
11. Ojala, T., Pietikainen, M., Maenpaa, T.: Multiresolution gray-scale and rotation invariant texture classification with local binary patterns. IEEE Trans. Pattern Anal. Mach. Intell. 971–987 (2002)
12. Heikkila, M., Pietikainen, M., Schmid, C.: Description of interest regions with local binary patterns. Pattern Recogn. **12**, 425–436 (2009)
13. Guillaume-Alexandre, B., Jean-Philippe, J., Nicolas, S.: Change detection in feature space using local binary similarity patterns. In: Computer and Robot Vision (CRV), pp. 106–112 (2013)
14. Silva, C., Bouwmans, T., Frélicot, C.: An extended center-symmetric local binary pattern for background modeling and subtraction in videos. In: International Joint Conference on Computer Vision, Imaging and Computer Graphics Theory and Applications (2015)

15. Deng, L., Yang, M., Qian, Y., Wang, C., Wang, B.: CNN based semantic segmentation for urban traffic scenes using fisheye camera. In: IEEE Intelligent Vehicles Symposium, pp. 231–236 (2017)
16. Cherian, A., Morellas, V., Papanikolopoulos, N.: Accurate 3D ground plane estimation from a single image. In: IEEE International Conference ICRA, pp. 2243–2249 (2009)
17. Jesús Osuna-Coutiño, J.A. de., Martinez-Carranza, J., Arias-Estrada, M., Mayol-Cuevas, W.: Dominant plane recognition in interior scenes from a single image. In: ICPR, pp. 1923–1928 (2016)
18. Jesús Osuna-Coutiño, J.A. de., Cruz-Martínez, C., Martinez-Carranza, J., Arias-Estrada, M., Mayol-Cuevas, W.: I want to change my floor: dominant plane recognition from a single image to augment the scene. In: ISMAR, pp. 135–140 (2016)
19. Craft, R.C., Leake, C.: The pareto principle in organizational decision making. IManagement Decis. **40**, 729–733 (2002)
20. Ng, A.: Coursera, Stanford, Machine Learning (2017). https://class.coursera.org/ml-003/lecture
21. Philipp, K., Vladlen, K.: Efficient inference in fully connected CRFs with gaussian edge potentials. In: Advances in Neural Information Processing Systems (2011)
22. Saxena, A., Sun, M., Ng, A.Y.: Make3D: learning 3D scene structure from a single still image. IEEE Trans. Pattern Anal. Mach. Intell. **31**, 824–840 (2009)

Automatic Contrast Enhancement with Differential Evolution for Leukemia Cell Identification

R. Ochoa-Montiel[1,2(✉)], O. Flores-Castillo[2], Humberto Sossa[1,3],
and Gustavo Olague[4]

[1] Centro de Investigación en Computación, Instituto Politécnico Nacional,
Av. Juan de Dios Bátiz and M. Othón de Mendizabal, 07738 Mexico City, Mexico
ma.rocio.ochoa@gmail.com
[2] Facultad de Ciencias Básicas, Ingeniería y Tecnología,
Universidad Autónoma de Tlaxcala, Tlaxcala, Mexico
omarflores8596@gmail.com
[3] Escuela de Ingeniería y Ciencias, Tecnológico de Monterrey,
Av. General Ramón Corona 2514, Zapopan, Jalisco, Mexico
humbertosossa@gmail.com
[4] CICESE Research Center, EvoVision Laboratory, Ensenada, Mexico
gustavo.olague@gmail.com

Abstract. Image enhancement techniques are needed to decrease the negative effects of blur or unwanted noise in image processing. In biomedical images, the quality of images is very important to achieve an adequate identification to detection or diagnosis purposes. This paper addresses the use of contrast enhancement to facilitate the identification of leukemia in blood cell images. Differential evolution algorithm is used to get parameters required to apply contrast enhancement specifically in the interest region in the image, which facilites the posterior identification of leukemic cells. Identification of leukemic cells is accomplished applying an edges extraction and dilatation. From this image, two types of neural networks are used to classify the cells like healthy or leukemic cells. In first experiment, a multilayer perceptron is trained with the backpropagation algorithm using geometric features extracted from image. While in the second, convolutional networks are used. A public dataset of 260 healthy and leukemic cell images, 130 for each type, is used. The proposed contrast enhancement technique shows satisfactory results when obtaining the interest region, facilitating the identification of leukemic cells without additional processing, like image segmentation. This way, computational resources are decreased. On the other hand, to identify the cell type, images are classified using neural networks achieving an average classification accuracy of 99.83%.

Keywords: Contrast enhancement · Differential evolution ·
Leukemia cells

© Springer Nature Switzerland AG 2019
J. A. Carrasco-Ochoa et al. (Eds.): MCPR 2019, LNCS 11524, pp. 282–291, 2019.
https://doi.org/10.1007/978-3-030-21077-9_26

1 Introduction

1.1 Background

A important aim for the scientific community is to endow the machines of the capability of processing an image the same way the human being. The goal of artificial vision is fulfill this objective, being the digital image processing a first phase for this purpose. Nowadays digital image processing has been applied in diverse areas like the robotics [1], surveillance [2], medicine [3], ecology [4], for mention a few. In these areas, the image identification and interpretation are fundamental tasks. An essential process to identify interest regions (ROI) in the image is to divide the image in two or more ROIs. Nevertheless, this process is notable affected when input image quality is low. Particularly in the medical area, the microscopic image processing in gray levels is useful to identify some biological specimens that typically highlight from the background. A type of images of special interest in medicine are the blood cells, this is because the morphological analysis of these images allows identifying pathologies like the leukemia and others hematological disorders. However, due to conditions for the images acquisition are not controlled, these images are generally of poor quality and with different properties for the same group of samples. Some causes are a poor illumination, lack of constant communication with the image sensor, or the wrong setting of lens during acquisition process, for mention a few.

Although, image enhancement techniques have been applied in analysis of leukemia cell images as in [5–7], the most not consider the particular properties of each one these, applying the same transformations to all images. Moreover, traditional enhancement approaches are highly dependent on the image, requiring a manual parameters adjustment. A technique commonly used to image enhancement is the contrast stretching, which consists in to expand the range of intensity levels in the image [8]. In this regard, some proposals to deal the problem of determining the adequate parameters for the image enhancement have been proposed. In [9] an Modified Differential Evolution algorithm is proposed for contrast and brightness enhancement, nevertheless it is computationally complex. Furthermore, in [10] two chaotic Differential Evolution schemes to contrast enhancement are proposed, here the enhancement is considered as a constrained nonlinear optimization problem. Nonetheless, the study uses only two images to test and it does not include an assessment of resulting images. Finally, in [11,12] enhancement techniques are applied to leukemia images, but the results are not reliable because their assessment is done only from a visual standpoint and without comparisons with others works.

Since the microscopic images analysis is a common technique in medical area, the image enhancement techniques are often required due to poor quality or lack of homogeneity in the images. This way, a enhancement technique should be adequate for each image to get satisfactory results in posterior phases of processing. This paper proposes the use of Differential Evolution (ED) to approximate a gaussian mixture model (GMM) to the image histogram. From this, some parameters used for contrast enhancement are computed. Edge detection and dilatation are applied to output image to isolate the cell nucleus region, from which geometrical features are extracted for classifying to the cell by using two types of neural networks.

The paper is organized as follows. Section 2 presents the theoretical fundamentals of proposed methodology. Section 3 describes the process of contrast enhancement with ED for detection of leukemia in blood cell images. Experimental results are shown is Sect. 4. Conclusions are drawn in Sect. 5.

2   Theoretical Fundamentals

2.1   Contrast Enhancement

The goal of image enhancement is to remove many unwanted aspects as posible, while retaining those aspects of the image that are critical to posterior processing. For this purpose an approach is by using per-pixel operations, where it is returned a single value corresponding to each pixel of the input image [13]. In this respect, a commonly used function is the contrast stretch which allows getting an image that covers a wider range of values in the image histogram. In a simple way, it is defined as (1),

$$y = A\frac{c - a}{b - a} \tag{1}$$

where A is the max value that it is wished pixels have, a and b are the bottom and upper limits and c is the gray value in the input image. Graphically it can be seen in Fig. 1. The estimation of values a and b can be done manually or by approximation.

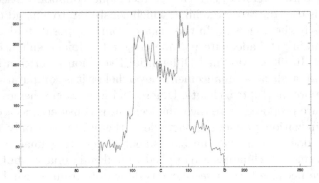

Fig. 1. Typical histogram

2.2   Approximation of Histogram with Gaussian Mixture Model (GMM)

In image processing, the GMM are commonly used for obtaining probabilistic data models. In the case of an image, the distribution of gray levels can be expressed as a histogram $h(gl)$. Considering L gray levels: $[0, \cdots, L-1]$, the histogram can be treated as a probability distribution function. For which, it is normalized dividing each gray level gl in the histogram over the total of pixels N in the image. Thus, the histogram $h(gl)$ can be contained in a mix of Gaussians (2),

$$p(x) = \sum_{i=1}^{K} P_i \cdot p_i(x) = \sum_{i=1}^{K} \frac{P_i}{\sqrt{2\pi}\sigma_i} e^{\frac{(x-\mu_i)^2}{2\sigma_i^2}} \tag{2}$$

where P_i is the probability a prior of class i, $p_i(x)$ is the probability distribution function of random variable x of gray level in the class i, K is the number of classes, μ_i and σ_i are the mean and standard deviation of the probability $i - th$ function. Moreover, there is a constraint that is referred to the sum of probabilities, which should be 1. The assessment of parameters for each mix is through the squared minimum error between the sum of Gaussians and the image histogram (3).

$$E = \frac{1}{n} \sum_{i=1}^{n} (p(x_i) - h(x_i))^2 \tag{3}$$

The problem of parameters estimation to minimize the error in (3) is complex, it is more difficult to solve if the number of mixtures increases. For this reason, the algorithm ED is used for estimation of parameters for each mix, which later are used to deduce the appropriate values of a and b in (1) for the contrast enhancement in the image.

2.3   Differential Evolution

Differential Evolution (DE) is a parallel direct search method which utilizes NP D-dimensional parameter vectors as a population for each generation G, where NP does not change during the minimization process as in (4). This is chosen randomly and should cover the entire parameter space [14].

$$x_{i,G}, i = 1, 2, ..., NP \tag{4}$$

DE is useful to solve optimization problems in continuous spaces where variables are represented by means of real numbers. Initial population is randomly generated and three individuals are selected to be parents, which one of them is the principal father and it is disturbed by the others two parents. If after a selection between the modified father and one of the others fathers, the first is fitter, it is conserved, else it is replaced. Therefore, DE's basic strategy includes the functions of mutation, crossover and selection. The strategy is as follows, For each vector $\overrightarrow{x_{i,G}}$, i = 1,2,...,NP, a mutant vector $\overrightarrow{v}$ is generated according to (5) :

$$\overrightarrow{v} = \overrightarrow{x_{r1,G}} + F \cdot (\overrightarrow{x_{r2,G}} - \overrightarrow{x_{r3,G}}) \tag{5}$$

with indexes randomly created $r_1, r_2, r_3 \epsilon [1, 2, 3, ..., NP]$, integer, mutually different and $F > 0$. The values r_1, r_2 and r_3 should be different from the running index i, so that NP must be greater or equal to four to allow for this condition.

F is a real and constant factor $\epsilon[0,2]$ which controls the amplification of the differential variation $(\overrightarrow{x_{r2,G}} - \overrightarrow{x_{r3,G}})$. In order to increase the diversity of the perturbed parameter vectors, crossover is used. For this purpose the trial vector u (6) is defined,

$$\overrightarrow{u_{i,G+1}} = (u_1 i, G+1, u_2 i, G+1, ..., u_D i, G+1) \tag{6}$$

where D is vector dimension. Trial vector u is formed according to (7):

$$u_{ji,G+1} = \begin{cases} v_{ji,G+1} & if(randb(j) \leq CR) or j = rnbr(i) \\ x_{ji,G} & if(randb(j) > CR) and j \neq rnbr(i) \end{cases} \quad j = 1, 2, ..., D. \tag{7}$$

In 7, $randb(j)$ is the jth evaluation of a uniform random number generator with outcome ϵ [0,1]. CR is the crossover constant ϵ [0,1] which is determined by the user. $rnbr(i)$ is a randomly chosen index ϵ 1,2, ..., D which ensures that $u_{i,G+1}$ gets at least one parameter from $v_{i,G+1}$. To select the individual of next generation $G + 1$, the trial vector $u_{i,G+1}$ is compared to the target vector $x_{i,G}$ using the greedy criterion. If vector $u_{i,G+1}$ yields a smaller cost function value than $x_{i,G}$ then $x_{i,G+1}$ is set to $u_{i,G+1}$; otherwise, the old value $x_{i,G+1}$ is retained.

Particularly, considering (3) as the objective function, the process described above is repeated until a ending criterion is attained or a predetermined generation number is reached.

3   Automatic Contrast Enhancement with Differential Evolution

In this section will be described the contrast enhancement process, which has the aim of highlight the area of interest (ROI) in images of blood cells. Considering

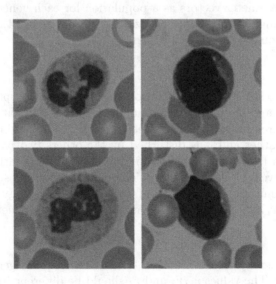

Fig. 2. Images of blood cells

that the cell nucleus is relevant to identify a cell type, the contrast enhancement is focused on highlight this region of cell. In Fig. 2 are shown healthy and leukemic cells images, in first column healthy cells, whereas in the second leukemic cells. As it can seen, the nucleus for each class is notably different. On the other hand, the typical histograms of blood cells contain at least three modes, which is shown in Fig. 3. This fact is considered to propose three mixes K in a model of gaussian mixes (GMM) for the histogram approximation of the image, which is used to get the values of variables a and b in 1. This way, by using 2, a GMM is obtained from the image histogram.

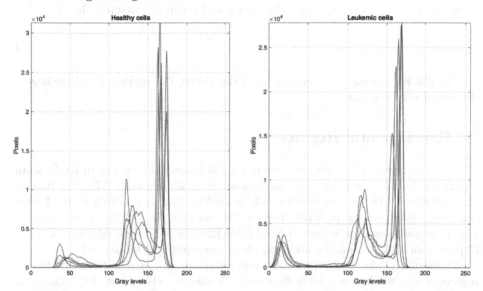

Fig. 3. Overlapping representative histograms of blood cells of a set of five images per class: healthy and leukemic cells.

It is worth to mention that the estimation of parameters for the mix is a complicated problem such that, the more it increases the number of components k, more complex is the estimation of these parameters. This way, the parameters estimation for each component of the mix is treated as an optimization problem as in 8.

$$Minimize\ f(E) = \frac{1}{n} \sum_{i=1}^{n} (p(x_i) - h(x_i))^2 \tag{8}$$

with design variables,

$$x = \{p_1, \sigma_1, \mu_1, p_2, \sigma_2, \mu_2, p_3, \sigma_3, \mu_3\} \tag{9}$$

subject to:

$$h_1(E) = (p_1 + p_2 + p_3) - 1 = 0 \tag{10}$$

From the above, each individual has the structure defined in 9. This is used by te ED algorithm to get the parameters for the GMM. The feasibility rules proposed by [15] are used to handling the constraint $h_1(E)$. These rules take into account the fitness and/or feasibility of each individual during the selection process in the evolutionary algorithm. From this approximation of histogram, and considering that the mode that is more on the left $M1$ in the representative histograms in 3 represents the darker regions in the image (i.e., the region of nucleus of the cell), to contrast enhancement in this region is pertinent to get the values of a and b from 1 solely for this mode $M1$. The calculation of these values is done taking into a count the 3-sigma rule, which about 99.7% of values from a normal distribution are within three standard deviations [16]. This means, from the values μ_1 and σ_1, the values for a and b can be gotten as in 11 .

$$a = \mu_1 - 3 * \sigma$$
$$b = \mu_1 + 3 * \sigma \tag{11}$$

Finally, enhancing the contrast from the above, the region of cell nucleus is delimited very accurately.

4   Experimental Results

The dataset used in this proposal includes 260 blood cells images in RGB, from which the half are healthy cells and remainder leukemic cells [17]. The images size is 600×600 pixels. For experiments is used G channel due to it shows better contrast, unlike image in level gray or the channels R and B, as is shown in Fig. 4. Algorithms were coded in MATLAB R2018a and executed on CPU Core i7 processor, 16GB memory and graphics processing unit Gforce 6.1.

Particularly, the goal of contrast enhancement proposed is to highlight the region of cell nucleus for identification of leukemic cells. First, DE algorithm estimates the parameters defined in 9 using the objective function in 8, which is subject to 10 with a tolerance $\epsilon = 1e^{-6}$. A population of 30 individuals is considered, whither each individual has the estructure defined in 9. This population is randomly initialized, whereas the DE algorithm uses a mutation factor $F = 0.3$ and crossover constant $CR = 0.8$. Number of generations is 200; all obtained experimentally. Deb's feasibility rules are used in constraints handling because search space can include parameters sets which might not be feasible solutions for the problem. Experiments are tested with 10 executions.

From the above, parameters gotten from approximation of image histogram are used to obtain the values of a and b for the mode $M1$, as is defined in 11 from Sect. 3. This way, contrast enhancement done from values of a and b previously gotten achieves to isolate the region of cell nucleus in the most of cases. On the other hand, to identify the leukemic cells from obtained image, a post processing with morphological operators were done to join some regions in the image for its posterior classifying. This way, the edges are extracted using the Robert's algorithm. Later, a dilatation is applied using a structuring element of disk with radius 5. The algorithm for edges extraction, the disk size and its shape were chosen by visual inspection. For which, methods like sobel, canny, prewitt and log for the edges extraction were applied. Whereas for disk geometries were tested

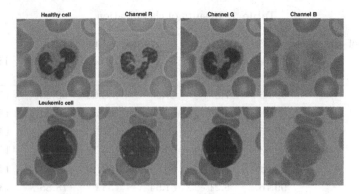

Fig. 4. Blood cells images. In first column images in gray level. Columns 2–4 images of channels R, G and B, respectively.

diamond, octagon and sphere shapes with sizes between 3 and 7. In Fig. 5, third column shows the results of previous process for an image per class. As it can be seen, the proposed enhancement allow us highlight only the interest area, unlike the other techniques like the histogram equalization. To determine that

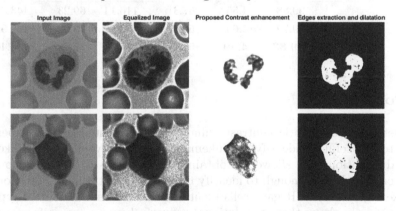

Fig. 5. Isolation of cell nucleus from the proposed contrast enhancement.

the contrast enhancement proposed is useful to identify leukemic cells, three types of neural networks were used: MLP, LeNet and AlexNet. In the former, 17 geometric features were extracted: area, diameter ratio, extent, eccentricity, orientation, solidity, rectangularity, euler number, perimeter, convex area and the 7 Hu's invariants. Whereas, in the convolutional networks LeNet and AlexNet the binary images obtained previously were used. In all cases 80% of data were used for training and remainder for test. Table 1 gives a summary of training outcomes, where we can see the proposed method for contrast enhancement has a good performance to identify the leukemic cells using a MLP network. Moreover, unlike of convolutional networks, the required time for classification is much shorter.

Table 1. Results of classification.

Number of execution	MLP		Convolutional networks			
	Accuracy	Time (s)	Accuracy LeNet	Time (s)	Accuracy AlexNet	Time (s)
1	99.83	7.38	57.69	153.63	69.23	158.45
2	99.88	4.20	55.77	150.33	86.54	144.81
3	99.85	4.18	50.00	157.33	73.08	142.22
4	99.83	5.21	50.00	156.72	75.00	143.63
5	99.81	5.44	50.00	152.19	78.85	147.91
6	99.76	5.21	61.54	153.67	78.85	137.16
7	99.85	4.02	50.00	154.48	82.69	143.91
8	99.83	4.00	50.00	164.31	86.54	146.16
9	99.85	4.92	63.46	154.67	78.85	139.55
10	99.85	4.11	40.38	157.94	86.54	144.09
11	99.81	4.39	50.00	157.64	84.62	144.31
12	99.82	4.44	48.08	148.23	84.62	145.81
13	99.77	4.12	50.00	134.39	73.08	144.19
14	99.88	4.55	67.31	116.14	69.23	143.84
15	99.79	5.66	59.62	132.64	73.08	139.95
Mean	**99.83**	**4.49**	53.59	153.63	78.72	144.40

5 Conclusions

The method of automatic contrast enhancement presented in this paper has shown to be useful for identifying leukemic cells. Evolutive algorithms like Differential evolution have allowed to obtain good solutions to achieve a contrast enhancement which is enough to identify the cells without using a posterior process like segmentation. Regard cells identification, the use of different types of neural networks shows that convolutional networks have a poor performance for classifying binary images, while a MLP is better for this task.

In brief, it is noticeable that the proposed method favours the use of computational few resources to identify leukemic cells in gray level images. Finally, the method could be used for whatever type of gray level images, considering a previous characterization theirs histograms.

Acknowledgements. This research was economically supported in part by the Instituto Politécnico Nacional, Mexico under projects SIP 20190007 and CONACYT 65 (Fronteras de la Ciencia); and in part by the Autonomous University of Tlaxcala, Mexico. R. Ochoa acknowledges CONACYT for the scholarship granted towards pursuing his PhD studies.

References

1. Maxwell, J.C.: A Treatise on Electricity and Magnetism, vol. 2, 3rd edn. Clarendon, Oxford (1892)
2. Liu, H., Feng, J., Qi, M., Jiang, J., Yan, S.: End-to-end comparative attention networks for person re-identification. IEEE Trans. Image Process. **26**(7), 6–13 (2017)
3. Kervrann, C., Sorzano, C., Acton, S., Marin, J.O., Unser, M.: A guided tour of selected image processing and analysis methods for fluorescence and electron microscopy. IEEE J. Sel. Top. Signal Process. **10**(1), 6–30 (2016)
4. Ma, B., Pu, R., Wu, L., Zhang, S.: Vegetation index differencing for estimating foliar dust in an ultra-low-grade magnetite mining area using landsat imagery. IEEE Access **5**(1), 8825–8834 (2017)
5. Toh, L.B., Mashor, M.Y., Ehkan, P., Rosline, H., Junoh, A.K., Harun, N.H.: Implementation of high dynamic range rendering on acute leukemia slide images using contrast stretching. In: 2016 3rd International Conference on Electronic Design (ICED), pp. 491–496 (2016)
6. Ravindraiah, R., Srinu, M.V.: Quality improvement for analysis of leukemia images through contrast stretch methods. Procedia Eng. **30**(1), 475–481 (2012)
7. Mokhtar, N.R.: Image enhancement techniques using local, global, bright, dark and partial contrast stretching for acute leukemia images. In: World Congress on Engineering, pp. 807–812 (2009)
8. González, R.C., Woods, R.E., Eddins, S.L.: Digital Image Processing Using MAT-LAB, 2nd edn. McGraw-Hill Education, New York (2011)
9. Suresh, H., Lal, S.: Modified differential evolution algorithm for contrast and brightness enhancement of satellite images. Appl. Soft Comput. **61**, 622–641 (2017)
10. Coelho, L.D.S., Sauer, J.G., Rudek, M.: Differential evolution optimization combined with chaotic sequences for image contrast enhancement. Chaos, Solut. Fractals **42**(1), 522–529 (2009)
11. Salihah, A.N.A., Mashor, M.Y., Harun, N.H., Rosline, H.: Colour image enhancement techniques for acute leukaemia blood cell morphological features. In: 2010 IEEE International Conference on Systems, Man and Cybernetics, pp. 3677–3682 (2010)
12. Toh, L.B., Mashor, M.Y., Ehkan, P., Rosline, H., Junoh, A.K., Harun, N.H.: Implementation of high dynamic range rendering on acute leukemia slide images using contrast stretching, pp. 491–496 (2016)
13. Prince, S.J.D.: Computer Vision: Models, Learning and Inference, 1st edn. Cambridge University Press, Cambridge (2012)
14. Storn, R., Price, K.V.: Differential evolution: a simple and efficient heuristic for global optimization over continuous spaces. Global Optim. **11**(1), 341–359 (1997)
15. Branke, J., Deb, K., Miettinen, K., Slowiński, R.: Multiobjective Optimization. Interactive and Evolutionary Approaches, 1st edn. Springer, Heidelberg (2008). https://doi.org/10.1007/978-3-540-88908-3
16. Grafarend, E.W.: Linear and Nonlinear Models: Fixed Effects, Random Effects, and Mixed Models, 1st edn. Walter de Gruter, Berlin (2006)
17. Labati, R.D., Piuri, V., Scotti, F.: All-IDB: the acute lymphoblastic leukemia image database for image processing (2011)

Enhanced Parallel Generation of Tree Structures for the Recognition of 3D Images

P. Real[1]([✉]), H. Molina-Abril[1], F. Díaz-del-Río[1], S. Blanco-Trejo[2], and D. Onchis[3]

[1] H.T.S. Informatics' Engineering, University of Seville, Seville, Spain
{real,habril,fdiaz}@us.es
[2] Dpto. Ingeniería Aeroespacial y Mecánica de Fluidos, University of Seville, Seville, Spain
sblanco1@us.es
[3] Faculty of Mathematics, University of Vienna, Vienna, Austria
darian.onchis@univie.ac.at

Abstract. Segmentations of a digital object based on a connectivity criterion at n-xel or sub-n-xel level are useful tools in image topological analysis and recognition. Working with cell complex analogous of digital objects, an example of this kind of segmentation is that obtained from the combinatorial representation so called Homological Spanning Forest (HSF, for short) which, informally, classifies the cells of the complex as belonging to regions containing the maximal number of cells sharing the same homological (algebraic homology with coefficient in a field) information. We design here a parallel method for computing a HSF (using homology with coefficients in $\mathbb{Z}/2\mathbb{Z}$) of a 3D digital object. If this object is included in a 3D image of $m_1 \times m_2 \times m_3$ voxels, its theoretical time complexity order is near $O(log(m_1 + m_2 + m_3))$, under the assumption that a processing element is available for each voxel. A prototype implementation validating our results has been written and several synthetic, random and medical tridimensional images have been used for testing. The experiments allow us to assert that the number of iterations in which the homological information is found varies only to a small extent from the theoretical computational time.

Keywords: 3D digital images · Parallel computing · Abstract cell complex · Homological Spanning Forest · Crack transport

1   Introduction

Using the analogy that a digital image can be seen as a puzzle of (initially, small) pieces, topological analysis and recognition problems can be rethought in terms

Work supported by the Spanish research projects TOP4COG, MTM2016-81030-P (AEI/FEDER,UE), COFNET (AEI/FEDER,UE), the VPPI of University of Seville and the Austrian Science Fund FWF-P27516.

© Springer Nature Switzerland AG 2019
J. A. Carrasco-Ochoa et al. (Eds.): MCPR 2019, LNCS 11524, pp. 292–301, 2019.
https://doi.org/10.1007/978-3-030-21077-9_27

of reconstructing the image as a puzzle of big pieces which are maximally stable with regards some connectivity criterion. This maximal stability of the regions mean that if one of these regions increase in size, the preservation of the topological criterion is lost. This perspective is not new [2,7,10] and exhibits nowadays fruitful results in object recognition. Working with a cell complex analogous of a 3D digital image, we are mainly interested here in using the topological invariant of homology (concretely, algebraic homology with coefficient in a field) as main argument in the topological criterion. Succinctly, a Homological Spanning Forest (HSF, for short) of a cell complex, notion developed in [1,8], is a set of trees, in which each of them is a path-connected representation of a maximal stable homological region, whose nodes are the cells of that region. In this paper, a parallel ambiance-based algorithm for computing a HSF is for the first time implemented and tested.

2   Enhanced Parallel Generation of MrSF and HSF

Given a 3D digital object D included in a 3D digital image I_D, the scenario in which we need to "embed" I_D based on cubical voxel is that of an abstract cubical cell complex (or ACC, for short), denoted $Cell(I_D)$, and having as 0-cells the voxels of I_D and as 3-cells the 0-dimensional corners of the voxels. In our parallel framework we define one processing element (PE) per voxel. The 0-cells inherit the properties (such as color; black or white from now on) of the actual voxels of I_D, the 1-cells are defined by the set of two 6-adjacent voxels, 2-cells by sets of four mutually 6-adjacent voxels and 3-cells by sets of eight mutually 6-adjacent voxels.

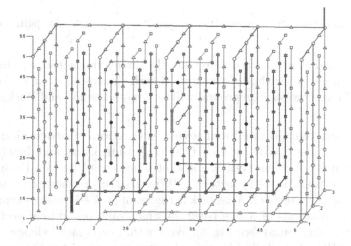

Fig. 1. A ring perpendicular to Y axis with an associated MrSF.

With the previous scenario of cells over the canvas, an initial HSF of the whole image, called Morse Spanning Forest ($MrSF(I_D)$ for short), is built. It is necessary to emphasize that our construction method may initially provide a set of graphs (not necessarily trees) that will be then pruned to be trees, so that parallel computing is promoted. An $MrSF(I_D)$ will be composed by a set of $(k, k+1)$-trees ($k = 0, 1, 2$) of size n, having as nodes cells of dimension k and (if $n > 1$) cells of dimension $k + 1$, and having as edges some incidence relations between these cells (called $(k, k+1)$-edges). In $MrSF(I_D)$, there is one $(0, 1)$-tree, one $(2, 3)$-tree and possibly several $(1, 2)$-trees.

In Fig. 1, a visual example of all the necessary cells and trees of the MrSF are depicted. The circles, triangles, squares and stars represent 0-cells, 1-cells, 2-cells and 3-cells, respectively. There are $(0, 1)$, $(1, 2)$ and $(2, 3)$ trees, represented by red, yellow and blue lines respectively.

The main steps of the complete construction process are shown in Fig. 2 and will be detailed in the sequel. From now on, and for clarity purposes, we restrict ourselves to work with 6-adjacency for any (background or foreground) voxel.

A complete implementation of the algorithm has been done in MATLAB / OCTAVE language [9]. This language has been chosen to favor an inherent parallel codifying and special care has been taken to promote element-by-element matrix operations whenever possible. These operations can be executed theoretically in a fully parallel manner. Only a few parts of the whole process cannot be executed with this kind of operations, thus diverging the theoretical timing order from $O(1)$, and yielding to a few loop structures including loop-carried dependencies (thus preventing ideal parallelism [4]).

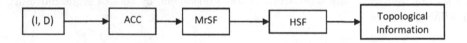

Fig. 2. Main steps of the parallel homological segmentation of a digital object.

The proposed algorithm is divided into the three following steps, which result to be close to the logarithm of the sum of each dimension, that is, $log_2(m_1 + m_2 + m_3)$. From now on, Foreground will be denoted as FG and Background as BG.

(a) MrSF construction at local level: Activation of processing units.
We construct $(k, k+1)$-edges of the $MrSF(I_D)$ using primal and dual $(k, k+1)$-vectors. Given two incidence cells c and c' of dimensions k and $k+1$ respectively, a primal (resp. dual) $(k, k+1)$ vector (c, c') (resp. (c', c)) connects the tail c (resp. c') with the head c' (resp. c). A k-crack is the set of $(k, k+1) - edges$ representing the boundary relations of a $k + 1$-cell, in which only one primal vector exists (being the rest dual ones) (see Fig. 3). We say that one crack belongs to the FG (resp. to the BG) if the tail of its primal vector is a cell of the FG (resp. of the BG).

We will limit ourselves to say that for three dimensional images, there are nine possible activation states for any **PE**. One of these states is pictured in Fig. 3.

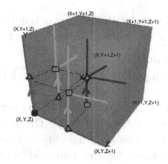

Fig. 3. An activation state of the processing unit showing its eight active cells, primal and dual activation vectors and associated cracks. The 0-cell (x, y, z) is drawn with a circle, the 1-cells with triangles, the 2-cells with squares and the 3-cell with a star. The active primal vectors are drawn with an arrow and using different colors depending on its dimension. (Color figure online)

Figure 1 shows an example of the final trees. FG cells are drawn with solid shapes (circle, triangles, squares and stars, depending on their dimension), and hollow shapes are used for BG cells. In this case, primal $(0, 1)$ vectors are represented with red lines inside each PE, and there is only one primal $(0, 1)$ vector for each voxel. Note that there is only one dual vector (going form triangles to circles towards positive directions) for each 1-cell belonging to the $(0,1)$ tree. Rules for the rest of dual vectors are similar; however in the case of the $(1,2)$ and $(2,3)$ trees, up to two dual vectors can go from a $(j + 1)$-cell to a j-cell.

An obvious tree preservation rule must be kept at this stage: only those dual vectors that connect the same dimensional tree are allowed. Bearing in mind 6-adjacency and in order to promote parallelism, cracks are only defined towards positive directions: $+X$, $+Y$, $+Z$. These cracks will allow to build the different trees for a given image. Note that dual inter-voxel connections can be extensive, that is, we can activate all the possible dual vectors that do not contravene the tree allocation for each cell. However, as we are interested in building trees (not graphs) for an efficient parallel processing of crack transports, some dual $(2,1)$ vectors must not be activated in our current implementation. More exactly, for those j-cells that can receive two dual vectors coming from $(j + 1)$-cells, only one of them is activated.

For activating in parallel all the processing units of $ACC(I_D)$, we use *local MrSF rules*. As each PE can compute its state with no dependencies to the rest of PE, this step is fully parallel, that is, $O(1)$. In this step we proceed so that the number of critical cracks in the MrSF is maintained to the minimum possible (considering only local interactions between neighboring voxels). Critical cracks, are those having on its border both, background and foreground cells.

Critical cracks are drawn using thicker lines (using the color convention in Fig. 1). In the case of a ring (Fig. 1), FG contains one critical 0-crack and one critical 1-crack, and BG contains one critical 0-crack, one critical 1-crack and one critical 2-crack.

The main advantage of this local MrSF construction method, is that it can be computed in a fully parallel manner for each voxel.

(b) Global MrSF construction

Once a local MrSF has been built, the MrSF global trees are to be computed and labelled.

This labeling consists of tracking the label from every cell to a new one. Most of these algorithms do this tracking by using the number of the label stored at each site [5]. That is, they compute label[i] = label[label[i]] until the label remains unchanged. In our case, we use two additional pieces of information: (a) The exact knowledge of which cracks are critical (whose labels will remain unchanged); (b) The magnitudes and directions of the hops from one cell to the root. Note that the first hop is immediately given by the MrSF local information.

In order to build trees in this stage, additional prunings within the resulting graphs might be done for the (1,2) cracks.

According to the definition of primal and dual vectors of previous stages, it is obvious that the maximum distance between two cells is $(m_1 + m_2 + m_3)$. Besides, using the process label[i] = label[label[i]], the hop magnitudes increases in a geometric manner of ratio 2. Hence the maximum time order for this stage is $log_2 (m_1 + m_2 + m_3)$ (Fig. 5).

(c) Final HSF construction via crack transports

The final step consists of minimizing the number of critical cracks, giving rise to a new MrSF. That means, that within this MrSF, if we only consider cells belonging to D, we have an HSF of D. From now on, this final MrSF will be named as $HSF(D)$. As an example, Fig. 4 (top) contains an MrSF and an $HSF(D)$ (bottom) of an object D composed of three parallel segments. The first MrSF contains three critical 0-cracks and two critical 1-cracks for the FG (drawn with thicker red and yellow lines, resp.) and the $HSF(D)$ contains only one critical 0-crack.

To clarify a transport operation, only one pair of the (0,1)-tree links that are to be transported have been rounded by a discontinuous oval in the MrSF. Those links are transported to the wider orange links (see the oval drawn at the HSF), so that they "close" correctly the (0,1)-tree. Another pair of (1,2)-tree links is also transported for this critical crack. Likewise, the same transport operations are done for the other pair of critical 0-crack and 1-crack. Obviously, the final HSF contains only one critical FG 0-crack, being the representative of the FG CC (connected component).

The key point for transforming an $MrSF(I_D)$ into an $HSF(D)$ is the achievement of the best parallelism degree. This is done as follows. For each critical MrSF 0-crack, we calculate in parallel the movements along (1,2) and (0,1) trees. Firstly, there are six possible paths leaving from each critical 0-cell and moving through the (1,2)-tree. One of them is selected for every critical MrSF 0-crack, and the (1,2)-trees (tracking frontier digital surfaces, which can be defined in a similar manner to [6]), fall onto the corresponding 2-cells. From these 2-cells, it is resolved what critical 1-crack has a primal vector to them. Then, every 1-cell has two incident 0-cells, and the two back movements for

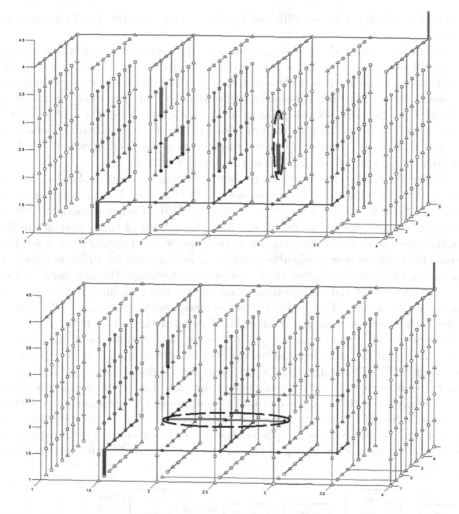

Fig. 4. A figure composed of three segments parallel to the axis (a total of 5 black voxels). Top: MrSF, which contains 3 critical 0-cracks and 2 critical 1-cracks for the FG (thicker red and yellow segments). Bottom: HSF, which contains only one critical FG 0-crack. (Color figure online)

these 0-cells are computed in parallel in order to determine if the couple of 0/1-cells can be eliminated, and so, the transport made. The movements of these 0-cells through the (0,1)-tree yield to three different cases (processed in an independent and parallel manner for each couple of 0/1-cells). These cases are: (a) the 1-cell can be deleted (a crack transport is done) with the initial critical 0-cell, because only one of its two (0,1) paths fell into the initial 0-cell; (b) the 1-cell is the representative of a tunnel (it is a true critical 1-cell), since these two (0,1) paths fell into the same 0-cell; (c) nothing can be determined, because the two (0,1) paths fell into two different 0-cells (in this case, the 1-cell remains the same).

Note that moving along trees guarantees that the uniqueness in the selection of the different couples of 0/1-cells is ensured, and therefore there is no need for synchronization primitives. In this sense, perfect parallelism is achieved in these six paths, thus, their time order can be considered as $O(1)$. Summing up, for each critical MrSF 0-crack, six set of paths must be computed (all the paths of each set in parallel). Likewise, for the pairing of couples of critical MrSF 1/2-crack, a similar parallel procedure can be performed, preserving time order as $O(1)$. The number of incident cells is inferior in this ulterior pairing.

Nevertheless, the transports along these six paths for couples of 0/1-cells and two paths for couples of 1/2-cells do not imply that complete pairing has been done and that these transports would give us the HSF. There are complex shapes that need some subsequent iterations. The exact form of these shapes will be studied elsewhere; for the present work, the experimental results of next section reveal that the number q of subsequent iterations needed for different types of images is less than 5 for most of the analyzed 3D images. Besides, some of the tested images required a sequential stage of 0/1 cell coupling that cannot be processed in parallel. This is due to the necessary pruning of some (1,2) vectors done in the previous stage (b) (Global MrSF construction). This pruning implies that some paths along the whole (1,2) tree are lost. As illustrated in the next section, the number of sequential transports (denoted as s_{01} in Fig. 5) represents less than 0.5% of the number of voxels even for random images, being around ten times inferior for the analyzed natural images. The pruning was also done for the inverse path 2/1/2, which means that some 1/2 transports can either be done in parallel (which number is denoted as s_{12} in Fig. 5). Nevertheless, for real or random 3D images the percentage of these sequential 1/2 transports is negligible. A further discussion of this aspect can be found in the next section.

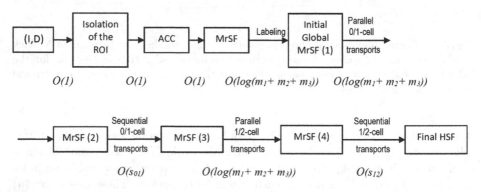

Fig. 5. Time orders for the different steps of HSF computation considering $m_1 \times m_2 \times m_3$ computation processors. s_{01} and s_{12} are the number of sequential cancellations of remaining 0/1 and 1/2 cells resp. (after the parallel cancellation of these pairs).

In summary, time order of one parallel step of this stage (c) is O(1). Besides, a small number q of parallel transport iterations is required for most of the images (see next section). Finally, time order would diverges from O(1) only for the small percentage of sequential transports. Figure 5 summarizes the time orders for the different steps of the whole HSF calculation considering $m_1 \times m_2 \times m_3$ computation processors. One final remark that highlights a practical significance to our method is that many useful geometric properties (area, perimeter, etc.) can be computed at the same time and also in parallel with the HSF.

3   Experimental Results and Conclusions

Firstly synthetic Menger sponges were used to test the results of the parallel algorithm by comparing the outputs with that of the algebraic AT-model [3]. Experiments were performed using fractal modifications of the Menger Sponge. The initial structures used to generate these new fractals were constructed filling planes (OX, OY and/or OZ) within the Menger Sponges of recursion 2 and 3 for different values of x, y and z. In all cases the first parallel transport iteration of 0/1 cell pairs yielded to the correct result. However, the results for the 1/2 pairs were very divergent. On one hand, for some sponges the final HSF was reached through our parallel transportation method; on the other hand, for some others the parallel transports produce moderate results (around a fifty percent of sequential 1/2 pair transports were required).

No doubt that synthetic images are very peculiar and the parallel processing of the HSF can present strange results. On the contrary, parallel computing is very efficient for random images, and even more for real medical images, as shown below. For small random images (up to $15 \times 15 \times 15$) the proposed method was almost perfect: the final HSF is completed in a fully parallel manner for almost 100% of the tested images. Table 1 (rows 1–3) shows the mean number of critical cracks for the first four parallel and last sequential transport iterations of 0/1 cell pairs, and for the following parallel and final sequential transport of 1/2 cell pairs for a set of five $30 \times 30 \times 30$ B/W random images (which were generated using a 50/50 probability for colors, and surrounded by six thin faces of BG voxels according to our working premises). Actually, a fifth iteration would transport another one or two 0/1 pairs more for two of the bigger tested images, although for the sake of simplifying the tables, it has not been exposed. The last three columns reveal patently the efficiency of our parallel processing: a first phase of parallel 0/1 transports reached more that three quarters of the total necessary transports. After the fourth parallel stage, this percentage reaches more that 90%, which supposes a sequential number of steps that is less than the 0.5% of the total amount of voxels for any random image. For the 1/2 pairs results are even better: almost all couples can be canceled in parallel.

Table 1. Mean number of critical cracks for the first four parallel and last sequential transport iterations of 0/1 cell pairs, and for the following parallel and final sequential 1/2 cell transport, for a set of five B/W $30 \times 30 \times 30$ random images with a 50/50 probability for colors, surrounded by six thin faces of BG voxels (rows 1–3). Rows 4–12: Same evolution of the number of critical cracks for three trabecular bone images of sizes $43 \times 43 \times 9$, $64 \times 64 \times 13$, and $43 \times 43 \times 9$ (rows 4–6, 7–9 and 8–12 resp.). The last three columns indicate the mean percentage of parallel transports achieved: in the first iteration for 0/1 pairs, after the fourth iteration for 0/1 pairs, and for the 1/2 pair transport, resp.

	Initial crit. cells (MrSF)	After 1st transp. of 0/1 cells	After 2nd transp. of 0/1 cells	After 3rd transp. of 0/1 cells	After 4th transp. of 0/1 cells	After sequential transp. of 0/1 cells	After parallel transp. of 1/2 cells	After seq. transp. of 1/2 cells (final HSF)	Percentage of parallel transp. in the 1st transp. (0/1 cells)	Percentage of parallel transp. (0/1 cells)	Percentage of parallel transp. (1/2 cells)
FG crit. 0-cells	1510.60	620.20	444.20	370.40	358.40	241.60	241.60	241.60	77.28	90.80	
FG crit. 1-cells	2746.40	1856.00	1680.00	1606.20	1594.20	1477.40	1401.00	1400.20	77.28	90.80	98.96
FG crit. 2-cells	77.20	77.20	77.20	77.20	77.20	77.20	0.80	0.00			98.96
FG crit. 0-cells	71	19	14	12	11	6	6	6	86.67	92.31	
FG crit. 1-cells	148	96	91	89	88	83	21	19	86.67	92.31	96.88
FG crit. 2-cells	106	106	106	106	106	106	44	42			96.88
FG crit. 0-cells	187	77	60	46	40	16	16	16	74.83	85.96	
FG crit. 1-cells	242	132	115	101	95	71	14	14	74.83	85.96	100.00
FG crit. 2-cells	60	60	60	60	60	60	3	3			100.00
FG crit. 0-cells	102	37	28	19	16	8	8	8	75.58	91.49	
FG crit. 1-cells	190	125	116	107	104	96	28	26	75.58	91.49	97.14
FG crit. 2-cells	101	101	101	101	101	101	33	31			97.14

Finally, a third set of tests were performed for three real binary 3D medical images. Clinical Micro Computer Tomography Images of trabecular bones (obtained by the ETH, Zurich) were selected because of their usually complex topology, consisting of many cavities and tunnels (see Table 1, rows 9–12). Results are similar to that of random images, that is, around a 90% of 0/1 pair transports and around 97% of 1/2 pair transports can be done in a fully parallel manner just in four iterations for the first pairs and in one iteration for the second ones. Because natural images are usually simpler than the random ones, less transports are necessary for them. In fact, the sequential number of steps for this set of medical images is around ten times inferior (less than the 0.05% of the total amount of voxels).

In conclusion, a new parallel algorithm for computing a HSF of a 3D digital object is designed and implemented. It has been demonstrated that its time complexity order is almost logarithmic (remaining only a linear term less than the 0.5% of the total amount of voxels even for random images). Several aspects to progress in a near future are: (a) To further improve the efficiency of some procedures of the algorithm: activation of processing units, crack transport, etc.; (b) To improve the results in object recognition of homology-based features via the definition of a "region-adjacency-graph" of the HSF and the proposal of new topological-based features; (c) To implement a 4D version of the algorithm for topological experimentation in this context.

References

1. Díaz-del-Río, F., Real, P., Onchis, D.: A parallel homological spanning forest framework for 2D topological image analysis. Pattern Recognit. Lett. **83**, 49–58 (2016)
2. Forman, R.: Morse theory for cell complexes. In: Advances in Mathematics, vol. 134, pp. 90–145 (1998)
3. González-Díaz, R., Jiménez, M.J., Medrano, B., Real, P.: A tool for integer homology computation: λ-AT-model. Image Vis. Comput. **27**(7), 837–845 (2009)
4. Hennessy, J.L., Patterson, D.A.: Computer Architecture: A Quantitative Approach, 5th edn. Morgan Kaufmann Publishers Inc., San Francisco (2011)
5. Komura, Y.: GPU-based cluster-labeling algorithm without the use of conventional iteration: application to the Swendsen-Wangmulti-cluster spin flip algorithm. Comput. Phys. Commun. **194**, 54–58 (2015)
6. Kovalevsky, V.: Multidimensional cell lists for investigating 3-manifolds. Discret. Appl. Math. **125**(1), 25–43 (2003)
7. J. Matas, O. Chum, M. Urban, T. Pajdla.: Robust wide baseline stereo from maximally stable extremal regions. In: Proceedings of British Machine Vision Conference, pp. 384–396 (2002)
8. Molina-Abril, H., Real, P.: Homological spanning forest framework for 2D image analysis. Ann. Math. Artif. Intell. **64**, 1–25 (2012)
9. Real, P., Díaz-del-Río, F., Molina-Abril, H., Onchis, D., Blanco-Trejo, S.: MATLAB implementation of Computing Homotopy Information of Digital Images in Parallel. version 1.0. https://es.mathworks.com/matlabcentral/fileexchange/66121-computing-homotopy-information-of-digital-images-in-parallel. Accessed Feb 2019
10. Xu, Y., Monasse, P., Géraud, T., Najman, L.: Tree-based morse regions: a topological approach to local feature detection. IEEE Trans. Image Process. **23**(12), 5612–5625 (2014)

Blood Vessel Analysis on High Resolution Fundus Retinal Images

Gemma S. Parra-Dominguez[1], Raul E. Sanchez-Yanez[1(✉)], and S. Ivvan Valdez[2]

[1] Universidad de Guanajuato DICIS, Salamanca, Mexico
{gs.parradominguez,sanchezy}@ugto.mx
[2] CENTROMET-INFOTEC, Querétaro, Mexico
ivvan.valdez@centromet.mx

Abstract. Image analysis is a relevant tool to improve the healthcare services. Fundus retinal image analysis allows the early detection of ophthalmic diseases such as diabetes and glaucoma. Thus, growing interest is observed on the development of segmentation algorithms for blood vessels in retinal images. For this purpose, Kernel-based approaches with Gaussian matched filters have been successfully used. Nowadays, improved image sensors and computers deliver high resolution images, and different parameter values are required for the efficient operation of such filters. In this work, an optimization system using genetic algorithms is designed to calculate those values. To evaluate our methodology, a segmentation algorithm is proposed and the outcomes are evaluated on the HRF image database. Performance measures are obtained and compared to those obtained using state of the art methods. This analysis represents a first step in the detection and classification of normal and abnormal eye conditions.

Keywords: Vessel enhancement · Vessel segmentation ·
Fundus retinal image · Matched filters · Parameter optimization ·
Genetic algorithms

1 Introduction

The analysis of medical images is a useful tool to diagnose, plan and execute treatment in different healthcare fields; for example, in ophthalmology, laryngology, oncology and neurosurgery [13]. In the human body, the vascular structure provides important information about the health and functioning of certain organs, therefore, detecting blood vessels or vessels-like structure occupies a remarkable place in the medical image segmentation field. A broad variety of algorithms and methodologies have been developed and implemented for the achievement of automatic or semiautomatic extraction of blood vessels, as reviewed in [3,7,13]. Particular concern is growing up in the area of ophthalmology, since detecting and analyzing vascular retinal pathologies may lead to early

© Springer Nature Switzerland AG 2019
J. A. Carrasco-Ochoa et al. (Eds.): MCPR 2019, LNCS 11524, pp. 302–311, 2019.
https://doi.org/10.1007/978-3-030-21077-9_28

diagnosis of various cardiovascular and ophthalmic diseases such as diabetes [7], which could have a big economic impact for the healthcare sector.

In the literature, vessel segmentation methods for fundus retinal images share three common stages. Previous to the processing stage, the pre-processing mainly aims to improve the image contrast, to convert to gray-scale levels and/or to suppress image noise; while the post-processing stage aims to reconnect vascular segments or remove image artifacts. The vessel segmentation algorithms can be classified as kernel-based techniques, vessel-tracking, mathematical morphology-based, multi-scale, model-based, adaptive local thresholding and machine learning [3]. Other authors classify the algorithms as vessel enhancement, machine learning, deformable models and tracking [13].

Prior to vessel segmentation, an enhancement process is performed to improve the quality of the vessel perception. Most enhancement algorithms use Gaussian matched filters, proposed by Chaudhuri *et al.* in [4]. Those algorithms are kernel-based methods, and operate on the assumption that a vessel intensity profile is modeled as a Gaussian curve. Later, a number of Gaussian matched filters have been proposed to enhance vessels in fundus retinal images and coronary angiograms. A Gaussian matched filter (MF) can be expressed as,

$$MF(x, y) = -\frac{1}{\sqrt{2\pi}\sigma} exp(\frac{-x^2}{2\sigma}) \ \forall |x| \leq 3\sigma, |y| \leq L/2 \qquad (1)$$

where, L is the length for which the vessels are assumed to have fixed orientation, σ is the spread of the Gaussian curve. Vessels are assumed to be aligned along Y-axis. We can think of this filter as a flume with a gaussian cross-section.

In the literature, the use of Gaussian derivatives to design filters has been proposed in [11,17]. There, the second order derivative, also known as the Laplacian (LoG) of a Gaussian, has also been employed for the detection of vessel and vessel-like structures. Authors argue that non-vessel retinal structures (abnormalities) may be modeled as uniform intensity regions, like ramps or step functions. When those regions are convolved with an LoG filter, they produce a zero response about its center, unlike vessel structures which respond with a high positive or negative value. Nowadays, the combination of MF and LoG filters is implemented to improve the classification rate between normal and abnormal retinal structures [9–11]. An LoG filter can be expressed as,

$$LoG(x, y) = \frac{1}{\sqrt{2\pi}\sigma} \frac{(x^4 - \sigma^2)}{\sigma^4} exp(\frac{-x^2}{2\sigma}) \ \forall |x| \leq 3\sigma, |y| \leq L/2 \qquad (2)$$

Most blood vessel segmentation algorithms are implemented and evaluated on two publicly available databases, the STARE [8] and DRIVE [16]. Both databases contain low resolutions images (of size 565×584 and 700×605 pixels, respectively) but, having now better image sensors and computers, it seems adequate to process newer high resolution images. Odstrcilik *et al.* [14] introduced a new High Resolution Fundus Retinal (HRF) image database, publicly available for development and comparison. The HRF is composed of 45 images, each one of size 3504×2336 pixels, divided in 3 categories: healthy (h), glaucomatous (g) and diabetic retinopathy (dr) patients; for each image, a mask containing the field of view and the manual segmentation are provided.

Recently, vessel enhancement research aims to optimize the filter parameters, hoping for higher detection rates [5]. Al-Rawi et al. [1] presented two strategies to optimize a single scale matched filter. They performed an exhaustive search to obtain better values and, later, proposed a genetic algorithm to improve the solutions, using the DRIVE [2] in both cases. Li et al. [12] explored the use of multiscale matched filters to enhance different size of vessels on STARE and DRIVE images, concluding that multiscale matched filters are better than single scale approaches. Other authors [14] introduced an improved matched filter by reshaping the Gaussian curves, generating different kernel masks to enhance the retinal image; those authors used the HRF, STARE and DRIVE databases. More recently, Sreejini et al. [15] presented an improved multiscale matched filter using a particle swarm algorithm on the STARE and DRIVE imagery.

The main motivation of this work is to explore the analysis of high resolution images using Gaussian filters and its derivatives. The use of a database containing images of different size requires the obtention of different filter value parameters. Then we aim to establish new value parameters to improve vessel enhancement algorithms on high resolution images. We focus our work on the parameter optimization using genetic algorithms. To evaluate our findings, we reproduce the vessel segmentation process proposed by Kumar et al. in [11] and compare the results to the work in [14]. The remain of this paper is organized as follows. We briefly describe the segmentation methodology in Sect. 2, and the optimization process in Sect. 3. In Sect. 4 we present results and analysis. Finally, the conclusions of this work are provided in Sect. 5.

2   Blood Vessel Extraction

The segmentation algorithm proposed in [11] is visually described in Fig. 1. First, the green channel of the input image is extracted [3]. Next, the image is equalized to increase the contrast between the background and the vascular structure. According to the authors, a Contrast Limited Adaptive Histogram Equalization (CLAHE) provides the best enhancement. Later, the processing stage refers to a filtering using MF and LoG filters. A bank of multiscale filters is computed according to Eqs. 1 and 2, using three values of σ to detect various sizes of vessels and 12 rotations to detect all possible vessels. Two images containing the maximum filters response, MFR and LoGR, are composed and compared. If $MFR(x, y)$ is maximum and $LoGR(x, y) > 0$, then (x, y) is labeled as a vessel pixel. Notice that each pixel has 3 labels (one for each σ), then a logical OR operation is performed to decide if the pixel is a vessel or a non-vessel pixel. Finally, morphological processing is performed to clean up the image and to reconnect missing pixels. An opening operation is performed on the image using linear structuring element, rotated in different directions. Reconstruction opening is performed between the opened image and the extracted vessel map.

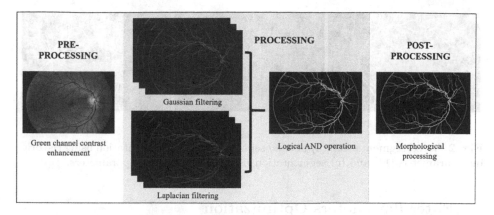

Fig. 1. Blood vessel segmentation method as proposed by Kumar *et al.* [11].

2.1   Implementation

Our segmentation algorithm was implemented using MATLAB R2017a® and evaluated using the HRF database. We believe that authors in [11] may have scaled the HRF images to work with the same parameters as the DRIVE and STARE, because we observed a low performance after preliminary evaluations. We also observed that they failed to report the value at which the filter response is considered maximum. In those preliminary tests, we decided to modify the filter parameters; the width was increased from $\sigma = \{1.5, 1.0, 0.5\}$ to $\sigma = \{4.5, 2.5, 0.4\}$; the kernel size from $L = 9$ and $L = 5$ to $L = 31$ for both filters; and the length of the linear structuring element from 11 pixels to 43 pixels. The reason can be observed in Fig. 2, where segmentation results are visually compared. Figure 2a shows the manual segmentation of an input image. Figure 2b shows the segmentation result using the filter parameters in [11], and Fig. 2c using our preliminary filter parameters. With these segmentation results, we have concluded that the first Gaussian curve does not cover the complete vessel, only the edges, therefore, wider Gaussian curves are required and specific filter parameters must be calculated. We followed a genetic algorithm-based approach for that purpose.

The outcome of the algorithm is compared to the manual segmentation of a database (ground truth). Measurement of the performance is always done only on pixels inside the field of view (FOV). Three performance measures are computed: accuracy (Ac), sensitivity (Sn) and $F1$-score ($F1s$). The accuracy indicates the fraction of correctly classified pixels, while the sensitivity indicates the fraction of vessel pixels correctly detected. The $F1$-score can be seen as a metric that gives more importance to the well-detected true positive pixels. In clinical applications involving retinal image analysis, detecting and extracting true vessel pixels is crucial to diagnose eye pathologies. We aim to increase the true positives rate of the segmentation, measuring it through the $F1s$.

Fig. 2. Vessel segmentation: (a) manual segmentation, (b) segmentation using the original parameters [11] and (c) segmentation using our preliminary parameters.

3   Filter Parameters Optimization

In our analysis, we have observed that the use of MF filters is intended to enhance vessel pixels, and the use of LoG filters is intended to discriminate among vessel and non-vessel structures as stated in the literature. Our optimization system is designed to look for optimal σ values using genetic algorithms. Genetic algorithms (GAs) belong to the family of evolutionary computation strategies that emulate genetic evolution. GAs are population-based methods [5], where each individual in the population is considered a potential solution. Each potential solution is gradually improved until a stopping criterion is satisfied. Individuals are improved using the evolutionary operators of selection (keep the best individuals), crossover (exchange information among the best individuals), and mutation (randomly introducing information in the population). As mentioned before, the use of GAs has been explored to obtain better solutions for low resolution images, hence it seems promising to use them for high resolution images.

In our optimization system, each individual is composed of 3 genes, each one representing a σ value. Those genes are used to create the bank of Gaussian filters, as described in Eqs. 1 and 2. Other parameters remained constant: $L = 31$, 12 rotations with $\theta = \{0, 15, \ldots, 165°\}$ and $SE = 43$. On each generation, the population size is set to 40 individuals, where 20% of the best previous individuals is kept. The initial population is randomly generated and individuals go through an evaluation to assess their fitness. In our approach, the evaluation of individuals refers to executing a segmentation using the genetic information. Its fitness is assessed using the $F1$-score, which is configured to be minimized. The individuals with the lowest values are considered the best possible solution.

3.1   Evaluation Function

Based on the implementation described in Sect. 2, a few modifications to the algorithm are proposed. Instead of seeking for the maximum filter response of the 12 directions, the image responses are added up, then high values increase and low values remain close to 0. Both image responses are thresholded, in separate, to obtain two binary images, later a logical OR is performed to conform the image vessel map. Morphological operations, as originally proposed in [11], are used to clean up the image and reconnect missing pixels. The algorithm is described on Algorithm 1. Note that reductions of the processing time and the use of computational resources are observed after these modifications.

Algorithm 1. Blood vessel analysis using Gaussian filters.

Require: Fundus retinal image input I_r and the filter parameters $\{\sigma_0, \sigma_1, \sigma_2, L\}$.
Ensure: Segmented binary image I_s.
    Create bank of filters b_{MF} for MF and b_{LoG} for LoG.
    Extract the green channel from I_r and then equalize it to obtain I.
    Filter I with b_{MF} and accumulate each response to obtain I_{MFR}.
    Filter I with b_{LoG} and accumulate each response to obtain I_{LoGR}.
    Obtain a threshold for I_{MFR} and for I_{LoGR}, then binaryze both images.
    Conform the vessel map I_{vm} by performing a logical OR with the binary images.
    Repeat from step 1 for each $\sigma = \{\sigma_0, \sigma_1, \sigma_2\}$.
    Perform logical OR on I_{vm0}, I_{vm1} and I_{vm2} to obtain the blood vessel map I_{bvm}.
    Perform morphological opening and reconstruction on I_{bvm} to obtain I_s.

---

4   Results and Analysis

In this image analysis, it was found that different values from the ones reported on the literature are needed to operate the Gaussian filters in high resolution images. Analytic results are described on Table 1, where we refer to the original configuration as the one proposed by [11], and adjusted configuration to our preliminary set up, as described on Sect. 2.1. Results on Table 1 are obtained after processing the HRF database according to the segmentation algorithm proposed by Kumar *et al.* With the original configuration, good accuracy levels were achieved, but the system fails considerably in detecting true vessel pixels, as reflected on the sensitivity and $F1s$ of the system. Our adjusted parameters increased considerably the sensitivity of the system, if compared with [11], which also increased the $F1s$ levels. Here, the overall false positives rate is of 0.1422, that is the reason the accuracy slightly decreases with our configuration.

Table 1. Comparison of the preliminary performance evaluation.

Configuration		Healthy group			Glaucomatous group			DR group		
		Ac	Sn	F1s	Ac	Sn	F1s	Ac	Sn	F1s
Original	Max.	0.933	0.329	0.467	0.945	0.279	0.402	0.944	0.304	0.375
	Min	0.909	0.127	0.223	0.931	0.054	0.099	0.905	0.158	0.238
	Mean	**0.922**	0.226	0.345	**0.938**	0.172	0.271	**0.928**	0.237	0.311
Adjusted	Max.	0.924	0.935	0.674	0.948	0.945	0.652	0.889	0.938	0.582
	Min	0.833	0.857	0.521	0.822	0.845	0.419	0.736	0.852	0.295
	Mean	0.881	**0.904**	**0.589**	0.893	**0.893**	**0.543**	0.810	**0.908**	**0.408**

After performing the optimization process, described on Sect. 3, we found better parameters with $\sigma = \{8.7589, 6.4611, 1.269\}$. Those were evaluated in our segmentation algorithm, described on Sect. 3.1, with processing parameters equal to $L = 31$, 12 rotations with $\theta = \{0, 15, \ldots, 165°\}$ and $SE = 43$. Analytic results are shown in Table 2, there, the performance for each image on each set is described. Maximum and minimum values are boldfaced on each column. If compared to results on Table 1, better accuracy and F1s are obtained in the three groups of the database. Although the sensitivity was decreased, it is worth to notice that the false positives rate dropped to 0.0166, meaning an increase on the F1s levels. To be compared with our previous analysis, Fig. 3 shows the segmentation results. A cleaner image is observed because the false positives rate was decreased, but some small vessels are missed as shown in Fig. 3c.

In Table 3 the performance of all configurations are compared, also the results presented by Odstrcilik *et al.* [14] are reported. The main contribution in [14] is the use of a manually reshaped Gaussian kernel with 5 scales to detect blood vessels. Notice that each image is filtered 60 times (5×12), we propose to filter each image only 36 times (3×12), requiring lower processing time. In general, the results are competitive, our algorithm obtained overall better accuracy levels, but the sensitivity of the system is lower if compared with [14].

Our implementation with optimized parameters still misses some hand-labeled vessel pixels, and further optimization could be performed to increase the true positives rate. As observed in the literature, authors usually do not report F1-score values. However, Dash *et al.* in [6] reported average values of 0.7240 and 0.7042 in other publicly databases. Our results indicate similar values for

Table 2. Performance evaluation on the HRF database using optimized values.

Image no.	Healthy group			Glaucomatous group			DR group		
	Ac	Sn	F1s	Ac	Sn	F1s	Ac	Sn	F1s
1	0.9538	0.6131	0.7299	0.9633	0.6314	0.6970	0.9564	**0.7818**	0.6457
2	0.9635	0.7548	0.8032	0.9605	0.7143	0.7293	0.9585	0.7106	0.6861
3	**0.9483**	**0.5871**	**0.7057**	**0.9701**	**0.6051**	0.7004	0.9512	0.6990	0.6337
4	0.9579	0.6662	0.7490	0.9689	0.6823	0.7386	0.9543	0.6668	**0.6225**
5	0.9662	0.7098	0.7911	0.9683	0.6129	0.7166	**0.9643**	0.7683	0.7280
6	0.9622	0.7320	0.7972	0.9663	0.7352	**0.7493**	**0.9468**	0.6021	0.6308
7	0.9649	0.6691	0.7725	0.9690	0.7092	0.7485	0.9564	0.7156	0.7185
8	0.9621	0.6880	0.7845	0.9657	0.7264	0.7420	0.9533	0.7084	0.6952
9	0.9641	0.6173	0.7279	0.9638	0.7677	0.7372	0.9582	**0.5997**	0.6600
10	0.9624	0.6818	0.7577	0.9674	0.6798	0.7325	0.9543	0.6502	0.7131
11	0.9671	0.7088	0.8010	0.9626	0.6760	0.7343	0.9576	0.7101	**0.7393**
12	0.9658	**0.7783**	**0.8270**	**0.9571**	**0.7714**	0.7482	0.9561	0.7057	0.6861
13	0.9616	0.6443	0.7448	0.9623	0.6882	0.7131	0.9629	0.6660	0.7105
14	0.9612	0.7080	0.7610	0.9578	0.6756	**0.6934**	0.9494	0.6664	0.6679
15	**0.9696**	0.76866	0.7986	0.9607	0.6931	0.7210	0.9526	0.6191	0.6306
Mean	0.9620	0.6885	0.7701	0.9643	0.6912	0.7268	0.9555	0.6847	0.6779
Std	0.0054	0.0573	0.0342	0.0041	0.0494	0.0190	0.0047	0.0538	0.0393

the healthy and glaucomatous group, although a direct comparison is impossible because the image databases are different. The DR group is harder to process due to the damage on the retina, which is visually depicted with dark and bright spots in the image. As a result, the segmentation algorithm got confused and might not be able to completely distinguished between vessel and non-vessel structures.

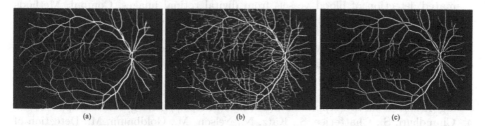

(a)   (b)   (c)

Fig. 3. Vessel segmentation results: (a) manual segmentation, (b) segmentation using the preliminary parameters and (c) segmentation using the optimized parameters.

Table 3. Comparison evaluation on the HRF database

Method	Ac h	Sn h	$F1$ h	Ac g	Sn g	$F1$ g	Ac dr	Sn dr	$F1$ dr
Kumar	0.9520	0.7485	–	0.9475	0.8028	–	0.9450	0.7574	–
Odstrcilik	0.9539	0.7861	–	0.9497	0.7900	–	0.9445	0.7463	–
Adjusted	0.8809	**0.9037**	0.5893	0.8925	**0.8934**	0.5426	0.8099	**0.9075**	0.4076
Optimized	**0.9620**	0.6885	**0.7701**	**0.9643**	0.6912	**0.7268**	**0.9555**	0.6847	**0.6779**

5 Conclusions

The combination of Gaussian filters is an appropriate technique to enhance blood vessels in fundus retinal images. Even more, the use of multiscale filters is crucial to enhance different size of blood vessels. The analysis of high resolution images with matched filters requires different value parameters from those used on low resolution images. Particularly, wider Gaussian curves are needed to cover all sizes of blood vessels, as shown in this work. We evaluated a segmentation algorithm, using the HRF image database, paying special attention to the vessel enhancement processing. We proposed an optimization system, using genetic algorithms to calculate improved filter parameters. Those parameters were found to be $\sigma = \{8.7589, 6.4611, 1.269\}$ with $L = 31$, 12 rotations with $\theta = \{0, 15, \ldots, 165°\}$ and $SE = 43$. As a result, the average vessel detection rate for our analysis is 96.20% for the healthy group, 96.43% for the glaucomatous group and 95.55% for the DR group. At the end of this work, it remains unknown the existence of another high resolution image database publicly available, then it was not possible to test our filter parameters in a different set of retinal images. This analysis represents a first step, in the detection and classification of normal and abnormal eye conditions.

Acknowledgment. The present research has been supported by the National Council of Science and Technology of Mexico through the scholarship 302076.

References

1. Al-Rawi, M., Karajeh, H.: Genetic algorithm matched filter optimization for automated detection of blood vessels from digital retinal images. Comput. Methods Programs Biomed. **87**(3), 248–253 (2007). https://doi.org/10.1016/j.cmpb.2007.05.012
2. Al-Rawi, M., Qutaishat, M., Arrar, M.: An improved matched filter for blood vessel detection of digital retinal images. Comput. Biol. Med. **37**(2), 262–267 (2007). https://doi.org/10.1016/j.compbiomed.2006.03.003
3. Almotiri, J., Elleithy, K., Elleithy, A.: Retinal vessels segmentation techniques and algorithms: a survey. Appl. Sci. **8**(2) (2018). https://doi.org/10.3390/app8020155
4. Chaudhuri, S., Chatterjee, S., Katz, N., Nelson, M., Goldbaum, M.: Detection of blood vessels in retinal images using two-dimensional matched filters. IEEE Trans. Med. Imaging **8**(3), 263–269 (1989). https://doi.org/10.1109/42.34715
5. Cruz-Aceves, I., Hernandez-Aguirre, A., Valdez-Peña, I.: On the performance of nature inspired algorithms for the automatic segmentation of coronary arteries using Gaussian matched filters. Appl. Soft Comput. **46**, 665–676 (2016). https://doi.org/10.1016/j.asoc.2016.01.030
6. Dash, J., Bhoi, N.: An unsupervised approach for extraction of blood vessels from fundus images. J. Digit. Imaging, April 2018. https://doi.org/10.1007/s10278-018-0059-x
7. Fraz, M., et al.: Blood vessel segmentation methodologies in retinal images – a survey. Comput. Methods Programs Biomed. **108**(1), 407–433 (2012). https://doi.org/10.1016/j.cmpb.2012.03.009
8. Hoover, A.D., Kouznetsova, V., Goldbaum, M.: Locating blood vessels in retinal images by piecewise threshold probing of a matched filter response. IEEE Trans. Med. Imaging **19**(3), 203–210 (2000). https://doi.org/10.1109/42.845178
9. Kar, S.S., Maity, S.P.: Automatic detection of retinal lesions for screening of diabetic retinopathy. IEEE Trans. Biomed. Eng. **65**(3), 608–618 (2018). https://doi.org/10.1109/TBME.2017.2707578
10. Kar, S.S., Maity, S.P.: Blood vessel extraction and optic disc removal using curvelet transform and kernel fuzzy c-means. Comput. Biol. Med. **70**, 174–189 (2016). https://doi.org/10.1016/j.compbiomed.2015.12.018
11. Kumar, D., Pramanik, A., Kar, S.S., Maity, S.P.: Retinal blood vessel segmentation using matched filter and Laplacian of Gaussian. In: 2016 International Conference on Signal Processing and Communications (SPCOM), pp. 1–5, June 2016. https://doi.org/10.1109/SPCOM.2016.7746666
12. Li, Q., You, J., Zhang, D.: Vessel segmentation and width estimation in retinal images using multiscale production of matched filter responses. Expert Syst. Appl. **39**(9), 7600–7610 (2012). https://doi.org/10.1016/j.eswa.2011.12.046
13. Moccia, S., Momi, E.D., Hadji, S.E., Mattos, L.S.: Blood vessel segmentation algorithms—review of methods, datasets and evaluation metrics. Comput. Methods Programs Biomed. **158**, 71–91 (2018). https://doi.org/10.1016/j.cmpb.2018.02.001
14. Odstrcilik, J., et al.: Retinal vessel segmentation by improved matched filtering: evaluation on a new high-resolution fundus image database. IET Image Process. **7**(4), 373–383 (2013). https://doi.org/10.1049/iet-ipr.2012.0455

15. Sreejini, K., Govindan, V.: Improved multiscale matched filter for retina vessel segmentation using PSO algorithm. Egypt. Inform. J. **16**(3), 253–260 (2015). https://doi.org/10.1016/j.eij.2015.06.004

16. Staal, J., Abramoff, M.D., Niemeijer, M., Viergever, M.A., van Ginneken, B.: Ridge-based vessel segmentation in color images of the retina. IEEE Trans. Med. Imaging **23**(4), 501–509 (2004). https://doi.org/10.1109/TMI.2004.825627

17. Zhang, B., Zhang, L., Zhang, L., Karray, F.: Retinal vessel extraction by matched filter with first-order derivative of Gaussian. Comput. Biol. Med. **40**(4), 438–445 (2010). https://doi.org/10.1016/j.compbiomed.2010.02.008

Pattern Recognition Techniques

The Mexican Conference on Pattern Recognition After Ten Editions: A Scientometric Study

Octavio Loyola-González[1]([⊠])(iD), Miguel Angel Medina-Pérez[2](iD),
José Fco. Martínez-Trinidad[3](iD), and Jesús Ariel Carrasco-Ochoa[3]

[1] Tecnologico de Monterrey, Vía Atlixcáyotl No. 2301,
Reserva Territorial Atlixcáyotl, 72453 Puebla, Mexico
octavioloyola@tec.mx
[2] Tecnologico de Monterrey, Carr. al Lago de Guadalupe Km. 3.5,
52926 Atizapán, Estado de México, Mexico
migue@tec.mx
[3] Instituto Nacional de Astrofísica, Óptica y Electrónica, Luis Enrique Erro No. 1,
Sta. María Tonanzintla, 72840 Puebla, Mexico
{fmartine,ariel}@inaoep.mx

Abstract. Scientific conferences are suitable vehicles for knowledge dissemination, connecting authors, networking, and research entities. However, it is important to know the impact of a determined conference for the international research community. The main way to do this is through a scientometric study of those papers derived from the conference. Therefore, in this paper, we introduce a scientometric study taking into account all papers published in each edition of the Mexican Conference on Pattern Recognition (MCRP) as well as all the papers published in special issues derived from MCPR. Our study is based on data taken from the SCOPUS database. We have extracted and analyzed several essential keys, such as acceptance and rejection rates, number of authors and top-productive institutions, and frequency of citations by other journals, with the aim of providing the impact of the papers derived from MCPR for the international research community. From our study, we report some important findings about the impact of the MCPR conference after ten editions.

Keywords: MCPR · Scientometrics · Information extraction

1 Introduction

Scientific conferences are the basic instruments in the process of knowledge dissemination by their short publication deadlines and their possibility of publishing incipient papers with important advances for the research community; at the same time, conferences are vehicles for connecting authors, networking, and research entities; among others.

© Springer Nature Switzerland AG 2019
J. A. Carrasco-Ochoa et al. (Eds.): MCPR 2019, LNCS 11524, pp. 315–326, 2019.
https://doi.org/10.1007/978-3-030-21077-9_29

Nowadays, there are several scientific conferences[1] promoting a space for the exchange of scientific results, experiences, new knowledge, and cooperation among research groups. Usually, the most relevant conferences promote to publish their oral presentations and posters on scientific journals, such as Lecture Notes Series, as conference proceeding.

The most common approach to measure the international relevance of a scientific conferences is to analyze the impact of their published papers through a scientometric study [10]. From this study, several key items are measured, such as acceptance and rejection rates, promptness of publication, and the number of citations by other journals, which provide an idea of the impact of the published papers on the international research community.

The Mexican Conference on Pattern Recognition (MCPR), organized every year since 2009 and published in Lecture Notes in Computer Science (LNCS) since 2010, aims to promote the development of the Pattern Recognition (PR) discipline among the Mexican and worldwide scientific community. MCPR has promoted several Special Issues (SIs), mainly fed from extensions of papers presented during their conferences, but also open to contributions of the international community working on PR areas. However, as far as we know, there is not a study showing the impact of this conference inside and outside of Mexico. Hence, in this paper, we introduce a scientometric study with the aim of measuring the impact of MCPR on the international research community. Our study relies on the SCOPUS database as a suitable source for extracting reliable information about the impact of MCPR. Our study presents findings on total citations, the rate of growth of citations excluding self-citation, number of authors, countries with more participation, and top-productive institutions and authors.

The remainder of the paper is organized as follows. Section 2 shows preliminaries for the MCPR and the Scientometric approach. Section 3 describes the methodology implemented for data acquisition and data extraction as well as a deep analysis and discussion of our study. Finally, Sect. 4 presents our conclusions and future works.

2 Preliminaries

In this section, we present an overview about MCPR as a forum for the exchange of scientific results and the foundations of the scientometric approach.

The MCPR is a forum for the exchange of scientific results, experiences, and new knowledge, as well as, promoting cooperation among research groups in PR and related areas in Mexico and around the world. MCPR is under the direction of the Computer Science Department of the National Institute for Astrophysics Optics and Electronics (INAOE) and other Mexican institutions. MCPR had international scientific committees, which contain well-known researchers. All

---

[1] https://scholar.google.com/citations?hl=es&view_op=search_venues&vq=conference &btnG=.

MCPR editions, excepting the first one, have been published on LNCS and several of them have published Special Issues (SI), (see Table 1).

Table 1. Editions of the Mexican Conference on Pattern Recognitions (MCPR)

Acro.	Place	Date	Vol	Count.	Cites	Cites^A	SI	Sponsors
MWPR 2009	Guadalajara, Jalisco	November 14, 2009	–		0	0	No	INAOE, CINVESTAV, IPN
MCPR 2010	Puebla, Puebla	September 27–29, 2010	6256	12	102	68	Yes	INAOE, IAPR, LNCS, MACVNR
MCPR 2011	Cancún, Quintana Roo	June 29–July 2, 2011	6718	11	126	84	Yes	INAOE, IAPR, LNCS, MACVNR, ITC
MCPR 2012	Huatulco, Oaxaca	June 27–30, 2012	7329	15	83	43	Yes	INAOE, IAPR, LNCS, MACVNR
MCPR 2013	Querétaro, Querétaro	June 26–29, 2013	7914	13	120	75	Yes	INAOE, IAPR, LNCS, MACVNR, IEEE, CONACYT, CONCYTEQ, IPN, CICATA
MCPR 2014	Cancún, Quintana Roo	June 25–28, 2014	8495	17	80	47	Yes	INAOE, IAPR, LNCS, MACVNR, BUAP
MCPR 2015	Mexico City	June 24–27, 2015	9116	12	33	13	Yes	INAOE, IAPR, LNCS, MACVNR, IPN
MCPR 2016	Guanajuato, Guanajuato	June 22–25, 2016	9703	10	26	10	Yes	INAOE, IAPR, LNCS, MACVNR, UGTO
MCPR 2017	Huatulco, Oaxaca	June 21–24, 2017	10267	13	12	3	No	INAOE, IAPR, LNCS, MACVNR, BUAP
MCPR 2018	Puebla, Puebla	June 27–30, 2018	10880	7	1	0	No	INAOE, IAPR, LNCS, MACVNR, BUAP

Table 1 shows for each MCPR edition its acronym (Acro.), place where the conference was carried out, date, volume in LNCS (Vol.), number of participating countries (Count.), total citations (cites), number of citations without self-citation (Cites^A), if it had an associated SI, and sponsors. At the conference website www.mcpr.org.mx into the section "previous MCPRs".

It is important for the organizing committee of MCPR to know if the conference is having an impact on the research communities inside and outside of Mexico. As a consequence, a study taking into account statistical data coming from a database of peer-reviewed literature, like SCOPUS, is needed.

In the last decades, journals have been indexed in databases and the indexation is determined by well-defined and quantifiable criteria, such as acceptance and rejection rates, promptness of publication, coverage by major abstracting and indexing services, high-confidence level of scientists using the journal in its contents, high frequency of citation by other journals (impact), and providing author(s) addresses (author reputation score); among others [15].

Scientometrics is the study of the quantitative aspects of science. It involves quantitative studies of scientific activities, including, among others, publication, and so overlaps bibliometrics to some extent [10]. As a consequence, a scientometric study should be based on reliable databases, like SCOPUS, which index the published papers on different journals.

Usually, the impact of a conference is measured by the number of citations to their published papers by papers from other journals, having more importance those with more citations, excluding self-citations (cites[4]). Also, the acceptance and rejection rates are important for evaluating the impact of a conference because, commonly, those conferences having high rejection rates include only high-quality papers that generate several citations, and they are considered as excellent forums for disseminating research results and for creating research collaboration networks. Also, other key items are taken into account such as the number of participating countries, research areas of the presented papers, and if the conference promotes the call for papers for special issues. Hence, all these items were taken into account in our scientometric study for evaluating the quality of MCPR.

3   Scientometric Study of MCPR

In this section, we show the methodology implemented for data acquisition and data extraction from SCOPUS regarding each MCPR edition published on LNCS and their SIs (Sect. 3.1), as well as a deep analysis and discussion of our study (Sect. 3.2).

3.1   Data Acquisition

In our study, data acquisition was designated to extract information from SCOPUS[2], a database of peer-reviewed literature. For this extraction, we use the Application Programming Interfaces (APIs) provided by Elsevier Developers[3], which allow obtaining up to 6,000 results[4] for each query. For each paper published in LNCS as well as each paper published in a SI, which are derived from MCPR editions and indexed by SCOPUS, we have extracted several features such as title, the name of authors, affiliations, number of citations, number of citations excluding self-citations, and keyword indexation. Besides, we obtained from the MCPR organizers the number of submissions and accepted papers for each LNCS book and SI. Also, from the Web of Science (webofknowledge.com), we got the h-index and the impact factor of those SI indexed into the Journal Citation Reports (JCR). Also, we contrast the information extracted from SCOPUS with the one provided by Google Scholar[5] at

---

[2] www.scopus.com.

[3] http://dev.elsevier.com/sc_apis.html.

[4] http://dev.elsevier.com/tecdoc_developer_faq.html.

[5] Google Scholar is a free web search engine that indexes published scientific papers.

the following URL: https://scholar.google.com/citations?hl=es&view_op=list_hcore&venue=pppC_Wi5EMQJ.2018. Finally, we have consulted with the organizing committee and the MCPR' web pages all those information which were not provided by SCOPUS, for example, keynote speakers, conference venue, among others.

3.2 Analysis and Discussion

The aim of this study is showing the impact of MCPR taking into account each edition published in LNCS as well as those SIs derived from MCPR.

Figure 1 shows the number of submissions, number of accepted papers, and citations for each MCPR edition published in LNCS (left side) as well as each SI derived from MCPR (right side). From this figure, we can see that from MCPR2010 to MCPR2014 the total of citations per edition is above 80 and the number of citations excluding self-citation (cites[4]) is above 50. Editions from MCPR2015 to MCPR2018 have fewer citations than older editions, which is normal because usually, the newer papers have fewer citations. Also, from this figure, we can see that for those editions published in the year 2013 are the most cited. In addition, it is important to highlight that MCPR has a rejection rate higher than 40% for LNCS and more than 70% for SI; which is a high-quality indicator for this type of conference and SI.

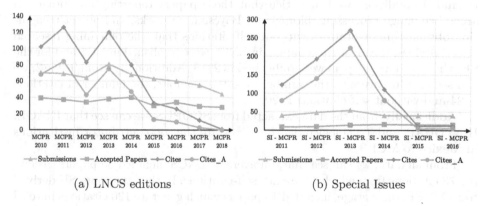

(a) LNCS editions   (b) Special Issues

Fig. 1. Graphic showing the number of accepted papers and citations for each LNCS and SI derived from MCPR.

Figure 2 shows two donut charts containing the countries participating in the LNCSs and SIs derived from MCPR. This information was extracted from the affiliation provided by each author in each one of the published papers. From this figure, we can notice that there are more Mexican researchers participating for both LNCSs and SIs derived from MCPR than from other nationalities. Although, analyzing this figure (left side) without taking into account Mexico, for LNCS there are more authors from Cuba, United States, and Spain than from the remaining countries. For the SIs derived from MCPR, there a similar behavior although there are more participation of authors coming from France, Italy, China, Brazil, and New Zealand than for authors participating in LNCS.

Figure 3 shows two donut charts containing the research areas of the papers published in the LNCSs and SIs derived from MCPR. From this figure, we can see that, for LNCS editions, there are more papers associated with the PR area than to the remaining areas. On the other hand, for SI derived from MCPR, there is a balanced distribution among the research areas, highlighting the areas of PR, classification of information, mathematical computing, clustering algorithm, optimization, data mining, image segmentation, feature extraction, time series, and learning systems [13]; among others.

Table 2 shows the most cited papers taking into account all LNCS and SI derived from MCPR; this table shows the top-ten papers for LNCS and the top-ten for SIs. In this table, we detailed for each paper, its title, research area, year of publication, country associated to each author, number of authors, reference (Ref.), total of citations, number of citations excluding self-citations (Cites^A), the ratio between cites and cites^A, and if it was published in a LNCS or SI edition.

From Table 2, we can see that those papers published in SIs have more citations and more citations without self-citations than those published in LNCS. Also, we can notice that most of the papers published in LNCS are from Mexican authors. On the other hand, for SIs, most of the papers are from Italy and Poland. In addition, we can notice that those papers reporting advantages in areas like image processing, biometrics, Bayesian networks, and object recognition obtained more citations without self-citations than the remaining research areas. Besides, the most cited papers in LNCS were published in 2011 and for the SIs, the most cited papers were published in 2015. Additionally, from Table 2, we can see that, on average, the number of authors is four, the number of citations is 24 and without self-citations is 20.

Additionally, from the data extracted from SCOPUS, we can see that INAOE, IPN, BUAP, and Tecnologico de Monterrey are the top-contributor institutions in Mexico to MCPR.

From all data, we can see that, on average, LNCS included 35 papers, receiving 73 citations from which 43 are not self-citations. In the same vein, SIs derived from MCPR, on average, included 13 papers which generate 120 citations in total from which 89 are not self-citations. From this, we can generalize that those papers published in LNCS could generate at least two citations from which one could be a non-self-citation and those papers published on a SI derived from MCPR, could generate, at least, nine citations from which seven could be non-self-citations.

It is important to highlight that there are some items which can not be collected by SCOPUS, but they are essential for an excellent conference such as high-level keynotes speakers, nice conference venue, international program committee, high-quality tutorials, and additional meetings during the conference like a postgraduate students' meeting. For MCPR, we have consulted the web pages

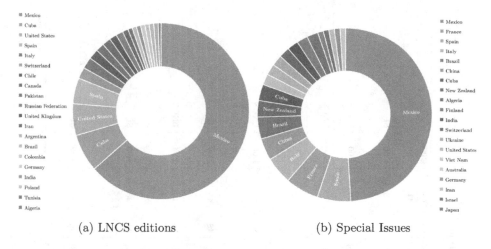

(a) LNCS editions   (b) Special Issues

Fig. 2. Donut chart containing the countries participating in the LNCSs and SIs derived from MCPR.

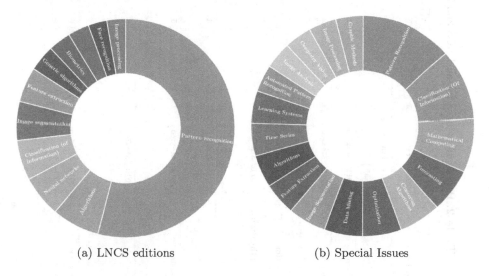

(a) LNCS editions   (b) Special Issues

Fig. 3. Donut chart containing the research areas with more papers published in LNCS and SIs derived from MCPR.

of each edition for extracting this information. Finally, based on the information provided by the MCPR's web pages and our scientometric study, we can conclude that MCPR is a high-quality conference on PR and related areas, with contributions from inside and outside of Mexico.

Table 2. Papers more cited for all LNCS and SI editions

Title	Area	Year	Country	Authors	Ref.	Cites	Cites^	Cites*	Edition
Traffic sign detection via interest region extraction	Computer vision	2015	Italy	5	[19]	41	41	1.00	SI
A subspace co-training framework for multi-view clustering	Clustering	2014	France	3	[23]	33	33	1.00	SI
People detection using color and depth images	Image Processing	2011	Mexico	2	[18]	25	25	1.00	LNCS
Thermal video analysis for fire detection using shape regularity and intensity saturation features	Video Processing	2011	Mexico	2	[2]	9	9	1.00	LNCS
Deep learning for emotional speech recognition	Speech recognition	2014	Mexico, Argentina	5	[20]	8	8	1.00	LNCS
Evolutionary multi-objective optimization: Basic concepts and some applications in pattern recognition	Evolutionary optimatization	2011	Mexico	1	[3]	8	8	1.00	LNCS
Local contrast phase descriptor for fingerprint liveness detection	Biometrics	2015	Italy	4	[9]	48	45	0.94	SI
Breaking reCAPTCHAs with unpredictable collapse: Heuristic character segmentation and recognition	Image Processing	2012	Mexico	5	[4]	16	15	0.94	LNCS
A fuzzy clustering algorithm with spatial robust estimation constraint for noisy color image segmentation	Image Processing	2013	Mexico	3	[14]	31	28	0.90	SI
Multi-label classification with Bayesian network-based chain classifiers	Bayesian networks	2014	Mexico, Australia, Spain	6	[22]	46	41	0.89	SI

(continued)

Table 1. (*continued*)

Spatial-based skin detection using discriminative skin-presence features	Object recognition	2014	Poland	2	[11]	51	44	0.86	SI
Breaking text-based CAPTCHAs with variable word and character orientation	CAPTCHAs	2015	Mexico	4	[21]	22	19	0.86	SI
Music genre classification: A semi-supervised approach	Semi-supervised Classification	2013	Mexico, United Kingdom, United States	5	[16]	12	10	0.83	LNCS
GANT: Gaze analysis technique for human identification	Face recognition	2015	Italy	5	[1]	37	30	0.81	SI
Genetic fuzzy relational neural network for infant cry classification	Neural network	2011	Mexico	3	[17]	13	10	0.77	LNCS
LIDAR and panoramic camera extrinsic calibration approach using a pattern plane	Image Processing	2013	Mexico	5	[8]	8	6	0.75	LNCS
Improving classification performance of breast lesions on ultrasonography	Computer aided diagnosis	2015	Brazil	3	[6]	19	12	0.63	SI
Automatic ultrasound image analysis in Hashimoto's disease	Image Processing	2010	Poland	3	[12]	16	9	0.56	LNCS
A new gaze analysis based soft-biometric	Biometric	2013	Italy	5	[7]	9	5	0.56	LNCS
Representing scenes for real-time context classification on mobile devices	Signal processing	2015	Italy	5	[5]	24	8	0.33	SI

4   Conclusions

In this paper, we presented a scientometric study of the publication derived from all MCPR editions; including their Special Issues in Journals, from 2010 to 2018. The analysis unveils findings on citations, number of authors, countries with more participation, and top-productive institutions and authors.

From our study, we can conclude that MCPR is becoming a prominent conference for the pattern recognition research community, including research areas such as image processing, biometrics, and neural networks. More than a half of the papers published in LNCS are from top-contributor institutions and authors in Mexico such as INAOE, IPN, BUAP, and Tecnologico de Monterrey, while the remaining are from outside of Mexico. This behavior changes for SIs derived from MCPR where there is more balance among the participating countries; although, the aforementioned Mexican institutions continue being those who most contribute. Also, we can conclude that SI publications generate more citations than LNCS publications, which makes sense because journals into the JCR have higher impact than those which are not included in the JCR. Although it is important to highlight that, on average, LNCSs derived from MCPR accept 35 papers, receiving 73 citations from which 43 are not self-citations. On the other hand, SIs derived from MCPR accept 13 papers, which generate 120 citations from which 89 are not self-citations.

Additionally, we can conclude that the most cited MCPR papers included in LNCS are from Mexican authors and the most cited papers included in SIs are from people with affiliation from Italy and Poland. In addition, for both LNCS and SI of MCPR, those papers in areas like image processing, biometrics, Bayesian networks, and object recognition attained more citations than papers in the remaining research areas.

Overall, in this paper, we have been able to analyze the scientometric behavior of the MCPR. To the best of our knowledge, it is the first work of its kind for this conference.

As future work, we plan to extract information from SCOPUS for the top-prominent conferences on PR in the world, and as a result, we will be able to extract contrast patterns from this information in order to show the main differences and similarities among them.

References

1. Cantoni, V., Galdi, C., Nappi, M., Porta, M., Riccio, D.: GANT: gaze analysis technique for human identification. Pattern Recogn. **48**(4), 1027–1038 (2015)
2. Chacon-Murguia, M.I., Perez-Vargas, F.J.: Thermal video analysis for fire detection using shape regularity and intensity saturation features. In: Martínez-Trinidad, J.F., Carrasco-Ochoa, J.A., Ben-Youssef Brants, C., Hancock, E.R. (eds.) MCPR 2011. LNCS, vol. 6718, pp. 118–126. Springer, Heidelberg (2011). https://doi.org/10.1007/978-3-642-21587-2_13

3. Coello Coello, C.A.: Evolutionary multi-objective optimization: basic concepts and some applications in pattern recognition. In: Martínez-Trinidad, J.F., Carrasco-Ochoa, J.A., Ben-Youssef Brants, C., Hancock, E.R. (eds.) MCPR 2011. LNCS, vol. 6718, pp. 22–33. Springer, Heidelberg (2011). https://doi.org/10.1007/978-3-642-21587-2_3

4. Cruz-Perez, C., Starostenko, O., Uceda-Ponga, F., Alarcon-Aquino, V., Reyes-Cabrera, L.: Breaking reCAPTCHAs with unpredictable collapse: heuristic character segmentation and recognition. In: Carrasco-Ochoa, J.A., Martínez-Trinidad, J.F., Olvera López, J.A., Boyer, K.L. (eds.) MCPR 2012. LNCS, vol. 7329, pp. 155–165. Springer, Heidelberg (2012). https://doi.org/10.1007/978-3-642-31149-9_16

5. Farinella, G., Ravì, D., Tomaselli, V., Guarnera, M., Battiato, S.: Representing scenes for real-time context classification on mobile devices. Pattern Recogn. 48(4), 1086–1100 (2015)

6. Flores, W.G., de Albuquerque Pereira, W.C., Infantosi, A.F.C.: Improving classification performance of breast lesions on ultrasonography. Pattern Recogn. 48(4), 1125–1136 (2015)

7. Galdi, C., Nappi, M., Riccio, D., Cantoni, V., Porta, M.: A new gaze analysis based soft-biometric. In: Carrasco-Ochoa, J.A., Martínez-Trinidad, J.F., Rodríguez, J.S., di Baja, G.S. (eds.) MCPR 2013. LNCS, vol. 7914, pp. 136–144. Springer, Heidelberg (2013). https://doi.org/10.1007/978-3-642-38989-4_14

8. García-Moreno, A.-I., Gonzalez-Barbosa, J.-J., Ornelas-Rodriguez, F.-J., Hurtado-Ramos, J.B., Primo-Fuentes, M.-N.: LIDAR and panoramic camera extrinsic calibration approach using a pattern plane. In: Carrasco-Ochoa, J.A., Martínez-Trinidad, J.F., Rodríguez, J.S., di Baja, G.S. (eds.) MCPR 2013. LNCS, vol. 7914, pp. 104–113. Springer, Heidelberg (2013). https://doi.org/10.1007/978-3-642-38989-4_11

9. Gragnaniello, D., Poggi, G., Sansone, C., Verdoliva, L.: Local contrast phase descriptor for fingerprint liveness detection. Pattern Recogn. 48(4), 1050–1058 (2015)

10. Hood, W., Wilson, C.: The literature of bibliometrics, scientometrics, and informetrics. Scientometrics 52(2), 291–314 (2001)

11. Kawulok, M., Kawulok, J., Nalepa, J.: Spatial-based skin detection using discriminative skin-presence features. Pattern Recogn. Lett. 41, 3–13 (2014). Supervised and Unsupervised Classification Techniques and Their Applications

12. Koprowski, R., Wrobel, Z., Zieleznik, W.: Automatic ultrasound image analysis in Hashimoto's disease. In: Martínez-Trinidad, J.F., Carrasco-Ochoa, J.A., Kittler, J. (eds.) MCPR 2010. LNCS, vol. 6256, pp. 98–106. Springer, Heidelberg (2010). https://doi.org/10.1007/978-3-642-15992-3_11

13. Martínez-Díaz, Y., Hernández, N., Biscay, R.J., Chang, L., Méndez-Vázquez, H., Sucar, L.E.: On fisher vector encoding of binary features for video face recognition. J. Vis. Commun. Image Represent. 51, 155–161 (2018)

14. Mújica-Vargas, D., Gallegos-Funes, F.J., Rosales-Silva, A.J.: A fuzzy clustering algorithm with spatial robust estimation constraint for noisy color image segmentation. Pattern Recogn. Lett. 34(4), 400–413 (2013). Advances in Pattern Recognition Methodology and Applications

15. Pisoschi, A.M., Pisoschi, C.G.: Is open access the solution to increase the impact of scientific journals? Scientometrics 109(2), 1075–1095 (2016)

16. Poria, S., Gelbukh, A., Hussain, A., Bandyopadhyay, S., Howard, N.: Music genre classification: a semi-supervised approach. In: Carrasco-Ochoa, J.A., Martínez-Trinidad, J.F., Rodríguez, J.S., di Baja, G.S. (eds.) MCPR 2013. LNCS, vol. 7914, pp. 254–263. Springer, Heidelberg (2013). https://doi.org/10.1007/978-3-642-38989-4_26
17. Rosales-Pérez, A., Reyes-García, C.A., Gómez-Gil, P.: Genetic fuzzy relational neural network for infant cry classification. In: Martínez-Trinidad, J.F., Carrasco-Ochoa, J.A., Ben-Youssef Brants, C., Hancock, E.R. (eds.) MCPR 2011. LNCS, vol. 6718, pp. 288–296. Springer, Heidelberg (2011). https://doi.org/10.1007/978-3-642-21587-2_31
18. Salas, J., Tomasi, C.: People detection using color and depth images. In: Martínez-Trinidad, J.F., Carrasco-Ochoa, J.A., Ben-Youssef Brants, C., Hancock, E.R. (eds.) MCPR 2011. LNCS, vol. 6718, pp. 127–135. Springer, Heidelberg (2011). https://doi.org/10.1007/978-3-642-21587-2_14
19. Salti, S., Petrelli, A., Tombari, F., Fioraio, N., Stefano, L.D.: Traffic sign detection via interest region extraction. Pattern Recogn. **48**(4), 1039–1049 (2015)
20. Sánchez-Gutiérrez, M.E., Albornoz, E.M., Martinez-Licona, F., Rufiner, H.L., Goddard, J.: Deep learning for emotional speech recognition. In: Martínez-Trinidad, J.F., Carrasco-Ochoa, J.A., Olvera-Lopez, J.A., Salas-Rodríguez, J., Suen, C.Y. (eds.) MCPR 2014. LNCS, vol. 8495, pp. 311–320. Springer, Cham (2014). https://doi.org/10.1007/978-3-319-07491-7_32
21. Starostenko, O., Cruz-Perez, C., Uceda-Ponga, F., Alarcon-Aquino, V.: Breaking text-based captchas with variable word and character orientation. Pattern Recogn. **48**(4), 1101–1112 (2015)
22. Sucar, L.E., Bielza, C., Morales, E.F., Hernandez-Leal, P., Zaragoza, J.H., Larrañaga, P.: Multi-label classification with bayesian network-based chain classifiers. Pattern Recogn. Lett. **41**, 14–22 (2014). Supervised and Unsupervised Classification Techniques and Their Applications
23. Zhao, X., Evans, N., Dugelay, J.L.: A subspace co-training framework for multiview clustering. Pattern Recogn. Lett. **41**, 73–82 (2014). Supervised and Unsupervised Classification Techniques and Their Applications

On the Use of Constructs for Rule-Based Classification: A Case Study

Manuel S. Lazo-Cortés[1,2]([⊠]), José Fco. Martínez-Trinidad[1], and Jesús A. Carrasco-Ochoa[1]

[1] Instituto Nacional de Astrofísica, Óptica y Electrónica, Puebla, Mexico
{mlazo,fmartine,ariel}@inaoep.mx
[2] SEP/SES/TecNM/Instituto Tecnológico de Tlalnepantla, Tlalnepantla de Baz, Mexico

Abstract. In Rough Set Theory, super-reducts are subsets of attributes that retain the ability of the whole set of attributes to discern objects belonging to different classes; reducts are minimal ones. On the other hand, constructs also allow discerning objects belonging to different classes but, at the same time, they retain similarities between objects belonging to the same. Therefore, constructs are a kind of super-reducts in whose definition inter-class and intra-class information is combined. This type of super-reduct has been little studied. In this paper, we present a case study, about the use of constructs instead of reducts for building decision rules useful for rule-based classification. Our results show the practical utility of constructs for rule based classification.

1 Introduction

Rough Set Theory makes an effort to examine whether a set of descriptive attributes is sufficient to classify objects into the same classes as the original partition. In this effort, super-reducts play an important role. Rough set theory performs analysis and reasoning about data in a data table, in which rows are objects, columns are attributes, and each cell is the value of an attribute on an object [9,10]. A decision table is a special data table such that the set of attributes is the union of a set of condition attributes and a set of decision attributes (most of the time, only one). The notion of super-reduct plays a fundamental role in rough set analysis. Pawlak [10] defined a super-reduct of a decision table as a subset of condition attributes that has the same classification ability as the entire set of condition attributes with respect to the set of decision attributes. Reducts are minimal super-reducts.

On the other hand, constructs [15] take into account more information, because they preserve discriminating relations between objects belonging to different classes and similarity relations between objects belonging to the same class. So, constructs are a kind of super-reducts in whose definition inter-class and intra-class information is combined.

Combining inter-class dissimilarity with intra-class similarity seems interesting because the resulting subsets of attributes (constructs) would ensure not only

© Springer Nature Switzerland AG 2019
J. A. Carrasco-Ochoa et al. (Eds.): MCPR 2019, LNCS 11524, pp. 327–335, 2019.
https://doi.org/10.1007/978-3-030-21077-9_30

the ability to distinguish objects belonging to different classes but also recognizing objects belonging to the same class. This type of super-reduct has been little studied and to the best of our knowledge, this is the first time the usefulness of constructs is studied for building classification rules.

In this paper, we present a case study about the use of constructs for building decision rules useful for a rule-based classifier. The rest of the document is organized as follows. Section 2 provides the formal definitions of reduct and construct. Section 3 presents a case study showing the experimental results that we obtained applying a rule-based classifier when rules are generated through reducts or constructs. A discussion about these results, as well as a comparison against other well known rule-based classifiers, is included in this section. Our conclusions are summarized in Sect. 4.

2   Theoretical Foundations

In this section, we introduce the definitions of reduct and construct under the same notation.

2.1   Reducts

The main data representation considered in this paper is a decision table, which is a special case of an information table [9]. Formally, a decision table is defined as

Definition 1 *(decision table). A decision table is a pair $S_d = (\mathcal{U}, A_t = A_t^* \cup \{d\})$ where $\mathcal{U}$ is a finite non-empty set of objects, A_t is a finite non-empty set of attributes. A_t^* is a set of conditional attributes and d is a decision attribute indicating the decision class for each object in the universe. Each $a \in A_t$ corresponds to the function $I_a : \mathcal{U} \to V_a$ called evaluation function, where V_a is called the value set of a. The decision attribute allows partitioning the universe into blocks (classes) determined by all possible decisions.*

Sometimes we will use D for denoting $\{d\}$, i.e. $(\{d\} = D)$.

A *decision table* can be implemented as a two-dimensional array (matrix), rows are associated to objects, columns to attributes and cells to values of attributes on objects.

When considering decision tables, it is important to distinguish between the so called *consistent* and *inconsistent* ones. A decision table is said to be *consistent*, if each combination of values of descriptive attributes uniquely determines the value of the decision attribute (i.e. objects for which their value of the decision attribute are different have a different description according to the descriptive attributes); and *inconsistent*, otherwise. For the purpose of this paper we only consider consistent decision tables.

It is important to introduce the definition of the indiscernibility relation.

Definition 2 *(indiscernibility relation). Given a subset of conditional attributes* $A \subseteq A_t^*$, *the indiscernibility relation is defined as* $IND(A|D) = \{(u,v) \in \mathcal{U} \times \mathcal{U} :$ $\forall a \in A, [I_a(u) = I_a(v)] \vee [I_d(u) = I_d(v)]\}$

The indiscernibility relation is an equivalence relation, so it induces a partition over the universe. Being $\mathcal{S}_d$ a consistent decision table, the partition induced by any subset of conditional attributes is finer than (or at maximum equal to) the relation determined by all possible values of the decision attribute d.

We can find several definitions of reduct (see for example, [8]), nevertheless, according to the aim of this paper, we refer to reducts assuming the classical definition of discerning decision reduct [10] as follows.

Definition 3 *(reduct for a decision table). Given a decision table* $\mathcal{S}_d$, *an attribute set* $R \subseteq A_t^*$ *is called a reduct, if* R *satisfies the following two conditions:*

(i) $IND(R|D) = IND(A_t^*|D)$;
(ii) For any $a \in R, IND((R - \{a\})|D) \neq IND(A_t^*|D)$.

All attribute subsets satisfying condition (i) are called super-reducts.

This definition ensures that a reduct has no lower ability to distinguish objects belonging to different classes than the whole set of attributes, being minimal with regard to inclusion, i.e. a reduct does not contain redundant attributes or, equivalently, a reduct does not include other super-reducts. The original idea of reduct is based on inter-class comparisons.

2.2   Constructs

As noted before, reducts are defined from an inter-class object comparison point of view. They ensure preserving the ability to discern between objects belonging to different classes. The novelty of the concept of construct (introduced by Susmaga in 2003 [15]) is the combination of inter-class and intra-class comparisons in such a way that a resulting subset of conditional attributes would ensure not only the ability to distinguish objects belonging to different classes, but also preserves certain similarity between objects belonging to the same class.

Let us now consider the following similarity relation defined between objects belonging to the same class in a decision table $\mathcal{S}_d = (\mathcal{U}, A_t^* \cup \{d\})$.

Definitions 4 and 5 were introduced by Susmaga [15], here we reformulate them for homogeneity in the notation.

Definition 4 *(similarity relation). Given a subset of conditional attributes* $A \subseteq A_t^*$, *the similarity relation is defined as* $SIM(A|D) = \{(u,v) \in \mathcal{U} \times \mathcal{U} : [I_d(u) = I_d(v)]$ *and* $\exists a \in A \, [I_a(u) = I_a(v)]\}$.

If a pair of objects belongs to $SIM(A|D)$ then these objects belong to the same class and they are indiscernible on at least one attribute from the set A.

The definition of construct may be stated as follows.

Definition 5 *(construct). Given a decision table S_d, an attribute set $C \subseteq A_t^*$ is called a construct, if C satisfies the following conditions:*

(i) $IND(C|D) = IND(A_t^*|D)$;
(ii) $SIM(C|D) = SIM(A_t^*|D)$;
(iii) *For any $a \in C, IND((C - \{a\})|D) \neq IND(A_t^*|D)$ or $SIM((C - \{a\})|D) \neq SIM(A_t^*|D)$;*

So, a construct is a subset of attributes that retains the discernment between any pair of objects belonging to different classes as well as the similarity of objects belonging to the same class. Alike reducts, a construct is minimal, which means that removing any attribute from it would result in making any (or both) of the conditions given by (i) and (ii) invalid.

Example 1. Given the decision table M, where $\mathcal{U} = \{u_1, u_2, u_3, u_4, u_5, u_6, u_7, u_8\}$, $A_t^* = \{a_1, a_2, a_3, a_4\}$ and $D = \{d\}$.

$$M = \begin{array}{c} \\ u_1 \\ u_2 \\ u_3 \\ u_4 \\ u_5 \\ u_6 \\ u_7 \\ u_8 \end{array} \begin{pmatrix} a_1 & a_2 & a_3 & a_4 & d \\ blue & 0 & TX & 0 & 1 \\ blue & 1 & NY & 1 & 1 \\ white & 0 & NY & 2 & 1 \\ white & 1 & TX & 0 & 1 \\ blue & 1 & IL & 3 & 2 \\ black & 1 & FL & 4 & 2 \\ red & 1 & AL & 3 & 3 \\ red & 0 & IL & 1 & 3 \end{pmatrix}$$

From this decision table, we have that $\{a_2, a_3\}, \{a_1, a_4\}, \{a_1, a_3\}$ and $\{a_3, a_4\}$ are the reducts. Notice that $\{a_2, a_3\}$ does not fulfill the definition of construct, since $0 = I_{a_2}(u_3) \neq I_{a_2}(u_4) = 1$ and $NY = I_{a_3}(u_3) \neq I_{a_3}(u_4) = TX$ being $I_d(u_3) = I_d(u_4) = 1$. In fact, none of the reducts is a construct for this decision table; the only construct for M is $\{a_1, a_2, a_3\}$. $\{a_1, a_2, a_3\}$ is a super-reduct because it contains $\{a_1, a_3\}$ which is a reduct (it also contains $\{a_2, a_3\}$), therefore $\{a_1, a_2, a_3\}$ fulfills condition (i) in Definition 5. For each pair of objects in the same class, we have that $blue = I_{a_1}(u_1) = I_{a_1}(u_2)$, $0 = I_{a_2}(u_1) = I_{a_2}(u_3)$, $TX = I_{a_3}(u_1) = I_{a_3}(u_4)$, $NY = I_{a_3}(u_2) = I_{a_3}(u_3)$, $1 = I_{a_2}(u_2) = I_{a_2}(u_4)$, $white = I_{a_1}(u_3) = I_{a_1}(u_4)$, $1 = I_{a_2}(u_5) = I_{a_2}(u_6)$ and $red = I_{a_1}(u_7) = I_{a_1}(u_8)$. Therefore, $\{a_1, a_2, a_3\}$ fulfills condition (ii) in Definition 5. Finally it is not difficult to verify that $\{a_1, a_2, a_3\}$ is minimal.

3   Case Study

In this section, we will show a case study about the use of constructs instead of reducts for building decision rules useful for a rule-based classifier.

To build the set of decision rules to be used in a rule-based classifier, we used the tools included in the software RSES ver. 2.2.2 [3], which has been widely used in the literature, see for example [2,11,12].

In RSES, once the reducts of a decision table have been computed, each object in the training sample is matched against each reduct. This matching gives as result a rule having in its conditional part, the attributes of the reduct, each one associated with the values of the currently considered object, and in its decision part it has the class for this training object.

At classifying an unseen object through the generated rule set, it may happen that several rules suggest different decision values. In such conflict situations a strategy to reach a final result (decision) is needed. RSES provides a conflict resolution strategy based on voting. In this method, when the antecedent of the rule matches the unseen object, a vote in favor of the decision value of its consequent is cast. Votes are counted and the decision value reaching the majority of the votes is chosen as the class for the object.

This simple method may be extended by assigning weights to rules. In RSES, this method (known as Standard Voting) assigns as weight for a rule the number of training objects matching the antecedent of this rule. Then, each rule votes with its weight and the decision value reaching the highest weight sum is considered as the class for the object.

In the same way that was explained above for reducts, in order to obtain a set of decision rules based on constructs, RSES was used. This was done by loading the set of constructs as if they were reducts, with the format corresponding to this type of file.

For our case study, we used the lymphography dataset, taken from the UCI Machine Learning Repository [1]. We selected this dataset to compare the results with those reported in [7]. We randomly generated two folds in order to perform two-fold cross validation. Characteristics of both the lymphography dataset and the folds used in our experiments can be seen in Table 1.

We used the sets of all reducts and all constructs for creating decision rules. Reducts and rules were computed by using RSES [14]. Constructs were computed by using the typical testor computation algorithm CT-EXT [13], following [6].

Table 1. Characteristics of the lymphography dataset and the two folds used in our experiments

Attributes	Classes	Objects	Objects per class			
			K_1	K_2	K_3	K_4
18	4	148	2	81	61	4
	Fold 1	74	1	40	31	2
	Fold 2	74	1	41	30	2

For each fold, we compute the sets of all reducts and all constructs. Table 2 shows the number of reducts and constructs computed for each fold.

The number of reducts and constructs is large enough to make it difficult to select the best ones. At this point, it is important to emphasize that, from a

Table 2. Number of reducts and constructs for each fold of the lymphography dataset

Fold	Reducts	Constructs
1	530	1431
2	317	970

practical point of view, the simple number of reducts and constructs is an informative indicator of the quality of the regularities found in the data. Although the reducts and constructs are few, the regularities can be strong. On the other hand, when the amount of reducts or constructs become large, the reducts and constructs generated are usually of low quality, since they tend to be a large number of combinations of attributes that satisfy the definitions. Of course, it is still possible that some of these reducts and constructs are really good, but detecting them is difficult due to the search in a large set is time consuming.

In Table 3, it can be seen the minimum, average, and maximum length of reducts and constructs, for both folds.

Table 3. Length of reducts and constructs for the lymphography dataset

Fold	Length	Reducts	Constructs
1	Minimum	5	6
	Average	7.3	8.1
	Maximum	10	11
2	Minimum	5	6
	Average	7	7.8
	Maximum	9	10

We can observe that, as previously reported in [15], this dataset produces more constructs than reducts, and also the constructs tend to contain more attributes than the reducts.

We generate a set of reduct-based rules for the set of all reducts, as well as a set of construct-based rules considering all constructs. Table 4 shows information about the sets of rules. The third column contains the number of rules, the subsequent four columns show the number of rules per class; and the three final columns show the minimum, average and maximum number of objects matching the antecedent of the rules (support of the rules). As it can be seen in these last three columns, for no rule more than seven objects matched the antecedent of the rule. Moreover, from the average (penultimate column), it can be seen that for most rules only one object matched the antecedent of the rule.

We apply, over the two folds, the RSES Standard Voting rule-based classifier and compute the average of the classification accuracy obtained in each fold.

Table 4. Characteristics of the rules generated for the lymphography dataset

Fold	Set	Rules	Rules per class				Support		
			K_1	K_2	K_3	K_4	Min	Mean	Max
1	Reducts	34958	530	18411	14957	1060	1	1.1	6
	Constructs	95797	1431	50585	41194	2862	1	1.1	6
2	Reducts	21138	317	11578	8620	623	1	1.1	5
	Constructs	62759	970	34913	25742	1914	1	1.1	7

Table 5 shows the results obtained in terms of accuracy in average when reduct-based rules were used in the Standard Voting classifier. Additionally, in Table 5, we show the confusion matrix as well as the true positive rate and the accuracy obtained by the Standard Voting rule-based classifier for each class. On average, the Standard Voting rule-based classifier using reduct-based rules obtained an accuracy of 0.73.

Table 5. Confusion matrix for the Standard Voting rule-based classifier for the lymphography dataset using reducts

	K_1	K_2	K_3	K_4	No. of objects	Accuracy
K_1	0	1	1	0	2	0.00
K_2	2	62	14	3	81	0.77
K_3	1	14	46	0	61	0.75
K_4	0	2	1	0	4	0.00
Total					148	**0.73**
True positive rate	0.00	0.78	0.74	0.00		

We repeat the procedure, but now considering constructs instead of reducts. Table 6 shows the results obtained in terms of accuracy in average when construct-based rules were used in the Standard Voting classifier. On average, the Standard Voting rule-based classifier using reduct-based rules obtained an accuracy of 0.78.

As we can see from Tables 5 and 6, when considering rules generated from constructs instead of reducts, the classification accuracy was improved.

Finally, taking into account that we are evaluating the practical utility of using constructs for a rule-based classifier, we wanted to compare the results obtained by rule-based classifiers based on reducts or constructs against those obtained with other well-known rule-based classifiers widely used in the literature. We select RIPPER [4] and SLIPPER [5]. These classifiers were run using the KEEL Software Suite [16].

Table 6. Confusion matrix for the Standard Voting rule-based classifier for the lymphography dataset using constructs

	K_1	K_2	K_3	K_4	No. of objects	Accuracy
K_1	0	1	1	0	2	0.00
K_2	2	69	9	1	81	0.85
K_3	2	13	46	0	61	0.75
K_4	0	1	2	0	4	0.00
Total					148	**0.78**
True positive rate	0.00	0.82	0.73	0.00		

Table 7 shows the results obtained by each compared classifier in ascending order. As we can see construct-based Standard Voting classifier got the best result.

Table 7. Accuracy of four rule-based classifiers for the lymphography dataset

Algorithm	Accuracy
RIPPER	0.69
Reducts based Standard Voting	0.73
SLIPPER	0.76
Constructs based Standard Voting	**0.78**

4   Conclusions

As we have discussed along the paper, reducts and constructs constitute two different contributions to the attribute reduction problem in Rough Set Theory.

The main purpose of the research reported in this paper is the discussion through a case study of the possible advantages that we can obtain when using constructs instead of reducts, for generating classification rules. Our experimental results allow concluding that constructs are an alternative for building rules which can improve the classification accuracy of the rules built from reducts. Even more, the classification results are better than other rule-based classifiers widely used in the literature. These results motivate to delve into the advantages of using either reducts or constructs, specially it may be interesting to study the development of methods to generate rules from a subset of reducts or constructs instead of considering the rules generated by the whole set.

References

1. Bache, K., Lichman, M.: UCI machine learning repository. University of California, School of Information and Computer Science, Irvine, CA (2013). http://archive.ics.uci.edu/ml
2. Barman, T., Rajesh, G., Archana, R.: Rough set based segmentation and classification model for ECG. In: Conference on Advances in Signal Processing (CASP), pp. 18–23. IEEE (2016)
3. Bazan, J.G., Szczuka, M.: The rough set exploration system. In: Peters, J.F., Skowron, A. (eds.) Transactions on Rough Sets III. LNCS, vol. 3400, pp. 37–56. Springer, Heidelberg (2005). https://doi.org/10.1007/11427834_2
4. Cohen, W.W.: Fast effective rule induction. In: Proceedings of the Twelfth International Conference on Machine Learning, Lake Tahoe California, USA, pp. 1–10 (1995)
5. Cohen, W.W., Singer, Y.: A simple, fast, and effective rule learner. In: Proceedings of the Sixteenth National Conference on Artificial Intelligence, Orlando Florida, USA, pp. 335–342 (1999)
6. Lazo-Cortés, M.S., Carrasco-Ochoa, J.A., Martínez-Trinidad, J.F., Sanchez-Diaz, G.: Computing constructs by using typical testor algorithms. In: Carrasco-Ochoa, J.A., Martínez-Trinidad, J.F., Sossa-Azuela, J.H., Olvera López, J.A., Famili, F. (eds.) MCPR 2015. LNCS, vol. 9116, pp. 44–53. Springer, Cham (2015). https://doi.org/10.1007/978-3-319-19264-2_5
7. Lazo-Cortés, M.S., Martínez-Trinidad, J.F., Carrasco-Ochoa, J.A.: Class-specific reducts vs. classic reducts in a rule-based classifier: a case study. In: Martínez-Trinidad, J.F., Carrasco-Ochoa, J.A., Olvera-López, J.A., Sarkar, S. (eds.) MCPR 2018. LNCS, vol. 10880, pp. 23–30. Springer, Cham (2018). https://doi.org/10.1007/978-3-319-92198-3_3
8. Miao, D.Q., Zhao, Y., Yao, Y.Y., Li, H.X., Xu, F.F.: Reducts in consistent and inconsistent decision tables of the Pawlak rough set model. Inf. Sci. **179**(24), 4140–4150 (2009)
9. Pawlak, Z.: Rough sets. Int. J. Comput. Inf. Sci. **11**, 341–356 (1982)
10. Pawlak, Z.: Rough sets. In: Theoretical Aspects of Reasoning About Data, pp. 315–330. Kluwer Academic Publishers, Dordrecht (1992)
11. Rana, H., Lal, M.: A rough set theory approach for rule generation and validation using RSES. Int. J. Rough Sets Data Anal. **3**(1), 55–70 (2016)
12. Rana, H., Lal, M.: A comparative study based on rough set and classification via clustering approaches to handle incomplete data to predict learning styles. Int. J. Decis. Support Syst. Technol. **9**(2), 1–20 (2017)
13. Sanchez-Diaz, G., Lazo-Cortes, M., Piza-Davila, I.: A fast implementation for the typical testor property identification based on an accumulative binary tuple. Int. J. Comput. Intell. Syst. **5**(6), 1025–1039 (2012)
14. Skowron, A., Bazan, J., Szczuka, M., Wroblewski, J.: Rough set exploration system (version 2.2.2). http://logic.mimuw.edu.pl/~rses/
15. Susmaga, R.: Reducts versus constructs: an experimental evaluation. Electron. Notes Theor. Comput. Sci. **82**(4), 239–250 (2003)
16. Triguero, I., et al.: KEEL 3.0: an open source software for multi-stage analysis in data mining. Int. J. Comput. Intell. Syst. **10**, 1238–1249 (2017)

Recognizing 3-colorable Basic Patterns on Planar Graphs

Guillermo De Ita Luna[(⊠)] and Cristina López-Ramírez

Fac. Cs. de la Computación, Universidad Autónoma de Puebla, Puebla, Mexico
deita@cs.buap.mx, cristyna2001@hotmail.com

Abstract. We recognize the wheel graphs with different kinds of centers or axle faces as the basic pattern forming a planar graph. We focus on the analysis of the vertex-coloring for these graphic patterns, and identify cases for the 3 or 4 colorability of the wheels. We also consider different compositions among wheels and analyze its colorability process.

If a valid 3-coloring exists for the union of wheels G, then our proposal determines the constraints that a set of symbolic variables must hold. These constraints are expressed by a conjunctive normal form F_G. We show that the satisfiability of F_G implies the existence of a valid 3-coloring for G. Otherwise, it is necessary to use 4 colors in order to properly color G. The revision of the satisfiability of F_G can be done in polynomial time by applying unit resolution and general properties from equalities and inequalities between symbolic variables.

Keywords: Wheel graphs · Polyhedral wheel graphs ·
Planar graphs · Vertex coloring

1   Introduction

By a proper coloring (o just a coloring) of a graph G, we refer to an assignment of colors (elements of a set) to the vertices of G, one color to each vertex, such that adjacent vertices are colored differently. The smallest number of colors in any coloring of G is called the chromatic number of G and is denoted by $\chi(G)$. When it is possible to color G from a set of k colors, then G is said to be k-colorable, while such coloring is called a k-coloring. If $\chi(G) = k$, then G is said to be k-chromatic, and every k-coloring is a minimum coloring of G.

The computation of the chromatic number $\chi(G)$ is polynomial computable if G is k-colorable with $k \leq 2$, but in other case the problem becomes NP-complete [4]. As a consequence, there are many unanswered questions related to the colouring of a graph.

Graph vertex colouring problem is an active field of research with many interesting subproblems and applications in areas like frequency allocation,planning, computer vision,scheduling, image processing, etc [2,7]. In this context, planar graphs play an important role in the graph theory area and complexity

© Springer Nature Switzerland AG 2019
J. A. Carrasco-Ochoa et al. (Eds.): MCPR 2019, LNCS 11524, pp. 336–346, 2019.
https://doi.org/10.1007/978-3-030-21077-9_31

theory since it involves the frontier between efficient and intractable computational procedures. In fact, planar graphs have several interesting properties: are four-colorables, scattered, and their inner structure is described elegantly and succinctly [1].

In the case of the vertex coloring problem, the 2-colorability is solvable in polynomial time. It has also been solved in polynomial time the 3-colorability for some graph topologies such as AT-free graphs and perfect graphs. Also the determination of $\chi(G)$ for some classes of graphs, for example: comparability graphs [10], chordal graphs, and interval graphs has been solved efficiently. In all those cases, special structures (patterns) have been found to characterize the classes of graphs that are colorable in polynomial time complexity.

In this article, we introduce for the first time what we believe are the basic graph patterns, that we have called *polyhedral wheels*, to form any planar graph. We have determined logical specification written as constraints that a set of symbolic variables must hold in order to recognize a valid 3-coloring for a polyhedral wheel. We consider different compositions among polyhedral wheels and analyze its chromatic number, in order to design a novel method for the recognition between 3 or 4-colorable polyhedral wheels.

2 Preliminaries

Let $G = (V, E)$ be an undirected simple graph (i.e. finite, loop-less and without multiple edges) with vertex set V (or $V(G)$) and set of edges $E(or E(G))$. We assume the reader is familiar with standar terminology and notation concerning graph theory and planar graphs in particular, see e.g. [8] for standard concepts in graph theory. Here we present only some notations that we will use.

If there is an edge $\{v, w\} \in E$ joining two different vertices then we say that v and w are adjacents. The Neighborhood of $x \in V$ is $N(x) = \{y \in V : \{x, y\} \in E\}$ and its closed neighborhood, denoted by $N[x]$, is $N(x) \cup \{x\}$. The cardinality of a set A is denoted by $|A|$. The degree of a vertex $x \in V$ is $|N(x)|$, and it will be denoted by $\delta(x)$,

We say that $G' = (V', E')$ is a subgraph of $G = (V, E)$ if $V' \subset V$ and $E' \subset E$. If $V' = V$ then G' is called a spanning subgraph of G. If G' contains all the edges of G that join two vertices in V' then G' is said to be induced by V'. In this way, $G - V'$ is the induced subgraph from $V - V'$. Similarly if $E' \subset E$ then $G - E' = (V, E - E')$. If $V' = \{v\}$ and $e = \{u, v\}$ then this notation is simplified to $G - v$ and $G - e$, respectively.

Given a graph $G = (V, E)$, $S \subseteq V$ is an independent set in G if for whatever two vertices v_1, v_2 in S, $\{v_1, v_2\} \notin E$. Let $I(G)$ be the set of all independent sets of G. An independent set $S \in I(G)$ is *maximal*, abbreviated as MIS, if it is not a subset of any larger independent set and, it is *maximum* if it has the largest size among all independent sets in $I(G)$.

A graph in which every pair of distinct vertices are adjacent is called a complete graph. The complete graph on n vertices is denoted by K_n.

By a proper coloring (o just a coloring) of a graph G, we refer to an assignment of colors (elements of a set) to the vertices of G, one color to each vertex, such that adjacent vertices are colored differently. The smallest number of colors in any coloring of G is called the chromatic number of G and is denoted by $\chi(G)$. When it is possible to color G from a set of k colors, then G is said to be k-colorable, while such coloring is called a k-coloring. Thus, every k-coloring is a minimum coloring of G.

If the vertices V of a graph $G = (V, E)$ can be partitioned into two disjoint sets U_1 and U_2 (called partite sets), which makes every edge of G join a vertex of U_1 to a vertex of U_2, then G is said to be a bipartite graph. If G is a k-chromatic graph, then it is possible to partition V into k independent sets $V_1, V_2, ..., V_k$ (the color classes), but it is not possible to partition V into $k - 1$ independent sets.

3   Planar Graphs

A drawing Γ of a graph G maps each vertex v to a distinct point $\Gamma(v)$ of the plane and each edge $\{u, v\}$ to a simple open Jordan curve $\Gamma(u, v)$, with endpoints $\Gamma(u)$ and $\Gamma(v)$. A drawing is planar if it can be embedded (or it has an embedding) in the space in a way that no two edges intersect except at an endvertex in common. A graph G is planar if G admits an embedding in the plane. A planar drawing partitions the plane into connected regions called faces. The unbounded face is usually called outer face or external face.

In general, a planar graph has many embeddings in the plane. Two embeddings of a planar graph are equivalent when the boundary of a face in one embedding always corresponds to the boundary of a face in the other. A planar embedding is an equivalent class of planar drawings and it is described by the clockwise circular order of the edges incident to each vertex. A maximal planar graph is one to which no edge can be added without losing planarity. Thus, in any embedding of a maximal planar graph G with $n \geq 3$, the boundary of every face of G is a triangle.

One of the most outstanding results is Kuratowski's theorem [5], which gives a criterion for a graph to be planar in the case that it contains no subgraph that is a subdivision of K_5 or $K_{3,3}$, where K_5 is the complete graph of order 5 and $K_{3,3}$ is the complete bipartite graph with 3 vertices in each of the sets of the partition, then the graph is planar. Similarly, the theorem of Wagner [11] states that a graph G is planar if and only if it does not have K_5 or $K_{3,3}$ as minor. However, both characterizations are different since a graph may admit K_5 as minor without having a subgraph that is a subdivision of K_5.

The famous Four-Color Theorem (4CT) says that every planar graph is vertex 4-colorable. Robertson et al. [9] describes an $O(n^2)$ 4-coloring algorithm. This seems to be very hard to improve, since it would probably require a new proof of the 4CT. On the other hand, to decide if a planar graph requires only three colors is a NP-hard problem. However, the Grötzsch theorem [3] guarantees that every triangle-free planar graph is 3-colorable. Then, the hard part in the coloring of planar graphs is to decide if an unrestricted planar graph is 3 or 4 colorable.

Not all graphs are planar. However planar graphs arise quite naturally in real-world applications, such as road or railway maps, electric printed circuits, chemical molecules, etc. Planar graphs play an important role in these problems, partly due to the fact that some practical problems can be efficiently solved for planar graphs even if they are intractable for general graphs [8]. In recent years, planar graphs have attracted computer scientists' interest, and a lot of interesting algorithms and complexity results have been obtained from planar graphs.

3.1   The Internal-Face Graph of a Planar Graph

A planar graph G has a set of closed non-intersected regions $F(G) = \{f_1, \ldots, f_k\}$ called faces. Each face $f_i \in F(G)$ is represented by the set of edges that bound its inside area. All edge $\{u, v\}$ in G, that is not the border of some face from G, is called an *acyclic edge*.

Two faces $f_i, f_j \in F(G)$ are adjacent if they have common edges, this is, $(E(f_i) \cap E(f_j)) \neq \emptyset$. Otherwise, they are independent faces. Notice that two independent faces can have common vertices but they do not have common edges. A set of faces is independent if each pair of them are independent.

An acyclic edge is adjacent to a face if they have just one common vertex. Two acyclic edges are adjacent if they share a common endpoint. We build an internal-face graph $G_f = (X, E(G_f))$ from G, in the following way:

1. Each face f_i has attached a node $x \in V(G_f)$.
2. Each acyclic edge from G has attached a vertex of G_f labeled by the label of its vertices.
3. There is an edge $\{u, v\} \in E(G_f)$ joining two adjacent vertices of G_f, when its corresponding faces (or acyclic edges) are adjacent in G.

G_f is the *internal-face* graph of a planar graph G. We must emphasize that G_f is not the dual graph of G since in the construction of G_f the external face is not considered. Notice that G_f is also a planar graph with vertices representing faces or edges from G (as we can see in Fig. 2). The internal-face graph G_f of G provides a mapping of the relation among the faces of G that is useful in the search for the 3-coloring pattern graphs.

A basic pattern in planar graphs is a wheel graph that is a single vertex (called the center vertex of the wheel) adjacent to vertices forming a cycle. Each face (called an axle of the wheel) is a triangle. There are two classes of vertices in a wheel; the center vertex and the vertices forming the cycle. Note that a wheel of a planar graph G is represented as a cycle in its internal-face G_f. Wheels with a number of even triangles are 3-colorable. Meanwhile any planar graph, containing K_4 or odd wheels, will request four colors in order to properly color those graphs. However, those topologies are not the unique 4-colorable cases.

We extend the class of wheels by considering any polygon as an axle face of the wheel. Such type of wheel is called a polyhedral wheel. This means that there are vertices in the cycle surrounding the center vertex which are not adjacent to the center. The center vertex is a common vertex to all axle face of the polyhedral wheel.

We differentiate the cycle's vertices in a polyhedral wheel as axle vertices if they are adjacent to the center vertex; and as extra-axle, when they are not

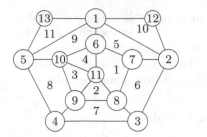 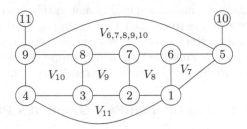

Fig. 1. Graph G with faces identified   **Fig. 2.** The internal-face graph G_f of G

adjacent to the center. In the case of the edges in a polyhedral wheel, we have the edges of the cycle and the edges incident to the center, which are called spoke edges. For example, in Fig. 1, a polyhedral wheel is formed by the edges: 10-6-7-8-9-10, whose center vertex is 11. All axle of this wheel is triangular with the exception of the face 1. The spoke edges are: $\{6, 11\}, \{10, 11\}, \{9, 11\}, \{8, 11\}$.

A polyhedral wheel of a planar graph G is represented as a cycle in its internal-face graph G_f. However, a cycle in G_f can also codify other kind of wheel of G. A wheel of G where the center is a polygon instead of a single vertex is called a polyhedral subgraph. For example, in Fig. 2 there are 5 polyhedral wheels whose centers are labeled by the single center vertex of the wheel. There is also a polyhedral subgraph whose center is the polygon formed by the set of vertices $\{6, 7, 8, 9, 10\}$. Any of these wheels is an odd wheel if it has an odd number of axle faces, otherwise, it is an even wheel.

4   Coloring Planar Graphs

It is easy (in linear-time on the size of the graph) to recognize if an input graph is 2-colorable, since it involves the recognition of only even cycles in the graph. Similarly, it is known by Grotszch's theorem [3] that any planar graph triangle-free is 3-colorable. However, the recognition of the 3-coloring of a planar graph is a classical NP-Complete problem [4]. It becomes difficult to recognize between the three or four coloring of a planar graph when it contains triangles, because there is not (at least until now) a sufficient condition to recognize the 3-colorability of a planar graph.

Let $Three = \{1, 2, 3\}$ be the set that contains three different colors. Given a planar graph G, let $x_{v,c}$ be the logical variable denoting that the vertex v has the color $c \in \{1, 2, 3, 4\}$. For each vertex $v \in V(G)$ a $Tabu(v)$ set is associated. $Tabu(v)$ indicates the prohibited colors for the vertex v. In fact, $Tabu(v)$ contains the variables associated to the vertices in $N(v)$ that have been already colored, i.e. $Tabu(v) = \{c : (x_{u,c}), \text{ and } \{u, v\} \in E(G)\}$.

We introduce a typical coloring for a wheel, where its center vertex is assigned the first color. The colors 2,3 are assigned in alternating way to the cycle's vertices. This coloring begins in any triangle face of the wheel, and follows an opposite clockwise direction from the cycle's vertices. Only when the last vertex of the cycle is visted, it is determined if a fourth color is necessary.

In this section, we start our analysis for searching basic graphic patterns, and analyzing if it is possible to determine if they are 3 or 4 colorable. We start considering the coloring of simple wheels, because the wheels are basic pattern to form planar graphs,

Lemma 1. *The union of even simple wheels, where its center vertices are independent, is 3-colorable.*

Proof. When all center vertices of the wheels form an independent set on the graph then the first color can be assigned to those vertices. Common edges between wheels are only given by the cycle's edges of the wheels. If the center vertices are removed of the graph, since they were already colored, the remaining subgraph is bipartite because it has only the cycle's edges. As only even cycles remain in the subgraph, then the subgraph is 2-colorable. We obtain a 3-coloring for this kind of planar graphs by using different colors between the center vertices and the cycle's vertices.

The lemmas to be developed in the next section guarantee the correctness of our proposal. We denote the function $Color(v)$ that assigns a unique color from Three to the vertex v.

Lemma 2. *An acyclic component is 3-colorable if all of its vertices have at most one color as a restriction.*

Proof. The acyclic component is considered as a tree rooted in v_r. A pre-order coloring is made from v_r, where $Color(v_r) = MIN\{Three - Tabu(v_r)\}$. If we advance in pre-order for each new level to be colored, all vertex y in the new level will have at most two restricted colors from its parent node and the color that could exist in $Tabu(y)$. Thus, a color has always been available of the three possible from $Three$. When all nodes of the tree had been visited in pre-order, our proposal has already colored all vertex.

Lemma 3. *Let $A = \{f_1, f_2, \ldots, f_n\}$ be a set of n non-adjacent faces where each face has at least one vertex that does not restrict color 3, then A is 3-colorable.*

Proof. As $A = \{f_1, f_2, \ldots, f_n\}$ is a set of non-adjacent faces, then some faces in A could share a common vertex at the most. The proof is developed by induction on the number of faces in A.

1. A single face is 3-colorable, since every cycle with at least one unrestricted vertex is 3-colorable.
2. Suppose that the hypothesis on the sets up to $n - 1$ faces is held.
3. Let A be a set of n faces where each face has at least one vertex that does not restrict color 3. If there is a face $f_a \in A$ that is independent (without common edges nor common vertices) from all other faces of A, then f_a is 3-colorable (as in the case 1), and it can be removed from A. The remaining set in A has

$n-1$ faces, and the inductive hypothesis is held.

Otherwise, the n faces in A share a common vertex. Let $x \in f_i : \forall f_i \in A$ be the common vertex. If $3 \notin Tabu(x)$, then by assigning the color 3 to x and removing it from the graph, all the faces in A become open and they form an acyclic graph, which is 3-colorable by Lemma 2.

Assuming $Tabu(x) = 3$, but $\forall f_i \in A$, there is $y_i \in V(f_i)$ such that $Tabu(y_i) = \emptyset$, by hyphotesis. By assigning color 3 to each one of these $y_i's$, and eliminating them from each $V(f_i)$, an acyclic component is formed and this component is 3-colorable by Lemma 2.

When G_f is a tree, we say that G (its corresponding planar graph) is a *polygonal tree* [6]. This means that, although G has cycles, all those cycles can be arranged as a tree whose nodes are polygons instead of single vertices of G. The following theorem show that it is enough an order to visit all faces from the planar graph in order to obtain an efficient procedure for the 3-coloring of G.

Theorem 1. *If the internal-face graph of a planar graph G has a tree topology, then G is 3-colorable.*

Proof. Let G_f be the internal-face graph of a planar graph G. As a face of G is a simple cycle then it is 3-colorable. Also, all acyclic edge of G is also 3-colorable, because all acyclic graph is 2-colorable. A 3-coloring procedure for G can be done by traversing the nodes of G_f in pre-order. The face of the father node of G_f is colored first and after, the faces of its children nodes. In each current level, the two adjacent faces (father and children in G) are considered. Both regions have two common extremal vertices x, y in its common boundaries.

Those common vertices are colored first, and then, the remaining vertices in both faces have two prohibited colors at the most. Notice that there is not a pair of adjacent vertices u and v in any of the two faces, such that $\{u, v\} \subseteq (N(x) \cap N(y))$. This happens because $\{x, y, u, v\}$ form K_4 and this subgraph can not be part of any polygonal tree. Thus, for all remaining vertices in both faces it is available at least one color of the three possible in *Three*. The 3-coloring process ends when all the nodes of the tree G_f have been visited in pre-order.

If a planar graph G has not a polygonal tree topology, this means that there are cycles in G_f and, therefore, wheels in G. For this kind of planar graphs, it is possible to recognize 3-colorable graphic patterns.

Lemma 4. *All polyhedral wheel is 3-colorable.*

Proof. If r_x is a polyhedral wheel, then there is an axle face that is not triangular. Therefore, there is at least one vertex $v_e \in V(r_x)$ that is not adjacent to the center vertex v_x of the wheel, otherwise all axle face would be triangular. The graph $R_{-v_e} = (r_x - v_e)$ is a polygonal array, and then it is 3-colorable by Lemma 3 and Theorem 1. Any typical 3-coloring for R_{-v_e} can be extended to a 3-coloring for r_x if v_e has the same color as v_x, because in a typical coloring the color of the center vertex is not used in the cycle's vertices. Therefore, the center's color has not been used for the vertices in $N(v_e)$.

The union of 3-colorable wheels is not necessarily 3-colorable. For example, each individual wheel in the graph of the Fig. 4 is 3-colorable, when the common face is assumed as part of each wheel. Therefore, each one of them is 3-colorable by Lemma 4. However, the final graph (union of the wheels) is 4-colorable as we will see in the following section.

4.1 Method for Determining the 3 or 4 Colorability of a Sequence of Wheels

We propose a logical method for recognizing between three or four colors for the colorabilty of the union of the wheels. Let G be a graph formed by the union of simple wheels sharing common faces. Our proposal is based on the construction of a propositional formula F_G expressed in conjunctive normal form, and whose satisfiability codify the three colorability of G. Otherwise, G would be 4-colorable.

In order to present our proposal, let us consider first a pair of simple wheels r_x and r_y sharing a common face that is denoted as $(r_x \cup_f r_y)$, where $f = (F(r_x) \cap F(r_y))$. The center vertices of the wheels are labeled by x for r_x, and a for r_y, as it is illustrated in Fig. 3. A triplet of symbolic variables $\{x, y, z\}$ is associated to $V(r_x)$, while the triplet of symbolic variables $\{a, b, c\}$ is associated to $V(r_y)$ in the following way.

1. The variable x is associated to the center vertex of r_x, while the variable a is associated to the center vertex of r_y.
2. The cycle's vertices of r_x are associated with the variables y and z in an alternating way. It begins with a triangular face adjacent to the common face f and follows the other triangular faces in r_x until all cycle's vertices are covered.
3. The cycle's vertices of r_y are associated with the variables b and c in an alternating way. It begins with a triangular face adjacent to the common face f and follows the other triangular faces in r_y until all cycle's vertices are covered.

The topology of $(r_x \cup_f r_y)$ defines the type of constrainsts forming F_G, in the following way.

(I) The vertices $V(f)$, that are common vertices between $V(r_x) \cap V(r_y)$, determine equality constraints among its corresponding variables: $(y \oplus z) = (a \oplus b)$, where $(\oplus)$ denotes the logical *xor* operator. This means that the vertices in $V(r_x) \cap V(r_y)$ define equal colors (variables with same values).

(II) An edge $e \in E(G)$, with endpoints in $V(r_x)$ and $V(r_y)$, define an inequality constraint between its corresponding variables: $(y \oplus z) \neq (a \oplus b)$. This means that adjacent vertices in $V(f)$ define different colors (variables with different values).

(III) F_G also considers that any pair of adjacent vertices must have different colors. This is codified as: $(x \neq y) \wedge (x \neq z) \wedge (z \neq y) \wedge (a \neq b) \wedge (b \neq c) \wedge (c \neq a)$.

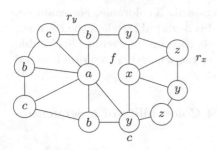

Fig. 3. A 3-colorable union of wheels

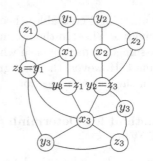

Fig. 4. A 4-colorable union of wheels

(IV) In F_G is also added the constraints defining that all vertice in $(V(r_x) \cup V(r_y))$ has to have one of the three possible colors, and this is codified as: $((x = a) \vee (x = b) \vee (x = c)) \wedge ((y = a) \vee (y = b) \vee (y = c)) \wedge ((z = a) \vee (z = b) \vee (z = c))$.

Notice that constraints type I and II are unitary clauses, and that any inequality can be considered as the negation of an equality constraint. Furthermore, a pair of contradictory unitary clauses implies the unsatisfiability of F_G. The satisfiability of F_G determines that $(r_x \cup_f r_y)$ is 3-colorable. Otherwise, $(r_x \cup_f r_y)$ is 4-colorable. When F_G is satisfiable, then a bijective function $f_R : \{x, y, z\} \rightarrow \{a, b, c\}$ exists. This determines the existence of a valid 3-coloring for the vertices in the pair of wheels.

The Figs. 3 and 4 illustrate the two different cases for the values of F_G. For the graph in Fig. 3, the constraints type II define that $(b \neq y) \wedge (a \neq y)$, and then $(c = y)$ is inferred due to the constraints type IV, as it is validated by the unique constraint type I. Since there are no more constraints type II, then the formula F_G can be satisfied by the assignments $((a = x) \wedge (b = z))$, or $((a = z) \wedge (b = x))$. Thus, the graph is Fig. 3 is 3-colorable. A valid 3-coloring is, for example, $(c = y) \wedge (a = x) \wedge (b = z)$, where $\{a, b, c\}$ represents any permutation of the values $\{1, 2, 3\}$.

Our proposal for reviewing the 3-colorabilty of a sequence of wheels works even when the centers of the wheels are not independent, or when the graph is formed by the union of two or more wheels.

For example, let us consider the graph in Fig. 4. In this case, we recognize three wheels and, therefore, the triplets $\{x_1, y_1, z_1\}, \{x_2, y_2, z_2\}, \{x_3, y_3, z_3\}$ are associated to $V(r_1), V(r_2)$, and $V(r_3)$, respectively. The constraints type I determine the equalities: $(y_3 = z_1) \wedge (z_3 = y_2) \wedge (z_3 = y_1)$. Meanwhile, the constraints type II determine the inequality: $(y_1 \neq y_2)$. It is not hard to infer $(y_1 = y_2)$ from the conditions: $(z_3 = y_2) \wedge (z_3 = y_1)$. However, this inferred equality contradicts the inequality type II: $(y_1 \neq y_2)$. Therefore, F_G is unsatisfiable. As F_G is unsatisfiable, then the planar graph is not 3-colorable and thus, it is necessary to use a fourth color to properly color the graph according to 4CT Theorem.

Notice that the revision of the satisfiability of F_G can be done in polynomial-time on the size of the graph G. This is possible, since it consists in the application of unit resolution of the constraints Type I and Type II versus all constraints in F_G, as well as the application of the transitivity of the equality constraints. If there is a contradiction in F_G, then it will be generated during the process of the unit resolution, implying that it is necessary 4 colors to color G.

5 Conclusion

We recognize the polyhedral wheels as the basic pattern graphs to form planar graphs. We analyze for these polyhedral wheels the possibility of determining its 3 or 4 colorability. We also consider different compositions among wheels, and we analyze its colorability process. We propose an efficient method based on the construction of a conjunctive normal form F_G, which is formed by the equalities and inequalities constraints defined by the relations of the vertices in a sequence of wheels of G.

Our method determines the conditions that a set of symbolic variables must hold when a valid 3-coloring exists for G. Thus, we show that the satisfiability of F_G implies the existence of a valid 3-coloring for G. Otherwise, it is necessary to use 4 colors to properly color G.

References

1. Cortese, P., Patrignani, M.: Planarity Testing and Embedding. Press LLC (2004)
2. Dvořák, Z., Král, D., Thomas, R.: Three-coloring triangle-free graphs on surfaces. In: Proceedings of the 20th ACM-SIAM Symposium on Discrete Algorithms, pp. 120–129 (2009)
3. Grötzsch, H.: Ein Dreifarbensatz fr dreikreisfreie Netze auf der Kugel, Wiss. Z. Martin-Luther-Univ. Halle-Wittenberg Math.-Natur. Reihe, vol. 8, pp. 109–120 (1959)
4. Johnson, D.: The NP-completeness column: an ongoing guide. J. Algorithms **6**, 434–451 (1985)
5. Kuratowski, K.: Sur le probleme des courbes gauches en topologie. Fund. Math. **15**, 271–283 (1930)
6. López-Ramírez, C., De Ita, G., Neri, A.: Modelling 3-coloring of polygonal trees via incremental satisfiability. In: Martínez-Trinidad, J.F., Carrasco-Ochoa, J.A., Olvera-López, J.A., Sarkar, S. (eds.) MCPR 2018. LNCS, vol. 10880, pp. 93–102. Springer, Cham (2018). https://doi.org/10.1007/978-3-319-92198-3_10
7. Mertzios, G.B., Spirakis, P.G.: Algorithms and almost tight results for 3-colorability of small diameter graphs, Technical report (2012). arxiv.org/pdf/1202.4665v2.pdf
8. Nishizeki, T., Chiba, N.: Planar Graphs: Theory and Algoritms, vol. 32, pp. 83–87. Elsevier, Amsterdam (1988)
9. Robertson, N., Sanders, D.P., Seymour, P.D., Thomas, R.: The four color theorem. J. Combin. Theory Ser. B **70**, 2–4 (1997)

10. Stacho, J.: 3-colouring AT-free graphs in polynomial time. In: Cheong, O., Chwa, K.-Y., Park, K. (eds.) ISAAC 2010. LNCS, vol. 6507, pp. 144–155. Springer, Heidelberg (2010). https://doi.org/10.1007/978-3-642-17514-5_13
11. Wagner, K.: Über eine Eigenschaft der ebenen Komplexe. Mathematische Annalen **114**, 570–590 (1937)

Inference Algorithm with Falsifying Patterns for Belief Revision

P. Bello$^{(\boxtimes)}$ and G. De Ita

Language & Knowledge Engineering Lab. (LKE), Faculty of Computer Science,
Benemérita Universidad Autónoma de Puebla, Puebla, Mexico
{pbello,deita}@cs.buap.mx

Abstract. Let K be a Knowledge Base (KB) and let ϕ be a query, the entailment problem $K \models \phi$ is crucial for solving the Belief Revision problem. The Belief Revision problem consists in incorporate new beliefs into knowledge base already established, changing as little as possible the original beliefs and maintaining consistency of the KB. A widely accepted framework for reasoning through intelligent systems is the knowledge-based system approach. The general idea is to keep the knowledge in some representative language with a well-defined connotation, particularly it we will be used prepositional logic for modelling the knowledge base and the new information.

This article shows that the use of falsifying patterns for expressing clauses help to determine whether an conjunctive normal form (CNF) is inferred from another CNF, and therefore, it allows us to construct an algorithm for belief revision between CNF's.

Our algorithm applies a depth first search in order to obtain an effective process for the belief revision between the conjuntive forms K and ϕ.

Keywords: Belief revision · Propositional inference ·
Falsifying patterns

1 Introduction

The belief revision problem consists on adding new beliefs to a database (KB) that is already established, while maintaining the original beliefs without interfering with its coherence. The best-known paradigm for the belief revision is the AGM model, where authors Alchourrón, Gärdenfors and Makinson in 1985 developed a model [5] for the change in beliefs. In this model, the revision operation puts emphasis on the new information over the existing beliefs in the agent knowledge; however, it's important to know the reliability of the source, just as quoted by Liberatore [19]. Afterwards, as indicated by Katsuno and Mendelzon [11] the different perspectives of semantic belief revision were unified and the AGM model was reformulated into the KM postulates.

© Springer Nature Switzerland AG 2019
J. A. Carrasco-Ochoa et al. (Eds.): MCPR 2019, LNCS 11524, pp. 347–356, 2019.
https://doi.org/10.1007/978-3-030-21077-9_32

From the point of view of the propositional logic, the revision of beliefs is seen as a process where reasoning in intelligent systems is the knowledge-based systems approach, which consists of maintaining knowledge in some representation language with well-defined connotation, according to Rúa and Sierra [15].

The knowledge of an agent is closed under logical consequence, denoted as $C_n(K)$, that is when an agent believes all the logical consequences of their beliefs. These sentences are stored in a knowledge database provided with a mechanism of deductive reasoning.

The propositional implication as mentioned in [8] is an important task in problems such as the estimation of the degree of belief and the update of beliefs in the applications of Artificial Intelligence. For example, it is important when working in the planning and designing of multi-agent systems, in logical diagnosis, in the approximate reasoning and in the counting of the number of solutions for satisfiability instances, as indicated in [2,18], among other applications.

In general, the propositional inference problem is a hard challenge in automatic reasoning and turns out to be in the class Co-NP complete [24]. Many other forms of reasoning have been shown to be hard to compute [4].

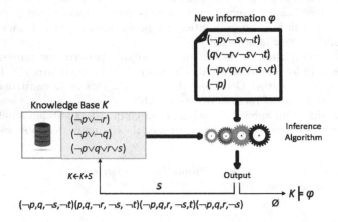

Fig. 1. Base model for propositional inference.

In this paper, it is applied a procedure based on falsifying patterns and the depth first search for belief revision. The basic model to determine if the new information is already present in our knowledge database is shown in Fig. 1. Thus, the objective of this research is to present an algorithm that allows determining if the new information should be added to the knowledge database or if it is not necessary as it can already be inferred.

2   Related Works

The problem of belief revision has been approached from different perspectives and different theories. Some authors consider important to pre-process the new information. For example, in [14] a study made of some of the computationally difficult problems is associated with the theory of belief revision, among them, the deduction in logical bases of knowledge is found.

It is expected that the complexity of the induction processes of NP-difficult problems can be reduced by pre-processing the input formulas. In addition, pre-processing could help determine what type of instances would unlikely be received or guided subsequently by deduction processes.

In [10] the direct relation of the problem of propositional implication between normal forms that can be reduced to the classic Co-NP-complete problem of reviewing the tautologicity of a disjunctive formula is described. Although propositional inference is a Co-NP problem in its general version, there are also different cases that can be solved efficiently.

When new information is available, the respective sets are modified differently to preserve parts of the knowledge during the review process. This approach allows for dealing with difficult and complex scenarios [16]. It is also important to know if the new information is reliable so it could save us some processing time. In [23] it is propose that when the new information comes from another agent, we must first determine if that agent should be reliable. Trust is defined as a step prior to processing the review. It is emphasized that trust in an agent is often restricted to a particular domain.

Liberatore [20] and Peppasa [21] propose to carry out the review of beliefs considering the plausibility of the information. Given a sequence of revisions and their result, a possible initial order is built according to how the sequence of revisions was generated.

It is important to note that the new information must be reliable before reviewing and updating the knowledge database, regardless of whether it is a database of one belief or multiple beliefs. As indicated in [22], the fusion of beliefs aims to combine pieces of information from different and possibly conflicting sources, in order to produce a single consistent belief database that retains as much information as possible.

In our work, we take as a basis the propositional inference to model the process of belief revision. For several authors that focus on beliefs' revision, logic has been the main subject of study [9]. In [13] an abstract theoretical model is presented characterizing the AGM and KM postulated for different logics, among which are: Propositional Logic (PL), Horn Logic (HL), First Order Logic (FOL) and Description logic (DL) in terms of minimum change between interpretations.

In [1] it is emphasized that the representation of knowledge and reasoning using propositional logic is an important component of artificial intelligence systems. A propositional formula in conjunctive normal form can contain redundant clauses, whose elimination of the formula does not affect the set of its models. The identification of redundant clauses is important because redundancy often leads to unnecessary calculations, wasted storage and can obscure the structure of the problem. The experimental results reveal that many instances of CNF obtained from the practical applications of propositional satisfiability problem (SAT) exhibit a high degree of redundancy.

Similarly, in [7] an algorithm based on decomposition is proposed for revision problems presented in the classic propositional logic. A set of decomposed rules are presented to analyze formulas' satisfiability considering a set of literals. A decomposition function is constructed to calculate all the satisfactory literal sets of a given formula since these will conforming to the models that satisfy the formula.

In [3], a general family of belief operators in a propositional environment is studied. Its operators are based on the formula/literal dependency, which is more refined than the notion of formula/variable dependency.

Several efforts have been made using mathematical logic to solve the problem of revision of beliefs [12, 17]. Our proposal is linked to the work reported in [10], where an operator is constructed using propositional logic. In this new version of the belief revision operator, a depth first search strategy is used in order to improve the complexity of the algorithm proposed in [10]. In addition, our algorithm considers the trust of the new information ϕ with a higher priority with respect to the information stored in the knowledge base, because the new information prevails in dynamic processes.

3   Preliminaries

Let $X = x_1, \ldots, x_n$ be a set of n Boolean variables. A literal denoted as *lit* is, a variable x_i or a denied variable $\neg x_i$. As usual, each $x \in X, x^0 = \neg x$ and $x^1 = x$. A clause is a disjunction of different literals. For $k \in N$, a *k-clause* is a clause with exactly k literals, and $(\leq k)$-*clause* is a clause with at most k literals. Sometimes, we consider a clause as a set of literals.

A *phrase* is a conjunction of literals. A *k-phrase* is a phrase with exactly k literals. A variable $x \in X$ appears in a clause C (or phrase) if x or $\neg x$ is an element of C.

A *conjunctive normal form* (CNF) is a conjunction of clauses, and *k-CNF* is a CNF containing only *k-clauses*. A *disjunctive normal form* (DNF) is a disjunction of sentences, and *k-DNF* is a DNF containing only *k-phrases*. A CNF F with n variables is a n-*ary* Boolean function $F:\{0,1\}^n \to \{0,1\}$. Rather, any Boolean function F has infinitely many equivalent representations, among these, some in CNF and DNF.

An *assignment* s for a formula F is a Boolean mapping $s : v(F) \to \{1,0\}$. An assignment s can also be considered as a non-complementary set of literals: $l \in s$ if and only if s assigns true to l and $\neg l$ false. s is a partial *assignment* for the formula F when s has determined a logical value only to variables of a proper subset of F, namely $s : Y \to \{1,0\}$ and $Y \subset v(F)$. A clause C is satisfied by an assignment s if $Lit(C) \subset Lit(s)$. Otherwise, if for all literal l in C it holds that $\neg l \in s$ then C is falsified by s. A CNF F is satisfied by an assignment s if each clause F is satisfied by s. A *model* of F is an assignment on $v(F)$ satisfying F. A CNF F is falsified by an assignment s, if it exists a clause of F that is falsified by s. $Mod(F)$ and $Fals(F)$ denote the set of models and falsifying assignments of the formula F.

Two independent clauses C_i and C_j have complementary pair of literals, therefore their falsifying assignments must also have complementary literals, that is, $Fals(C_i) \cap Fals(C_j) = \emptyset$.

Given two falsifying strings A and B each of length n, if there is an $i \in [0, n]$ such that $A[i] = x$ and $B[i] = 1 - x$, $x \in \{0, 1\}$, it is said that they have the *independence* property. Otherwise, we say that both strings are *dependent*.

Given a pair of dependent clauses C_1 and C_2, if $Lit(C_1) \subseteq Lit(C_2)$ we affirm that C_2 is subsumed by C_1.

The propositional logic as indicated in the book [6] is used to analyze formally valid reasonings, starting from propositions and logical operators in order to construct formulas operating on the propositional variables.

4   Inference Algorithm with Falsifying Patterns

In the search to reduce the required amount of computational resources in the belief revision process, this new algorithm is presented based on the depth first search. The algorithm reported in [10] it is based on a table of $|K| \times |\phi|$ that is adjusted dynamically depending on the number of new clauses to be generated. In this way, the table is scanned by row to row. While the new algorithm traverses the nodes of a tree in depth, but with a limited depth value $|k|$, this avoids the risk of being indefinitely interned in a non-finite branch, as well as the need to save all the expanded nodes.

Let K be the Knowledge Base and let ϕ be the new information, we say that K scmantics inferences implies ϕ, written as $K \models \phi$, if ϕ is satisfied for each model (Mod) of K, i.e., if $Mod(K) \subseteq Mod(\phi)$. The belief revision seen as propositional inference have the following facts:

- $K \models \phi$ iff $\mathrm{Mod}(K) \subseteq \mathrm{Mod}\,(\phi)$
- $K \models \phi$ iff $\mathrm{Fals}(\phi) \subseteq \mathrm{Fals}\,(K)$

Thus Fals() represents the truth values inverted for each literal in each clause K and ϕ. Given a clause $C_i = (x_{i_1} \vee ... \vee x_{i_k})$, then the value at each position from i_1-th to i_k-th of the string A_i is fixed with the true value falsifying each literal of C_i. E.g., if $x_i \in C_i$, the i_j-th element of A_i is set to 0. On the otre hand, if $\neg x_i \in C_i$, then the i_j-th element is set to 1. The literal which do not appear in C_i are represented by the symbol $*$, meaning that they could take any logical value in the set 0,1. We call *falsifying patterns* to the string A_i representing the set of falsifying assignments of a clause C_i.

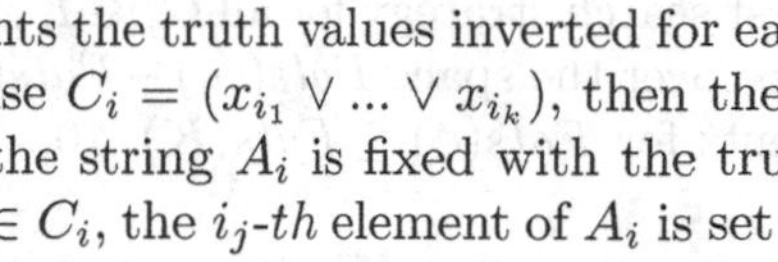

$$(\neg p \vee q \vee \neg s) \qquad (q \vee r \vee \neg s \vee t)$$
$$\downarrow \;\swarrow\; \swarrow \qquad\qquad \searrow\; \downarrow\; \swarrow$$
$$(\,1\; 0\; *\; 1\; *\,) \qquad (\,*\; 0\; 0\; 1\; 0\,)$$

Fig. 2. Transforming by falsifying patterns

Let a KB $K = \bigwedge_{(j=1)}^{m} C_j$ and $\phi = \bigwedge_{(i=1)}^{k} \phi_i$ where each $C_j \in K$ and each $\phi_i \in \phi$ are expressed clauses in the same set of n boolean variables. The clauses $(\neg p \vee q \vee \neg s)$ and $(q \vee r \vee \neg s \vee t)$ are transformed using falsifying patterns as shown in the Fig. 2 considering the space of variables: p, q, r, s, t.

The main procedure for the belief revision process between the new information ϕ and the knowledge base K returns a set S of clauses deduced from ϕ. This procedure contemplates the following subprocesses:

- $Pre(F, K, S)$: This function performs a pre-processing of the knowledge base K with respect to each of the clauses of the new information ϕ, in order to eliminate subsumed and independent clauses.
- $sort(K, F)$: sort K based on the differences with Fi using the function $Dif(F, C)$ which computes the difference $|Lit(F_i) - Lit(C_i)|$ between the literals of a clause ϕ and a clause of the Knowledge Base K.
- $DFS(\phi, K, S)$: This function (Algorithm 1) allows the generation of the depth first search tree for each clause in ϕ.

Subsumed	Independent	Difference
$K = (\ast\ast00\ast11\ast)$	$K = (000\ast\ast\ast1)$	$K = (\ast\ast00\ast11\ast)$
$\varphi = (\ast\ast00\ast110)$	$\varphi = (\ast01\ast\ast11)$	$\varphi = (\ast1\ast0\ast\ast11)$

Fig. 3. Operations between clauses considered in the development of the Algorithm

Figure 3 describes the main operations that are applied in the general procedure as well as in Algorithm 1. The set S of clauses generated by the proposed algorithm contains exactly the necessary clauses that allow to infer each $\phi_i \in \phi$. When applying depth first search strategy for all $C_j \in K$, we obtain that $K \models \phi$, and in this way allows to cover the space $Fals(\phi_i) - Fals(C_j)$, which is the minimum space of assignments for $Fals(\phi) \subseteq Fals(K)$ [10].

5   Results

The following is the result of applying the general procedure with the depth first search described in Algorithm 1 using falsifying patterns.

Example 1. Let $K = \{(r \vee s \vee \neg u \vee \neg v) \wedge (r \vee \neg s \vee \neg u \vee v \vee \neg w) \wedge (\neg q \vee \neg s \vee \neg t \vee u \vee \neg w) \wedge (\neg q \vee \neg r \vee \neg s \vee \neg w) \wedge (\neg q \vee r \vee t \vee u \vee \neg w) \wedge (p \vee q \vee r \vee w)\}$ and $\phi = \{(\neg q \vee \neg s \vee \neg v \vee \neg w) \wedge (\neg w) \wedge (r \vee s \vee \neg u \vee \neg v \vee w)\}$.

Expressing the above formulas via falsifying patterns: $K = \{C_1, C_2, C_3, C_4, C_5, C_6\} = \{(\ast\ast00\ast11\ast), (\ast\ast01\ast101), (\ast1\ast110\ast1), (\ast111\ast\ast\ast1), (\ast10\ast00\ast1), (000\ast\ast\ast\ast0)\}$ and $\phi = \{(\ast\ast00\ast110), (\ast\ast\ast\ast\ast\ast\ast1), (\ast1\ast1\ast\ast11)\}$. In Fig. 4, the complete processing tree is shown.

Algorithm 1. Function $DFS(\phi, K, S)$

---

if (ϕ is *empty*) **then**
   Return S
end if
if (K is *empty*) **then**
   $S \leftarrow S + Pop(\phi)$ {The S set is updated}
end if
$Fi \leftarrow Pop(\phi)$
$C \leftarrow Pop(K)$
if ($Ind(Fi, Ci)$) **then**
   $Push(\phi, Fi)$ {independent Fi is added to ϕ }
else
   $K\_dif \leftarrow Dif(Fi, C)$ {it obtains difference between literals }
   if ($K\_dif > 0$) **then**
     $K \leftarrow K - C_i$
     $Gen(\phi, Fi, C, K\_dif)$ {it generates new clauses }
   end if
end if
$K \leftarrow K - C$
$S = DFS(\phi, K, S)$ { recursive call }

Table 1 shows some results of the execution of the algorithm reported in [10] against the new algorithm proposed in this paper. In each of the cases it is noted that the new algorithm performs less processing to determine the process of interference, which is due to the use of the depth first search strategy.

- The main process starts applying the procedure $Prep()$. In this step is determined that ϕ_1 is a clause subsumed by C_1 because its difference is zero.
- The process restarts considering the clause ϕ_2. The pre-processing determines that C_6 is deleted because it is independent with ϕ_2.
- The knowledge base K is sorted and it is based on the difference ($Dif()$) with ϕ_2, obtaining the base $K = \{C_4, C_1, C_2, C_3, C_4, C_5\}$.

Table 1. Algorithms processing results

Variables	$|K|$	$|\phi|$	Processing	
			Previous algorithm	New algorithm
5	4	4	20	16
5	4	4	36	24
5	3	4	15	6
6	6	2	23	14
7	6	2	23	17
8	6	3	45	26
15	5	5	35	22

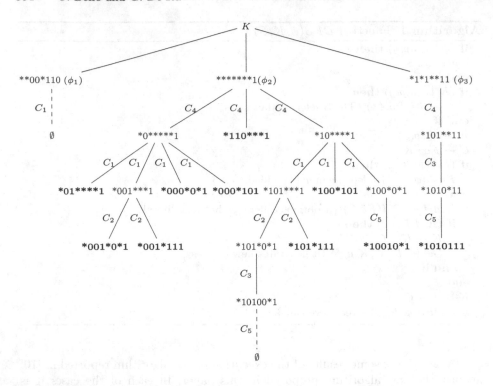

Fig. 4. Generating the Depth First Search tree by $DFS\_BR()$

- The reduced knowledge base K is sorted by subtracting with ϕ_1, resulting $K = \{C_4, C_3, C_5\}$.
- The recursive process (Algorithm 1) starts by generating the center branch in the Fig. 4, at each edge, it is marked the clause that is applied. The dashed line shows which clause was subsumed.
- The procedure continues considering the clause ϕ_3, and by generating the branch that is shown on the right of the tree. In this case, the clauses C_1, C_2 and C_6 were deleted from K because they are independent clauses with ϕ_3.
- The pre-processing finishes when all clauses are evaluated from ϕ and the trees' leaves represent the final clauses that will form S. For this example, we have that $(K \wedge S) = \{(*01****1), (*001*0*1), (*001*111), (*000*0*1), (*000*101), (*110***1), (*101*111), (*100*101), (*10010*1), (*1010111)\}$.

The time function for the algorithm that determines $(K \models \phi)$ will be denoted by $T_0(|\phi|, |K|)$. This process depends mainly on the runtime of the procedure $DFS(\phi, K, S)$ which is obtained from a recursive computation of $Gen(\varphi_i, C, n)$, with $\varphi_i \in \phi, C \in K$ and $n = |Dif(\varphi_i, C)|$.

The time complexity for the $DFS(\varphi_i, K, S)$ process is of order $O(|K| \cdot n \cdot f(|\varphi_i|, |K|))$, where $f(|\varphi_i|, |K|)$ is an integer function, that given a clause φ_i and a CF K, counts the number of clauses to be formed by $Gen(\varphi_i, C, n)$.

Analyzing the possible maximum number of clauses that can be generated through $Gen(\varphi_i, C, n)$. In some cases, $Gen(\varphi_i, C, n)$ generates the empty set (when $n = 0$, because $C \models \varphi_i$). However, in the worst case, the time complexity of calculating $Gen(\varphi_i, C, n)$ depends on the length of the sets: $Dif(\varphi_i, C_j) = S_{ij} = \{x_1, x_2, \ldots, x_p\} = Lit(C_j) - Lit(\varphi_i)$.

As it was noted previously, given $\varphi_i \in \phi$, it is relevant to sort the clauses $C_j \in K$ according to the cardinality of the sets $Dif(\varphi_i, C)$ from lowest to highest, and eliminating the clauses that are independent with φ_i. When there is no independent clauses with φ_i, the time complexity for calculating $DFS(\varphi_i, K, S)$ is bounded by the number of resulting clauses. In other words, $|DFS(\varphi_i, K, S)| \leq |S_{i1}| * |S_{i2}| * \ldots * |S_{is}| * Poly(n, m), s \leq m$. Where $Poly(n, m)$ summarizes a polynomial time due to the matching strings process and the sorting of the clauses in K.

Then, we infer an upper bound for the function $f(|\varphi_i|, |K|)$, given by

$$Max\{|S_{i1}| * |S_{i2}| * \ldots * |S_{is}| : \forall \varphi_i \in \phi\} \tag{1}$$

Furthermore, $Dif(\varphi_i, C)$ arranges logical values for a set of variables that do not change their values during the process $DFS(\varphi_i, K, S)$, and then $|S_{i1}| + |S_{i2}| + \ldots + |S_{is}| \leq n - |\varphi_i|$.

6   Conclusions

The belief revision allows modeling a very general aspect of human reasoning about how we store our knowledge by keeping the new information. One of the mechanisms we make of rational way is to apply inference, i.e., if the new information can be inferred from some prior knowledge then it is no longer necessary to save it.

It is proposed a method that works on the set of falsifying assignments of the involved formulas, in order to review: $K \models \phi$.

It is presented a method for belief revision using conjunctive normal forms. Since K and ϕ are CNF's, the belief revision process between K and ϕ (K infer ϕ) is reduced to make the revision between each $\phi_i \in \phi$, and each $C_i \in K$.

A logical algorithm is proposed and it is based on the depth first search in order to obtain a set S of clauses whose falsifying assignments cover the space $Fals(S) = Fals(\phi_i) - Fals(C_j)$, and in this way, we can be determine if $K \models \phi$.

In general we assume that the knowledge base K represented in FNC is satisfiable, that is, there is a set of models that satisfy K. When new information ϕ is added to carry out the belief revision process, in fact we are eliminating models. Thus, K and ϕ could become in an unsatisfiable knowledge base. The revision of the consistency of the dinamic knowledge bases in terms of falsifying patterns is considered as a future work.

References

1. Belov, A., Janota, M., Lynce, I., Marques-Silva, J.: Algorithms for computing minimal equivalent subformulas. Artif. Intell. **266**, 309–326 (2014)

2. Darwiche, A.: On tractable counting of theory models and its application to truth maintenance and belief revision. Appl. NonClassical Logics **11**, 11–34 (2001)
3. Herzig, A., Lang, J., Marquis, P.: Propositional update operators based on formula/literal dependence. ACM Trans. Comput. Logic **14**, 1–31 (2013)
4. Selman, B.: Tractable default reasoning. Ph.D. dissertation, Department of Computer Science University of Toronto (1990)
5. Alchourrón, C., Gärdenfors, P., Makinson, D.: On the logic of theory change: partialmeet contraction and revision functions. J. Symbolic Logic **50**, 510–530 (1985)
6. Pons, C., Rosenfeld, R., Smith, C.: Lógica para informática, Buenos Aires, Argentina: Universidad Nacional de La Plata, Ed. Universidad de La Plata (2017)
7. Jiang, D., Li, W., Lou, J., Lou, Y., Lia, Z.: A decomposition based algorithm for maximal contractions. J. Front. Comput. Sci. **7**, 801–811 (2013)
8. Cresto, E.: Revisón de creencias y racionalidad. Cuadernos del CIMBAGE **5**, 133–156 (2002)
9. Boella, G., Pigozzi, G., Van der Torre, L.: AGM contraction and revision of rules. J. Logic Lang. Inf. **25**, 273–297 (2016)
10. De Ita, G., Marcial, R., Bello, P., Contreras, M.: Belief revisions between conjunctive normal forms. J. Intell. Fuzzy Syst. **34**, 3155–3164 (2018)
11. Katsuno, H., Mendelzon, A.: On the difference between updating a knowledge base and revising it. In: KR 1991, Cambridge, MA, USA, pp. 387–394 (1991)
12. Delgrande, J., Jin, Y., Pelletier, F.J.: Compositional belief update. J. Artif. Intell. Res. **32**, 757–791 (2008)
13. Aiguier, M., Atif, J., Bloch, I., Hudelot, C.: Belief revision, minimal change and relaxation: a general framework based on satisfaction systems, and applications to description logics. Artif. Intell. **256**, 160–180 (2018)
14. Cadoli, M., Donini, F.M., Liberatore, P., Schaerf, M.: Preprocessing of intractable problems. Inf. Comput. **176**, 89–120 (2002)
15. Rúa, M.G., Sierra, A.M.: Algunas lógicas modales asociadas al razonamiento de agentes inteligentes. Ingeniería y Ciencia **4**, 23–45 (2008)
16. Korpusik, M., Lukaszewicz, W., Madalińska-Bugaj, E.: Consistency-based revision of structured belief bases. Fundamenta Informaticae **136**, 381–404 (2015)
17. Creignou, N., Ktari, R., Papini, O.: Belief update within propositional fragments. J. Artif. Intell. Res. **61**, 807–834 (2018)
18. Doubois, O.: Counting the number of solutions for instances of satisfiability. Theor. Comput. Sci. **81**, 49–64 (1991)
19. Liberatore, P.: The complexity of iterated belief revision. In: Afrati, F., Kolaitis, P. (eds.) ICDT 1997. LNCS, vol. 1186, pp. 276–290. Springer, Heidelberg (1997). https://doi.org/10.1007/3-540-62222-5_51
20. Liberatore, P.: Revision by history. J. Artif. Intell. Res. **52**, 287–329 (2015)
21. Peppasa, P., Willians, M.A., Choprac, S., Foo, N.: Relevance in belief revision. Artif. Intell. **229**, 126–138 (2015)
22. Pozos-Parra, P., Chávez-Bosquez, O., McAreavey, K.: A belief merging tool for consensus support. J. Intell. Fuzzy Syst. **34**, 3199–3210 (2018)
23. Booth, R., Hunter, A.: Trust as a precursor to belief revision. J. Artif. Intell. Res. **61**, 699–722 (2018)
24. Khardon, R., Roth, D.: Reasoning with models. Artif. Intell. **87**, 187–213 (1996)

Analytical Hierarchy Process Based Model for Safety Assessment of Coastal Touristic Locations

Alberto Daniel Dávila–Lamas[(✉)], José J. Carbajal–Hernández,
Luis P. Sánchez–Fernández, and César A. Hoil–Rosas

Centro de Investigación en Computación, Instituto Politécnico Nacional,
Juan de Dios Bátiz s/n, Nva. Industrial Vallejo, 07738 Ciudad de México,
Gustavo A. Madero, Mexico
addavlam@gmail.com, {jcarbajalh,lsanchez}@cic.ipn.mx,
cesarhoil_92@hotmail.com

Abstract. Touristic Mexican beaches are highly visited places where safety is one of the most important priorities. In this work, a computational model based on the Analytical Hierarchy Process is proposed to evaluate main coastal characteristics, providing a safety index score. Parameters such as: wind, tide, temperature and bathymetry are studied using an importance weighment procedure. Beaches located at La Paz, South Baja California, Mexico are measured, and assessed to show the proposed model performance, providing a good alternative to impulse tourism.

Keywords: Analytical Hierarchy Process · Signal processing · Tourism · Safety · Beach

1 Introduction

Tourism is one of the fastest growing industries worldwide, and coastal areas are the most important sources of income. In Mexico, 73% of the economic income associated with tourism comes from beach areas [1]. Despite the attractive beach conditions for tourism, natural events such as red tide or sea conditions, could avoid the development of touristic activities. At present, there are no metrics to define if the coastal conditions are adequate for the practice of tourism activities. Actions to define security in coastal tourist areas are based only on monitoring tide by color coding. It is necessary to create tools to identify undesirable situations and places unsuitable for tourism. Annually, a large number of accidents are reported in tourist coastal zones due to the lack of safety signs, and the lack of knowledge of tourists to interpret signs when they exist. In this sense, warning signs do not reflect the real safety conditions present in the zone.

Some studies have carried out evaluations of coastal areas from different perspectives. Leatherman in 1992 [2] presented a comparison of beaches, evaluating quantitatively 50 physical, biological and human parameters that influence beach quality using the Leopold approach [3], which was originally designed for the evaluation of rivers scenery. Another quantitative assessment is presented in [4], taking into

© Springer Nature Switzerland AG 2019
J. A. Carrasco-Ochoa et al. (Eds.): MCPR 2019, LNCS 11524, pp. 357–367, 2019.
https://doi.org/10.1007/978-3-030-21077-9_33

consideration 5 relevant beach parameters (safety, water quality, facilities, scenery and litter) in the region of Andalucia, Spain. In this work, one of the evaluated parameters is safety; however, this indicator is formed from subjective observations of the evaluator, such as safe environment beach and infrastructure features, considering the possibility of area access with emergency vehicles. Both of these works qualify the data obtained from subjective observations; therefore, the preferences and perspectives of the evaluator influence the results.

Coastal landscape assessment has been the object of study by some researchers. In Ergin [5], 26 parameters have been defined to evaluate coastal scenery through surveys of tourists and landscape perception experts in Turkey and UK. For each parameter, 5 range of values or attributes were established. All parameters are integrated to perform a general assessment using a Fuzzy Logic Approach (FLA), to overcome the subjectivity and uncertainty detected in other models. In another paper, Ergin [6] presents the results obtained by the methodology in a particular application case by comparing 34 coastal zones in the Western Black Sea region.

Due to the lack of quantitative evaluations of coastal security, the generation of an index is necessary to allow the identification of undesirable situations and places unsuitable for tourist activity. The purpose of this paper is to design a computational model to assess ideal zones in beaches, were tourists can perform their activities with the best possible safety. This model is based on geographical characteristics, natural events, and physical factors, such as tide and wind. The beach safety depends on several factors, but the ones just mentioned above are the most relevant in order to generate an evaluation. The Analytical Hierarchy Process (AHP) methodology is used to assign the relative importance of each parameter. A FLA is proposed to calculate the safety index, since it has proven to overcome uncertainty and subjectivity.

This paper considers La Paz Bay as a case study; this tourist destination is located on the east coast, south of Baja California peninsula, in Mexico. La Paz City is located on the south of the bay and is the capital of Southern Baja California State. Due to the presence of the city in the bay, there are a large number of sensors monitoring different physical, chemical and biological parameters constantly. Additionally, some researchers have characterized the Bay seabed [7]. Some of this data and infrastructure is taken to feed the evaluation model. Parameters selected for analysis were bathymetry, wind, tide, temperature and a biological index.

In Sect. 2 we define the coastal characteristics. In Sect. 3 we present the model building. In Sect. 4 we give results. In Section we describe the conclusions.

2   Coastal Characteristics

Commonly, touristic beaches should have some recommendations about safety for tourists. Different criteria have been defined to generate areas for touristic activities and are represented by a set of parameters, which is the study case of this work. According to this, the following sections explain the needed information about the main characteristic of a touristic coast.

2.1 Geographic Site

La Paz is a popular tourist destination with a hot, dry climate located in the coordinates 24.14222, −110.31083. Beaches of this destination are the main attraction, with turquoise waters ideal for swimming, sun-bathing, enjoyable scenery and the practice of aquatic sports. Facilities provide information about weather and ocean measurements, and closeness of different touristic places are ideal for this study purpose. Figure 1 shows the geographic characteristics of the sampling site.

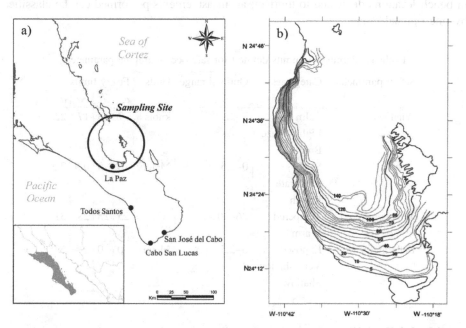

Fig. 1. (a) Sampling site monitored in La Paz Bay, located at Southern Baja California, Mexico. (b) Bathymetry measurements obtained from Del Monte in 2005 [8].

2.2 Factor Analysis

Usually, a problem depends on several factors, where involved parameters have different importance according to their behaviors and characteristics. This paper considers 3 principal factors to assign the importance of the parameters. The first factor is *measurement facility*; some parameters are difficult to quantify or require a previous processing. The next considered factor is the *dangerousness*; the risk associated to each parameter is not equal for all the parameters. The last factor is *infrastructure facilities*; data obtained from other sources could be obtained to feed the evaluation model. Factors are identified as follows:

- *F1*: Measurement facility
- *F2*: Dangerousness
- *F3*: Infrastructure facilities

The safety index proposed is functioned in 4 parameters, which were defined as the most relevant in this discipline according to the factors just mentioned. These parameters are: bathymetry, tide, temperature and wind speed. The first two parameters are associated with the risk of drowning [9–11], and the last are associated with the presence of red tide.

A classification for all the parameters is presented in Table 1. This classification is based on the international scales and information collected from other research works [12–14]. The categories defined in Table 1, include the different types of status present in beach locations dedicated to tourism; all measurements performed can be classified by one optimal range.

Table 1. Permissible limits defined for safe oceanographic parameters.

Safety parameters	Categories	Optimal range	Units	Fuzzy limits			
				a	b	c	d
Wind (s)	Calm	7–22	knots	7	13	17	22
	Light breeze						
	Breeze						
Tide (d)	Slight	0–2.5	Meters	0	0	0.5	2.5
	Moderate						
	Rough						
Temperature (t)	Tempered	26–30	°C	25	28	28	31
	Warm						
Bathymetry (b)	Exposed	0–2.5	Meters	0	0	2.5	6
	Very shallow						
	Shallow						

3   Model Building

3.1   Fuzzy Inputs

The purpose of the fuzzy assessment is to evaluate each parameter according to its own scale and optimal level, transforming the measured values into a [0–1] range. This normalizes all parameter ranges and scales [15]. To make this transformation, fuzzy expressions were created for each parameter, d refers to tide, b refers to bathymetry, s refers to wind and t refers to temperature; the expressions are defined as follows:

$$\mu(d) = max\left\{ min\left(1, \frac{2.5 - x}{2.5 - 0.5}\right), 0 \right\} \tag{1}$$

$$\mu(b) = max\left\{ min\left(1, \frac{5 - x}{5 - 2.5}\right), 0 \right\} \tag{2}$$

$$\mu(s) = max\left\{ min\left(\frac{x-7}{13-7}, 1, \frac{22-x}{22-17}\right), 0\right\} \tag{3}$$

$$\mu(t) = max\left\{ min\left(\frac{x-25}{28-25}, 1, \frac{31-x}{31-28}\right), 0\right\} \tag{4}$$

3.2 AHP Model

The safety evaluation on beaches can be defined according to the importance of each oceanographic involved parameter. For this purpose, an analysis of parameters with high impact in the safety assessment and the reasons why they are important are analyzed as proposed. This work uses the Analytic Hierarchy Process methodology, created by Saaty [16]. In the AHP, a relative importance level is assigned to each parameter according to Table 2.

Table 2. Importance scale interpretation according to Saaty [18].

Scale	1	2	3	4	5	6	7	8	9
Importance	Equal	Weak	Moderate	Moderate+	Strong	Strong+	Very	Very+	Extreme

The first step is to create a pairwise matrix $(A = a_{ij})$ where the importance priorities given by Saaty [15] can be assigned between parameters (w_a/w_b). This is a positive reciprocal $n \times n$ matrix and is constructed as follows:

$$A = \begin{array}{c} \\ P_1 \\ P_2 \\ \vdots \\ P_n \end{array} \begin{array}{cccc} P_1 & P_2 & \cdots & P_n \\ \begin{bmatrix} a_{11} & a_{12} & \cdots & a_{1n} \\ a_{21} & a_{22} & \cdots & a_{2n} \\ \vdots & \vdots & \ddots & \vdots \\ a_{n1} & a_{n2} & \cdots & a_{nn} \end{bmatrix} \end{array} = \begin{bmatrix} \frac{w_1}{w_1} & \frac{w_1}{w_2} & \cdots & \frac{w_1}{w_n} \\ \frac{w_2}{w_1} & \frac{w_2}{w_2} & \cdots & \frac{w_2}{w_n} \\ \vdots & \vdots & \ddots & \vdots \\ \frac{w_n}{w_1} & \frac{w_n}{w_2} & \cdots & \frac{w_n}{w_n} \end{bmatrix} \tag{5}$$

The eigenvector proposed by Perron in 1907 [17] must be computed to determine the priority weights that will be used for computing the Safety index (SI). According to this, the square matrix **B** must be computed as follows:

$$\mathbf{B} = \begin{bmatrix} a_{11} & a_{12} & \cdots & a_{1n} \\ a_{21} & a_{22} & \cdots & a_{2n} \\ \vdots & \vdots & \ddots & \vdots \\ a_{n1} & a_{n2} & \cdots & a_{nn} \end{bmatrix} \times \begin{bmatrix} a_{11} & a_{12} & \cdots & a_{1n} \\ a_{21} & a_{22} & \cdots & a_{2n} \\ \vdots & \vdots & \ddots & \vdots \\ a_{n1} & a_{n2} & \cdots & a_{nn} \end{bmatrix} \tag{6}$$

The sum of the rows is determined according to:

$$C_i = \sum_{j=1}^{n} B_{ij} \; \forall i = 1, 2, \ldots, n \tag{7}$$

The priority weights are obtained by normalizing the C_i vector according to:

$$W_i = \frac{C_i}{\sum_{j=1}^{n} C_j} \; \forall i = 1, 2, \ldots, n \tag{8}$$

An additional criteria step is to validate the matrix consistency as follows:

$$CR = \frac{\lambda_{max} - n}{(n - 1)RI} \tag{9}$$

where λ_{max} is the maximum eigenvalue of the pairwise matrix, n is the matrix size, CR is the Consistency Ratio and RI is the Random Consistency Index (Table 3) [18]. The calculation of the Consistency rate evaluates the confidence level inconsistencies found in the pairwise matrix building. A limit of $CR = 0.1$ was defined as the maximum acceptable inconsistency.

Table 3. Random consistency index.

Matrix size	1	2	3	4	5	6	7	8	9	10
RI	0	0	0.52	0.89	1.11	1.25	1.35	1.4	1.45	1.49

3.3 Safety Index

The Safety Index (SI) is a value in a [0–1] range and is defined by involving the complete parameter assessments. Importance weights define the negative impact of each parameter, generating a score concerning the good or bad safety in that place. The SI index can be described as follows:

$$SI = \sum_{i=1}^{n} \mu_i(k) W_i^k \tag{10}$$

where k refers to a parameter, W is the ith importance weight obtained in the AHP process and $\mu_i(k)$ is the fuzzy value obtained with the expressions defined in Sect. 3.1. By replacing each parameter in Eq. (10), then we have the following expression:

$$SI = \mu(t)W^t + \mu(d)W^d + \mu(b)W^b + \mu(s)W^s \tag{11}$$

where t refers to temperature, d refers to tide, b refers to bathymetry and s refers to wind.

If beach safety conditions are optimal, the index has a score of "1"; otherwise, when one or more parameters present non optimal values, the final score decreases, being "0" in the worst case.

4 Results and Discussions

4.1 Parameter Assessment

Based on expert criteria, comparisons between factors and parameters related to safety assessment were defined. Table 4 shows comparisons between factors, comparing them according to the importance scale and criteria defined for safety impact. Pairwise matrix uses the fractional values to compute the weights. Normalized columns can be used as a partial solution for weight assignment; however, the largest eigenvalue has been demonstrated to be the most accurate solution in the AHP. Tables 5, 6 and 7 have the respective pairwise matrices of each parameter, where comparisons were made taking into consideration the factor as decision criteria. Consistency ratios show values in acceptable levels.

Table 4. Factor comparison with a CR = 0.04501.

Factors	F1	F2	F3	Normalized	Eigenvector
F1	1	1/9	1/2	0.0709	0.0738
F2	9	1	8	0.7917	0.8044
F3	2	1/8	1	0.1374	0.1218
		Column sums		1	1

Table 5. Parameter comparative according to measurement Facility and with a *CR* = 0.09217.

Parameters	Tide	Temp	Wind	Depth	Normalized	Eigenvector
(*d*) Tide	1	1/8	1/3	3	0.1135	0.0897
(*t*) Temp	8	1	4	9	0.5599	0.6385
(*s*) Wind	3	1/4	1	7	0.2863	0.2295
(*b*) Bathymetry	1/3	1/9	1/7	1	0.0403	0.0423
			Column sums		1	1

Table 6. Parameter comparative considering Dangerousness and a $CR = 0.06174$.

Parameters	Tide	Temp	Wind	Depth	Normalized	Eigenvector
(d) Tide	1	9	7	1	0.4302	0.44
(t) Temp	1/9	1	1/3	1/9	0.0372	0.0403
(s) Wind	1/7	3	1	1/7	0.1024	0.0797
(b) Bathymetry	1	9	7	1	0.4302	0.44
			Column sums		1	1

Table 7. Parameter comparative considering Infrastructure facilities and a $CR = 0.09454$

Parameters	Tide	Temp	Wind	Depth	Normalized	Eigenvector
(d) Tide	1	5	3	1/5	0.2465	0.2027
(t) Temp	1/5	1	1/3	1/9	0.0441	0.0457
(s) Wind	1/3	3	1	1/7	0.1199	0.0942
(b) Bathymetry	5	9	7	1	0.5895	0.6574
			Column sums		1	1

The final weight priorities are obtained by combining all particular results according to the sum of the weight multiplication, having a global sum of the unity, which means that weights are balanced. Table 8 shows these results.

Table 8. Parameter comparative considering all factors and weights.

Parameter / Factors	d	t	s	b	Factor weights	d	t	s	b
F1	0.0897	0.6385	0.2295	0.0423	0.0738	0.007	0.047	0.017	0.003
F2	0.44	0.0403	0.0797	0.44	0.8044	0.354	0.032	0.064	0.354
F3	0.2027	0.0457	0.0942	0.6574	0.1218	0.025	0.006	0.011	0.08
Final score					1	0.386	0.085	0.092	0.437

4.2   Safety Index Assessment

The safety index (SI) calculation was made over a database of collected measurements at sampling site. This database includes values of temperature, wind speed, tide and bathymetry. It has 976 samples, taken every 15 min from the 1st to 11th of January 2016. Figure 2. shows the parameter behavior in the corresponding sampling period.

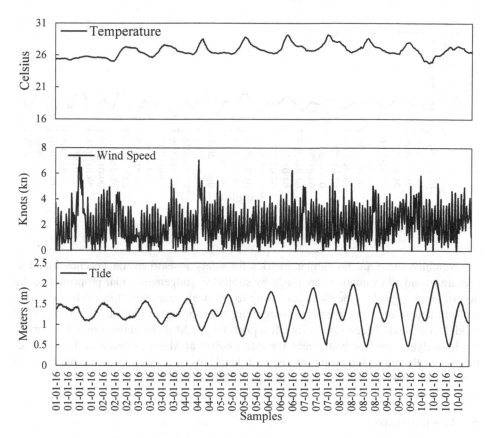

Fig. 2. Parameter signals used for safety assessment.

As can be seen in Fig. 2, wind conditions are out of the optimal ranges described in Table 1, so the probability of red tide presence increases, and this condition will affect the SI score. The temperature presented a highly variable behavior. The height of the waves increased over time, but never reaching values out of the optimal ranges. According to Fig. 1, the bathymetry area is estimated considering zones lower that 5 m depth, since deeper zones are not adequate for touristic practices. Parameter behaviors can be observed in Fig. 3, where the SI index assessment is performed.

Variations in temperature and wind speed can be observed; however, those changes, have not a significant influence in the safety index response. Tide variations largely affect the behavior of the index, due to the tide weight obtained in the AHP process is significantly higher than the rest of the parameters. The safety index variations were from 0.10 to 0.47 with a medium value of 0.28. This means that the safety conditions during the test dates, in the sampling site were bad.

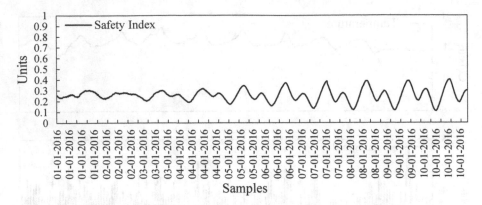

Fig. 3. Safety assessment using the SI index proposed at the sampling site.

Actually, there are no similar metrics for safety assessment on beaches found in literature, and all evaluations are made by subjective judgements. Our proposal had the aim of assessing safety locations according to physical parameters that can be measured and studied in an objective way, integrating oceanographic data in a computational model to evaluate beach safety. Result reports for the SI index show a new framework for identifying good or bad places for safe tourism at Mexican beaches. This characteristic is the most important strategy of local governments trying to obtain more tourists as a way to increase the economy of the region.

5 Conclusions

The safety index presented in this paper evaluates the beach safety conditions present at La Paz Bay, considering temperature, wind speed, bathymetry and tide. According to Literature, similar models have been developed in order to evaluate visual characteristics; however, our proposal has been developed in order to provide information about excellent or bad places for touristic activities on beaches. This tool is a novelty approach for assessing safety in touristic coastal locations; helping people to avoid risk areas, preventing accidents and increasing safety in touristic beaches. Although this research studied a Mexican place, it can be used for assessing another beaches by only replacing input data with those of the interest place. As a future work, more parameters have been proposed to be studied and analyzed such as: harmful wildlife, solar radiation or ocean aspects, integrating other techniques and computational models for better analysis to improve touristic care.

References

1. Banco de México: Extracto del Reporte sobre las Economías Regionales Enero – Marzo, pp. 10–13 (2018). http://www.banxico.org.mx/
2. Leatherman, S.P.: Beach rating: a methodological approach. J. Coast. Res. 253–258 (1997)

3. Leopold, L.B.: Quantitative Comparison of Some Aesthetic Factors Among Rivers, vol. 620. US Geological Survey (1969)
4. Micallef, A., Williams, A.T., Gallego Fernandez, J.B.: Bathing area quality and landscape evaluation on the Mediterranean coast of Andalucia, Spain. J. Coast. Res. 87–95 (2011)
5. Ergin, A., Karaesmen, E., Micallef, A., Williams, A.T.: A new methodology for evaluating coastal scenery: fuzzy logic systems. Area **36**(4), 367–386 (2004)
6. Ergin, A., Özölçer, İ.H., Şahin, F.: Evaluating coastal scenery using fuzzy logic: application at selected sites in Western Black Sea coastal region of Turkey. Ocean Eng. **37**(7), 583–591 (2010)
7. Urcádiz-Cázares, F.J., Cruz-Escalona, V.H., Nava-Sánchez, E.H., Ortega-Rubio, A.: Clasificación de unidades del fondo marino a partir de la distribución espacial de los sedimentos superficiales de la Bahía de La Paz, Golfo de California. Hidrobiológica **27**(3), 399–409 (2017)
8. Del Monte-Luna, P., Arreguín-Sánchez, F., Godínez-Orta, L., López-Ferreira, C.A.: Batimetría actualizada de la Bahía de La Paz, Baja California Sur, México. CICIMAR Oceánides **20**(1–2), 75–77 (2005)
9. Castelle, B., Scott, T., Brander, R.W., McCarroll, R.J.: Rip current types, circulation and hazard. Earth Sci. Rev. **163**, 1–21 (2016)
10. Drozdzewski, D., et al.: Surveying rip current survivors: preliminary insights into the experiences of being caught in rip currents. Nat. Hazards Earth Syst. Sci. **12**(4), 1201–1211 (2012)
11. Drozdzewski, D., Roberts, A., Dominey-Howes, D., Brander, R.: The experiences of weak and non-swimmers caught in rip currents at Australian beaches. Aust. Geogr. **46**(1), 15–32 (2015)
12. Alonso Rodríguez, R.: Hidrología y condiciones ambientales que determinan la proliferación de dinoflagelados causantes de marea roja en la Bahía de Mazatlán, Sin., México (2004)
13. Rodríguez, L.: Revisión del fenómeno de Marea Roja en Chile. Rev. Biol. Mar. **21**, 173–197 (1985)
14. Kim, D.I., et al.: Effects of temperature, salinity and irradiance on the growth of the harmful red tide dinoflagellate Cochlodinium polykrikoides Margalef (Dinophyceae). J. Plankton Res. **26**(1), 61–66 (2004)
15. Gutiérrez, J.D., Riss, W., Ospina, R.: Lógica Difusa como herramienta para la bioindicación de la calidad del agua con macroinvertebrados acuáticos en la sabana de Bogotá - Colombia/Application of fuzzy logic as bioindication tool for the water quality with aquatic macroinvertebrates in the Sabana de Bogotá-Colombia. Caldasia 161–172 (2004)
16. Saaty, T.L.: Decision making with the analytic hierarchy process. Int. J. Serv. Sci. **1**(1), 83–98 (2008)
17. Perron, O.: Grundlagen f'ur eine Theorie des Jacobischen Kettenbruchalgorithmus. Math. Ann. **64**, 11–76 (1907)
18. Saaty, T.L.: Decision making—the analytic hierarchy and network processes (AHP/ANP). J. Syst. Sci. Syst. Eng. **13**(1), 1–35 (2004)

Signal Processing and Analysis

Modeling of a Simplified 2D Cardiac Valve by Means of System Identification

Carlos Duran-Hernandez[✉][iD], Rogelio Perez-Santiago[iD], Gibran Etcheverry[iD], and Rene Ledesma-Alonso[iD]

Universidad de las Americas Puebla, 72810 Puebla, Mexico
{jose.duranhz,rogelio.perez,gibran.etcheverry,rene.ledesma}@udlap.mx

Abstract. The function of a heart valve is to maintain the correct circulation of blood from the heart to the entire Cardiovascular System (CVS). The CVS has become a main target in the health science and engineering, due to the importance of the detection anomalies or pathologies. Some techniques that deal with these problems, like Magnetic Resonance Imaging (MRI), Ultrasound and Electrocardiography (ECG) among them, require important investments to acquire measurement instruments. Numerical simulations have arisen as an alternative, by means of Fluid-Structure Interaction (FSI) analysis. The combination of computational methods, such as Finite Element Method (FEM) and Incompressible Computational Fluid Dynamics (ICFD), have allowed the development of FSI software, which leads to design versatility and economic advantages. However, computational time is high even for simplified designs. Lumped models appear as another solution. They consist in simplified zero-dimensional models that allow to mimic the Cardiovascular System (CVS) with low computational cost and good approximations. Nevertheless, they require a parameter identification and the calculation process for each scenario, which becomes increasingly complicated when the number of parameters is high. Therefore, an alternative approach is proposed in the present manuscript. Taking the volumetric flow rate and the Pressure Difference (PD) as the input and output parameters, respectively, of the flow across a heart valve of simple geometry, a System Identification (SI) is performed. The proposed methodology requires low computational cost and provides a good approximation. Results obtained guarantee a 99.76% of goodness of fit.

Keywords: Cardiac valves · Cardiovascular System · Fluid-Structure Interaction · ARMAX · System identification

1 Introduction

Within the CVS, the purpose of a heart valve is to maintain the correct circulation of blood, from the heart to the entire body. Pathologies presented in one or more of the four heart valves can lead to a critical malfunctions of the heart, such as stenotic or back-flow complications. Many of these pathologies arise as

© Springer Nature Switzerland AG 2019
J. A. Carrasco-Ochoa et al. (Eds.): MCPR 2019, LNCS 11524, pp. 371–380, 2019.
https://doi.org/10.1007/978-3-030-21077-9_34

consequences of an increment of the magnitude of the shear stresses acting on the valves, due to the blood flow.

For these reasons, many attempts to create artificial valves have been tried, with special interest on Biological Heart Valves (BHV) and Mechanical Heart Valves (MHV). MHV are usually fabricated with inorganic and stiff materials, whereas BHV are obtained directly from animals or fabricated with organic and flexible tissues. According to [25], BHV has outstanding mechanic and hemodynamic properties due to the bio-materials used for their construction. Contrary to BHV, MHV designs minimize back-flow and last longer lifespans, but they produce deficient physiological flow conditions such as high stress levels that lead to the destruction of red blood cells [14,21].

Considering that the design of MHVs is based on mathematical modeling, they can be tested by using numerical simulations. The methodology employed to simulate the performance of valves is known as computational FSI, and consists of a combination of ICFD to calculate the fluid motion and a force balance to compute the leaflets rotation. This alternative allows us to modify and create new geometries by using a Computer-Aided Design (CAD) software. Studies on the flow across MHVs have been carried out in [2,9,10,12]. Nevertheless, a numerical simulation of flexible leaflet materials is completely different, since their motion depends strongly on the interaction with the fluid. In this case, the dynamics of the mechanical valve can be simulated using time-dependent FEM combined with ICFD. Many works using this strategy are found in literature using different techniques [1,8], for instance an Arbitraty Lagrange-Eulerian (ALE) [6] method, the Fictitious Domain Method (FDM) and the Boundary Method (IBM) in [4,5,21] and [19,22], respectively.

Another approach to represent the CVS is by using the zero-dimensional lumped models. They are based on simple ordinary differential equations and they consider an average value of the CVS local variables (pressure and velocity) within each of their components (organs and blood vessels). Different variations, such as the Windkessel Model (WM) allows to mimic the systemic arterial tree [3,7,17,18,20,23,24]. However, their main disadvantage in these approaches is the need to identify and calculate all the parameters to adjust to a particular physiological condition.

Considering all previous methods, the main contribution of this work relays on the implementation of an alternative method using SI to estimate the behavior of a cardiac valve under certain blood flow rate inside of a channel. This method allows to replicate the output, pressure difference PD measured across the valve, with a lower computational cost than the one required by FSI, and with no requirement of parameters identification and calculations, as required by the lumped models such as WM.

In Sect. 2, a new approach to study them using AutoRegressive (AR) system identification is proposed. A comparison between the results obtained with FSI and AR is shown in Sect. 3. Finally, future work and conclusions of this paper are listed in Sect. 4.

2   Theoretical Background and Methodology

2.1   Computational FSI

As mentioned in the previous section, computational FSI is one of the main alternatives to understand how the heart valves behave under certain fluid conditions. As a first step, a simplified 2D cardiac valve has been studied by means of a numerical simulation, which corresponds to the geometry and flow conditions presented in a previous experimental work [11]. Parameters used for the experiment can be described as (a) Fluid domain $(\Omega_f) \in \{U_f, V, f, \rho_f, \mu\}$, where the elements are inlet velocity, stroke volume, frequency, fluid density and dynamic viscosity, respectively, and (b) Solid domain $(\Omega_s) \in \{d, l, E, \rho_s, PR\}$, where the elements are leaflet thickness, length, elastic modulus, material density and Poisson ratio, respectively.

The simulation has been performed with the following boundary conditions for the fluid domain (see Fig. 1): **Inlet Wall** representing the entrance for the fluid, **Outlet Wall** where the fluid goes away and the pressure reaches zero, **Non-Slip Condition Wall** representing that the fluid has zero velocity relative to the boundary. The valve is also configured as a Non-Slip Condition Object.

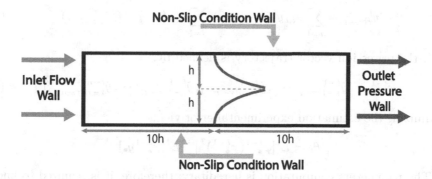

Fig. 1. Boundary conditions used for a channel with a simplified cardiac valve design inside. The channel is in terms of semi-height h, where $h = 15\,\text{mm}$, width $w = 50\,\text{mm}$.

Inlet velocity curve is formed by the two stages during the cardiac cycle. Systole t_s is the positive velocity pushing forward the volume V during $0.35Tc$ and diastolic part t_d is a momentary negative pulse that moves back the fluid and then goes to zero velocity at the end of cardiac cycle. Magnitude of the negative pulse is controlled by a scale factor $\frac{\alpha}{\gamma}$, where $\alpha = \frac{ts}{td}$ and γ is a scalar positive value. The velocity used for the experiment is obtained by initially considering the following volume formula:

$$V = A \int_0^{Tc} U \cdot g(t)dt \tag{1}$$

where $g(t) = 1$ during t_d (represents a unitary pulse) and $g(t) = -\alpha$ during t_s (see Fig. 2a), A is the cross-sectional area $A = hw$. By solving the integral divided into the two stages, we obtain the following:

$$U_s = \frac{V}{At_s} \qquad\qquad U_d = \frac{V}{A\alpha t_d} \qquad (2)$$

2.2   System Identification

The hereditary identification principle uses the same idea by taking the experimental *expectation* instead of the mathematical one [16]. In this case, the distance among estimated trajectories is minimized. Hence,

$$E^t[x_\bullet] = \frac{1}{t}\sum_{\tau=1}^{t} x_\tau \qquad (3)$$

is the trajectory x_τ experimental expectation over $[1,t]$ and $x_\bullet = \{x_\tau, \tau = 1, ..., t\}$. Considering the optimal estimator trajectory $\hat{y}_\tau^t$ at instant t for data over $[1,t]$ and the past estimator values:

$$\hat{y}_{\tau|\tau-1}^t = \sum_{i=1}^{n} a_{i,t}\hat{y}_{\tau-i|\tau-i-1}^{t-i} + \sum_{i=1}^{n} k_{i,t}(y_{t-i} - \hat{y}_{t-i|t-i-1}^{t-i}) \qquad (4)$$

If the regression vector trajectory is defined by:

$$\varphi_\tau^{t-1} = [\hat{y}_{\tau-1|\tau-2}^{t-1}, \cdots, \hat{y}_{\tau-n|\tau-n-1}^{t-n}, \tilde{y}_{\tau-1|\tau-2}^{t-1}, \cdots, \tilde{y}_{\tau-n|\tau-n-1}^{t-n}] \qquad (5)$$

minimizing the estimation experimental error yields:

$$\theta_t = E^t[\varphi_\bullet^{t-1}(\varphi_\bullet^{t-1})^T]^{-1} E^t[\varphi_\bullet^{t-1} y_\bullet] \qquad (6)$$

The parameters computation is hereditary; therefore, it is required to know the experimental autocorrelations of φ_τ^{t-1}, plus φ_τ^{t-1} and y_τ inter-correlations. Hence, to compute the system parameters at instant t, it is necessary to keep in memory all the past trajectories $\hat{y}_{\tau|\tau-1}^{t-1}, \cdots, \hat{y}_{\tau|\tau-1}^{t-n}$.

2.3   ARMAX Model

The hereditary algorithm can be extended when a system exogenous measured input is available [15]. It is then necessary to consider the following estimator model:

$$\hat{y}_{\tau|\tau-1}^t = \sum_{i=1}^{n} a_{i,t}\hat{y}_{\tau-i|\tau-i-1}^{t-i} + \sum_{i=1}^{n} k_{i,t}(y_{t-i} - \hat{y}_{t-i|t-i-1}^{t-i})$$
$$+ \sum_{i=0}^{n} b_{i,t} u_{t-i} \qquad (7)$$

If we define two vectors x_τ, y_τ external product such as:

$$\langle x_\bullet | y_\bullet \rangle^t = \frac{1}{t} \sum_{\tau=1}^{t} x_\tau^T y_\tau \tag{8}$$

The optimal estimator can be seen as the output trajectory projection over the following trajectories:

$$\hat{y}_\tau^t = P_\tau^t(y_\bullet | \hat{y}_{\bullet-1|\bullet-2}^{t-1}, \tilde{y}_{\bullet-1|\bullet-2}^{t-1}, u_\bullet, \cdots, \hat{y}_{\bullet-n|\bullet-n-1}^{t-n}, u_{\bullet-n+1}) \tag{9}$$

It is important to note that the criterion minimization task is quadratic; as a result, it is not necessary to derivate it. The nonlinear parameters dependence is solved by the hereditary algorithm linear augmenting memory.

2.4 Hereditary Identification Algorithm

1. Initialization. As data before $t = 1$ is unknown, the projection over it is zero (division by a covariance à priori infinite). It is then possible to think of it as zero:

$$\hat{y}_{\tau|\tau-1}^{1-i}, \quad \forall \tau < 1, \forall i = 1, \cdots, n \tag{10}$$

2. At instant $t - 1$ we have data from the already optimized trajectories $\hat{y}_{\tau|\tau-1}^{t-i}, \forall \tau = 1, \cdots, t-1, \forall i = 1, \cdots, n$

3. At instant t, new data y_t, u_t are available in order to update the experimental correlation matrix and the inter-correlation vector, both defined in Eq. (6), by hereditary computation:

$$E^t[\varphi_\bullet^{t-1}(\varphi_\bullet^{t-1})^T] = \frac{1}{t} \sum_{\tau=1}^{t} \varphi_\bullet^{t-1}(\varphi_\bullet^{t-1})^T$$

$$E^t[y_\bullet \varphi_\bullet^{t-1}] = \frac{1}{t} \sum_{\tau=1}^{t} y_\bullet \varphi_\bullet^{t-1} \tag{11}$$

4. We obtain the new system parameters at instant t by inverting:

$$\theta_t \hat{=} E^t[\varphi_\bullet^{t-1}(\varphi_\bullet^{t-1})^T]^{-1} \times E^t[y_\bullet \varphi_\bullet^{t-1}] \tag{12}$$

5. Hereditary part. With the obtained parameters, it is then possible to compute the new estimator trajectories $\hat{y}_{\tau|\tau-1}^{t-1}$ based on the trajectory $\hat{y}_\tau^{t-i}$ computed at the preceding stage by employing the model $\forall \tau = 1, \cdots, t$:lh

$$\hat{y}_{\tau|\tau-1}^t = \sum_{i=1}^{n} a_{i,t} \hat{y}_{\tau-i|\tau-i-1}^{t-i} + \sum_{i=1}^{n} k_{i,t}(y_{t-i} - \hat{y}_{t-i|t-i-1}^{t-i}) + \sum_{i=0}^{n} b_{i,t} u_{t-i} \tag{13}$$

6. Return to step 2.

3   Results

Parameters for this simulation are the following. $(\Omega_f) = \{0.09641\,\mathrm{m/s},\ 3.8$ $x10^{-5}\mathrm{m}^3,\ 0.666\ \mathrm{Hz},\ 1000\,\mathrm{kg/m}^3,\ 0.001\ \mathrm{Pa\cdot s}\}$ and $(\Omega_s) = \{0.0004\ \mathrm{m},\ 0.26\ \mathrm{m},$ $2.15\ x10^6\ \mathrm{Pa},\ 1070\ \mathrm{kg/m}^3,\ 0.47\}$. The cardiac cycle for this test is $Tc{=}1.5015$ *seconds* and by substituting Eq. (2) we can find that $|U_s| \approx |U_d| = 0.09641\ \mathrm{m/s}$. The curve is designed using hyperbolic tangents trying to fit the respective systole and diastole duration (see Fig. 2a). The magnitude of this curve is unitary and multiplied by U_s and $\frac{U_d\alpha}{\gamma}$, depending on the stage.

FSI results are compared with experiments in [11] by measuring two parameters. Opening Area (OA), indicates how much the valves opened during systole stage (see Fig. 2b). Pressure difference is also measured into two locations of the channel, $x = [-5h, 5h]$ and $y = 0$ (before and after the valves).

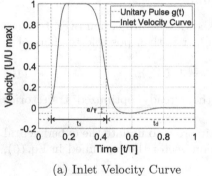

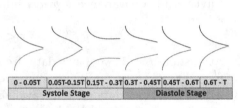

(a) Inlet Velocity Curve

(b) Steps followed by the valve during FSI simulation.

Fig. 2. (a) The curve describes two stages of the cardiac cycle. *ts* and *td* represents systole and diastole time respectively. α/γ represents the scaling factor for the negative pulse. (b) Opening and closure steps of a heart valve during cardiac cycle.

Considering that our simplified valve only moves along the $x - y$ plane, the fluid only interacts into two directions and not along the width as in the experiment. This could lead to some variations as the ones seen in magnitude for the OA observed in Fig. 3a or the falling part during diastole in the pressure difference (blue curve) of Fig. 3b. Another consideration to consider is that the experiment results are taken from a Particle Image Velocimetry (PIV) system during certain time-steps and the number of samples of the output signal is very limited compared to the ones obtained in simulations. Despite these considerations, results seen are qualitative correlated to the experimental 3D set-up.

In order to implement the SI method, it is necessary to conduct more simulations to have a test/validation process. Hence, a set of simulations are conducted by changing the frequency of the fluid $f = [0.1, 0.2, 0.3, ..., 0.666, ..., 0.8, 0.9, 1]Hz$ (these f change the velocity U_f as well) and leaving all the remaining parameters as they were.

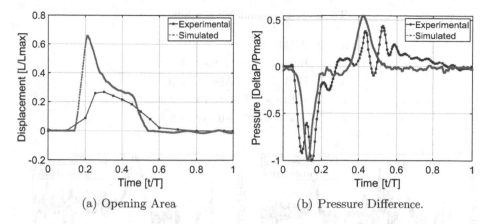

(a) Opening Area   (b) Pressure Difference.

Fig. 3. (a) As it can be seen in Figure 2b the maximum opening area occurs between $0.15Tc - 0.3Tc$ which approximately represents half of the systole. (b) PD observed in both curves during the first stage is almost identical. The falling part seen during diastole in the simulation curve is cleaner due to lack of external uncontrollable disturbances that were present in experimental test. Experimental data is retrieved from [11]. (Color figure online)

3.1 Identification Results

The figure of merit considered in this work, called the *multiple correlation coefficient*, assesses the algorithm quality by indicating the percentage of y_τ that has been well explained by $\hat{y}_\tau^t$ [13]:

$$R = \left(1 - \frac{\sum\limits_{\tau=1}^{t}(y_\tau - \hat{y}_\tau^t)^2}{\sum\limits_{\tau=1}^{t} y_\tau^2}\right) \times 100 \tag{14}$$

The 11 set of samples obtained from the set of simulations were concatenated in order to use 45% of them for training the model and 55% to validate it afterwards.

3.2 Validation

The identified ARMAX transfer function (see Eq. (15)) used for validation deals with two components, one for the input plus another for tracking the error or innovations within the process and its respective polynomials are given in Table 1.

$$ARMAX(s) = \frac{B(s)}{1 - [A(s) - K(s)]} + \frac{K(s)}{1 - [A(s) - K(s)]} \tag{15}$$

The identification process employed a dimension $n = 2$, given the CVS behavior did not require further exploration (Fig. 4).

Table 1. Polynomials for validation

n = 2	ARMAX		
	Input	Output	Innov.
	B(s)	A(s)	K(s)
s^{-1}	-2.13×10^6	1.876	2.092
s^{-2}	2.13×10^6	-0.889	-0.849

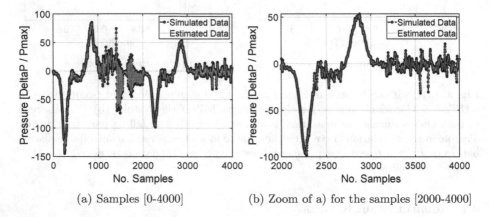

(a) Samples [0-4000]   (b) Zoom of a) for the samples [2000-4000]

Fig. 4. (a) Difference of pressure observed for the cardiac valve during the first two sets of simulation. (b) Estimation of the output signal for the second set of simulations.

4   Conclusions

SI has proved to be a suitable alternative to estimate how a valve is going to behave under certain conditions. By using an inlet flow rate curve as the only input, the method can be trained to obtain a good approximation on the pressure difference, the only output, without any complications. It is important to remark that this method only works if any of the parameters inside (Ω_f) changes; hence, by changing only the frequency f ($|U_f|$ is directly affected), the proposed method can obtain results with a 99.76% of goodness of fit with the FSI simulations, between a set of frequencies established for the same elasticity modulus. In order to solve this limitation, future work includes the implementation of a method that considers changes not only in the fluid but in the solid as well. This will guarantee to achieve estimations; for example, for different elasticity modulus or densities and even changes in physical properties such as density or length.

References

1. Baccani, B., Domenichini, F., Pedrizzetti, G.: Model and influence of mitral valve opening during the left ventricular filling. J. Biomech. **36**(3), 355–361 (2003)

2. Bluestein, D., Li, Y., Krukenkamp, I.: Free emboli formation in the wake of bi-leaflet mechanical heart valves and the effects of implantation techniques. J. biomech. **35**(12), 1533–1540 (2002)
3. Catanho, M., Sinha, M., Vijayan, V.: Model of aortic blood flow using the windkessel effect. University of California of San Diago, San Diago (2012)
4. De Hart, J., Peters, G., Schreurs, P., Baaijens, F.: A three-dimensional computational analysis of fluid-structure interaction in the aortic valve. J. Biomech. **36**(1), 103–112 (2003)
5. De Hart, J., Peters, G.W., Schreurs, P.J., Baaijens, F.P.: A two-dimensional fluid-structure interaction model of the aortic value. J. Biomech. **33**(9), 1079–1088 (2000)
6. Horsten, J.B.A.M.: On the analysis of moving heart valves: a numerical fluid-structure interaction model. Ph.D. thesis, Technische Universiteit Eindhoven (1990)
7. Huang, H., Shu, Z., Song, B., Ji, L., Zhu, N.: Modeling left ventricular dynamics using a switched system approach based on a modified atrioventricular piston unit. Med. Eng. Phys. **63**, 42–49 (2019)
8. Khalili, F., Gamage, P.T., Mansy, H.: Prediction of turbulent shear stresses through dysfunctional bileaflet mechanical heart valves using computational fluid dynamics. arXiv preprint arXiv:1803.03361 (2018)
9. King, M., Corden, J., David, T., Fisher, J.: A three-dimensional, time-dependent analysis of flow through a bileaflet mechanical heart valve: comparison of experimental and numerical results. J. Biomech. **29**(5), 609–618 (1996)
10. Krafczyk, M., Cerrolaza, M., Schulz, M., Rank, E.: Analysis of 3D transient blood flow passing through an artificial aortic valve by lattice-boltzmann methods. J. Biomech. **31**(5), 453–462 (1998)
11. Ledesma-Alonso, R., Guzmán, J., Zenit, R.: Experimental study of a model valve with flexible leaflets in a pulsatile flow. J. Fluid Mech. **739**, 338–362 (2014)
12. Lemmon, J.D., Yoganathan, A.P.: Three-dimensional computational model of left heart diastolic function with fluid-structure interaction. J. Biomech. Eng. **122**(2), 109–117 (2000)
13. Ljung, L.: System Identification: Theory for the User. Prentice-Hall, Upper Saddle River (1987)
14. López-Zazueta, A., Ledesma-Alonso, R., Guzman, J., Zenit, R.: Study of the velocity and strain fields in the flow through prosthetic heart valves. J. Biomech. Eng. **133**(12), 121003 (2011)
15. Monin, A.: Armax identification via hereditary algorithm. IEEE Trans. Autom. Control **49**(2), 233–238 (2004)
16. Monin, A., Salut, G.: Arma lattice identification: a new hereditary algorithm. IEEE Trans. Signal Process. **44**(2), 360–370 (1996)
17. Pant, S., Corsini, C., Baker, C., Hsia, T.Y., Pennati, G., Vignon-Clementel, I.E., of Congenital Hearts Alliance (MOCHA) Investigators, M., et al.: Data assimilation and modelling of patient-specific single-ventricle physiology with and without valve regurgitation. J. Biomech. **49**(11), 2162–2173 (2016)
18. Peña Pérez, N.: Windkessel modeling of the human arterial system. B.S. thesis, Universidad Carlos III de Madrid (2016)
19. Peskin, C.S.: Flow patterns around heart valves: a numerical method. J. Comput. Phys. **10**(2), 252–271 (1972)
20. Pironet, A., Dauby, P.C., Chase, J.G., Docherty, P.D., Revie, J.A., Desaive, T.: Structural identifiability analysis of a cardiovascular system model. Med. Eng. Phys. **38**(5), 433–441 (2016)

21. Stijnen, J., De Hart, J., Bovendeerd, P., Van de Vosse, F.: Evaluation of a fictitious domain method for predicting dynamic response of mechanical heart valves. J. Fluids Struct. **19**(6), 835–850 (2004)
22. Wang, Z., Yuan, Q., Shen, B., Tang, D., Zhang, X.: Mathmatic abstraction for fluid-structure interaction analysis of bioprosthetic heart valves with immersed boundary method. DEStech Trans. Eng. Technol. Res. (mcemic) (2016). ISBN: 978-1-60595-352-6
23. Westerhof, N., Lankhaar, J.W., Westerhof, B.E.: The arterial windkessel. Med. Biol. Eng. Comput. **47**(2), 131–141 (2009)
24. Xu, P., et al.: Assessment of boundary conditions for CFD simulation in human carotid artery. Biomech. Model. Mechanobiol. **17**(6), 1581–1597 (2018)
25. Yoganathan, A.P., He, Z., Casey Jones, S.: Fluid mechanics of heart valves. Annu. Rev. Biomed. Eng. **6**, 331–362 (2004)

Sound Source Localization Using Beamforming and Its Representation in a Mixed Reality Embedded Device

Aldo Valencia-Palma$^{(\boxtimes)}$ and Diana-Margarita Córdova-Esparza$^{(\boxtimes)}$

Facultad de Informática, UAQ, Universidad Autónoma de Querétaro,
Av. de las Ciencias S/N, Campus Juriquilla, 76230 Querétaro, Mexico
aldo.valencia.palma@gmail.com, diana_mce@hotmail.com

Abstract. Acoustic localization is a technique that allows measuring the intensity and direction of a sound source. A popular technique for its calculation is the beamforming algorithm "Sum-and-Delay" which generates an approximate angle of its location while reducing noise in the signal. Combining this technique with advances in mixed reality environments it is possible to develop essential applications both in the industry and beyond. However, these systems can be too large and expensive. In this work, a method was designed to approximate the sound direction of arrival using a beamforming technique to represent it in mixed reality environment using an embedded device, achieving to approximate it with an average error of 2.5% in distances up to 3 m long. Among its main advantages is that it is a portable and low-cost system in which applications of great utility can be developed, such as mixed reality conversation assistants capable of generating subtitles in real-time to assist people with deafness in a classrooms that do not have a translator, or to incorporate a translation service to understand speakers in different languages.

Keywords: Sound source localization · Direction of arrival ·
Mixed reality · Beamforming · Embedded hardware

1 Introduction

The process of locating the source of acoustic waves by recording the propagating acoustic signals through various sensors and properly analyzing them is known as the acoustic source localization technique [1]. The components of a sound source that can be estimated are two: the angle of arrival and the distance of the source. Obtaining these parameters can be crucial for applications that require such estimates in subsequent processing stages, such as sound source separation [2], audio source classification [3] and automatic voice recognition [14].

With the rapid advances in technology, comes the ability to improve how we acquire, interact and display information within the world that surrounds us. We can blend knowledge from our senses and mobile devices, and in this way

© Springer Nature Switzerland AG 2019
J. A. Carrasco-Ochoa et al. (Eds.): MCPR 2019, LNCS 11524, pp. 381–388, 2019.
https://doi.org/10.1007/978-3-030-21077-9_35

create virtual environments [4]. One of these environments is the mixed reality, where the user can see useful information anchored to real points in the space that coexist and interact in real time, making it possible to treat them as real [5].

Several applications have taken advantage of the of sound source localization mainly in video conferencing systems [6], actuators control in robotics [7] and security systems [8]. In regards to the industry, the representation of sound in mixed reality is applied in acoustic cameras for prototype development and fault detection and diagnosis [9]. The disadvantage is that this type of equipment is usually specialized and it may be large and expensive for the average consumer electronics users.

Out of the industrial field prototypes have been developed that make use of acoustic localization to assist people with deafness, since conventional cochlear implants only amplify the signal but do not help to locate the source of the sound source [10, 11].

In recent years, an augmented reality system has been developed, consisting of a matrix of microphones and a head-mounted display that alerts the user if a person is talking and points to the direction of the sound, and in this way, the user can read the lips of the emitter [11]. The biggest problem with the prototype was that the direction of the sound shown to the user was relative to the location of the microphone array, which was fixed on the table, and not to the movement of the screen. Therefore, the information was not practical for the user since it was not easy to interpret.

The proposal of this work consists in locating acoustic events indoors, to visualize the presence and direction of sound in real-time through the mixed reality in an embedded device. In this way, create a base system for the development of applications in embedded devices that can assist users in conversations in mixed reality by including voice-to-text processing services and translation services. A possible application of this system is a mixed-reality conversation assistant for deaf people in which a display points at a speaker's direction and after processing the signal the system generates and displays subtitles in real-time. In this way, the user could be assisted in classrooms that do not have a sign language translator.

2   Description of Beamforming Technique

In the location of sound sources, the beamforming technique is popular for its versatility since it functions as a type of spatiotemporal filter. That is, it manipulates the signals in the time domain. This is allowing to extract a signal at a specific address in an environment subject to interference. The algorithm "Sum-and-Delay" [13], within the beamforming category, requires an array of sensors for determining the angle of arrival of a signal and then synchronizing all channels to enhance the signal coming from a certain angle. The result is that signals from a particular direction experience a constructive superposition, while others experience destructive interference. Usually, this algorithm is used to filter stationary, non-coherent noise signals so it can be applied in low ambient noise environments (see Fig. 1).

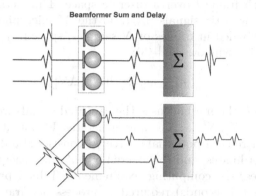

Fig. 1. The signal of interest is amplified by pointing the beam to the desired signal.

The calculation of the coefficients in a circular uniform array in the frequency domain for a microphone is expressed as (1):

$$W_n(\omega) = e^{-i\frac{\omega}{c}\frac{d}{2}\cos(\varphi - \phi n)} \tag{1}$$

and for the whole array (2):

$$W(\omega) = \frac{1}{N}\sum_{n=1}^{N} e^{-i\frac{\omega}{c}\frac{d}{2}\cos(\varphi - \phi n)} \tag{2}$$

Where ω is the angular frequency, N is the number of microphones, c is the speed of sound d is the diameter of the array, ϕn is the angle of the microphone index n and φ is the angle at which it must be addressed to process the desired signal.

Another powerful feature of the beamforming technique is the ability to electronically steer the beam without physically manipulating the array of microphones. The calculation can be performed dynamically when it detects new sound sources and continuously generates values of an angle to the sound source [12].

There exist a number of techniques to estimate the direction of arrival of signals of interest which are used to steer the beamformer. One of these methods is the Steered Response Power with Phase Transform for Hierarchical Search with Directivity model and Automatic calibration (SRP-PHAT-HSDA) [15].

The method scans the 3D space over a coarse resolution grid and then refines search over a specific area. It includes a Time Difference of Arrival uncertainty model to optimize the scan accuracy using various grid resolution levels applying open and closed microphone array configurations. These characteristics provide efficient tracking of multiple sound sources and make the method convenient for low-cost embedded hardware achieving fewer computations.

The underlying mechanism of SRP-PHAT-HSDA is to search for V potential sources for each frame l over a discrete space. The method first captures synchronously the acoustic signals x_m from the M microphones in the array. These signals are divided in frames of N samples, spaced by ΔN samples and multiplied by the sine window $w[n]$ (3):

$$x_m^l[n] = w[n]x_m[n + l\Delta N] \tag{3}$$

For each frame l, the method uses the captured signals from the M microphone array $X^l = X_1^l, X_2^l, ..., X_M^l$ and generates V potential sources $\Psi^l = \{\psi_1^l, \psi_2^l, ..., \psi_V^l\}$ where each potential source ψ_v^l consists of a direction of arrival λ_v^l in cartesian coordinates, and the steered beamformer energy level Λ_v^l.

To better express the computing requirements, Table 1 presents simulation results of the time (in seconds) required to process one frame l, with various values of N and M, on a Raspberry Pi 3.

Table 1. Processing time in sec/frame for SRP-PHAT-HSDA.

M	$N = 256$	$N = 512$	$N = 1024$	$N = 2048$
8	1.8E−4	3.3E−4	7.1E−4	1.6E−3
16	7.6E−4	1.4E−3	3.1E−3	6.9E−3

3   Methodology

In this section, we described each of the stages that were carried out to implement the acoustic localization method that allows representing the origin of sound in a mixed reality environment through embedded devices.

3.1   Hardware Description

We used a Raspberry Pi 3 model B+ with the Matrix Creator developer board that contains a circular array of 8 microphones and an FPGA for signal processing; a module of the raspberry pi V2 camera and a 7-inch monitor (see Fig. 2).

3.2   Procedure

First, the acoustic signal is captured by the microphones at a frequency of 16000 Hz, and then the direction of arrival of the sound wave is calculated using the SRP-PHAT-HSDA implemented in the ODAS (Open embeddeD Audition System) library that returns the cartesian coordinates of potential sources [15].

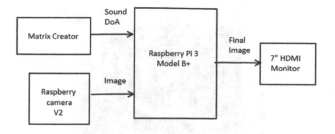

Fig. 2. Hardware components

Then the steering angle for the beamformer "Sum-and-Delay" described in the Sect. 2 is calculated by taking two of the axis values parallel to the monitor plane with the formula (4) and sent to the Raspberry Pi via the GPIO port.

$$\theta = \arctan \frac{y}{x} \tag{4}$$

The proposed algorithm takes the output signal from the camera and creates a plane on which the angles of the potential sound sources are represented.

Finally, the resulting image of the algorithm is sent to the monitor to show an approximation of the sound source localization in a mixed reality environment (Fig. 3).

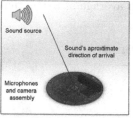 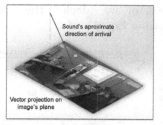 

(a) signal processing and vector generation

(b) vector projection in image plane

(c) approximation of sound direction of arrival

Fig. 3. System operation.

It is important to mention that to have congruence between the angle of the sound origin and the displayed image, the center of the microphone array, camera lens and monitor screen must be coincident (see Fig. 4).

To calibrate the prototype, it is necessary to generate the Direction of Arrival of at least two sources and draw the angles form the center of the image plane. These angles have to point at the sources in the screen. If they don't, the origin of the angles has to be adjusted by changing the coordinates in the software until the angles match the sources.

It is also important to mention that the prototype is not meant to be a head mounted display and therefore there is no motion sickness related issues.

Fig. 4. Center alignment.

3.3 Error Calculation

To perform the error calculation is necessary to get an average approximate angle that will be used for the measurements. This value is obtained by generating a buffer with the last ten measurements and saving it in the instant where a picture is taken, and then averaging the values. Next, this angle is projected and drawn in the final picture from the center of the image plane.

Subsequently, we manually drew a second angle from the same center to the sound source and measured the difference between the two values (see Fig. 5). Once we obtain the absolute error, we calculate the mean average of percentual error (MAPE) with the following Eq. (5):

$$MAPE = \sum_{i=1}^{n} \frac{\frac{|Expectedvalue_i - Realvalue_i|}{|Expectedvalue_i|}}{n} \tag{5}$$

Fig. 5. Measuring the absolute error.

4   Results

We performed measurements in a room of 4×6 m at distances of 3, 2 and 1.5 m from the sound source with low ambient noise and with a speaker as a sound source. The method proved to be capable of representing the approximation of an audio source in real-time in a mixed reality environment using an embedded device and having results with an average error of 2.5% better working for distances of less than 3 m (see Table 2).

A system constraint is that the device presents problems when locating sound sources with distances greater than 4 m because it fails to resolve the arrival direction angle and cannot generate the vector. We also observed a high percentage of error in the approximations of the angles 0–90 (left side) against the measurements of the angles 91–180 (right side), caused by a gap between the centers of the microphone array, camera lens, and monitor screen. Possible solutions to resolve this issue are designing a more robust method or implement a calibration system.

However, the system also has significant advantages such as being based on a low-cost embedded device, is portable and it can continue to be improved by the implementation of other types of algorithms that may add new functionalities like image processing or voice processing services.

Table 2. Testing results.

Distance	Approximate angle	Real angle	Absolute error	Error %
3 m	139°	136°	3°	2.16%
	36°	32°	4°	11.11%
2 m	129°	128°	1°	0.78%
	26°	26°	1°	0.0%
1.5 m	139°	137°	2°	1.44%
	139°	139.5°	0.5°	0.36%
	36°	34°	2°	5.56%
	36°	36°	0°	0.00%
			MAPE	2.51%

5   Conclusions

The method proved to have low error rates and the ability to continue improving, taking advantage of the versatility of embedded systems. The work lays the groundwork for applications based on sound source localization and mixed reality using an embedded device. An example is the creation of a mixed-reality conversation assistant where it identifies a person who is talking to later process the signal using voice-to-text conversion services and represent the information in mixed reality as subtitles in real-time. In this way, people with deafness could be assisted in classrooms that do not have a translator. In a similar way, a translation service can be incorporated to understand speakers who speak another language.

Acknowledgements. The authors wish to acknowledge the financial support for this work by the Consejo Nacional de Ciencia y Tecnología (CONACYT) through financial support scholarship number 494038. We also want to thank Universidad Autónoma de Querétaro (UAQ) through project number FIF-2018-06.

References

1. Kundu, T.: Acoustic source localization. Ultrasonics **54**(1), 25–38 (2014). https://doi.org/10.1016/j.ultras.2013.06.009
2. Rascon, C., Meza, I.: Localization of sound sources in robotics: a review. Rob. Auton. Syst. **96**, 184–210 (2017). https://doi.org/10.1016/j.robot.2017.07.011
3. Dong, B., Antoni, J., Pereira, A., Kellermann, W.: Blind separation of incoherent and spatially disjoint sound sources. J. Sound Vibr. **383**, 414–445 (2016). https://doi.org/10.1016/j.jsv.2016.07.018
4. Huang, Z., Hui, P., Peylo, C., Chatzopoulos, D.: Mobile augmented reality survey: a bottom-up approach. CoRR, abs/1309.4413, p. 1 (2013)
5. Noor, A.: The Hololens revolution. Mech. Eng. **138**(10), 30 (2016). https://doi.org/10.1115/1.2016-oct-1
6. Wang, H., Chu, P.: Voice source localization for automatic camera pointing system in videoconferencing. In: 1997 IEEE International Conference on Acoustics, Speech, and Signal Processing (1997). https://doi.org/10.1109/icassp.1997.599595
7. Zhong, X., Sun, L., Yost, W.: Active binaural localization of multiple sound sources. Rob. Auton. Syst. **85**, 83–92 (2016). https://doi.org/10.1016/j.robot.2016.07.008
8. Huang, Y., Benesty, J., Elko, G.: Passive acoustic source localization for video camera steering. In: 2000 IEEE International Conference on Acoustics, Speech, and Signal Processing. Proceedings (Cat. No.00CH37100) (2000). https://doi.org/10.1109/icassp.2000.859108
9. Lanslots, J., Deblauwe, F., Janssens, K.: Selecting sound source localization techniques for industrial applications. Sound Vib. (2010). http://www.sandv.com/home.htm. Accessed 15 Feb 2019
10. Azar, J., Abou Saleh, H., Al-Alaoui, M.: Sound visualization for the hearing impaired. Int. J. Emerg. Technol. Learn. (iJET) **2**(1) (2007). International Association of Online Engineering, Kassel, Germany. https://www.learntechlib.org/p/45106/. Accessed 15 Feb 2019
11. Jain, D., et al.: Head-mounted display visualizations to support sound awareness for the deaf and hard of hearing. In: Proceedings of the 33rd Annual ACM Conference on Human Factors in Computing Systems, CHI 2015 (2015)
12. Greensted, A.: Delay Sum Beamforming - The Lab Book Pages (2012). http://www.labbookpages.co.uk/audio/beamforming/delaySum.html
13. Pessentheiner, H.: Beamforming Using Uniform Circular Arrays for Distant Speech Recognition in Reverberant Environment and Double-Talk Scenarios. Bachelor of Science, Graz University of Technology (2012)
14. Acero, A., Stern, R.: Environmental robustness in automatic speech recognition. In: International Conference on Acoustics, Speech, and Signal Processing. https://doi.org/10.1109/icassp.1990.115971
15. Grondin, F., Michaud, F.: Lightweight and optimized sound source localization and tracking methods for opened and closed microphone array configurations. Rob. Auton. Syst. (2019). https://doi.org/10.1016/j.robot.2019.01.002

Using Morphological-Linear Neural Network for Upper Limb Movement Intention Recognition from EEG Signals

Gerardo Hernández[2]([✉]), Luis G. Hernández[1], Erik Zamora[2],
Humberto Sossa[1,2], Javier M. Antelis[1], Omar Mendoza-Montoya[1],
and Luis E. Falcón[1]

[1] Tecnológico de Monterrey en Guadalajara,
Av. Gral. Ramón Corona 2514, 45201 Zapopan, Jalisco, Mexico
{luisg.hernandez,mauricio.antelis,omendoza83,luis.eduardo.falcon}@tec.mx
[2] Instituto Politécnico Nacional - CIC,
Av. Juan de Dios Batiz S/N, Gustavo A. Madero, 07738 Ciudad de México, Mexico
gerardohernandez.hernandez@gmail.com, ezamorag@ipn.mx, hsossa@cic.ipn.mx

Abstract. This study aims to compare classical and Morphological-Linear Neural Network (MLNN) algorithms for the intention recognition to perform different movements from electroencephalographic (EEG) signals. Three classification models were implemented and assessed to decode EEG motor imagery signals: (*i*) Morphological-Linear Neural Network (MLNN) (*ii*) Support Vector Machine (SVM) and (*iii*) Multilayer perceptron (MLP). Real EEG signals recorded during robot-assisted rehabilitation therapy were used to evaluate the performance of the proposed algorithms in the classification of three classes (*relax*, movement intention A *Int A* and movement intention B *Int B*) using multi-CSP based features extracted from EEG signals. The results of a ten-fold cross validation show similar results in terms of classification accuracy for the SVM and MLNN models. However, the number of parameters used in each model varies considerably (the MLNN model use less parameters than the SVM). This study indicates potential application of MLNNs for decoding movement intentions and its use to develop more natural and intuitive robot assisted neurorehabilitation therapies.

Keywords: Brain-computer interfaces ·
Morphological-linear neural network · Movement planing ·
Machine learning · Electroencephalogram

1 Introduction

Brain-Computer Interfaces (BCI) is a technology developed for the purpose of providing people with neurological disabilities with an alternative communication channel to activate robot-assisted neurorehabilitation therapy devices. To achieve this goal, BCI systems based on non-invasive electroencephalographic

© Springer Nature Switzerland AG 2019
J. A. Carrasco-Ochoa et al. (Eds.): MCPR 2019, LNCS 11524, pp. 389–397, 2019.
https://doi.org/10.1007/978-3-030-21077-9_36

signals (EEG) need to recognize information from mental tasks. Currently, for the development of BCI systems, conventional methods of supervised classification algorithms such as Linear Discriminant Analysis and Support Vector Machines or SVM are implemented [1]. These types of algorithms has provided satisfactory performance in controlled laboratory settings.

The next step in the development of BCIs based on EEGs is the use of these systems in applications during real and everyday activities. This requires greate precision in the detection of mental MI tasks carried out by the user. We propose to explore new classification models such as the Morphological-Linear Neural Network.

This work evaluates the performance of 3 classification algorithms: (i) Morphological - Linear Neural Network (MLNN), (ii) Support Vector Machine (SVM) and (iii) Multilayer Perceptron (MLP) in a three-class classification scenario using Multiclass Common Spatial Patterns (CSP) based features extracted from the EEG signals during motor movement intention and presents a comparison of their performance. The results show that although the classification percentages are similar, the MLNN model uses a smaller number of learning parameters, which means that this model can be used in limited and portable hardware by using fewer resources.

This work shows that Morphological-Linear Neural Network (MLNN) algorithm can be an effective classification model to obtain highest confident classification accuracy in three different movements states of upper limbs. The rest of this paper is organized as follows. Section 2 describes details about how dataset was recorded and prepared, how attributes are calculated to extract relevant information from the EEG signals. Section 3 describes the different classification algorithms used and the performance evaluation process. Section 4 describes the accuracies obtained on three-class classification scenario.

2   Recognition of Movement Intention from EEG Using MLNN

2.1   Data Recording

Seven healthy subjects voluntarily participated in this study. The experiment was conducted in accordance to the Helsinki declaration. All participants were duly informed about the research goals. The participants were asked to carry out a upper limb rehabilitation therapy session using the neurorehabilitation device Tee-R on passive mode [2]. The rehabilitation actions consisted of self-selected and self-paced movements of the right arm. The movements were (A) supination/pronation of the forearm and (B) flexion/extension of the arm. During the execution of the experiment, EEG signals were recorded from 21 scalp locations associated with motor brain activity according to the international 10/20 system using a g.USBamp with active electrodes (g.tec medical engineering GmbH, Austria). The reference and ground electrode were placed over left earlobe and AFZ, respectively. In addition, two digital signals from Tee-R were also recorded which indicated the movement type and the movement onset. The EEG signals were acquired at a sampling frequency of 1200 Hz and not filtering was applied.

2.2 Experimental Paradigm

The therapy session consisted of several trials which was controlled by three visual cues (See Fig. 1). The first cue showed during 3 s was an image with the text "relax" indicating to stay relaxed with the robot in the home position. The second cue showed during 12 s was an image with a "cross" indicating to perform any of two movements (self-selected). The subjects were asked to initiate the movement whenever they desired (waiting around 6 s after the cross was first displayed while avoiding any mental count). This means that they decided when to initiate the movement (self-initiated). The last cue showed during 3 s was an image with the text "rest" which indicated to rest, move or blink.

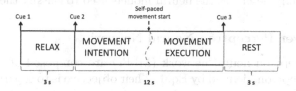

Fig. 1. Description of the experimental paradigm for self-selected and self-initiated movements.

2.3 Data Preprocessing

Visual artifact rejection processing was applied to rule out noise-contaminated trials. EEG signals were low-pass filtered at a cutoff frequency of 45 Hz using a 2nd-order Chebychev-type filter and then common average referenced (CAR) method was applied. Subsequently, EEG signals were shortened to 15-s duration trials, starting from the first visual cue to the second visual cue. For each trial the motion onset signals obtained from the Tee-R used as time zero reference. EEG signals were aligned with this time reference.

All trials have the same reference to the movement onset ($t = 0$) but the trial starting point (t_{ini}) and the trial ending point (t_{end}) are different for all of them. According to this, the time segment [$t_{ini}+1$, $t_{ini}+3$) and [-2, 0] correspond to relax and movement intention, respectively. Finally, the time segments of all the trials were labelled according to the motor stage (i.e., *Relax*, *Int A*, *Int B*) to construct the EEG dataset.

2.4 Attributes

The Common Spatial Pattern (CSP) algorithm was used as feature extraction method. CSPs is a technique commonly used in bi-class classification scenarios for brain activity information based on EEG signals. CSP allows to find a set of spatial filters that maximize the separability between the variances of signals of two conditions. CSP algorithm has been extended to a multiclass approach. In this work we use the One-Versus-the-Rest (OVR) algorithm which is a multiclass extension of CSP algorithm [3]. CSP features corresponding to *Relax* state were extracted from the interval $[t_{ini} + 2, t_{ini}+1)$ and CSP features corresponding to *Int A* and *Int B* states were extracted from $[t_{ini} + 2, t_{ini}+1)$ CSP filters were designed for the frequency window 7–30 Hz and the log-variance of the CSP-filtered signals were used as features. The application of this multiclass CSP resulted a feature vector of 60 (used as input for MLNN, SVM and MLP). The number of spatial filters and the number of features were selected in accordance to prior studies with CSP features [4,5].

3 Classifiers

This section briefly describes the neural models used to classify the EGG signals.

3.1 Multilayer Perceptron Neural Network

Multilayer perceptron neural network (MLPs) are composed of a computation unit called perceptron, defined by Eq. 1. Their objective is to separate two classes through a hyperplane.

$$O(\boldsymbol{x}) = F(\sum_{i=1}^{n} x_i w_i + b) \tag{1}$$

where x_i represents the ith element of the input $\boldsymbol{x}$ vector. $\boldsymbol{w}$ are the synaptic weights, b is the bias and F represents a non-linear activation function [6–8]. In our case, the *tanh* function. A MLP network usually consists of more than two intermediate layers, each layer of a variable Perceptron number, as shown in Fig. 2. These networks are trained by stochastic gradient descent.

3.2 Support Vector Machine (SVM)

A SVM is a discriminative classifier, whose objective is to look for a separation hyperplane between two classes, defined by Eq. 2. This maximizes the separation distance between two classes. SVM uses non-linear transformation functions, or kernels. The two most common kernel functions are: the linear (L_k), Eq. 3, and the radial basis (G_k), Eq. 4, like gaussians [9,10].

$$D(x) = \sum_{k=1}^{p} \alpha_k K(\boldsymbol{x}_k, \boldsymbol{x}) + b \tag{2}$$

where α_k are the parameters to be adjusted, $\boldsymbol{x}_k$ is the training pattern. The K function, is a predefined kernel and $\boldsymbol{x}$ is the support pattern.

$$L_k = (x \bullet w) \tag{3}$$

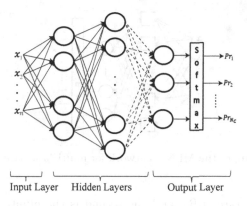

Input Layer   Hidden Layers   Output Layer

Fig. 2. MLP classic architecture.

$$G_k = e^{\frac{-||x - \mu_j||^2}{\sigma_j^2}} \qquad (4)$$

where x is the training pattern, μ is the center of the Gaussian, σ the variance, and • is the dot product.

3.3 Morphological-Linear Neural Network

The Morphological-Linear Neural Network (MLNN) is a new hybrid model, introduced in [11], which consists of two layers mainly, the first layer composed of morphological neurons, and the second layer composed of perceptron-like neurons. The first layer works as a feature extractor, and the second layer as a classifier. The architecture of this model is defined by the following equations:

$$h_k(\boldsymbol{x}) = min \left(min \left(\boldsymbol{x} - \boldsymbol{w}_{min}, \boldsymbol{w}_{max} - \boldsymbol{x} \right) \right), \qquad (5)$$

$$f(\boldsymbol{x}) = \sigma \left(h_k(\boldsymbol{x}) \right), \qquad (6)$$

where h_k specifies the kth morphological neuron of the middle layer of the network, $\boldsymbol{w}_{min}$ and $\boldsymbol{w}_{max}$ specify the initial and final limit of the hyperbox, $\boldsymbol{x}$ specifies the training pattern, and the function $f(\boldsymbol{x})$ specifies an activation function. For our specific case, the $tanh$ function. Figure 3 shown the architecture of this network.

3.4 Classification Scenarios and Evaluation Procedure

In this section, we describe the evaluation methodology used for the brain signals classification. For the three models of neural network the same methodology was used, methodology proposed by [12], which establishes that to obtain a set of optimal classification hyperparameters, it is necessary to generate a random valued search grid. MLNN network has two configuration hyperparameters, the

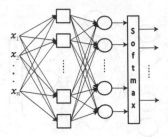

Fig. 3. Architecture of the MLNN network for multiclass classification problem.

first is the learning rate (LR), and the second is the number of morphological neurons in the intermediate layer. The grid that was used for the number of morphological neurons consists of 50 values with a uniform distribution on a logarithmic scale in a range of $[1, 500]$ and 50 values in a range of $[0.0001, 0.1]$ for the learning rate using the same distribution. This gives us a search grid of $2, 500$ combinations. For the SVM a similar grid was generated with $2, 500$ combinations, 50 values of each hyperparameter μ and σ of the radial base kernel. And finally for the MLP search grid, which consists of three configuration hyperparameters, the learning rate was defined in a range of $[0.001, 0.1]$, the number of intermediate layers in a range of $[1, 3]$ and the number of perceptrons per layer in a range of $[1, 250]$ generating a search grid of 3000 combinations.

Classification performance was assessed independently for each subject through a 10-fold cross-validation procedure. For each fold, the performance metric was classification accuracy which was computed as:

$$accuracy = \frac{TP + TN}{TP + TN + FP + FN} \tag{7}$$

where TP is the true positive rate, TN is the true negative rate, FP is the false positive rate and FN is the false negative rate. Therefore, average and distributions of classification accuracy were obtained for each subject.

4   Results

In this section, we present the results for EEG signal classification with three different types of classifiers the MLNNs, SVMs and MLPs. The results in Table 1 show that, on average, the classification of this type of signals is feasible with MLNN and SVM-RBF models; since the two models obtain similar classification percentages, on average 80% of classification on ten-fold validation sets.

The main difference between these two models is the number of learning parameters, while the SVM uses 4234 learning parameters distributed in 146 support vectors (each vector with 29 dimensions), the MLNN model uses 1223 learning parameters distributed among 20 morphological neurons in the intermediate layer and 3 perceptrons with their respective bias in the output layer.

Based on the experimental results from Table 1 we conclude that the MLNN classifier is the best option for this type of classification problem.

Table 1. Classification results for EGG signals using MLNNs.

Dataset	MLNNs		SVM-RBFs		MLPs	
	P_n	A_{va}	P_n	A_{va}	P_n	A_{va}
S2	1223	0.8	4234	0.783	9900	0.725
S3	1223	0.846	4234	0.84	9900	0.786
S4	1223	0.762	4234	0.840	9900	0.681
S5	1223	0.8	4234	0.791	9900	0.737
S6	1223	0.82	4234	0.83	9900	0.756
S7	1223	0.837	4234	0.787	9900	0.691
S8	1223	0.8	4234	0.772	9900	0.684
Avrg	**1223**	0.80	4234	**0.806**	9900	0.723

Table 1 shows the average classification rates A_{va} of the 10 folds for each subject, the column P_n shows the number of parameters used in each model. The last row the parameter average used for classification is shown, as well as the classification average for the seven subjects.

5 Conclusion

In this work, the performance of three classification algorithms was evaluated in a three-class classification scenario using of EEG movement intention signals. Real EEG signals recorded during robot-assisted rehabilitation therapy over seven healthy participants. Common spatial patterns were calculated for the three classes: *Relax, Int A, Int B* and the log-variances of the CSP-filtered signals were used as attributes.

For classification and performance evaluation, a three-class classification scenario was followed to asses the classification accuracy with the proposed models. The results showed that the accuracy average of the MLNN technique is superior than the other techniques implemented. The better results can be observed for subject 3 (84.6%), 7 (83.7%) and 8 (80.0%); While using a lesser number of training parameters, 340% less parameters than the SVM.

This work shows that the MLNN technique allows to obtain a confident classification accuracy in three different movement states for upper limbs. This is important since the accurate recognition for motor planning can be used in BCI area to control neurorehabilitation devices. So, the detection of the intention to execute a movement of a limb and the recognition of the type of movement is essential to enhance the performance of robot-assisted rehabilitation.

These results cannot be compared against the related state of the art due to there are several differences with others works [4,13,14], as experimental setup (execution of different movements), different state of participants (with some motor injury) and different attributes to classify (frequency domain features). Finally, we consider this work can be a starting point in two ways; (i) to evaluate diverse MLNN architectures that allow to improve the three class MI classification (ii) to explore the classification of motor planning using the MLNN models in others classification contexts, such as on-line classification scenario.

Acknowledgments. This work was partially supported by the National Council of Science and Technology of Mexico (CONACYT) through grant PN2015-873 and scholarship 291197. H. Sossa and E. Zamora would like to acknowledge the support provided by CONACYT grant number 65 (Frontiers of Science) and SIP-IPN (grant numbers 20180180, 20190166 and 20190007). G. Hernández acknowledges CONACYT for the scholarship granted towards pursuing his PhD studies.

References

1. Vega, R., et al.: Assessment of feature selection and classification methods for recognizing motor imagery tasks from electroencephalographic signals. Artif. Intell. Res. **6**(1), 37 (2017)
2. Figueroa-Garcia, I., et al.: Platform for the study of virtual task-oriented motion and its evaluation by EEG and EMG biopotentials. In: 2014 36th Annual International Conference of the IEEE Engineering in Medicine and Biology Society, pp. 1174–1177, August 2014
3. Dornhege, G., Blankertz, B., Curio, G., Muller, K.: Boosting bit rates in noninvasive EEG single-trial classifications by feature combination and multiclass paradigms. IEEE Trans. Biomed. Eng. **51**(6), 993–1002 (2004)
4. Shiman, F., et al.: Classification of different reaching movements from the same limb using EEG. J. Neural Eng. **14**(4), 046018 (2017)
5. Yong, X., Menon, C.: EEG classification of different imaginary movements within the same limb. PLOS One **10**(4), 1–24 (2015)
6. Van Der Malsburg, C.: Frank Rosenblatt: principles of neurodynamics: perceptrons and the theory of brain mechanisms. In: Palm, G., Aertsen, A. (eds.) Brain Theory, pp. 245–248. Springer, Heidelberg (1986). https://doi.org/10.1007/978-3-642-70911-1_20
7. Rumelhart, D.E., Hinton, G.E., Williams, R.J.: Neurocomputing: Foundations of Research, pp. 696–699. MIT Press, Cambridge (1988)
8. Rumelhart, D.E., Hinton, G.E., Williams, R.J.: Parallel Distributed Processing: Explorations in the Microstructure of Cognition, vol. 1, pp. 318–362. MIT Press, Cambridge (1986)
9. Cortes, C., Vapnik, V.: Support-vector networks. Mach. Learn. **20**(3), 273–297 (1995)
10. Boser, B.E., Guyon, I.M., Vapnik, V.N.: A training algorithm for optimal margin classifiers. In: Proceedings of the Fifth Annual Workshop on Computational Learning Theory, COLT 1992, pp. 144–152. ACM, New York (1992)
11. Hernández, G., Zamora, E., Sossa, H.: Morphological-linear neural network. In: 2018 IEEE International Conference on Fuzzy Systems (FUZZ-IEEE), pp. 1–6, July 2018

12. Bergstra, J., Bengio, Y.: Random search for hyper-parameter optimization. J. Mach. Learn. Res. **13**(1), 281–305 (2012)
13. Ofner, P., Schwarz, A., Pereira, J., Müller-Putz, G.R.: Upper limb movements can be decoded from the time-domain of low-frequency EEG. PLoS One **12**(8), e0182578 (2017). PONE-D-17-04785[PII]
14. Pereira, J., Sburlea, A.I., Müller-Putz, G.R.: EEG patterns of self-paced movement imaginations towards externally-cued and internally-selected targets. Sci. Rep. **8**(1), 13394 (2018)

Evaluation of Five Classifiers for Children Activity Recognition with Sound as Information Source and Akaike Criterion for Feature Selection

Antonio García-Domínguez[(⊠)], Laura A. Zanella-Calzada[(⊠)],
Carlos E. Galván-Tejada[(⊠)], Jorge I. Galván-Tejada[(⊠)],
and José M. Celaya-Padilla

Unidad Académica de Ingeniería Eléctrica,
Universidad Autónoma de Zacatecas,
Jardín Juarez 147, Centro, 98000 Zacatecas, Zac, Mexico
{antonio.garcia,lzanellac,ericgalvan,gatejo,jose.cpadilla}@uaz.edu.mx

Abstract. The recognition and classification of children activities is a subject of novel interest in which different works have been presented, where the data source to perform this classification is crucial to define the way of working. This work uses environmental sound as data source to perform the activities recognition and classification, evaluating the accuracy of the k-Nearest Neighbor (kNN), Support Vector Machines (SVM), Random Forests (RF), Extra Trees (ET) and Gradient Boosting (GB) algorithms in the generation of a recognition and classification model. In the first stage of experimentation, the complete set of features extracted from the audio samples is used to generate classification models. Then, a feature selection process is performed based on the Akaike criteria to obtain a reduced set of features used as input for a second generation of these models. Finally, a comparison of the results obtained from the data of models of both approaches is carried out in terms of accuracy to determine if the model contained by the features selected improves the performance in the classification of children activities.

1 Introduction

The human activity recognition and classification is a subject of recent interest, on which many works have been presented and proposed different applications [1–5], in order to facilitate the daily life of human beings by promoting an automated interaction with their environment.

An important aspect to be considered in human activity recognition is the data source to be used. As a data source, the use of different types of sensors has been proposed, as in the work presented by Arnon [6]. In recent years, in the topic of recognition and classification of children activities, has been proposed the use of different data sources, such as video cameras, accelerometers, and radio-frequency devices, as in the work presented by Kurashima et al. [7]. Most

© Springer Nature Switzerland AG 2019
J. A. Carrasco-Ochoa et al. (Eds.): MCPR 2019, LNCS 11524, pp. 398–407, 2019.
https://doi.org/10.1007/978-3-030-21077-9_37

of the works described in this area collect information for analysis by embedding the sensor directly into a child's garment to record activity data as is proposed by Nam et al. [8]. This way of data capture has the disadvantage that the devices or sensors used, which are placed in the garments, can interfere directly with the natural action of the children, not allowing them to perform normally the activities to be analyzed.

One way to solve the problem mentioned above is to change the data source to one that does not interfere with the activities to be performed by the study subjects. Under this idea, environmental sound has been used as data source to recognize and classify human activities, as in the works presented by Leeuwen [9] and Galván-Tejada et al. [10], since data capture passes inadvertently to the study group, thus not interfering with the activities to be analyzed.

Environmental sound as data source in child activity classification models is a major challenge due to the complexity of the audio signal analysis process as well as due to the different environmental factors that may interfere during the data capture process, causing that the samples taken do not have the necessary features for their analysis. Therefore an adequate data processing (audio samples) and the choice of an appropriate model that optimizes the process of recognition of the activities becomes of vital importance.

For the correct audio signals processing it is necessary to perform a feature extraction on which the classification model will be based. Given these features, it is possible, with a set of training examples (samples), to label the classes (type of sound to which the samples belong), construct and train a model that predicts the class of a new sample. Once the classification model is constructed, it is possible to perform the process of recognizing an activity through an audio signal, passing the signal through the model so that it can predict which kind of sound it belongs to, based on the information with which the model was trained. In the present work, the accuracy of 5 classification algorithms, Support Vector Machines (SVM), k-Nearest Neighbors (kNN), Random Forests (RF), Extra Trees (ET) and Gradient Boosting (GB) is compared, in the generation of a model of recognition and classification of children activities using environmental sound as a data source.

The activity classification models are constructed by executing the classification algorithms with the data obtained from the audio samples in the feature extraction stage. In the first phase of the methodology proposed, these models are built using the 34 extracted features present in the dataset. Nevertheless, in order to develop a more efficient classification model that can be used in mobile applications, a feature selection is performed to reduce the number of features. Therefore, in this proposal Akaike criterion is applied to re-generate the models with a reduced set of features, finally comparing the results obtained in terms of accuracy.

This paper is organized as follows, in the present section is presented an introduction to children activity recognition. Materials and methods are described in Sect. 2. Section 3 reports the results obtained from the methodology.

The discussion and conclusions of this proposal are described in Sect. 4. Finally, future work is reported in Sect. 5.

2   Materials and Methods

To compare the efficiency of the classification algorithms SVM, kNN, ET, RF and GB in the generation of a model of recognition and classification of children activities using environmental sound data, and a feature selection process using the Akaike criterion, 5 main stages were performed: data acquisition, feature extraction, classification analysis based on the complete set of features, feature selection, classification analysis based on the set of selected features.

The feature extraction was performed using the programming language, Python [11], while the feature selection and the classification analysis were performed using the free software environment, R [12].

2.1   Data Description

In the majority of the works presented about children activity recognition, is common to analyze detectable activities through movement, such walking or running, because these works use motion sensors like accelerometer as data source, as in the works presented by Boughorbel et al. [13] and Nam et al. [8]. In order to analize different kind of activities, in the present work, the dataset is composed of recordings from four activities commonly performed by children from 12 to 36 months in a residential environment: crying, running, walking and playing (manipulating plastic objects), two of which are not detectable through motion sensors (crying and playing). For the conformation of the dataset, 10% of the sounds was generated and 90% was acquired from the Internet [14,15] through a search of audio clips about children activities carried out on October 3, 2018.

Table 1 shows the description of the activities analyzed in this work.

Table 1. General description of activities.

Activity	Description
Crying	Emitting crying sound in reaction to some event
Playing	Handling plastic pieces
Running	Moving quickly from one place to another
Walking	Moving from one place to another at medium speed

Recording Devices. To make the recordings of the audio clips corresponding to the part of the generated data, the devices used were a Lanix Ilium s620 (MediaTek MT6582 quad-core, Android 4.2.2) and a Motorola Moto G4 (Snapdragon 617, Android 6.0.1).

Metadata. From the process of recording the audio clips using different devices and different configurations, as well as considering the recordings taken from the Internet, the dataset of this work includes audio clips with a sample rate between 44100 Hz and 96000 Hz, in stereo and mono channels. Table 2 shows the metadata of the audio clips in the dataset for each activity. The features presented in Table 2 ensure an acceptable quality for recorded audio files, and they define the parameters required for future recordings in order to expand the dataset.

Table 2. Audio clips metadata per activity.

Activity	Sample rate	Encoding format	Channels
Crying	44100 Hz–96000 Hz	mp3, wav	Mono, Stereo
Playing	44100 Hz–96000 Hz	mp3, wav	Mono, Stereo
Running	44100 Hz–48000 Hz	mp3, wav, flac	Mono, Stereo
Playing	44100 Hz–96000 Hz	mp3, wav, flac, aiff	Mono, Stereo

2.2 Feature Extraction

The feature extraction is the process by which information is obtained from audio clips. This information is used to differentiate the type of activity to which the recording belongs, since for each type of activity, the audio clips contains different measurements for their extracted features.

Because the dataset contains audio files of different lengths, these were divided into 10-s clips, causing that all the analyzed samples have the same length. Each 10-s clip is transformed into an array, where each position represents the magnitude of the corresponding feature for that audio clip. Table 3 shows the set of 34 features extracted for each audio 10-s clip. To prevent problems with the difference in the channels of the recordings (Mono and Stereo), all the samples were converted to the Mono type.

It is important to mention that this set of features was chosen because they have been commonly used in related works of audio processing [16–19], especially the mel-frequency spectral coefficients, being one of the most robust features in the area of recognition and classification of activities using sound [20–24].

2.3 Classification Analysis Based on the Features Extracted

For the classification analysis, the 34 extracted features were subjected to five classification algorithms, SVM, kNN, RF, ET and GB, generating five children activities classifications models, one for each algorithm used.

The classification algorithms used in this work are supervised learning algorithms, being necessary to be previously trained with known data, using a

Table 3. Features extracted.

Feature ID	Feature name	Description
1	Zero Crossing Rate	The rate of sign-changes of the signal during the duration of a particular frame
2	Energy	The sum of squares of the signal values, normalized by the respective frame length
3	Entropy of Energy	The entropy of sub-frames normalized energies. It can be interpreted as a measure of abrupt changes
4	Spectral Centriod	The center of the gravity of the spectrum
5	Spectral Spread	The second central moment of the spectrum
6	Spectral Entropy	Entropy of the normalized spectral energies for a set of sub-frames
7	Spectral Flux	The squared difference between the normalized magnitudes of the spectra of the two successive frames
8	Spectral Rollof	The frequency below with 90% of the magnitude distribution of the spectrum is concentrated
9–21	MFCCs	Mel Frequency Cepstral Coefficients form a cepstral representation where the frequency bands are not linear but distributed according to the mel-scale
22–33	Chroma Vector	A 12-element representation of the spectral energy where the bins represent the 12 equal-tempered pitch classes of western-type music (semitone spacing)
34	Chroma Deviation	The standard deviation of the 12 chroma coefficients

training dataset (70% of the total samples), to later be able to classify new data automatically, based on a blind test using a testing dataset (30% of the remaining total samples).

Finally, each classification model was evaluated obtaining its accuracy, to be compared with each other.

2.4   Feature Selection

In this stage, a feature selection process based on the Akaike criterion (AIC) [25, 26] is performed to reduce the number of features, selecting those that present the most significant information to differentiate the classes to which the audio samples belong.

The principle of this technique is based on the generation of models constructing all the possible combinations of the 34 features extracted through a stepwise regression, a forward selection and a backward elimination, calculating subsequently the AIC for each of these models. Then, the models are ranked according to their AIC, being the best of them the one with the lowest AIC [27].

2.5 Classification Analysis Based on the Features Selected

The classification analysis based on the features selected was carried out only with the set of features that belong to the combination of those with the lowest AIC, since they are the ones that best describe the difference between the analyzed classes.

Finally, as well as in the classification analysis based on the total extracted features, a validation to compare the accuracy of each model is performed in order to evaluate which classification approach presents the most significant results, the classification based on the total number of features extracted or the classification based on the selected features.

3 Results

From the data acquisition, a total of 146 recordings were obtained (considering both the own recordings and those taken from the Internet), which were divided into 2,716 10-s clips. Table 4 shows the number of recordings obtained for each activity as well as the number of 10-s clips generated.

Table 4. Audio clips per activity.

Activity	Generated		Taken from Internet		Total	
	Recordings	Clips	Recordings	Clips	Recordings	Clips
Crying	8	72	33	532	41	604
Playing	9	67	17	636	26	703
Running	9	81	30	611	39	692
Walking	10	65	30	652	40	717

A total of 34 features were extracted for each 10-s clip, so the database for the comparison of the classifying algorithms was contained by 2,716 records with 34 features each one.

Then, from the classification analysis based on the total set of features extracted, in Table 5 are shown the true positives obtained from each classification technique and Table 6 summarizes the accuracy by activity. Table 7 shows the average accuracies of each technique considering the whole set of activities analyzed.

All classifiers achieve an accuracy equal or greater than 0.90.

In the feature selection stage, a set of 27 features was selected, shown in Table 8.

Table 5. True positives for each classification technique based on the features extracted.

	True positives				
	SVM	kNN	RF	ET	GB
Crying	167	170	175	177	175
Playing	177	191	185	191	190
Running	180	194	193	195	194
Walking	196	199	209	211	211

Table 6. Accuracy for each classification technique based on the features extracted.

	Accuracy				
	SVM	kNN	RF	ET	GB
Crying	0.8743	0.9497	0.9665	0.9779	0.9615
Playing	0.8592	0.9139	0.9257	0.9502	0.9548
Running	0.9424	0.9417	0.9847	0.9898	0.9652
Walking	0.9245	0.9660	0.9372	0.9548	0.9633

Table 7. Average accuracy for the features extracted.

	Average accuracy
SVM	0.90
kNN	0.9425
RF	0.9525
ET	0.9675
GB	0.9612

Table 8. Features selected.

Feature name
Zero Crossing Rate
Energy
Entropy of Energy
Spectral Centriod
Spectral Spread
Spectral Entropy
Spectral Rollof
MFCCs (1, 3–13)
Chroma Vector (2, 4, 6–10)
Chroma Deviation

Table 9. True positives for each classification technique based on the features selected.

	True positives				
	SVM	kNN	Random Forests	Extra Trees	Gradient Boosting
Crying	169	168	177	177	174
Playing	177	189	189	193	190
Running	178	185	193	198	193
Walking	194	200	207	209	209

Table 10. Accuracy for each classification technique based on the features selected.

	Accuracy				
	SVM	kNN	Random Forests	Extra Trees	Gradient Boosting
Crying	0.8989	0.9545	0.9620	0.9833	0.9721
Playing	0.8551	0.8915	0.9220	0.9324	0.9179
Running	0.9468	0.9343	0.9948	0.9851	0.9747
Walking	0.8940	0.9346	0.9539	0.9858	0.9676

Table 11. Average accuracy for the features selected.

	Average accuracy
SVM	0.8975
kNN	0.9275
Random Forests	0.9575
Extra Trees	0.9712
Gradient Boosting	0.9575

From the classification analysis based on the features selected, the true positives obtained are shown in Table 9, while Table 10 summarizes the accuracy by activity. Table 11 shows the average accuracies for each classification technique.

All classifiers achieve an accuracy between 0.89 and 0.97.

4   Discussion and Conclusions

The objective of this research is to compare the efficiency of five classification techniques based on the generation of a recognition and classification model of children activities using environmental sound data, comparing the classification accuracy of a specific set of extracted features and a reduced set of selected features through an AIC approach.

From the results presented in Sect. 3, it can be observed that, initially, for the four analyzed activities, on average the best model is the one generated by the ET classification technique, followed by GB, RF, kNN and SVM, respectively, all with an accuracy equal or greater than 0.90. These five initial models were generated using the 34 extracted features of the audio samples, which represents 100% of the data.

In the next phase the process feature selection was performed, selecting a set of 27 according to the AIC, which represents the reduction of 20% of the data used for the development of the classification models.

For the generation of the recognition and classification models of activities using the reduced dataset, the results show a practically equal behavior in the accuracy of the classifying techniques, besides that the RF and ET techniques presented an improvement in their accuracy values.

According to this results, the set of 27 selected features classify activities with a similar performance as the complete dataset contained by 34 features, managing to reduce the amount of data needed by 20% and practically maintaining or improving the accuracy of the models.

The reduction in the number of features is important because when the classification techniques are subjected to large amounts of information, the response time is usually long in a significant way, increasing the computational cost, in addition to the fact that the recognition and classification of activities models are usually designed to be implemented in mobile applications, so it is important to optimize the amount of data with which the user will work and reduce the cost of processing.

5   Future Work

As part of the future work, it is proposed to add to the analysis more common activities in children with the established age range, as well as perform a validation analysis of the dataset to establish if the number of features and samples is optimal for the type of study that is being done.

Another important aspect is to improve the process of feature selection, finding a mechanism that further reduces the set of features needed to describe the phenomena or activities analyzed, and thus, reducing the size of the database with which the algorithms work and the models are generated.

References

1. Masuda, A., Zhang, K., Maekawa, T.: Sonic home: environmental sound collection game for human activity recognition. J. Inf. Process. **24**(2), 203–210 (2016)
2. Shaikh, M.A.M., Hirose, K., Ishizuk, M.: Recognition of real-world activities from environmental sound cues to create life-log. In: The Systemic Dimension of Globalization, January 2011
3. Aggarwal, J., Xia, L.: Human activity recognition from 3D data: a review. Pattern Recogn. Lett. **48**, 70–80 (2014)
4. Chen, B., Fan, Z., Cao, F.: Activity recognition based on streaming sensor data for assisted living in smart homes. In: 2015 International Conference on Intelligent Environments (2015)
5. Vrigkas, M., Nikou, C., Kakadiaris, I.A.: A review of human activity recognition methods. Front. Robot. AI **2**, 28 (2015)

6. Arnon, P.: Classification model for multi-sensor data fusion apply for human activity recognition. In: 2014 International Conference on Computer, Communications, and Control Technology (I4CT) (2014)
7. Kurashima, S., Suzuki, S.: Improvement of activity recognition for child growth monitoring system at kindergarten. In: IECON 2015–41st Annual Conference of the IEEE Industrial Electronics Society (2015)
8. Nam, Y., Park, J.W.: Child activity recognition based on cooperative fusion model of a triaxial accelerometer and a barometric pressure sensor. IEEE J. Biomed. Health Inform. **17**(2), 420–426 (2013)
9. Salomons, E., Havinga, P., Leeuwen, H.V.: Inferring human activity recognition with ambient sound on wireless sensor nodes. Sensors **16**(10), 1586 (2016)
10. Delgado-Contreras, J.R., García-Vázquez, J.P., Brena, R.F., Galván-Tejada, C.E., Galván-Tejada, J.I.: Feature selection for place classification through environmental sounds. Procedia Comput. Sci. **37**, 40–47 (2014)
11. Python.org. https://www.python.org/
12. The R project for statistical computing. https://www.r-project.org/
13. Boughorbel, S., Breebaart, J., Bruekers, F., Flinsenberg, I., Kate, W.T.: Child-activity recognition from multi-sensor data. In: Proceedings of the 7th International Conference on Methods and Techniques in Behavioral Research - MB 10 (2010)
14. Freesound. https://freesound.org/
15. Youtube. https://www.youtube.com/
16. Scheirer, E.D.: Tempo and beat analysis of acoustic musical signals. J. Acoust. Soc. Am. **103**(1), 588–601 (1998)
17. Wang, H., Divakaran, A., Vetro, A., Chang, S.-F., Sun, H.: Survey of compressed-domain features used in audio-visual indexing and analysis. J. Vis. Commun. Image Represent. **14**(2), 150–183 (2003)
18. Zhang, T., Kuo, C.-C.: IEEE Trans. Speech Audio Process. **9**(4), 441–457 (2001)
19. Verhaegh, W.F.J., Aarts, E.H.L., Korst, J.: Algorithms in Ambient Intelligence. Kluwer Academic, Dordrecht (2004)
20. Stork, J.A., Spinello, L., Silva, J., Arras, K.O.: Audio-based human activity recognition using non-Markovian ensemble voting. In: 2012 IEEE RO-MAN: The 21st IEEE International Symposium on Robot and Human Interactive Communication (2012)
21. Galván-Tejada, C.E., et al.: An analysis of audio features to develop a human activity recognition model using genetic algorithms, random forests, and neural networks. Mob. Inf. Syst. **2016**, 1–10 (2016)
22. Markakis, M.: Selection of relevant features for audio classification tasks (2011)
23. Salamon, J., Bello, J.P.: Unsupervised feature learning for urban sound classification. In: 2015 IEEE International Conference on Acoustics, Speech and Signal Processing (ICASSP) (2015)
24. Mascia, M., Canclini, A., Antonacci, F., Tagliasacchi, M., Sarti, A., Tubaro, S.: Forensic and anti-forensic analysis of indoor/outdoor classifiers based on acoustic clues. In: 2015 23rd European Signal Processing Conference (EUSIPCO) (2015)
25. Akaike, H.: A new look at the statistical model identification. In: Parzen, E., Tanabe, K., Kitagawa, G. (eds.) Selected Papers of Hirotugu Akaike. Springer Series in Statistics, pp. 215–222. Springer, New York (1974). https://doi.org/10.1007/978-1-4612-1694-0_16
26. Snipes, M., Taylor, D.C.: Model selection and akaike information criteria: an example from wine ratings and prices. Wine Econ. Policy **3**(1), 3–9 (2014)
27. Akaike, H.: Akaike's information criterion. In: International Encyclopedia of Statistical Science, p. 25 (2011)

Natural Language Processing
and Recognition

Exploring the Use of Psycholinguistic Information in Author Profiling

Delia Irazú Hernández Farías[(✉)], Rosa María Ortega-Mendoza,
and Manuel Montes-y-Gómez

Instituto Nacional de Astrofísica, Óptica y Electrónica (INAOE),
Santa María Tonantzintla, Puebla, Mexico
{dirazuherfa,mortega,mmontesg}@inaoep.mx

Abstract. Identifying profile characteristics of the author of a given text
is the aim of the *Author Profiling* (AP) task. In this paper, we explore
the use of two well known psycholinguistic dictionaries, the *Linguistic
Inquirer and Word Count* and the *General Inquirer*, with the objective
to capture relevant information for recognizing the age and gender of
the author of a given text. The contribution of this paper is two-fold.
Firstly, we introduce the use of General Inquirer in the AP task. Secondly, we propose different text representations based on these dictionaries, which help to analyze their relevance and complementariness to
accomplish author profiling. We experiment with benchmark corpora on
AP. The obtained results are competitive with state-of-the-art, validating the usefulness of psycholinguistic information for recognizing profile
attributes of authors.

Keywords: Author Profiling · Psycholinguistic dictionaries · LIWC ·
General Inquirer

1 Introduction

Identifying the gender, age, personality, or native language of the people based
on their writings is the aim of *Author Profiling* (AP) [6]. This task attempts to
analyze texts in order to predict various attributes related to its author. AP has
attracted the attention of the research community due to the many applications
that can benefit from it, ranging from forensic to marketing methods and tools.

From a computational linguistics perspective, AP has been addressed as a
text classification problem. There are many approaches attempting to tackle this
task. Some of them use stylistic features such as the bag of words, presence of
URLs, punctuation marks, POS-tags labels, etc. [3,10]. Others take advantage of
more sophisticated techniques such as topic-based representations [1] and word
embeddings [4]. Furthermore, since 2013 each year a shared task[1] dedicated to
identify different aspects of author profiling has been organized.

---

[1] https://pan.webis.de/tasks.html

© Springer Nature Switzerland AG 2019
J. A. Carrasco-Ochoa et al. (Eds.): MCPR 2019, LNCS 11524, pp. 411–421, 2019.
https://doi.org/10.1007/978-3-030-21077-9_38

From a different perspective, research in related areas such as Sentiment Analysis, Personality Recognition, and Emotion Detection has been taken advantage of lexical resources. For AP, where the use of particular linguistic aspects could shed light on the differences among distinct types of authors, the use of such resources has also shown to be beneficial. We believed that the use of language and also psychological aspects (psycholinguistic characteristics) of people are involved in their writings, which can be studied to distinguish traits of authors. For example, the way of authors reflect basic emotional and cognitive dimensions reveal cues for recognizing classes of authors. In this context, there is one psycholinguistic resource that has been widely exploited: the *Linguistic Inquirer and Word Count* (hereafter LIWC) [9].

LIWC is a dictionary of words labeled according to different categories covering grammatical and psycholinguistic aspects. It includes more than four thousand words belonging to at least one of 64 categories, which consider, among others, *social processes* (words related to family, friends, etc.), *effective processes* (words associated to positive and negative emotions), *personal concerns* (words related to work, home, leisure, etc.), and *biological processes* (words associated with body, health, ingest, etc.). In AP, information from LIWC categories is commonly used to generate feature vectors [1]. Also, representations based on LIWC have been combined with other lexical resources [5] and with stylistic features [2].

There are other psycholinguistic resources considering different kinds of categories such as the *General Inquirer* [11] (hereafter GI). GI has been already used in various NLP tasks, but never in Author Profiling. It is a dictionary composed by 182 categories[2] developed for analyzing language considering several aspects, ranging from cognitive to emotion-laden words. The categories in this dictionary cover words associated to pleasure and pain, regarding roles and forms of interpersonal relations, and associated to places and locations, among others.

In this paper, we aim to evaluate the performance of both dictionaries when they are used to characterize aspects related to age and gender identification. Thus, the main contributions of this work can be summarized as follows: (*i*) it proposes three representations based on psycholinguistic information for the AP task; (*ii*) it uses for the first time –to the best of our knowledge– the *General Inquirer* lexicon in AP; and (*iii*) it presents a qualitative and quantitative analysis of the kind of information relevant for AP that is captured by these two dictionaries, paying special attention to their differences and similarities.

2   Psycholinguistic-Based Representations for AP

The AP task has been traditionally tackled as a supervised text classification problem, where a classifier is trained to assign predefined author classes to a collection of documents. Recently, the use of psycholinguistic dictionaries, such

---

[2] A complete list of categories and their description is found in http://www.wjh. harvard.edu/~inquirer/homecat.htm.

as LIWC, has been explored. In this paper, we consider information from LIWC and GI by means of three different representations, as described below.

Let $D = \{d_1, \ldots, d_{|D|}\}$ denote the collection of documents, and $V = \{t_1, \ldots, t_{|V|}\}$ its term vocabulary, where the terms correspond to word n-grams of different sizes. Also, let $C = \{C_1, \ldots, C_{|C|}\}$ represents the set of categories in a given dictionary (e.g. LIWC or GI), where each category is a set of words (lexical unigrams) denoted by $C_f = \{w_1, \ldots, w_{|C_f|}\}$.

Traditional Term-Based Representation. In this representation, each document d_i is modeled by a vector $\mathbf{d_i^w}$:

$$\mathbf{d_i^w} = <v_{i,1}, \ldots, v_{i,|V|}> \tag{1}$$

where $v_{i,j} = f(d_i, t_j)$ represents the number of occurrences of the term t_j in the document d_i.

Rep 1. Category-Based Representation. This representation exclusively relies on the information provided by the dictionary. Therefore, each document d_i is represented by a vector $\mathbf{d_i^c}$, whose feature space is determined by the categories compressed in the resource:

$$\mathbf{d_i^c} = <v_{i,1}, \ldots, v_{i,|C|}> \tag{2}$$

where $v_{i,j} = \sum_{s=1}^{|C_j|} f(d_i, w_s)$ represents the sum of occurrences of words belonging to category C_j of the dictionary in the document d_i.

Rep 2. Term-Category Based Representation. Term and category based representations are quite different, the former has good coverage but it is ambiguous and imprecise, whereas the latter is the opposite. For taking as much benefit as possible from both of them, we decide to combine them. Let $\mathbf{d_i^w}$ and $\mathbf{d_i^c}$ be the vector representations for a document d_i based in terms and categories respectively, the enriched vector $\mathbf{d_i^e}$ is the result of their concatenation.

$$\mathbf{d_i^e} = \mathbf{d_i^w} \parallel \mathbf{d_i^c} \tag{3}$$

where $\parallel$ indicates the vector concatenation operation. Therefore the dimensionality of the enriched vector $\mathbf{d_i^e}$ corresponds to $|\mathbf{d_i^e}| = |\mathbf{d_i^w}| + |\mathbf{d_i^c}|$.

Rep 3. Category-Masked Term-Based Representation. It consists in transforming the original text by "masking" the words that belong to a certain category in the resource. The masking process is done as follows: each word in the text is replaced by its corresponding category(ies) in a given dictionary. Words out of the dictionary's vocabulary are kept in their same position. Therefore, this representation avoids having redundant information by including the same knowledge more than once in the feature space (i.e., terms and their respective category, as in the previous representation). Following we present an example of a sentence and its masked version.

- Original text: *"Lovely hotel, comfortable room"*
- Masked text[3]: *"social-affect-posemo hotel, affect-posemo space-relativ-home"*

Once the texts are masked, we build their term-based representation. However, in this case there is a new vocabulary $V' = \{t'_1 \ldots t'_k\}$, where each t'_j represents a n-gram that may include words and categories. For instance, from our example, the vocabulary will include the unigrams "social-affect-posemo" and "hotel", and also the bigram "social-affect-posemo hotel".

Formally, a document d_i is represented by the enriched vector, $\mathbf{d_i^m}$:

$$\mathbf{d_i^m} = <v_{i,1}, \ldots, v_{i,|V'|}> \tag{4}$$

where $v_{i,j} = f(d_i, t'_j)$ represents the number of occurrences of the new term t'_j in the document d_i.

3   Experiments

3.1   Evaluation Datasets

For evaluation purposes, we used the corpora from the *2nd* and *5th International Competitions on Author Profiling*, hereafter *PAN2014* and *PAN2017*, respectively. The PAN2014 corpus includes collections of blogs (*Blogs*), hotel reviews (*Reviews*), tweets (*Tw14*), and social media posts (*SMedia*), which are different kinds of social media data allowing us to assess the proposed approach over distinct domains. On the other hand, the PAN2017 corpus only includes a collection of tweets written in different languages and annotated according to gender. In this paper we only consider the English partition of this dataset (*Tw17*). For the sake of the comparison, we used the same training and test data partitions than in the aforementioned competitions. Table 1 shows the distribution for each label in the used corpora.

3.2   Experimental Settings

We applied a preprocessing process consisting in replacing all urls, Twitter marks (mentions and hashtags), emoticons, and emojis, by a corresponding label. We also coverted all texts to lowercase. Additionally, we lemmatized all words from texts and psycholinguistic dictionaries (LIWC and GI). Once built the representations described in the previous section, we normalized them by applying the L2 norm. Finally, we addressed the AP task as a classification problem by means of a Support Vector Machine. In line with the shared tasks on AP, as well as with most work in the state-of-the-art, we evaluated our approach using the *accuracy* measure.

---

[3] The sentence in the example was processed with LIWC. The word *Lovely* belongs to three categories: social, affect, and posemo. The word *comfortable* belongs to two categories: affect and posemo. The word *room* belongs to three categories: space, relativ, and home.

Table 1. Data distribution of the Author Profiling corpora.

	Blogs		Reviews		Tw14		SMedia		Tw17	
	Train	Test	Train	Test	Train	Test	Train	Test	Train	Test
Female	73	39	2,080	821	153	77	3873	1,688	1,800	1,200
Male	74	39	2,080	821	153	77	3873	1,688	1,800	1,200
18–24	6	10	360	148	20	12	1,550	680	-	-
25–34	60	24	1,000	400	88	56	2,098	900	-	-
35–49	54	32	1,000	400	130	58	2,246	980	-	-
50–64	23	10	1,000	400	60	26	1,838	790	-	-
65-xx	4	2	800	294	8	2	14	26	-	-
Total	147	78	4,160	1,642	306	154	7746	3376	3,600	2,400

3.3   Results

Comparing LIWC and GI

The purpose of this experiment is to evaluate the relevance of using psycholinguistic information in the AP task. We decided to take advantage of the *Category-based* representation by exploiting two settings: each dictionary individually (denoted as **GI** and **LIWC**, respectively) and by combining both resources into a single one (denoted as **GI+LIWC**). The first one allows to evaluate the performance of each resource at its own, while the second one also serves to analyze how complementary the dictionaries are. Table 2 shows the obtained results.

Table 2. Results from the *Category-based representation* (Rep 1).

	Gender					Age			
	Blogs	Reviews	Tw14	SMedia	Tw17	Blogs	Reviews	Tw14	SMedia
GI	0.602	**0.641**	**0.681**	0.499	0.608	0.333	**0.295**	0.389	0.263
LIWC	0.538	0.632	0.558	0.505	0.623	**0.384**	0.258	**0.402**	0.219
GI+LIWC	**0.628**	0.64	0.668	**0.514**	**0.715**	0.307	**0.295**	0.324	**0.285**

In general, results show that the categories of each dictionary contain words that help to reveal the profile of authors. Regarding the gender classification, GI slightly outperforms LIWC, whereas, for age classification, results indicate that both resources obtained the best performance in two collections. From these results, we can infer that these resources capture psycholinguistic information in a different way, which is highly related to the traits of profiles. For example, several categories of LIWC correspond to popular topics mentioned by people of a certain age range, such as *work*, *past*, and *home*. On the other hand, GI has a greater number of categories than LIWC, thus different dimensions are captured benefiting to the binary problem on gender identification.

Regarding the combination of the dictionaries, our results show that when both resources are used together, there is no a clear advantage with respect to using each dictionary on its own. This indicates that both resources are not complementary, maybe due to the redundancy (or overlap) of the words belonging to their categories. One example of this is the high overlap between the positive and negative effective categories from both dictionaries.

Combining Lexical and Psycholinguistic Information

As shown in the previous experiment, using only information from the dictionaries increases the probability of missing important clues for identifying users' profiles. On the other hand, it has been recognized that lexical features, such as word n-grams, are good discriminators of profiles. Nevertheless, many of them are not covered by the psycholinguistic dictionaries. One example are slang terms, which are very popular is social media texts. In order to take advantage of both kinds of information, the following experiments consider their combination by means of the *Term-category based representation* (referenced as **Rep2**), and the *Category-masked term-based representation* (denoted as **Rep3**). Both representations were instantiated with information from the GI and LIWC dictionaries. Table 3 shows the obtained results. It also shows two baseline results, namely, the results from the *Traditional term-based representation* (**Traditional**), as well as the best result from the *category-based representation* (**Rep1**), when using a single dictionary.

Table 3. Obtained results when combining lexical and psycholinguistic information, using the proposed representations.

	Gender				Age				
	Blogs	*Reviews*	*Tw14*	*SMedia*	*Tw17*	*Blogs*	*Reviews*	*Tw14*	*SMedia*
Traditional	0.576	0.704	0.623	0.530	0.768	0.346	0.315	0.357	0.308
Rep1	0.602	0.641	0.681	0.505	0.623	0.384	0.295	0.402	0.263
Rep2-GI	**0.705**	0.697	**0.681**	0.529	0.729	0.358	0.308	**0.402**	0.325
Rep2-LIWC	0.653	**0.708**	0.597	0.520	0.767	0.333	**0.316**	0.376	0.239
Rep3-GI	0.666	0.660	0.675	0.507	0.726	0.371	0.294	0.402	0.242
Rep3-LIWC	0.602	0.635	0.675	0.522	0.615	0.358	0.283	0.324	**0.335**

The results from Table 3 indicate that the combination of lexical and psycholinguistic information works. In 7 out of 9 collections, this combination outperformed the baseline results. It is also possible to notice that GI obtained slightly better results than LIWC, demonstrating its usefulness for the AP task. This advantage could be caused by its broader coverage of terms used in formal communications such as the ones from social media. Finally, these results show a clear disadvantage of the Rep 3 with respect to Rep 2, confirming the relevant role of lexical information for the task of AP in social media.

Comparison with State of the Art

As mentioned before, for comparison purposes we used the same datasets than in the PAN2014 and PAN2017 shared tasks. In Table 4 we present the obtained results[4]. Concerning to *Blogs* collection, we improved the best performing approach for gender classification. This is an encouraging result because of size of the collection, which represents a great challenge. Overall, the obtained results at the PAN2014 collections are very competitive against those from the shared task, particularly if we consider that the proposed approach is quite simple and straightforward. With respect to the PAN2017 collection (*Tw17*), we ranked on the 12th position, but our result is higher than the average performance of the share task participants. Furthermore, despite the simplicity of our approach, it showed a similar performance than other methods based on novel techniques such as word embeddings and deep learning[5]. For further details on the best ranked systems in the shared task, see [7] and [8] for the *2014* and *2017* editions, respectively.

Table 4. Comparison of the obtained results with the state of the art

Dataset	Gender				Age			
	BestTeam	AvgPerf	OurRes	Rank	BestTeam	AvgPerf	OurRes	Rank
Blogs	0.679	0.567	**0.705**	1	0.461	0.332	0.384	2
Reviews	0.725	0.606	0.708	2	0.35	0.274	0.316	5
Tw14	0.733	0.586	0.681	3	0.506	0.378	0.402	5
SMedia	0.542	0.524	0.529	5	0.365	0.307	0.335	6
Tw17	0.823	0.757	0.767	12	-	-	-	-

4 Analysis

Content Analysis. The purpose of this analysis is to explore the use of words from the different dictionaries' categories regarding to each profile trait. Specifically, we investigated what are the categories mostly used according to a profile group. For each dataset, we grouped the texts according to gender and age. Then,

---

[4] Table 4 shows the best performing approach in each dataset (in the 2nd column), the average performance of all the participating teams (3rd column), the higher accuracy achieved by our proposal (4th column), as well as the ranking corresponding to our best result (5th column).

[5] Just to mention, three of the methods exploiting such kind of approaches have accuracy rates around 0.78, only 0.02 above the best score achieved in our experiments.

we calculated the frequency of the words included in each category. Finally, we manually selected a subset of the most frequent categories and analyzed their content with respect to the each class.

In general, as it was expected, the categories most frequently used in each dataset comprise words referring to prepositions, pronouns, articles, adverbs, verbs, etc. We also observed that by using either of the dictionaries, it is possible to catch clues related to the use of personal information, that have been recognized as a key feature for AP [6]. Particularly, we observed several categories associated to some particular profiles. Table 5 summarizes the most frequent categories for each of the profile traits in the used datasets, showing some

Table 5. A subset of the most frequent categories used in the AP corpora.

Task	Resource	Category and some words included on it
Female	GI	Afill: *love, son, side, thank, friend, care, team, helpful, friendly*, etc.
		ABS: *need, think, right, idea, learn, reason, holiday, cause, pace*, etc.
	LIWC	percept: *ear, thin, hot, see, look, hear, feel, view, feeling, listen*, etc.
Male	GI	Means: *war, say, make, live, free, ready, hand, job, order, build*, etc.
		Strong: *king, own, win, able, great, make, gain, love, show, game*, etc.
		ECON: *job, business, price, money, tax, project, custom, company,* etc.
	LIWC	quant: *some, every, each, most, best, many, enough, worst, plenty,* etc.
18–24	GI	Overst: *just, great, right, last, always, amazing, full, quite, high*, etc.
		Afill
	LIWC	work: *staff, working, office, report, meeting, publish, interview*, etc.
		percept
25–34	GI	Afill, ECON, and Overst
	LIWC	quant
		achieve: *win, top, goal, lost, effect, gain, success, challenge, effort,* etc.
35–49	GI	ECON
		ECON@: *own, fee, rent, market, shop, social, fill, serve, import*, etc.
	LIWC	work
50–64	LIWC	home: *room, bath, family, garden, kitchen, studio, garage, door*, etc.
		motion: *walk, visit, trip, travel, went, move, arrived, walking, drive,* etc.
65–xx	GI	Afill and ABS
		Underst: *only, small, never, something, suggest, care, nothing*, etc.
	LIWC	home and achieve
		past: *ate, was, did, met, been, stayed, won, made, loved, went, told,* etc.

intuitive and interesting aspects. For example, regarding LIWC, words related to perceptual processes ("*percept*" category), such as *ear, thin, hair, look, feel,* and *eye,* are more used by female than by men. Instead, men use more quantifiers. According to GI, female use more words related to supportive ("*Afill*" category) than males. Similarly, terms related to economy (*rent, earn, shop,* etc.) tend to characterize people within 25–49 age range.

Discriminative Analysis. To deeply understand the contribution of the evaluated dictionaries, the most discriminative attributes were identified. For achieving it, information gain was calculated on the *Term-Category based representation* for each problem in each dataset. Table 6 shows some of the features with the highest information gain per dataset.

As it can be observed, word unigrams emerged as more relevant than bigrams or trigrams. There are some intuitive categories from GI appearing among the most discriminative for gender identification: "*Female*" and "*Male*", both contain words[6] referring to women/male and social roles associated to them. Some categories including words related to negation and negative feelings ("*negate*",

Table 6. Some of features with the highest information gain rate per dataset according to gender and age traits. Words in italic font represent lexical n-grams from Rep 2. Category tags are listed per dictionary.

Dataset	Top discriminative features	
	Gender	Age
Blogs	TERMS: *publish, sinc,* and *internet*	TERMS: *wife, husband,* and *love*
	GI: EnlOth, EnlTot, and Know	GI: Goal
	LIWC: work	
Reviews	TERMS: *wife, husband,* and *love*	TERMS: *amaz*
	GI: SklAsth, Our	GI: Self, Ovrst, and Strong
	LIWC: sexual, we	LIWC: i, pronoun, funct
Tw14	TERMS: *play, beat*	TERMS: *me, emoticon,* and *haha*
	GI: Know, Male, and Ovrst	GI: Self, NegAff
	LIWC: negate, negemo, tentav	LIWC: swear
SMedia	TERMS: *here, live,* and *2012*	TERMS: *me, individu,* and *repost*
	GI: Tool, IAV	GI: WltTot, MeansLw, Econ@
	LIWC: funct, incl	LIWC: quant, achieve
Tw17	TERMS: *love, my,* and *emoji*	
	GI: Female, AffOth	
	LIWC: i	

---

[6] Some terms included in these categories are: *aunt, girl, lady, bride, boy, dad, gentleman, son,* etc.

"*negemo*", and "*NegAff*") were identified as very discriminative for age identification. Furthermore, it is possible to observe that there are various categories ("*our*", "*self*", "*i*", and "*we*") reflecting personal pronouns found among the most relevant ones. It is also important to mention that there are some onomatopoeic expressions as well as non verbal elements used in social media for enriching written communication; ("*haha*", "*emoticon*", and "*emoji*") emerged as very discriminant (maybe for identifying young people). Such kinds of terms are hard to be found in dictionaries like LIWC or GI. This points out the relevance of combining lexical and psycholinguistic information for AP.

5   Conclusions

In this paper we assessed the performance of two psycholinguistic dictionaries in the AP task: Linguistic Inquirer and Word Count (LIWC) and General Inquirer (GI). The knowledge in such resources was exploited by three novel text representations attempting to capture psycholinguistic information for distinguishing the age and gender of a given user, by considering only her/his written texts. Several experiments were carried out, demonstrating the usefulness of taking advantage of psycholinguistic dictionaries as well as the viability of the proposed representations for AP. Particularly, this paper introduces the use of GI in AP. The results provide evidence that the categories in this resource allow to wrap peculiarities of users which help to profile classification.

The experimental evaluation showed that the categories from both dictionaries, LIWC and GI, incorporate relevant discriminative information for the AP task. However, we observed that there is not a clear evidence allowing to state than one is better than the other. Besides, it seems that they are not complementary resources. Each one captures information associated to specific traits of profiles (for example, GI outperformed LIWC in the gender problem, whereas the opposite happens in the age case). Finally, according to our findings, it can be stated that the combination of lexical and psycholinguistic information is very relevant for AP.

As future work, it could be interesting to incorporate the information coming from psycholinguistic dictionaries into systems considering other kinds of techniques, such as with deep learning and word embeddings. Furthermore, evaluating the performance of lexical resources available in different languages in a cross-lingual setting for Author Profiling is also matter of future work.

Acknowledgments. This research was funded by CONACYT (project FC 2016-2410 and postdoctoral fellowship CVU-174410).

References

1. Álvarez-Carmona, M.A., López-Monroy, A.P., Montes-y-Gómez, M., Villaseñor-Pineda, L., Meza, I.: Evaluating topic-based representations for author profiling in social media. In: Montes-y-Gómez, M., Escalante, H.J., Segura, A., Murillo, J.D. (eds.) IBERAMIA 2016. LNCS (LNAI), vol. 10022, pp. 151–162. Springer, Cham (2016). https://doi.org/10.1007/978-3-319-47955-2_13
2. Bartoli, A., De Lorenzo, A., Laderchi, A., Medvet, E., Tarlao, F.: An author profiling approach based on language-dependent content and stylometric features. In: 2015 Labs and Workshops, Notebook Papers. CEUR Workshop Proceedings (2015)
3. Basile, A., Dwyer, G., Medvedeva, M., Rawee, J., Haagsma, H., Nissim, M.: N-GrAM: new groningen author-profiling model. CoRR abs/1707.03764 (2017)
4. Bayot, R.K., Gonçalves, T.: Author profiling using SVMs and word embedding averages. In: Working Notes of CLEF 2016 - Conference and Labs of the Evaluation forum, Évora, Portugal, 5–8 September 2016, pp. 815–823 (2016)
5. Marquardt, J., et al.: Age and gender identification in social media. In: 2014 Labs and Workshops, Notebook Papers. CEUR Workshop Proceedings (2014)
6. Ortega-Mendoza, R.M., López-Monroy, A.P., Franco-Arcega, A., Montes-y-Gómez, M.: Emphasizing personal information for author profiling: new approaches for term selection and weighting. Knowl.-Based Syst. **145**, 169–181 (2018)
7. Pardo, F.M.R., et al.: Overview of the author profiling task at PAN 2014. In: Working Notes for CLEF 2014 Conference, pp. 898–927 (2014)
8. Pardo, F.M.R., Rosso, P., Potthast, M., Stein, B.: Overview of the 5th author profiling task at PAN 2017: gender and language variety identification in Twitter. In: Working Notes of CLEF - Conference and Labs of the Evaluation Forum (2017)
9. Pennebaker, J.W., Francis, M.E., Booth, R.J.: Linguistic Inquiry and Word Count: LIWC 2001, vol. 71. Lawrence Erlbaum Associates, Mahway (2001)
10. Posadas-Durán, J.P., et al.: Syntactic N-grams as features for the author profiling task: notebook for PAN at CLEF 2015. In: CLEF (2015)
11. Stone, P.J., Hunt, E.B.: A computer approach to content analysis: studies using the general inquirer system. In: Proceedings of the May 21–23, 1963, Spring Joint Computer Conference, AFIPS 1963 (Spring), pp. 241–256. ACM (1963)

Abstractive Multi-Document Text Summarization Using a Genetic Algorithm

Verónica Neri Mendoza, Yulia Ledeneva$^{(\boxtimes)}$ (iD),
and René Arnulfo García-Hernández (iD)

Autonomous University of the State of Mexico,
Instituto Literario No. 100, 50000 Toluca, Mexico
veronica.nerimendoz@gmail.com, yledeneva@yahoo.com,
renearnulfo@hotmail.com

Abstract. Multi-Document Text Summarization (MDTS) consists of generating an abstract from a group of two or more number of documents that represent only the most important information of all documents. Generally, the objective is to obtain the main idea of several documents on the same topic. In this paper, we propose a new MDTS method based on a Genetic Algorithm (GA). The fitness function is calculated considering two text features: sentence position and coverage. We propose the binary coding representation, selection, crossover and mutation operators to improve the state-of-the-art results. We test the proposed method on DUC02 data set, specifically, on Abstractive Multi-Document Text Summarization (AMDST) task demonstrating the improvement over the state-of-art methods. Four different tasks for each of the 59 collection of documents (in total 567 documents) are tested. In addition, we test different configurations of the most used methodology to generate AMDST summaries. Moreover, different heuristics such as topline, baseline, baseline-random and lead baseline are calculated. The proposed method for AMDTS demonstrates the improvement over the state-of-art methods and heuristics.

Keywords: Multi-Document Text Summarization (MDTS) ·
Language-independent methods · MDTS methodology · Genetic algorithm ·
Heuristics

1 Introduction

The extensive use of Internet has caused the enormous growth in the usage of digital information. Currently, there are a great variety of users of online information services with a huge amount of unstructured digital information [9, 18]. The user accesses the information through queries, but the precision is always an issue due to the information overload. One way to resolve this issue is by generating summaries [6, 12].

The general process of summarization consists of rewriting the full text into a brief version [19]. Automatic Text Summarization (ATS) is a task of Natural Language Processing (NLP). ATS consists in selecting the most important units which could be paragraphs, sentences, part of sentences or keywords from a document or collection of documents using the state-of-the-arts methods or commercial systems.

© Springer Nature Switzerland AG 2019
J. A. Carrasco-Ochoa et al. (Eds.): MCPR 2019, LNCS 11524, pp. 422–432, 2019.
https://doi.org/10.1007/978-3-030-21077-9_39

ATS methods can be abstractive or extractive. In the abstractive text summarization, the summaries are composed from fusing and generating new text that describes the most important facts [10]. In the extractive text summarization, the sentences or other parts of a text are extracted and concatenated to compose a summary [14, 18].

Depending on the number of documents, summarization techniques can be classified in two tasks: Single-Document Text Summarization (SDTS) and MDTS. The main goal of the MDTS is to allow to the users to have an overview about the topics and important information that exists in collection of documents within relatively a short time [1, 3, 22]. The MDTS has gained interest since mid-1990s [4], starting with the development of evaluation programs such as Document Understanding Conferences (DUC) [23] and Text Analysis Conferences (TAC) [26].

In this paper, we consider the methodology for building the final summary that considers all sentences of all documents [2, 18, 21, 29]. In this paper, a new MDTS method based on a GA is proposed.

The organization of the paper is as follows: the Sect. 2 describes the proposed method. The Sect. 3 shows experimental configuration and results. Finally, in the Sect. 4 the conclusions are presented.

2 Proposed Method

2.1 Pre-processing

The proposed method consists of three steps. In the first step, the documents of the collection were chronologically ordered, then the original text is adapting to the entry of the format of the GA, where the original text is separated in sentences. Also, the text pre-processing is applied to the collection of documents. Firstly, the text was divided into words separated by commas, then some tags were placed in the text to be able to differentiate quantities, emails, among others, and finally the lexical analysis is carried out [8, 20].

2.2 Text Model

The goal of text modeling is to predict the probability of natural word sequences. It assigns high probability on word sequences that occur, and low probability on word sequences that never occur. The simplest and most successful form for text modeling is the n-gram model. n-gram is defined as a subsequence of consecutive elements in a given sequence [15, 20].

2.3 Genetic Algorithm

The basic configuration of GA is defined as follows [5]: the initial population is randomly generated, while the population of other generations are generated from some selection/reproduction procedure. The search process terminates when a termination criterion is met. Otherwise a new generation will be produced, and the search process continues. The termination criterion can be selected as a maximum number of generations, or the convergence of the genotypes of the individuals. Genetic operators are constructed according to the problem to be solved, so the crossover operator has been applied to the generation of summaries.

Encoding. The binary encoding is used for each individual, where each sentence of the document constitutes a gene. The values 1 and 0 determine if the sentence will appear or no in the final summary. The initial population is randomly generated [8, 20].

Selection Operator. *Roulette* selects individuals from a population according to their aptitude, and is intended to select stronger individuals (with greater value in the fitness function) [20].

Crossover Operator. This operator has been used in [8]. It was designed for ATS, where each individual represents a selection of sentences. The process of cross over is randomly select parents, only those with genes with a value of 1, and this value is assigned to the new individual. Genes with a value of 1 in both parents will be more likely to be chosen. To meet the condition of the summary, a gene is selected to be part of a new individual, the number of words is counted [20].

Mutation Operator. This operator performs the mutation according to a certain probability as described in [8, 20].

Stop Condition. The stop condition that was applied for the term of the GA is the maximum number of generations. For the execution of the GA, consideration must be given to the number of words that the summary must have. In this case, the lengths of 10, 50, 100 and 200 words were used.

The number of individuals and the number of generations are automatically calculated by the GA through the Eqs. 1 and 2 respectively. The number of individuals is determined by the number of sentences that the document contains by means of the following equation [20]:

$$Number\ individuals = Number\ Sentences * 2 \tag{1}$$

The number of generations is calculated trough the following equation:

$$Number\ Generations = 4 * 15 * Number\ Sentences \tag{2}$$

Fitness Function. The fitness function was used in the method [8, 20]. In this fitness function are evaluated two features, position sentences and coverage. The main idea is that if all the sentences (see the Eq. 3) had the same importance, it is could draw a line with the points that make up those coordinates as it is showed in Eq. 4.

$$\{X_1, X_2, X_3, \ldots X_n\} \tag{3}$$

$$\{(X_1, y), (X_2, y), (X_3, y), \ldots (X_n, y)\} \tag{4}$$

The idea for assigning more importance for the first sentences, would be consider the first sentence with the importance X_n, the second with importance $X_n - 1$.

Since the placement of the line indicates its importance, the midpoint of that line can be used to determine the slope of the line; thus, softening the importance of sentences. This would allow us to know how important a sentence is with respect to the following. For this can use the general equation of the slope of the line.

For a text with n sentences, if the sentence i is selected for the summary then its relevance is defined as $t(i-x)+x$, where $x = 1+(n-1)/2$ and t is the slope to be discovered. With the objective to normalize the measurement of the position of the sentence (*Sentence Importance*), the importance of the first k sentences is calculated, where k is the number of selected sentences. Then the formula to calculate the importance of the first sentences would be as follows:

$$Sentence\ importance = \frac{\sum_{|c_i|}^{n} = 1^{t(i-x)+x}}{\sum_{j=1}^{k} t(j-x)+1}, x = 1+\frac{(n-1)}{2} \qquad (5)$$

However, it is not the only value by which the GA should be governed since it would try to obtain only the first sentences. It is also necessary to evaluate that the summary has different ideas, that is, it is not repetitive, but at the same time it has important words (*Precision − Recall*). To measure both things the fitness function makes the summation of the frequencies of the n-grams that the summary weigh how significant are the n-grams obtained is the same but considering the original text, in this case only the most frequent n-grams according to the number of minimum words. This weighing are Precision and Recall. Precision defines as a sum of the frequencies of the n-grams consider the original text, expressed as follows:

$$\sum Original\ text\ frequency \qquad (6)$$

Recall defines as a sum of the frequencies of the different n-grams of summary:

$$\sum Frequency\ Summary \qquad (7)$$

Therefore, the formula for obtaining Precision-Recall is:

$$Presicion - Recall = \frac{\sum Original\ text\ frequency}{\sum Frequency\ Summary} \qquad (8)$$

Finally, to obtain the value of the fitness function, the following formula is applied, which is multiplied by 1000.

$$FA = Presicion\_Recall * Sentence\ Importance * 1000 \qquad (9)$$

3   Experimental Results

We test the proposed method based on the MDTS using the dataset provided in DUC [23]. We use ROUGE[1] to evaluate the proposed method, which is widely applied by DUC for performance evaluation [16]. It measures the performance of a summary by counting the unit overlaps between the candidate summary and two reference summaries.

Dataset. In order to empirically evaluate the summarization results, DUC02 dataset is used. This corpus contains 59 clusters of news texts documents, every cluster contains from 5 to 14 text documents. The summary lengths are 10, 50, 100, and 200 words [17].

Experiment Configuration. In each experiment, we followed the standard sequence of steps explained in the Sect. 2. The Table 1 presents the best obtained result of the proposed method with different slop value, for four different summary lengths, and selection operator *(Roulette)*. The sentence selection considered parameter is *k-best +first* which consists in selecting the first sentences of the text, until the desired size of the summary is reached [13, 14].

In the Sects. 3.1, 3.2 and 3.3, we describe and compare the best obtained results of the proposed method to the state-of-the-art methods, commercial systems and heuristics.

3.1   Description of the State-of-the-Art Methods

R2N2 [6]: Recursive Neural Networks (R2N2) to rank sentences for MDTS were presented. This is a supervised method because analyzes the syntactic structure of an input sentence and produces a sentence parse tree. The R2N2 are used to automatically learn ranking features over parsing tree, and used features as POS, named entity, sentence depth, among other. Two sentence selection methods were used: **R2N2_G:** uses greedy algorithm G which selects the most salient sentences with a similarity threshold. **R2N2_ILP:** The sentence selection is based on Integer Linear Programming (ILP). ILP is intended to find the global optimum. In addition to the previous selection methods in [6] were used three support machine regression baselines: **UR:** Unigram regression with G selection. **SR:** Sentence regression with G selection. **U+SR:** ILP method assigns weights to the words of the sentences that are measured by related regressions.

LexRank [29]: It computes sentence importance based on the concept of centrality in a graph representation of sentences. In this model, a connectivity matrix based on intra sentence cosine similarity is used.

WF (Word Frequency) [18]: The sentences that contains the words with the most frequency from the source document (without stop-words) are considered for the final summary. **TE** (Textual Entailment) [18]: It consists of using textual implication in ATS that has been considered as a useful approach for obtaining a preliminary summary,

---

[1] ROUGE (Recall-Oriented Understudy for Gisting Evaluation) version 1.5.5.

Table 1. The best obtained results with several parameters of the proposed method.

Summary length	Value of slope	Selection operator	Elitism	Results		
				Recall	Precision	F-measure
10 words	−0.20	Roulette	3	16.312	15.465	15.840
50 words	−0.70	Roulette	3	28.383	28.170	28.268
100 words	−0.70	Roulette	3	35.377	35.063	35.214
200 words	−0.72	Roulette	3	42.728	42.332	42.526

where the sentences have not associated with any other sentence of document. **TE + WF** [18]: This method applies prior recognition of the textual entailment as a previous step to the words frequency in the summarization process.

GS, Knapsack, ILP [21]: This work considers tree inference global algorithms, the first is a greedy approximate method **GS**, the second is a dynamic programming approach based on solutions to the knapsack problem **Knapsack**, and the third is an exact algorithm that uses an Integer Linear Programming formulation of the problem **ILP**.

MFS (Maximal Frequent Sequences) [11]: This method analyses several options for language-independent features and corresponding term weighting feature based on units larger than one word.

3.2 Description of Heuristics

Topline [25]: It is a heuristic that allows to obtain the maximum value that any state-of-the-art method can achieve due to the lack of concordance between evaluators, since it selects sentences considering one or several gold-standard summaries.

Baseline-First [25]: It is a heuristic that take the first sentence in the 1st, 2nd, 3rd, etc. document collection in chronological sequence until you have the target summary size.

Baseline-Random [25]: It is the state-of-the-art heuristic that randomly selects sentences to present them as an extractive summary to the user.

Baseline-First-Document: It is a heuristic that take the first sentences in the 1st document of a document collection, until you have the target summary size. This heuristic is proposed in this work.

Lead Baseline [18]: It is a heuristic that take the first 10, 50, 100, and 200 words in the last document in the collection, where documents are assumed to be chronologically ordered.

3.3 Description of Systems

Svhoong Summarizer [12]: This system is available online. The text should be copied to the web page. The final summary is the text underlined in the same page.

Pertinence Summarize [12]: This system is available online. For each document, Pertinence automatically calculates percentages depending on the number of words in the document.

Tool4noobs Summarizer [12]: This system is available online and it uses three steps: extraction of text, identification of the key-words, and identification of sentences and generation of summary.

Copernic Summarizer [12]: The system was exclusively developed for the generation of automatic summaries. The version 2.1 was used on the Microsoft Windows operating system.

Microsoft Office Word Summarizer [12]: This system can be found in versions of Microsoft Office Word 2003 and Microsoft Office Word 2007.

3.4 Experimental Results (4 MDTS Tasks)

It is considered that any method can be worse than randomly choosing sentences (baseline-random), so the advance of baseline-random can be recalculated as 0%. The best possible performance is called topline and it is considered as 100% of advance. Using baseline-random and topline is possible to recalculate F-measure results in order to see the advance compared to the worst and the best results. In the Tables 2, 3, 4 and 5, the results of F-measure of ROUGE-1, ROUGE-2 and Advance are presented.

10 Words Task: The summary length of this task is 10 words. This task is rarely tested in the state-of-the-art, because of the difficulties related to find less words to describe the most important information. We calculate all heuristics: topline, baseline-first, baseline-random, baseline-first-document and lead-baseline (see Table 2) where we show the results of all state-of-art method and heuristics. The topline shows an enormous margin which exists between the best method and the best possible result to obtain. The difference is 62.09%. We hope that these experimental results serve as a reference for the future works.

Table 2. Comparison of the results to other methods for 10 words.

Type of Method	Method	ROUGE-1	ROUGE-2	Advance (%)
Unsupervised methods	Proposed	15.840	3.699	27.50%
Heuristics	Topline	37.636	16.732	100%
	Baseline-first	18.970	5.994	37.91%
	Baseline-first-document	18.970	5.994	37.91%
	Lead baseline	12.869	3.675	17.62%
	Baseline-random	7.570	1.226	0%

50 Words Task: The summary length of this task is 50 words. Several state-of-the-art unsupervised methods are 5 heuristics are presented in Table 3 (3 are calculated in the state-of-the-art: topline, baseline-first and baseline-random, and 2 heuristics are calculated in this paper: baseline-first-document and lead-baseline). In the Table 3, we see that the proposed method overcome the results of all state-of-art method and heuristics. As topline heuristic shows an extensive margin exists between the best method and the best possible result to obtain. The difference is 68.79%.

Table 3. Comparison of the results to other methods for 50 words.

Type of method	Method	ROUGE-1	ROUGE-2	Advance (%)
Unsupervised methods	Proposed	28.268	6.084	31.21%
	ILP [21]	28.100	5.800	30.42%
	Knapsack [21]	27.900	5.900	29.48%
	GS [21]	26.800	5.100	24.34%
Heuristics	Topline [25]	42.967	16.084	100%
	Baseline-first [25]	26.939	5.241	24.99%
	Baseline-first-document	25.286	4.331	17.25%
	Lead baseline	22.587	3.733	4.62%
	Baseline-random [25]	21.599	2.298	0%

100 Words Task: The summary length of this task is 100 words. The task of 100 words summary length is the most tested in the state-of-the-art. We can see several unsupervised and supervised methods, commercial tools, heuristic calculated in the state-of-the-art such as topline, baseline-first and baseline-random, and heuristics calculated in this paper such as baseline-first-document and lead baseline. In the Table 4, we see that the proposed method overcome the results of the state-of-art method, heuristics and commercial systems. However, only one supervised method from [2] overcome results of the proposed method, our conclusion is because the usage of language-dependent features. As topline result shows, an enormous margin exists between the best method and the best possible result to obtain. The difference is 55.47%. The summaries of commercial systems were provided by the authors and were evaluated.

Table 4. Comparison of the results to other methods for 100 words.

Type of method	Method	ROUGE-1	ROUGE-2	Advance (%)
Unsupervised methods	Proposed	35.214	8.145	31.41%
	LexRank [29]	35.090	7.510	30.82%
	Knapsack [21]	34.800	7.300	29.44%
	ILP [21]	34.600	7.200	28.48%
	GS [21]	33.000	6.800	20.84%
	MFS [11]	32.640	5.987	19.12%
	WF [18]	29.620	5.200	4.69%
Supervised methods	R2N2_ILP [2]	37.960	8.800	44.53%
	R2N2_G [2]	36.840	8.520	39.18%
	Ur + Sr [2]	35.130	8.020	31.01%
	Sr [2]	34.230	7.810	26.71%
	Ur [2]	34.160	7.660	26.38%
	TE + WF [18]	31.333	5.780	12.87%

(continued)

Table 4. (*continued*)

Type of method	Method	ROUGE-1	ROUGE-2	Advance (%)
Heuristics	Topline [25]	49.570	18.998	100%
	Baseline-first [25]	33.385	7.042	22.68%
	Baseline-first-document	30.170	5.326	7.32%
	Lead baseline	28.770	5.097	0.63%
	Baseline-random [25]	28.637	3.798	0%
Commercial systems	Copernic [12]	32.489	5.692	18.40%
	Svhoong [12]	31.555	6.121	13.93%
	Word 2007 XP [12]	29.383	5.930	3.56%
	Word 2003 7 [12]	28.792	5.055	0.74%
	Word 2003 XP [12]	28.792	5.055	0.74%
	Word 2003 Vista [12]	28.792	5.055	0.74%
	Word 2007 Vista [12]	28.713	6.172	0.36%
	Word 2007 7 [12]	28.284	4.975	0.36%
	Pertinence [12]	27.377	3.495	−6.01%
	Tool4noobs [12]	26.688	3.143	−9.31%

200 Words Task: The summary length of this task is 200 words. Several unsupervised and supervised methods, and 4 heuristics calculated in the state-of-the-art such as topline, baseline-first, lead baseline and baseline-random and 1 heuristic calculated in this paper is baseline-first-document. In the Table 5, we see that the proposed method overcome the results of all the state-of-art methods and heuristics. The topline result shows an extensive margin exists between the best method and the best possible result to obtain. The difference is 67.37%. We logically understand that the MDST task needs the summary of more length, so our proposed method could find the most important ideas to compose the summary and obtain the best result in the task where the summary of bigger length is required.

Table 5. Comparison of the results to other methods for 200 words.

Type of method	Method	ROUGE-1	ROUGE-2	Advance (%)
Unsupervised methods	Proposed	42.617	11.67	32.63%
	ILP [21]	41.500	10.300	27.06%
	Knapsack [21]	41.200	10.000	25.57%
	GS [21]	40.100	9.500	20.08%
Supervised method	TE + WF [18]	37.762	8.004	8.42%
Heuristics	Topline [25]	56.120	23.682	100%
	Baseline-first [25]	41.118	10.362	25.16%
	Baseline-first-document	36.739	8.042	3.31%
	Baseline-random [25]	36.074	6.308	0%
	Lead-baseline [25]	34.716	6.497	−6.77%

4 Conclusions

In this paper, we proposed the method for AMDTS based on GA. The fitness function was calculated considered sentence position and coverage. We proposed the binary coding representation, selection, crossover and mutation operators. Four different tasks for each of the 59 collection of documents of DUC02 data set (specifically AMDST task) were tested. We tested different configurations of the most used methodology to generate AMDST summaries. Moreover, different heuristics such as topline, baseline, baseline-random and lead baseline were calculated. The proposed method for AMDTS demonstrates the improvement over the state-of-art methods and heuristics.

As future work we will use more language-independent features as redundancy reduction, sentence length and similarity with the title [28]. Also, we will consider other text models like sn-grams [27] and MFS [7], and other language [24].

References

1. Bakkar, H., et al.: Multi-document summarizer (2018)
2. Cao, Z., Wei, F., Dong, L., Li, S., Zhou, M.: Ranking with recursive neural networks and its application to multi-document summarization, vol. 7 (2015)
3. Carbonell, J., Goldstein, J.: The use of MMR, diversity-based reranking for reordering documents and producing summaries. In: SIGIR 1998, pp. 335–336 ACM Press, New York (1998)
4. Das, D., Martins, A.F.T.: A survey on automatic text summarization (2007)
5. Du, K.L., Swamy, M.N.S.: Search and optimization by metaheuristics: techniques and algorithms inspired by nature (2016)
6. Ferreira, R., et al.: A multi-document summarization system based on statistics and linguistic treatment. Expert Syst. Appl. **41**(13), 5780–5787 (2014)
7. García-Hernández, R.A., Martínez-Trinidad, J.F., Carrasco-Ochoa, J.A.: A new algorithm for fast discovery of maximal sequential patterns in a document collection. In: Gelbukh, A. (ed.) CICLing 2006. LNCS, vol. 3878, pp. 514–523. Springer, Heidelberg (2006). https://doi.org/10.1007/11671299_53
8. García-Hernández, R.A., Ledeneva, Y.: Single extractive text summarization based on a genetic algorithm. In: Carrasco-Ochoa, J.A., Martínez-Trinidad, J.F., Rodríguez, J.S., di Baja, G.S. (eds.) MCPR 2013. LNCS, vol. 7914, pp. 374–383. Springer, Heidelberg (2013). https://doi.org/10.1007/978-3-642-38989-4_38
9. Kaushik, A., Naithani, S.: A comprehensive study of text mining approach (2016)
10. Kumar Bharti, S., et al.: Automatic keyword extraction for text summarization in multi-document e-newspapers articles (2017)
11. Ledeneva, Y., García-Hernández, R., Gelbukh, A.: Multi-document summarization using maximal frequent sequences, vol. 47, pp. 15–24 (2010). ISSN 1870-4069
12. Ledeneva, Y., et al.: Experimenting with maximal frequent sequences for multi-document summarization, vol. 45, pp. 233–244 (2010). ISSN 1870-4069
13. Ledeneva, Y., Gelbukh, A., García-Hernández, R.A.: Terms derived from frequent sequences for extractive text summarization. In: Gelbukh, A. (ed.) CICLing 2008. LNCS, vol. 4919, pp. 593–604. Springer, Heidelberg (2008). https://doi.org/10.1007/978-3-540-78135-6_51

14. Ledeneva, Y.N., García-Hernández, R.A.: Generación automática de resúmenes - Retos, propuestas y experimentos (2017)
15. Ledeneva, Y.N., Gelbukh, A.: Automatic Language-Independent Detection of Multiword Descriptions for Text Summarization. Instituto Politécnico Nacional (2013)
16. Lin, C.-Y.: ROUGE: a package for automatic evaluation of summaries, vol. 34, no. 12, pp. 1213–1220 (2011)
17. Lin, H., Bilmes, J.: Multi-document summarization via budgeted maximization of submodular functions, 912–920 (2010)
18. Lloret, E., et al.: Incorporating textual entailment recognition in single-and multi-document summarization systems (2008)
19. Mani, I., Bloedorn, E.: Multi-document summarization by graph search and matching (1997)
20. Matías, M.G.A.: Generación Automática De Resúmenes Usando Algoritmos Genéticos. Universidad Autónoma del Estado de México (2013)
21. McDonald, R.: A study of global inference algorithms in multi-document summarization. In: Amati, G., Carpineto, C., Romano, G. (eds.) ECIR 2007. LNCS, vol. 4425, pp. 557–564. Springer, Heidelberg (2007). https://doi.org/10.1007/978-3-540-71496-5_51
22. Nayeem, M.T., Chali, Y.: Extract with order for coherent multi-document summarization (2017)
23. Over, P., Dang, H.: DUC in context. Inf. Process. Manag. **43**(6), 1506–1520 (2007)
24. Rojas-Simón, J., Ledeneva, Y., García-Hernández, R.A.: Calculating the upper bounds for portuguese automatic text summarization using genetic algorithm. In: Simari, G.R., Fermé, E., Gutiérrez Segura, F., Rodríguez Melquiades, J.A. (eds.) IBERAMIA 2018. LNCS (LNAI), vol. 11238, pp. 442–454. Springer, Cham (2018). https://doi.org/10.1007/978-3-030-03928-8_36
25. Rojas Simón, J., et al.: Calculating the upper bounds for multi-document summarization using genetic algorithms. Comput. Sist. **22**, 1 (2018)
26. Saggion, H., Poibeau, T.: Automatic text summarization: past, present and future. In: Poibeau, T., Saggion, H., Piskorski, J., Yangarber, R. (eds.) Multi-source, Multilingual Information Extraction and Summarization, pp. 3–21. Springer, Heidelberg (2013). https://doi.org/10.1007/978-3-642-28569-1_1
27. Sidorov, G.: N-gramas sintácticos no-continuos. Polibits **48**, 69–78 (2013)
28. Vázquez, E., et al.: Sentence features relevance for extractive text summarization using genetic algorithms. J. Intell. Fuzzy Syst. **35**(1), 353–365 (2018)
29. Wang, D., et al.: Multi-document summarization using sentence-based topic models. In: ACL and AFNLP, p. 297 (2010)

Soft Bigram Similarity to Identify Confusable Drug Names

Christian Eduardo Millán-Hernández⬤,
René Arnulfo García-Hernández(✉)⬤, Yulia Ledeneva⬤,
and Ángel Hernández-Castañeda⬤

Autonomous University of State of Mexico, 50000 Toluca, Mexico
ceduardo.millan@gmail.com, renearnulfo@hotmail.com,
yledeneva@yahoo.com, angelhc2305@gmail.com

Abstract. Look-alike and Sound-alike drug names are related to medication errors where doctors, nurses, and pharmacists prescribe and administer the wrong medication. Bisim similarity is reported as the best orthographic measure to identifying confusable drug names, but it lacks from a similarity scale between the bigrams of a drug name. In this paper, we propose a Soft-Bisim similarity measure that extends to the Bisim to soften the comparison scale between the Bigrams of a drug name for improving the detection of confusable drug names. In the experimentation, Soft-Bisim outperforms others 17 similarity measures for 396,900 pairs of drug names. In addition, the average of four measures is outperformed when Bisim is replaced by Soft-Bisim similarity.

Keywords: LASA drug names · N-gram similarity · Orthographic similarity

1 Introduction

A medication error that involves confusable drug names occurs as result of weak medication system and human errors-related factors [1–3]. Many human factors are related to the Look-Alike and Sound-Alike drug names (LASA) problem like visual perception error, auditory perception error, short term memory error, and motor control are errors. However, the similarity between confusable drug names is a detectable root-cause. Drug names like *cycloserine* and *cyclosporine* are involved in LASA errors. LASA pairs normally sound similar and have a similar spelling [4]. Sometimes the confusion happens when the names are communicated in prescriptions handwritten, for example, the drugs *Avandia* and *Coumadin* [5]. In other cases, the confusion occurs in verbal communication when the pronunciation sounds similar. For example, *Zantac* and *Xanax* [6].

Nowadays, the Institute for Safe Medication Practice (ISMP) publishes a list that contains LASA pairs that were previously reported [7–10]. Regulatory agencies, including the Food and Drug Administration (FDA), the World Health Organization (WHO), and the Joint Commission are implementing strategies to identify and to prevent a LASA error.

String-matching algorithms are used to measure the distance or the similarity between two drug names and to identify a priori potential confused drug names. For

© Springer Nature Switzerland AG 2019
J. A. Carrasco-Ochoa et al. (Eds.): MCPR 2019, LNCS 11524, pp. 433–442, 2019.
https://doi.org/10.1007/978-3-030-21077-9_40

example, *Edit Distance* (ED) measures the minimum of the insertion, elimination and substitution operations to transform a string to another [11]. For example, the LASA pair *cycloserine* and *cyclosporine* has a distance of two because there are needed at least two edit operations (a substitution $p{\rightarrow}e$ and an elimination of letter o) to transform *cycloserine* in *cyclosporine*.

Longest Common Subsequence (LCS) measures the maximum possible length of the longest common subsequences between two drug names. NLCS represents the Normalization of LCS that is obtained by dividing the maximum length of the longest drug name. In the previous example, /cyclos-rine/ is the LCS and the NLCS is 0.833. NLCS presents a weakness to ignore subsequences that does not represent a similarity between drug names. For example, the no-LASA pair *Benadryl* and *Cardura* have the LCS /adr/ [6].

Ngram similarity represents a drug name as the set of all its contiguous subsequences (grams) of size n [12, 13]. For example, the bigrams for the LASA pair *cycloserine* and *cyclosporine* are {*cy, yc, cl, lo, os, se, er, ri, in, ne*} and {*cy, yc, cl, lo, os, sp, po, or, ri, in, ne*}, respectively. In this case, eight bigrams are shared, and the number of bigrams is 10 and 11, respectively. Therefore, the similarity is $(2 \times 8)/(10+11) = 0.762$. However, the Ngram similarity of the LASA pair *Verelan* and *Virilon* is zero [6].

Nsim similarity [14] extends to NLCS but it manages the n-grams of a drug name with a scale of similarity. The predefined scale of similarity between a pair of n-grams is computed by counting the identical matching letters in each position and normalized by n. *Bisim* is a specific case of *Nsim* with a predefined scale of similarity. For example, the bigrams *cy* and *cy* have a similarity of $2/2 = 1$ and the bigrams *se* and *sp* of $1/2 = 0.5$. The similarity scale presents a weakness when computes values for bigrams like *sp* and *ps*, or *sp* and *es*; because it misplaces completely the common letters in previous or next positions. This issue is a common root-cause when a visual or auditory perception error happens [15–17]. Even the pairs of bigrams {*aa*}{*aa*} and {*ac*}{*ac*} computes the same similarity, it is clear that in the first example the letter a match all the letters of the bigrams showing a higher similarity. In this manner, commonalities characteristics that are presented in LASA pairs [18] needs to be considered to adjust a softened similarity scale.

In this paper, we propose a new softened similarity measure based on Bisim that increase the accuracy to identify LASA pairs. For this, different cases that form the scale of bigrams are identified, and a proposed methodology based on an evolutionary algorithm to soften the scale of the similarity is described. Therefore, this paper is based on the hypothesis that an evolutionary approach can adjust better the weights of the scale of similarity between n-grams.

2 Definitions

String matching algorithms recover the common correspondences between the drug names that are used to determinate a similarity or a distance measure. Measures are classified as distance (as closer to zero as more related are the names) or similarity (as greater is the value as more related are the names). A normalized similarity/distance measure keeps a scale between different similarity values.

Similarity and distance measures detect the particular look-alike (orthographic cause) and sound-alike (phonetic case) issue. In this sense, the measures are classified as orthographic or phonetic in relation to the used approach to detect the confusion.

2.1   Orthographic Distance Measures

Edit distance (ED). Given the drug names X and Y as sequences of size n and m, respectively, ED (also called *Levenshtein*) refers to the minimum cost of editing operations (insertion, deletion and substitution) to convert the sequence X into Y [11, 19–21]. In this paper, all editing operations have a cost of 1. In this case, the edit distance between X and Y is given by edit (n, m) computed by the following recurrence:

$$edit(i,j) = \begin{cases} max(i,j) & i = 0 \vee j = 0 \\ edit(i-1,j-1) & x_i = y_j \\ min \begin{cases} edit(i-1,j)+1 \\ edit(i,j-1)+1 \\ edit(i-1,j-1)+cs(x_i,y_i) \end{cases} & x_i \neq y_j \end{cases} \tag{1}$$

A Normalized ED (NED). NED is computed by dividing the ED between the length of the longer sequence [6, 21–25].

2.2   Orthographic Similarity Measures

Prefix Similarity. Given the drug names X and Y as sequences of size m and n respectively, *Prefix* represents the ratio of the longest contiguous common initial letters [6], see Eq. 2. The common prefix for drug names *Accutane* and *Accolate* is Acc ($|Acc| = 3$), and the normalized prefix similarity is 0.375.

$$Prefix(X,Y) = \frac{|x_1 = y_1, x_2 = y_2, \ldots, x_i = y_i|}{max(X,Y)} \tag{2}$$

N-gram Similarity. Represents a sequence of the set of all its contiguous subsequences (grams) of size n [12]. For example, if $|X| = m$ and $n = 2$ (bigrams), then $X' = \{x_1x_2, x_2x_3, \ldots, x_{m-1}x_m\}$ [6, 14, 26]. Given the sequences X and Y, the *n-gram similarity* is defined as the *Dice similarity* [27] between the sets X' and Y' in the next way:

$$Dice\left(X', Y'\right) = \frac{2|X' \cap Y'|}{|X'| + |Y'|} \tag{3}$$

N-gram similarity presents a weakness because it is well-known that the prefixes and suffixes of the drug names are involved in their confusion [6, 18]. For increasing the sensitivity of the *N-gram similarity* some variations with respect to initial and final letters area applied. Lambert [14] proposes to add spaces (or a letter not included in the names) (B)efore and (A)fter in both drug names to make that the initial or final letters appear in one or more *n*-grams. Lambert experimented with the variants of Bigram-(1B, 1A, 1B1A and 1A) and Trigram-(1B, 1A, 1B1A, 2B, 2A, 2B2A, 1B2A and 2B1A) [14, 17, 28].

Normalized LCS (NLCS). *NLCS* similarity lets to maintain an order in the common matching letters. Given the sequences X and Y of size n and m, respectively, the *NLCS similarity* is defined as the ratio of the length of the longest common subsequences between X and Y, $NLCS = |lcs(n, m)|/max(m, n)$, where $lcs(n, m)$ can be calculated by the recurrence in Eq. (4) [6, 14, 23–25, 29].

$$lcs(i, j) = \begin{cases} 0, & i = 0 \vee j = 0 \\ lcs(i - 1, j - 1) + 1, & x_i = y_j \\ max(lcs(i, j - 1), lcs(i - 1, j)) & x_i \neq y_j \end{cases} \quad (4)$$

Nsim Similarity. It is proposed by Kondrak [6, 23, 24] and it combines features implemented by grams of size β, non-crossing-links constraints and the first letter it is repeated at the begging of the drug name. A specific case of *Nsim* is the measure *Bisim* [6]. Given the sequences (with the first repeated letter) X and Y representing the drug names of size n and m, respectively, *Bisim similarity* is defined as:

$$Bisim(X, Y) = \frac{nsim(n, m)}{max(n, m)}$$

$$nsim(i, j) = \begin{cases} 0, & i = 0 \vee j = 0 \\ max \begin{cases} nsim(i, j - 1), \\ nsim(i - 1, j), & in \\ nsim(i - 1, i - 1) + & other \\ s(x_i x_{i+1}, y_j y_{j+1}), & case \end{cases} \end{cases} \quad (5)$$

$$s(x_i x_{i+1}, y_j y_{j+1}) = \frac{1}{2} \sum_{k=0}^{1} id(x_{i+k}, y_{j+k}) \quad (6)$$

$$id(a, b) = \begin{cases} 1, a = b \\ 0, a \neq b \end{cases} \quad (7)$$

2.3   Related Work

Using a list of 1,127 LASA pairs and 1,127 non-LASA pairs, Lambert [14] evaluates 22 measures with ten-fold cross-validation technique and concludes that Trigram2B, NED and Editex [20] are the best measures to identify LASA pairs.

Kondrak [6, 23–25] proposes the orthographic Nsim similarity and the phonetic Aline similarity [30, 31] where the recall metric is used to evaluate the results of 12 measures with the USP LASA list [32] of 360 unique drug names. Kondrak [6] concludes that Bisim is the best orthographic measure. Bisim is used to create automated warning systems to identify potential LASA errors in prescription electronic systems [4, 33] and in the software POCA by the FDA [6]. Furthermore, the average of Bisim, Aline, Prefix, and NED measures outperform to Bisim [6].

3   Proposed Method

In this paper, a Soften Bigram Similarity measure (Soft-Bisim) is proposed. First, the cases of bigrams involved in the scale of similarity in Soft-Bisim are described. After that, the fitness function used to find the weights in the scale of similarity by a genetic algorithm is described. Our hypothesis is that an evolutionary approach defines better the levels in the scale of similarity compared to the original similarity scale proposed by Kondrak in Bisim (cf. Eqs. 7 and 8). In other words, we consider this problem as an evolutionary approach for optimizing the internal parameters of the similarity scale.

3.1   Definition of Soft-Bisim Similarity

Given the drug names X and Y as sequences of size n and m, respectively, Soft-Bisim is defined as:

$$Soft - Bisim(X, Y) = \frac{Bisim(n, m)}{max(n, m)} \tag{8}$$

$$Bisim(i, j) = \begin{cases} 0, & i = 0 \lor j = 0 \\ max \begin{cases} Bisim(i, j-1), \\ Bisim(i-1, j), \\ Bisim(i-1, i-1) + \\ s\left(x_i x_{i+1}, y_j y_{j+1}\right), \end{cases} & \begin{matrix} in \\ other \\ case \end{matrix} \end{cases} \tag{9}$$

Where the proposed scale of similarity for Soft-Bisim is defined as:

$$s\left(a_i a_{i+1}, b_j b_{j+1}\right) = \begin{cases} w_1, a_{i+1} = b_{j+1} \neq a_i \neq b_j \\ w_2, a_i \neq a_{i+1} \neq b_j \neq b_{j+1} \\ w_3, a_i = a_{i+1} = b_j \neq b_{j+1} \lor a_i = b_j = b_{j+1} \neq a_{i+1} \\ w_4, a_i = b_{j+1} \land a_{i+1} = b_j \\ w_5, a_i = b_{j+1} \neq a_{i+1} \neq b_j \lor a_{i+1} = b_j \neq a_i \neq b_{j+1} \\ w_6, a_i = a_{i+1} = b_{j+1} \neq b_j \lor a_{i+1} = b_j = b_{j+1} \neq a_i \\ w_7, a_i = b_j \neq a_{i+1} \neq b_{j+1} \\ w_8, a_i = a_{i+1} = b_j = b_{j+1} \\ w_9, a_i = b_j \land a_{i+1} = b_{j+1} \end{cases} \tag{10}$$

For increasing accuracy to identify confusable drug names it is needed to find the set of weights $W = \{w_1, w_2, \ldots, w_9\}$ of the scale of similarity of Soft-Bisim. For this, a Genetic Algorithm is used [34–36].

3.2   Finding the Scale of Similarity for Soft-Bisim

The fitness function of the Genetic Algorithm is designed to evaluate each individual in relation to the objective to optimize.

The FDA reviews the similarity of a new drug name with all drug names that were previously registered. Therefore, the f-measure evaluation widely used in the information retrieval is used as the fitness function [37]. Given a LASA pair $(d_i, d_j) \in$ List of LASA pairs, the f-measure for the query d_i evaluates the size of the set of retrieved drug names in ranking one (most similar drug names to the query d_i), but if d_j does not appears in the last set, the f-measure add the size of the retrieved drug names in the next ranking, until appears d_j. In this way, f-measure evaluates the ability to find a relevant drug name from a query. The f-measure could be obtained at every ranking (r). In fact, we desire to improve the f-measure in the top four rankings. Therefore, the fitness function computes a macro-averaging f-measure for the queries of all different drug names (set D) based on the sum of the first four rankings, see Eq. 11. In other words, the fitness function gives more relevance to the combination of weights in W (Eq. 10) that, after retrieving the queries of all different drug names with the Soft-Bisim measure, produces the best sum of the first four f-measure evaluation.

$$fitness(D) = \sum_{r=1}^{4} f - measure(D, r) \qquad (11)$$

4   Results and Discussion

In all the experiments, the ground truth USP-858 collection with 858 LASA pairs is used. The USP-858 contains 630 unique drug names, and it can generate 36,900 pairs of drug names. That means that 0.3% of LASA pairs must be recovered.

4.1   Calculating the Scale of Similarity for Soft-Bisim

Although, the genetic algorithm only optimizes the macro-averaging f-measure for the top four positions, the comparison in Table 1 shows an improvement, with respect to Bisim, in all positions of ranking to retrieve LASA pairs. As it is possible to observe, the weight w_9 for Soft-Bisim maintains a higher relevance than w_8 while in Bisim w_8 and w_9 are the same. On the contrary, the case when all the letters are different the weight is not zero.

Table 1. Comparison of the macro-averaging f-measure evaluation for Bisim and Soft-Bisim with the USP-858 collection where the resulting weights for Soft-Bisim are: $w_1 = 0$, $w_2 = 0.1$, $w_3 = 0.4$, $w_4 = 0$, $w_5 = 0$, $w_6 = 0.2$, $w_7 = 0.4$, $w_8 = 0.6$ and $w_9 = 0.8$; and the implicit weights for Bisim are: $w_{1...3} = 0$, $w_{4...7} = 0.5$, $w_7 = 0$, and $w_8 = w_9 = 1$. *In the last row the ten-fold cross-validation results are showed.

Ranking		1	2	3	4	5	6	7	8	9	10
Bisim	F-Meas.	48.86	39.78	29.74	22.45	17.18	13.44	10.64	8.75	7.24	5.96
	ΣF-Meas.	48.86	88.65	118.40	140.86	158.04	171.49	182.14	190.90	198.14	204.11
Soft-Bisim	F-Meas.	51.07	45.20	39.03	33.45	28.89	25.75	23.08	20.93	19.07	17.52
	ΣF-Meas.	51.07	96.27	135.31	168.76	197.65	223.41	246.49	267.42	286.50	304.03
Soft-Bisim*	F-Meas.	51	44.75	38.79	33.51	29.18	25.97	23.33	21.21	19.38	17.85
	ΣF-Meas.	51	95.75	134.53	168.05	197.23	223.2	246.53	267.74	287.12	304.97

4.2 Evaluation of Orthographic Measures

In Fig. 1, Soft-Bisim is compared to all orthographic measures presented in Sects. 2.1 and 2.2. In this case, Trigram-2B maintains the relevance indicated by Lambert but Bisim is more relevant that Trigram-2B. It is worth to mention that Trigram-2B2A and Trigram-2B1A are more relevant that Bisim. However, Soft-Bisim obtains the best performance with the adjusted similarity scale.

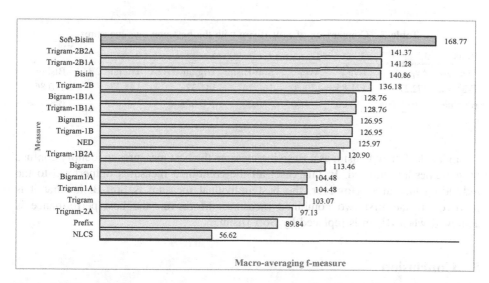

Fig. 1. Ranking obtained for each orthographic measure according to sum of top four positions of macro-averaging f-measure.

4.3 A Combined Measure with Soft-Bisim

Using the Average of Prefix, NED, Bisim and Aline, Kondrak [6] proposes a combined measure that outperform to Bisim: $\text{Avg}_{\text{Bisim}}$(Prefix, NED, Bisim, Aline). In this paper, we propose two combined measures, in the first one, Soft-Bisim is added to the average Avg_{all} (Prefix, NED, Bisim, Aline, Soft-Bisim), and the second one, Bisim is replaced by Soft-Bisim in the average, $Avg_{SoftBisim}$(Prefix, NED, Aline, Soft-Bisim). In Table 2, the comparison of original combined proposed by Kondrak and our proposed combined measures are presented.

Table 2. Macro-averaging f-measure evaluation for Avg_{Bisim}, Avg_{All} and $Avg_{SoftBisim}$.

Ranking	Avg_{Bisim}		Avg_{All}		$Avg_{SoftBisim}$	
	F-Measure	ΣF-Measure	F-Measure	ΣF-Measure	F-Measure	ΣF-Measure
1	51.36	51.36	51.63	51.63	51.70	51.70
2	44.69	96.05	45.56	97.20	45.42	97.12
3	39.63	135.68	39.78	136.98	40.01	137.13
4	35.11	**170.80**	34.87	**171.85**	35.13	**172.27**
5	30.79	201.59	30.72	202.58	30.89	203.16
6	27.55	229.15	27.76	230.34	27.85	231.02
7	25.04	254.19	25.05	255.39	25.10	256.12
8	22.81	277.00	22.87	278.27	22.86	278.98
9	20.84	297.85	20.92	299.19	21.06	300.04
10	19.31	317.17	19.45	318.64	19.47	319.52

Table 3. Comparison of Soft-Bisim with the best previous measures.

Rank	1	2	3	4	5	6	7
Measure	$Avg_{SoftBisim}$	Avg_{all}	Avg_{Bisim}	Soft-Bisim	Trigram-2B2A	Trigram-2B1A	Bisim
F-Meas.	172.27	171.85	170.80	168.76	141.37	141.27	140.86
p-value	0.005	0.005	0.005	0.005	0.005	0.005	Baseline

In Table 3, using Bisim as a Baseline measure the best measures to identify confuse drug names are showed. In this case, all the combined measures outperform to the individual measures. However, the best individual measure is Soft-Bisim that it is involved in the first two combined measures. Moreover, the best performance is achieved when Bisim is replaced by Soft-Bisim.

5 Conclusion

The problem of confusion of drug names needs attention because it is still growing. All measures presented in this paper (except by Nsim) are designed or adjusted to different application or domain. In this sense, Nsim takes into consideration characteristics that take part on confusable drug names like the fact that the initial letters are frequently involved in a confused drug name. In this paper we propose to Soft-Bisim measure that it is a new orthographic measure for identifying LASA pairs based on Nsim similarity with an extension to soften the scale of similarity between the bi-grams that conforms a drug name. In specific, nine combinations of weights were calculated. For this, the sum the first-four macro-averaging f-measure of the retrieved pairs is proposed as the fitness function in a genetic algorithm.

According to the experimentation, Soft-Bisim increases the accuracy with respect to Bisim in a retrieved list of potential LASA pairs in all the ranking positions. Furthermore, Soft-Bisim outperforms significantly to the others 17 orthographic measures used in this problem. In this paper, we found that the measures Trigram-2B2A and Trigram-2B1A are good measures since outperform to the Bisim measure.

In addition, a new average combination of four measures using Soft-Bisim is proposed. This new average combination outperforms to the previous average that use Bisim measure. Even thought, we only use a list of drug names Soft-Bisim can be used to retrieve other cases of confusions like in proper names or brand names.

References

1. Billstein-Leber, M., Carrillo, C.J.D., Cassano, A.T., Moline, K., Robertson, J.J.: ASHP guidelines on preventing medication errors in hospitals (2018). https://www.ashp.org/Pharmacy-Practice/Policy
2. Cohen, M.R., Domizio, G.D., Lee, R.E.: The role of drug names in medication errors. In: Medication Errors, pp. 87–110. American Pharmacists Association, Washington, DC (2007)
3. Medication Without Harm.: World Health Organization, Geneva (2017)
4. Rash-Foanio, C., et al.: Automated detection of look-alike/sound-alike medication errors. Am. J. Heal. Pharm. **74**, 521–527 (2017)
5. Tittemore, L.M.: The name game (2017). https://sunsteinlaw.com/l-tittemore/
6. Kondrak, G., Dorr, B.: Automatic identification of confusable drug names. Artif. Intell. Med. **36**, 29–42 (2006)
7. FDA: FDA and ISMP Work to Prevent Medication Errors 2017 (2012)
8. Craigle, V.: MedWatch: the FDA safety information and adverse event reporting program. J. Med. Libr. Assoc. **95**, 224–225 (2007)
9. Gershman, J.A., Fass, A.D.: Medication safety and pharmacovigilance resources for the ambulatory care setting: enhancing patient safety. Hosp. Pharm. **49**, 363–368 (2014)
10. Getz, K.A., Stergiopoulos, S., Kaitin, K.I.: Evaluating the completeness and accuracy of MedWatch data. Am. J. Ther. **21**, 442–446 (2014)
11. Wagner, R.A., Fischer, M.J.: The string-to-string correction problem. J. ACM **21**, 168–173 (1974)
12. Pfeifer, U., Poersch, T., Fuhr, N., Vi, L.I.: Searching proper names in databases. In: HIM, pp. 259–275. Citeseer (1995)
13. Pfeifer, U., Vi, L.I.: Searching proper names in databases, vol. 20, pp. 1–13, October 1994
14. Lambert, B.L., Lin, S.J., Chang, K.Y., Gandhi, S.K.: Similarity as a risk factor in drug-name confusion errors: The look-alike (orthographic) and sound-alike (phonetic) model. Med. Care **37**, 1214–1225 (1999)
15. Schroeder, S.R., et al.: Cognitive tests predict real-world errors: the relationship between drug name confusion rates in laboratory-based memory and perception tests and corresponding error rates in large pharmacy chains. BMJ Qual. Saf. **26**, 395–407 (2017)
16. Lambert, B.L., et al.: Listen carefully: the risk of error in spoken medication orders. Soc. Sci. Med. **70**, 1599–1608 (2010)

17. Lambert, B.L.: Predicting look-alike and sound-alike medication errors. Am. J. Heal. Pharm. **54**, 1161–1171 (1997)
18. Shah, M.B., Merchant, L., Chan, I.Z., Taylor, K.: Characteristics that may help in the identification of potentially confusing proprietary drug names. Ther. Innov. Regul. Sci. **51**, 232–236 (2017)
19. Levenshtein, V.I.: Binary codes capable of correcting deletions, insertions, and reversals. In: Soviet Physics Doklady, pp. 707–710 (1966)
20. Zobel, J., Box, G.P.O., Dart, P.: Phonetic string matching: lessons from information retrieval. In: Proceedings of 19th Annual International ACM SIGIR Conference Research and Development in Information Retrieval, pp. 166–172 (1996)
21. Elmagarmid, A.K., Ipeirotis, P.G., Verykios, V.S.: Duplicate record detection: a survey. IEEE Trans. Knowl. Data Eng. **19**, 1–16 (2007)
22. Chen, S., Liu, Y., Wei, L., Guan, B.: PS-FW: a hybrid algorithm based on particle swarm and fireworks for global optimization. Comput. Intell. Neurosci. **2018**, 1–27 (2018)
23. Kondrak, G., Dorr, B.: Identification of confusable drug names: a new approach and evaluation methodology (2004)
24. Kondrak, G., Dorr, B.J.: A similarity-based approach and evaluation methodology for reduction of drug name confusion. Alberta University, Edmonton (2003)
25. Kondrak, G.: N-Gram similarity and distance. In: Consens, M., Navarro, G. (eds.) SPIRE 2005. LNCS, vol. 3772, pp. 115–126. Springer, Heidelberg (2005). https://doi.org/10.1007/11575832_13
26. Chen, L.-C., Chen, C.-H., Chen, H.-M., Tseng, V.S.: Hybrid data mining approaches for prevention of drug dispensing errors. J. Intell. Inf. Syst. **36**, 305–327 (2011)
27. Adamson, G.W., Boreham, J.: The use of an association measure based on character structure to identify semantically related pairs of words and document titles. Inf. Storage Retr. **10**, 253–260 (1974)
28. Lambert, B.L., Chang, K.-Y., Lin, S.-J.: Effect of orthographic and phonological similarity on false recognition of drug names. Soc. Sci. Med. **52**, 1843–1857 (2001)
29. Lambert, B.L., Yu, C., Thirumalai, M.: A system for multiattribute drug product comparison. J. Med. Syst. **28**, 31–56 (2004)
30. Kondrak, G.: Phonetic alignment and similarity. Comput. Hum. **37**, 273–291 (2003)
31. Kondrak, G.: Algorithms for language reconstruction (2002)
32. USP: USP quality review (76). US Pharmacopeia. (2001)
33. Or, C.K.L., Wang, H.H.L.: Examining text enhancement methods to improve look-alike drug name differentiation accuracy. In: Proceedings of the Human Factors and Ergonomics Society, pp. 645–649 (2013)
34. Goldberg, D.E.: Genetic Algorithms in Search, Optimization, and Machine Learning. Addison Wesley, Reading (1989)
35. Holland, J.H.: Adaptation in Natural and Artificial Systems: an Introductory Analysis with Applications to Biology, Control, and Artificial Intelligence. MIT Press, Cambridge (1992)
36. Mitchell, M.: An Introduction to Genetic Algorithms. Cambridge, Massachusetts, London, England, Fifth Printing (1999)
37. Croft, B., Metzler, D., Strohman, T.: Search Engines: Information Retrieval in Practice. Addison-Wesley Publishing Company, Boston (2009)

Author Index

Printed in the United States
By Bookmasters